The Cities

Ditch

y from Aldgate

EAST SMITH FIELD.

Hog Lane

East Smith Field

The place where the Pound stood

The Cage

Mount

AG

G H I

K

W

Y

L

K

The Queens Lodgings

The Barrs to keep the Carts from the Ditch

Jewel house

The Hall decay'd

R

M

Queens Gallery

The Privy Garden

Q N

O P

The Iron Gate

The way to the Flemish Church

E

...of the DRAUGHT of the TOWER LIBERTIE Surveyd in the year 159 by GULIELMUS HAIWAR and J. GASCOYNE.

A Note of the Boundaries of ye Libert of the Tower as appears in the Leet A 27. Hen. 8.

The Liberties of the Tower beginning a Water Gate next the Ram's Head in Petty W doth extend straight North to the end of Tow Street and direct North to the Mud Wall call Pikes Garden on this side the Crutched Fryers so straight East to the Wall of London with the Gardens above the Postern and above the Broken To right unto the midst of Hog Lane and and so stra broad South to the Stone Corner and so on to ye Tha and according to the former abutting a green lir drawn about the said liberties.

Where there is not sufficient room for Names of ces to be written, the names of such places are ted with letters and are to be referr'd to ye Alpha ical table here under written.

These are the Marks of the Several Towers.

A. The Middle Tower.
B. The Tower at the Gate.
C. The Bell Tower.
D. Buecamp Tower.
E. Devilin Tower.
F. Flint Tower.
G. Bowyar Tower.
H. Brick Tower.
I. Martin Tower.
K. Constable Tower.
L. Broad Arrow Tower.
M. Salt Tower.
N. Well Tower.
O. The Tower leading to the Iron Gate.
P. The Tower above Iron Gate.
Q. The Cradle Tower.
R. The lanthorn Tower.
S. The Hall Tower.
T. The Bloody Tower.
V. St Thomas Tower.
W. Cæsar's, or White Tower.
X. Cole Harberte
Y. Warderoap Tower.

These are the Marks for the Boundaries of the Liberties

A B. The House at the Water Gate call'd the Rams Head.
A C. The place where the Mud Wall was call Pike's Garden.
A D. The City Wall at the North East of the Nine Gardens
A E. The place where the Broken Tower was
A F. Hog Lane end.
A G. The House call'd the Stone corner House

THE WHITE TOWER

THE WHITE TOWER

Edited by

Edward Impey

With contributions by:

Jeremy Ashbee, John Crook, Philip Dixon
Roland B. Harris, Edward Impey, Anna Keay
Daniel Miles, Julian Munby, Robin Sanderson
Abigail Wheatley and Bernard Worssam

Yale University Press ∼ New Haven and London
in association with
**Historic Royal
PALACES**

Designed by Sarah Faulks

Printed in Singapore

Library of Congress Cataloging-in-Publication Data

Impey, Edward.
The White Tower / Edward Impey.
p. cm.
Includes bibliographical references and index.
ISBN 978-0-300-11293-1 (cl : alk. paper)
1. White Tower (Tower of London, London, England) 2. Castles – England – London. 3. Historic
buildings – England – London. 4. London (England) – Buildings, structures, etc. 1. Title.

NA7746.L626147 2008
728.8'1094215 – dc22

2008037695

A catalogue record for this book is available from The British Library

Endpapers: The Tower of London in 1597 by William Haiward and John Gascoyne,
a copy of the lost original made in 1741.

Frontispiece: Aerial view of the Tower of London from the south-east in 2004, showing
the White Tower at the heart of the castle.

Contents

Contributors

Jeremy Ashbee

Dr Jeremy Ashbee FSA read Archaeology and Anthropology at Downing College, Cambridge and the Archaeology of Buildings at York University. He was an Assistant Curator of Historic Buildings at Historic Royal Palaces between 1996 and 2003, based at the Tower of London. In 2006 he completed his doctoral thesis on the Tower's role as a royal residence between 1066 and 1400, and has published widely on the architecture and function of medieval palaces and castles. He is currently the Head Properties Curator of English Heritage.

John Crook

Dr John Crook FSA read Modern Languages at Oxford, and after teaching for some years at Eton and in Winchester returned to Oxford to write a doctoral thesis on 'The Architectural Setting of the Cult of Saints'. He is an independent scholar in the field of historic buildings, medieval archaeology, and ecclesiastical art and architecture, with a particular interest in the Romanesque. He has published many books and papers on a variety of historical subjects. He is Cathedral Archaeologist at Winchester, and also a widely published architectural photographer and occasional radio and recording performer in Old French music and literature.

Philip Dixon

Professor Philip Dixon FSA FRHS was for thirty years lecturer and Reader in Medieval Archaeology at the University of Nottingham, and is now Director of an architectural and archaeological consultancy company. He holds research fellowships at two universities, and is visiting professor of archaeology at the University of Aarhus, Denmark. He is Past President of the Council for British Archaeology and is currently Hon. Vice President of that body and Vice President of the Royal Archaeological Institute. He has directed excavations in Britain on a variety of sites for over forty years, and is the author of more than 150 books and articles.

Roland B. Harris

Dr Roland B. Harris BA DPhil FSA MIFA read History of Art and Medieval Archaeology at University College London, and undertook his doctoral research on medieval townhouses at the University of Oxford. At the time of the White Tower Recording and Research Project he was Director of the Historic Buildings Recording Unit, University of Reading, and is now an independent buildings archaeologist. He is Norwich Cathedral Archaeologist and an archaeological consultant to Historic Royal Palaces, with responsibility for the recording and research programme during the current major conservation works on the White Tower (2008–10).

Edward Impey

Dr Edward Impey studied history and then archaeology at the University of Oxford, and held a British Academy Post-Doctoral Research Fellowship at Oriel College from 1991–5. From 1995 until 1997 he was Historic Buildings Curator at Historic Royal Palaces, and Curator from 1997–2002. Since then he has been an Executive Board Director of English Heritage, with responsibilities including research and conservation. His publications and research interests have focused on monastic history and medieval domestic and military architecture in England and France.

Anna Keay

Dr Anna Keay was educated at Magdalen College, Oxford, and London University where she completed her doctoral thesis in 2004. She was for seven years an Assistant Curator at Historic Royal Palaces, where she worked extensively on the post-medieval history of the Tower of London. She published *The Elizabethan Tower of London: The Haiward and Gascoyne Plan of 1597* in 2001 and *The Magnificent Monarch: Charles II and the Ceremonies of Power* in 2008. She is currently Properties Presentation Director at English Heritage.

Daniel Miles

Dr Daniel Miles FSA is a partner in the Oxford Dendrochronology Laboratory and runs a firm specialising in the conservation of historic timberwork. He is an Honorary Research Associate at the Research Laboratory for Archaeology and the History of Art, Oxford University, and completed his doctoral thesis in Archaeological Science at Hertford College, Oxford in 2005. In addition to the White Tower, he has also undertaken extensive studies of historic woodwork at Salisbury Cathedral, Windsor Castle, and Westminster Abbey.

Julian Munby

Julian Munby FSA studied archaeology at the Institute of Archaeology, London, and is head of Buildings Archaeology at Oxford Archaeology. He has a special interest in medieval roof carpentry and town houses and has published numerous papers on these topics. Currently he is researching the archaeology (and carpentry) of medieval carriages and early coaches, and most recently has participated in the rediscovery of

Edward III's Round Table building buried in the Upper Ward at Windsor Castle.

Robin W. Sanderson

Robin Sanderson, BSc, CGeol, FGS studied geology at Birkbeck College, London and followed a career as petrographer with the British Geological Survey. His work included analysis of mainly British stone types for the FGS field surveys and curation of the rock collections which in part developed from the Parliamentary Commissioners' 1839 collection of stones considered for the rebuilding of the Houses of Parliament. Following retirement in 1992 he has surveyed and advised on the sources and decay of building stones for conservators and historians, notably for Historic Royal Palaces at Hampton Court Palace and the Tower of London.

Abigail Wheatley

Dr Abigail Wheatley gained her Ph.D. from the Centre for Medieval Studies, University of York, in 2002. Her work focused on the medieval castle as an architecture of ideas, examining literary and artistic depictions of castles and their influence on, and response to, contemporary castle architecture. Since then she has published articles on the mythological and symbolic associations of several specific British castles and published the book: *The Idea of the Castle in Medieval England* in 2004.

Bernard C. Worssam

Dr Bernard C. Worssam, BSc, DSc, FGS after studying geology at University College London, Bernard pursued a career in the British Geological Survey. His work included the geological mapping of large parts of the Weald, notably around Maidstone and Haslemere, and studies of the geology of the south Midlands. Since retirement in 1985 he has developed an interest in medieval building stones, and carried out studies such as that of Rochester Cathedral in conjunction with Tim Tatton-Brown. He was awarded a London University Doctorate in 1995.

Foreword

One of the many pleasures which accompanied my service as Resident Governor of HM Tower of London was that so much was being learnt, during that period, about its history, its surroundings and its buildings. It was therefore particularly exciting to keep abreast of the archaeological and historical discoveries extracted from the White Tower, the very heart of the castle, and a building which dominated the view from my home, the Queen's House. And at a personal level, as a former Engineer-in-Chief of the British Army, I always felt an affinity with Gundulf of Rochester, whose skills may very well have been exercised on this building. I know that this volume represents a major step forward in our understanding of the White Tower and indeed the Tower of London as a whole, of value to scholars and as a starting-point for other works, and stands as a worthy tribute to what must be one of the most remarkable buildings in the world.

Major General Geoffrey Field, CB CVO OBE
Resident Governor and Keeper of the Jewel House,
HM Tower of London, 1994–2006

Acknowledgements

The authors and editor are extremely grateful to a number of organisations and individuals – in addition to those whose assistance is acknowledged at the end of individual chapters – who have been fundamental to the realisation of this volume. Historic Royal Palaces, responsible for the management and conservation of the Tower of London, funded the key contractors, provided staff time, and subsidised the publication. Its staff, David Beeton (Chief Executive, 1989–98), Dr Simon Thurley (Curator, 1989–96), Major-General Geoffrey Field (Resident Governor of the Tower of London, 1994–2006) and Charlotte Clackson (Head of Finance, 1994–7) made the decisions and provided the authority and encouragement needed to proceed; Clare Murphy (Publications Manager) managed the bulk of the administrative work prior to its handover for publication with characteristic expertise and calm; Annie Heron, Susan Mennell and Louise Nash, in the Publications Team, procured images and permissions. The Historic Buildings Recording Unit at the University of Reading, directed by Dr Roland Harris with the support of Dr John Crook, carried out in an exemplary fashion the archaeological survey and analysis of the White Tower on which its structural history, as presented here, is based; Monika Hauth carried out many months of unpaid work transcribing documents in the National Archives and Dr Lucy Vinten-Mattich, also unpaid, carried out an exhaustive literature search on the subject and its context at the beginning of the project. Final thanks must go to Yale University Press for their sustained commitment during the long period of preparation, and the skill and tenacity of Gillian Malpass, Sarah Faulks and Delia Gaze in steering this book through to publication.

Den Tower van London

Introduction

EDWARD IMPEY

The Tower of London is one of the best-known castles in the world. At its centre stands one of the most notable monuments in Europe, the White Tower, so called since at least the fourteenth century, and which, within a few years of 1100, had given the castle its name. It is of course remarkable as the best preserved of any secular Romanesque building on anything approaching this scale, and for the opportunity this provides for study and appreciation. But its real importance stems from qualities that have been there from the beginning and ensured its significance, impact and preservation: its sheer size and presence, its innovative design, its place in the development and proliferation of the tradition to which it belongs, its royal status, and above all the success with which it has served as a symbol of authority, and of national and civic identity, for 900 years.

Although this book, in discussing its most important component, necessarily contributes to our understanding of the castle as a whole, its subject is emphatically the White Tower, not the Tower of London. For although they cannot and should not be studied as entirely separate entities, the White Tower stands as a great and individual architectural set piece, designed both to be structurally independent and to serve an independent function: it both preceded the construction of any other surviving medieval building on the site and has remained substantially unaltered. In historical and architectural terms, too, it also has a place and significance quite independent of the post-eleventh-century history and development of the cas-

tle that grew up around it. For it is the supreme example of a 'great tower', 'keep', *donjon* or *tour maîtresse*, a tradition that originated in tenth-century France, was reinvigorated with the building of the White Tower, flourished throughout the twelfth century, and remains the best-known, most durable and most distinctive form produced by the secular architecture of northern Europe in that period.

The Tower of London is, as a whole, as much studied as any monument in England. Since the appearance of the first scholarly description of the site by John Bayley in 1821,[1] at least forty publications have appeared on the Tower, and dozens more that mention it. Particularly important steps were made with the compilation of the Royal Commission account of 1930,[2] Brian Davison's excavations of 1963,[3] and the work of Reginald Allen Brown, Howard Colvin and Arnold Taylor in the *History of the King's Works*, which established the essential chronology and process of the castle's medieval and early modern development.[4] A spate of archaeological work in the late 1970s and 1980s, largely written up by Geoffrey Parnell,[5] and excavations in and around the Tower moat in the years 1995–8 have added much since.[6] Little of this, however, set out to improve or contributed to our understanding of the White Tower. Significant discoveries from the 1820s to the mid-1990s, at least concerning its original fabric, were confined to the identification of the original entrance, of Roman remains underneath the building, and of evidence of its original roof, although the last was not published:[7] the most impor-

Facing page: detail of fig. 59

tant suggestions and reinterpretations have been that the existing top floor was a post-Norman insertion;[8] that the apse was an afterthought;[9] and that the building's plan form was arrived at in stages.[10] Meanwhile, since the 1960s and 70s, interest in the 'great tower' in general had been gathering momentum, fuelled by the publications of Derek Renn, Reginald Allen Brown and André Châtelain, and by Michel de Boüard's discoveries at Doué la Fontaine in 1967.[11] The 1980s, and still more so the early 1990s, saw a rapid increase in the growth of interest in the 'great tower' in general, and important advances in the understanding of, and range of questions concerning, its origins, functions and 'typology'. The process was aided by a series of studies of major buildings, including Loches and Langeais in France,[12] and Hedingham, Norham and Colchester in England,[13] and the synthetic work, in particular, of Philip Dixon and Jean Mesqui.[14] Few authors have omitted to mention the White Tower, although sometimes as little more than a long-accepted anchor-point in the chronology of Romanesque architecture, trusting the start date of 1078 suggested by John Stow in 1598 but since accepted as a fact.[15] But as studies of the type and of other buildings raised questions concerning the White Tower that the existing literature could not answer, the need for a modern study became increasingly apparent.

The impetus and opportunity to do this came in 1995. First, the decision made in 1991 to move the bulk of the Royal Armouries' collections from the Tower to Leeds, requiring the White Tower to be emptied for repairs and the installation of new displays,[16] was by then being carried out. As it happened, the once-in-a-generation opportunity for study that this offered was soon enhanced by the launch of a comprehensive repair programme to the south front of the White Tower, carried out in 1997–8.[17] Second, having recently completed fieldwork at Langeais and Ivry-la-Bataille, in 1995 the editor joined the Historic Royal Palaces Agency (HRPA), responsible for managing the Tower, with a research project already in mind.[18] With encouragement from the then Curator, Simon Thurley, and with the help of Jeremy Ashbee, proposals for a multi-disciplinary study of the building and its significance began to take shape. By autumn 1996 the White Tower Recording and Research Project (WTRRP) had been defined, funding over two years had been secured, and a contract for digital recording and an archaeological analysis let by competitive tender to the Historic Buildings Recording Unit (HBRU), attached to the Department of Archaeology at the University of Reading under Roland Harris. The HBRU team included John Crook, who carried out a detailed analysis of the chapel of St John, and Helen Jones, who developed a three-dimensional computer model of the White Tower, used to aid and present its analysis; the HRP team consisted of the author and Jeremy Ashbee, shortly thereafter joined by Anna Keay, with the support of the Surveyor of the Fabric's Department. Throughout the fieldwork and research stages, invaluable help was provided by a number of volunteers, while Geoffrey Parnell, in charge of crucial aspects of the Royal Armouries' re-presentation project, provided essential assistance and made many important contributions and observations. The initial findings of the recording and research were presented at a conference held at the Society of Antiquaries of London on 16 April 1999.

The core objective of the project was the creation of 'as complete a record as is possible within the constraints of access, finance and current technology',[19] and, based on this, an improved understanding of the building's original form, date and structural history. Central questions included whether the plan of the building as completed had been intended from the outset, the position of the original roof and the date of the existing one. But it was also intended to consider or reconsider the functions the building was intended to serve; why it took the particular form it did; and the functions it actually served, both during the continued *floruit* of the 'great tower' up to *circa* 1200 and in the remainder of the Middle Ages. Since the very existence of the White Tower today is owed to its continued usefulness and prestige after the early Tudor period, the account of its medieval history is followed by a study of its subsequent functions and structural alterations, and its part in the functions and life of the castle as a whole. This forms the core of the present study, but this would be inadequate without considering the building in a fuller context. Accordingly, we have included a study of the site and origins of the Tower of London before the building of the White Tower, and examinations of the ancestry of the 'great tower' before its construction, of its impact on the 'great tower's' development thereafter, and on popular and literary perceptions of the building in the Middle Ages.

Much discussion was had about alternative ways to order the content. Given its complexity, we felt it would be useful to provide, at the beginning of the book, a description and illustrations of the anatomy of the White Tower itself; given also the important relation between the White Tower and its surroundings, this is followed with a brief and up-to-date synopsis of the history and development of the castle as a whole. The book then falls into two main sections. Thanks to its position in the chronological sequence and the 'background' nature of its content, the first starts with the chapter on London before the White Tower, followed by the seven chapters presenting and discussing the building itself, in chronological order. The chapters dealing with the broader issues of context and significance, as opposed to the structure and functions of the White Tower itself, and which would otherwise interrupt the broadly chronological narrative, are then grouped together to form the second main section. Throughout, although the chapters inevitably differ in style according to writer and content, the intention has been to sort and arrange the material and arrive at a consistency of argument and analysis that allows it to be read as a single work by many authors, rather than as a collection of essays.

The substance of the book therefore begins with the exploration of the Tower of London site before the Conquest and the history and context of its creation, addressing such questions as when the initiative to found this and London's other early castles was taken, the form of the early defences, and why it should have been there that the Conqueror chose to build the White Tower. The first of the following chapters, by Roland Harris, presents the bulk of the archaeological analysis of the structure, drawing on a range of petrographic, dendrochronological and stylistic techniques and material. It discusses the form, construction and dating of the original building, the role of Gundulf of Rochester, and establishes, among other things, that building began *circa* 1075–9, was interrupted in the 1080s and completed by 1100; that its plan was decided from the start; and that the roof was originally steeply pitched and at the level of the existing top floor. Interdependent with this is John Crook's contribution on St John's Chapel, which although an entirely integral and original part of the building, has an independent standing as one of the masterpieces of Anglo-Norman construction. Crook describes the structure and phasing of the chapel, discussing the significance of its form and decoration and its place in Anglo-Norman ecclesiastical art and architecture in general.

In the chapter that follows, Jeremy Ashbee examines how the White Tower may have been intended to function, both in itself and in relation to other buildings in the castle and beyond, particularly the royal palace at Westminster. Since written sources relating to the White Tower in this period consist of little more than odd mentions in chronicles, Ashbee concentrates on the abundant material provided by the structure itself, and by related structures and sources. Previous accounts had concluded that the two main floors of the building were intended to provide lodgings of similar layout but differentiated grandeur for two households, those of the constable and the king. Ashbee concludes that the layout was intended to provide a single, coordinated whole, designed for residential and ceremonial use. Ashbee's second chapter discusses the functions of the building, and changes to its structure from *circa* 1150 to 1485. It was in this period, during which royal lodgings were constructed and elaborated in the Inner Ward below the White Tower, that it began to be used and adapted for the huge variety of functions that were to characterise its history thereafter, and in which, in 1240, it is first recorded painted white.

In the next three chapters, following a chronological sequence but addressing the White Tower's new and continued functions in each period, Anna Keay and Roland Harris continue the story up to the end of the millennium. The period begins with the construction of the existing roof and of a new floor beneath it, the most radical alteration to the building in its entire history and one of a scale and virtuosity so far little understood or recognised. Thereafter, although structural alterations did little to change the basic fabric of the building, the almost overwhelming abundance of documents enables a minute picture to be drawn up of the building's changing form and use, contributing in the process to understanding the development of the institutions that used it, public perceptions of and interest in the past, and aspects of military technology and museography. Some of this material, particularly the ever-increasing abundance of drawings created from the 1720s onwards, is vital also to our understanding of its original form. The continued practical use of the White Tower has of course ensured, uniquely amongst eleventh-century great towers, its continued maintenance up to the present day. But another function of the building – and this time one intended by its builders – was its power as a symbol. And this, as these chapters show, was encouraged and reinforced in this period as much as ever, for example, by the massive refurbishments of the 1490s, the blatantly triumphant improvements to its skyline in the 1530s, and the remodelling and whitewashing for Charles I in the 1630s.

The next section opens with a chapter on the origins, proliferation and development of the 'great tower' tradition before 1066, and the possible sources and precedents for the essentials of the White Tower's plan; it is suggested that the origins of the tradition lie in the Paris area in the tenth century, and that of the White Tower itself in developments that took place in Normandy in the first part of the eleventh. Philip Dixon then explores the impact the White Tower had on the building of 'great towers' in England and on the Continent in the twelfth century, identifying its role in the 're-endorsement' of the type, and the creation and design of the second generation of such buildings under Henry I and its final, magnificent expression under Henry II. The final chapter of the section, by Abigail Wheatley, explores a quite different aspect of the White Tower – its place in medieval myth and legend, and what this can tell us about the prestige of the building, how it accumulated, and what people really thought or were prepared to believe about its origins and antiquity – including attributions to the Trojans, the mythical British king Belinus and Julius Caesar, and its adoption by Arthurian legend.

The fourth part of the book, 'Methodological and Technological Appendices', provides information on techniques (survey, dendrochronology and petrography) used to gather primary data, test hypotheses and provide evidence used in the main chapters, but which it would not be appropriate for them to include. It finishes with a substantial study of medieval and later carpentry in the White Tower, expanding on aspects of structural detail and context, which would have been less appropriate elsewhere. The work presented has made a crucial contribution to the overall analysis of the building and serves as a reminder of the importance of studying masonry and timber fabric with equal rigour. The final section consists of a series of extracts from written sources repeatedly referred to in the text, unpublished or not available in an accessible and modern edition.

Taken as a whole, it is hoped that the book will be of value to the study of castles, of the 'great tower', and of allied subjects. But is also hoped that it will – if not immediately – raise as many questions as it answers, and stimulate further work on these general subjects, on the Tower of London and on the White Tower itself.

Facing page: detail of fig. 127

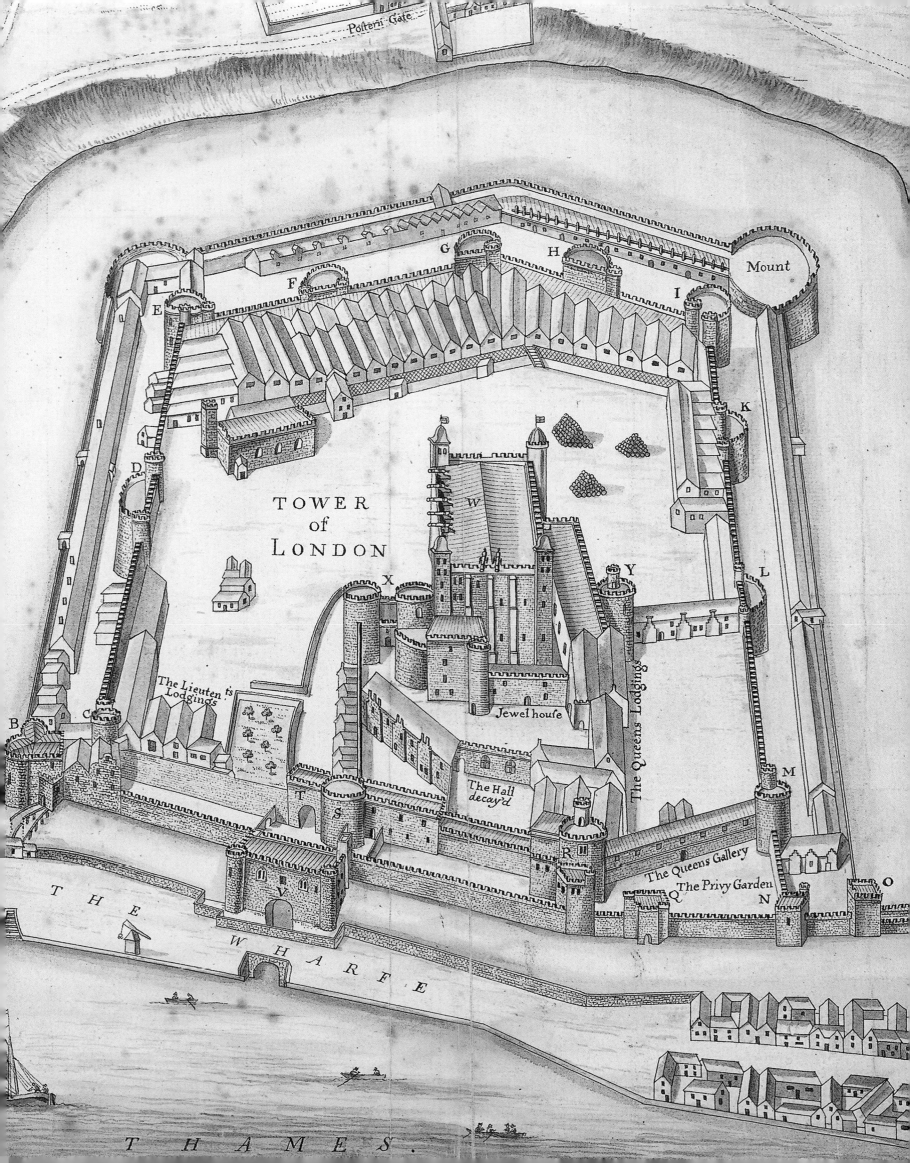

Postern Gate

TOWER
of
LONDON

Mount

F   G   H

E   I

K

D

L

The Lieuten ts
Lodgings

W

X   Y

The Queens Lodgings

B

C

Jewel house

The Hall
decay'd

M

T

S

R

The Queens Gallery

V

The Privy Garden

Q   N   O

THE   WHARFE

THAMES.

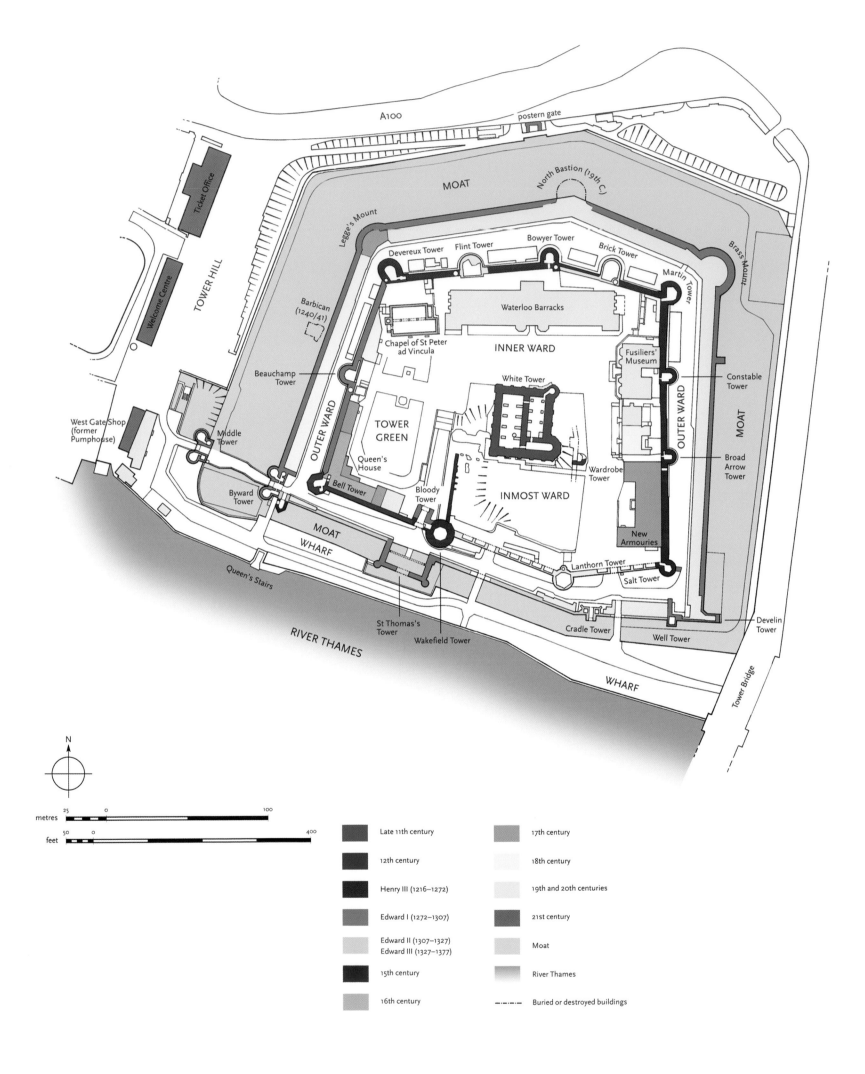

A100

postern gate

MOAT

North Bastion (19th C)

Legge's Mount

Brass Mount

Devereux Tower

Flint Tower

Bowyer Tower

Brick Tower

Martin Tower

Ticket Office

TOWER HILL

Welcome Centre

Barbican (1240/41)

Waterloo Barracks

INNER WARD

Fusiliers' Museum

Chapel of St Peter ad Vincula

Beauchamp Tower

Constable Tower

OUTER WARD

White Tower

West Gate Shop (former Pumphouse)

TOWER GREEN

OUTER WARD

MOAT

Middle Tower

Queen's House

Broad Arrow Tower

Byward Tower

Bell Tower

Bloody Tower

Wardrobe Tower

INMOST WARD

New Armouries

MOAT

WHARF

Lanthorn Tower

Salt Tower

Queen's Stairs

St Thomas's Tower

Cradle Tower

Well Tower

Develin Tower

RIVER THAMES

Wakefield Tower

WHARF

Tower Bridge

N

metres 25 0 100

feet 50 0 400

Late 11th century

12th century

Henry III (1216–1272)

Edward I (1272–1307)

Edward II (1307–1327)
Edward III (1327–1377)

15th century

16th century

17th century

18th century

19th and 20th centuries

21st century

Moat

River Thames

– – – – Buried or destroyed buildings

Summary History of the Tower of London

EDWARD IMPEY

The original form and function of the White Tower and subsequent changes to them, which form the substance of this book, cannot easily be understood without some appreciation of the development of the castle as a whole and the institutions that shaped it (fig. 1). In addition, following the detailed history of the White Tower itself requires a grasp of its three-dimensional anatomy and familiarity with the names of its component parts. The brief summary that follows is intended to make these processes easier.

Before the White Tower

London had been provided with defensive walls, largely still standing in 1066, by the Romans. The early castle, established in 1066, that became the Tower of London occupied the south-east corner of the Roman circuit, where the land wall joined the wall along the river (fig. 2), so that its defences to the south and east were provided ready-made. The angle between the walls was occupied by an enclosure of approximately 5,000 sq. m defined to the north and west by a ditch, identified by excavation in the 1960s,[1] and presumably by a bank and palisade. This seems to have been accompanied by a vast but relatively short-lived outer bailey to the west and north, approximately coextensive with the area subsequently known as the Tower Liberties.

The White Tower

Function and Date

The White Tower belongs to a broad category of building usually known as the 'great tower', originat-

ing in France in the tenth century, and intended in varying proportions to impress, to serve as a stronghold, to provide accommodation and to act as a venue for ceremonial. The White Tower's construction has traditionally been held to begin *circa* 1078, based on the documented involvement of Gundulf, Bishop of Rochester, and his appointment to the see in 1077. Building may in fact have begun as early as 1067, but more probably started between *circa* 1075 and *circa* 1079. In the 1080s, when building had reached approximately 1.5 m above the level of the first floor, the work was interrupted for several years, but was completed by 1100. These two campaigns of construction are described as Phase 1 and Phase 2.

Plan

Externally, the White Tower measures 35.5 m north–south and 30.0 m east–west, with an apsidal projection at the south end of its east wall and a circular turret at the north-east corner (figs 3a, 3b). The interior is split into three main parts at all levels – a room occupying the whole of the western half of the building, with a smaller one and an apsidal-ended space to the east of a north–south spine wall. Some twentieth-century scholars have suggested that this arrangement was arrived at by a series of changes in plan while building, or that the apsidal projection, at least, was an afterthought.[2] These claims are, however, flatly contradicted by the analysis of the structural evidence presented here: its plan as executed was clearly intended from the start. This is in keeping with the existence of a building of fundamentally similar plan in Nor-

2 The castle viewed from the south-west as it might have looked during the early stages of the White Tower's construction, and showing the suggested form of the defences of 1066 within which it was built. To the west of the castle (foreground) lay an outer bailey, which, it is suggested below, formed an original part of the defences. The church of St Peter ad Vincula is shown to the left.

Facing page: 3a   Plans of the White Tower at all four levels in 1996. Minor alterations have been made since.

mandy by about 1020, which also demonstrates that the keep at Colchester was not – as has been suggested – the model for the White Tower, or where the crucial shared features of their layout were first arrived at.

Floor and Roof Levels (As Built)

As built, the White Tower had three interior levels. The apsidal room was vaulted at all levels, with timber floors to the other upper rooms. The lowest, partly under ground, is referred to below as the basement. The main entrance to the building opens into the floor above this, referred to as the entrance floor, and above this is the first floor. Since the early twentieth century it has been recognised that the existing second floor is an insertion, although the original roof was considered to be at its present level, covering double-height rooms overlooked, as at Hedingham and Rochester, by a mural gallery.[3] The present study has shown, however, that the original roof was not set at

its existing (late fifteenth-century) level, but within and screened by the topmost tier of the external walls. Only the chapel, as is shown by its gallery and vault, was roofed at the present level.

Circulation, Fenestration and Interior Detail (As Built)

The basement was accessible internally only, via the north-east stair or 'great vice'. It was lit by narrow loops and contained a well in its western room. An eastward-opening door linked the two main volumes, and another, northward-opening, led to the chapel basement.

The only known entrance to the White Tower opened into the floor above (the entrance floor), at the western end of the south wall, and was approached by a wooden stair, a landing and steps within the wall thickness. The western room, into which it opened, was lit by five single-light windows to the west and

BASEMENT

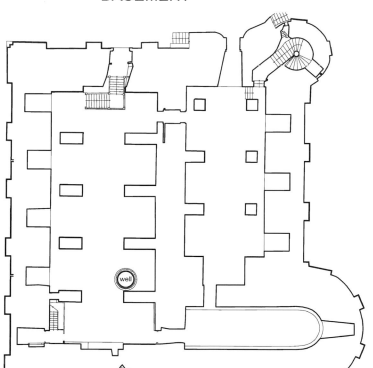

well

ENTRANCE FLOOR

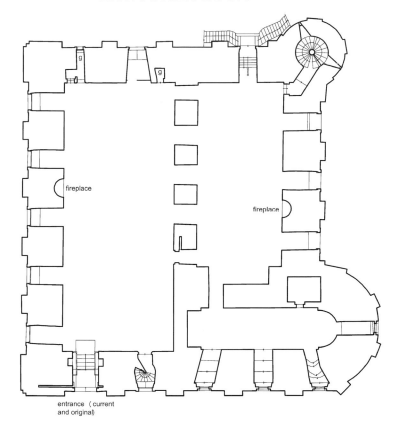

g

g

fireplace

fireplace

entrance (current
and original)

FIRST FLOOR

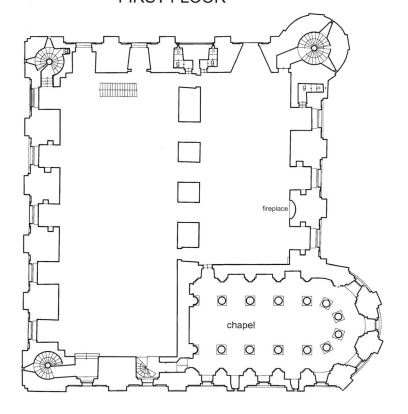

g

g

g

fireplace

chapel

SECOND FLOOR

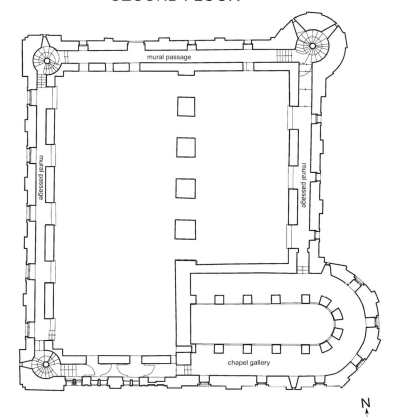

mural passage

mural passage

mural passage

chapel gallery

g = garderobe/latrine

0 METRES 5

N

west

east

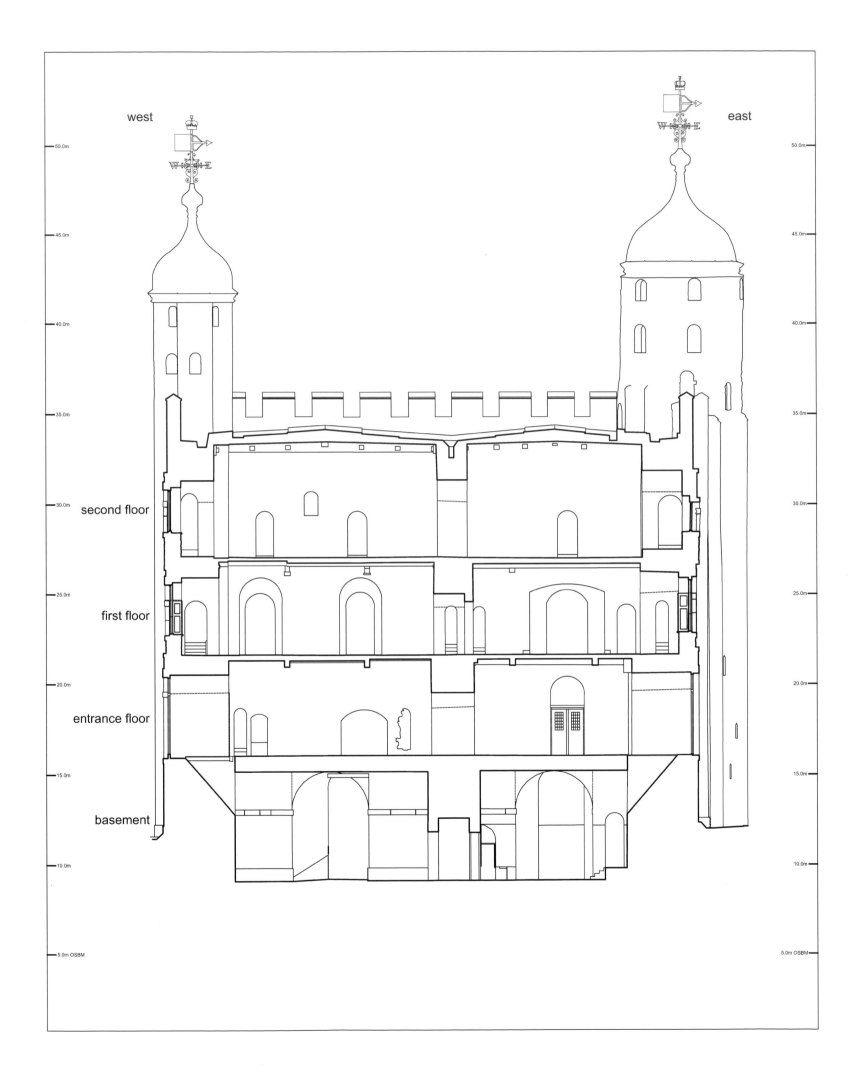

50.0m

45.0m

40.0m

35.0m

second floor 30.0m

first floor 25.0m

entrance floor 20.0m

15.0m

basement

10.0m

5.0m OSBM

50.0m

45.0m

40.0m

35.0m

30.0m

25.0m

20.0m

15.0m

10.0m

5.0m OSBM

one to the south; it had two latrines to the north and a fireplace to the west. Doorways at each end of the spine wall led to the eastern room, lit by four windows, one facing north and three to the east, with a fireplace on the east wall. The spine wall contained three east-facing arched recesses. To the south lay the apsidal-ended room under the chapel.

The first floor was reached by the great vice, opening into its eastern room. This had two latrines, a fireplace, a north-facing window and three windows to the east. A door in its south-west corner led to the magnificent chapel, lit by eight windows to the south and east and provided with a full ambulatory and gallery. The western chamber, reached through a westward-opening doorway at the north end of the spine wall and an eastward-opening one to the south, had a fireplace in its west wall.[4] Two double-light windows were provided at each end and five of the same form to the west. Spiral stairs in the wall thickness of the south-west and north-west corners led up to the wall passage within the screen wall at the top of the building.

Within the thickness of the screen wall was a vaulted passageway, provided with narrow outward-facing openings and broad inward-facing embrasures, facing the roof slopes. The chapel gallery completed the circuit around the building. The spine wall at this level, narrowing in thickness towards the north, took the form of an open arcade of five openings.

Above this there was a wall-walk carried by the screen wall, with four corner turrets, containing rooms at wall-walk level, rising above it. The wall-walk was accessible by the great vice and stairs in the south-west and north-west turrets.

The Late Eleventh and Twelfth Centuries

The creation of the White Tower apart, very little is known about the development of the castle in the late eleventh century, although the *Anglo-Saxon Chronicle* relates that William Rufus (1087–1100) built a 'wall around the Tower' in 1097.[5] Probably from shortly after the Conquest, the castle was governed on the king's behalf by a 'custodian', an office that has existed with minor interruptions, if greater changes in function, ever since. At various times and in various combinations, it may also have been the seat of the Sheriff of Middlesex, London, Essex and Hertfordshire.[6]

No activity is recorded under Rufus's successor, Henry I (1100–1135), although the first known use of the castle as a prison dates from the first year of his reign. During the civil wars between King Stephen (1135–54) and Henry's daughter, Matilda – in which the castle and its custodian, Geoffrey II de Mandeville, changed sides more than once – the castle was strengthened, but how is not clear. By 1171–2, well into the reign of Henry II (1154–89), the castle contained 'houses for the King',[7] by then in need of repair, and thus perhaps the work of Rufus or of

Henry I. It may have been under Henry II that the square forebuilding (shown by the present study to post-date Phase 1 and probably Phase 2) was built up against the White Tower's south side to dignify and protect its entrance. Destroyed in 1674, this is known from a number of views (figs 60, 128, 104, 124).

The main works of the twelfth century, however, were carried out from 1190 to 1193, on behalf of King Richard I (1189–99) by his chancellor, William Longchamp, Bishop of Ely. The scale of the work is shown by the £2,881 that it cost, but what it bought is less clear.[8] The fabric of the Bell Tower (figs 105, 106), however, dates it to this period, and marks an extension and reinforcement of the inner bailey, accompanied, perhaps, by a strengthening of the outer bailey (fig. 4).[9] A contemporary source tells us that the bishop 'had a deep ditch dug around the Tower' early in 1190,[10] and a source of *circa* 1250–55 that it had failed to fill with water.[11]

Henry III (1216–72)

The reign of Henry III, by or during which the early outer bailey must have fallen out of use, saw the first of the two great thirteenth-century reinforcements of the inner defences and a number of important works to its domestic buildings and the White Tower. Activity began in the 1220s with the construction of the Wakefield and Lanthorn towers, standing on the castle's southern rampart, then still fronting the river. The aim was to reinforce the defences, but also to supplement the nearby domestic buildings, in turn remodelled or replaced in the years 1232–6, with the creation of a double-aisled Great Hall, a new kitchen and new chambers.[12] This complex – the 'royal lodgings' – continued to be improved and remained fit for royal use until the mid-sixteenth century.

In the late 1230s attention turned again to the defences, and by 1238 a new wall had been built running north from the Wakefield Tower, along with the Coldharbour Tower, a massive twin-towered gatehouse (destroyed), to the Inmost Ward, up against the west face of the White Tower. Vastly more ambitious, however, was the creation of the existing inner curtain wall and the Inner Ward it encloses, a process begun in 1238. To the east, the riverside wall was extended approximately 50 m east of the Roman wall, terminating in the Salt Tower (a name acquired, like those of most towers in the castle, long after it was built); from there the wall ran north to the Martin Tower, reinforced by the D-shaped Broad Arrow and Constable towers, and then west to the Devereux Tower, punctuated by the Brick, Bowyer and Flint towers. From there the new defences turned south to meet – and probably replace – the late twelfth-century western rampart.[13] The landward sides were surrounded by a new moat, and the work was substantially complete by the early 1240s. Problems, meanwhile, had

Facing page: 3b East–west section of the White Tower, looking north. Shown as it was in 1996.

5

4 Reconstructed view of the castle from the south-west after the completion of the new inner defences *circa* 1193. The White Tower had by then received the addition of the 'forebuilding' covering the main entrance, perhaps under Henry II. The new ramparts were reinforced at their south-west corner by the existing Bell Tower – the main survival from this period. The buildings shown to the south of the White Tower represent, conjecturally, the 'Kings Houses' known to have existed there in the 1160s. The early outer bailey (not shown) may conceivably also have been reinforced at this time.

been encountered with the castle's new western entrance. That a new 'noble gateway' and its 'outworks' had collapsed in 1240 was recorded at the time, but not their location: excavations in the years 1995–7, however, revealed the footings of a collapsed barbican tower, dated by dendrochronology to 1240–41, clearly part of the missing complex (fig. 5). The 'noble gate' to which it led probably stood on or near the site of the Beauchamp Tower.[14]

The White Tower, meanwhile, had not been neglected. In 1240 a timber *hourd* was built out over the tower's southern parapet, and in March of the same year it was whitewashed inside and out, a process that, at least in the case of the exterior, was maintained until the seventeenth century and gave the building its name. Improvements were also made inside it, particularly to the decoration of the chapel. These were probably prompted by the king's desire to increase its amenities if and when required as a place of refuge.

Henry's reign is of importance also in the history of the institutions that were to shape the function and

fabric of the castle. It saw, in particular, the creation of the Wardrobe as an office of state independent of the Chamber, previously responsible both for royal finances and portable property. By the 1230s the Wardrobe itself had split into two parts – one responsible for foodstuffs and perishable goods and the other, the Great Wardrobe, for chattels, furnishings, jewels and weapons. The known origins of the Tower Menagerie date from 1235, with the arrival of three leopards presented by Louis IX of France.

Edward I (1272–1307) and Edward II (1307–27)

Under Edward I the Tower acquired the existing outer wall and moat (fig. 6). The digging of the moat began in 1275, along with the partial backfilling of the old one to form the new Outer Ward and to carry a low rampart. A new western entrance was created close to the river's edge, defended on the far side by the half-moon Lion Tower, leading via a twin-towered gatehouse (the Middle Tower) across a fortified causeway to a second gatehouse (the Byward Tower) and the

5 View of the Tower of London as it might have looked on the eve of the collapse of 1240 or 1241, showing the reinforcement of the castle and the digging of the new moat in progress. The White Tower had been whitewashed, perhaps for the first time, in 1240, and the palace buildings to the south (right) remodelled in the previous decade.

new Outer Ward. A postern gate (the Develin Tower) mirrored it at the castle's south-eastern corner. A fourth arm to the Inner Ward was created by reclaiming land from the river (Water Lane) and building a wall along its outer edge. Access from the river was provided by St Thomas's Tower (or 'Traitors' Gate'), constructed in front of its precursor (the Bloody Tower), now high and dry. By 1281 the site of Henry III's 'noble gate' was occupied by the massive Beauchamp Tower. The only major work in the castle was the rebuilding of St Peter's church in 1286–7, and accommodation for the Mint, installed, probably in the Outer Ward, by King Edward.

Under Edward II the heightening of the landward stretches of the outer wall, probably begun in the previous reign, was completed. The use of St John's Chapel in the White Tower for the storage of state papers in the early 1320s is the first known instance of a function that the castle was to serve until the mid-nineteenth century.[15] Edward II also appears to have begun, or formalised, the tradition whereby kings and queens spent the night at the Tower before processing to their coronations, last observed in 1558.[16]

Edward III (1327–77) to 1485

The most important building work undertaken in this period was the creation of the riverside wharf, separated by a narrow moat from the outer curtain. This had its origins in the thirteenth century and by the 1320s had extended as far east as the Byward Tower, but in 1339, spurred on by the demands of the French war, it was extended eastwards as far as St Thomas's Tower, and further still in 1360 and in 1369. Meanwhile, the Cradle Tower – a private water gate – had been built in the years 1348–55, and the superstructure of the Bloody Tower shortly after 1360.

Since the early nineteenth century Edward III has also been credited with building the large courtyard structure attached to the east side of the White Tower (destroyed in 1879: figs 127, 139, 159),[17] although the building is first recorded only in 1597[18] and its origins are uncertain. Domestic buildings were also im-

6 View of the castle as it might have looked *circa* 1320, following the completion of the major expansion begun in 1272. The White Tower and the Inmost Ward and royal lodgings to the south (right) were now surrounded by two curtain walls and the moat, which, although drained, survives today. In the foreground is the complicated Western Entrance and beside it the first stages of the Tower wharf.

proved, including the Great Hall, remodelled in 1336–7. The constable's lodgings (on the site now occupied by the Queen's House) were rebuilt. Within the White Tower, new doors were provided for the basement doorway at some stage shortly after 1346.

In the 1360s the Wardrobe was again subdivided to create the Great Wardrobe, which set up elsewhere, and the Privy Wardrobe, which retained a presence at the Tower and made use of several parts of the royal lodgings, including St Thomas's Tower. During the fifteenth century further changes were made to the Tower's institutions. The last Keeper of the Privy Wardrobe appeared in 1405, and some of his functions were assumed by the 'keeper of the King's Armour in the Tower'. After 1414 the rest were entrusted to the 'Master of guns and of the ordnance', a position that increased in importance with that of firearms, and whose requirements and personnel were to have a major influence on the structural and functional history of the castle until 1855. Major building works

were confined to the creation of additional defences on Tower Hill (the Bulwark) under Edward IV (1471–83) and the south-facing turret and postern beside the Byward Tower (fig. 7).

1485–1642

Under Henry VII (1485–1509), in the years 1488–90, the White Tower was provided with the existing second floor and roof, and in 1508 a new store was built against its south front for the use of the Jewel House, an institution separated off from the Privy Wardrobe in the middle of the previous century. In 1502 the king added a new turret beside the Cradle Tower, and in 1506 a gallery crowning the wall between the Lanthorn and Salt towers, overlooking a new garden. These were the last improvements to the royal lodgings with a view to anything but very brief use for particular occasions.

Major repairs to the castle were begun in 1532, extended and accelerated a year later to prepare for the

7 View of the Tower of London *circa* 1550, after the completion of major works under Henry VIII. The White Tower's roofs, rebuilt at a higher level in the 1490s, now covered an additional top floor, and its turrets had received the familiar ogival caps. To the north of the White Tower stands the Long House of Ordnance, a munitions store built in the years 1545–7, and the chapel of St Peter ad Vincula, as rebuilt in 1512. The wharf had been extended along the entire length of the castle's river frontage in the late fourteenth century.

pre-coronation visit of Anne Boleyn: substantial work was done to the White Tower's roof and parapets and the existing ogival caps added to the turrets; St Thomas's Tower was re-roofed and partly reconstructed. The chapel of St Peter ad Vincula was rebuilt in 1519–20, and from 1532 a new Wardrobe storehouse linked the Wardrobe and Broad Arrow towers. In the years 1545–7 the stores and administration of the Ordnance Office were rehoused in a vast building to the north of the White Tower, which survived until 1688. In 1540 a house (today the Queen's House) was built for the lieutenant, a position to which constables had occasionally delegated duties since the twelfth century and regularly did so from the sixteenth, particularly those relating to the custody of state prisoners.

Only modest additions were made during the second half of the century. New workshops, scattered across the castle, were provided for the Mint, and the White Tower was fitted out in the years 1568–70 and the 1590s for the storage of records and gunpowder,

the latter involving major repairs to the top floor, implemented in 1605 under James I (1603–25).[19] The first known reports of guided tours of the castle, and of displays of weapons arranged for visitors, date from the last decades of the sixteenth century.

By 1603 the royal lodgings, last and very briefly used that year, were in such poor condition that the Great Hall was given a temporary roof to accommodate the new king's pre-coronation visit. In the next reign (Charles I: 1625–49) most of the medieval window architraves to the White Tower were renewed (1637–8), the building newly whitewashed, additional powder storage spaces fitted out within it, and doorways pierced in its north side for easier loading.

1642–1855

During the Civil War (1642–51) the Tower was held, with London, by Parliament. Ambitious refortification schemes considered after the Restoration (1660) in the end led only to the revetment of the Tower

9

moat. The dangers of storing vast quantities of powder in the White Tower, emphasised by the Great Fire of 1666, led to the removal, except for the eastern annexe, of the buildings attached to it. Amongst these was the temporary home of the re-created Crown Jewels, which were moved to the Martin Tower in 1669, under the control of the Master of the Jewel House. The Wardrobe's presence at the Tower, briefly revived in 1660, ceased in 1685. Increasing needs for weapons storage space, however, prompted the creation of what came to be known as the New Armouries building, in the south-east corner of the Inner Ward, in 1663–4. In 1688–9 the gigantic Grand Storehouse replaced the decaying Tudor buildings to the north of the White Tower, although in the event, thanks to the creation of new Ordnance stores further afield, its contents were arranged as much for display as any practical purpose. Meanwhile, reorganisation of the army and the Tower garrison had led, in 1669, to the creation of the castle's first purpose-built barracks.[20] Further major building works followed only in the years 1774–92, with the creation of storehouses and offices that obliterated the Lanthorn Tower, a stretch of medieval curtain wall, and remnants of the royal lodgings, which included the shell of the Great Hall.

The first half of the nineteenth century saw the start of the long exodus of the Tower's historic institutions, beginning in 1810 with the removal of the Mint. The Menagerie followed in 1835; the decision to move the Record Office was made in 1838, while the Ordnance Survey headquarters departed in 1841. Meanwhile, the decline in the Tower's defensive capacity was hastened with the draining of the moat in the years 1843–5, although some rearming followed in the 1850s and '60s. A continued military presence, however, was reaffirmed by the replacement of the Grand Storehouse, burnt in 1841, by the gigantic Waterloo Barracks. The Ordnance Office, its shortcomings revealed in the Crimean War, was dissolved in 1855 and its duties transferred to the War Office, which delegated the charge of its collections in 1892 to the newly formed Tower Armouries.

1855–2000

In the second half of the nineteenth century the administrative and military value of the Tower further diminished as its status as a great national icon and tourist attraction increased. The demise of the Board of Ordnance and increased use of storage and administrative facilities elsewhere led to a gradual withdrawal of these functions from the castle; in 1856 the Record Office too departed. Prompted by public and aesthetic interest in the Middle Ages and their legacy, the castle was soon undergoing a vigorous programme of 're-medievalisation', under the architect Anthony Salvin and, after 1878, Sir John Taylor. The vast complex of Ordnance buildings on the south side of the castle was demolished and the Lanthorn Tower and its adjacent curtain reconstructed: mutilated and built-over medieval structures were exposed and refaced, and others destroyed.[21]

In 1902 control of the Tower's fabric, and two years later its collections, was transferred from the War Office to the Office of Works. Ever increasing space and effort were now given to satisfying visitors: the Crown Jewels were rehoused in the Wakefield Tower in 1867, again in 1967 in the Waterloo Barracks, and by the present Jewel House in 1994. From the 1860s an increasing area of the White Tower had been opened to visitors, after 1892 under the direction of the newly constituted Tower Armouries: the re-display of 1913–16, extending throughout the building, remained until the 1960s. Reconstituted in 1993 as the Royal Armouries, it was their initiative in the 1990s to renew entirely their displays in the White Tower that provided the opportunity for archaeological recording and analysis, around which the present study is based.[22]

PART I

Before the White Tower

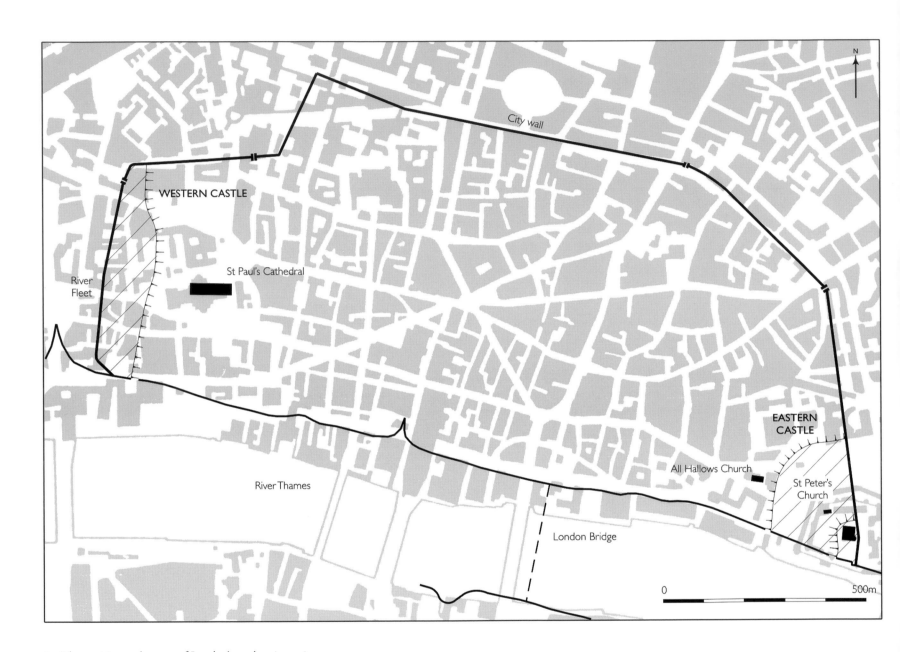

8   The position and extent of London's castles *circa* 1080.

CHAPTER ONE

London's Early Castles and the Context of their Creation

EDWARD IMPEY

The White Tower, defining architectural symbol of the Norman Conquest, was begun as much as twenty years after that event. Since the Conquest itself, however, there had been a castle on its future site, and another, precursor to Baynard's and Mountfichet's, at the opposite, western end of the city. Their creation, bound up in the political and military events of 1066–7, is also the opening chapter of the White Tower's history, for their location, form and status were all to have a bearing on its siting, and the need for its creation.

This chapter describes the aspects of London's topography on the eve of the Conquest that were to influence the siting of the early castles and summarises the historical sources bearing on their creation and the city's submission in 1066. It then discusses the reasons behind the siting of the early castles and offers an interpretation of their layout and defences, concentrating in particular on those of the early castle on the Tower site. Finally, it considers the reasons behind the Conqueror's creation of a great tower in London, for the choice of the eastern castle for its construction, and for the positioning of the new building within it.

THE TOWER SITE: LAND USE AND TOPOGRAPHY TO 1066

The Roman City and its Defences

The first Roman settlement on the site of London, probably established in the very earliest days of the occupation, had become a thriving city by the time of Boudicca's revolt in AD 60 or 61.[1] Known as *Londinium* at least as early as AD 70, by the early second century it had a forum, a vast basilica, an amphitheatre, public baths and, to the north-west, what is referred to today as the Cripplegate fort.[2] The core of the occupied area lay near the basilica (straddling modern Gracechurch Street), crossed by a road leading northwards from the bridge and by an east–west route to Newgate. Roughly parallel with this to the south, a second major route, less well understood, ran from Ludgate to beyond the bridge, perhaps extending eastwards over the Tower site. By the second half of the second century, however, the occupied area clearly had been extended over that of the future castle, and a large stone building had been erected on a site beside and under the White Tower.[3] But it was with the construction of the city wall, datable on archaeological grounds to AD 190–220,[4] that the enduring topography of the Tower's site really began.

The first walls were on the landward side only, but within the period AD 255–70 they were extended along the river's edge.[5] In the middle of the fourth century the land wall, and perhaps also the river wall, was reinforced by u-shaped bastions built against its outer face.[6] Meanwhile, at some stage shortly after AD 350 a basilican building, apparently similar in plan to the church of Santa Tecla in Milan, and perhaps equally enormous, was put up to the north of the future Tower Hill, between modern Pepys Street and Trinity Square.[7]

In the late fourth century the riverside defences at the extreme east end of the Roman city, close to the position of the existing Lanthorn Tower, were radically altered: a massive wall some 3.2 m thick was put up approximately 4 m south of the existing one, then still evidently in good condition, but which it presumably replaced. About 14.5 m west of the third-century north–south landward wall it turned north to connect with the earlier riverside wall, creating a fortified projection at the corner of the city walls.[8] Coin evidence securely dates its construction to a period after 388, making it the latest known Roman defensive wall in Britain.[9] The exact purpose of the remodelling is unknown, but the projection could have accommodated a west-facing postern gate in the angle where the new wall returned north, or have provided a platform for catapults commanding the approaches by the river and along its edge.[10]

Anglo-Saxon London

Romano-British town life in anything like recognisable form seems to have ended in London by the middle of the fifth century AD. From then until the early seventh century the written sources tell us nothing, other than the tradition recorded in the *Anglo-Saxon Chronicle* that the defeated Britons took refuge within the walls in 457;[11] archaeological evidence, meanwhile, shows that much of the walled area was under cultivation.[12] Yet by 600 the East Saxon kings had established a power base in the vicinity, and in 604 London's renewed significance was confirmed by the foundation of the bishopric,[13] while Bede refers to the city at that time (although possibly in his own time, *circa* 720) as the capital of the East Saxons and an '*emporium* of many people coming by land and sea'.[14] There are indications of a port at London in the 670s;[15] coins were minted there under Offa (757–96) and Coenwulf (796–821), and from the reign of Egbert (802–39) began to bear the city's name. Since the early 1980s, however, it has been realised that the centre of commerce and population lay to the west, along the course of the Strand, an interpretation recently reinforced by the discovery of a gold coin of Coenwulf inscribed DE VICO LUNDONIAE.[16] As a consequence, the cathedral, probably established on its present site in 604[17] – although more certainly so from the time of Bishop Erkenwald, 675–91[18] – is the only known development of this period that was to have a bearing on the character of the intramural area in 1066: the church of All Hallows, immediately to the north-west of the Tower site, once thought to date from as early as the time of Erkenwald,[19] is now considered to be of eleventh-century origin.[20] Whether there was a royal palace in the city in the seventh century is not clear, but if so it probably lay to the north of St Paul's, rather than, as once thought, in the Cripplegate area.[21]

Activity and population returned to the walled area after King Alfred's refortification of the city, now thought to be in his hands from 883, and the reorganisation of its interior in 886, perhaps in response to a renewal of the Viking threat in the previous year.[22] The reconstruction of the bridge and the fortification of a bridgehead at its south end may also date to his reign,[23] although there can be no certainty of their existence much before 1014.[24] Aethelred, the Mercian nobleman to whom Alfred entrusted the city, may have had a base in the area of St Mary Aldermanbury, outside the east gate of the Cripplegate fort and close to the Roman amphitheatre: certainly, his name came to be associated with a riverside landing-place directly to the south.[25] From at least the early eleventh century, however, a palace does seem, once again, to have existed within the city – close to the wall to the north of St Paul's.[26] To what extent a regular grid of streets was established under Alfred, still less whether it extended over the Tower site, remains unclear.[27]

The Tower Site on the Eve of the Conquest

In spite of the important hypotheses put forward by Jeremy Haslam in the 1980s,[28] the geography and administrative arrangements of the city's south-eastern quarter on the eve of the Conquest remain poorly understood. With regard to its churches, all that can be said with any confidence is that All Hallows was established in or by the early eleventh century, and that St Mary and St Peter ad Vincula were probably in existence by or soon after *circa* 1050.[29] If, as is by no means certain, the boundaries of the city parishes were sufficiently well defined by 1066, the Tower site would have lain within St Peter's; possibly this extended, as Haslam suggested, over an area to the east of the city wall,[30] although twelfth-century disputes between the Tower's *custos*, its priests and Holy Trinity Aldgate indicate that this more probably belonged to the parish of St Botolph's, whose property the priory had absorbed.[31] Nothing is known of the domestic or commercial occupation of the site, while the loss or absence of a London Domesday deprives us of any information of the kind available, for example, for Lincoln, York and Shrewsbury as to the number of houses or households swept away to create the early castle.[32] The presence of the churches, however, suggests that the area was inhabited and that some clearance must have been required, if not for the small 'campaign' castle of 1066 then surely for the much larger outer bailey that soon accompanied it (see below, pp. 20–2; fig. 9).

Churches apart, the most prominent landmarks were presumably the Roman walls, which, certainly on the landward side, had been kept in repair since the ninth century. Whether the river wall was still functional is less clear. In describing London as protected 'on the north by walls, on the south side by the river', the 'Song of the Battle of Hastings' (*Carmen de Hastingae proelio*: below) may imply that it had gone.[33] William Fitz Stephen, about seventy years later, wrote that the wall had been undermined by the river,[34] a process confirmed at its far western end by excavation, although both there and again near Upper Thames Street it had been deliberately toppled northwards, not, as he put it, 'washed away',[35] while stratigraphy suggests that this occurred after the Conquest.[36] On balance, there is no need to assume that the river wall in the Tower area, massively rebuilt after AD 388, was unusable in 1066, while its survival in some form is indicated by the reuse of its footings in the mid-thirteenth century. Whether other Roman remains were visible in 1066 is unknown, although massive Roman foundations were certainly encountered in digging the early castle's ditches and the foundations of the White Tower.[37] Excavations in 1963–4, however, appear to have revealed a late Saxon ditch running north-west to south-east across the Parade Ground to the north-west of the White Tower,[38] later intersected almost at right angles by the first defences of the Norman castle (below). A continuation of the same ditch further north, up to 5 m deep, has been identified in engineers' drawings of 1845, showing how the footings of the Waterloo Barracks were to be built up from the solid ground beneath its fill.[39] The full extent and purpose of the ditch remain entirely unknown. Its alignment at 45° to the Roman walls suggests that it was not part of a defensive complex that made use of them, unlike the early Norman castle, but a defensive purpose of some sort remains a possibility, and it would have been a prominent feature at the time of the Conquest. Nevertheless, it seems to have had no influence on the form or siting of the early castle on the Tower site.

THE EARLY CASTLES: THE CONTEXT OF THEIR CREATION

The Sources

Just as William the Conqueror's possession of London secured his possession of England, so the building of his London castles secured the possession of the city. The means by which he achieved this, and the events immediately leading up to it, have not so far, perhaps, been considered by historians in sufficient detail: what follows is an attempt to do so.

Consideration of these events sheds light on William's motivation for building castles in the first place, the timing and relative timing of their foundation, and, in parallel with the city's topography, where he chose to site them – and so ultimately on the inception and siting of the White Tower.

The London part of the campaign is known from a range of written sources, of which the most important are contemporary or near-contemporary: the *Carmen de Hastingae proelio* ('Song of the Battle of Hastings') by Guy of Amiens;[40] the *Gesta Normannorum ducum* ('Deeds of the Dukes of the Normans') by William of Jumièges;[41] the *Gesta Guillelmi* ('Deeds of William') by William of Poitiers;[42] and the various versions of the *Anglo-Saxon Chronicle*, in particular the 'D' or 'Worcester' narrative.[43] In addition to the literary material, there is the evidence contained in the Domesday Book of the Normans' routes across the country, although this is less convincing than proposed by Francis Baring in 1909,[44] and there are also fragments of archaeological evidence that need to be considered (below, p. 18). The most famous and vivid source for events preceding the Conquest and for the Battle of Hastings, the Bayeux Tapestry, does not cover the capture of London, although it may have done so when complete.[45]

The *Carmen*, now firmly attributed to Guy, Bishop of Amiens (1058–74/5), and written in 1068,[46] is the earliest of the three main 'French' sources and gives the fullest account of events at London. According to this, having received the submission of Winchester at Dover, William marched on London, laying waste to the country as he went. The 'obstinate men who had been defeated in battle', having retreated to the city, had meanwhile consecrated Edgar Aetheling as king.[47] Hearing of this, William 'surrounded the walls on the left side [i.e., the north] with encampments, set close together, and kept the enemy alert for battle'.[48] He then established himself at the palace or hall (*aula*) of Westminster, and the siege of London began in earnest. Guy tells us that:

> To overthrow the city he built siege engines (*moles*) and made battering rams with horns of iron as well as machines for mining. Then he thundered forth menaces and threatened punishment and war. He vowed that, given the chance, he would raze the walls, level the bastions, and reduce the high tower to rubble.[49]

William also, it seems, either at the same time as or immediately following the actual assault, offered terms to the Londoners' leader, Ansgar, who, persuaded, offered his compatriots a bleak summary of their situation:

> You see the walls assailed by powerful assaults and encompassed by countless disasters. The siege engine that has been erected overtops the bastions. The walls, split by the blows of its rocks, are falling down. From the many breaches ruin threatens on every side.[50]

Having set the scene, Ansgar persuaded the Londoners to buy time by feigned cooperation, but the messenger was taken in by William's promises, which the Londoners in turn accepted. They then proceeded to Westminster, with Edgar Aetheling, to offer their submission. The new king's coronation followed a few days later, on 25 December.

William of Jumièges, in the *Gesta Normannorum ducum*, gives only the briefest account of events between Hastings and the duke's arrival: 'he came to a first stop at Wallingford', and

> From there he moved on to London, where upon entering the city some scouts, sent ahead, found many rebels determined to offer every possible resistance. Fighting followed immediately and thus London was plunged into mourning for the loss of her sons and citizens. When the Londoners finally realised they could resist no longer, they gave hostages and surrendered themselves and all they possessed to the most noble conqueror and hereditary lord.[51]

The account was written, perhaps at the king's request, in the years 1067–70.[52] It was subsequently much revised and extended, notably by Orderic and Robert of Torigny, although the passage concerning London is original. For the events of the Conquest William of Jumièges seems to have relied on oral reports available as events were still unfolding,[53] and for events at London on an eyewitness report.[54]

William of Poitiers, a Norman and former knight, was among the Conqueror's chaplains, and although not with him during the campaign of 1066, is variously considered to have relied on eyewitness accounts and on William of Jumièges.[55] His work was written between 1071 and 1077.[56] The first activity he reports in the environs of the city was an attack on what must have been the Southwark bridgehead and the burning of houses outside the defences.[57] Confusingly, he then claims that the duke 'crossed the river by a ford and bridge' *before* arriving at Wallingford, but here he was clearly wrong, as is shown by the Domesday evidence: in fact, he approached Wallingford from the west, without yet having crossed the river at all.[58] It was there that William received the homage of Stigand, Archbishop of Canterbury, and he then advanced, by a roundabout route, to take up 'a position near London, where he heard that they most often held their meetings',[59] by which the author presumably meant either the shire *mootstow* at 'Oswulf's stone' (in the modern Park Lane area),[60] or Westminster itself, as Guy of Amiens believed. Once in sight of the city, he says, its chief men came out and submitted and implored the duke to take the crown. Following a debate with his knights, William agreed, in the hope 'above all that once he had begun to reign, any rebels would be less ready to challenge him and more easily put down'. His next action, of crucial importance in the present context, was to send 'men ahead to London to build a fortress in the city and make many preparations for royal dignity, while he himself remained in the neighbourhood'. By then, William of

Poitiers tells us, 'all opposition was so remote that he could, if he wished, spend his time in hunting and falconry'.[61] The coronation then duly took place, and the author embarks on a eulogy, ending with the statement that 'all the first acts of his reign were righteous'.[62] The next sentence, however, adds:

> Leaving London, he spent a few days in the nearby place of Barking [*Bercing*], while fortifications were being completed in the city as a defence against the inconstancy of the numerous and hostile inhabitants. For he saw that it was of the first importance to constrain the Londoners strictly. It was there that Edwin and Morcar came to submit to him.[63]

The *Anglo-Saxon Chronicle* version 'C' ends with the Battle of Stamford Bridge,[64] while 'E' makes no reference to London at all. The 'Worcester' or 'D' manuscript tells us that William left Hastings, 'went inland and ravaged all the region until he came to Berkhamsted', where Aldred, Archbishop of York, Edgar, Edwin and Morcar 'and all the chief men of London' came and submitted to him.[65]

Of the slightly later sources, the most important is the lively 323-line account of the Norman Conquest written *circa* 1100 by Baudri, a monk of Bourgueil in Touraine, for King William's daughter, wife of the Count of Flanders.[66] Called *Adelae Comitissae* ('To the Countess Adela'), this ends with the capture of a city that, although unnamed, he must have intended to be taken for London: he describes the men 'high on the towers' sighting the Norman army, the hasty and inadequate attempt to man 'what fortifications there were', the acceptance of the duke's terms and his welcome into the city.[67] Although Baudri's credibility is not strengthened by his placing of the city's capitulation on the day after Hastings, the poem is now considered to be a historical source of real value, although the London events are probably based on the *Carmen*.[68] John of Worcester, writing at about the same time, tells us that the Londoners, wanting to make the Aetheling king, prepared to fight the Normans, while 'Earl William laid waste Sussex, Kent, Hampshire, Middlesex and Hertfordshire, and kept on slaying men until he came to the township called Berkhamsted', where Edwin, Morcar and others surrendered to him: in mentioning Berkhamsted he follows the *Anglo-Saxon Chronicle*, but for the itinerary he is the only early authority.[69]

Best known amongst the twelfth-century sources is the *Historia ecclesiastica* of Orderic Vitalis, written at the Norman abbey of St Evroul in the 1120s. Orderic's version of events omits William's order to prepare a fortification in the city before his coronation, but reproduces William of Poitiers' wording concerning the completion of 'fortifications' (*firmamenta*) in the city whilst at, or on the way to, Barking.[70] Although written between 1114 and 1120, the *Brevis relatio de*

Guillelmo nobilissimo comite Normannorum ('Brief Account of the Most Noble William, Count of the Normans') is an important source for the Hastings campaign, but tells us only that William made for London after Hastings and that there the English submitted.[71] William of Malmesbury's *Gesta regum anglorum*, of the 1120s, describes only how, on his arrival in London, 'the citizens . . . burst out in waves from every gate to welcome him';[72] Henry of Huntingdon's *Historia anglorum* ('History of the English People'), written in the 1130s, relates merely that William 'was received peacefully'.[73] None of the remaining twelfth-century accounts of the campaign, by Eadmer, Geoffroi Gaimar, Simeon of Durham and Wace, provides any independent or additional information on the capture of London.[74]

The Capture of London and the Origins of its Castles

The importance of London, both as a threat and as a future power base, must have been clear to the Conqueror before the invasion. The city's political importance had been clearly demonstrated in the not too distant past, particularly in the succession crises of 1013–16, which had seen Edmund Ironside chosen as king by the Londoners under siege by Cnut.[75] The duke is also likely to have been aware, at least in general terms, of its strategic importance, ensured by the convergence at the river crossing of the roads from Yorkshire, East Anglia and the Midlands, from where they led to Dover and the south-coast ports and thus to the Continent.[76] The city's concentration of wealth and population, too, was well known. William of Poitiers relates that London 'abounds in a large population famous for their military qualities',[77] and Guy of Amiens that it was 'a most spacious city, full of evil inhabitants, and richer than anywhere else in the kingdom'.[78] That the citizens were likely to oppose William after Hastings must have been obvious from the headlong flight to London of his surviving opponents, if from nothing else. Thus although aware of the importance of Winchester,[79] it was London, as William of Jumièges explains,[80] that was the Conqueror's ultimate goal; the long, menacing approach was a deliberate technique – and one that he had used three years earlier at Le Mans.[81]

William of Jumièges and William of Poitiers are in agreement that the immediate descent on London was made from Wallingford. Baring traced the route to Wallingford from Hastings and accepted it as the crossing point,[82] and although Domesday reveals no waste in an area where the Normans clearly paused for several days,[83] its place in the Normans' itinerary remains unchallenged. Important differences between the written accounts, however, emerge as the city is encountered. Actual hostilities at London are mentioned by Guy of Amiens and William of Jumièges,

and a siege only by Guy, but neither the *Anglo-Saxon Chronicle* nor John of Worcester records these events, while William of Poitiers presents an entirely peaceful handover. Barking is mentioned only by William of Poitiers (*Bercing*), while among the early sources Berkhamsted is introduced only in the *Anglo-Saxon Chronicle* (*Beorh ham stede*) and by John of Worcester (*Beorhchamstede*). William of Poitiers' is the only account to mention castle building in London. Historians have therefore generally adopted a synthetic acceptance and rejection of sources to produce a coherent narrative, essentially as follows: the duke marched from Wallingford to Berkhamsted, received the city's peaceful submission, and ordered the preparation of his coronation and of a fortress in London; once crowned, he retired to Barking in Essex while the fortress (or fortresses) was being completed.[84] This, however, evades a number of important questions with a bearing on the origins of London's castles.

The first of these concerns the point of departure for the immediate descent on London. William of Poitiers and Guy of Amiens lead us to believe that the duke took up a position to the west of the city, and the former that he received the submission of the city's leaders 'as he came in sight of' it. The *Anglo-Saxon Chronicle*, however, followed by John of Worcester, tells us that the duke settled at Berkhamsted before descending on London and took there the submission of its 'chief men'. Fortunately, these itineraries are not fundamentally incompatible if we accept that the French sources simply omitted or were ignorant of the Berkhamsted incident, while its very definite mention in the much briefer *Chronicle* entry, by an author to whom English geography would have been better known and more important, must carry more weight.

Assuming, then, that a place called Berkhamsted was involved, there remains the question of which of the two Berkhamsteds (Great or Little, both in Hertfordshire) it was. Francis Baring identified it as Little rather than Great Berkhamsted, which lies 25 miles further east.[85] For several reasons, however, this long-accepted interpretation[86] can now be considered implausible: first, not only would such a greatly extended and circuitous approach to Little Berkhamsted have been unnecessary after the submission at Wallingford, but a much more direct one to Great Berkhamsted – up the Icknield Way and along Akeman Street eastwards through the Chilterns – was easily available. Second, the submission of the English leaders at Great Berkhamsted a few days after that at Wallingford makes more sense than a submission several weeks later, as Baring's much longer route would have required. Finally, Great Berkhamsted was a borough and the seat of Edmer Atule, a major landholder and a thegn of King Harold,[87] and thus a place where a meeting might have been deliberately planned rather than improvised as the Norman and English parties converged. Finally, the obvious route to London from Great Berkhamsted, along Watling Street, would have ended in an approach from the west, and been consistent therefore with the accounts of William of Poitiers and Guy of Amiens. There need be little doubt, therefore, that Great Berkhamsted was the duke's first stopping point; that a 'submission' took place there (if not fully representative of the citizens' position); and that it was from there that he approached the city.

A second important question is whether there were any hostilities on arrival at or entry into London. A major objection, clearly, is the absence of any mention of conflict by William of Poitiers, who might be expected to have made the most of it, unless it was somehow to the duke's discredit. Another is simply that all sources imply the submission of the English in advance of the duke's arrival at its gates: arms, therefore, would have been taken up only by Londoners still not reconciled to defeat. Nevertheless, at least three factors suggest that the actual seizure of the city was more complicated than William of Poitiers or the *Chronicle* implies. Most important, of course, is the testimony to this effect of Guy of Amiens and William of Jumièges, which cannot simply be ignored. In addition, it is inherently likely that elements of the 'famously large and warlike' population of London, augmented by men who had encountered William in the field, aware of the duke's still-vulnerable position and within the security of its walls, would have been tempted to reject an agreement made by their leaders. Finally, a struggle in 1066 at least provides a plausible explanation for the dismembered skeletons buried under a cairn in the Fleet valley in the late eleventh century.[88] That there was a great set-piece siege, as indicated if not necessarily as described by Guy of Amiens, therefore remains a possibility, and certainly William was no stranger to siege warfare. Siege or not, however, both the *Carmen*'s story of complex negotiations and William of Jumièges' indication of fighting *within* the city suggest that the actual capitulation followed further resistance once the walls or gates had been forced.[89]

A final question, potentially with an important bearing on the Conqueror's future strategy for London's castles, is Guy of Amiens' reference to a 'high tower' (*elatam turrim*), in so far as it might suggest that the city already possessed some sort of citadel. This could be taken as a literal reference to a tower, and if so perhaps a church tower incorporated in the defences, as in the case of St Michael's tower in Oxford,[90] or an independent building, such as St George's tower, also in Oxford and now thought to be pre-Conquest.[91] The *turris* could also, as David Stocker has suggested, have been the late Roman work on the future site of the Tower,[92] or indeed some other Roman structure. More probably, though, the reference owes more to a preconception that formidable cities had

great towers – Guy's home town being no exception – than the existence of any such thing in Anglo-Saxon London.[93]

Of more immediate importance in the present context, however, is the sequence of events that followed and the identification of the point at which the city's early castles were created. William of Poitiers, the only source to mention the Conqueror's fortifications, tells us that his order 'to build a strongpoint [*munitio*] in the city' followed the submission of the Londoners, but preceded, and accompanied the preparations for, his coronation. The plausibility of this need not be doubted: creating a stronghold within the newly conquered city would have been a natural first act in consolidating his position, as it had been at Dover, and as was soon to be repeated at Winchester and elsewhere. Nor is there anything in other accounts, beyond omission, to suggest otherwise. In this, traditionally, has been seen the origin of the Tower of London.[94] Nevertheless, the story is complicated by the same author's statement that, after his coronation, the king 'retired to Barking while certain defensive positions [*firmamenta*] were being completed in the city'. The use of the plural suggests that although the strongpoint of the first initiative may have been among those being 'completed' after the coronation, in the immediate aftermath the Conqueror had ordered the creation of at least one more. As it happens, not only is the existence of a further castle by *circa* 1100, at the west end of the city, proven both by archaeological and documentary evidence, but there are also indications that both this and the early castle on the Tower site date from the campaign period: since the western castle took up the whole of the intramural area west of St Paul's (below), it is unlikely to post-date William's charter to the Londoners,[95] and was clearly in decay or being reduced in size by 1111; the castle on the Tower site, meanwhile, was exactly of the 'ringwork' type that might be expected during the primary consolidation of power (below, pp. 19, 20). That more than one metropolitan castle was created to consolidate the Norman hold on London in 1066–7, as implied by William of Poitiers, therefore seems highly likely. His narrative, however, also implies that one was established, if not completed, before the other, and if so the ease with which the eastern castle could have been created, compared with the effort required to lay out its vast western counterpart, would make it the best candidate. A feature of William of Poitiers' narrative, however, may in fact suggest that not only was there no 'second order', but that he was over-complicating the king's movements after the coronation. The feature in question is William I's alleged sojourn at Barking, for which a reason is neither given nor, beyond perhaps a desire to complete a symbolic encirclement of the city, easy to imagine.[96] Is it not more likely that the similarities between the names of the two places led William of Poitiers to identify the obscure Berkhamsted, rendered in the *Anglo-Saxon Chronicle* as *Beorh ham stede* but equally frequently at the time as *Beorcham*,[97] as Barking, much better known and much closer to London?[98] If so, it would explain why the author, who understood the duke to have approached London directly from Wallingford, had to place the 'Barking' incident *after* the coronation, and, requiring a reason for this, might state that it took place while the city was being secured. It would also explain why he had to place the submission of Edwin and Morcar, which the *Chronicle* places at Berkhamsted, after the coronation, and that of the 'chief men of London' before it. The foundation of both London fortresses might then have been a simultaneous action, taken, as would have been logical and expedient, immediately after the city's capture. The king's second rural sojourn, meanwhile, acknowledged by modern scholars in order to accommodate both the *Anglo-Saxon Chronicle* and William of Poitiers, need never have taken place at all. Instead, he could have remained at Westminster, where the Confessor's palace would have provided a more comfortable, dignified and appropriate position from which to supervise the completion of London's castles.

THE FORM AND SITING OF THE EARLY CASTLES

The Early Castle on the Tower Site

Siting

The first question concerns the choice of the general location of the early castle (fig. 8), for there were certainly alternatives. London could, for example, have been furnished with a castle occupying a central commanding site, as at Colchester, or it could have superseded the palace occupied by previous dynasties near St Paul's Cathedral. The placing of this castle at an extremity of the city, however, must have been linked to the placing of another at the other end, resulting from a deliberate intent to divide the internal threat in two and doubly reinforce the city's defences. This scheme was presumably William's own, in addition, probably, to the exact positioning of the individual castles, as it was at Saint-James de Beuvron (Manche) in 1064,[99] and at Exeter in 1068, where he 'selected a spot within the walls for the erection of a castle'.[100]

This is not to say that the early castle at the east end of London was necessarily that in which the White Tower was later built, and not another nearby, subsequently obliterated. Nevertheless, a site to the north or west is unlikely, since command of the river and landward approaches would have been seriously reduced. In addition, an initial site immediately *outside* the walls, as suggested by Braun in the 1930s[101] and a common arrangement at other towns,[102] is not supported by the literal sense of William of Poitiers'

account, and is more or less ruled out by the possession of the crucial extramural area in the early twelfth century by the English *Cnihtengild* rather than the king.[103] A location within the corner of the walled area would also have reproduced that of the castles or ducal residences at Avranches, Bayeux, Evreux[104] and Rouen, a factor that might be expected, either consciously or subconsciously, to have affected the Conqueror's decision. But the more immediate reasons for choosing a site in the angle of the city wall were no doubt those that had prompted this arrangement on the Continent and were to do so all over England in the months and years to follow – at Cambridge, Cardiff, Chichester, Exeter, Lincoln, Leicester, Rochester, Shrewsbury, Wallingford and Winchester: first, it offered a position within the town but without the vulnerability of envelopment; second, and of more immediate importance in the case of a city in a newly conquered land, was the simple fact that the right-angled junction of upstanding Roman walls offered a fortress half ready-made.

Layout and Defences

The most important evidence for the form of the first castle on the Tower site, within which the White Tower was implanted, was obtained by excavation in 1963–4, prior to the building of the underground Jewel Chamber.[105] So far, unfortunately, this has not been fully published.[106]

The crucial discovery was a ditch, encountered in four trenches, about 8 m across, 3.5 m deep and v-shaped in profile, running north-east to south-west across the Parade Ground to the north of the White Tower before turning southward just beyond the White Tower's north-west corner.[107] Another stretch of ditch was discovered in excavations in 1974–5 to the north of the Wakefield Tower, outside of, but roughly parallel to, the surviving thirteenth-century western wall of the Inmost Ward. The two ditches are on slightly different alignments,[108] but it has been suggested that the misalignment could have been intended to provide a gateway re-entrant (approximately on the site of the thirteenth-century Coldharbour Gate: see fig. 1), or, perhaps more convincingly, to avoid Roman remains encountered in this area.[109] But assuming that the ditches did join up, they would have defined an enclosure approximately 100 by 50 m in the angle of the Roman wall. Since the ditch revealed in 1974–5 had been regularly scoured up to *circa* 1200, the dating of the enclosure depends on pottery 'of 11th-century date' in the fill of the northern arm, and its origins are therefore uncertain, but on balance the excavator identified it as 'one of the garrison forts of 1067'.[110]

The known primary fortifications of the early castle thus comprised an enclosure of about half a hectare (1.25 acres), defended to the south and east by Roman

9 The defences of the early castle on the Tower site and related topographical details as they may have existed *circa* 1080. The inner bailey and the course of its defences are known or inferred from archaeological evidence and assumed to be those of 1066. Documentary evidence suggests that an outer bailey was created at the same time or very soon after, and that it covered an area more or less coextensive with what later became the intramural area of the Tower Liberties. Note that the courses of the Lorteburn (at least to the north of All Hallows), of Chicke Lane and of the streets to the north and west are those they are understood to have followed *circa* 1270, and that the plans of All Hallows and St Peter's are indicative only. The outer edge of the Tower's late thirteenth-century defences, the outer edge of the existing moat and the river's edge are shown for scale and orientation.

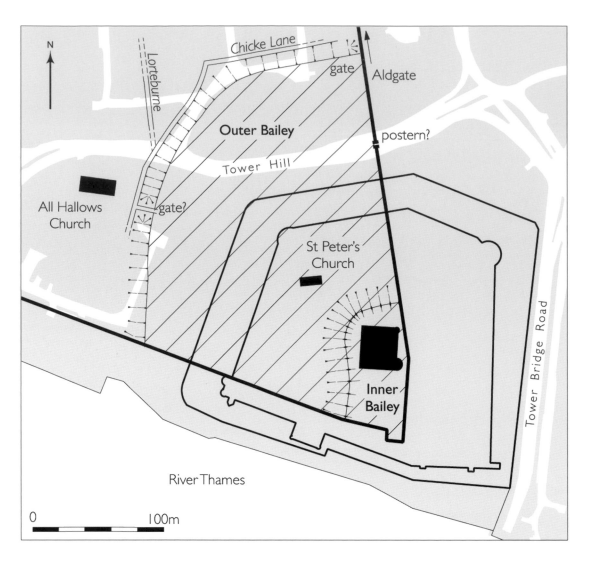

walls and on the north and west sides by a new rampart.[111] There must presumably have been a gate opening towards the town, although its site is unknown, and there is also likely to have been at least a postern opening through the Roman river wall.

As such, the early castle would have belonged to what has been identified as the most typical castle form of the Conquest period – the 'ringwork', an enclosure without a motte – of which 190 have been counted, among them William's castles at Exeter (1068) and Winchester (1067).[112] Many of these, however, subsequently acquired a motte, as perhaps at Winchester, or an outer bailey, as at Exeter. The creation of a motte within or associated with the 'ringwork' on the Tower site and its replacement by the White Tower therefore remains a remote possibility, although no hint of this has been discovered archaeologically. It does appear, however, that the 'ringwork' was accompanied by an outer bailey – perhaps contemporary, perhaps a little later, but certainly well before what has so far been understood as the first expansion of the castle in the late twelfth century.[113] The evidence for this is associated with the history and location of St Peter ad Vincula (fig. 9), which, as understood so far, was not included within the castle until the reign of Henry III. First, a reference of 1128–

34 to Dermanus (who is named in a slightly later document as 'the priest of St Peter's') as the 'priest of the Tower' (*sacerdos de Turre*)[114] not only tells us that the priest served the castle but also implies that his church lay within it, as does a description of the church in the late twelfth century, with reference to an event in 1154, at the 'king's chapel'.[115] Second, and more important, is the description of St Peter's church as 'of the bailey' ('Sancti Petri de Ballio') in 1157,[116] and third is its description as 'St Peter's in the bailey of the Tower', or close variations of the same, twice in 1237, once in 1239 and twice again in 1240.[117] In the past the word *ballium* as used here has been held to mean 'jurisdiction' or jurisdictional area rather than 'bailey' in the sense of a physically defined enclosure,[118] and the former was indeed the sense of the old French word from which it was adopted in the eleventh century. In the twelfth and thirteenth centuries the word *ballium* and its variant *ballivus* continued to be used as legal terms, but also in numerous contexts – including that of the Tower – where 'bailey' in the castellogical sense was certainly intended.[119] That this was the intended sense in naming and situating the chapel of St Peter, given the status of its priest and the physical implications of *in* and *infra*, must be the probability.

The existence of an early outer bailey at the Tower – and, importantly, that such an important feature could subsequently disappear from the urban landscape – is also supported by the existence of similar features and similar sequences elsewhere. An example is London itself, where the sites of Baynard's and Mountfichet's castles as they existed in the mid-twelfth century had once been included in an enormous intramural enclosure (below). Another is Nottingham, where the eleventh-century castle was flanked by a far larger bailey extending to the north and east.[120] At Rochester, it now seems that the area to the south of the existing castle (and roughly equal in size), known as the 'Boley' since at least the late thirteenth century and more recently 'Boley Hill', was at one stage a second outer bailey.[121] At Chester, the inner and outer baileys of the castle as they survived into recent centuries were surrounded by a 'Fee', coextensive with the area later known as Gloverstown, and which is also considered to have originated in a defensible outermost bailey.[122] More exact analogies are offered by Lincoln and Norwich. At the former, not only did the original castle extend over the entire area of the Roman upper city before shrinking to its present size in the twelfth century,[123] but it also bestowed the suffix 'in the bail' on the churches inside it – St Paul's, St Clement's and All Saints.[124] At Norwich, the core of the castle of 1067–70 was surrounded from the start by a vast area enclosed by a bank and a ditch up to 8 m wide and 3.5 m deep, taking in a pre-existing church still described at the time of its demolition in the sixteenth century as St Martin *in Balliva*.[125] The otherwise unexplained name of St Peter the Bailey at Oxford may also indicate the existence of an outer enclosure to the east of the castle, perhaps extending as far as New Inn Hall Street and St Ebbes, either abutting or taking in a part of the defended area of the pre-Conquest town.[126] As at the Tower, these outer enclosures were subsequently reabsorbed into the townscape – in London by the mid-twelfth century; at Rochester by the early 1480s; at Lincoln by the mid-twelfth century; at Nottingham under King John;[127] and at Norwich by a deliberate act in 1345.[128] In all these cases the later castle consisted of what had been the nucleus of the early defensive complex, massively reinforced before and after the bailey's abandonment.[129]

Finally, the existence of an early outer bailey at the Tower is supported by the hitherto rather inconvenient and puzzling mention of the 'small castle that was Ravengar's' ('parvum castellum quod fuit Ravengeri') when it was granted by the Empress Matilda to Geoffrey II de Mandeville, along with the custody of the Tower (*turris*), in 1141.[130] Of Ravengar himself we know only that he had been a minor landholder in Essex at some stage before Domesday,[131] but he could, as Colvin and Brown suggested, have been the castle's custodian in the years immediately after the Conquest,[132] and further elucidation of his career and connections might shed light on the precise functions and governance of the early castle. But for present purposes it is the identification and differentiation of the 'tower' and the 'small castle', and particularly the description of the latter, that is important. As Round pointed out in 1892,[133] the terms *turris* and *castellum* were used in the mid-twelfth century to describe towers and their attendant baileys, as they were, in various ways, with reference to Arques (1123),[134] Caen (1118),[135] Colchester (1101)[136] and Gloucester (1137 and 1155).[137] *Castellum* was used in the same sense with reference to Hereford and Worcester, although in these cases the bailey was accompanied by a motte (*mota*), not a tower:[138] *castellum* in the sense of bailey was also the intended meaning of *chastel* when used with reference to Dublin, Carlisle and Appleby, just as *dungon* took the place of *turris*.[139] There can be little doubt, therefore, that the *castellum* of 1141 (and what can only have been the same entity, described in a second charter of the same year as *subtus* the Tower of London,[140] and in near-identical terms in a charter of Stephen)[141] was the primary enclosure in which the White Tower stood. While this might be taken as an indication that this was in fact the castle's only bailey, or that Ravengar's *castellum* was a distinct fortification,[142] the use of *parva* is more likely to have been used to distinguish it from a larger bailey adjoining it. The same words were used to describe what was probably a similar arrangement in Robert of Torigny's description of the capture of the castle at Torigny-sur-Vire (Manche) except for the 'tower and small castle which is around it' ('turrem et parvum castellum circa eam'),[143] likely to have been a small *chemise* or curtain wall at the foot of the tower, a typical twelfth-century configuration.

If the existence of an outer bailey is accepted, important questions remain as to its extent, the form of its defences, its date and its longevity. With regard to the first, we know that it was large enough to take in St Peter's, so that its northern rampart must at the very least have followed the same route as the existing thirteenth-century inner curtain, although this would have created only a narrow and improbable-looking enclosure to the north of the late twelfth-century rampart. Evidence, however, not only of its greater size, but also of its actual boundaries, is contained in a description of the boundary of the Soke of Aldgate purporting to be that confirmed by Queen Matilda, but which, although compiled in the fifteenth century, clearly preserves earlier elements.[144] According to this, the boundary ran 'from the gate of Aldgate down to the gate of the bailey of the Tower which is called *Cungate*, and along the whole length of the lane called Chicke Lane towards Barking church as far as the cemetery',[145] before threading its way northwards back to the gate. Since the Cungate led into the bailey, and was the point at which the boundary turned westwards from the city wall along Chicke Lane, the lane must have followed the boundary between the Soke and the bailey; and since Chicke Lane ran westwards across the north end of (what became) Tower Hill before turning south towards the cemetery,[146] the bailey must have been almost precisely coextensive with the intramural area of the Tower Liberties, loosely defined in writing as early as 1382,[147] and which the Haiward and Gascoyne plan of 1597 so clearly delineates (see fig. 127). This interpretation is also at least consistent with the probable course of the Lorteburn, a stream that joined the Thames at the point marked today by Tower Dock,[148] and which could therefore have served as a moat reinforcing the western rampart of the bailey.

The Cungate, meanwhile, must have been a gate or postern hard against the Roman wall, presumably spanning what had been an intramural street, standing approximately where the post-medieval Liberty boundary met the wall, and therefore in or to the south of the yard behind numbers 8–10 and 42–3 Coopers Row, where a stretch of Roman wall in fact survives.[149] The otherwise rather puzzling opening through the Roman wall to the north of the thirteenth-century postern, marked on the plan of 1667 of the Tower and Liberties and which then stood 'in the manner of an arch thro' which carts must pass', may conceivably have been created to provide direct access to the outer bailey from the extramural area.[150]

In total, the early castle would therefore have covered an area of about 4 hectares (9.8 acres) – large, but well within the range of the urban castles to which it has already been compared: Chester covering 3.7 hectares (9 acres), Lincoln 15 hectares (37 acres), Nottingham 4.5 hectares (11.1 acres) and Norwich 5 hectares (12.3 acres), or with William's own foundation of the early 1060s at Caen, which covered more than 5 hectares (12.3 acres).[151]

With regard to its origins, it is possible that the outer bailey post-dated the White Tower, perhaps dating from as late as 1128–34, when its existence is first inferred. Conceivably, this was the *weall* that the *Anglo-Saxon Chronicle* tells us was built 'around the Tower' at such grievous cost in 1097, although this is at least equally likely to have been a reinforcement either of an outer bailey already in existence or of the inner enclosure.[152] An origin much sooner after the Conquest or during the process itself is more likely, however, if only because this is the case with most of the other early outer baileys, while carving out such a large area of the city much after William's confirmation of the citizens' rights and privileges, usually dated to very early in the reign,[153] would have been difficult and might be expected to have left some trace in the historical record. Whether the outer bailey was con-

temporary with the 'ringwork' is unclear, but the huge undertaking of creating it, even if relatively lightly defended, is more likely to have followed than accompanied the building of the 'campaign' castle of 1066.

How long the outer bailey may have survived is, of course, unknown. While it could have remained intact after the extension and reinforcement of the inner defences in the 1190s, it is unlikely to have existed much longer as a defensible entity. The fact that the 'new works' of 1238 needed to be protected by a palisade[154] suggests that they were vulnerable to attack, while the compensation paid out for loss and damage caused by the works (although most of this probably related to the extramural area) implies that private rights had already encroached on the bailey area.[155] If not, the definitive loss of the early outer bailey, or at least its defensive purpose and capacity, would almost certainly have followed the refortification and extension of the castle's inner kernel, for which these works were undertaken, in 1241:[156] the suffix *infra ballio* that was attached to St Peter's in 1242 must in this case have become part of its name rather than used as a literal description, as indeed it may have been for several decades.[157] But while the defences of the outer bailey disappeared and its physical integration with the castle was lost, the approximate definition of its boundaries and a close administrative relationship with the Tower lived on in the Tower Liberties, a development that neatly mirrors those at Norwich, Chester and elsewhere.

In conclusion, it can be suggested that the earliest castle on the tower site consisted of an earthwork fortification of 'ringwork' type created to reinforce the Conqueror's grip on London in 1066. To this was soon added a vast outer bailey approximately coextensive with the intramural Liberties, and with a gate – in addition presumably to one facing west – at its northeast corner. It was into this two-part castle that, a few years later, the White Tower was to be implanted.

The Western Castle

The Royal Castle

The creation of a second castle in London during the Conquest period has been referred to above, but its precise location, extent and early history, which had a bearing on the future of the eastern castle and its selection for the building of the White Tower, remain to be discussed (fig. 10). So too does the origin, siting and form of the castles that succeeded it, Mountfichet's and Baynard's, whose existence formed such a crucial part of London's townscape during the first century of the White Tower's existence.

The evidence for the early castle's extent is almost entirely archaeological, consisting of a north–south ditch, of natural origin but artificially enlarged, and for which a defensive function is the only plausible

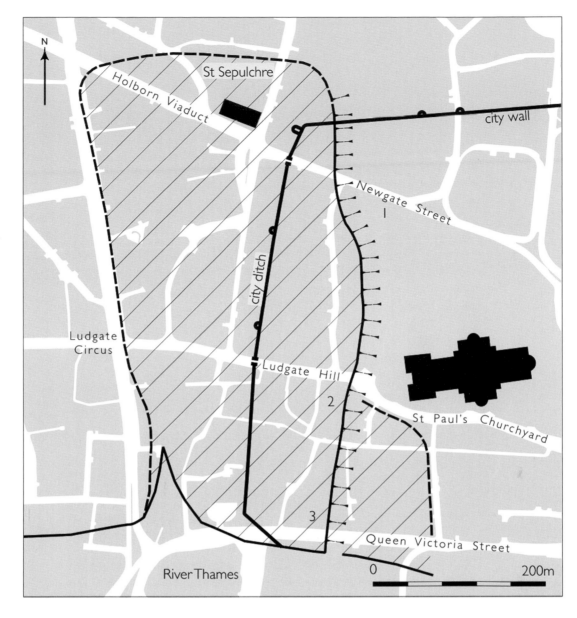

10 The likely extent and boundaries of the western fortification, which, it is suggested, was created in 1066–7 and administered as a royal castle until *circa* 1087. Numbers indicate points at which the part-natural, part-artificial watercourse that is taken to have been its eastern ditch has been identified archaeologically, with the precise location drawn in where the information is available. Marked in a dotted line to the west are the possible limits of a second fortified area, later known as the 'old bailey', which in the early years may have been considered as part of the same complex. To the east, a second additional area may have lain between the main ditch and the approximate line of modern Godliman Street. Indications of the modern street pattern and the position of the existing cathedral are given for orientation.

explanation, running approximately parallel to the city walls and between 100 and 150 m to the east.[158] This was encountered in 1907 on the Greyfriars' site in Newgate treet, in the early 1960s in Paternoster Square, and in the mid-1980s on the south side of St Paul's Churchyard, at the bottom of Addle Hill (immediately to the east of St Andrew by the Wardrobe), and at the medieval riverbank.[159] This would have carved out of the city an intramural area of more than 6 hectares (14.8 acres), making it the second largest urban castle in England. Its total area may, however, have been larger still: in particular, it has been suggested that the name of the 'Bailey', in use by the 1160s, in 1190 and in the 1240s[160] for what later became 'Old Bailey', and the suffix of 'in the Bailey' attached to St Sepulchre's church by 1243 indicate that it extended beyond the city wall.[161] It has also been suggested that the substantial building discovered in the early 1990s on the site of the Fleet prison (with dimensions of 12.5 by 10.5 m and what appear to be turret bases at its corners)[162] formed part of its defences,[163] while the east bank of the Fleet river

would have made an obvious course for the associated rampart. In addition, the extent of the Soke of the Lord of Baynard's castle, as it existed in the fourteenth century, suggests that the early defences may also have taken in, at the south end, an additional intramural area to the east of the ditch, extending eastwards to modern Godliman Street.[164]

The break-up of the vast early castle and the creation of the later ones probably followed a fire in 1087, which according to the *Anglo-Saxon Chronicle* destroyed St Paul's and 'the noblest part of the city',[165] leading to a major reordering of the quarter. Since the London *castellum* for which the king required services in the years 1094–7 must have been the Tower, this too suggests that the western castle had lost its significance as a royal stronghold by that period.[166] This was certainly the case by 1111, when Henry I granted the Bishop of London

as much of the ditch of my castle on the south side [of St Paul's] as was needed to make a [precinct] wall of St Paul's, and as much of the ditch as was required for making a way outside the wall, and, on the north side of the church, as much as the bishop destroyed of the same ditch.[167]

The Formation, Tenure and Abandonment of the 'Successor' Castles

The earliest and the best known of the 'successors' to the royal fortification was Baynard's Castle. Its existence as an independent stronghold – if still held of the king and within the confines of the former royal castle – is known from 1111, the year in which, according to the mid-thirteenth-century entry in the *Chronicle of Dunmow*, William Baynard lost the Honour of Baynard's Castle ('Castrum Baynardi').[168] How long it had existed is unclear, but perhaps from at least *circa* 1100, by when William Baynard was a king's minister,[169] and it may perhaps be identified with the London house (*domus*) he is known to have possessed by 1106.[170] Possibly, however, the Baynards' association with the site was even earlier, dating from the lifetime of Ralph Baynard, probably William's uncle,[171] who had been Sheriff of Essex in the years 1076–81, of Middlesex in the years 1075–85,[172] and holder of vast territories in eastern England in 1086:[173] if so, he may have held an official position relating to the castle. Following William Baynard's forfeiture, however, Henry I granted his properties to Robert Fitz Richard of Clare, whose family retained possession of the castle or property on its site until 1275. It was probably following the marriage of Fitz Richard's niece to William Mountfichet in the 1120s or early 1130s[174] that the Mountfichets gained some sort of tenure of a subdivision of the Baynards' castle, and to which their family name then became attached. This had clearly happened before Fitz Richard's death in 1137, as is shown by evidence brought before a jury in the early thirteenth century to settle a dispute over fishing rights, which not only refers to Mountfichet's Castle ('castellum de Munfichet'), but to its lord, and even suggests that he may have sided against the Clares.[175] By then, Mountfichet's Castle, occupying the northern part of the site (below), had probably become a genuinely independent fortress, and had clearly done so in or before 1173–4, when, according to Jordan Fantosme's contemporary poem about the Young King's rebellion that year, it was reinforced in his cause by Gilbert Munfichet.[176] The distinct identities of the castles by the late twelfth century are also underlined by William Fitz Stephen's reference of *circa* 1180 to 'two strongly fortified castles to the west',[177] and more explicitly by Gervase of Tilbury's mention in the early thirteenth century of the 'two castles (*castella*) constructed with magnificent ramparts (*aggeres*) on the western side of the city, one being Baynard's Castle, while the other belongs by right to the barons of Monfiquit'.[178] Reference to the *castellum de Munfichet* in contexts that imply it was a major and well-estab-

lished landmark is also made in three charters of 1180 to *circa* 1203.[179] Nevertheless, the Clares seem to have retained ultimate possession of Mountfichet's Castle, since Richard de Mountfichet was proved in 1276 not to have been the owner of the 'tower called Mountfichet', 'the site of the castle called "Castelbaynard"' being 'entire and undivided as of the right and possession' of Robert Fitz Walter.[180] By then, however, the existence of the two castles as viable fortresses had ended or was soon to do so: according to the anonymous author of the early thirteenth-century *Histoire des ducs de Normandie et rois d'Angleterre*, Baynard's Castle had been demolished (*abbatu*) by the self-proclaimed 'barons' of London at the king's orders in 1212.[181] In 1275 Robert Fitz Walter received licence to make over the site of Baynard's Castle to the Dominicans,[182] the name being subsequently adopted by a succession of important buildings on a site slightly further east.[183] By 1278 it is clear that Mountfichet's Castle must have been largely demolished, and its site was being considered, once again, as part of the former Baynard's Castle.[184]

The Form and Extent of the 'Successor' Castles

The area that was to become or be included in Baynard's Castle very likely originated as the fortified nucleus of the vast eleventh-century castle, equivalent to the inner defences of the Tower of London as they existed at the demise of its outer bailey (fig. 11). Since Mountfichet's Castle originated as a subdivision of Baynard's Castle, occupying its northern half, its northern boundary must originally have been that of the earlier castle. This has been placed by Henry Johns and John Schofield, largely on the basis of thirteenth-century documentary evidence, parallel to and a little to the south of Ludgate Hill.[185] The crucial document is a late twelfth- or early thirteenth-century charter referring to property

> in the corner opposite the land of St Paul's [the Deanery], between the land of David Long, chaplain, to the north and the southern road which leads towards the city wall following beside (*secus*) the ditch of the Castle of Montfichet.[186]

From this Johns deduced that the ditch followed Carter Lane and that the castle lay to the north, occupying the area between the lane and Ludgate Hill.[187] The discovery of a ditch to the north of Carter Lane in the late 1980s, as first cut containing fill of *circa* 1050–1200 and as re-cut as much as 16 m wide and containing fill of *circa* 1150–1350, and of a second ditch to the south of Ludgate Hill, seemed to corroborate this entirely.[188] Derek Keene has suggested, however, that it was the ditch by the lane, and not the other one further north, that marked the northern boundary of the castle,[189] partly because the other ditch (if

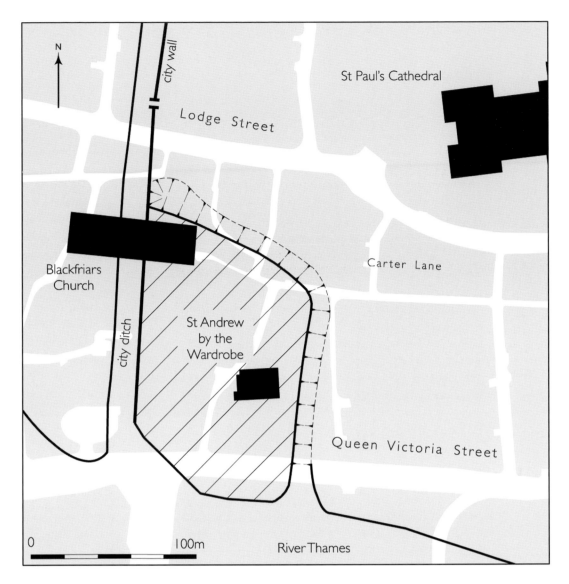

medieval at all) seems too slight, and partly on the basis of information contained in an agreement of 1278, by which the Archbishop of Canterbury gave the Dominicans land

> . . . in the area known as Baynard's Castle . . . to build a new church and other suitable buildings . . . so that the chancel of the said church shall be of such length as to be the largest chancel which the said friars have been able to build in England, and twenty feet [of land] beyond the chancel, provided that the northern side of the said chancel is not built, towards the gate of Ludgate, beyond the old foundation of the Tower of Mountfichet.[190]

While Bruce Watson's interpretation that the chancel of the Dominican church stood 'outside', or 'up against' the footings is not impossible,[191] the most probable interpretation is that the new building was not to extend beyond the former limits of the castle (below). In this case, since the chancel of the church lay hard against but to the south of Carter Lane,[192] so must the castle within whose footprint it was built. This would be perfectly in keeping with the other documents cited by Johns, describing plots to the west of the 'Atrium' of St Paul's or the Deanery as 'near' or 'against' Mountfichet's.[193] In all probability, therefore, the northern rampart lay just to the south of modern Carter Lane, the castle's north–south extent therefore being rather less than Johns supposed (fig. 11). The eastward extent of Baynard's Castle can be assumed to be marked by the known section of the eleventh-century north–south ditch, although, as suggested above, it may have covered some additional ground in this direction.[194] The western boundary of the complex was formed by the city wall, although it seems that at least by 1279 this was pierced by a gate, defended by a barbican to the west.[195]

With regard to Mountfichet's Castle, very little, other than that it occupied the northern part of the enclosure formerly entirely taken up by Baynard's Castle, can be said about its layout or defences, although the rounded inner corner of the junction of St Andrew's Hill and Carter Lane as they existed in the late seventeenth century may conceivably follow the base of a motte or its ditch.[196] It is also possible that a reference to the *turris* of Mountfichet in 1279 recalled the former existence of a 'great tower', which, if so, presumably inspired the representation of a tower at the west of the city on the common seal of the citizens of London (see fig. 222) of *circa* 1220.[197]

THE WHITE TOWER: ORIGINATION AND SITING

It is now clear that the city within which the White Tower was to be constructed possessed a powerful royal castle at both its western and eastern extremities. A number of questions as to the relationship between the existence and the nature of these castles, and the creation and siting of the White Tower, remain to be explored. First, given the extent and likely strength of the early castles, why did the Conqueror decide to build a great tower in London at all? Second, why was its chosen site within the eastern, not the western castle? Third, why was the White Tower positioned as it was within the eastern castle?

The answer to the first question must lie largely in the symbolic potential of a great tower, deriving essentially from its appearance, and which a castle consisting of relatively inconspicuous ditches, banks, walls and palisades – however effective in practice – could not achieve. But it is likely that for William and his adherents the great tower possessed a particularly powerful status and symbolism, of a kind that their subsequent proliferation, inspired by the White Tower itself, was later to dilute.[198] This derived from the strict association of the three or four great towers that stood in Normandy by 1066 with its great *vicomtés* and the ducal family itself, an exclusivity that had been maintained by the absence of any further tower building since the first decades of the century.[199] It is also underlined by the fact that the only tower that William does seem to have created on the Continent, at Le Mans, was built following the capture of the city and the county of Maine in 1063.[200] Its potential as a long-established symbol both of conquest and of the ducal dynasty, combined with an unprecedented requirement and opportunity for its use, are likely to have been the deciding incentives for the building of the White Tower.

Various explanations can be suggested as to why the White Tower was built within the eastern castle, not its western counterpart. First, as suggested above, the western castle may just conceivably have already possessed a great tower. Second, placing the tower in the eastern castle, directly overlooking the Thames, enabled it to confront traffic going upstream with an immediate impression of armed strength within the city, which the western castle's siting would not have allowed: a related factor may have been the situation at Rouen, the Conqueror's principal Continental base, where a celebrated tenth-century tower stood in an

exactly analogous position at the south-east corner of the city, although overlooking the approaches from upstream, in Duke Richard's time the source of greatest danger.[201] A third factor may have been the position of the eastern castle at the opposite end of the city from St Paul's, if only because its western counterpart would have been psychologically, if not yet physically, dominated by the pre-1087 cathedral.

Finally, and perhaps most important, were the locations of the castles in relation to the palace of Westminster: while, as seems likely, the growing importance of the palace usurped the importance of the western castle as a royal power base, this would have tended, if anything, to increase the importance of the other. If so, the placing of the White Tower in the favoured eastern castle can be seen as an affirmation of the distinct but complementary roles that Westminster and the Tower of London were to play throughout the Middle Ages and beyond – one as the great royal palace, the other as the great royal fortress.

Why the White Tower was sited precisely as it was within the early castle is perhaps easier to assess. Although, as at Colchester, there are Roman footings underneath the White Tower, these were not of enough practical or symbolic value to have influenced its siting,[202] and the main consideration must have been the position and layout of the pre-existing defences. If it is accepted that the early castle had two baileys, placing the great tower in the inner one would have followed normal practice: the fact that this placed the White Tower very close to the Roman wall is no surprise, as other examples of this and similar arrangements in England and Normandy attest.[203] The choice of the northern half was made, no doubt, to take advantage of the rising ground and its contribution to the White Tower's most important and enduring function – the domination of the city and its river-borne approaches.

Acknowledgements

I am very grateful to the many people, including the other contributors to this volume, who have read drafts of this chapter and provided guidance and information. Amongst them I owe particular thanks to Dr Jeremy Ashbee, Professor David Bates, Dr Hugh Doherty, Karen Lundgren, Dr Derek Renn, Professor Richard Sharpe, Dr David Stocker and Professor Derek Keene, the last of whom has been particularly generous in advising on aspects of pre-Conquest London that he will himself be discussing in a forthcoming publication.

PART II

The Structure and Function of the
White Tower to 2000

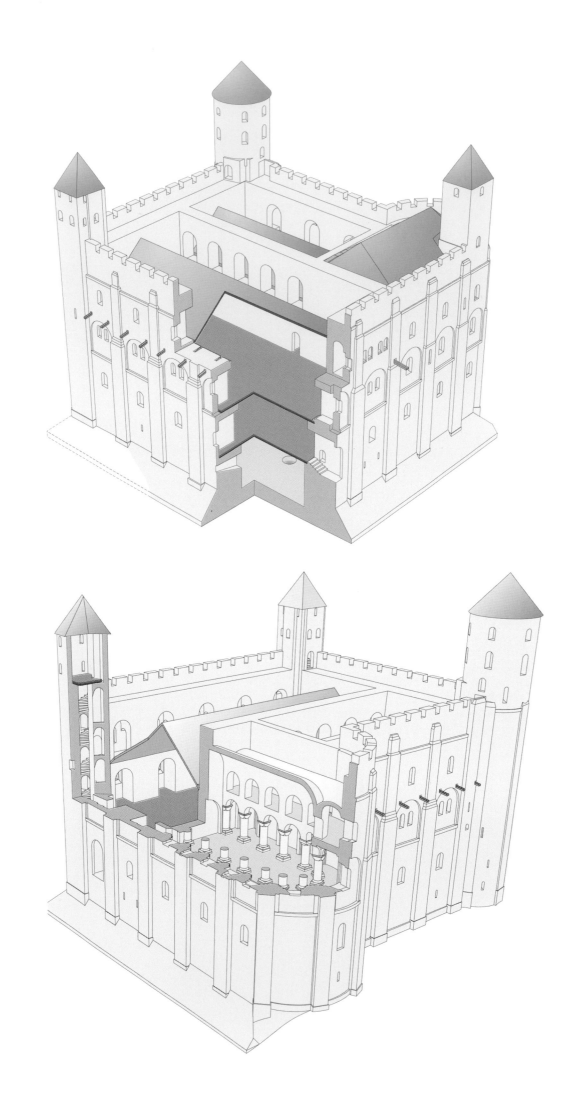

CHAPTER TWO

The Structural History of the White Tower, 1066–1200

ROLAND B. HARRIS

It has long been accepted that the White Tower is a building that survives largely intact from the late eleventh century, except for the replacement of quoins and architraves with Portland stone, the insertion of brick vaults in the basement and the addition of a floor at the level of an original gallery.[1] Over the years other interpretations have been advanced. Of these, the most complex and least sustainable is that of gradual evolution, beginning with a ground-level residence comprising the east room and chapel only, followed by the addition of the west room and the heightening of the building in stages.[2] Recently, the evolutionary theory has reappeared in a more compelling manner: it has been proposed that the White Tower was initially built a storey lower, except for the chapel, and that, shortly after, this gabled structure was heightened by the addition of the mural passage.[3]

The structural history reasoned here is based on the first systematic scrutiny of the fabric (in the course of the White Tower Recording and Research Project) and is neither as simple as the traditional interpretation nor as complex as the evolutionists would have it (fig. 12). Three important findings of this study need to be stressed, and are explored both in this chapter and, insofar as they are relevant to St John's Chapel, in the next chapter, by John Crook. First, the present form of the White Tower as expressed by its masonry is not only largely that achieved by completion circa 1100, but as conceived from the outset: this includes the walls, buttresses, four turrets and the projecting apse. Second, the one lasting major alteration made to the

building comprised the raising of the roofs of the east and west rooms by a storey, with a new floor added at the level of the former rafter feet and roof drains. There is no evidence of this higher roof before circa 1490; previously, the roofs of the east and west rooms were screened by the second-floor walls of the White Tower. Third, there was a substantial pause in the primary construction, midway through the building of the first floor (i.e., that with the chapel). This break is marked by minor changes in material and technique, and, most importantly for the study of late eleventh-century architecture, in the sculptural detail of St John's Chapel. The identification of a major building break is intimately bound up with a reassessment of the date of the White Tower, for so long confidently cited as circa 1078: a combination of scientific, documentary and architectural evidence suggests that the primary construction of the White Tower began around 1075–9 and was completed by 1100, with the long building break beginning circa 1079–83 (and most probably circa 1080) and ending circa 1090–3.

The confirmation of the primary nature of the general form of the White Tower today (bar the later raising of the roof) and the identification of the building break are dependent on the analysis of the surviving fabric, and both are closely related to the chronology of construction. The dating of the building works, and the architectural elements that help determine this, also have implications for identification of the historical figures responsible. This chapter begins with such matters, and thus provides a basis for

Facing page: 12 Three-dimensional cut-away reconstruction from the south-west (top) and from the south-east (bottom).

subsequent discussion of the form and detail of the primary building. This discussion concludes with the complex – and much misunderstood – nature of the primary roof construction. The construction of the square entrance tower, or forebuilding, against the south face of the White Tower is also discussed, since, if not part of the initial construction, it was of Norman build. An analysis of aspects of the geometry and proportion used in the design of the White Tower forms an annexe to the chapter.

THE DATING OF THE PRIMARY CONSTRUCTION AND THE ROLE OF GUNDULF

Documentary Evidence

The castle on the Tower site was probably established in the weeks before King William's coronation on 25 December 1066,[4] but it is highly unlikely that the White Tower was begun in this period or even soon after.[5] Nevertheless, by the date of the earliest unambiguous reference to the Tower of London the White Tower clearly was in existence or well advanced: in the course of an explanation of how the cathedral church of Rochester came to possess several London properties from Eadmer the Cripple, the *Textus Roffensis*[6] relates that 'Gundulf, by command of King William the Great, was supervising the work of the great tower of London'.[7] Since Gundulf was appointed to the see of Rochester on 19 March 1077, it has become something of a tradition to date the construction of the White Tower to 1078,[8] or *circa* 1080. The *Textus Roffensis*, however, does not imply that the bishop initiated the works, or that they were in progress immediately after his appointment, but simply that Gundulf was involved with the building of the White Tower between becoming bishop in 1077 and the death of William I on 9 September 1087.[9] That the building was well under way by 1097 is clear from an entry in the *Anglo-Saxon Chronicle*, which records that in that year

> many shires whose labour was due at London were hard pressed because of the wall that they built about the Tower (*túr*), and because of the bridge [i.e., London Bridge] that was nearly all carried away by a flood, and because of the work on the king's hall, that was being built at Westminster, and many a man was oppressed thereby.[10]

Together with a charter of 1093–7 by which William II confirmed the exemption of St Paul's demesne from work on the 'castle of London, the wall, the bridge and the bailey, as the writ of my father ordered',[11] these sources confirm that the castle was still under construction in the 1090s, with the implication that the White Tower itself was complete, or well advanced, by 1097 and that work on an enclosing wall was in progress.

The completion of the White Tower is also implied by the accounts in the *Anglo-Saxon Chronicle* and by

Orderic Vitalis of the famous escape from the castle by William Rufus's chief minister, Rannulf Flambard, in 1101.[12] The *Anglo-Saxon Chronicle* records the prison as the 'ture on Lunden', while Orderic uses the term 'arce Lundoniensi': both almost certainly refer to the White Tower. Additionally, Orderic recounts how Rannulf organised a great feast and then, while the guards slumbered drunkenly, escaped down a rope tied to a shaft in the middle of a window ('columnam quae in medio fenestrae'). Double windows in the Romanesque White Tower featured only on the first and second floors,[13] so, if Orderic is to be believed in every detail, the building must have been substantially complete at the time of the incident. Despite the near-contemporary nature of the account and Orderic's undeniable eye for detail, however, such minutiae as the form of the windows should be treated with caution. More significant is the fact that Orderic's references to the building imply that the White Tower was complete, and this concurs with the more general inference that can be drawn from Rannulf's imprisonment: that the building was fit for use as a prison and for feasting. It is unlikely that a half-completed building, let alone an active building site, would have provided secure or suitable accommodation. If it is to be accepted that Rannulf was imprisoned in a great tower that was near, if not wholly, complete, then the dating of his escape at Candlemas (2 February) 1101 means that the building was finished by 1100: a building season in 1101 would not have begun as early in the year as Candlemas. Moreover, since Rannulf Flambard was sent to the Tower by Henry I in August or early September 1100, this would imply that works were completed by that date. This interpretation is supported by a condition in Henry I's treaty with Robert II of Flanders, which was concluded at Dover on 10 March 1101, that, should he break it, hostages would be imprisoned in the Tower of London ('Turri London'). This is also the earliest date by which the White Tower is known to have given its name to the whole castle.[14]

Architectural Evidence

The Building Break in the Primary Construction (Phase 1)

There is overwhelming evidence for a substantial building break of several years, at which point construction had reached the level of approximately 1.5–2.3 m above the first floor: that is, at 22.7–23.5 m OSBM.[15] This break was first suspected during the analysis of St John's Chapel, where John Crook identified various anomalies in the construction.[16] The subsequent survey programme identified more widely distributed and clearer evidence that includes a fundamental change in the bedding mortar type from one with a very high concentration of small bivalve shells (Type 1: see fig. 69)[17] to one with little or no such shell, but with large pieces of unburnt chalk (Type 2). The mortars are obscured in much of the interior by the modern repointing and, in the chapel, by Salvin's repointing of 1864,[18] but areas of primary mortar remain visible. In the chapel, the two types of mortar meet at approximately 23.0 m OSBM, although the nineteenth-century repointing leaves the point of the junction visible in only a few places. The best place in the interior for locating the horizon between the two mortar types, however, is in the stair turrets at the north-east, north-west and south-west corners. In the south-west turret the mortar change occurs at approximately 22.7–23.0 m OSBM; in the north-west turret the break occurs at approximately 22.9 m OSBM; and in the north-east turret shelly mortar occurs up to approximately 22.8 m OSBM. The change can also be seen at 23.0 m OSBM in the two garderobes at the north end of the spine wall, but the junction of the two mortars is difficult to identify with precision in the north-east garderobe. It was during the repair and repointing of the south elevation in 1997–8, however, that the most overwhelming evidence of the change in mortar type was observed, with the removal of stone permitting a rare opportunity for viewing and sampling the primary bedding mortars deep into the wall. Understandably, the raking out of modern pointing was determined by the programme of conservation rather than by archaeological concerns, and did not penetrate far enough to allow the precise mapping of the junctions of the two mortars in the three eastern bays. In the two western bays and on the south-west turret raking out went deeper, but these areas had been previously deeply repointed at this level, almost certainly in the post-medieval period. The shelly mortar, however, was identified up to a height of 23.2 m OSBM in the western bay, and the evidence of the three eastern bays is consistent with such a height for the junction. More importantly, the repairs to the south elevation revealed that above and below this approximate line each of the two mortar types was consistent and ubiquitous wherever the bedding mortar was visible (fig. 13).

The change in mortar type that marks the building break is echoed in the geological variation of the building stones.[19] While Kentish Ragstone is the predominant building stone, other geological types are present in significant amounts. Some, most obviously Portland stone, are related to later repair programmes, but others are clearly primary, and the opportunity for geological mapping of the stones of the south elevation has proved informative. None of the subsidiary stone types is spread entirely evenly across the height of the elevation, although Caen stone comes closest (fig. 14).[20] Reigate stone and dolomitised Chalk from the Seine valley are very much exclusive to the lower half of the elevation (fig. 15), while the sparser Taynton limestone is found only in the upper part. Inter-estingly, on the south elevation Quarr stone and Bembridge limestone (sometimes known as Binstead stone by architectural historians) are concentrated in the vicinity of the building break, although not exclusively so (fig. 16). This pattern is more consistent on the interior, where the responds of the chapel aisles change from Quarr stone to Bembridge limestone at the level of the break as mapped by the mortar types, with the Bembridge limestone in turn succeeded by Caen stone.[21] Similar banding occurs in the ashlar in the other first-floor rooms, and, given the evidence for the height of the break provided by the stair turrets and garderobes, it is clear that the top of the band of Quarr stone marks the level of the break.

Of course, the banding of stone types need only reflect variation in supply during a major building project and does not of itself imply a building break. The coincidence of geological banding with the break in the construction at the White Tower, however, reveals that the restarting of works was associated with several changes in stone supply. Most importantly, the banding of the stone types confirms that construction advanced at the White Tower in a series of well-defined and level horizons,[22] and that no major element of the surviving building represents addition.[23]

More tangible and, again, hitherto unrecognised evidence for a building break is seen in a corresponding and abrupt reduction in the use of ashlar. This is especially clear in the three spiral stairs where the ashlar lining gives way to rubble, in the north-east turret at 22.84 m OSBM; in the north-west turret at 22.93 m OSBM; and in the south-west turret at 22.73 m OSBM (fig. 17). The reduced use of ashlar is also visible externally in the bays between the buttresses where there are ashlar quoins to the internal, or re-entrant, angles at the lower two storeys only: the additional angle order of the blind arcading of the first floor means that the break is obscured, but the second floor has no ashlar quoins. More obvious still, clear junctions of ashlar and rubble facework can be seen on the wide north-west buttress of the chapel apse at 21.40 m OSBM (fig. 18); on the north and west faces of the north-west turret (22.62 m OSBM and 22.05 m OSBM, respectively); and the south and west faces of the south-west turret (22.54 m OSBM and 21.22 m OSBM, respectively). Clearly, there is some variation in the height of the top of the exterior ashlar, even on adjacent faces of turrets. Moreover, the height reached by the exterior ashlar of the turrets is below that of the interior ashlar of the staircases. The significance of this, if any, is not immediately apparent, since detailed examination was necessarily restricted to the south elevation,[24] and this did not reveal either of the primary mortar types above the ashlar: later repair possibly associated with the demolition of the fore-building had resulted in repointing to a greater depth than that required in 1997–8.[25] What does seem ap-

Mortar type 1 (shelly Romanesque)   Mortar type 3 (with Portland)   Mortar type 5

Mortar type 2 (non-shelly Romanesque)   Mortar type 4 (Roman cement)   Mortar type 6

Mortar type 7

13   South elevation showing primary bedding mortars revealed during works of 1997–8.

Distribution of Caen stone in the south elevation.

50.0m

45.0m

40.0m

35.0m

30.0m

25.0m

20.0m

15.0m

10.0m

5.0m OSBM

50.0m

45.0m

40.0m

35.0m

30.0m

25.0m

20.0m

15.0m

10.0m

5.0m OSBM

Caen stone

50.0m

45.0m

40.0m

35.0m

30.0m

25.0m

20.0m

15.0m

10.0m

5.0m OSBM

dolomitized Chalk

Reigate stone

15   Distribution of Reigate stone and dolomitised Chalk in the south elevation.

50.0m 50.0m

45.0m 45.0m

40.0m 40.0m

35.0m 35.0m

30.0m 30.0m

25.0m 25.0m

20.0m 20.0m

15.0m 15.0m

10.0m 10.0m

5.0m OSBM 5.0m OSBM

☐ Quarr stone

☐ Bembridge limestone

16   Distribution of Quarr stone and Bembridge limestone in the south elevation.

17   (*right*) Junction of rubble and ashlar walling in the south-west stair turret.

18   (*far right*) Transition from ashlar to rubble on the wide buttress on the north side of the apse.

parent from much of the exterior evidence is that there was a transition from well-cut ashlar to precisely coursed sub-ashlar, and then to less carefully coursed rubble at this point. Given the evidence of the change of mortar type on the exterior and interior, and the evidence of the abrupt cessation of ashlar in the spiral stairs, it must be suspected that either the wall-heads were left lower on the outside at the break (possibly to assist the run-off of rain water from what was a wide wall-head) or that the lack of ashlar that distinguishes the work above the break was anticipated before it. The variation in the heights reached by external ashlar, even in adjacent faces, favours the argument for a ragged and sloping wall-head at the point of a broadly horizontal break, but only newly begun analysis of the north, east and west elevations during repointing and repairs in 2008–10 will be able to determine this (fig. 19).

Notwithstanding possible anticipation prior to the break, it is difficult to conceive that the reduction in the use of ashlar was planned from the outset, not least because some of the effects it produces are bizarre. For example, the north-west and south-west spiral stairs only begin at the first floor and thus are lined with ashlar for just approximately 1.8 m before their construction changes to rubble. Such a transition from ashlar to rubble at a seemingly illogical point with no correspondence to storey heights or string-courses is

typical of the White Tower, and distinguishes it from the well-conceived and executed changes from ashlar to rubble, or vice versa, that are known in near-contemporary buildings elsewhere.[26] Moreover, the unusually sparing use of ashlar in the construction of St John's Chapel,[27] which was built almost entirely after the break, is less surprising if not an original intention of the design. It may be that stone supply was a problem, which would seem contrary to the evident success of Norman quarrying and distribution. This could reflect, however, the lower priority given to military rather than ecclesiastical projects in the late eleventh century: certainly a similar absence of ashlar is found in the upper half of Colchester Castle. More probably, speed, cost or labour supply were important factors in the second phase of the primary construction of the White Tower.

While no significant modifications to the design are apparent following the building break, the changes in technique, mortar type and stone supply, and the remarkably horizontal level of the break across the whole building, suggest that the pause in construction was more than a normal seasonal break. At near-contemporary Colchester Castle a pause in construction just above the level of the existing first floor was sufficiently substantial for the building to be battlemented at this lower level and justifies doubt as to whether the putative final three-storey height of

Facing page: 19   The extent of essentially primary ashlar on the south elevation.

50.0m

45.0m

40.0m

35.0m

30.0m

25.0m

20.0m

15.0m

10.0m

5.0m OSBM

50.0m

45.0m

40.0m

35.0m

30.0m

25.0m

20.0m

15.0m

10.0m

5.0m OSBM

☐ probable in situ primary ashlar

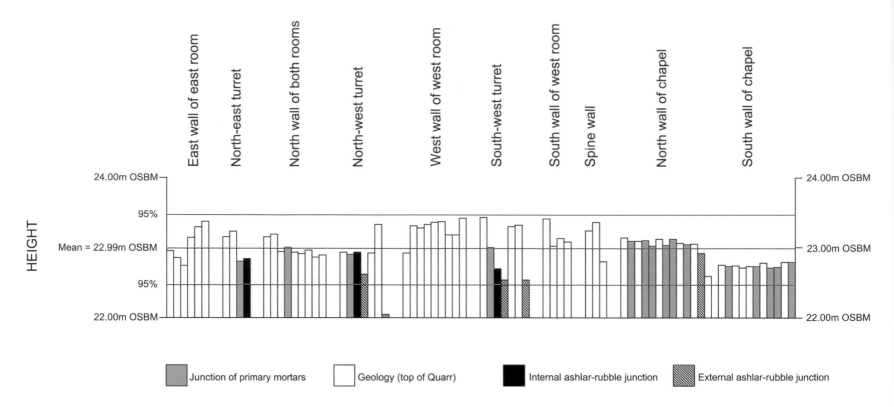

LOCATION OF OBSERVATION OF EVIDENCE FOR LEVEL OF THE BREAK

East wall of east room · North-east turret · North wall of both rooms · North-west turret · West wall of west room · South-west turret · South wall of west room · Spine wall · North wall of chapel · South wall of chapel

HEIGHT

24.00m OSBM — ... — 24.00m OSBM
95%
Mean = 22.99m OSBM — ... — 23.00m OSBM
95%
22.00m OSBM — ... — 22.00m OSBM

■ Junction of primary mortars   □ Geology (top of Quarr)   ■ Internal ashlar-rubble junction   ▨ External ashlar-rubble junction

20   Graph showing the heights OSBM of the break around the White Tower, as evidenced by the cessation of ashlar, mortar-type change and the top of the band of Quarr stone.

Colchester was originally intended.[28] There is no such evidence for the use of the White Tower on the completion of Phase 1, and the level of the break midway through a storey, but too high for battlements, positively suggests that this was not the case.[29] Furthermore, the fact that the first floor, with its two-storey chapel and north-west and south-west stairs, was begun before the break reveals that the Phase 2 fabric was not in any sense an afterthought, but fully part of the original design. Rather, the implication is that the break represents nothing more than a pause in construction, or that it reflects a change of master mason or some other fresh impetus (fig. 20).

The differences between the primary construction above and below the break are made all the clearer by the fact that the fabric of each of the two phases is in itself remarkably homogeneous. This homogeneity is seen in the uniformity of construction technique, mortar type and stone supply, and suggests that each construction phase was continuous and rapid. The number of identifiably primary stone types used on the south elevation is constant in the lower, middle and upper parts, at around six, and the geological variety of the ashlar could reflect the speed of construction. Moreover, the haste of Phase 2 can be inferred from the lack of ashlar in the upper half of the building.

Both the implications for Phase 1 and Phase 2 being rapid and for the break being considerably more significant than an annual pause are important considerations in the dating of the initial construction of the White Tower.

Absolute Dating

The chronology indicated by the documentary sources and the extended building campaign implied by the building break are broadly corroborated by the architectural evidence. The combination of a tower of double-pile construction with multiple storeys and a projecting apsidal chapel has long been considered restricted to Colchester Castle and the White Tower,[30] but it is now certain that at least one well-known great tower of this type and scale, at Ivry-la-Bataille in Normandy, existed in the early eleventh century.[31] That at least two other examples from northern France are known from the twelfth century[32] simply confirms that the overall design of the White Tower tells us little of the precise date of its construction.

Turning to the architectural detail, the immediate problem is similar, in that most of the features of the design are not closely datable. This does not reflect a current lack of understanding of the absolute chronologies of such features, but rather the fact that many of the details at the White Tower are extremely simple and robust. Of course, it is possible that the replacement of windows has deprived us of much of the more diagnostic masonry. Many of the features that do survive had a long usage in Romanesque architecture. This is demonstrated by the building break, which although accompanied by significant changes in the use of ashlar and mortar, is not marked by equally obvious changes in the treatment of architectural detail. It could be argued that this simply reflects the brevity of the break, but the longevity of many of the design features and techniques that appear in the White Tower suggests that the stylistic analysis of such a plain building cannot in itself determine the whole chronology of construction. Features at the White Tower that can be identified simply as symptomatic of Norman construction prior to the early to mid-twelfth century include the vaulting in the two rooms below the chapel, the garderobes and the mural passages; the pilaster buttresses, of which we know only the general form; the fireplaces, which have lost their hoods; the plain non-rebated doorways; and the spiral stairs with rubble vaults rather than structural steps.[33]

Other problems with stylistic dating abound. Some elements of the design are insufficiently well known to provide evidence for a construction date: in spite of so much post-medieval replacement, enough survives or is recorded to show that almost all the windows represent primary openings, but there is insufficient evidence of their precise form to allow close dating. Other features are unusual, but not therefore more datable: into this category must go the recesses in the spine wall on the entrance and first floors, and the round-headed niches in the side walls of the entrance. There are also features for which dated parallels can be found but which, it must be suspected, are insufficiently distinctive to be used as grounds for dating the White Tower: an example is the double course of ashlar immediately above the junction of plinth and wall, which is found at the castles of Canterbury (*circa* 1100–20)[34] and Colchester (probably 1080s),[35] but which probably represents a more widely used feature in rubble construction.

More distinctive is the use of blind arcading on the first floor of all four external elevations and the chapel apse. Shallow blind arcading in itself is not especially diagnostic, in that it is found in Anglo-Saxon architecture[36] and, on a more comparable scale, nearby on the west elevation of the undercroft of the dormitory range at Westminster Abbey (late 1060s–70s),[37] and on the north elevation of Westminster Hall (1090s).[38] In these two local examples, however, the blind arcading does not form a frame for the windows as it does at the White Tower, and it is closer to the ground-level blind arcading found at the west end of the abbey church at Jumièges in Normandy (1052–67).[39] The blind arcading that encloses the gallery windows at St Etienne, Caen, is a more convincing parallel for the White Tower.[40] In view of the rather obvious similarities in the designs of St Etienne and Lanfranc's cathedral at Canterbury, it is perhaps unsurprising that blind arcading enclosing the windows is found at the latter as well. In this case fragments of blind arches survive on the west face of the north transept; at the junction of the north-west transept and the north side of the nave; and at the junction of the south-west tower and the south side of the nave. The use of blind arches to surround the windows of the clerestory marks a departure from St Etienne, but it is likely, as Richard Gem suggests, that Canterbury also adopted a similar external treatment for the gallery windows.[41] Although represented as segmental in the most recent analysis of Lanfranc's cathedral,[42] examination of the *in situ* evidence shows that there can be little doubt that the arches were like those at the White Tower in that they were approximately semicircular. The similarity extends to scale, with the arches of the Canterbury clerestory spanning 3.6 m and those at the White Tower having a mean span of 3.78 m.[43] While the arches of the blind arcading at the White Tower are above the building break, they spring from an angle order between wall and buttress that begins below the break, so that the blind arcading was fully intended in Phase 1 and simply completed in Phase 2. Given the precise dating of Lanfranc's cathedral to 1071–7,[44] this could suggest a similar date for the lower half of the White Tower, but gives no clue as to the length of the building break or the date of completion.

To the dating evidence of these architectural features can be added that of the ashlar itself.[45] Rough diagonal tooling at the White Tower pre-dates the introduction of claw-chisel techniques, but is simply typical of Romanesque work in general. Smaller blocks of ashlar with wide pointing, however, are more diagnostic, since they are typical of Norman construction of the late eleventh century and would seem to preclude construction of the White Tower before *circa* 1070.[46] While there is no evidence of a change from extremely wide joints to more refined Romanesque masonry analogous to that found at Winchester Cathedral, which has allowed the work of 1079–93 there to be distinguished from the fabric rebuilt after the collapse of the central tower in 1107,[47] the size and shape of the ashlars and the jointing at the White Tower are perhaps indicative of a date before 1110, if not before 1100. This dating is corroborated by the petrography of the primary ashlar at the White Tower, since the substantial use of Quarr stone in the upper part of the Phase 1 fabric provides good evidence that construction up to this level at least was completed by 1120.[48] The use of Quarr[49] and Caen[50] stone also confirms that the White Tower is post-Conquest.

These architectural features and stone types, then, provide good but perhaps not entirely conclusive grounds for supposing that the White Tower was begun no earlier than 1070 and finished by 1100–10. Moreover, the evidence of the blind arcading suggests that the lower half of the building belongs to the 1070s. This provides the background for consideration of the well-known stylistic dating evidence of the chapel of St John. Here, study of the bases, capitals and responds of the arcade, and of the side-aisle abaci, confirms that construction of the chapel was indeed

interrupted by a significant building break. Inevitably, it is the capitals that have proved most datable, and they have been the subject of a thorough re-examination in the course of the present study. A detailed analysis of the sculpture is provided by John Crook in Chapter Three, and this concludes that the capitals date from both before and after the building break. The eight chamfered block capitals and the single free-standing volute capital, all from Phase 1, are best paralleled by other examples from the mid- to late 1070s. This is in contrast to the remaining capitals of Phase 2, which can be dated to the early 1090s.[51] This dramatically refines the dating limits of *circa* 1070–1110 for Phase 2 suggested by the rest of the upper part of the White Tower, particularly when it is borne in mind that Phase 2 necessarily began with the carving of these capitals. Most of Phase 2 post-dates the insertion of the capitals, and this work includes the construction of the aisle vaults, the chapel gallery (if not the entire second floor), the south-east turret (if not the other three turrets) and the chapel roof (if not all the roofs). The consistency in the masonry of Phase 2 has been discussed above,[52] however, and implies rapid and near-continuous construction that makes it difficult to argue for a completion date significantly later than that provided by the stylistic date range of the chapel capitals. It is probable, therefore, on this combination of stylistic and structural evidence, that the masonry component at least would have been completed by *circa* 1100.

Scientific Dating: Dendrochronology[53]

Given the building break and the lack of other dating evidence for the lower part of the White Tower, it is fortunate that the Phase 1 fabric includes enough datable primary timbers for dendrochronology to play a part in determining the construction chronology. Felling dates have been determined for boards lining the drawbar sockets for doorways in the basement (after 1068), the main entrance (after 1050) and the spine wall of the entrance floor (with a heartwood/sapwood boundary, giving the only precise range of the series, to 1049–81). The linings to the drawbar sockets were so constructed that they must have been placed in position as the wall around them was being built.[54] While they cannot have been inserted, it is possible that they were converted and stored before use, but the normal use of green oak and the consistency in the dates suggest that the felling of the timbers was contemporary with the primary construction of the White Tower. If the four timbers from which these dates have been derived were felled at the same time for use in a single phase of construction (as seems most probable), this gives a felling date range of 1068–81 for the timber supply to the lower two storeys of the White Tower. There is Phase 1 masonry both above and below these drawbar sockets that must be accounted for, and, thus, the outer limits for the dating of Phase 1, by dendrochronology, extend beyond this range. The building break occurs 6.63 m higher than the uppermost dendrochronological samples, so, assuming that work on the upper part of the entrance floor and the lower part of the first floor followed on immediately from the rest of the Phase 1 construction, something in the order of two years must be added to this range. Likewise, the lowest of the sampled drawbar socket linings is 1.21 m above the primary basement floor level that, in turn, is on top of foundations more than 2.20 m deep: this suggests that the lower limit should be extended by a year at least.[55] Limits of *circa* 1067–83 are thus reasonable for the construction up to the building break, insofar as this campaign can be dated by dendrochronology.

In this context, it is interesting to consider dates for the primary lintels positioned around the level of the building break. Timber lintels are found in the small square cupboards in the window embrasures flanking the two fireplaces on the first floor, and the dated lintels come from the embrasures immediately to the north of the fireplace in both the eastern and western rooms (fig. 21). In the western room the dated lintels are at 22.95 m OSBM, which is consistent with the lintels of the other cupboards in this room (these have a mean height of 22.98 m OSBM, and a range of 22.90–23.08 m OSBM). This places the sampled lintels only a matter of 40 mm below the mean height of the building break. The adjacent ashlar quoins of the embrasures, however, provide a better guide to the exact level of the break in this part of the building than an average value. We have seen (above) how the break is marked by the top of the band of Quarr stone, and this occurs in the embrasure quoin immediately adjacent to the sampled lintels at a height of 23.33 m OSBM. The mean value for the top of the Quarr stone in this room only is 23.32 m OSBM. With the primary lintels thus appearing to fall 380 mm below the local height of the building break, there are good grounds to suppose that they belong to the first phase. Fortuitously, one of the lintels produced a heartwood/sapwood boundary at 1046, giving a felling date range of 1055–87. This is completely consistent with the other dendrochronological dating for Phase 1 construction, but since it is wider in range than the limits of *circa* 1067–83 argued above, this does not help us to refine the dating further. Most importantly, it does provide a secure, though largely superfluous, *terminus ante quem* of 1087 for the completion of Phase 1, with the caveat, albeit unlikely, that the timbers may have been stored before use. In the cupboards of the east room the lintels average 23.22 m OSBM, while the top of the band of Quarr stone in this room occurs at an average of 22.92 m OSBM, suggesting that in this case the lintels belong to Phase 2. One of the lintels here produced a heartwood/sapwood boundary at 1063, giving a felling date range of 1072–1104. This suggests a *terminus post quem* of 1072 for Phase 2 and, indeed, a completion date by the early twelfth century, allowing for almost the entire Phase 2 work above the lintels. The proximity of the dated lintels to the building break, however, means that attribution of either lintel to a particular phase is not absolutely certain, especially since it might be expected that all the lintels were fitted at the same time. In the case of the lintel in the western room, its function as provider of a *terminus ante quem* for Phase 1 is not altered if, indeed, the cupboard lintels prove to have marked the start of Phase 2 construction. Equally, if the eastern room lintels do in fact belong to the very end of Phase 1, then there is no conflict with the dendrochronological dating of the lower part of the White Tower. The lower limit of the date range of 1072–1104 for the lintel is only four years later than that of the combined drawbar sockets (1068–81) and, given that the socket defining the lower limit of 1068 is in the basement, would not require modification of the *terminus post quem* of Phase 1.

Above the level of the probable Phase 2 lintels of the eastern room, the fabric of the White Tower is singularly lacking in primary timbers suitable for scientific dating. While a dendrochronological match was achieved for one of the wooden drains at the primary eaves level, this had no heartwood/sapwood boundary, and thus the timber simply dates from after 1101. Given the latest likely completion date of 1100 (that is, of fabric substantially higher than the level of this drain) and the fact that the timber used for the scupper could well date from substantially later than 1101, it would be a misuse of dendrochronology to ex-

tend the period of construction of the White Tower to meet the earliest possible date for the felling of this timber: it is almost certainly secondary.[56] Perhaps significantly, the east wall drain timber giving this dating is a simple board approximately 100 mm (4 in.) wide, in contrast to the carefully channelled drains surviving in the west wall (dated to after 1014: evidently significantly later).

With its ashlar showing rough diagonal tooling, the well in the western room of the basement is obviously primary, and this has been confirmed as dating from after 1082 by sampling of a beech template supporting the bottom course of the stone lining. A mortar sample taken during the analysis of the well carpentry had a single small bivalve shell only, and lacked the density of shells that defines the Type 1 mortar of Phase 1. This suggests that the well was not built until Phase 2. Even disregarding the significant evidence of this single mortar sample, it is unlikely that the well could belong to Phase 1: the only precise dendrochronological range from a sample belonging to the pre-break construction is that of 1049–81 (from one of the entrance-floor drawbar sockets) and, as we have seen, this indicates completion of Phase 1 by *circa* 1083. Although it is likely that the beech planks used in the well lost few annual growth rings in conversion (there being no discernible sapwood in beech), these cannot be estimated accurately and, thus, the well timbers do not help to refine the dating of Phase 2.[57]

A New Chronology

Combining the three diverse, and less than ideal, sources of evidence for the dating of the White Tower demands caution. The early documentary references strongly suggest that work was completed by 1100, but do not provide such a convincing *terminus post quem*. If the connection between Gundulf and the Tower is accepted, it is still not immediately clear when he was involved, or indeed whether he inherited responsibility for an existing construction project. In this light, the date range for the building of the lower part of the White Tower (Phase 1) provided by dendrochronology has particular significance, since it gives a more precise outer limit for the start of construction: 1068 minus perhaps one year to allow for the foundations, giving *circa* 1067. The dendrochronological dating of the lower part of the White Tower also provides us with the latest likely date for the building break: 1081 plus perhaps two years to allow for the 6.63 m of Phase 1 walling above the highest drawbar socket dendrochronological sample, giving *circa* 1083. The dated lintel in the western room around the level of the break means that at the very latest Phase 1 was completed by 1087, although this would represent improbably slow construction of the walling above the entrance-floor drawbar sockets, or, even, the storage of timber prior to use. Stylistic dating provides some evidence for Phase belonging to the 1070s, with the chamfered block capitals and the free-standing volute capital having closest parallels in the mid- to late 1070s. Such comparative dating of sculptural detail is more precise as a means of dating the Phase 2 capitals in St John's Chapel to the early 1090s. On reasonable structural grounds, the upper part of the White Tower must have been finished soon after, and this accords well with the latest completion date of 1100 suggested by the documentary sources. Thus ranges of *circa* 1067–83 and *circa* 1090–1100 almost certainly contained the two primary construction phases of the White Tower.

Needless to say, this does not imply that construction in Phase 1 lasted fully seventeen years or that Phase 2 lasted eleven years. The dendrochronological and stylistic date ranges that play such important roles in defining the chronological limits of Phase 1 and Phase 2 do not indicate that timber was felled or that capitals were carved over comparably long periods. Rather, it is likely that these activities occurred at precise points (almost certainly in single years) within these ranges, and it is only a wider understanding of medieval building practice that determines that each phase must have taken several years to complete. Studies by Derek Renn[58] and John Harvey[59] agree that the rate of tower or keep construction during this period was typically 10–12 ft (3.1–3.7 m) per year, so it might be expected that Phase 1 lasted as little as five years, especially in the light of the evidence for rapid construction discussed above. Phase 2 involved more complex architectural detail, inherently more laborious work at height and more complex carpentry and roofing, and, given the mid-height break, may be supposed to have taken a little longer. Of course, the aforementioned evidence for the rapidity of progress in Phase 2 (especially, the lack of ashlar) may mean that even this phase was also as short as five years. Possible corroboration of the rate of construction in Phase 2 is provided by what appear to be annual building breaks visible on the interior of the upper part of the north-east turret of the White Tower, at 24.85 m OSBM and 27.65 m OSBM (i.e., 2.8 m for one year). These putative annual break lines are visible as slight changes of mortar mixes and by horizontal joints in the mortar that are more obvious than the junctions of what appear to be single sessions of building (most probably single days), typically of approximately 240–300 mm.

Placing the possible, if not probable, construction period of the Phase 1 fabric within the limits of *circa* 1067–83 necessarily must be based on the historical and architectural context of the works. Architecturally, there is very little that survives elsewhere of comparable form from the period of William 1's rule and which is well dated. The double-pile tower with projecting apsidal chapel was a form that we now know existed prior to the Conquest at Ivry-la-Bataille, and, thus, the general design of the White Tower is not closely dat-

able.[60] While the surviving architectural detail of the basement and entrance floors is rudimentary, the external blind arcading was begun in this phase, and, in view of the similarity with the clerestory at Canterbury Cathedral,[61] would suggest a date in the 1070s. Likewise, the chamfered block capitals and the single free-standing volute capital in St John's Chapel are most closely paralleled in works of the mid- to late 1070s, yet presumably these capitals were carved at the end of the Phase 1 works. Given that the dendrochronological range allows for the start of construction as early as *circa* 1067 and that the stylistic evidence of the Phase 1 capitals (at the very end of this phase) points to manufacture in the mid-1070s, the possibility must be entertained that the White Tower was begun a few years after the Conquest. It seems reasonably certain, however, that the castles erected in 1066–7 to secure London were symptomatic of a first wave of Norman castle building in England that was marked by the rapid creation of timber and earth defences in response to urgent strategic requirements. Programmes of similar castle construction were begun in 1067 on William's behalf by his half-brother Odo, Bishop of Bayeux, and William Fitz Osbern,[62] and, following William's return from Normandy in December 1068, under his own supervision.[63] The scale, sophisticated design and masonry construction of the White Tower sit at odds with these works, but identifying a date by which the victory at Hastings had been consolidated sufficiently to allow such a major building project is highly subjective. Furthermore, greater stability than the immediate aftermath of the Conquest may not have been a prerequisite for construction of the White Tower, since, for example, William began his new hall and palace to the west of the Old Minster and the New Minster in Winchester within four years of the Conquest.[64] This complex was certainly a major undertaking and less strategically, even politically, important than the White Tower, and it is an example that cautions us against placing the start of works on the White Tower later on these grounds alone.

Convincing grounds for arguing for a later start date are to be found, however, in Gundulf's involvement: given the new evidence for phasing and dating the primary construction of the White Tower, the oft-quoted *Textus Roffensis* assumes a new significance. If Gundulf was involved in supervision of the construction of the White Tower after his appointment to the see of Rochester and before the death of William 1, then Phase 1 must have been still under way at some point within the period 1077–87. As we have seen, dendrochronology provides the basis for a *terminus ante quem* of *circa* 1083 for completion of Phase 1, prior to William's death, and thus permits the refinement of the chronological limits of Gundulf's work for the Conqueror at the White Tower to 1077–83. Furthermore, for Gundulf to be so firmly associated, whilst Bishop of Rochester, with the works in the time of William I, it is fair to assume that Phase I extended into this period by a year or two at the very least, suggesting that Phase I could hardly have finished prior to, say, 1079. Since the structural evidence appears to rule out an extended building campaign, an early start date is thus unlikely. Taking our postulated five-year campaign for Phase I, this would give an earliest likely construction period of 1075–9, through to a latest likely construction period of 1079–83. Given the stylistic dating of the blind arcading and, more importantly, the fact that the Phase I capitals in St John's Chapel are likely to have comprised the last work undertaken before the break, something corresponding to the earlier range is more probable. Either range is compatible with the dendrochronological dating of the cupboard lintels of the first-floor eastern room (1072–1104), if these do in fact mark the end of Phase I rather than the resumption of work after the break. It is significant that the chapel capitals determine the most likely dating of the Phase I building campaign – that is, the second half of the 1070s – since this means that the chronology is not dependent on the, generally wholly reasonable, assumption that medieval timber was used green and not stored for several years.

The shorter date limits of *circa* 1090–1100 mean that there is less uncertainty for Phase 2. On the basis of the dating of the Phase 2 capitals of St John's Chapel, which must have been amongst the first work when construction resumed, any shorter period of actual construction is most likely to have started in the early 1090s, but not before 1090. Again assuming five years for this work, this would suggest that date ranges of 1090–4 to, say, 1093–7 are more likely to represent the actual period of construction of the upper part of the building than the end of the decade. Such a chronological framework certainly accords well with those documentary references that seem to imply that the White Tower itself was complete by 1097. Therefore, while lacking the robustness of our more general chronological framework – which dictates that construction of the White Tower began no earlier than *circa* 1067, had finished by 1100, and saw a major pause in construction in at least the years between *circa* 1083 and *circa* 1090 – there are good grounds to suppose that we can achieve something very near to the actual chronology of the construction programme. Such diverse evidence as we can draw upon suggests that the somewhat extended period of primary construction at the White Tower began around 1075–9, was completed by 1100, with a break probably beginning *circa* 1079–83 (and most probably *circa* 1080) and ending *circa* 1090–3. The break, then, is unlikely to have been less than seven years in duration and may have been as much as fourteen years (fig. 22).

The Historical Context of the Building Break

The substantial building break is a newly discovered factor in the construction history of the White Tower, and its suggested dating to a period between 1079–83 and 1090–3 raises the question as to what identifiable external factors could have caused such a pause in construction. Whatever the precise start and end dates of Phase I, the building break is unlikely to have begun later than 1083, and thus the death of William the Conqueror is ruled out as a possible reason for the cessation of works by a considerable margin. Alternative reasons are not easy to identify. The hostilities that marked the final years of the reign are well known, and were a huge financial burden that gave rise to the Domesday survey. Certainly, such military expenditure would have justified halting major construction projects, but these hostilities were very much concentrated between the autumn of 1085 and William's death in September 1087, and thus occurred too late to explain the building break at the White Tower.[65] Likewise, the burning of the 'largest and noblest part of all the city' of London in 1087, reported in the *Anglo-Saxon Chronicle*, appears to be too late to be relevant.[66] However, while the difficulties of the closing years of the reign, the death of William and his succession all occurred after the early 1080s, it is possible that they caused an earlier pause in construction to become something more substantial. Phase 2 postdates the accession of William Rufus, and the new reign provides a variety of reasons for the resumption of works.

The Role of Gundulf

Given the discovery of a lengthy building break and the establishment of a new chronology for the White Tower, it is perhaps surprising that the traditional identification of Gundulf as the organisational force behind its construction should still stand up to scrutiny. Of course, the pause in the later years of William I's reign, followed by completion of the building works during the reign of William Rufus (1087–1100), may mean that Gundulf was not involved in the later stages of the project. His construction of the stone castle at Rochester for Rufus in the opening years of the new reign, however, must have been a convincing demonstration of his continuing, even heightening, skills in the administration of such major building works.[67] Indeed, throughout the 1090s he continued to demonstrate his worth in this area at Rochester Cathedral and in his foundation of a nunnery nearby at Malling. Since Gundulf did not die until 1108, and thus well after the completion of the White Tower, he must remain the prime, if not the only, candidate for overseeing the Phase 2 works as well.

Some form of supervisory role in the construction of the White Tower does not imply that the bishop was the architect in the sense of designer and project

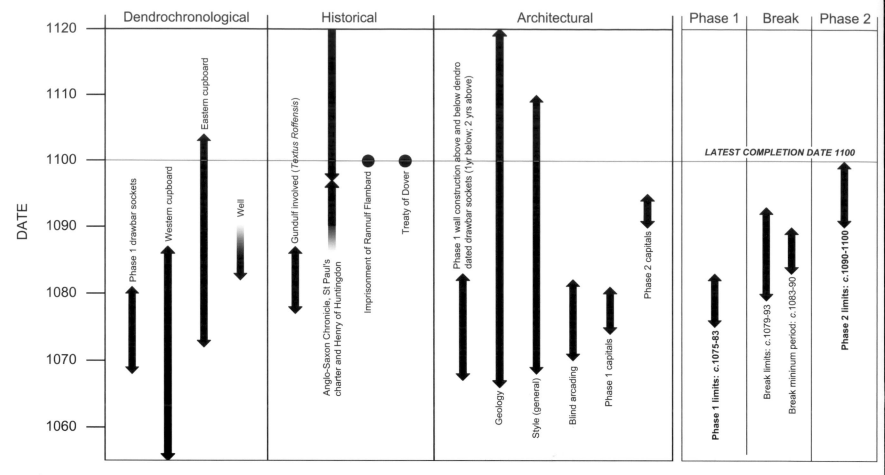

22   Graph summarising the diverse evidence for the chronology of the primary construction of the White Tower.

manager. Indeed, Gundulf's life prior to his appointment to the see of Rochester in 1077 does not reveal a background likely to have produced a trained mason, engineer or architect, and there is no explicit reference to his involvement in any architectural projects during these years. Rather, the evidence indicates that Gundulf was primarily a conscientious and efficient ecclesiastical administrator.[68] Born *circa* 1024 in the Vexin (east of Rouen) and schooled in Rouen, where he was a clerk in the cathedral, Gundulf arrived at the abbey of Bec *circa* 1057. In the 1050s the school of Bec was at the forefront of training the administrators demanded by the rapid expansion of the area under Norman control.[69] At Bec Gundulf became close to both Lanfranc and Anselm, and assumed the office of sacrist soon after taking his vows. He followed Lanfranc and other monks from Bec to William the Conqueror's new foundation at St Etienne, Caen, in 1063, where Lanfranc became abbot and Gundulf his assistant.[70] When Lanfranc was appointed Archbishop of Canterbury in 1070, Gundulf again followed him as his coadjutor, and, until 1077, bore the burden of the temporal administration of the archbishopric. Even after his appointment to the see of Rochester, Gundulf continued his supportive role to Canterbury: during his episcopate the Bishop of Rochester assumed the role of coadjutor-bishop of

Canterbury. Moreover, during the long *inter regnum* of 1089–93 Gundulf administered the archiepiscopal see *in spiritualibus*, and, later (1097–1100 and 1103–6), when Anselm was in exile, the archbishop received support from Gundulf, who again took charge both of the temporal and spiritual administration of the archbishopric. Although not explicitly linked to building works prior to his appointment at Rochester, it is noteworthy that during his early years at Rouen the construction of the Romanesque cathedral was in progress (consecrated 1063); at Bec he witnessed the first half of the rebuilding of Herluin's small monastery (*circa* 1060–73);[71] at Caen he was possibly prior from the foundation of William the Conqueror's great church of St Etienne (in the early 1060s),[72] and left when work was presumably well advanced (there were dedications in 1073, 1077 and 1081);[73] and at Canterbury he had not only been present as coadjutor when Lanfranc rebuilt the entire cathedral from 1071 to 1077, but his later involvement in the administration of the archbishopric and the close links between Rochester and Canterbury meant that he would have been at least aware of Ernulf's and Anselm's rebuilding of the eastern arm (begun 1093–6[74] and substantially complete by 1110,[75] even 1107).[76]

The known facts of the life of Gundulf are thus sufficient to demonstrate that even by 1077 his knowledge of administration would have included an awareness of the organisation of major building programmes. Moreover, at both St Etienne and Canterbury Cathedral he assumed a role second only to Lanfranc, and, since this role was very much administrative, his involvement in the building programmes was almost inevitable. As Lanfranc's coadjutor at Canterbury, Gundulf could well have been an obvious choice as supervisor of one of William the Conqueror's more ambitious architectural enterprises. Lanfranc's own loyalty and closeness to William I is well established,[77] and Gundulf's parallel career, even origins, would have made him similarly suited to the Conqueror. What remains unclear is the contribution, if any, of Gundulf to the design of the White Tower. While such ambiguity is to be expected at this date in even the great cathedrals and abbeys, the situation is complicated at the White Tower because Gundulf was not the patron in the manner of an abbot, prior or bishop in his own establishment, and any patronal input to the design may have come from elsewhere: either William the Conqueror himself or, conceivably, by another crucial, hidden, figure.

Since we have no evidence that Gundulf was definitely supervising the construction of the White Tower from its conception, and since we know that William I was frequently outside his kingdom during the 1070s, the possibility of involvement of a figure other than the king merits some consideration. William Fitz Osbern was a close associate of William I, an experienced castle builder and familiar with the only known prototype for the White Tower,[78] but his death in 1071 would appear to rule him out. That William I de Mandeville is recorded in 1100 as the first known keeper of the Tower of London could suggest earlier involvement of his family: his father, Geoffrey, was one of the most important Norman barons in England, with a massive fiefdom in Essex.[79] However, Lanfranc's role as the administrator of England in the absence of the king, and the Gundulf connection, mean that a better case can be made for the archbishop. Lanfranc's involvement at the highest level of affairs of state around the time of the start of works on the White Tower is illustrated by his regency for William in 1075, during which he successfully squashed the English rebellion.[80] Quite feasibly, then, Gundulf's role at the Tower of London could have been at the request of Archbishop Lanfranc, William I directly or, even, one of William's barons experienced in military construction.

As with any medieval building, conscious or unconscious influence on the design also results from the selection of an architect, master mason or group of craftsmen. The sculptural detail of St John's Chapel strongly supports links with the architecture of the institutions in which Gundulf spent time, especially Canterbury Cathedral. Although these links relate to the work of the 1090s, the initial construction, with which Gundulf is more firmly connected, also had similar associations expressed both in the form of the chapel and in the use of the external blind arcading. Therefore, it is quite possible that Gundulf facilitated the employment of masons known to him from previous, even current, projects elsewhere – most logically from Canterbury or Rochester. There remain, however, no grounds to suppose that he was in any practical sense the architect of the White Tower and, as with so many other great buildings, the actual designer must remain something of a mystery. In the absence of an identifiable architect, or mason, we can undertake only the ultimately more rewarding task of examining the architectural milieu from which the White Tower arose and the evidence provided by comparable castle and church design. This evidence for the origins of the design of the White Tower as a whole is examined in Chapter Nine, and with specific regard to St John's Chapel in Chapter Three.

THE FORM AND EXTENT OF THE PRIMARY BUILDING

The close analysis of the fabric and other evidence during the White Tower Recording and Research Project led to the identification of the building break and the confirmation that most of the masonry dates from the primary construction that began between 1075 and 1079, and which was completed by 1100, as discussed above. This study, however, did not simply refine the chronology of the initial construction: it also comprised a reassessment of the form of the White Tower as originally built. Accordingly, this section of the chapter considers the evidence for the form and extent of the Romanesque building.

The Exterior Elevations

The South Elevation: A Detailed Case Study (fig. 23)

The coincidence of repairs to the south elevation with the duration of the White Tower Recording and Research Project[81] enabled analysis and recording to be undertaken prior to the works being carried out; it also permitted a watching brief to take place during the raking out of modern mortar and the replacement of decayed stone.[82] In view of the periodic repairs to the external faces of the White Tower – seen most obviously in the Portland stone dating from the seventeenth and eighteenth centuries – the careful scrutiny of this one elevation has enabled us to test the extent of rebuilding and to determine the appearance of the elevation as built by 1100.

The south elevation comprises five bays separated by pilaster buttresses; it is flanked to the west by the south-west corner buttress and turret, and to the east by the projection of the chapel apse. The south-east

50.0m

45.0m

40.0m

35.0m

30.0m

25.0m

20.0m

15.0m

10.0m

5.0m OSBM

50.0m

45.0m

40.0m

35.0m

30.0m

25.0m

20.0m

15.0m

10.0m

5.0m OSBM

turret simply rises from the top of the easternmost bay, and is not expressed on the elevation below battlement level. There are windows to each bay on every floor level above the basement, with the exception of the entrance floor of Bay 1,[83] which contains the only known primary entrance to the White Tower. Evidence for the basement fenestration is found in a part-surviving, but blocked and mutilated, window in Bay 2. Additionally, two windows to the chapel aisle and one to the gallery puncture the buttresses between Bays 3 and 4, and Bays 4 and 5. Both these windows and the double windows on the second floor of Bays 1 and 2 are eleventh-century openings, albeit refaced externally, and, together, they make this elevation the most densely fenestrated of the White Tower.[84] In view of the fact that the south elevation faces the river and the larger part of the bailey in which it was built, this relative proliferation of windows is not surprising.

Buttresses

The south elevation is articulated by pilaster buttresses that continue eastwards around the apse. To the west, the elevation ends in a great corner buttress of similar projection to the pilaster buttresses, and, higher up the elevation, this breaks free to form the south-west turret. The use of Portland stone for quoins shows that the buttresses have been at least partially refaced, if not wholly rebuilt, and the study of the petrography and bedding mortar of the rubble facework of the buttresses confirms that this too is mostly repair work. There is sufficient evidence, however, to reveal that not only was the White Tower externally divided into bays by buttresses, but that they were broadly of the form that survives today. Although little primary bedding mortar was observed in the buttresses during the recent repair programme, Type 1 mortar was found on the western buttress, where there is a large area of Caen stone. Similar concentrations of Caen stone are to be found on the other buttresses and the south-west turret at this level (approximately 11.0–17.0 m OSBM). That on the turret is not only bedded in Type 1 mortar, but also preserves the marks of rough diagonal tooling typical of Romanesque masonry, the good state of preservation here doubtless aided by the abutment of the south forebuilding between the twelfth and seventeenth centuries. Interestingly, the Caen stone changes from small blocks to large blocks at 14.2 m OSBM on the south-west turret and the two westernmost buttresses, and this consistency in the banding of the Caen stone supports the identification of all this ashlar as predominantly eleventh century. A similar banding of ashlar across the turret and buttresses is seen in the distribution and block size of the dolomitised Chalk, which is situated immediately above the Caen stone: this stone type is associated only with Phase 1 fabric (see below). Further evidence, if needed, for the originality of the buttresses is provided by the quoins that form the internal angles between the bays and the sides of the buttresses. These are predominantly of Caen stone, which is set in Type 1 mortar and which preserves rough diagonal tooling. Moreover, on the east side of the second buttress from the west, the primary quoins continue around the side of the buttress (12.58–13.61 m OSBM). All these observations, which show that the present buttresses preserve the position and much of the fabric of their eleventh-century predecessors, are concentrated in the lower half of the elevation, where the buttresses are wider and deeper. Higher up, the buttresses have suffered more than the renewal of quoins, since removal of stones for replacement in 1997–8 revealed that the repairs from the seventeenth century onwards had left less, if any, primary fabric *in situ*. Since the form of the buttresses is different on each elevation, such a lack of evidence for originality in those on the south elevation might be problematic, were it not for the survival of Phase 2 bedding mortar in the facing masonry immediately flanking the buttresses. This suggests that any upper sections of the primary buttresses cannot have been wider than they are today, although they could have been narrower, or non-existent. Of course, the upper part of the western buttress is narrower than the others, but it is most likely that this was designed to accommodate the symmetrical arrangement of second-floor double windows in the two western bays. As for the height reached by the original buttresses, the change in level of the upper string-course between the two western bays was a feature of the Romanesque building (see below) and almost certainly would have occurred at a buttress, as it does today. There is every reason to suppose, therefore, that the buttresses on the south elevation perpetuate the positions and dimensions of the primary pilaster buttresses, although details such as the precise angle and form of the weatherings are likely to have changed during the various repair programmes.

Doorway

While no longer the sole entrance to the White Tower, the doorway in the westernmost bay of the south elevation provided the only known primary external entrance,[85] raised roughly 6.4 m above the external ground level, as it is today.[86] The location of the entrance on the south side probably reflected the greater importance attached to the elevation facing the river, and would have opened into the larger part of the bailey that is known to have surrounded the building. The position of the doorway in the westernmost bay implies that the external stair ran eastward, parallel to the façade, as it does today. Perhaps we can assume that this was still the case in the later twelfth century, when the south forebuilding that protected the top of this stair was almost certainly in existence.[87] Significantly, similar arrangements are found in the square

47

24   The chamfered stone of the western jamb revealed during restoration of the original doorway in 1973.

keeps at Canterbury, Corfe, Norwich, Rochester and Castle Rising.

The doorway itself probably ceased to be the principal entrance to the White Tower at, by or with the building of the Jewel House (in existence by 1508), which required the removal of the external stair (assuming that the stair had survived the building of the Constable's Hall by the early fourteenth century).[88] Although it continued, presumably, to link the western room of the White Tower to the forebuilding, with the latter's demolition in 1674[89] the door was simply blocked.[90] The doorway was converted to a window with Portland stone dressings, almost certainly during the refitting of the western entrance-floor room as a repository for 'sea service' arms in the years 1734–6,[91] but it was reinstated in 1973 and provided with the present timber external stair, echoing what is likely to have been the original arrangement.[92] The works of 1973 involved lowering the sill to its original height of 14.54 m OSBM and extending the Portland stone external jambs to this level. During the course of the works remains of stone steps were discovered: these were necessary to rise the 800 mm from the original threshold up to the level of the entrance floor. As with the window embrasures, the remodelling of the doorway in Portland stone had little effect beyond the depth of the new architraves, and thus the primary embrasure is preserved largely

intact. While the threshold of the eleventh-century doorway is now known, however, its height is less easily determined. The front of the soffit of the barrel vault has been rebuilt, almost certainly to accommodate the higher apex of the opening of 1736. If the jambs and arch were concentric with the embrasure, the surviving primary jambs suggest that the apex of the present doorway is 130 mm higher than that of the eleventh century. At the White Tower, however, none of the primary doorways that open into barrel-vaulted passages is concentric in this manner, since the doorway arches spring from a lower level than the embrasure arches, in effect creating a tympanum. Following similar proportions to the preserved doorways, it must be suspected that the apex of the principal entrance was approximately 800 mm lower than it is today. In this light it is perhaps significant that the upper courses of the jambs are not eleventh-century work.

The door jambs are evidently a primary feature because they display tooling of apparently identical form to that of the adjacent primary reveals. More significantly still, the ashlar of the jambs matches the coursing of the earlier walls and is also of the distinctive dolomitised Chalk. Details of the construction of the primary door jambs were exposed by the works of 1973. These uncovered the alternating use of chamfered and keyed-in stones at the junction of the jambs and the reveals (fig. 24). Drawbar sockets are located 60–80 mm to the rear of the jambs, showing the means by which the primary door was secured. One of the planks that lined these drawbar sockets has been dated by dendrochronology to after 1050. As with the drawbar sockets of the internal doors, those in the entrance can hardly be a later insertion since one socket is 3.50 m (11 ft 6 in.) deep.

Although the doorway passage is not ornamented, the use of ashlar, with the exception of the rubble vault, gives it special treatment. Moreover, in the side walls there are niches measuring, on the west, 735 mm wide, 490 mm deep and 1,510 mm high, and, on the east, 745 mm wide, 465 mm deep and 1,440 mm high. That on the west is set back from the door jambs by 1,705 mm, and that on the east by 1,680 mm. These niches are now rectangular in form, but evidence of their original round-headed arches is preserved, and they bear comparison to the single example at Colchester Castle.

Fenestration

While there is no evidence that there were ever windows in the south wall of the apsidal basement room, there was at least one basement window on the south elevation. Evidence for this can be seen in the second bay from the west (Bay 2), where, on the interior face of the wall, there survives the western half of a rear arch, with its splay intact to a depth of 660 mm

25 Remains of the partly blocked primary window visible in the south wall of the western room of the basement.

(fig. 25). The rear arch and splay permit the reconstruction of the form of the window, and this is identical to two basement windows in the west wall of the White Tower recorded in plans made prior to their blocking in 1733.[93] That is, a window with a rear arch 1.5 m (5 ft) in width with a steep splay rising and tapering through the 4.31 m (14.14 ft) thick wall to an outer window only 200 mm wide and 850 mm high. The apex of the outer window arch would have been 330 mm above that of the rear arch, and, at 14.67 m OSBM, immediately below the entrance floor. The blocking of the window with rough masonry set back from the internal wall face pre-dates the insertion of the vault in 1732–4. Moreover, it is evident that the blocking of this window occurred at, or by, the time of the creation of the adjacent intramural spiral staircase, since three-dimensional computer modelling of the stair and the reconstructed window during this project demonstrated wholly unambiguous interference: that is, the window and the stair could not have coexisted.[94] The window appears to have existed in the late 1350s when 'ferramenta' were ordered.[95] Late medieval origins for the staircase are possible, therefore, and it was certainly rebuilt in 1676.[96] Considering the early disappearance of the window, it is remarkable that the two sill stones of the eleventh-century outer window can still be identified. A piece of L-shaped ashlar bedded in the shelly Type 1 mortar of Phase 1 coincides almost exactly with the projected position of the western jamb and sill of the outer window. Another L-shaped ashlar, in this case inverted or reversed, is to be found bedded in Portland-type mortar, just below the *in situ* sill fragment, and could represent the other half of the Romanesque sill: it certainly displays rough diagonal tooling. That both these pieces of ashlar should be of the same dolomitised Chalk adds further credibility to this identification, since, as we have seen, this stone type is known only in the work of Phase 1 at the White Tower. A third piece of dolomitised Chalk is to be found 200 mm below the putative *ex situ* sill stone and has evidently been used in the packing around the seventeenth-century Portland stone doorway: it is a reused ashlar and could well come from the jamb of the eleventh-century basement window.

While there can be no doubt that the spiral stair in Bay 2 is later than the basement window, this removes a convenient explanation for the eccentric location of the latter. It is placed 1.12 m to the west of the centre of the 4.23 m-wide bay, whereas the two known basement windows of the west elevation were placed centrally to their respective bays. With or without a forebuilding and with or without a staircase rising across the south elevation, this window would have been clear of obstruction, either placed where it is or placed centrally, and thus no explanation is provided by the access arrangements. Likewise, the location of the east wall of the western room of the basement has no significance, because it lies 3 m to the east of the reconstructed rear arch. In the absence of any obvious cause for the eccentric position of this window, we must consider whether it really is eccentric: internally, it could have provided a symmetrical arrangement to the south end of the western basement if in conjunction with a window in Bay 1; or it could have been balanced externally by a second window, also in Bay 2. There is no evidence for the former presence of either, but the level of the threshold of the entrance and the necessity for a staircase or landing in this area would appear to rule out a basement window in Bay 1. Indeed, a doubling up of basement windows in Bay 2 could have been the result of the difficulty of placing a basement window in Bay 1. The suggestion gains some credibility from the fact that the south elevation has a degree of fenestration not seen on the other elevations.

With the exception of the westernmost bay, which contains the principal doorway to the White Tower, each bay of the entrance floor on the south elevation now has a window. The three straight bays adjacent to the apse mark the position of the room below the chapel, and, in common with the floors above, have Bath stone windows of pseudo-Romanesque form. However, while the chapel windows date from Salvin's restoration of 1864, these lower windows date from the restoration of *circa* 1880–2.[97] They replaced earlier Portland stone windows that probably dated from immediately after the demolition of the Jewel House, which abutted the south elevation until 1668–9. Although it is not clear whether the late medieval Jewel House obscured the entrance-floor windows, the internal remains of the pre-Salvin jambs match similar details on the windows built after the demolition of the adjacent south forebuilding in 1674.[98] The only primary window of the room below the chapel for which there is a record is that at the apex of the apse, but the embrasure for this is much smaller than those in the straight bays of the south elevation.[99] The embrasures of the straight bays and the apse, however, all have stepped floors that could imply higher sills: thus, all these windows could have been small. Between the windows of the room below the chapel and the doorway of Bay 1 there is a Portland stone window that dates from the years 1674–1754,[100] the Romanesque precursor of which opened into a wide barrel-vaulted embrasure that typifies the windows of the east and west rooms at this level and on the first floor.[101] The primary window in this bay, therefore, was almost certainly of identical form to those throughout the two principal rooms at this level. Unfortunately, there is no unambiguous evidence of the form of the main Romanesque window type on the entrance floor, since all the embrasures are devoid of primary window openings and these were all replaced before adequate record was made. However, the mean width of the embrasures for the east and west rooms is 1.87 m, and this is only slightly narrower than that of the three south-facing windows of the room below the chapel (1.98 m). This could suggest that all the entrance-floor windows were of similar dimensions and form, but there is no evidence that the stepped floors of the apsidal room were echoed in the main rooms. Thus, there may well have been a distinction between the different rooms similar to that which we know was the case at the level of the chapel (see below). Any similarity between the entrance-floor windows of the east and west rooms and those of the first floor, about which we know so much more, is improbable: the embrasures at the higher level have a mean width of 2.34 m, and this additional 470 mm almost certainly reflects the fact that only the upper floor had double windows (see below). Moreover, when William Mills undertook the first and most extensive remodelling of the quoins and windows of the White Tower with Portland stone in the years 1638–40, the detailed accounts for the repairs on the west side describe what we have every reason to suppose was the Romanesque arrangement: from bottom to top, the bands of fenestration comprised 'lower windowes', 'duble windows' and 'upp windowes'.[102]

At first-floor level it is evident that single windows again dominated the primary south elevation, since the narrow Romanesque window embrasures of the chapel were simply reused by Salvin in his restoration of 1864.[103] In the course of this work, Salvin replaced the windows of St John's Chapel with the Bath stone pseudo-Romanesque ones that survive today, removing Portland stone windows that almost certainly dated from 1638.[104] The remarkable fact that for the most part the internal splays up to about 300 mm from the external wall face are of undisturbed primary fabric confirms that the re-fenestration in both 1638 and 1864 simply reused eleventh-century embrasures. Moreover, it also shows that in general form and dimensions the chapel windows were quite unlike other windows in the White Tower. This is especially the case with the windows positioned in buttresses.

However correct Salvin was in the disposition and dimensions of his windows, the intervening phase of Portland stone windows means that he had no more hard evidence than we to determine the precise external appearance of the eleventh-century chapel windows. Salvin's choice of relatively elaborate windows with nook shafts was not based on any idea that the chapel alone should have such sophisticated treatment, since he planned to introduce similar windows throughout the entire White Tower,[105] but the argument would be a reasonable one. However, one early voussoir does survive that is likely to come from an external arch of a chapel window, and this suggests that the chapel windows were simpler than those reconstructed by Salvin. This voussoir is of Quarr stone, has diagonal tooling, and is almost certainly primary. It is now placed ex situ in the stone-work used to make good the internal splay of the window at the apex of the ambulatory at gallery level. It is unclear as to whether the voussoir arrived in its current position in 1638 or 1864, but the projected diameter of the arch from which it comes is 1.09–1.73 m, and consistent with local reuse: that is, it is most likely to derive from the window where it is reused. The fact that the reconstructed range of diameters fits the primary windows of both levels of the chapel is suggestive, although it could also derive from the single windows elsewhere on the second floor. A complete absence of mouldings on the visible parts of this voussoir could indicate that the chapel windows were of simple form similar to the other primary windows at the White Tower.[106] Nevertheless, while we have grounds to suspect that Salvin's reconstructed windows may be over-elaborate, the evidence for a plainer type is evidently insubstantial, and, in the way that they distinguish the chapel windows from the other windows of the White Tower, Salvin's windows perpetuate an important aspect of the primary design.

The differentiation of the chapel windows from those of the east and west rooms applies to the first and second floors, but is more pronounced at the former: the Romanesque chapel windows at first-floor level would have averaged approximately 1 m in width compared with 1.88 m for the other first-floor windows. In addition to the different widths of the first-

26 (*above left*) *In situ* primary voussoirs of a Romanesque double window at the northern end of the first-floor western room.

27 (*above right*) *In situ* primary jamb stones in the south elevation, adjacent to the later Portland stone jamb: the only surviving external detail of the Romanesque double windows of the first floor.

floor windows inside and outside the chapel, there is ample evidence that the windows of the east and west rooms had double lights (fig. 26). Of course, the narrow width of the chapel windows does not rule out the use of two-light windows, but it certainly makes it extremely unlikely.

On the south elevation, the wide barrel-vaulted embrasures to the two western windows at first-floor level lit the western room. They are identical to the other primary embrasures of the east and west rooms and are likely to have had double windows too. Indeed, the only external structural evidence for the first-floor windows is found in the westernmost bay of the south elevation, where a primary jamb was discovered during the course of the White Tower Recording and Research Project (fig. 27). Four of the quoins are Quarr stone and one is an undifferentiated oolite. Quarr stone is found only in eleventh-century work at the White Tower and, as we have seen, this stone type was not used outside its immediate hinterland after the early twelfth century.[107] That the jamb is primary is confirmed by the use of Type 1 bedding mortar, and the uppermost quoin marks the very limit of the Phase 1 fabric in this area. That the jamb belonged to a window rather than a doorway into the upper room of the south forebuilding is suggested both by its primary nature (the forebuilding was an addition of Phase 2 or later[108]) and its position. The quoins lie 910 mm from the centre line of the bay, thus giving a reconstructed opening 1.82 m in width, if symmetry is assumed. The arris of the jamb in this case is likely to represent the actual edge of the window, since removal of one of the blocking stones showed that these quoins ran back into the wall and did not return to create a space for a nook shaft. The surviving quoins suggest a simple window form for the first floor that is corroborated by eighteenth-century measured drawings. These record double

windows, which were destroyed around 1800 (possibly the subject of 'cutting out walls' in 1805[109]), on the east, west and north elevations that, at a span of around 1.88 m, approximately matched the reconstructed dimensions of this example on the south elevation.

The double windows that survived to be recorded in detail have been identified previously as the Romanesque originals,[110] but there are good grounds to suppose that many, if not all, of these windows had been rebuilt in Portland stone in the seventeenth century. There is an unambiguous account of the replacement of the western double windows at this level in 1638,[111] and what appears to be a similar account for the replacement of the eastern windows in 1639.[112] The fitting out of a new powder room in 1608, however, included the 'making of ix^en double windowes, each windowe haveing double leaves, wth other Carpente^rs worke thereunto'.[113] The nine windows suggest that this refers to the western room of the first floor, and, therefore, that the White Tower had double windows prior to the Portland stone repairs. More conclusive evidence is found in the second embrasure from the west in the north wall of the western room, where there survive the rear arches of a double-light window, the voussoirs of which are chalk with Romanesque diagonal tooling and, therefore, clearly not part of the Portland stone repairs of 1638.[114] Given the correspondence between these rear arches, the jamb on the south elevation and the windows recorded in the eighteenth-century measured drawings,[115] it can be inferred that not only were there double windows to the east and west rooms of the first floor in the late eleventh century, but that the 1638 repairs were confined to replacement of the decayed external architraves with new Portland stone (fig. 28).

The positioning of the double-window sills at perhaps 22.60 m OSBM on the south elevation, and

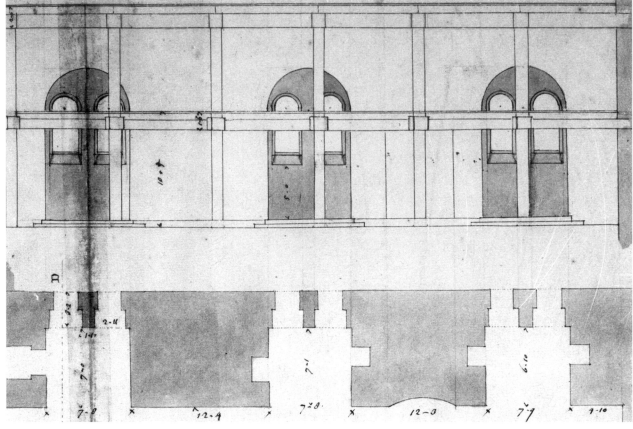

28 The first-floor double windows of the eastern room as recorded in 1721. While it is almost certain that the external quoins had been replaced in 1638, the form of the windows and the internal detail survived from the eleventh century (detail).

23.04 m OSBM elsewhere, means that the windows of the east and west chambers were 2.69–3.13 m above floor level. Even the lower south windows would have been well above eye level, and, as with the basement windows, a near-contemporary parallel for this is to be found at Canterbury Castle (*circa* 1100–20). Here, the single-light windows of the first, or principal, floor are placed at a height of 3.3 m.[116] The embrasures to the Canterbury windows differ from those of the White Tower, however, in that they are four-stepped horizontally and vertically, so that the embrasures reduce from the large rear arches to the smaller window apertures in a series of broadly concentric steps. A similar arrangement, with less concentric steps but certainly with stepping of the floor of the embrasure, survives throughout at Colchester Castle. In both these near-contemporary examples this had the effect of rendering the embrasure entirely redundant: it neither allowed use of the space as an extension of the room nor made provision for window seats. The first-floor embrasures at the White Tower, however, show no evidence of such stepping, and the primary cupboards in four of the embrasures in the side walls of the east and west rooms confirm that these spaces were utilised.

On the second floor, the chapel gallery follows the plan of the aisles and ambulatory below and this results in similar fenestration, albeit with slightly smaller windows and only one buttress window.[117] Again, Salvin's restoration is correct in the position and dimensions of the chapel windows. To the west of the three chapel bays, the south elevation at this upper level does not simply comprise bays and fenestration typical of the rest of the storey, for Bays 1 and 2 have pairs of double windows that quite clearly did not exist on the other elevations. The four distinctive double-light windows appear to represent the eleventh-century arrangement, although they were rebuilt in 1638.[118] The single rear arches of the windows are of Caen stone with rough diagonal tooling, and thus evidently Norman fabric, but the jambs of the double lights themselves were part of the 1638 rebuilding. The easternmost double window is now blocked, and the fact that the western light was built blind has led to this window being seen as a feature of the eleventh-century design.[119] Examination of the arch and jambs, however, reveals that the Romanesque window was not blocked in any way. The only *in situ* primary fabric in this window is the rear arch, and all the stonework within the compass of the rear arch is bonded with mortars that are quite different from those used in the primary construction of the White Tower. In other words, the diagonally tooled voussoirs of the easternmost light are reset.

Turret windows first appear on the south elevation at this level: the lowest is on the south-west turret, slightly below the level of the second-floor double windows. As with most of the other splayed windows opening onto the three spiral stairs of the White Tower, the internal detail of the window has escaped modification and is evidently a primary feature. The four windows above this staircase window light the top of the south-west turret and are similar to the fenestration of the upper levels of all the turrets at the White Tower. They are of unsplayed form, rebuilt externally in Portland stone, largely rebuilt internally or obscured by brickwork added in later strengthening of the turrets,[120] but are essentially Romanesque in position, number and form. Evidence for their primary nature comes from pictorial sources such as the fifteenth-century view of the White Tower from the south-west (see fig. 104), and from visible fabric such as the Romanesque voussoirs and jambs visible on the interior of the east window of the south-west turret.

Blind Arcading and String-Courses

The exterior emphasis given to the first floor of the White Tower by the use of double windows was exaggerated by the use of blind arcading to enclose the windows of each bay. Although this feature is represented on the south elevation entirely by quoins and voussoirs of Portland stone from the seventeenth and eighteenth centuries,[121] its primary nature can be established. Most importantly, the areas enclosed by the blind arcading are recessed approximately 200 mm from the plane of the wall above, and, since the rubble both above and below the arches is for the most part primary, evidently this feature was part of the eleventh-century building. Moreover, the Portland stone voussoirs and the additional angle order from which the arches spring represent direct replacement of Romanesque ashlar: the less exposed east and north elevations preserve *in situ* non-Portland ashlar in both these features, much of which is primary.[122]

Similar evidence reveals that the Portland stone string-courses of the south elevation are also straightforward replacements of eleventh-century equivalents. A string-course across all five bays at approximately 20.85 m OSBM marks the position of the first floor, and again emphasises it. Here, the primary walling above the string-course is recessed approximately 70 mm from that below, and the pattern is repeated on the other elevations. Another string-course across all five bays is to be found at the top of the second floor. This too marks an offset (about 50 mm) in the eleventh-century wall faces and, therefore, it also represents the replacement of a primary feature. The offset, and thus the argument for its originality, applies to Bay 1, where the string-course sits 1.54 m higher than in the other bays.

In addition to these string-courses, which perpetuate the primary arrangement, there is a feature on the south elevation that may represent the fragmentary *in situ* survival of a Romanesque string-course. Immediately east of the lowest window of the south-west turret (at 26.26 m OSBM) three blocks of oolitic limestone survive. The bedding mortar for these stones was not revealed by the recent repairs, but the stone type alone suggests that they pre-date the Portland stonework and, thus, are potentially primary work. Moreover, the fact that the surface of the stones is worn and that they are arranged in a precise horizontal band with a uniform height of 260 mm suggests that they were part of an earlier string-course: the use

of shelly oolites would be typical for this in a Romanesque context. If this was a string-course, it differs from the other, primary, examples on the south elevation in that it does not mark a change in the plane of the main wall face. The location is perhaps significant, however, since it coincides with the approximate position of the roof of the south forebuilding that was demolished in 1676 (see below).

Plinth

The rebuilding of the plinth in 1955–6 followed an investigation by Dr D. E. Strong that, although not a thorough archaeological excavation, was sufficient to provide a good understanding of the evolution of this part of the building, and the present form of the plinth represents a reconstruction of the original form. By removing the easily identifiable nineteenth-century repairs, it was possible to demonstrate that the earlier plinth joined the vertical wall immediately below the double course of ashlar and that it was primary. Dr Strong's interpretation is evidently reliable, because surviving photography shows that the south wall and the buttresses have no face work below the point where the batter of the plinth meets the wall. Moreover, the 'roughly-coursed ragstone and sandstone lumps' of the plinth were set in a 'shelly lime-mortar':[123] almost certainly, our Type 1 mortar. The plinth of the south side terminated in the mitred corner seen in restored form today. The investigations revealed that the primary form was a smooth batter similar to that at Colchester Castle, and differing from stepped plinths, such as that partly preserved at Canterbury Castle. Along the western part of the south elevation the plinth was of uniform construction, but this changed at the eastern side of Bay 2: east of this point the plinth was built in large steps, with the stonework of the batter not keyed into it. Strong considered that the lack of keying explained the disappearance of primary masonry on top of these steps, and took their clean-cut form as a good indication that they were a primary feature (fig. 29). His explanation of this feature was that the steps provided a solid base for scaffolding, with the batter finished off later. The change in construction after the two western bays was explained in terms of the forebuilding, but this is not a satisfactory explanation: the forebuilding did not extend across Bay 2 and, if the forebuilding was primary, then there would be no reason to continue the battered plinth across the entire south elevation. Some connection with the position of the main entrance is possible, and it could be that the steps relate to the lower part of entrance stairs across the south elevation. Whatever their function, it is likely that the steps are primary, since the point where they start is marked by a change in the form of the primary buttresses: the two western buttresses and the south-west corner buttresses have plinths at a higher level than those to the east.

29 Excavation of the plinth during restoration in 1955–6, showing the primary stepping that from the outset underlay a plain batter. The stepping stops at the original mitred south-east angle of the plinth, which can be seen immediately below the first of the angled buttresses of the apse.

Turrets

The repairs of 1997–8 to the south elevation provided a rare opportunity to examine the fabric of the south faces of the south-west and the south-east turrets. The consistency of the petrography with walling below the turrets, and the use of Type 2 mortar, confirm that the two turrets were part of the initial construction of the White Tower as completed by *circa* 1100, and internal examination corroborates this. This is hardly surprising in the case of the south-west turret, since it is clear that its construction was intended from the completion of the plinth, if not earlier: the massive corner buttresses made provision for the turret from basement level, even if its spiral stair rises from the first floor only. The status of the south-east turret has been more contentious,[124] presumably on the grounds that it is not matched by a wide buttress below and is not very square in plan, and that this corner of the building has been viewed as suspect since the apse was misconstrued as an addition.[125] Because it is not surprising that the turret does not manifest itself on the lower part of the south elevation, since this was never a corner of the building, the only unusual feature is its irregular plan. Far from being the result of poor setting out, however, its plan responds to its position above the ambulatory of the chapel: the east face of the turret is precisely angled so that it loads onto the piers of the gallery and the main arcades of the chapel

below. That structural considerations were necessary here is made obvious by the present outward lean of the south-east corner of the White Tower. A less carefully designed turret would have exacerbated the problems caused by the thinner walls of the chapel, perhaps to the point of failure (fig. 30).

Battlements and Wall-Walk

Of all the primary features on the south elevation, and indeed all elevations, the battlements and the wall-walk are the least known. The repairs of 1997–8 to the south elevation confirmed that the quoins and copings of the battlements were completely rebuilt when the Portland stone was added. The petrography revealed an unsuspected concentration of Caen stone at this level, which proved to result from the reuse of earlier coping stones.[126] These were devoid of Romanesque tooling, however, and, given the profiles, are likely to be remnants of the Caen stone battlements that we know were built in 1532.[127] Of earlier battlements nothing physically survives, and the earliest documentary referevnce to them is as late as 1312,[128] but it can be reasonably assumed that they were a feature of the eleventh-century building. As to the form of the primary battlements, the very exposure of such stonework to the weather and to modifications in response to defensive requirements and fashion means that few eleventh-century battlements

54

30 Base of the south-east turret from the west, showing the careful loading of the arches onto the vault above the gallery piers below.

have been preserved. Those at Colchester Castle are probably of the 1080s, since they were preserved when the walls were raised soon after the primary phase. They are distinguished by wide and low merlons.

The wall-walk that would have provided access to the primary battlements was positioned above what is now the second-floor mural passage.[129] While the width of the wall-walk can be reconstructed at approximately 2.3 m (7 ft 6 in.), as the width of the wall less the likely depth of the battlements,[130] the height is not so evident, since the re-roofing of *circa* 1490 and 1962–5 means that pitched roofs abut the north and south battlements, and the east and west battlements are accessible via gutters only. The examination of the south elevation, however, showed that the battlements can hardly have been located lower than they are at present, since Phase 2 fabric extends up to the point of the rebuilt merlons.

Stone

The White Tower is almost entirely built of rubble, most of which is Kentish Rag. This rubble forms the core, most of the internal elevations and a large proportion of the exterior. While the distribution of the Kentish Rag and the other rubble geologies supports the argument that the building was not the result of modification and addition, albeit with a substantial midway building break,[131] it is the sparser ashlar that provides us with the greater insight into the structural history of the White Tower. The wider use of ashlar in the lower half of the external elevations has already been cited as evidence for the building break, and the recent scaffolding of the south elevation provided an opportunity for closer analysis. The ashlar on the south that is feasibly primary is typical of all four elevations in that it is mixed and chiefly comprises Caen, Reigate and dolomitised Chalk, with some Bembridge limestone and Quarr stone. Stone types such as Portland

stone and igneous rock quite obviously belong to post-medieval repairs, while others, although not improbable in a Romanesque context, are demonstrably not primary. For example, the use of a Bath-type oolite is restricted to Salvin's restorations. Further complexity is caused by the documented use of one of the principal primary ashlar types, Caen stone, in the sixteenth-century rebuilding of the battlements and again in more recent repairs:[132] indeed, this stone type may have been used in earlier repairs. Other stone types are more reliably identifiable as primary. Quarr stone ceased to be used outside Hampshire and western Sussex after the early twelfth century. Bembridge limestone is known to have been used throughout the Middle Ages, but its distribution on the south elevation and, internally, in St John's Chapel so closely follows that of the Quarr stone that it must be suspected that both these Isle of White stones (which are immediate geological stratigraphic neighbours) are part of the primary construction only. The dolomitised Chalk is found only in the lower half (i.e., Phase 1 fabric) of the elevation and, coming from the Seine valley near Rouen, may well represent a single shipment of the stone.[133] Reigate does appear later at the Tower and elsewhere, but its use in the south elevation is again restricted almost exclusively to the lower half and, thus, would appear to be mostly, if not entirely, of eleventh-century date. The use of Reigate for the distinctive double coursing at the bottom of the elevations and internally is consistent with this.[134]

We have seen that while the geological banding of several stone types does not in itself indicate a building break, it does suggest strictly horizontal progress on all the walls of the White Tower. It is interesting to note that this banding is paralleled by variation in the size of the ashlar used. Analysis of all four external elevations reveals three bands of ashlar that can be differentiated by size. On the south elevation this is found in the south-west turret, where small squarish blocks are succeeded by larger blocks at 14.61 m OSBM. These extend up to 18.04 m, where recent patching with paving sets replaces primary ashlar until 21.90 m OSBM; here three more courses of small blocks of primary ashlar extend up to the point at which construction turns to rubble (22.53 m OSBM). While the junction of the upper band of small blocks and the large blocks is missing on the south elevation, near-identical banding on the other elevations shows that it falls around 18.20–18.45 m OSBM. Elsewhere on the south elevation, the restoration of the buttresses has left only the lower junction visible on the two western buttresses at, from west to east, 14.20 m OSBM and 14.16 m OSBM. The quoins that mark the internal angles formed between these three buttresses and the rubble panels also show this banding.

The consistency of the banding and the fact that much of this ashlar is identifiably primary, on the

55

grounds of its Type 1 bedding mortar and rough diagonal tooling, confirm that the variation in ashlar size is not a result of later repair. Likewise, it is further proof that the plan of the White Tower was not achieved by addition: construction advanced in a strictly horizontal manner across the whole building. The appearance of occasional courses of larger or smaller blocks within otherwise consistent bands of ashlar means that there is no complete internal consistency within each band. That these odd courses should reflect an atypical stone type is noteworthy: the courses of larger ashlar found in the lower band of smaller Caen stone are almost entirely of Reigate, while smaller courses towards the top of the band of larger blocks are of Caen stone, in contrast to the predominant dolomitised Chalk. Indeed, this raises the question as to whether the dolomitised Chalk should be differentiated from the Caen stone that forms the rest of this band of larger ashlar: the dolomitised Chalk blocks are slightly larger than those of Caen stone. Irrespective of such possible finer banding, the more general small–large–small banding is important because it shows that the size of ashlar at the White Tower cannot be used to determine chronology. A wider significance may be suggested by the connections between geology and stone size, for this raises two possibilities about stone supply. First, it is possible that the ashlar used at the White Tower was cut to size at the quarries, and that the variance in size is similar to, and often in concert with, the successive batches of different stone supply. Contemporary documentation of such pre-cutting of stone is very limited, but the practice did occur in a building closely associated with the White Tower: Lanfranc is recorded as importing squared stone for building from Caen for his work at Canterbury Cathedral in the 1070s.[135] Alternatively, but less probably, the variation in stone size could simply reflect practice by the masons on site, either as a result of successive teams of masons with slight variations in technique or the masons' response to the different stone types.

Mortar

We have seen that the recent repair and repointing of the south elevation provided a rare opportunity to study the bedding mortar and that this revealed overwhelming (and otherwise corroborated) evidence for a building break around 23 m OSBM. Although the viewing and sampling of the bedding mortar were dictated by the repair programme, a reasonably complete picture was gained of the mortars behind the post-medieval repointing and repairs. Moreover, since the works involved the removal of whole stones for replacement, observations were not restricted to viewing mortar in joints, but included bedding mortars used deep within the wall and more reliably original. The results were impressive, for they supported observations made earlier during analysis of the interior of

the White Tower, namely, that the lower half used a lime mortar distinguished by a very high shell content, absent in the mortar of the upper half. In addition to providing evidence of the building break, both mortars were distinctive and largely consistent above and below it. Above all, they confirmed what is shown by the geological and archaeological analyses of the ashlar and rubble stonework. That is, despite its post-medieval details, the form of the south elevation as it survives today is essentially the same as when first built. Taken in conjunction with the internal evidence (see below), this preservation of the original arrangement extends to the bay spacings, buttress forms, the position of windows, the offsets in the wall face, the string-courses and both turrets. Indeed, the only major feature of the south elevation for which there is no direct evidence of a Romanesque equivalent is the battlements, and there is no reason to doubt that these had precursors dating back to the eleventh century.

The North, East and West Elevations

The absence of repair programmes on the north, east and west elevations of the White Tower during the life of the White Tower Recording and Research Project precluded intensive examination: conservation work began on these elevations in 2008 and includes a new programme of archaeological recording and research (by the author) and petrographic survey (by Robin Sanderson and Bernard Worssam). Since many of the features on these elevations are found on the south elevation, they have already been discussed, so the summaries for the other elevations are restricted to other anomalies or idiosyncrasies.

The North Elevation (fig. 31)

The north elevation is unique in several aspects of its original design, but is the most altered: doorways have been created in previously blank walls, windows converted to doorways, two flights of steps built against it, and all masonry above the upper string-course refaced. William Mills's repairs in Portland stone of 1638–40 included this elevation, but the surviving doorways and windows are of the eighteenth century and later. The only earlier doorway has itself been replaced, and is that in the second bay from the west on the entrance floor: this probably dates from the sixteenth century or the early seventeenth.[136] It is clear from the position of a primary garderobe, which the splay of the doorway renders redundant, that there could never have been a Romanesque main window or doorway placed centrally in this bay. Since all the other principal window embrasures and the south doorway are central to the external bays, this indicates that the only openings in this bay were the garderobe window and chute, and, thus, it mirrored the western bay.[137] This is confirmed by the fact that the apex of the sixteenth- or early seventeenth-century embrasure

is 2.0 m lower than the eleventh-century embrasures in the same room, yet has no evidence of blocked masonry above. The eastern entrance-floor doorway is again later, but opens into a primary embrasure. Since this embrasure is identical in form and dimensions to the others in the eastern room at this level, there is every reason to suppose that it was designed to house a window rather than a doorway. Likewise, it would appear that the three eighteenth-century doorways on the first floor reuse eleventh-century window embrasures. Certainly, the two western doorways reuse embrasures of identical form and date to those of the Romanesque windows elsewhere in the same room, although the eastern of these has been modified to take a splay. Nevertheless, the rear arch preserves primary quoins and, uniquely, it is this bay that preserves the *in situ* remains of the rear arch of an eleventh-century double window of the type that dominated this storey.[138] That the eastern doorway at this level occupies the position of a Romanesque window is not so evident, since the creation of a wide-splayed embrasure, most probably in 1636,[139] has removed any eleventh-century rear arch. The segmental arch of this opening, however, is 730 mm lower than the primary embrasures elsewhere in the eastern room, and an area of patching above the seventeenth-century voussoirs corresponds exactly with the necessary blocking of a taller Romanesque window embrasure. The single doorway on the second floor represents the final stage in the post-medieval remodelling of the north elevation to provide external access at all levels, and it can be safely assumed that this also occupies the space of an eleventh-century window, even though it has obliterated any remains.[140]

The north elevation has a deceptive appearance: five of its eight doors open into reused Romanesque window embrasures, and the other three have been cut through bays previously devoid of major openings. As far as we can determine it, then, the original scheme was as follows: basement – no evidence for windows and very possibly none, given that the garderobes were concentrated above;[141] entrance level – garderobe windows and chutes in the two western bays, followed by a blank bay, then a main window in the eastern bay; first floor – main (double) windows in the two western bays, followed by a bay with two garderobe loop windows and chutes, then a main (double) window in the eastern bay; second floor – small single-light windows to each bay.

This dearth of windows when compared with the other elevations results from the location of the spine wall, here roughly aligned with the centre of a bay, and the provision of garderobes. It could be argued that these characteristics are linked, since the two garderobes on the first floor open off the north end of the spine wall and thus make use of a bay that would otherwise be blind. That the garderobes of the entrance floor, however, do not do this but occupy instead the two western bays suggests that the intention was, understandably, to avoid the stacking of garderobes and their windows one above the other.[142] It is on this wall that the building's garderobes are concentrated, even that in the north-west tower discharging through the north elevation on the first floor: only one is found elsewhere, and even this is at the very northern extremity of the east elevation.

In view of the austere and rather functional aspect to the north elevation before post-medieval modifications, it is surprising to find that the two turrets that flank it are the most heavily windowed. Of course, to suggest that the north-east turret presents a north elevation ignores its cylindrical form, but it does present thirteen Romanesque windows to the strictly orthogonal view from the north compared with ten to the east. More significant is the square north-west turret, which presents seven Romanesque windows to the north and only five to the west. This contrasts with the south-west turret, which presents six windows to the west and five to the south, and the differences cannot be explained in terms of the orientation and geometry of the spiral stairs.

The blind arcading and string-courses of the north elevation follow the general pattern of the other elevations. Interestingly, all three garderobe chutes on the first floor are placed immediately above the lower string-course. As with all elevations, the surviving string-courses and blind arcading are of Portland stone, but tantalising remnants of earlier ashlar survive. In the lower string-course the older ashlar is preserved below the thresholds of the eighteenth-century architraves of the three doorways. The ashlar of this earlier string-course is yellow-coloured and of smaller size than the Portland work. Similar ashlar appears in the additional angle order of the blind arcading in all four bays, and suggests that the north elevation escaped complete replacement of quoins in the seventeenth and eighteenth centuries.[143] Of course, that the ashlar appears to pre-date the Portland stone repairs does not mean that it is primary, and even if it is Caen stone, it could well belong to Thomas Cromwell's repairs of 1532, or another date altogether.

The buttresses on the north elevation are like their southern counterparts in general dimensions and height, but, in their current form at least, are distinguished by having two additional stages. Given the evidence for the continuity of form of the pilaster buttresses on the south elevation between the eleventh and seventeenth centuries,[144] it must be suspected that the Portland stone repairs to the northern buttresses were similarly conservative. Certainly, the lower parts of the buttresses are of their original width, since primary internal angle quoins are preserved. These confirm that the western buttress is 150 mm narrower than its eastern counterparts. There is no obvious reason for this, although the narrowness of the angle orders to the blind arcading in the second bay from the east suggests that it is the two eastern buttresses that have been widened. More obvious is the reason why, of all the outward-looking faces of the western turrets, it is only the north elevation of the north-west turret that has an angle order on its inner (in this case north-east) corner. This enables the main face of the turret to be narrower as it runs the height of the elevation, and permits the bays of the north elevation to be wider than would otherwise be the case. Since the design of the White Tower means that the bays of the north elevation are the narrowest, any such attempt to increase their width is wholly understandable.

The West Elevation (fig. 32)

With its square turrets and corner buttresses at both ends, the west elevation has the distinction of being the only symmetrical face of the White Tower, although the north–south slope of the ground does provide some irregularity.[145] Given the evidence of the plinthless east wall, such a slope probably existed from the outset, perhaps leaving the western plinth partly buried (fig. 33). The only significant asymmetry on this elevation is provided by an additional window in the south-west turret.

The west elevation has undergone as much restoration of windows and quoins in Portland stone as any other, yet it is unique in preserving the entire external architraves of two loops of basement windows. Although these are of Portland stone and thus date from the seventeenth- or eighteenth-century repairs, they are likely to represent bona fide primary windows, because, prior to the construction of the brick vaults in the years 1732–4, they are recorded as opening into splayed embrasures identical to that which partly survives in the south wall and which has been discussed above. The entrance floor is now distinguished by tall glazed doors that reuse primary barrel-vaulted window embrasures. The enlargement of the windows can be dated to 1715,[146] and would have involved the removal of the wall with the smaller, and presumably primary, window openings. Disturbed masonry shows that the thickness of the wall at the outer ends of the window embrasures was approximately 850 mm, but the size of the windows can only be surmised. We have seen that the narrower embrasures of the entrance-floor windows, and the documentary evidence, suggest that the double windows of the first floor were not used on that below: a more modest single light is probable. Above the well-attested double windows of the first-floor,[147] the west elevation had single windows to the mural passage. On this elevation, however, the primary windows were almost certainly given Portland stone architraves in 1638, and, more drastically, enlarged in 1812.[148]

The buttresses of the west elevation are similar to those on the south. There is a minor difference where they thin at the level of the external blind arcading, however, since on the west elevation this is marked by the weathering achieving the transition in two stages rather than one. While the general form is likely to represent the primary pilaster buttresses, such detailing may result from the heavy restorations of 1638 and later. There are some grounds for supposing that this detail is primary, nonetheless, since the two-stage weatherings mark a narrowing that is more comparable to the western buttresses of the south elevation. Perhaps significantly, the plinths of the buttresses on the west elevation match the level of the western buttresses of the south elevation.

The East Elevation (fig. 34)

While preserving something nearer its eleventh-century appearance than the north elevation, the east face of the White Tower is the most asymmetric, with its projecting apse at the southern end and the circular turret to the north. The space between these is insufficient for four flat bays and, as a consequence, the three bays of the east elevation are not only the widest on the White Tower, but also include a strip of blank masonry, akin to a buttress, between the northernmost bay and the north-east turret.

The fenestration follows the pattern established for the White Tower. Although there are no basement windows today on this elevation, a loop window formerly existed in the apsidal basement room, where an eighteenth-century widening has destroyed the medieval window.[149] The apse semi-dome vault here, however, necessitated a smaller and lower rear arch than in the timber-ceiled east and west rooms. Additionally, the splay of this apsidal loop followed a curved profile, possibly with the intention of increasing the transmission of light in what is an east-facing window (fig. 35). Of the other basement-level windows we have no evidence, since none was recorded prior to the insertion of the vault in the years 1732–4, but we can assume that there were splayed loops similar to that which partly survives in the south wall of the west room.[150] On the evidence of the arrangement of the basement windows of the west elevation, it is likely that there were at least two loop windows to the basement on the east elevation.

There are no explicit references to the building of the present windows of the entrance floor, but the distinctive projecting architraves of the Portland stone and the absence of any sills is shown on the plan of 1729[151] and later ones. Since they are identical to the western equivalents, it is assumed that they also date from 1715. Again, the rear arches and much of the side walls and barrel vaults of the embrasures are part of the primary construction, and disturbance in the masonry suggests that the thickness of the wall pene-

33 The western plinth as exposed
in 1954: the existence of plinths
along the northern part of the west
wall and along the north wall
remains unknown.

trated by the original windows was approximately 900
mm. The narrower embrasures throughout this level,
compared with those of the first-floor double windows, and the documentary evidence have been discussed, and it is probable that the entrance-floor
windows were all single lights. It is unlikely that all
the entrance-floor windows were alike, however, for it
is evident that the east window of the apse at this level
was smaller than the other windows in the apsidal
room. Although turned into a passage to the eastern
annexe, probably in 1734,[152] what appears to be its
Romanesque form was recorded in 1729.[153] As we have
seen, in common with the other windows in this room,
the embrasure had a stepped floor, and, notwithstanding the fact that the straight-bay embrasures
were of similar width and form to those of the east
and west rooms, the steps could indicate that the
windows throughout the apsidal room were smaller
than elsewhere at entrance level.

At first-floor level, the evidence for double windows
extended to the straight bays of the east elevation,
although the windows recorded in great detail in

1721[154] may have been partly rebuilt (see above). The
windows of the chapel apse, however, were clearly of
different form: as we have seen, the restorations by
Salvin and his predecessors touched only the outer 300
mm or so of the deep embrasures, and they are otherwise of primary construction. The windows of the apse
were in general terms identical to those of the bays of
the south elevation, although their position allowed for
wider splays. There is a difference in the fenestration
of the apse, however, since here there are no windows
in the buttresses. The reason for the difference is simple: the buttress windows in the south elevation are
required to ensure that each of the four bays of the
south aisle of the chapel is lit, while no such windows
are necessary in the apse, with its equal number of
internal and external bays. Significant distortions,
however, in the splays of the ambulatory windows are
necessary to achieve a balanced effect, since the internal responds and external buttresses are less than perfectly matched.[155] The northernmost external bay of the
apse is abutted midway by the east wall of the White
Tower, so no window is provided there. At gallery level

50.0m

45.0m

40.0m

35.0m

30.0m

25.0m

20.0m

15.0m

10.0m

5.0m OSBM

50.0m

45.0m

40.0m

35.0m

30.0m

25.0m

20.0m

15.0m

10.0m

5.0m OSBM

the smaller size of the windows allows an extra window
to be included at this point, although it is of necessity
still narrower than the others. The other windows of
the apse at this level are identical to those of the south
wall, and survive intact other than for Salvin's slightly
fanciful restored external jambs and arches.

The buttresses of the east elevation are more varied
than the others, largely as a result of the different elements of which it is made up. The three straight bays
are separated by a pair of buttresses that, with their
staggered mid-height weatherings, are similar to those
on the west elevation. To the north of these are the
plain buttresses of the north end of the main elevation and the north-east turret. The buttresses of the
apse are similar to those of the main elevations, and
follow in their detail the form of those of the south
elevation. Again, on the basis of the close investigation of the south elevation, it can only be assumed
that these buttresses follow the form of their eleventh-
century predecessors.

Plans

Foundations and the Basement (fig. 36)

As with all levels of the White Tower, the basement
comprises three spaces: a room measuring 25.91m by
10.75 m occupies the whole of the western half, while
the eastern half is occupied by one room measuring
20.47m by 8.16 m, and, to the south, a smaller barrel-
vaulted space with a projecting apse measuring 14.12m
by 4.32 m. The insertion of brick vaults in the larger
two rooms in the years 1732–4 considerably altered the
appearance of the basement floor and resulted in the
loss of most of the original fenestration. The internal
doorways survive, however, and it is clear that the only

primary access to this storey was via the spiral stair
turret, or great vice, in the north-east corner.

The Foundations, the Plinth and the Question of the Apse

The analysis of the primary fabric of the lowest parts
of the White Tower is complicated by the effects of the
insertion of brick vaults in the basement in the years
1732–4, the whitewashing of the interior at this level,
and the repointing of the building inside and out
during the 1960s. On the exterior, however, the repointing and repair of the south elevation in 1997–8
permitted examination of the bedding mortar down to
the level of the top of the plinth at 11.2 m OSBM, and
this revealed a consistent use of the Type 1 shelly
mortar. While the restoration of the plinth in 1954–6
was accompanied by only limited archaeological
recording, the use of a shelly lime mortar was noted,
confirming that the Type 1 mortar extended to 7.09m
OSBM, and almost certainly below this. Limited evidence for mortar types from inside the basement suggests that the shelly mortar continues down to the
foundations: for example, the lowering of the basement floor to 8.40 m OSBM[156] has revealed that the
mortar below the ashlar of the doorway passage at the
north end of the spine wall is of Type 1. This passageway provides another link with the lowest parts of the
external fabric, for here again the lowest courses are of
Reigate ashlar: on the south there are two courses
(upwards from 9.13 m OSBM), while on the north there
are three courses (upwards from 9.23 m OSBM).

The implication of such observations is that the
lowest parts of the White Tower, including much that
is subterranean, were built using the same materials
and techniques as the visible Phase 1 work, which
appears to have followed on without break or modification in design. Something of a tradition has emerged, however, in which it is supposed that the
south-east apse was added to the White Tower after
the construction of both the foundations and the
lowest storey.[157] While the idea of such a modification
to the design after the completion of the basement is
extremely unlikely, since the current, and primary,
disposition of buttresses was determined by this stage
and cannot be reconciled with a plan *sans* apse, the
possibility of a change in plan before building reached
the top of the plinth needs to be considered. Eager-
ness for such an evolutionary theory for the design of
the White Tower is easily explicable, given that previous
scholars were unaware of the existence of square great
towers with apsidal projections other than at Colchester Castle and the Tower of London.[158] It was accepted, on minimal evidence, that the former owed its
existence to underlying Roman remains, yet the White
Tower appeared to have been begun earlier and, thus,
was easier to explain if its plan was achieved by subsequent modification inspired by Colchester. Whatever
the preconceptions, structural evidence is cited as a

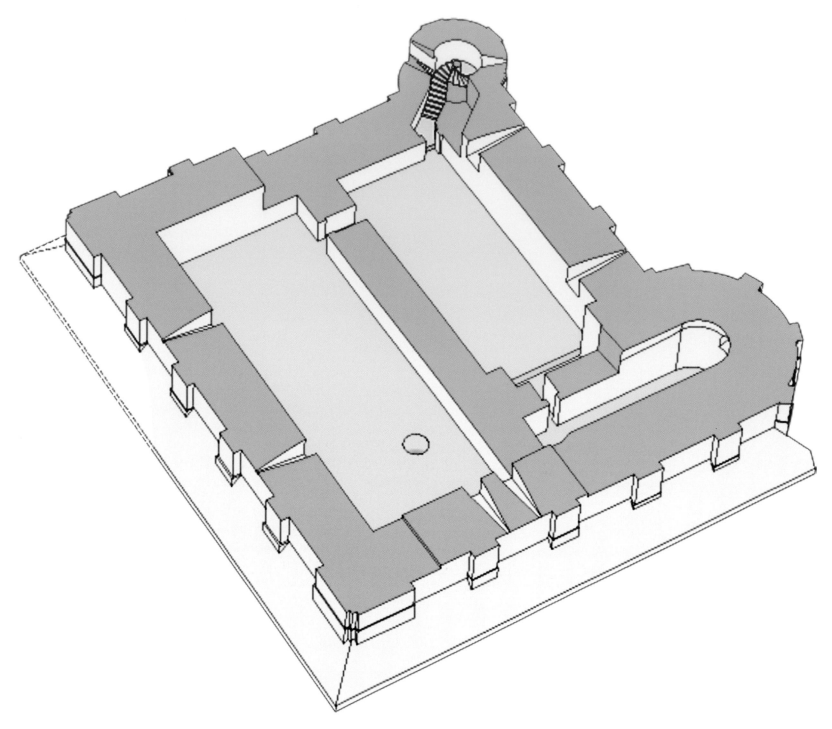

36 Basement: three-dimensional
reconstruction of the primary form.

Facing page. 37 Basement plans –
present (bottom) and reconstructed
circa 1100 (top).

basis for the apparent two phases of work in the lowest
parts of the White Tower and it is a re-examination of
this alone, rather than circular argument, that must
form the basis for interpretation (fig. 37).

Investigations of foundations in the area of the apse
occurred at the time of the restoration of the plinths
on the south and west sides of the White Tower in
1955–6, and again in 1965. The earlier investigations
were concerned with the exterior, and comprised the
examination of the plinth and the lower part of the
main walls. These were followed by more formal
archaeological excavations on the east side of the
White Tower in 1956–7, although these concentrated
firmly on remains of the Roman period.[159] The best
evidence for the form of the plinth, however, comes
from photographs taken during its restoration, and

these show a slight discontinuity in the coursing at the
junction of foundations of the apse and the east wall
(fig. 38). This discontinuity does not of itself suggest
that the apse abuts the east wall: rather, the apse and
the east wall foundations show the same banding,
albeit at slightly different levels, positively suggesting
that they are of the same build.

The similarity in the construction of the lower parts
of the apse and the east wall extends to the fact that
neither had a plinth, and this would tend to support
the argument that they are contemporary. As has been
noted above, the original form of the plinth was
revealed by the investigations of Dr D. E. Strong, in
1955–6, prior to the reconstruction in the form it has
today. His work showed that the 2.86 m-tall plinth of
the south wall ended in a mitre, now restored. While

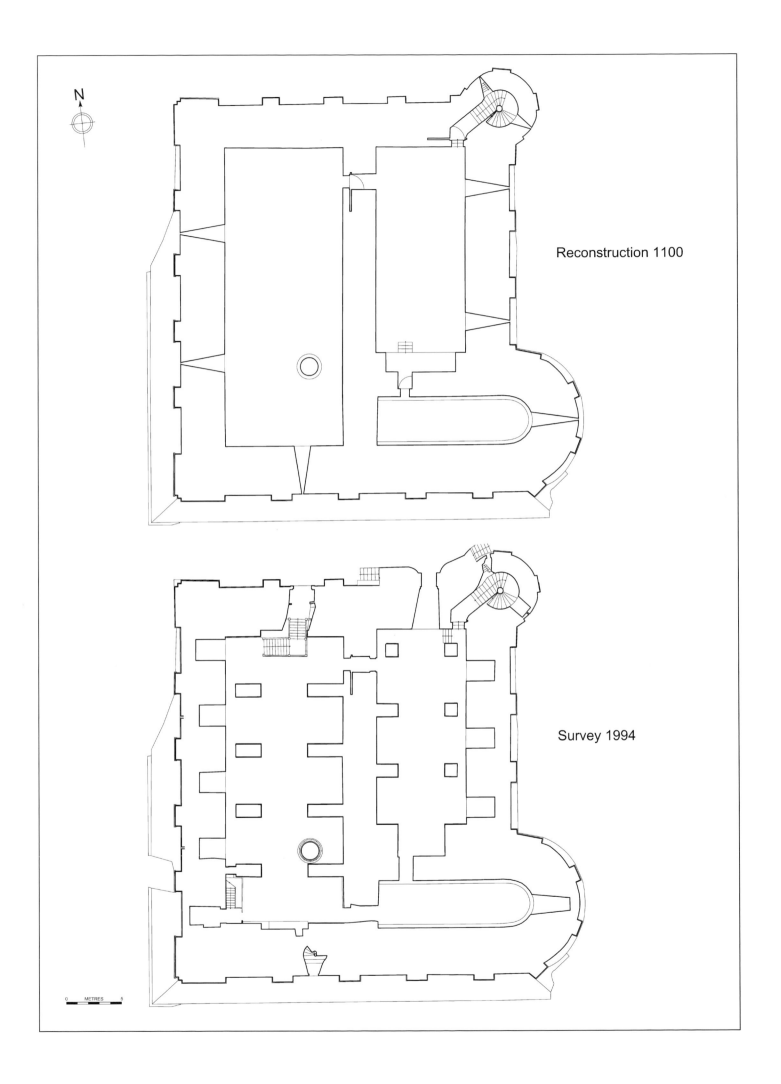

N

Reconstruction 1100

Survey 1994

0 METRES 5

38 The foundations of the apse, and the absence of a plinth on the east side, revealed during works in 1955–6. The incomplete excavation has left soil against the foundations, giving the illusion of different depths for the east wall (to the right) and the apse (to the left).

Strong avoided the error, other scholars have used this detail of construction as evidence for a change in plan, with the argument on the following lines: the mitre must mark a corner, the plinth returning northwards along the east side of the White Tower, with the plinthless apse a de facto addition. This ignores the fact that Strong was able to demonstrate that the plinth did not turn the south-east corner and continue along the east side. From the mitred corner, the plinth made a smooth transition into the near-vertical foundations of the apse. Equally importantly, the putative original corner was in the wrong place: scholars in favour of the addition of the apse have failed to account for the fact that this corner is a substantial 1.7 m east of the position required to match the line of the east wall. That the south-east mitre should be followed in what might otherwise appear an eccentric angling of the buttress that marks the junction of the south wall and the apse shows that, far from being a relic of an earlier abandoned design, the mitre was an integral part of a coherent design. There are no grounds, then, to doubt Strong's interpretation that the plinth returned at the south-east corner only to change to the quite clearly below-ground foundations of the apse, the entire east side requiring no plinth, since the sloping ground between the east wall of the White Tower and the Roman city wall was made level.[160]

Archaeological excavation of the interior of the apsidal basement room followed in 1965. The principal discoveries of this excavation were the surviving lower courses of the lost jambs of the internal doorway to this room, an offset running around the entire room at what the doorway suggests was the primary floor level, and a north–south wall or revetment. The last appears to be part of the primary construction, but it is too far to the west to be identified as the surviving eastern wall prior to the addition of the apse. Indeed, the evidence of the excavations of 1965 inside the White Tower is noteworthy for the implication of consistency in construction: not only was there no evidence of any discontinuity in the fabric, but there was also, in the uniform presence of a 390 mm-wide offset, strong evidence for the apse being integral with the rest of the room (fig. 39).

While it is possible that more rigorous archaeological excavation in the future will produce new evidence, it is clear that to date the only indication that the apse could be secondary is a minor discontinuity at the junction of the foundations of the apse and east wall. That this relates to the lowest levels of two walls that otherwise show remarkable consistency in their banding of rubble and in their lack of plinths suggests that this anomaly does not indicate two separate phases of construction. Indeed, the primary nature of the apse is positively supported by the facts that the short length of plinth running north from the south-east corner of the White Tower terminates against the wall of the apse, and the neatly mitred corner of this plinth lies too far to the east to align with the east wall. Likewise, the identification of the Phase 1 shelly

mortar elsewhere in the basement as low as 8.40 m OSBM, and as low as 7.09 m OSBM on the plinth of the south wall, means that there is a strong case for rapid and continuous construction from foundations to the first-floor building break. Finally, when the design implications of adding an apse are considered fully in terms of both the external bay divisions of the White Tower and the precise and related geometry of the first-floor chapel,[161] it is even more apparent that the idea of the apse being added to the White Tower has no basis in structural analysis.

Fenestration

Although the introduction of brick vaults in the years 1732–4 was accompanied by adaptation of the lighting, so that each of the east and west bays had a borrowed light opening via a grille into the entrance-floor embrasures, we have seen that windows were recorded prior to this work in the west room. In the south wall another loop window partly survives, and may have been one of a pair.[162] Another was recorded in the south-east apsidal room prior to widening in the eighteenth century, and remains of another are visible at the bottom of the spiral stair in the north-east turret. No evidence is visible for basement windows in the north elevation, nor have any been recorded there, and it must be suspected that the concentration of garderobes has ruled these out. The most likely scheme, then, for basement fenestration is that presented in the reconstructed plan.

Doorways

There are currently two external doorways in the north wall of the basement and, until recently, there was another in the south-west corner. None of these is medieval, and all three were cut through the primary wall. In the absence of any evident blocking elsewhere, there is no evidence of an original external entrance to the basement of the White Tower. Thus, access to the basement was via the staircase in the north-east turret that extends the full height of the building. The doorway at the end of the passage that links this stair to the eastern room of the basement is a primary feature, with jambs arranged so that the flush-mounted door opened from the room into the passage. Two other Romanesque internal doorways survive in varying degrees, both having seen replacement of flush-mounted doors by rebated doors at the other ends of the passages, probably in the fourteenth century.[163]

That at the northern end of the spine wall between the east and west rooms is typical of the Romanesque doorways in the White Tower in that it is located at one end of a passage in the thick wall (here 2.92 m wide).[164] The jambs of the doorway are 1.11 m apart, and somewhat narrower than the passage. This leaves an offset of 145 mm to the rear of each jamb and, while not a rebate as such, this provided a relatively snug fit for a door opening into the passage. The doorway has a drawbar socket 2.01 m deep matched by a shallower recess opposite, to receive the shot drawbar. A lining

40   Doorway into the basement
from the north-east spiral staircase,
showing the flush fitting over the
jambs and the absence of a
concentric rebate.

plank survives at the top of the southern socket, and the length of this precludes later insertion due to the narrowness of the passage. Dendrochronological analysis has produced a felling date of after 1068.[165] As with the other unblocked drawbar sockets in the White Tower, the deeper one has the larger cross-section. The surviving 25 mm (1 in.) thick top plank in the longer slot, with its impressions of the two side planks, provides the obvious explanation for the difference: only the deeper socket into which the drawbar was withdrawn was lined with timber.

A similar doorway led from the eastern chamber into the basement apsidal room, although the jambs have been removed, probably at the fitting of the present door (dated to after 1345).[166] The ashlar toothing of the eleventh-century jambs survives, however, marking their location 1.51 m south of the north end of the door passage. Below the flooring the surviving lowest courses of these jambs were uncovered in 1965, and this confirmed that the doorway was similar to that in the spine wall. There are significant differences, because the doorway passage to the apsidal room is of rubble, with ashlar confined to the jambs and to two courses at the bottom of the passage walls, whereas the entire walls of the spine-wall doorway are of ashlar. Despite the mutilation of the original jambs, the blocked remains of a drawbar socket are still discernible. More significantly, the present floor (at approximately 8.4 m OSBM) sits slightly above the level of the Romanesque threshold of the apsidal room doorway, while the same floor level has been achieved in the spine-wall doorway passage only by lowering the floor between 770 and 830 mm.[167] The dropping of the latter appears to be the result of digging out the basement floor in the post-medieval period, but this fails to explain why the eleventh-century doorway to the apsidal basement room, and its fourteenth-century replacement, was so much lower: evidently, there was a minor variation in height in the primary floor level of the basement.

The doorway to the north-east turret is similar to the others in that the door was flush-mounted on the rear face of the jambs, and opened into a passage. As with that in the spine wall, this passage is of ashlar and has evidence for a drawbar in the form of a recess for the shot bar, 1.21 m above the present floor: a stone without Romanesque tooling occupies the position of the supposed drawbar socket. That this marks a blocked primary drawbar socket is supported by the fact that the socket must pre-date the hanging of the present door, which has been dated to after 1457, possibly from *circa* 1475:[168] the doorway has a hinge at this height that is supported by a pintle set into the stone blocking the drawbar socket. Again, this doorway provides evidence for the lowering of the floor, in this case by 790 mm (fig. 40).

The Well

The western basement room contains a well towards its southern end. Internal wells are a feature of other great towers (such as Beaugency, Canterbury, Loches, Norwich and Rochester), and the early date of the example at the White Tower is evident from the rough diagonal tooling of the ashlar lining. The well has a diameter of approximately 1.7 m and descends more than 12 m, with the ashlar in neat courses ranging from 150 to 200 mm, forming a lining approximately 230 mm thick. During investigation in 2005, the well was drained and a beech template (supporting the descending masonry sleeve during digging) located at the bottom. This produced a dendrochronological date of after 1082, which, though it does not refine the chronology of the construction of the White Tower,[169] at least confirms the primary nature of the well and its surviving carpentry.[170] The dating probably places the sinking of the well within Phase 2, or, just conceivably (and contrary to the evidence of its non-shelly mortar[171]), at the end of Phase 1. Either way, if construction was to take advantage of natural light, this suggests that the entrance and first floors were not actually floored until Phase 2: this is to be expected in any case.

Entrance Floor (figs 41, 42)

Other than the main entrance, the internal arrangement of the entrance storey replicates that of the basement, although the spine wall has a doorway at the

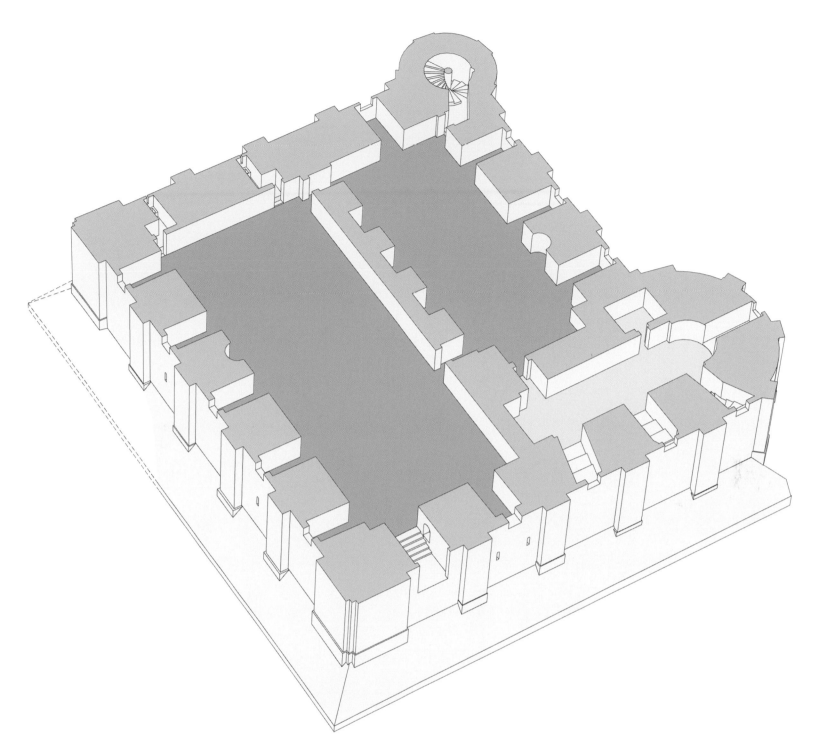

41 Entrance floor: three-dimensional reconstruction of the primary form.

southern end in addition to that at the north. Offsets at floor-joist level mean that the east and west rooms are slightly larger than those below, at 20.81m by 8.74m and 27.63m by 11.32 m, respectively. Likewise, the apsidal room is larger than the one below, at 15.34m by 4.23 m, mainly due to the 1.42 m-deep recess in the west wall: again, this has a barrel vault. As at basement level, the east room is distinguished by a recess at its southern end, although on the entrance floor it is shallower (1.80 m) and wider (6.12 m). Above the springing of the arch of this recess, at 2.75 m above modern floor level, there are slots for a plank approximately 500 mm deep and 52 mm (2 in.) thick. Examination of these slots, however, shows that they were cut in after construction, and, together with three other sockets for vertical studs above this level, they probably represent the insertion of a screen. A similar but shallower recess forms the west wall of the apsidal room. The increased sophistication of this room compared to its counterpart in the basement is also seen in the treatment of the apse, with its more extensive use of ashlar, in the fenestration that is extended to include three windows on the south side, and the small unlit chamber (3.37 m by 2.56 m) that opens off the north wall. Unlike their basement equivalents, the east and west rooms have preserved something of their primary internal arrangement in that they have timber arcades, with the posts supporting the wide span of the floors. The surviving posts are post-medieval, however, and it remains a matter of pure conjecture as to whether any primary supports took the form of single or, as now exists, paired arcades.[172]

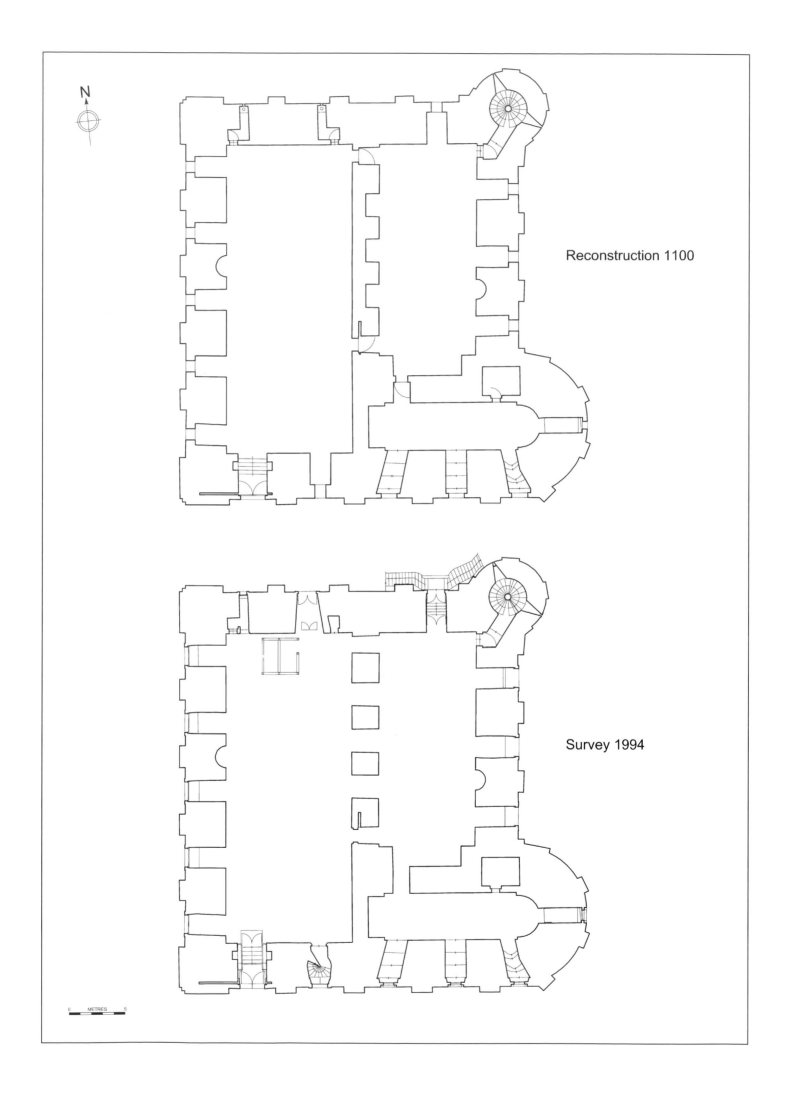

N

Reconstruction 1100

Survey 1994

0   METRES   5

Internal Access and Doorways

The entrance floor has the only primary external doorway of the White Tower,[173] appropriately larger and more elaborate than the other doorways. Access to the other floors of the White Tower is provided by the spiral stair of the north-east turret, which rises the full height of the building. The stair is connected to the east room via a dog-legged passage, similar to that below except that the doorway is in the east wall rather than the north. The primary jambs of this doorway again fall short of the full height of the passage, so that the door closes against jambs and a wide tympanum rather than into a concentric rebate. There is no evidence of a drawbar socket.

As in the basement, there is a primary doorway at the northern end of the spine wall, but at this level there is also a southern counterpart. The northern doorway has suffered the removal of its jambs, but the 520–40 mm scar of these is plainly visible at the west end of the passage. To the east of this the surviving, but heavily repointed, primary stonework suggests the presence of a blocked drawbar socket, 1.50 m above the floor. This matches the height of the surviving example in the doorway at the southern end of the spine wall. Although better preserved, this has had its southern jamb entirely rebuilt and the west face of the whole doorway later rebated for a square-headed door. The eleventh-century northern jamb is intact and the drawbar socket even has all four of its original lining planks.[174] The socket is located 1.46 m above floor level and 64 mm back from the jamb, and, at 1.32 m, is not so deep as the example in the basement.[175] Both of the passages behind these doorways are of rubble, with ashlar restricted to the quoins at the eastern openings and the western jambs.

The basement plan is replicated to the extent that there is a doorway to the apsidal room from the south-west corner of the east room. Here, again, the projecting jamb has been removed, but the remains of the cut-back western jamb are still proud of the passage, and show the jamb to have been placed at the northern end, 1.83 m from the southern end.[176] Some attention to detail is seen in the use of a single course of ashlar at the bottom: some of these stones are replacements, but others reveal typical Romanesque rough diagonal tooling. The doorway to the small chamber off the apsidal room is largely intact, although some of the exterior jamb stones have been replaced. Sadly, the fact that the door opened inwards, and could not therefore be barred from the outside, makes nonsense of the inevitable sinister suggestions as to the chamber's purpose.

Spine Wall

The spine wall on the entrance floor differs from the solid wall below in that it is penetrated by three wide plain openings and the two doorways at the extremi-ties. The soffits and reveals indicate that the arched recesses were formerly blocked on the western side, and this is corroborated by the complete absence of Romanesque quoins and voussoirs on that side.[177] That the blocking of the arches was on the western side is in direct contradiction of even recently published plans,[178] and it must be suspected that this error derives from the fact that after the arches were opened out, they were blocked again but on the east side. A plan of 1729 shows them unblocked but with the new blocking pencilled in on the east:[179] like most pencilled features on this plan, this seems to relate to the creation of the Sea Armoury in 1736,[180] and the new blocking was certainly drawn in designs of 1734 for this refitting.[181] This secondary blocking had gone by the time of Nash's plans of 1815.

Garderobes

The provision for garderobes on the entrance floor comprised two at the northern end of the west room only. The eastern of these was mostly obliterated during the construction of the splayed opening to the north doorway in the sixteenth century,[182] but the eastern jamb, five voussoirs and part of the passage survive to show that it was a mirror-image of its western counterpart. The latter has also seen modification in that a larger and higher window was inserted, probably in the years 1734–6. Apparently at the same time an internal window, or borrowed light, was inserted immediately to the east of the Romanesque doorway to the garderobe.[183] The original form, then, of the two garderobes was dog-legged. At the rear of the western garderobe, the Caen stone voussoirs of an approximately 600 mm-wide arch rise 260 mm above the modern floor, and this marks the location of the waste chute itself, eccentrically placed to the west.

Fireplaces

Both east and west rooms have fireplaces (fig. 43). That in the east room has been restored, while the other is in a less doctored but more ruinous state. The wall over the latter projects slightly, raising the possibility of a more subtle version of the conical hoods found at Loches,[184] but the evidence is far from conclusive and there may have been no more than an arch spanning the fireplace on the plane of the wall. The flue in each case slopes outwards and is of oval form, but is blocked and no outlets are visible. It must be suspected that smoke outlets were placed in the angles of the buttresses.

The First Floor (figs 44, 45)

The first floor replicates the three volumes of the two floors below, although the progressive offsets mean that at this level the west room measures 12.04m by 29.20m and the east room 9.29m by 19.69m. Lateral fireplaces in both east and west rooms duplicate those

below and intercommunication follows the pattern of the entrance floor. Minor differences are to be found in the absence of a recess at the southern end of the east room, an additional doorway linking the apsidal room to the western room, and in the distribution of the garderobes, with both rooms here provided with a pair. More significant differences are to be found in the greater number of windows, and in the provision of staircases in the north-west and south-west corners. Although the east and west rooms now have post-medieval timber arcades, in this case supporting the floor above, the absence of a second floor in the original building strongly suggests that these rooms contrasted with those below in that they were uncluttered by posts: but it is possible that the primary roofs used mid-span supports.[185] The third, apsidal, room shows the greatest difference from its entrance-floor equivalent, for at this level the aisled chapel of St John rises up through two storeys to include a gallery and a stone barrel vault. Although it saw secular use from the early fourteenth century and was thereafter adapted for a variety of functions – notably a store for records – the chapel remained largely intact. As a result, the restoration by Salvin in the years 1864–6 involved little more than the removal of a spiral stair from the ambulatory, the replacement of aisle-respond abaci lost to shelving and replacement of seventeenth-century Portland stone windows with what he considered more appropriate designs.[186] The form of the chapel, its famous capitals and its art-historical context have been studied anew

in the course of the present project and are considered in detail by John Crook in Chapter Three. To avoid repetition, here the chapel is considered only where relevant to the discussion of the other rooms.

Access and Doorways

The access to the first floor from the north-east spiral stair is identical to that in the basement in that a dog-legged passage leads to a doorway in the north wall of the east room. The jambs are again positioned so that the door opened into the passage and there is no evidence of a drawbar socket.

The spine wall has doorways at either end, of similar form to those below except for the surprising fact that the northern doorway has its jambs at the east end of the passage and not at the west. Rather than implying a different circulatory route at this level, it may reflect nothing more than that it allowed access from the west room to the western garderobe leading off this doorway passage, even if the door between the two main rooms was closed.[187] Again, there is no evidence of drawbar sockets.

The chapel is distinct from the apsidal rooms below in that it is provided with two doorways, and both are quite clearly primary features. Access to the chapel from the west room is provided by a short east–west passage at the west end of the south aisle. Although this is now linked by a spiral staircase to the entrance floor and, ultimately, to the main external stair to the White Tower, the spiral stair is, as we have seen, a later insertion. Thus, the eleventh-century passage simply opened into the easternmost window embrasure of the south wall of the west room. A shallow rebate on the northern jamb and the arch of the opening into this embrasure are secondary. At the east end of the passage the vault has been altered to accommodate the top of the present door. If there was originally a door here, it was presumably face-mounted, like so many of the other doors in the White Tower, and opened into the chapel. The second doorway connects the east room and the chapel, and occupies the westernmost bay of the north aisle. There is no rebate, which again suggests a flush-mounted door: although the inner (south) face of the wall has a concentric order suitably sized for a door rebate, there is no evidence for iron-work and, in the absence of any other primary door rebates in the White Tower, it must be suspected that this concentric order is for decorative effect only.

Spine wall

The spine wall of the first floor echoes the arrangement of the floor below, with three plain arches flanked by doorways to the north and south. Here, again, the soffits of the plain arched openings show that they were originally built as recesses, and this is confirmed by the Romanesque tooling, which is restricted to the quoins and voussoirs of the eastern face.[188]

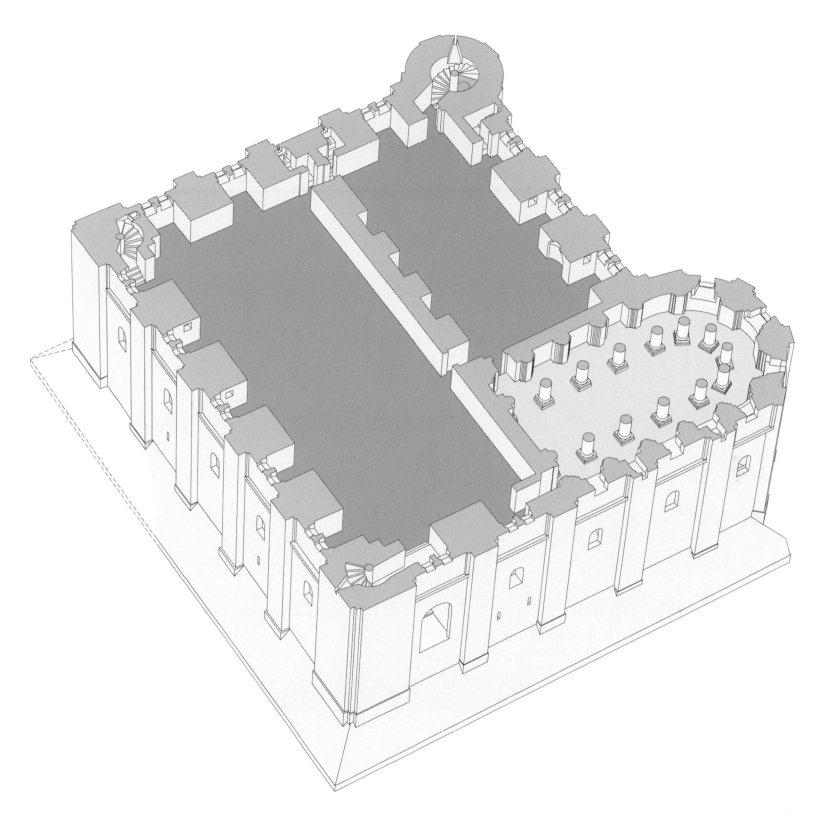

44　First floor: three-dimensional reconstruction of the primary form.

Garderobes

The provision for garderobes on the first floor is the most generous in the White Tower. While the example located a few steps up the north-west stair may relate to use from above (fig. 46), the remaining three open off the main east and west rooms. All are substantially intact primary features. Two take advantage of the fact that the spine wall joins the north wall near the middle of a bay, ruling out a large window at this point. They form a symmetrical pair of mirrored dog-legs, the eastern garderobe opening immediately east of the spine wall (fig. 47), and the western one opening into

the passage of the doorway that penetrates its northern end. The fourth garderobe is placed towards the northern end of the east wall, its dog-legged passage opening off the side of a window embrasure. Its window and well-preserved waste chute are located in the wide buttress-like feature that abuts the north-east turret.

Fireplaces

Both east and west rooms at this level are equipped with lateral fireplaces, immediately above those in the rooms below. That in the west room is blocked, which explains why it has previously passed unnoticed.[189]

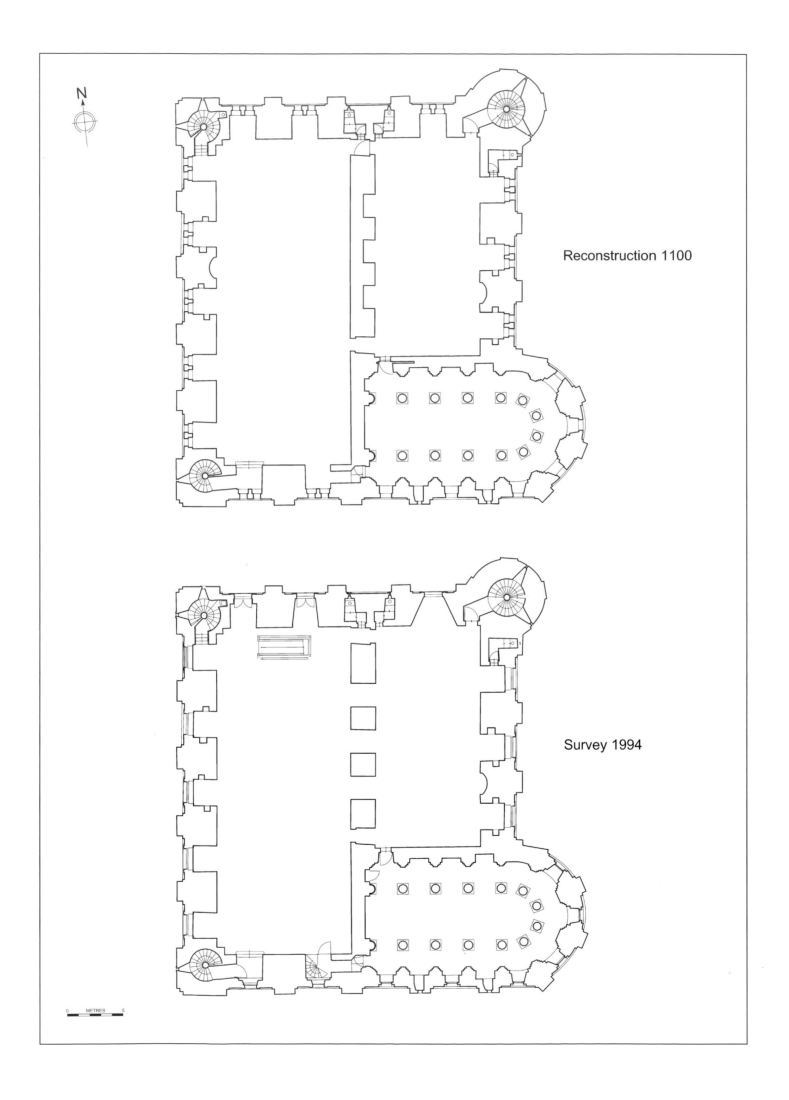

N

Reconstruction 1100

Survey 1994

0   METRES   5

46 (*right*) First-floor garderobe opening off the north-west spiral stair.

47 (*far right*) First-floor garderobe adjacent to the passage of the north doorway in the spine wall.

The arrangements for the smoke outlets appear identical to that of the fireplaces below. There is no clear evidence of blocking, however, suggesting that the fireplaces were redundant by the time of the renewal of the quoins with Portland stone.[190]

Reference has been made above in the discussion of the building break to the eight cupboards in the sides of the window embrasures on the first floor. These small square cupboards are unique to this storey and are restricted to the embrasures on each side of the fireplaces in the two main rooms. They have plain timber lintels, two of which have produced dendrochronological dates linking them to the primary construction. These cupboards are around the level of the building break.

The Second Floor, Roof and Turrets (figs 48, 49)

Today, the second, or top, floor of the White Tower differs from the other storeys in matters of detail only. With the first-floor chapel rising through two storeys, there is, of course, no self-contained apsidal room at this level, but the barrel-vaulted gallery instead. The chapel gallery forms part of a mural passage that makes a complete circuit of the White Tower, cutting through window embrasures that are otherwise similar to those below. The east and west rooms are present again, and are also separated by a massive spine wall: offsets at floor level make these rooms a little larger than those below at 29.23m by 12.36m and 19.74m by 9.36m.[191] Some elements of the floors below are missing, however, for the second floor has no garderobes or fireplaces. Moreover, some of the detail is less sophisticated. For example, the voussoirs of the

embrasures and spine-wall openings (the latter were never merely recesses here) are of rubble, not ashlar. The north-east, south-west and north-west stairs reach this level and continue further up the corner turrets, which then break free of the building. In the chapel roof space a fourth turret rises from the top of the barrel vaults, giving the White Tower a degree of symmetry it would otherwise lack.

While the arrangement of the second floor of the White Tower has a certain logic to it, and a general consistency with the storeys below, it has been viewed for many years as a substantial modification of the original design. The most consistently presented view of the primary form has been one in which the first-floor east and west rooms rose through two storeys in the manner of the chapel.[192] The second-floor mural passage then becomes akin to a clerestory passage, overlooking the principal rooms. Such a model explains the absence of garderobes and fireplaces, and, indeed, the need for a mural passage, but has been overtaken by new discoveries. This section of the chapter examines all the evidence now available for the upper part of the White Tower, and presents a new and quite different interpretation.

The Form and Position of the Primary Roof

The extent of the primary construction of the White Tower has been the subject of debate in the last few years, largely as a result of the recent rediscovery of a soot imprint of a former roof in the east room, the roof apparently springing from the floor level of the current top storey (fig. 50).[193] Identification of scarring left by a similar roof in the west room was followed by archaeological investigation of eaves drains,

Facing page: 45 First-floor plan: present (bottom) and reconstructed *circa* 1100 (top).

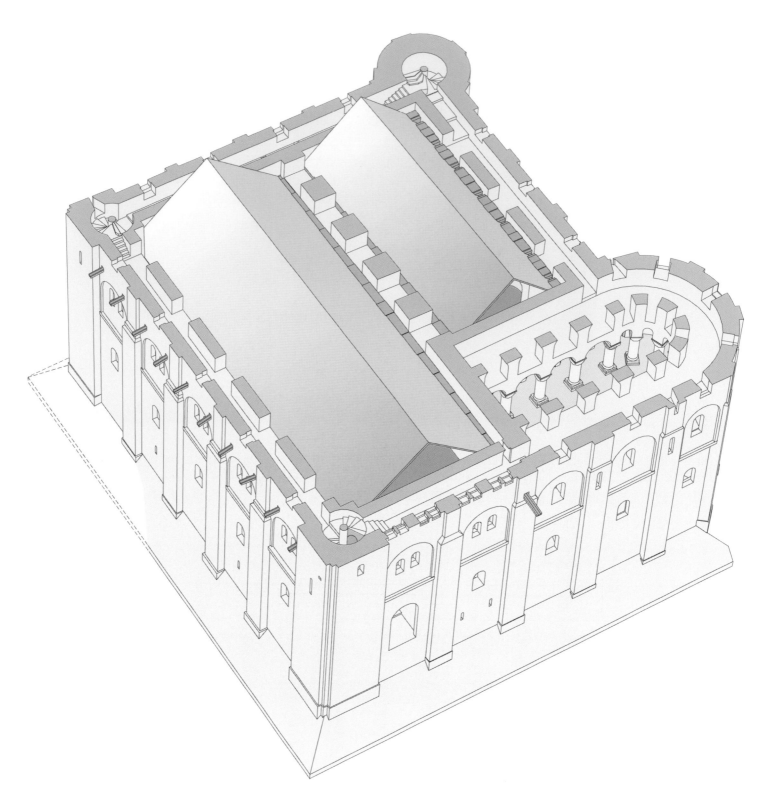

48 Second floor: three-dimensional reconstruction of the primary form.

Facing page: 49 Second-floor plan: present (bottom) and reconstructed *circa* 1100 (top).

or scuppers, under the floor of the mural passages (fig. 51).[194] These lead-covered wooden drains penetrated the entire thickness of the east and west walls (and presumably projected to throw rainwater clear) and, since they were quite clearly primary, confirmed that the soot mark and scars record the position and pitch of the earliest roof of the White Tower. The discoveries led to the suggestion that the building was gabled in the first instance, with a battlemented wall-walk converted into a mural passage only during the twelfth century. In one interpretation this was associated with the creation of the second floor and the

raising of the roof to its present level.[195] In the other, the mural gallery formed part of a false storey enclosing the earlier roof.[196] While the discoveries used to support these hypotheses are of great significance, a wider body of structural evidence is used here to show that the reality was less complex and consistent with the evidence from the south elevation for uniform and unmodified construction (see above).

The North and South Walls: Evidence for Gables?

Details of the north and south walls have been interpreted as evidence for primary gables, later modified to

76

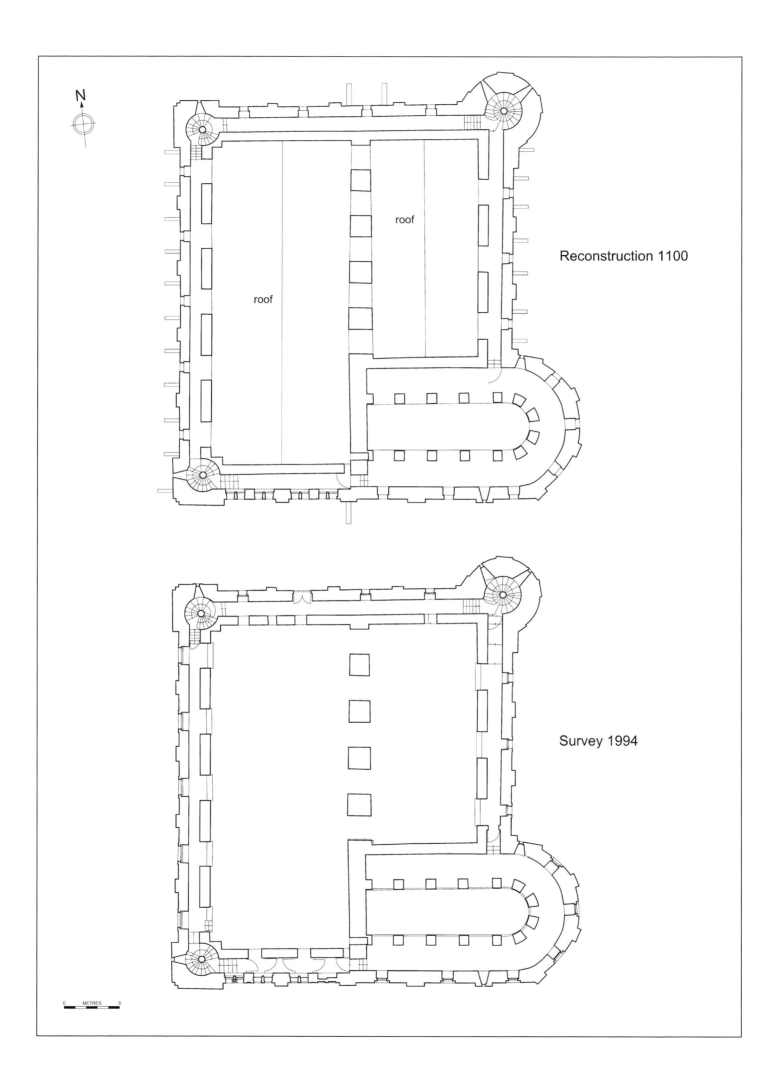

N

roof

roof

Reconstruction 1100

Survey 1994

0   METRES   5

50 Soot imprint of an earlier and lower roof, discovered on the south wall of the eastern room of the second floor in 1966, and still visible today.

51 Evidence for the drains was found by excavation of the east and west mural passages (top), which permitted the identification of the function of the long-visible, but apparently unnoticed, external drain holes (bottom).

their present form:[197] the use of pitched stones in the roof scar at the north end of the west chamber; the survival of a gable 'window' in this same wall; an area where the wall above a roof scar is offset from the rubble below; the imperfect form of the doorway in the south wall of the west room that apparently opened into the central roof valley; and the survival of what appears to be another drain outlet on the west face of the south-west turret.[198] Few of these points stand up to scrutiny.

Careful analysis of the rubble walling of the end walls of the two rooms shows that it courses consistently, which could hardly be expected if gables were later built up to create the walls we have today (fig. 52). Indeed, such continuity in coursing across rubble walling of different phases would be remarkable in any context, but especially so here since the courses cross the point of abutment of a roof; a painstaking matching of the coursing of the rubble would have been pointless because of the presence of the roof itself. Furthermore, the consistency in the walling is such that the north wall of the east room shows no evidence of a roof scar at all. This implies that the eastern roof simply abutted the north wall, as we know that it did at the south. The pitched stones in the north wall of the west room can hardly be coping stones for an original gable since they are small pieces of rubble only, and are more reasonably explained as the infilling of the primary roof scar after the removal of the lower roof. Finally, for the end walls of the east and west rooms to be secondary requires that the spine wall at this level is also secondary, yet the coursing of the rubble on the west face shows complete continuity where it continues the line of the unambiguously primary west wall of the chapel.[199]

The 'window' in the north wall of the west room is certainly primary, but rather than confirming the former presence of a gable, it suggests the reverse. The semicircular-headed opening is off-centre to the roof scar, and the reason for this position is clearly determined by the vaulting and fenestration of the mural passage, which, in turn, is dictated by the bay divisions of the north elevation. If this opening had indeed been a window and had overlooked a battlemented wall-walk there would have been no reason for it to be off-centre. A further point to note is that this primary opening has no external ashlar dressings or offset jambs consistent with it having been an exterior window. As for its possible function, if the mural passage was also primary, it is the only known second-floor opening in the west room (the north and south doorways are not primary) and could have let a little light into the roof, or provided a view for security purposes, access to the collar level of the roof or access for ceremonial functions, such as lowering of banners, or for a musician. That it was not required as a smoke vent is evident, since a primary fireplace has now been identified in the first-floor west room.[200] Two sockets in the reveals above the external sill of this opening are likely to have been for a timber and may relate to the fixing of a step or ladder for access, because the opening is 2.13 m above the floor of the mural passage (fig. 53).

The small area of offset masonry above the roof line in the south wall of the west room is the most sug-

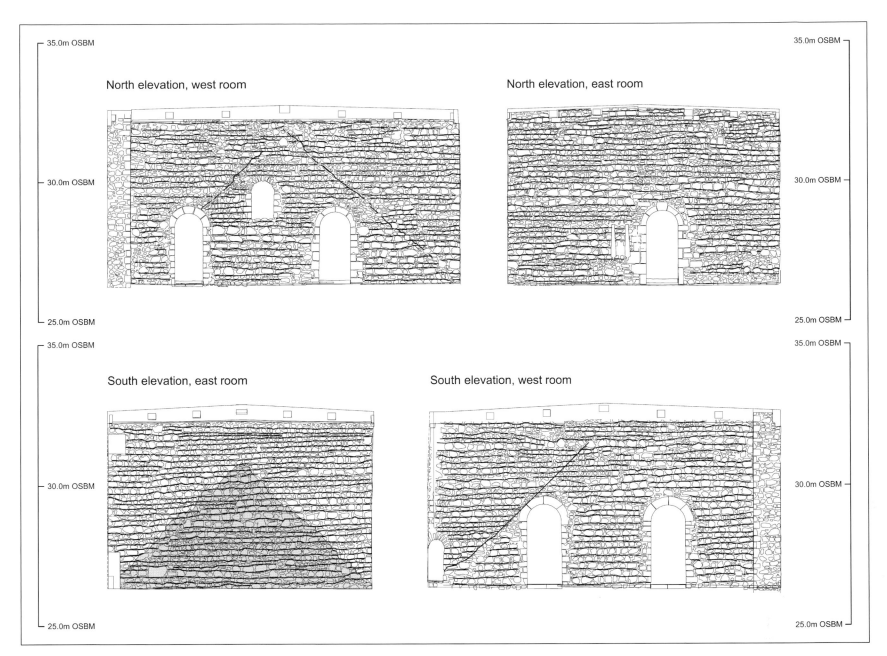

North elevation, west room

35.0m OSBM

30.0m OSBM

25.0m OSBM

North elevation, east room

35.0m OSBM

30.0m OSBM

25.0m OSBM

South elevation, east room

35.0m OSBM

30.0m OSBM

25.0m OSBM

South elevation, west room

35.0m OSBM

30.0m OSBM

25.0m OSBM

52 End elevations of the second-floor rooms showing the rough but consistent coursing of the rubble stonework. This strongly suggests that the walls are largely of primary date, and are not the result of gables later built up.

gestive feature in support of original gables at the White Tower, but it is a very small anomaly on which to base such a grand theory. Moreover, since the primary roofs occupy the same position in the gabled interpretation and in a model in which the mural passage is primary, the anomaly does not favour gables. Rather, it appears that the change in plane results from the correction of a deformation, or mis-alignment, of the fabric below the roof line in this area, and, since a chasing for the roof was clearly created in the west room, correction of this non-vertical walling at this point cannot on its own provide a sufficient basis for identifying a free-standing gable.

The form of the doorway to the central roof valley in the south wall of the west room is similarly uninformative. True, it is set slightly into the west face of the east wall of the room, but there is no structural evidence that it is cut into a pre-existing wall. In view of the confined area for such an access at this point, such setting in would appear to be essential and, thus,

could equally be primary or secondary, depending on which interpretation is preferred. What it quite clearly does not provide is structural evidence for either model.

The possible drain outlet in the west face of the south-west turret does not imply a free-standing gable, since it is positioned well to the south of the primary roof, meaning that any association between the two is by no means certain. It could be argued that the positioning of a drain this far south was easier to achieve in the absence of a stair, but there can be no doubt that all the spiral stairs in the White Tower are primary and, from the outset, were intended to reach at least the level of the mural passage.[201] Indeed, we have seen that there is good evidence for the primary construction of all the corner turrets and, thus, the continuance of stairs beyond this level.[202] Given the undoubted originality of the spiral stair here, it is interesting to note that this possible drain outlet is so positioned that it could indeed drain the

79

south-west corner of the western valley, or gutter: its position, at approximately 200 mm lower than the other sloping drain outlets, is simply consistent with the fact that the west face of the turret is proud of the main face of the west wall, and a diagonal channel drawn from the outlet to the south-west corner of the west room passes neatly through the vault of the spiral stair. Such an idea might appear a little far-fetched, except that no other obvious function can be deduced, save some possible but unlikely connection with the south forebuilding, which abutted the south elevation around this level. Moreover, an exact parallel is to be found for this arrangement at Rochester Castle, where one of the main roof valleys drained out of the end wall, crossing the primary spiral stair on its way (fig. 54).

The Mural-Passage Floors and Drains (fig. 55)

The archaeological investigation at the level of the mural-passage floor is undoubtedly of crucial importance in establishing the location of roof drains and, thus, the primary roofs of the east and west rooms, but it also provides evidence of the phasing of the side walls of the present second-floor rooms, and the phasing and dating of beam sockets along the inner edge of these walls.

Of particular interest is the blocking of the drains by a band of mortar (layer 139 on fig. 56) that represents the rebuilding of the entire inner edge of the floor

surface of the mural passage (layer 106), and which contained beam or joist sockets.[203] Evidently, the drains ceased to function at, or before, this blocking, with their demise most obviously caused by the raising of the roof. The fact that the band of mortar is overlain by the east wall of the Romanesque mural passage, however, does not require that the building of the latter post-dates the blocking of the drains. In fact, the fine and creamy lime mortar of the blocking band is quite different from the coarse primary mortar types seen at the White Tower or in other Romanesque buildings. It must be suspected that the band of mortar simply results from the removal of wall fabric for the insertion of beam or joist sockets. Significantly, the mortar matches that used in the internal thickenings of the west and apse walls of the chapel roof space, and these thickenings were almost certainly required to take the present high-level roof. Given this correspondence and the fact that the mortar above and below the blocking band is of the type that typifies the Phase 2 work of the primary construction of the White Tower, the building of the present roof *circa* 1490 provides the most likely point for the raising of the roof and the creation of the top-floor rooms.

Interestingly, a few early floorboards have been discovered at second-floor level in the spine-wall openings. These appeared to have survived *in situ* from flooring prior to the post-medieval rebuilding of the east and west rooms and, significantly, were dated by dendrochronology to *circa* 1488.[204] This strongly suggests that the second floor was built, or re-boarded, at the same time as the existing roof was built. In the complete absence of any evidence of an earlier roof or floor, the simplest and most probable interpretation is that the raising of the roof and the creation of the second floor were the products of a single phase, *circa* 1490. Further confirmation that the creation of the floor-beam sockets and the raising of the roof could not be an early modification was provided by the excavations themselves: medieval roof tiles formed the primary lining of the beam sockets and, given that roof tiles (even in their primary usage) are not reliably

datable prior to *circa* 1150,[205] this would require, at the earliest, a date for the construction of the mural passages in the second half of the twelfth century, which is quite contrary to the architectural evidence.[206]

Since there are good grounds to suppose that the mortar band containing the beam or joist sockets does not represent an early modification, it is necessary to consider whether the construction of the gallery piers (the inner wall of the passage) themselves led to the disuse of the eaves drains. The structural relationship of the two does not rule out continued use, and, given the case for the low-level roof surviving the creation of the mural passages, they would have had an identical function as before: that is, to provide discharge at regular intervals along the east and west elevations from what was presumably a stepped gutter or valley. Indeed, if the low-level roof survived the creation of the mural passages it can be assumed only that the drains remained in use. Equally, and ultimately more probably, it could be that the combination of low-level roof and mural passages was the reason for creating these drains in the first place.

The removal of the flooring in the openings in the spine wall revealed a seemingly primary surface of rubble and mortar similar to that found in both mural passages, but closest to that of the east passage in that 'it was extremely hard in consistency and not prone to erosion'.[207] On both sides of the mortared surface there were strips of different material, approximately 600 mm wide,[208] and the junctions between these and the

primary surface were marked by cracks and voids. As with its counterpart in the western mural passage, the western band along the spine wall contained beam or joist sockets. These sockets were of the same dimensions and spacing as those of the west mural passage and, again, the implication is that these relate to a floor inserted some time after the primary construction, and presumably at the point of the raising of the roof.

Thus, while the results of the archaeological investigations on the second floor have provided us with a wealth of knowledge as to the draining of the outer sides of the primary roofs of the east and west rooms, they do not provide a sufficient basis to support any argument for the construction of a primary building with gables on the north and south, to which mural passages, a second floor and a higher roof were all added within a few decades at most. Quite clearly, most of the evidence used to support this interpretation can be more convincingly related to the construction of the present roof and the carpentry of a second floor *circa* 1490.

Other Evidence for the Primary Roof and Second-Floor Construction

The scrutiny of possible evidence for a gabled form for the White Tower as first built is useful in that it suggests a more likely alternative: that the primary roofs of the east and west rooms were contained by the false storey of the mural passages and a higher wall-walk from the outset. While compelling reasons for this will have become obvious during the discussion above, there is additional structural evidence that supports this new and simpler model. Most important is the evidence from the south elevation, where we have seen that the repair programme of 1997–8 permitted a close analysis of the fabric. This concluded that, on either side of the break, the construction of the White Tower was remarkably homogenous. Certainly, there was a complete absence of evidence for a substantial modification of the upper parts of the building, from one with gables to one with a high screen wall. To this can be added several other pertinent observations.

First, there is the evidence of the spiral stairs. These stairs start on the first floor (or, in the case of the north-east turret, the basement) and were begun in Phase 1. After the resumption of work in Phase 2, the form and fabric of these stair turrets are wholly consistent until brickwork is encountered at the highest level. The spiral stairs open into the window embrasures of the mural passages via short lengths of barrel-vaulted passage. These vaulted exits from the stair turrets are of consistent construction technique and material with the stair turrets themselves and with the vaults to the rest of the mural passage. Perhaps most importantly, however, it is clear that such exits from the stair turrets were planned originally and were

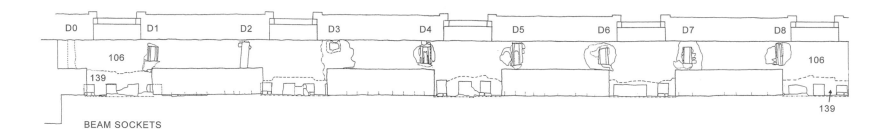

D0　D1　D2　D3　D4　D5　D6　D7　D8

106

139

106

139

BEAM SOCKETS

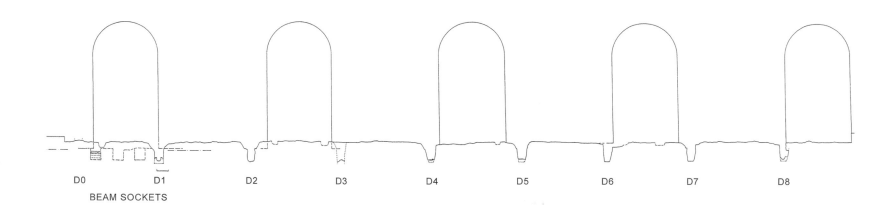

D0　D1　D2　D3　D4　D5　D6　D7　D8

BEAM SOCKETS

0　　　METRES　　　5

D = DRAINAGE CHANNEL

56 Plan of archaeological excavations of the western mural passage (based on site records by Oxford Archaeology).

facing page: 57 The turrets of the White Tower from the roof: clockwise from the north-east turret (top right).

unlikely to have been added when a later mural passage was created. The stairs within the north-west and south-west turrets are not placed centrally within the turrets, but are located towards the inner faces to such a degree that the cylinder of the stair is only 100 mm from the north face of the south-west turret and 130 mm from the south face of the north-west turret. It is inconceivable that such thin walls could have been contemplated, but with the projection of barrel-vaulted passages of 900 mm and 1,100 mm there is no problem. Significantly, these short passages form an integral part of the mural passages. Other aspects of the spiral stairs that need to be considered are the fabric and construction techniques, which are consistent above and below this level, revealing that the stairs continued upwards in their primary form. This consistency is seen internally, but has been witnessed most clearly in the petrography and bedding mortar of the south face of the south-west turret, during the recent works on the south elevation. The upper part of the stairs not only provided access to the mural passages but also to the battlemented wall-walk above the mural passage. The doorway at the higher level from

the north-east turret remains in use, while those from the north-west and south-west turrets survive, albeit partially blocked and now used as windows. Of course, these doorways could have been added to the spiral stairs if gables were later built up, but the structural evidence for the turrets being built to their present height in one campaign after the break between Phase 1 and Phase 2 means that it is hard to countenance an arrangement whereby the turrets rose clear of the rest of the building for 13 m of their 30 m height (fig. 57).

Second, the mural passage requires consideration. Its exterior wall both internally and externally is of uniform build at least to the level of the springing of the vault, and clearly does not incorporate any battlements from a previous wall-walk.[209] This could imply that any battlements were simply removed down to the floor level of what is now the mural passage on the grounds that they were too insubstantial to be incorporated within a later wall, although this would contradict observations made during the recent investigations that considered the primary floor surface and the outer wall of the mural passage to be contempo-

rary.[210] Again, scrutiny of the south elevation during the works of 1997–8 was informative, for this showed consistency in the geologies, mortar type and construction technique above and below the putative battlement level. Further evidence suggesting that the mural passage was not previously a wall-walk is provided by the positioning of the primary roofs. On the clear evidence of the roof scars and soot mark, these were placed entirely within the east and west rooms of the present second floor, with wall plates, tie-beams and rafter feet largely accommodated by the offsets (up to 340 mm wide) formed by the progressively thinning walls of the White Tower.[211] Since these side walls would not have had a gable occupying 820 mm of the approximately 3 m-wide wall-heads, in the manner of the north and south walls, there would have been ample room to have footed a roof in a conventional fashion on top of the wall, still leaving room for a wide wall-walk and crenellations. The implication of not footing the roofs on the wall-heads must be that the wall-heads were not available and that the roofs were originally boxed in on all sides. The final piece of evidence from the mural passage comes from the excavated primary drains or scuppers. These drains penetrated the entire thickness of the east and west second-floor walls and presumably drained valleys placed alongside the inner faces of the walls. Not only did these drains pass well below the level of the mural passage, or putative wall-walk, but they were also sealed from them. In other words, there was no provision for drainage of any wide battlemented wall-walk open to the elements.

Third, access has to be considered in evaluating the merits of any model for the primary construction of the upper parts of the White Tower. Whereas a mural passage carrying a wall-walk provides good access to all upper parts, as it does today, the gabled interpretation raises serious problems. Access to the chapel gallery is the most problematic, in that the two primary doorways to the gallery would have opened from external wall-walks. It would be surprising if the unusually sophisticated barrel-vaulted gallery to the chapel was to have access only via an open wall-walk, and it is difficult to accept on these grounds alone that the mural passage linking the chapel gallery to the south-west stair and thence the west room below is not primary. Indeed, the presence of Romanesque double windows along this length of passage is unique at this level and is indicative of the importance attached to this route at an early date.[212] Another access problem arising from the gabled model of the White Tower is that of the south-east turret. The asymmetric plan form of the turret has been cited as evidence for it being an addition, but such an interpretation has been based on a misunderstanding. We have seen that far from being a haphazard addition, this turret was carefully designed so as not to load

onto the chapel vaults alone.[213] Access to this primary tower would have been required and could have been only via a wall-walk on top of the chapel, as it is today. In the gabled model of the White Tower, this chapel wall-walk would have been a storey higher than the rest of the wall-walk – an oddity, incidentally, that takes some explaining – yet there is no evidence of any access. At the point where access could have been provided from the lower wall-walk (i.e., the south wall-walk immediately west of the chapel, and the east wall-walk immediately north of the chapel), there were doorways into the chapel gallery that would have been blocked by any stairs. The only point of access remaining would have been the unlikely one from the spine wall, or valley, between the two roofs. Given the evidence for the primary nature of the spine wall,[214] it is hardly surprising that the archaeological investigation of the spine wall did not reveal evidence of a stair. This leaves the doorway high in the east wall of the west room, which, until it was blocked *circa* 1490, opened into the chapel roof space,[215] and thus would have given access to the south-east turret. That such a convoluted route via a small doorway into a gutter and another still more awkward doorway opening from the top of a ladder into a confined roof space should have been the only access to one of the turrets beggars belief, and, more to the point, renders redundant the primary doorway in the north face of this turret.

The evidence for the form of the second floor of the White Tower by *circa* 1100 is both considerable and conclusive. That the White Tower had primary roofs at a lower level is without doubt. That these were contained within walls from the outset is equally clear: there is no evidence for an earlier gabled form that was only later built up into the second-floor walls as we know them today. To the contrary, there is good evidence (from the homogeneity of the fabric of the closely studied south elevation, the stairs, the turrets, the mural passage, the spine wall and the end walls of the two rooms) to show that any gabled model is untenable. The form of the original design argued here should not prove surprising to any student of Romanesque keeps, for boxed-in roofs are something of a norm and existed, for example, at Norwich (*circa* 1095–1115),[216] Montrichard (*circa* 1109–31),[217] Portchester (*circa* 1100–30),[218] Richmond (*circa* 1125–50),[219] Rochester (*circa* 1130)[220] and the south-west gatehouse at Sherborne Old Castle (by 1135).[221] That the walls rising above the eaves of an enclosed roof could be given false fenestration is also seen at Hedingham.[222] Parallels are important, for they reduce the urge to create additional interpretations. One such hypothesis could be that the original intention was to roof the White Tower at the higher level, and that this was reduced at a late stage in construction. Certainly, this would partly address the less than fully understood role of the primary spine wall and the fact that the east roof simply abutted its end walls. Such complexity and apparent conservatism are not sustainable, however, since they ignore the very important evidence of the subtle tapering of the spine wall (see below) and the primary nature of the side-wall drains, both of which imply that the lower roof was anticipated before the second-floor walls were begun. Another, and even less plausible, hypothesis has actually been advanced in which the low boxed-in roofs were designed to be temporary, with a high roof both planned and perhaps built (giving a pair of two-storey rooms).[223] Even ignoring the improbably elaborate provision for a temporary roof (such as the doorway giving access to the valley, now at the south end of the west room) or the unlikely connection between the two rooms at the inaccessible upper level through the large arches of the primary spine wall (the arches on the principal floor below being only recesses), this is also contrary to the evidence of the taper of the spine wall (see below) and does not account for the crudeness of the window and spine-wall arches of the second floor. More tellingly, it is wholly implausible that lower roofs were built as a necessary temporary feature within the surrounding screen of the second-floor walls when a higher roof could have been built equally easily in the first place. Needless to say, there is no evidence at all for any steeply pitched early medieval roof at the higher level, nor is it clear how such a wide roof as that of the western room would have been contained by the fabric of the White Tower: a roof at this level was achieved only *circa* 1490 by a remarkably flat pitch, inconceivable in an eleventh-century context.

With the loss of all earlier roof carpentry at the building of the surviving roof of *circa* 1490, it is a matter of pure conjecture as to the detailed form of the primary roofs or, indeed, any possible pre-1490 successor. The few details of the abutment of the roofs in the west room and the east room give mean pitches of 42.5° and 43.5° respectively. The 12.03 m[224] span of the western roof is substantial for the period, and this raises the possibility of intermediate support, as would have been inevitable for the similarly wide span of the floor joists of the entrance and first floors. An upward continuation of floor-supporting posts, or arcades, could have resulted in an arcaded roof structure at the first-floor level. It is unlikely, however, that the structural benefits of the boxed-in roofs of the White Tower would have been unrecognised by the builders: the great mass of walling provided by the false second storey was all above the springing point of the roofs of the east and west rooms, and would have been sufficient to prevent the spreading of much simpler free-spanning roof forms. The more modest span of 9.29 m[225] for the eastern room would hardly have required intermediate support even without the struc-

tural effect of the false second storey, and this, perhaps, strengthens the case for the adjacent western room having a self-supporting roof.[226] The absence of intermediate supports, if this were the case, would have had a considerable effect on the principal floor of the White Tower – the first floor – by freeing it of the arcade posts necessary at the lower levels.

Access and Doorways

While the suggested primary form and subsequent development of the upper parts of the White Tower are consistent with the structural evidence, this interpretation does not of itself solve the interesting problem of provision for doors. Considering that the mural passage was apparently constructed as a feature open to the exterior,[227] it is surprising that none of the doorways from the spiral staircases of the turret that open onto the mural passage has rebates or any other indication of the hanging of doors. This also appears to apply to the junction of the east mural passage and the chapel gallery. Here, the present rebated doorway is post-medieval, and the higher and wider arch for a doorway (more correctly simply the end of a barrel-vaulted passage) can be seen above. It is just possible that the post-medieval doorway replaces a Romanesque doorway, but the visibility of the voussoirs of the barrel vault above the door head, and the analogy with the other openings into the mural passage, suggest otherwise. The apparent oddity of these doorways is increased by the fact that the openings from the two western spiral stairs on the floor below (i.e., the principal floor) also have no rebates or other evidence of former doors, nor is there any sign of doorways on the stairs between the two levels. This could be taken as suggesting that the false-storey model is improbable, but there are good grounds to argue the reverse: the lack of doorways in this position is unlikely in any model of the structural history of the White Tower; and, more importantly, there are no rebated primary doorways anywhere else in the building. The only rebate on an original doorway is that to the basement apsidal room, but we have seen that this is plainly an insertion, probably at the time of the construction of the surviving door (after 1345). Other doors were simply made larger than the doorway and hung on one face of the jambs, a rebate-like effect created in most instances by a rear arch or a barrel-vaulted passage. This arrangement for door closure falls short of the snug fit of rebated doorways, but is manifestly adequate. It is only a small step from this type of surface-mounted doorway in a rear arch, or passage, to a workable arrangement for the spiral stairs: that is, surface-mounted doors on flat walls.

In the absence of a primary floor at the level of the present second floor, it is to be expected that the doorways to the chapel gallery are positioned differently from the floors below. The gallery is not provided with

any direct access from the main level of the chapel, but rather completes the circuit of the roof-level mural passage. To this end, there are doorways at the end of the south aisle of the gallery and, on the north side, at a point approximating to the chord of the apse. The gallery is lower than the mural passage in both cases, and the requisite three steps are contained within the doorway passages. The present door to the south-west opening is flush-mounted on the outer (west) face and there is no indication of an alternative previous position. The northern doorway is now provided with jambs at the northern end of the passage, but the ashlar of this work is recent,[228] and it appears that here also there were no jambs or rebate: any door was mounted flush.

Spine Wall (fig. 58)

As we have seen, the continuity of the coursing at the junction between the spine wall and the west wall of the chapel demonstrates that the spine wall is primary. The differences in the construction of the spine wall at this level from those below are explicable in terms of function: there are no recesses or doorways, but five simple round-headed openings, since the wall did not separate rooms. Likewise, the arches of the spine walls have rubble voussoirs that contrast with their ashlar counterparts in the spine-wall recesses below. A similar change in the construction of the rear arches of the window embrasures at this level has the same explanation, in that all these arches simply opened onto the roofs. Perhaps the most interesting feature of the spine wall at second-floor level, however, is its taper from a

width of 2.17 m at the south end to 1.68 m at the north. In the longer, western room, this is matched by a similar angling of the west face of the west wall of the chapel, so that what is now a second-floor room has a slightly waisted plan. Given the evidence that the spine wall coexisted with the lower roofs, this taper is wholly explicable, since there can be little doubt that it relates to the roof valleys, or gutters, on either side of the spine wall, necessary to drain the two enclosed roofs. The gutter for the east roof drained entirely from the northern end, while the gutter for the west roof could have drained both north and south. At 19.81 m for the single eastern gutter and 14.60 m for the two half-length western gutters, both would have required a substantial drop to flow correctly, and would have generated considerable volumes of run-off, so that an increase in width at the draining ends would have been desirable. Given this possible explanation, it is interesting to note that the spine wall tapers by 276 mm on the east side, whereas on the west side the northwards taper measures 200 mm and the southwards one measures 221 mm. That the western tapers should average 76 per cent of the eastern taper corresponds neatly to the different length of the gutters: the half-length western gutters are each 74 per cent of the length of the single eastern gutter.

The usefulness of the tapering of the spine wall can only be guessed at, since the drop of the gutters is unknown. Modern standards are for a minimum fall of 1:60, to which should be added a figure of, say, 50 mm for drips at the junctions of lead sheets:[229] over the longest gutter of 19.18 m and working with a normal 3 m-length sheet, this would give a total fall of 630 mm. With the angle of pitch of the White Tower eastern roof, this means that such a fall would have narrowed the gutter by approximately 600 mm. Therefore, the taper would have increased the width of the gutter at its narrowest by a useful 50 per cent. Indeed, since it is quite possible that the original gutters fell below modern standards, it is likely that the gain was greater. All this strongly suggests that the builders of the spine wall and the west wall of the chapel at this level took into account the considerable problems of draining enclosed roofs, and reduced the drainage problems by careful design of the masonry. Moreover, that the spine wall and the west wall of the chapel make the same subtle provision for the roof drainage adds yet further credibility to the primary nature of the spine wall.

THE SOUTH FOREBUILDING

The south forebuilding at the White Tower was demolished in 1674, the event being marked by the famous discovery of the skeletons of two children identified at the time as those of the Princes in the Tower.[230] The building was the rectangular tower immediately in front of the main entrance to the White

Tower, recorded in numerous panoramas of London and more detailed views of the Tower of London before this date. Such a forebuilding would have provided additional protection to the main entrance, but was too small to have housed an entrance stair itself.

Graphical Evidence

In the absence of any known remains of the forebuilding, even below ground,[231] the graphical evidence is of crucial importance. The earliest, but by no means the sketchiest view is that of *circa* 1500 from the south-west (see fig. 104). The forebuilding appears in the form of the upper half to two-thirds of a rectangular tower slightly inset from the south-west corner of the White Tower and as high as the sill of the lower windows of the south face of the turret. It appears slightly wider than deep, and occupies the width of the south face of the turret and the westernmost bay of the south elevation. The forebuilding is crenellated, and the only opening shown is a two-light window with semicircular heads on the south side. Further views of the forebuilding in plans and panoramas by Wyngaerde (*circa* 1544: see fig. 121), Ralph Agas (1560–70) and Braun and Hogenburg (1572) show the same form, but in less detail. The survey of the Tower Liberties in 1597 by Haiward and Gascoyne is the first to show the full height of the forebuilding, but the clumsy rendering of detail (at least in the eighteenth-century copies on which, due to the loss of the original, we rely)[232] means that the additional windows shown on the south face cannot be relied on (see fig. 127). More importantly, although both copies show the forebuilding extending as far east as the middle of the second bay of the south front, the engraving based on one of them shows it no more than one bay wide. Since a wider structure would have blocked the windows in this bay,[233] and drawings made after 1597 also show a narrower structure, this too can be regarded as a copyist's mistake.

One significant element that is shown for the first time in the two known versions of the survey is a turret at the south-east corner of the forebuilding, in this case drawn as circular with a doorway to the Inmost Ward at the bottom. Colvin has suggested that this turret was the 'Ludwyktoure', newly built in 1399, but this is unlikely.[234] It is clear, however, that it is not an original part of the south forebuilding, since it was referred to as the 'brick tower' in 1663:[235] bricks were used en masse very early at the Tower, but not until 1276–8.[236]

The corner turret, albeit square in form, appears again on the three versions of a view of the Tower of London from the south-west across the Thames by Hollar (*circa* 1640–60: fig. 59). As with the British Library manuscript view of *circa* 1500, this shows only the upper part of the forebuilding, but is much more

reliable than the Haiward and Gascoyne survey. The height is again around the level of the super-arches, although the lower window of the south face of the south-west turret is not shown, or is hidden from view. Interestingly, the west face of the forebuilding is depicted as having a central pilaster buttress, of reasonably convincing Romanesque appearance. In a portrait of Sir John Robinson of *circa* 1662,[237] the west face of the forebuilding is depicted almost face on, but there is little detail and the buttress is obscured by a chimney in the foreground (see fig. 136).

These various views of the Tower of London record the south forebuilding with considerable consistency, if with a frustrating lack of detail. The dimensions can be reasonably reliably determined by reference to the surviving fabric of the White Tower: the fact that the west wall of the forebuilding is shown as slightly inset from the south-west corner of the White Tower probably simply reflects the staggering of quoins on the main angles of the White Tower; the eastern wall coincided with the western buttress; and the height coincided with the level of the sill of the lowest window of the south face of the south-west turret. Unexpected confirmation of the last may well survive in the form of what appear to be the remains of an oolite string-course (or weathering) immediately to the east of this window and 150 mm above the sill.[238] Very possibly, this represents the limit of upstanding leadwork from the lead roofing of the forebuilding, with the window looking out onto the battlements and gutters of the forebuilding (fig. 60).[239]

The layout of the forebuilding can also be determined. With probable internal dimensions in the range of approximately 6.4m by 6.7m and with the principal doorway positioned 6.3 m above ground, it is inconceivable that the staircase was housed within the forebuilding itself. Rather, the forebuilding would have covered a landing and possibly the upper steps only of an external stair, as was the case also at the keeps of Rochester and Castle Rising, amongst others. The fact that the survey of 1597 provides the only view of the structure down to ground level, along with its deficiencies, has been noted, but the fact that it does not show such a substantial feature as a south-facing doorway can probably be relied on. Meanwhile, the proximity of Coldharbour Gate and the presence of the central pilaster buttress would appear to rule out a doorway and stair on the west side. This leaves the unrecorded east face, surely the most obvious location for the stair in any case. The lack of structural evidence for a stair descending west to east against the south elevation is to be expected if the stair was later than the wall (see below). Moreover, that such a stair did exist in the Middle Ages is suggested by the location of the doorway to the spiral stair in the second bay from the west. This is placed at such a level that the modern stair (modelled on this proposed arrange-

Den Tower van London

59 View of the White Tower from across the Thames by Wenceslaus Hollar, *circa* 1640–60. Although the view is limited, it is the most reliable record of the south forebuilding.

ment) passes it at exactly the right height. Of course, we have seen that this spiral stair was built after the late 1350s, but its location could have been determined by the original arrangement for the external stair.[240] Similarly arranged external entrance stairs at Norwich and (at the rear of) Colchester were at least partly of stone, but there is little evidence at the White Tower other than the tantalising references to the removal of massive stone footings to a stair in the demolition work of 1674.[241]

Phasing and Dating

The limited stylistic evidence suggests pre-1200 origins, but does not allow for more accuracy. Nevertheless, the forebuilding has become firmly identified in the literature as a secondary feature of the later twelfth century.[242] The exact reasoning behind such a dating is difficult to determine, but it must be suspected that it reflects in part a general assumption that forebuildings were late twelfth-century phenomena. A re-examination of the considerable evidence of forebuildings elsewhere in England and on the Continent demonstrates that such a late dating cannot be sustained on these grounds alone. The castles at Monmouth, Corfe, Norwich, Portchester, Kenilworth, Rochester, Sherborne, Castle Rising and, most precociously, at Loches[243] show that forebuildings were common in the earlier twelfth century, and known in the early eleventh. The dating of the forebuilding at the White Tower must therefore be based on the available structural evidence.

Examination of the south elevation confirms that the south forebuilding must post-date the construction of the lower half of the White Tower, since the areas of primary ashlar below the building break on the south face of the south-west turret reveal no trace of the building. Indeed, the expanse of primary *in situ*

ashlar here is sufficient to confirm that the west wall of the south forebuilding simply abutted the Phase 1 walling of the White Tower and was not keyed in. Similarly, on the buttress to the east of the south-west turret (the location of the junction between the east wall of the forebuilding and the White Tower proper), there are areas of primary Caen ashlar that also confirm later abutment rather than coeval, keyed-in, construction. This implies that the main entrance and the blocked window above were also built in advance of the south forebuilding.

While it is evident that the forebuilding abutted primary ashlar on the lower part of the south elevation, and is therefore of later date, it is not equally apparent that it was added to the upper half of the building. Of the anomalies in this part of the south elevation, the double windows of the second floor, and the necessarily narrower upper part of the buttress between them, need not reflect the entrance arrangements but simply the prestigious and more private entrance to the chapel gallery. The string-course above these windows, however, is higher than elsewhere on the south elevation over the western pair of double windows only. Since this is not applied to both bays of double windows, it is perhaps more likely to reflect the only feature unique to the westernmost bay – the entrance. Since there are no comparable anomalies at first-floor level and the raised string-course is 15 m above the doorway, there could be more reason to believe that the anomalous treatment of the string-course reflects the forebuilding rather than the entrance alone.

If the forebuilding were of Phase 2, some evidence might be expected of bonded masonry. Certainly, it rose above the building break, but only by approximately 1.8 m (approximately 23.2–25.0 m OSBM). On the south-west turret, most of this area was distin-

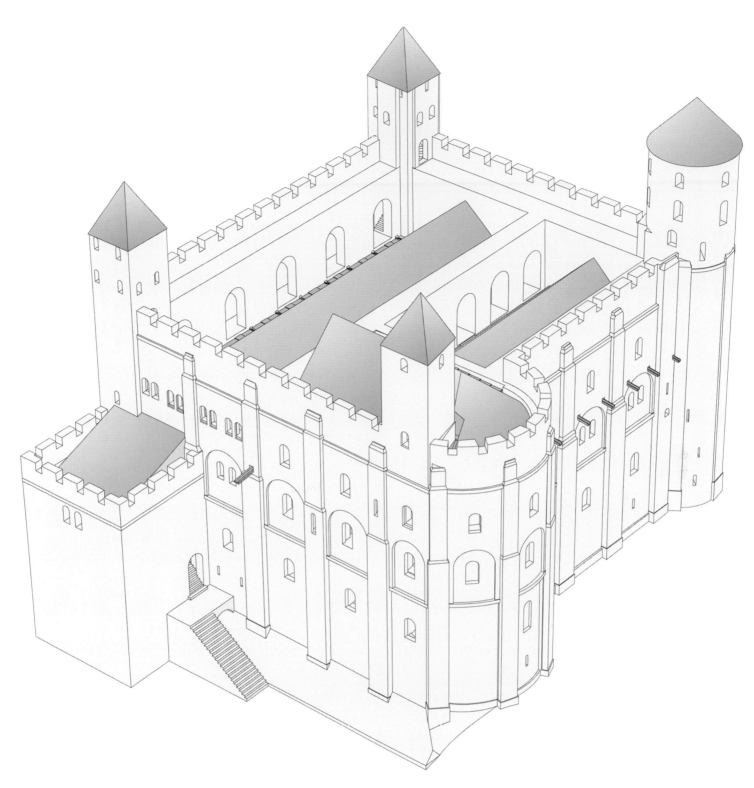

60 Three-dimensional reconstruction from the south-east with forebuilding.

guished by Type 6 mortar associated with patching that is consistent with, but not the slightest proof of, the repair required following the removal of a forebuilding structurally bonded with the main elevation at this level. The buttress that marks the eastern wall of the forebuilding is faced entirely with Portland stone at this level, and is less informative still. Likewise, it is unclear whether the design of the western bay of the south elevation was modified after the break to take account of the forebuilding. This would have rendered the first-floor window and the blind arcading of the western bay quite unnecessary, yet there is evidence for both. The evidence for the window, however, consists

of a western jamb only and this does not continue above the level of the Phase 1 fabric, and thus may never have been completed. As for the blind arcading in this bay, it is just possible that this was first created in the years 1674–6 on the removal of the forebuilding, since the rubble above the primary window jamb is distinguished by a uniquely high density of chert in what appears to be a post-medieval mortar.

Thus, the case for the phasing and dating of the forebuilding is far from conclusive. Certainly, the structural and contextual evidence would allow for the forebuilding to belong to Phase 2 of the primary construction of the White Tower, but the same evi-

89

61 The overall geometry of the
White Tower: a hypothesis.
Basement plan with superimposed
square and north–south centre-line.

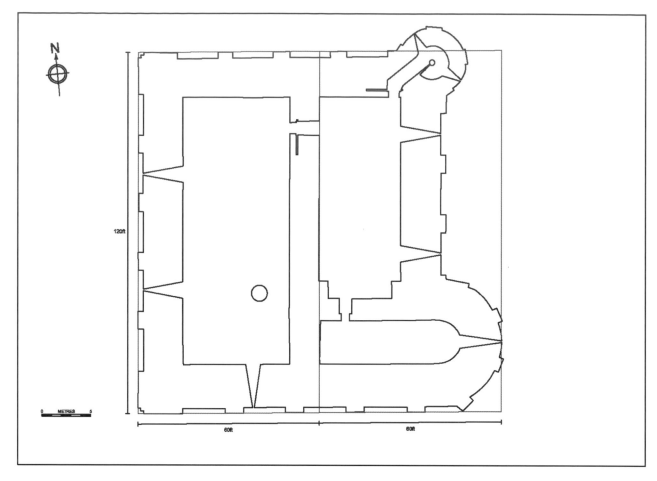

dence allows for it to be a twelfth-century addition.
Given that the evidence for the rest of the building
repeatedly indicates a great tower constructed to a
consistent design from foundations to turrets, irrespective of the building break, it must be suspected
that the forebuilding was not a modification of the
1090s, but, rather, an addition of the twelfth century.

ANNEXE: GEOMETRY AND PROPORTION

It is with some wariness that a dimensional analysis of
the White Tower is approached here (figs 61, 62). Elsewhere, such study has often acquired a poor reputation, largely resulting from the misleading use of
inaccurate measurements derived from small-scale
plans.[244] Of course, we can hardly avoid considering
the dimensional component of the design of the
White Tower, and, given the quality of the record made
during the 1990s, there is the opportunity to adopt an
approach that ensures that the study is based on
dimensions that withstand scrutiny. This has been
achieved in several ways: all measurements are taken
from the controlled tacheometric survey of the White
Tower, so there are none of the inaccuracies that arise
from taped measurements or other casual field observations; all measurements are of the surviving primary
fabric or repaired fabric where it is evident that repair
has not modified the original dimensions; the survey
data is held as plans, sections and elevations, within a
CAD (Computer Aided Design) program, so there are
no errors introduced by reduction to scale drawing

and subsequent scaling off; and wherever a measurement can be repeated (e.g., room widths), multiple
observations are combined to give a mean value and
a standard deviation, thus giving a clear indication of
the regularity of the surviving fabric and also pre-
venting the selection of measurements to fit the argument. Perhaps the most important result of the CAD-
based metric survey is that it has been possible to
explore the angular dimensions of the building as
easily as the more conventional linear dimensions.[245]

In examining the White Tower for any underlying
dimensional or geometric logic, it is essential that we
work from well-founded premises. First, any linear
module must operate within common multiples of
the English foot of 304.8 mm: no other value for the
foot is tenable in Anglo-Norman London. Second,
proportional and geometric relationships should be
from the known canon of design systems available to
the eleventh-century Anglo-Norman architect. Most
typically, these comprise the square, the relationship
of the diagonal to the side of the square ($\sqrt{2}$), the regular triangle and the regular pentagon.[246]

St John's Chapel

Given the obvious attention to its construction, it is
perhaps not surprising that the dimensional logic
underlying the design of St John's Chapel is that which
can be most readily reconstructed. First, there is ample
evidence of a 5, 10 or 20 ft module, to which has been
applied $\sqrt{2}$ (i.e., the diagonal of a square): the central

facing page: 62   The geometry of St
John's Chapel. A) Root two ($\sqrt{2}$)
modules; B) 60° angles.

90

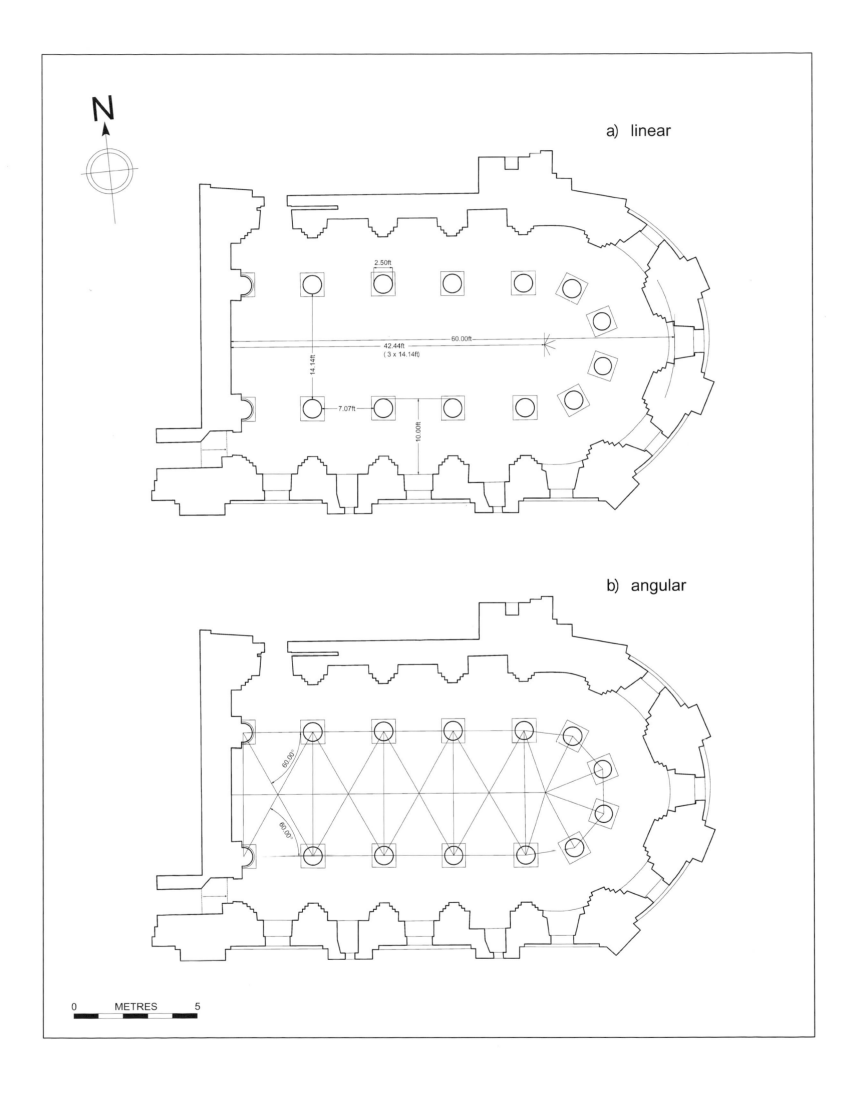

N

a) linear

2.50ft

60.00ft

42.44ft
(3 x 14.14ft)

14.14ft

7.07ft

10.00ft

b) angular

60.00°

60.00°

0   METRES   5

vessel is 14.14 ft wide (√2 of 10 ft);[247] the arcade piers are at 7.07 ft spacings (√2 of 5 ft);[248] the arcade piers are 10 ft high; the apse cord is 12.935 m (42.44 ft) from the west wall (i.e., 3 x 14.14 ft); the aisle width plus arcade is 10 ft;[249] and the total internal length of the chapel is 60 ft. The last dimension is especially interesting, because it is half the length of the sides of the 120 ft squared plan of the White Tower (see below). Second, examination of the angular dimensions of the chapel is revealing. While no discernible linear module can be identified between the centres of the arcade piers, the centres are set out at a precise angle of 60°.[250] On first consideration this may not appear to signify much, but when it is remembered that the inter-pier spacing along the arcade follows a 7.07 ft (√2 of 5 ft) module, then it is apparent that an extremely subtle design is in evidence: the slightest thickening or thinning of the 2.5 ft pier (itself consistent with a 5, 10 or 20 ft module) would remove the capability for the angular and linear systems to coexist.

Overall Proportions

The exterior of the White Tower is dominated by the sheer corner towers, and it is understandable that they, and the identically aligned buttresses, appear to be the face of the building adopted for the overall proportional scheme. The starting point for analysis is that the White Tower sits neatly within a square placed along the main walls, and taking in the apse. Of course, the fact that the circular north-east tower straddles the square could undermine this scheme were it not for two significant pieces of evidence. First, the east face of the spine wall sits exactly along the centreline of the square. Given the offsets that progressively narrow the walls of the east and west rooms, it is only at basement level that the match is perfect, and this suggests that, if the square is valid, any general scheme of proportions should work at this level. Second, the square has sides of almost exactly 120 ft.[251] Taken together, there seems to be sufficient basis for the rather modest claim that the White Tower is set out within a 120 ft square.

The consistency of the linear measurements, in which opposing sides match to within 30 mm, is not matched by the angular setting out, since the building is slightly rhomboidal in plan. The rhomboid angle of 0°28'37" translates to a misalignment along the 120 ft sides of approximately 1 ft.[252] Of course, setting out even simple right angles on this grand scale (and on a sloping site) is problematic with rudimentary equipment, and the angular error is not outside what might be expected. Whilst imperceptible on site, the misalignment does need to be taken into account when undertaking this type of analysis: any proportional scheme must work within these outside errors, but, if it depends on theoretically true right angles for the overall square, it can hardly expect to offer perfect correlation.

The encompassing 120 ft square, and any derived purely linear scheme, does not account for the position of the east wall. The inter-buttress wall face of this is set back by approximately 20 ft from the nominal 120 ft square. We have seen, however, that for a 120 ft square to have any relevance to the plan of the White Tower, measurements should be made to the faces of the buttresses and corner towers, and the eastern buttresses are positioned 101.46 ft east of the western wall. Given the fusion of linear (square and √2) proportions and angular geometry (60° triangles) in St John's Chapel, such a scheme can be tested on the grander scale of the whole White Tower. The results are remarkable, for it is immediately evident that 60° angles (or regular triangles) struck from the north-west and south-west corners of the 120 ft square intersect at the line of the east wall buttresses. The same exercise repeated for the south-west and south-east corners gives lines intersecting at the inner face of the north wall, and the same regular triangle from the south-east and north-east corners provides an intersection on the inner face of the east wall. Thus, in the absence of an alternative scheme and given the abundance of evidence for an angular setting out in the chapel, it must be suspected that the 60° angle, or regular triangle, was consciously used in the design of the overall ground plan of the White Tower. The rhomboidal misalignment of the building is such, however, that there can be no certainty.

It is clear that the four external faces have little consistency in bay dimensions, and the reason for this must surely be the anomalies that project from them – the chapel apse and the circular north-east turret. The western wall is alone in having neither of these projections and thus presents a regular face to what is arguably the prime direction – towards the city. It is not surprising, therefore, that only this side shows clear evidence of regular design, with the buttresses spaced at 20 ft centres. The other external walls have bays smaller or larger than this, depending on whether the bays have to be stretched (on the east and the south) or compressed (on the north).

The use of proportion in the elevations of the White Tower is neither obvious nor, perhaps, open to analysis, since the widely varied external ground level means that there is no obvious datum to work from. If the interior basement floor level of approximately 8.4 m OSBM is adopted, then the overall height to the top of the surviving and recorded primary fabric is 33.59 m (110.20 ft). This is close (within 200 mm) to the apex height of a regular tetrahedron made of regular triangles with sides of 120 ft, but this is hardly a serious proposition: to the ambiguity of the ground level we must add the variability in the turret heights, which measure 40.41 m OSBM (south-west), 41.32 m OSBM (south-east), 42.02 m OSBM (north-east) and 40.31 m OSBM (north-west). With battlements rebuilt at least twice since the eleventh century, we also lack a precise height for the wall between the turrets, and the reconstructed wall-head/wall-walk at 32.80 m OSBM is not obviously meaningful. The external horizontal string-courses and buttresses are similarly devoid of discernible proportions.

Other instances of the use of linear (square and √2) proportions and angular geometry (60° triangles) can be found within the White Tower. These may be consequences of the relationships already identified here or vice versa, since, outside the chapel, it is difficult to determine the actual thinking or procedure followed by the designer or builder. What is sufficiently clear from this study of the dimensions of the primary fabric, however, is that these different systems of linear proportions and angular geometry were consciously combined with absolute imperial measurements (seen in the 5, 10, 20 or 120 ft modules), and that this is most notable in the plan form of the building and, especially, within its most sophisticated component – the chapel of St John.

Acknowledgements

Members of the Historic Buildings Recording Unit (HBRU)/University of Reading team (Helen Jones, John Crook, Andrew Walker, Sharon Hall, Cheryl Bishop and the late Bruce Sellwood); present and former staff at Historic Royal Palaces/Tower of London (Anna Keay, Edward Impey, Jeremy Ashbee, Bridget Litchfield, Jane Holmes, Jane Spooner and the White Tower Wardens); and Martin Brett, Alan Vince, Sandy Heslop and the late Martin Caroe.

63　Interior view of St John's Chapel, facing east.

CHAPTER THREE

St John's Chapel

JOHN CROOK

St John's Chapel (fig. 63) enjoys a well-justified reputation as one of the most complete surviving examples of early Anglo-Norman ecclesiastical architecture.
Even though the chapel was subsequently used for
secular purposes for several hundred years, this did
not cause irreversible damage to the primary fabric,
and the building was easily restored to its original state
in the mid-nineteenth century.[1] The primary decorative elements, so important as indicators of the date
when the chapel was first built, have survived relatively unscathed, the main replacements being the
impost mouldings of the responds in the north aisle,
which were hacked back to allow post-medieval
presses to lie flush against the aisle wall. The vault of
the ambulatory at the apex of the apse was also damaged when a spiral stair was inserted, as shown in
Lemprière's east-west section of 1729 (see fig. 147).
Ironically, much of the worst damage to the fabric
probably occurred during Anthony Salvin's 'conservation' work of 1864. Some of the chapel's stonework
was evidently scraped at this time, notably the pier
shafts and their capitals; the shafts were totally repointed, as were the side walls. Further repointing
seems to have occurred more recently.

Considering the acknowledged importance of the
chapel, the bibliography specifically devoted to it is
surprisingly sparse. One reason for this may be the
perceived simplicity of its constructional history:
no disjunctions in the building sequence had been
detected prior to our detailed examination of the
chapel, and so it was thought to be of a single phase.
It is, furthermore, a building where all appears accessible, transparent and plain to the eye. Consequently,
the chapel has tended to be cited in studies of Anglo-
Norman architecture for its value as a structure of supposedly secure date rather than as an interpretative
challenge in its own right. Yet significant constructional anomalies emerge as soon as one begins to
examine the fabric more closely, raising questions
about the chronology of construction. The date of the
chapel is not as clear-cut an issue as has hitherto been
assumed. This chapter opens with a broad structural
overview of the chapel; its component parts are then
examined in greater detail, including an analysis of the
anomalies that allow its constructional history to be
refined. The second section of the chapter is concerned with stylistic features, the date of the various
phases of construction, and the place of the chapel,
and especially of its quasi-sculptural decorative elements, in the broader context of Anglo-Norman
ecclesiastical architecture. Finally, we offer a few suggestions as to how the chapel was used, though in the
absence of documentary evidence this must remain
very sketchy.

STRUCTURE, ANOMALIES AND BUILDING SEQUENCE

Structural Description

The chapel of St John is located in the south-east
corner of the White Tower, at first-floor ('main') level
and rising through the second floor. Figure 64 shows
a simplified plan of the chapel, and the numbering
system employed in this chapter. The plan is expressed

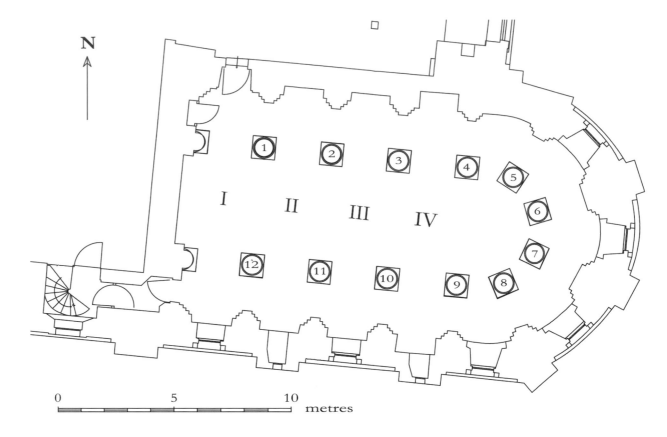

N

0   5   10
                    metres

externally in the apsidal projection at the south end of the east side of the tower (fig. 65). This apse is demonstrably part of the primary design from the foundations upwards,[2] and the plan of the outer walls of the chapel must therefore have been envisaged from the outset. It is unlikely that such an apsidal plan could have been intended for any room other than a chapel.[3]

The southernmost part of the eastern half of the White Tower, of which the chapel occupies the two uppermost storeys, contains the only solid, masonry floors in the tower, the others being of timber construction from entrance level upwards. Below the chapel are two storeys of vaulted rooms, but it is uncertain that the room beneath the chapel (sometimes called the 'crypt') had an ecclesiastical function as has often been supposed. There is no direct communication between the chapel and the lower room, the southern staircase being a later insertion, and this would seem to invalidate the use of the lower room as a crypt to the chapel at main level. It might, rather, have served as a 'lower chapel' in its own right, though in the absence of physical or documentary evidence this interpretation remains entirely hypothetical.[4]

As Richard Gem has observed,[5] the general form of St John's Chapel is 'closely similar to the eastern arm of a great church, bereft of transepts and nave'. Its plan resembles that of the choir of a church of apse-and-ambulatory design (though of course without any radial chapels), comprising four straight bays terminating in a five-bay apse. The chapel is two-storeyed, with a continuous gallery (locally called the 'triforium'), but no clerestory.

Outer Walls

The west wall of the chapel consists of the southern third of the north–south spine wall that divides the White Tower at all levels (see fig. 147). The western face of this wall is almost exactly aligned to that of the wall at entry level below, with only a slight offset of 120 mm. The main feature of the east side of the wall (fig. 66) is a recess occupying the entire width of the central vessel of the chapel; there is a similar recess in the room beneath the chapel. Again, the rear faces of the two recesses are almost exactly aligned over each other, with a small offset of only approximately 80 mm.[6] The apex of the recess is at the same height as that of the arches of the main arcade, presumably for aesthetic effect, so the geometry requires the recess arch to spring from a level well below that of the abaci of the adjacent western responds. The masonry at the back of the western recess is disturbed to a height of about 450 mm above floor level. This is too high for a plinth, but the disturbance might represent the removal of a dais.

The north wall of the chapel consists of the upper part of the east–west cross wall that rises throughout the entire White Tower, separating the southern third of the tower from the rest of the building. The north face of this wall is exactly aligned to that of the storey below, without any offset. Within the chapel, the wall is articulated by the vaulting responds of the north aisle groin vault. This articulation continues around the apse and the south aisle of the chapel, and along this aisle the relationship of the vaulting rhythm to that of the main articulation of the outer walls of the

65   The White Tower from the
south-east, showing the projecting
apse of the chapel and the floors
below it.

White Tower is not immediately apparent.[7] The inner face of the chapel is further characterised by the absence of a plinth and by round-headed recesses under wall arches of the same profile and height as those of the main arcade. In terms of structural logic, the face of the aisle wall should be defined as the front of the recesses, and this plane continues, in a more or less accurate semicircle, around the ambulatory in the blind north-east bay and beneath the windows in the other curved bays. Working forwards from this plane, the aisle responds (fig. 67) have three elements supporting in turn: (1) a small wall arch built in rubble rather than ashlar, answering to the arch of the main arcade; (2) the springing of the aisle groin vault; (3) the transverse arch. The recesses in Bay IV, west of the apse chord, are twice the depth of the others in the straight bays (750 mm compared with 370 mm).

Elevations of the Central Vessel

The main elevation is of two storeys: a main arcade of round-headed arches supported on stout cylindrical columns of coursed masonry, and an upper tier of similar arches opening into a gallery. The elevation lacks any kind of vertical articulation, though this would not be expected in a nave whose barrel vault is without transverse arches. There is a simple chamfered string-course at the gallery floor level, but the main barrel vault springs directly from the head of the walls without an impost course. The upper parts of the wall show a sparing use of ashlar, rubble being used to fill the spandrels between the main arches and the gallery floor; this reduced use of ashlar at a higher level is a feature discussed elsewhere.[8]

Main Arcade

The position of the main arcade, unlike that of the north and west walls, does not obviously correspond to any supports in the storey beneath the chapel. On the contrary, the arcade piers slightly oversail the inner, vertical face of the apsidal 'crypt' at entrance level; they sit on the haunches of the massive barrel vault of that room. Piers 6–7 and 10–11 are placed on the corners of the great window embrasures on the east and south side of the crypt; Piers 9 and 12 sit less comfortably over two of the crypt window embrasures. It is therefore not immediately clear that consideration was given to the position of the chapel arcade piers when those crypt embrasures were constructed.

The arcade columns have moulded bases displaying a variety of rather shallow profiles, and four different types of capitals (most being chamfered block capitals decorated with tau crosses). These quasi-sculptural features clearly have implications for the date of the construction of the chapel and are discussed in detail below. They support round-headed arches of a single, plain order. These arches are of necessity stilted in the five-bay apse, whose six pillars are more closely spaced than those of the straight bays.

97

The arrises of the main arcade have ashlar only on the side facing the central vessel; those on the aisle side are formed simply of rubble.

Gallery

The gallery opens into the main vessel through plain, round-headed arches that are also of a single order and identical in profile to those of the main arcade below; consequently, the width of the rectangular gallery piers matches the diameter of the main columns beneath them. A chamfered string-course at the gallery floor level emphasises the two-storeyed nature of the main elevation.

As discussed in greater detail below, the gallery (fig. 68) has a continuous barrel vault, which springs directly from the side walls, the springing line being marked merely by a slight set-back. A consequence of the choice of a barrel, rather than a groined, vault is that the outer walls of the gallery do not display the bay divisions expressed at lower level by the aisle responds. The inner faces of the north and south walls are aligned to the rear face of the recesses in Bays 2 and 3 of the aisles, while the outer (north) face of the north wall simply continues the plane of the storeys below. In the apse the face of the gallery wall is set back slightly with respect to that of the ambulatory beneath, on a line approximately coinciding with the offset of the first sub-arch of the ambulatory window embrasures.

Vaults

The main vessel is roofed by a barrel vault, constructed in rubble, which still shows the imprint of its centring boards. The vault terminates in a semi-dome at the eastern end. The aisles and ambulatory are groin-vaulted in rendered rubble, and their transverse arches are also of rubble rather than well-cut ashlar (fig. 67). The transverse arches in the straight bays are unusually narrow, their width being determined by that of the aisle responds, but in the curved bays of the ambulatory the transverse arches widen outwards, and are supported on broader responds against the external wall. As already noted, the gallery, which forms a complete circuit at upper level, is roofed in a continuous barrel vault formed of flattish, irregular voussoirs, which were then rendered.

The extrados of the main barrel vault is visible in the roof space, where it protrudes above a floor of loosely consolidated rubble approximately at the level of the upper surface of the aisle vaults. The chapel seems originally to have been covered by its own roof running east–west a storey higher than the roof over the remainder of the building.[9]

Doors

Given the resemblance of the chapel to the eastern arm of a church, a central entrance doorway might have

67 North aisle, vault of Bay IV, showing the articulation of the north wall (right), the groin vault (centre) and the soffit of the main arcade (left).

68 Eastward view along the south gallery.

been expected in the western wall of the chapel. The occurrence of primary mortar in the rubble fabric of this wall shows, however, that the recess was always blocked. Instead of a grand western doorway there are two rather unassuming, asymmetrically placed lateral entrances into the aisles.[10] One of these is in the aisle wall on the north side of Bay 1. In place of the recess found in the other straight bays, the wall here is simply pierced by a short, round-headed passage to the adjacent chamber. The present door of this entrance is located at the north end of the passage and opens towards the chapel, and this was probably the position of the original door. The door arch does not rise to the full height of the end wall of the passage, and the door is simply face-mounted against the wall, without any rebate. Remains of a drawbar socket are visible in the embrasure. A rebate at the south end of the entrance passage dates from the thirteenth or fourteenth century on tooling evidence, and is associated with the evident replacement of masonry at the angles of the jambs.

The other entrance at the main level is a low east–west passage leading to the chapel from the flank of the south-east window embrasure of the main, western chamber of this storey. The vault of the passage appears to be Romanesque, and it retains the imprint of the centring boards used in its construction. On this evidence the recess cut to accommodate the head of the door when open is also original, proving that this was the primary position of the door, which closes against the entrance arch at the east end of the passage. A shallow rebate on the northern jamb and arch at the western end of the passage, indicating that there was a second door here, is almost certainly secondary: it cuts clumsily through blocks near to vertical joints and the claw-chisel tooling suggests a thirteenth- or fourteenth-century date.

At the west end of the north aisle is a shallow, round-headed recess, now fitted with modern doors and used as a book cupboard. Unlike the south-west door, it is centrally placed and its apex is considerably higher than the arch of the south-west door. The modern timber lining of the recess prevents further examination of the masonry behind it; rubble would be expected.

There are two entrances to the gallery, in the north-east and south-west corners, a position presumably determined by a concern to continue the circuit provided by the mural passage that runs around the rest of the tower at roof level. The gallery is, in fact, lower than the mural passage. The north-east entrance, in Bay IV, consists of a short passage, with three modern steps descending from the eastern mural passage through the north wall. There is a modern door at the north end of the passage, hanging from nineteenth-century jambs, and the quoins at the south end of the passage are also modern, but the rubble-built short barrel vault sloping down into the chapel gallery is

Romanesque and there can be no doubt that this entrance is an original feature.

The other entrance at gallery level is located at the west end of the south gallery, a passage whose south wall continues the line of the gallery wall; thus the door is offset tight against the outer wall rather than being centrally located within the end wall of the gallery. Again, three modern steps are required to account for the difference in level between the gallery floor and the mural passage. The door (also modern) is flush-mounted on modern pintles at the east end of the passage, and opens into the south mural passage.

Windows

The windows of the chapel were much affected by Salvin's restoration of 1864, particularly externally, and these works are discussed more fully in Chapter Two.[11] At the main level the recesses in the outer walls are pierced by windows on the south side and in four of the curved bays of the ambulatory. Since the internal straight bays of the chapel are roughly half the length of the external bays of the White Tower, two windows, corresponding to Bays II and IV of the chapel, coincide with buttresses of the south elevation, and cut through those buttresses. The plan of the splays is adjusted so that the innermost arch of the window in Bay II is centrally located within the bay; the south window in Bay IV is eccentrically displaced towards the east end of that bay. The form of the windows seems to have been simpler than those of the remainder of the White Tower, comprising single lights rather than the subdivided windows that were a feature of the east and west rooms at first-floor level.[12]

Floor

The present floor surfaces of St John's Chapel, at both main and gallery levels, result from restorations by Salvin as well as earlier campaigns, discussed more fully elsewhere. The main floor level was repaved in rather bland large modern limestone slabs in 1967–8.[13] These slabs replaced the nineteenth-century floor scheme, which survives in the gallery, comprising diagonally set yellow to buff-coloured earthenware tiles decorated with an incised, geometrical repeating pattern. No areas of Romanesque flooring survive. As already noted, the outer walls of the chapel have no plinth, nor have the aisle responds. The height of the plinths both of the free-standing piers and the western responds indicates, however, that the floor is still at its Romanesque level, and this is confirmed by photographs taken when the floor was re-laid. The recent survey has shown that the present floor slopes upwards by 120 mm from the western responds to the apex of the apse, and this probably reflects a similar slope in the original substrate below the modern floor. Although the eastward rise might be a deliberate feature,[14] it could equally result from subsidence at the west end, given that the levels of the piers and the string-course at gallery floor level are also higher towards the east. On the other hand, the piers appear to be vertical rather than leaning westwards, as might be expected had subsidence occurred at the west end of the chapel.

There are two original drains at floor level: one between Responds 4 and 5, the other on the south side of the chapel, in the westernmost bay. These might have been intended to evacuate rainwater during construction, or could have served for periodic cleaning of the chapel floor after the chapel was completed.

Building Stone Petrography and Mortars

Ashlar

As indicated above, the use of materials shows some concern for economy, ashlar being employed for the load-bearing elements and as dressings for those arrises visible from the nave; rubble for the main walling and vaults, and also, more unusually, for the transverse arches of the aisles. At the main level of the chapel all the window reveals are of rubble, with ashlar quoins.

The principal material for ashlar work is Caen stone, the famous Normandy limestone of Middle Jurassic (Bathonian) age. This creamy white peloidal limestone was a fairly new stone in English buildings at the time that the Tower of London was being constructed. It was used, notably, in Lanfranc's work at Canterbury Cathedral (1071–7),[15] but some pre-Conquest use of Caen stone has been claimed, particularly in coastal Sussex.[16] Other stones are, however, discernible at the White Tower. Most obviously, eight of the twelve cylindrical piers of the main arcade contain significant amounts of Quarr stone, a Tertiary limestone from the Bembridge Formation, quarried near Fishbourne on the Isle of Wight. This has a characteristic 'featherbed' texture resulting from the recrystallisation of calcite, replacing the originally aragonite gastropod shell fragments and partially infilling the voids between the shell fragments.[17]

Quarr stone also occurs in a discrete band in the aisle responds. This band plays an important role in our interpretation of the development of the White Tower as a whole. At the top of this feature there is a particularly significant second band of two or three courses of another stone from the Bembridge Formation. This stone, called 'Binstead limestone' by Anderson and Quirk (a nomenclature that has not been adopted by geologists),[18] succeeds Quarr in the Bembridge beds. In this chapter the term 'Bembridge limestone' is used for the 'normal' limestone, and 'Quarr stone' for the shelly facies. The first is a fine-grained pale grey or white limestone containing fossilised shells of freshwater or terrestrial molluscs, though in St John's Chapel the blocks only occasionally exhibit the most characteristic feature of this

stone: small, dark cavities, 1 to 2 mm in diameter, left by nucules of the algal water-plant *Chara*. It was used, *inter alia*, for the tower of Bosham church, West Sussex, where the stone contains recent marine borings, indicating that it was quarried from the foreshore at Bembridge.[19]

In conjunction with these Isle of Wight limestones, another, completely different, stone occurs in the responds of the apse and south aisle: Reigate stone, which is used sporadically throughout the tower.[20] This is a fine-grained sandstone from the Upper Greensand formation, pale grey, sometimes greenish in colour, containing small flecks of glauconite and, frequently, flakes of mica. It was used extensively shortly before the Conquest at Westminster Abbey, and subsequently for St Paul's Cathedral and the buildings of the medieval Palace of Westminster. The petrographical analysis of the exterior of the south face of the White Tower in 1997–8 showed that this stone was abundantly used at lower levels, notably in two courses immediately above the plinth; thereafter it was employed sporadically, though its use tended to die out at the main level of the chapel.

For the specialist work of bases and capitals a somewhat shelly oolitic limestone of a straw-yellow colour was employed, identified as Taynton stone, from the Great Oolite Group of the Middle Jurassic.[21] The medieval quarries were at Taynton, near Burford in Oxfordshire; one of them, Lees Quarry, is still open and occasionally operational. As argued below, the distribution of this stone, and the way it was eked out towards the end of the building project, suggests that it may have arrived at the Tower in a single consignment.[22] It is not possible to state with certainty that the similar lithography of this stone throughout the Tower indicates that it came from the same bed of the same quarry. This stone is characterised by current-bedding, which manifests itself as darker stripes of calcite-cemented shell fragments seen on the worked faces (probably due to differential adhesion of dirt), and by worm burrows forming dark spots. The presence of current-bedding enables the original orientation of each block to be determined, and it is interesting to note that in areas where the deposits are graded, changing from a coarse, shelly facies to a 'quieter' facies typical of deeper water, the sculptors seem to have attempted to ensure that mouldings were cut into the finer part of the stone, reserving the rougher areas for the plane faces; this means that blocks were sometimes used upside down with regard to their true bedding.[23]

At gallery level the rectangular piers of the straight bays are faced with ashlar on all four sides, up to the springing level of their arches. In the curved bays, however, the faces of the piers on the gallery side are of rubble with ashlar quoins; the rubble of the pier faces contains a great mixture of stone types. Ashlar is

69 Close-up of the shelly mortar characteristic of Phase I.

also used for the arrises of both sides of the gallery arches, but in the curved bays the arris voussoirs on the gallery side are very roughly cut in comparison with those of the arches of the five straight bays. The gallery window reveals are mostly of rubble with ashlar quoins, with the exception of the windows in Bays I and II, which have reveals built totally of ashlar. Caen stone is employed almost exclusively for all this ashlar work, the only exceptions being a few blocks of Quarr stone.

Mortars

The mortars used in the chapel, as elsewhere in the White Tower, are an important diagnostic feature. Two quite distinct and easily recognisable mortars are found in St John's Chapel. The earlier (fig. 69) is characterised by the presence of numerous bivalve shells, sometimes fragmentary but often whole; evidently the sand used to make the lime mortar was rich in marine shells. Poorly sorted, well-rounded, black and deep red gravels are also present, ranging in size from 0.5 to 2 mm. The later mortar lacks the characteristic shell debris, though it retains poorly sorted black or red gravel, up to 5 mm in diameter. It also contains, notably at second-floor level, quite large lumps of un-burnt chalk (up to 8 mm in diameter), presumably deriving from incomplete burning of the lime.

The provenance of the constituents of these mortars has not been discovered. A highly shelly mortar similar to that of Phase I occurs, however, throughout Rochester Castle. It is possible that the gravel for the earlier mortar at the White Tower was brought by water from a sand and gravel bank of Recent age in the Thames Estuary.

Decorative Features

Quasi-sculptural features within the chapel are limited to the capitals, abaci and bases of the main arcade (including the western responds); the imposts of the aisle responds; and a chamfered string-course at the foot of the gallery openings. These features are discussed in detail below. The building relies for its aesthetic effect above all on the satisfying equilibrium of its volumes, and this in turn is a consequence of the geometrical relationships employed in its design.[24]

Constructional Anomalies: The Evidence

The chapel as described thus far appears simple in its design and construction. In fact, a closer examination reveals several anomalies indicating that the structural development of the chapel was more complicated than has hitherto been supposed. These findings have important implications for the development of the White Tower as a whole.

The Major Building Break

Many of the constructional anomalies may be linked to what appears to have been a major pause in the constructional work on the entire White Tower. The identification of this building break was one of the most important discoveries to emerge from our study of the chapel. It was in St John's Chapel that the discontinuity of the building sequence first became apparent, rapidly corroborated by observations elsewhere in the building. It is most obviously identified by an abrupt change from the 'shelly' to the 'chalky' mortars described above. By this means the break may be traced around the internal walls of the chapel in places where the medieval mortar is visible through gaps in the post-medieval repointing. Occasional occurrences of shell fragments above the break do not invalidate the general trend.

The break is also apparent from a change in the character of the walling between the responds, a change that is particularly evident on the north side. Below the break, the fabric consists of roughly cut, rectangular blocks, approximately laid to courses. Above, the blocks are more irregular in shape; they are not laid to a true horizontal. Consequently, the yellow sandy mortar employed by Salvin appears more abundant above the break, where it was used in an attempt to transform the irregular wall into a flatter surface.

It is clear that this change in mortar is more significant than a mere seasonal pause or change in the supplier of materials. Once the building break had been identified, various other anomalies could be linked to it, both of construction and execution, notably a pattern of variations in the type of stone used both for the outer walls and for the piers, as well as the diversity of design of the pier capitals. The latter, quasi-sculptural features provide the best available evidence for the date both of the break itself and the resumption of building, but discussion of the dating evidence must be deferred until the constructional anomalies of the chapel have been fully described.

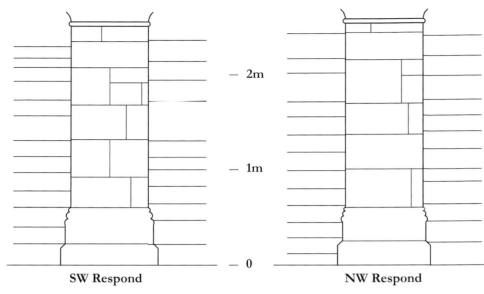

71 (*above*) Diagram showing the heights of the courses of the western responds and of the main west wall of the chapel.

70 (*left*) South side of the south-west respond, and south-west entrance to the chapel.

The Western Responds

The semicircular responds (figs 70, 71) at the west end of the arcade are of the same diameter as the arcade piers. The responds are composed of Caen stone, each course typically comprising two blocks of unequal size rather than complete semi-drums. The height of the masonry courses varies, with a maximum of 460 mm (Table 1). These responds are supported on bases of Taynton stone, broadly similar in design to the other Taynton bases and capitals in the chapel. The respond bases comprise two courses. A chamfered plinth is formed of a single block (unlike most of the free-standing piers, whose plinths are made up of at least two blocks); above the plinth is a monolithic stylobate comprising a rectangular block integral with a semicircular base moulding. The respond bases appear

to retain their Romanesque tooling, whereas the masonry of the respond half-shafts has been retooled. The respond capitals, also of Taynton stone, are the most carefully formed in the chapel.

While the Taynton bases appear to be consistently bonded with the masonry of the western wall, the blocks forming the respond half-shafts do not course with the wall masonry. Figure 71 shows in schematic form the position of the horizontal joints of the responds compared with those of the adjacent masonry of the west wall. The discrepancy suggests that the respond blocks were inserted into pre-existing masonry, and this interpretation is supported by the way that toothings have been cut in some of the ashlar blocks of the wall in order to accommodate the respond blocks. Figure 72 shows an instance of

Table 1. *Course heights (mm) of responds and pier shafts, working upwards from the top of the moulded bases*

Pier	Total	1	2	3	4	5	6	7	8	9	10
NW respond	1945	390	365	330	460	280	120	–	–	–	–
Pier 1	1935	220	215	200	200	180	210	180	180	190	160
Pier 2	1930	190	200	200	185	195	225	200	185	180	170
Pier 3	1915	240	200	185	225	200	215	200	215	235	–
Pier 4	1945	245	200	200	190	220	205	195	185	180	125
Pier 5	1930	245	180	185	215	180	215	200	185	200	125
Pier 6	1925	230	195	220	200	215	235	220	200	210	–
Pier 7	1960	210	200	180	205	185	200	200	205	185	190
Pier 8	1930	250	225	215	185	185	215	225	200	230	–
Pier 9	1920	230	235	175	220	200	200	215	215	230	–
Pier 10	1915	245	235	215	200	230	235	180	180	195	–
Pier 11	1910	240	215	225	210	200	180	220	210	210	–
Pier 12	1925	215	220	240	200	195	200	240	200	215	–
SW respond	1925	330	390	365	390	285	165	–	–	–	–

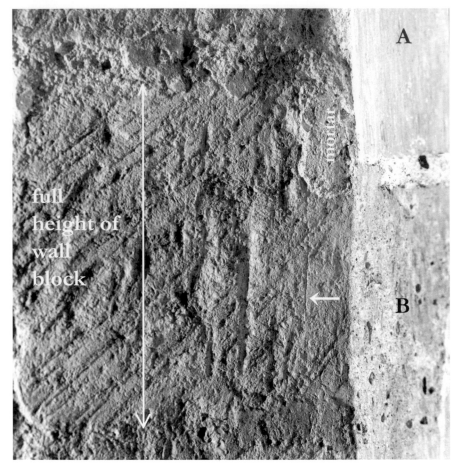

72 (*above left*) Close-up of the junction of the south-west respond and the west wall of the chapel. The top right-hand corner of the main wall block has been cut away along the line of the vertical marking-out line (arrowed) in order to accommodate the upper block (A) of the respond.

73 (*above right*) South aisle, facing east-south-east, showing Respond 11 in foreground. The building break occurs at the top of the ninth course above the pavement. The next three courses are mainly of Bembridge limestone; thereafter, light-coloured Caen stone predominates.

this, where the mason's marking-out line on the wall for the toothing of one of the respond blocks is visible.

It should be noted that the horizontal joints of the wall blocks on either side of the respond do not match up with each other either. One should not therefore envisage that, before the responds were inserted, coursed masonry originally ran continuously between the central recess and the ends of the aisles. The areas between the ashlar dressings of the central recess and the coursed ashlar at the ends of the aisles were probably left empty to a suitable depth, in preparation for the subsequent insertion of each respond.

When the anomalies in jointing of the western responds were first noted, it was supposed that they reflected the major building break, which had just been identified, and that the responds had been inserted after the break. In fact, the responds are almost entirely bedded in the shelly mortar characteristic of the masonry immediately preceding the major break. Thus the insertion of the western respond half-shafts (though not their capitals, which are bedded in the chalky mortar of Phase 2) forms part of the first major phase; the lack of coursing may indicate no more than the fact that the large blocks forming the half-shafts – architectural 'specials', unlike the ordinary wall ashlar – were prepared without regard to the coursing of the wall into which they were to be inserted. A similar lack of coursing is a commonplace in the architecture of the later medieval period, where door and window jambs are inserted in a similar way.

The building break defined by the change in mortar appears to occur immediately below the top two courses of the south-west respond, and below the shallow top course of the north-west respond. The top course of this respond also shows a lithographical change, being formed of Reigate stone. Higher still, the respond capitals were undoubtedly built in during Phase 2 and appear to be properly bonded with the adjacent walls. Above the level of the western respond capitals, the rubble masonry of the main elevations of the chapel, roughly laid to courses, bonds satisfactorily with that of the western wall of the chapel: that is, the stones forming the angles between this main elevation and the end wall are alternately bonded, and are bedded in the same mortar.

The use of Taynton stone for the western respond bases, which undoubtedly precede the major building break, is important. The occurrence of this stone in the bases of the western responds indicates that it had arrived on site before the major building break; furthermore, the way it was subsequently used may suggest that only one consignment of Taynton stone was ever ordered for the works at the Tower. This point has implications for the likely date of other sculptural features, notably the fourteen decorative capitals discussed more fully below.

The Aisle Responds

The building break, reflected in the change in mortar type, is also indicated by a significant pattern of varia-

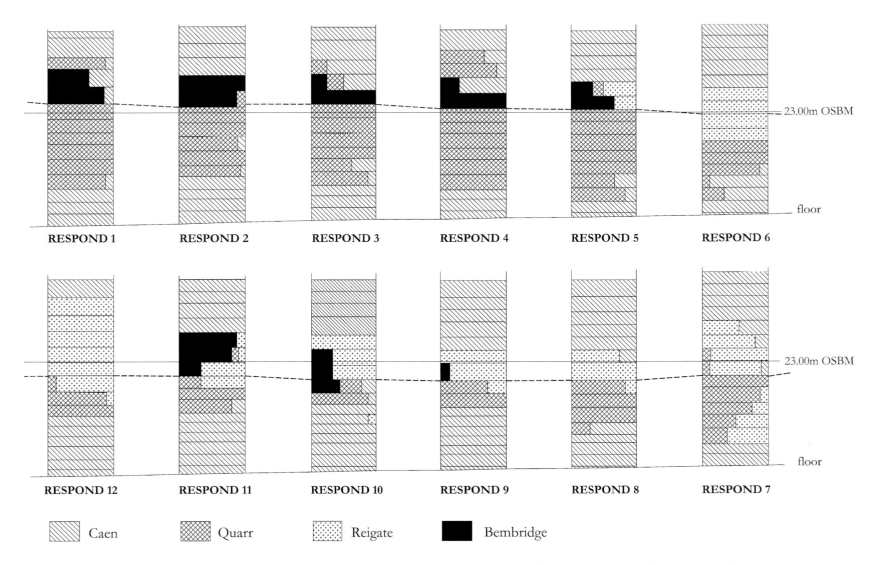

RESPOND 1   RESPOND 2   RESPOND 3   RESPOND 4   RESPOND 5   RESPOND 6

— 23.00m OSBM

— floor

RESPOND 12   RESPOND 11   RESPOND 10   RESPOND 9   RESPOND 8   RESPOND 7

— 23.00m OSBM

— floor

Caen   Quarr   Reigate   Bembridge

74 Schematic representation of the proportion of four different stones within each course of the responds. The pecked line indicates the approximate position of the building break.

tions in the stone types found in the aisle responds (figs 73, 74). The stone types used were described above; this section treats their distribution more thoroughly, and its significance. The lower courses (varying from two to seven courses) all round the chapel are predominantly of Caen stone, often in quite small blocks. Then there is an increase in block size. In itself, this feature is not necessarily diagnostic; such periodic changes in block size are characteristic of the ashlar of the White Tower throughout its height, occurring in bands that may each correspond to a new supply of cut stone.[25] But in this case the change in block dimensions coincides with a change in stone type. The most obvious feature is a distinctive band of Quarr stone, together with Reigate. These stones are of darker colour than the Caen stone below and above. The Quarr stone blocks are often chipped, and defects are made good in the shelly mortar diagnostic of Phase 1. The band of Quarr was, indeed, the last masonry to be laid before the major building break, whose line, defined by the change in mortar, is also indicated in figure 74.

The first masonry after the building break is also characterised by the use of another Isle of Wight stone, namely Bembridge limestone, found only in one to three courses immediately above the junction.[26] Thereafter, pale yellow Caen stone predominates, and

these later blocks of Caen are well cut and notably better laid than any of the masonry lower in the wall, perhaps indicative of improved technical skill when work resumed.

The building break is also reflected in joint thicknesses. The joints of the responds below the major building break are uneven, ranging from 17 to 23 mm, and this thickness seems mainly to result from the need to compensate for quite crude variations in the sizes of blocks used within each course. Above the break, where the masonry is more accurately cut, the joints are more consistent, and narrower, averaging 15 mm. Conversely, as already noted, the walling between the responds is less carefully done above the break.

The Piers

Anomalies also occur in the twelve piers of the arcade. These are built of coursed masonry, with blocks similar in size and proportions to those of most of the aisle responds. Each shaft comprises nine or ten courses (Table 1). Each course is composed of seven to eleven blocks, the average being nine blocks.

Stone Type

Two types of limestone are used for the piers: Caen and Quarr. The proportion of each of these stones

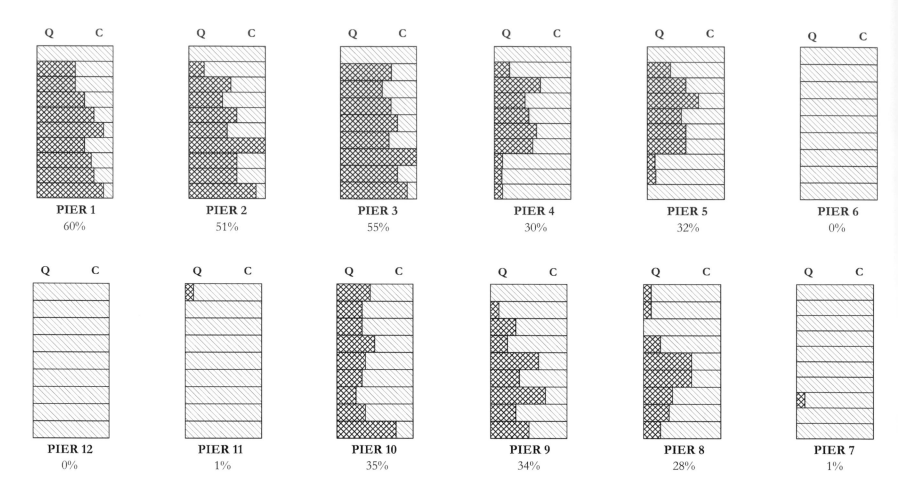

Q	C	Q	C	Q	C	Q	C	Q	C	Q	C
PIER 1 60%		**PIER 2** 51%		**PIER 3** 55%		**PIER 4** 30%		**PIER 5** 32%		**PIER 6** 0%	

Q	C	Q	C	Q	C	Q	C	Q	C	Q	C
PIER 12 0%		**PIER 11** 1%		**PIER 10** 35%		**PIER 9** 34%		**PIER 8** 28%		**PIER 7** 1%	

75 Schematic representation of the proportion, within each course of the piers, of Quarr stone (cross-hatched) and Caen stone (single hatch).

used is illustrated schematically in figure 75. Four piers in particular command attention, being built entirely of Caen stone. These comprise the two piers at the apex of the apse (Piers 6 and 7, which also differ from the other pier shafts in that they are more slender) and the two westernmost piers on the south side (Piers 11 and 12).

Most of the piers contain a mixture of the two stone types, in various proportions. Within some of these 'mixed' piers less obvious variations in the relative amounts of the two stones may be discerned. In the case of Piers 4 and 5, for example, Caen stone predominates for the first three courses, after which the amount of Quarr stone increases. Piers 1–3, on the other hand, show a slight but consistent upward reduction in the amount of Quarr used. No such pattern is discernible in Piers 8 to 10, each of which employs Quarr and Caen in roughly equal proportions without an obvious change higher up the column.

What figure 75 does not show is the distribution of the two stone types within each course of the pier shafts. As far as possible, the builders appear to have attempted to avoid placing two stones of the same type side by side, although in practice there are few examples where the average of nine blocks per course are equally distributed between four blocks of one material and five non-contiguous blocks of the other. The alternation is not, however, sufficiently regular for one to be able to argue that it was done as a

decorative feature, even though such alternation used decoratively is frequently encountered in architecture of this period.[27]

The uppermost course of each pier is composed entirely of Caen stone; it is perhaps a levelling course, echoing the predominant use of Caen in the upper courses of the aisle responds. As argued more fully below, it seems most probable that the 'mixed' piers, employing both Caen and Quarr stone, were erected before the major building break.

Variations in Pier Diameter

As already noted, the piers at the apex of the apse (Piers 6 and 7) are also anomalous in their diameter, being significantly thinner than the others (Table 2). The mean diameter of Piers 6 and 7 is 714 mm, compared with a mean of 758.4 mm for the other ten piers. The values of 717 mm and 711 mm for Piers 6 and 7 fall well outside two standard deviations from the mean of the rest ($\sigma n = 10.06$ mm), and there can be little doubt that their different diameter is intentional. The next pair westwards (Piers 5 and 8) are two of the smallest of the remainder of the piers (with diameters of 754 mm and 745 mm, respectively), but these measurements fall well within two standard deviations of the means of Piers 1–4 and 9–12. Moreover, Pier 4, with a diameter of 742 mm, is even thinner than Pier 8, and Pier 5 is thicker than Piers 4 and 9. Thus it is unlikely that Piers 5 and 8 were deliberately made thinner than the roughly standard piers to the west.[28]

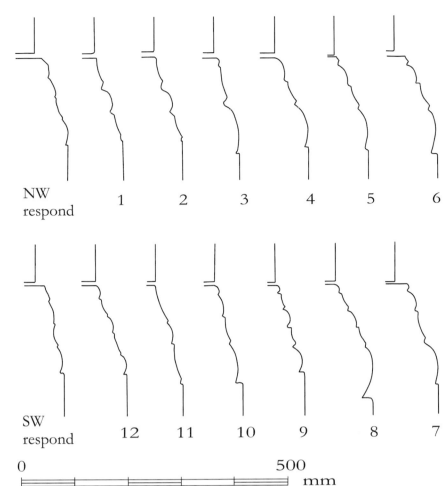

NW
respond   1   2   3   4   5   6

SW
respond   12   11   10   9   8   7

0   500
                                          mm

76 (*above left*) Base of Pier 9, from east-south-east.

77 (*above right*) Moulding profiles of the bases of the piers and western responds.

Base Types (figs 76, 77)

Each pier base may be regarded as comprising two elements: a chamfered plinth, one course deep, invariably made up of two blocks with a joint running parallel to the aisles; and the actual base effecting the transition from the square plinth to the circular column. In the case of Pier 10 the entire base is a monolith above the plinth; the bases of Piers 6 and 8 are formed of two elements: a large square block above the plinth and a separate monolith for the circular portion. Piers 11 and 12 have a different pattern again; in each case the square and circular portions are composed of two blocks, with joints perpendicular to the aisles. The remaining piers have a shallow, single course composed of several blocks above the plinth, above which a monolithic element comprises both the upper part of the square portion and the circular part of the base.

The mouldings of the bases display a variety of profiles (fig. 77), but this is not significant: similar variations are found in other contemporary structures, such as the transepts of Winchester Cathedral and the Romanesque bases excavated from the walls of Westminster Hall in the 1820s. It is illusory to imagine that these base mouldings may be placed in a meaningful typological sequence. Such variation in base types within a single building is a commonplace in Anglo-Norman architecture of the post-Conquest period; notions of consistency in base design would be more rigorously applied in the twelfth century.

Capital Types

The most obvious anomaly of the pier design is the variety of capitals used. The sources and date of these capitals are discussed fully below, but in order to tackle the question of the constructional sequence of the piers, and their relationship to the building break, the broad classification of capital types must be introduced at this point. There are five main types:

- Chamfered block capitals with tau crosses (Piers 1–4, 6, 7, 9, 10)
- One volute capital with tau crosses (Pier 8)

Table 2. *Pier diameters in millimetres* (Roland Harris)

Pier	bottom	middle	top	mean
Pier 1	761	761	767	763
Pier 2	767	764	774	768
Pier 3	770	774	783	776
Pier 4	739	742	745	742
Pier 5	751	754	758	754
Pier 6	719	716	716	717
Pier 7	710	710	713	711
Pier 8	742	745	748	745
Pier 9	754	748	751	751
Pier 10	761	761	767	763
Pier 11	764	764	767	765
Pier 12	758	754	758	757

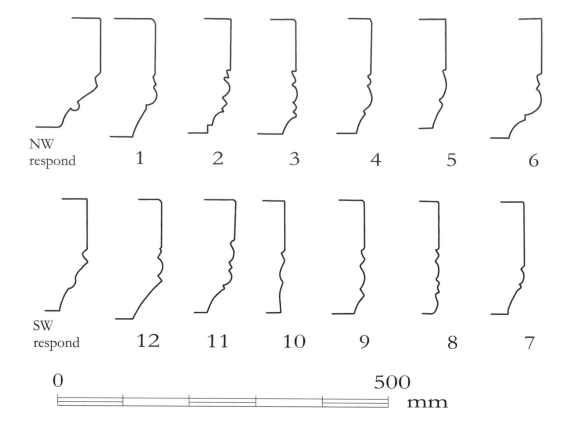

NW respond 1 2 3 4 5 6

SW respond 12 11 10 9 8 7

0   500

mm

- Double cushion capitals (proto-scallops) (Piers 11, 12)
- A single cushion capital with mitred corners, formed of several pieces of stone (Pier 5)
- In addition, the western responds are volute types with tau crosses

The pier abacus mouldings do not display the same diversity of forms as the capitals (fig. 78). A variety of profiles is employed, but all could well have been made in a single campaign. As argued below, the capitals supporting them may date from both of the major phases of the White Tower; the abaci, on the other hand, could well be of a single phase, that is, Phase 2.

Anomalies Above the Building Break

The building break, found throughout the White Tower, as discussed more fully by Roland Harris,[29] corresponds to a reduction in the amount of ashlar used. As already noted, only the lower courses of the aisle and ambulatory walls of St John's Chapel seem to have been started at the time of the building break, the arcade being entirely of Phase 2; thus the chapel as a whole is notable for its minimal use of ashlar. Ashlar is exclusively used in the main piers and the arrises of the main arches (and there, only on the nave side). Above the piers of the straight bays are four to five courses of poorly laid ashlar blocks, after which rubble fills the spandrels above Piers 1–3 and 9–12; the spandrel above Pier 4 is an exception, being totally of ashlar. Ashlar is used up to the gallery floor level in the spandrels above the apse piers. Within the north-west entrance ashlar gives way to rubble four courses above floor level, but this change in material may not be related to the building break since it also occurs in the corresponding entrance passage on the floor below. The window reveals at the main level are of rubble with ashlar quoins. In the gallery ashlar is used even more sparingly, as already described, the main use being for the gallery piers in the straight bays.

This sparing use of ashlar is in striking contrast with other ecclesiastical buildings of the late eleventh century to the early twelfth. The crypt at St Augustine's, Canterbury, and the transepts of Winchester Cathedral, for example, are completely ashlar-faced, rubble being used only for core-work. In this context, the sparing use of ashlar in St John's Chapel appears surprising, the more so given its waterside location favouring the easy transport of stone.

Interpretation of the Evidence

The evidence discussed in the previous pages suggests that the constructional sequence did not run as seamlessly as has hitherto been supposed. Various questions arise: notably, whether the design of the chapel was modified as a result of the building break; whether or not the piers had been constructed at the time of the break; and the date of the building break.

The Design of the Chapel

The chapel could not have been an afterthought, because its apsidal plan is found in the very foundations of the White Tower. The simplest design conforming with this outline plan would have comprised a large un-aisled space with an apsidal east end. The provision of integral responds in the chapel aisles, however, clearly indicates an intention to build groin-vaulted aisles. The three orders of these responds were intended to support the wall-arches, the groins and the transverse arches, respectively. Careful examination of the bonding of the responds and the side walls shows that the junction is as consistent as one might reasonably expect, given that the responds are of coursed masonry but the walls are of roughly coursed rubble; there are no indications that they were inserted in Phase 2. This evidence that groin-vaulted aisles were envisaged at least from the time the tower walls reached chapel floor level means that the arcade was likewise planned by then. Indeed, it is most probable that a decision to include an aisled chapel had been made by the time the foundations of the White Tower were laid out.

Building Sequence: the Piers

The Construction of the Piers and the Building Break

The use of Quarr stone in most of the piers, a material that in the aisles is used for the ashlar work immediately preceding the major building break, is a compelling reason for supposing that the piers were also constructed before the break: as noted above, the use of Quarr stone in the chapel, and indeed throughout the White Tower, falls off markedly after the building break. Furthermore, this conjecture appears also to be supported by other anomalies of the piers and their bases and capitals, discussed below. It is not, however, possible to prove that the piers were constructed before the break on the grounds of mortar type, which is the most reliable feature for distinguishing the phases of the outer walls, because of the large amount of repointing that has taken place. Although the mortar joints of the piers are noticeably thinner than those of the first phase of the outer walls, typically measuring 10–15 mm, such narrow joints are also a feature of the western responds, which are certainly bedded in the shelly mortar of Phase 1; the narrower joints may simply reflect the load-bearing intention of the piers and the greater care taken in cutting the stones for these important constructional elements.

No building interruption is discernible in the piers, which implies that at the time of the major building break they rose nearly to their full intended height. It is unlikely that their capitals were placed in position on top of the piers in Phase 1, however, since levelling courses of Caen stone occur immediately below each capital, and this use of Caen is a feature of the upper parts of the aisle responds of Phase 2.

The Caen Stone Piers

It has been noted that most piers are constructed of Caen and Quarr stone, a mixture that is a feature of the masonry of the chapel immediately prior to the constructional break. This is an important initial reason for supposing that those piers, like the western responds, formed part of Phase 1. Yet four of the piers are constructed totally of Caen stone; and these four piers may be further subdivided into two pairs of anomalous piers, the thinner pair at the head of the apse (Piers 6–7), and the pair with double cushion (proto-scallop) capitals at the west end of the south arcade (Piers 11–12).

PIERS 6 AND 7
The major difference between Piers 6 and 7 and the others is most simply explained as a design consideration, resulting from their special position at the apex of the apse. As already noted, the apse piers are quite close together, and it may have been felt that a less enclosed effect would be obtained by reducing the thickness of the piers themselves. It should be noted that their capitals, both of the chamfered block variety, make no concession to the smaller diameter of the shafts, which means that the astragals oversail the shaft in a somewhat clumsy way. Perhaps even more significantly, the bases are also of dimensions suited to full-width columns, which means that an incongruous shelf is left around the shaft at the top of the base (fig. 77, Bases 6 and 7); the base and shaft diameters of the other piers are carefully matched. Furthermore, the curvature of the individual blocks of Piers 6 and 7 is too shallow, which means that the piers are not truly circular, but composed of curved facets. All this suggests that the smaller diameter of the piers was a modification to the original design, introduced after the bases and capitals, and indeed the ashlar blocks, had been produced. It lends weight to the conjecture that the Caen stone piers were built with slimmer profiles as an afterthought in Phase 2.

PIERS 11 AND 12
Piers 11 and 12 are also built almost entirely of Caen stone, and their double cushion capitals also set them apart from the piers of the other straight bays. As with the piers at the crown of the apse, the uniform use of Caen stone indicates that they were built in a later phase than the columns with a mixture of Caen and Quarr stone, that is, immediately after the building break. This conjecture receives support from the probable date of the double cushion capitals, which are typologically later than the majority of capitals in the chapel.[30]

It would be difficult to invoke reasons of style to explain the features that set Piers 11 and 12 apart from most of the other piers; the notion, for example, that these piers flanked some kind of ceremonial entrance from the south aisle is difficult to sustain. It seems more likely that these piers were not built in Phase 1, a conjecture supported by the different construction of their bases, and the style of their base mouldings. One highly speculative possibility is that the two piers in question were not built in the first instance because deferring their construction would have allowed better access to the chapel during the early stages of the building works. Unlike ground-level churches, major components, in particular the massive monolithic capitals, probably had to be hoisted some 15 m from ground level and over the rising south wall of the White Tower. This would have been an easier means of entry than lifting the material through the inside of the building, and certainly more practical than using the stair turrets at the north end of the tower. There could therefore have been an advantage in delaying the construction of the two piers at the west end of the south side of the chapel. This conjecture receives partial support from the distinctive way in which their bases are constructed of two blocks above the plinth, as already described. Furthermore, damage has occurred to the corners and interfaces of the stones forming the base of Pier 11 in a way that could suggest that these stones had been in a vulnerable location for some time before they were put in place.

CHRONOLOGY

It is to be hoped that the preceding analysis of the structural sequence of the chapel adequately demonstrates its two-phase character, echoing that of the White Tower as a whole. In the question of the date of the two phases, the sculptural work in Taynton stone is crucial. It is possible that all the Taynton stone arrived from the quarry in one consignment at the very end of Phase 1. As we have seen, the western respond bases certainly form part of the Phase 1 work, being set in the mortar characteristic of that phase and being fully integrated with the surrounded masonry. The bases of the free-standing piers are also probably of Phase 1, together with the shafts of eight of the piers. All the capitals and abaci, on the other hand, appear to have been set in place *after* the break, so stockpiling of the Taynton stone may have occurred; it is therefore important to determine whether the capitals were actually carved just before the break, or whether some of them at least were made when work resumed.

Dating Evidence: Sculptural Details and Mouldings

The only features of St John's Chapel that lend themselves to dating on art-historical grounds are the capitals and bases of the western responds and main arcade, and the mouldings of the aisle respond imposts.

The Bases (figs 76, 77)

The various ways in which the pier bases are constructed have already been described. Their mould-

ings are perfectly consistent with the broad, late eleventh-century period of the chapel, but do not possess characteristics permitting a more precise date range. There is no obvious pattern in the distribution of the base profiles, though the moulding profiles of the pair at the apex of the apse do suggest that they were created as a matching pair.

The Capitals

Three major types of capitals are represented: (1) chamfered block capitals; (2) a single volute capital together with western responds of comparable form; and (3) a single cushion capital and a pair of double cushion (proto-scallop) capitals – a derivative form of the cushion capital. This third group represents a completely different sculptural tradition. All the capitals have suffered considerable scraping, but restoration work appears, thankfully, to have stopped short of actual retooling.

The Chamfered Block Capitals

The largest group of capitals (Piers 1–4, 6, 7, 9, 10: figs 79, 80) comprises a simple type with fluted chamfers to the corner and so-called tau crosses on the main faces. Since these represent the earliest class of capital in the chapel, both typologically and, probably, in point of actual date, they should be discussed first.

In these capitals the transition from the circular section of the column to the rectangular plan of the abacus is achieved by cutting away the lower corner of the capital block in a curved, triangular configuration resembling an inverted fan. Such block capitals are a commonplace in pre-Romanesque and Romanesque architecture and are encountered, for example, in the crypt capitals of St Bénigne, Dijon, of *circa* 1000 (fig. 81a). The type is of long standing, and chamfered block capitals on their own are of little value as dating indicators.

At St John's Chapel, however, the capitals have some decorative elements that may permit a more precise dating. The chamfers are enriched with shallow fluting rising to a point, which should probably be regarded as a simplified form of the corner foliage of Corinthian capitals, transmitted via the more immediate lineage of the volute capitals discussed in the following section. Most of the capitals in the chapel have four concave flutes at the angles, but that of Pier 3 (fig. 79c) has six on each of its four corners, as does the north-east corner of the Pier 4 capital. In most cases the fluted chamfers are detached from the body of the capital by a simple quirk; the capitals of Piers 2 and 9 have a double quirk in this position. These differences probably indicate that the various capitals were carved by different hands, but it is unlikely that there is any further significance; the distribution of the various forms within the chapel appears to be completely random, and the variety

79   (A) Capital 1, from south-east.
    (B) Capital 2, from south-west.
    (C) Capital 3, from south-west.
    (D) Capital 4, from south-west.

reflects that lack of concern for uniformity already noted in the base moulding profiles.[31]

The other decorative elements of these capitals are the T-shaped projections formed in high relief on their four main faces; this relief is created by the way the faces are angled back slightly towards the centre in a swept-back configuration. These crosses are found on nine of the free-standing pier capitals. They show some variety of treatment, notably the presence or absence of a chamfered element beneath the arms, and whether or not the foot of the cross is clearly defined by an offset or simply chamfered off (as in the capitals of Piers 6 and 7). These crosses have often been taken as the most significant feature of the St John's Chapel capitals, causing them to be regarded as part of a special 'tau cross' group. A Lombardic origin has been claimed, justified by examples such as those in the rebuilt nave of San Vincenzo in Prato, Milan (probably dating from

80 (A) Capital 6, from south-west. (B) Capital 7, from west-south-west. (C) Capital 9, from north-west. (D) Capital 10, from north-west.

the first half of the eleventh century).[32] The influence of such distant traditions cannot be excluded, but the tau-cross motif at the Tower is first and foremost a variant of the square consoles found on the face of eleventh-century volute capitals, such as those seen (admittedly mostly in the form of nineteenth-century replicas) at St Etienne, Caen (fig. 81b): these consoles may be understood as the ultimate simplification of the rosette or palmette usually featuring in this position in classical Corinthian capitals. A minimalist view of the

London tau-cross motif was expressed by Victor Ruprich-Robert, writing in 1884, who illustrated the south-western respond capital of St John's Chapel and commented: 'The console is even doubled by another, smaller one', without mentioning the tau-cross form.[33] Given the care of the St John's Chapel masons in incorporating the motif not only in the block capitals but also in the single volute capital and the western responds, it seems likely that the masons were fully aware of the symbolic importance of the cross motif.

81 (A) Capital, crypt of St Bénigne, Dijon. (B) Capital, nave of St Etienne, Caen. (C) Capital from the dorter, Westminster Abbey, now *ex situ*. (D) Capital in dorter undercroft, Westminster Abbey.

The tau-cross motif undoubtedly enjoyed a certain popularity in the first phase of Anglo-Norman architecture. Examples of plain chamfered block capitals with tau crosses with very thin arms were formerly visible in the capitals of the window shafts of the dorter range at Westminster Abbey. Unfortunately, they were replaced during restoration work in the early twentieth century. One of them is preserved in the Abbey lapidarium (fig. 81c), and is probably the one removed by Lethaby in 1925.[34]

The construction of the dorter range at Westminster Abbey is undocumented. In 1910 Bilson proposed a date in the mid-1070s for the undercroft, suggesting that it was perhaps the work of Abbot Vitalis (from 1076).[35] A slightly earlier date, before the mid-1070s, seems more likely, based on the form of the undercroft capitals (fig. 81d).[36] Furthermore, construction would not have reached the level of the first-floor windows for two to three years after that; the earlier date casts doubt on Professor Zarnecki's suggestion

113

82 (A) Jumièges, abbey church. Capital on north side of the nave (centre of first double bay to the west of the crossing). (B) Jumièges, abbey church. Double capital on south side of the west arch of the western entry block. (C) Capital 8, from west-north-west. (D) Caen, St Etienne. Volute capital in nave.

that the Westminster capitals derived from those previously used at the White Tower.[37] It is perhaps more probable, however, that the inspiration for the decorative features of both buildings came directly from Normandy at roughly the same time.

Though lacking the tau-cross motif, the best parallels for the Tower block capitals occur in the nave of the abbey church of Jumièges.[38] The cylindrical piers at the centre of the first double bay west of the crossing (fig. 82a) have capitals of this type. The chamfers are plain rather than fluted, thus forming a useful field for polychrome, traces of which adhere. Fluted chamfers are, however, found in a small pair of capitals at the springing of the western arch of the western entry block of the church (fig. 82b). All the Jumièges examples occur in the second phase of construction, that is, the work on the nave initiated by Abbot Robert in 1052. The nave had presumably just been completed when the church was consecrated in 1067.[39]

On their own, the chamfered block capitals do not provide a closely defined date for St John's Chapel. But the best extant parallels are to be found in mainland Normandy or in the first generation of Anglo-Norman architecture, and a date in the later 1070s seems on balance most probable.

The Free-Standing Volute Capital (fig. 82c)

The appearance of a single volute capital amongst the block capitals, on Pier 8, is at first surprising. The basic shape of this capital is recognisably related to that of the chamfered block capitals; but in the volute capitals the chamfers are faceted rather than fluted,

and each chamfer takes the form of a large, flat leaf that terminates in a fat volute rather than merely coming to a point. The design is so contrived as to give the effect of a rolled leaf-end when viewed from one side or the other, though it would in fact be geometrically impossible to roll a single leaf into such a configuration. Above the astragal is a single row of flat leaves (two are missing, probably broken off and later retooled). The main faces of the capital are almost flat, rather than swept back towards the centre of the block, and are decorated with very shallow tau crosses with chamfered feet.

The immediate sources of the type occur at Caen rather than Jumièges, in the various churches erected in that town under the patronage of William, Duke of Normandy and his consort Matilda. A rich diversity of such capitals is found in the churches of La Trinité (started 1059–60),[40] the ruins of the Chapelle Ste-Paix (probably founded by Duke William in 1061),[41] St Etienne (probably after 1066)[42] and St Nicholas (started in the 1080s). Unfortunately, many of the capitals at St Etienne and La Trinité have been subject to radical retooling or even replacement,[43] making close comparative analysis more difficult. Nevertheless, rows of leaves about the astragal somewhat resembling those of St John's Chapel occur in the nave at St Etienne, the main difference being that the flat leaves at the Tower are better defined, being more deeply cut and separated from each other; their squatter appearance echoes the generally squatter format of the Tower capitals. Figure 82d shows an example from the nave at St Etienne; assuming that it is original rather than a re-

placement, the obvious retooling may nevertheless have altered the form of the volutes at the ends of the flat leaves, which are otherwise similar to those found in the Tower capital. An unrestored capital half-buried by the secondary vault of the north transept at St Etienne, with similar volutes to the Tower example, is dated by Baylé to the period 1060–70 on typological grounds.[44] However, the better parallels for the capital as a whole are the later examples in the nave at St Etienne, where the double rows of leaves seen on the transept capital tend to be simplified to a single row above the astragal–the configuration found at the Tower.[45] This simplification might point to a slightly later date for the Tower capital–again perhaps in the later 1070s.

In the churches at Caen, the consoles are occasionally plain (presumably providing a flat field for painting), but more commonly they are moulded or carved into human or animal heads, or into more elaborately sculpted panels at La Trinité. Likewise, some of the volutes at St Etienne and a rather larger number at La Trinité are modified to figurative sculpture.

Volute capitals probably also deriving from Caen are found in a number of Anglo-Norman buildings. Amongst the earliest examples may be those in the church at Bramber (West Sussex), perhaps dating from as early as 1073 (fig. 83a):[46] this is of interest, since there is documentary evidence that the capitals were imported from Caen as rough-outs, even perhaps ready carved.[47] More securely dated are the capitals of the crypt at St Mary's church at Lastingham (North

Yorkshire), started soon after the arrival there in 1078 of Stephen, Abbot of Whitby, to set up a new monastery. The crypt capitals (fig. 83b) must therefore date from around 1080. They are quite squat, with better-developed volutes.

Volute capitals also occur on the exterior of the western tower block at Lincoln Cathedral (the best examples, fig. 83c, are now preserved in the Morning Chapel subsequently constructed around the north-west corner of the tower block), perhaps begun in the late 1070s, and in the eastern tower arch of the nearby church of Harmston (fig. 83d). A respond capital in the south aisle of Canterbury Cathedral crypt as rebuilt under Archbishop Anselm in the 1090s shows a fussier treatment of the theme (fig. 84a),[48] and a similar free-standing capital is found within the main vessel of the same crypt. Other relevant examples include the chapel of Durham Castle (started 1072), a capital in the north nave arcade of Blyth Priory, Nottinghamshire (*circa* 1088–1100),[49] and those of the entrance doorway to Colchester Castle (fig. 84b). The general form survived into the twelfth century and is found, in conjunction with cushion capitals, in the main internal elevations of Norwich Cathedral, but there the tall capitals lack the collar of leaves typical of the Caen and early Anglo-Norman examples.

The Western Respond Capitals (figs 85a, b)

The western respond capitals of St John's Chapel are also of the volute type. The immediate impression is one of greater sophistication than the free-standing

example in the apse. They, too, are decorated with tau crosses on three sides; the motifs on the north and south faces are displaced eastwards so that each cross is entirely visible. There can therefore be no doubt that these capitals are true responds rather than submerged capitals; they could never have been free-standing.

As with the block capitals, the faces of the tau crosses are in the vertical plane, standing out against the body of each capital, the more so because the faces of the capitals are not only swept back, like those of the block capitals, but also curve inwards at the top with a rotundity lacking in the free-standing block capitals of the arcade. The feet of the crosses terminate in a set-back above a chamfer extending down to the astragal, and similar chamfered elements fall away below the arms of the cross, just as they do on some of the block capitals.

At the corners of the western responds are wide, flat leaves, terminating in volutes of the kind already considered. The treatment of the volutes of the two responds is sufficiently different to suggest the work of two sculptors: those of the north-west respond are characterised by flat, deeply incised scrolls; those of the south-west respond are more bulbous and shallower.

The corner leaves are also differently decorated. The mid-ribs of those of the north-western respond comprise a line of thin billets; and the same motif appears in the hollow chamfer of the abacus, suggesting that the two components were designed together. The mid-ribs of the leaves of the south-west respond are decorated with a device that, when viewed square on, resembles a series of nested chevrons, but which when seen from the side may be read as a cable moulding, a device used in the hollow chamfer of the abacus. The south-east corner of this capital shows greater complexity, having a short cross-bar near the base of the leaf, terminating in double scrolls; below this the final chevron in the series is inverted (fig. 85a). Apart

from the cable moulding already mentioned, the vertical faces of the abacus of this capital are decorated in a chip-carved pattern resembling an interpenetrating alternation of saltires and Roman crosses.

The best parallel for the western respond capitals at the tower is the well-known pair in the crypt ambulatory at Canterbury Cathedral (fig. 85c, d).[50] They are clearly not in their original position, but serve as somewhat intrusive supports to the penultimate pair of piers at the east end of the Gothic presbytery of William of Sens at the main level of the cathedral (*circa* 1178). It has not, I think, previously been noted that the reused capitals derive from several originals, of slightly differing design, which have been pieced together in a somewhat rough-and-ready manner. A further, recarved capital from the same series is reused further to the west in the crypt. The pair in the crypt ambulatory are characterised by very large, bulbous volutes, at the end of multiple flat leaves occupying the entire body of each capital, and tau crosses whose outline is emphasised by an additional band. These capitals have in the past occasionally been attributed to Lanfranc, but, as Deborah Kahn and many other observers have pointed out,[51] the fact that they clearly derived from an ambulatory (one of the abaci is curved), together with stylistic features such as the geometrical pattern on one side of the abacus of the north-east capital, indicates that these reused piers came from Archbishop Anselm's 'Glorious Choir' of the 1090s.

The Cushion Capitals

1. THE SINGLE CUSHION CAPITAL (fig. 86a)
The capital of Pier 5, opposite the volute capital (Pier 8), is equally unusual within the context of the capital design of St John's Chapel. It is a cushion capital with mitred corners, a type that became widespread in Anglo-Norman architecture (one is seen in the background of fig. 83b). Its most surprising feature is that it is com-

85 (a) St John's Chapel. South-
west respond capital, from east.
(b) North-west respond capital,
from east. (c) Canterbury
Cathedral. Crypt ambulatory, facing
north, showing pier reused as a
support to the new choir piers.
(d) Canterbury Cathedral. Crypt.
South-east pier in the ambulatory,
from the east, with capital
reassembled from reused
components from Archbishop
Anselm's 'Glorious Choir'.

posed not of a single block, but of several pieces of
stone, in two courses. The lower course consists of a
single, somewhat shallow block of Taynton stone; the
upper course has a large piece of Taynton facing into
the chapel, on the more visible side, while the aisle
side comprises five pieces of stone: two of Quarr and
three of Caen. The cushion form without sculptural
adornment was probably selected for its simplicity.
The mixture of stone also lends support to the notion
that all the Taynton stone had arrived on site before
the building break, and that not enough was available

in order to carve as a monolith the last capital to be
made. A small number of pieces of Taynton stone
amongst the rubble facing of the south wall of the
White Tower are presumably waste fragments from
the creation of the various capitals.

The origins of the cushion capital have been often
discussed and the evidence need not be repeated here.
Suffice it to say that the earliest examples appear to
occur in the Rhineland; those in Lombardy are of generally later date, such as the nave at Sant'Abbondio,
Como, dating from as late as the 1090s. The earliest

known English cushion capitals of the type found at the Tower are the lost capitals from the crypt of St Augustine's, Canterbury, now represented only by a photograph, and those at the west end of Lanfranc's crypt at Canterbury Cathedral (fig. 86b). Both these sets of capitals date from the earliest years of the 1070s and were possibly imported ready carved from Marquise in the Pas-de-Calais, as already noted.[52]

II. THE DOUBLE CUSHION (PROTO-SCALLOP) CAPITALS
(Piers 11, 12; figs 87a, b)

The double cushion capitals, which represent a development of the cushion type, are of greater significance for the date of the building phases of St John's Chapel. Such capitals are unknown in Normandy until well after the Conquest.[53] Maylis Baylé, writing before the building break had been identified, was of the opinion that 'the first known examples [of scallop capitals] in the Anglo-Norman world are the big capitals in St John's Chapel at the Tower of London, *circa* 1080'.[54] This date was presumably based on the traditional interpretation of the passage in the *Textus Roffensis* relating to Gundulf's involvement, which has been taken as unequivocal evidence both that he initiated work on the Tower and also that he did so soon after his appointment to the see of Rochester in 1077. The passage is reassessed by Roland Harris in this volume.[55] Similarly, in a passage relating proto-scallops to the parent cushion type, Baylé again opted for a date of *circa* 1080: 'The appearance of scalloped capitals alongside cushion capitals in St John's Chapel at the Tower of London in around 1080...seems to confirm the formal lineage that considers scalloped capitals as a subdivision of elements of cushion ones.'[56] In the same work she also discussed in detail the possible role of the Tower scallop capitals as a source for those in Normandy at Lessay.[57] More broadly, she considered that the appearance of such forms in Normandy was a result of the experiments at the Tower.

A date of 1080, however, is somewhat earlier than the first more securely dated examples. Amongst the earliest are those of the wall shafts of Abbot Serlo's crypt at Gloucester Cathedral (then St Peter's Abbey, begun in 1089);[58] of the chapter house arcade of Winchester Cathedral (probably shortly before the first consecration of the cathedral in 1093); and a single capital in the crypt of Archbishop Anselm's choir at Canterbury (after 1093) (fig. 87c), together with marking-out on a single cushion capital there in apparent preparation for subdivision into the double type.

Two other early examples of proto-scallops are less securely dated. The broad inner orders of the main nave arcade of Chichester Cathedral are supported on wide double capitals; and similar capitals are found at gallery level. Double cushions are also found in the surviving Romanesque gallery arches of the choir. It is traditionally claimed that this church was started by Bishop Ralph Luffa (1090/91–1123) shortly after his appointment to the see, that is, some fifteen years after the decision to move the see from Selsey had been promulgated at the Council of London (1075). The only evidence that Bishop Ralph started the church is William of Malmesbury's admittedly incidental reference to his having 'made [his] church from new' (*a novo*);[59] according to the *Winchester Annals* Chichester Cathedral was dedicated in 1108, which seems consistent with a start of works in the 1090s.[60] Richard Gem has argued, however, that the construction of the cathedral may have begun soon after the transfer of the see from Selsey after the decision of the Council of London in 1075, an argument that requires a downplaying of William of Malmesbury's reference to the reconstruction of the church.[61] The basis of Gem's argument is the 'primitive' character of the earliest surviving masonry and the implausibility of a delay of fifteen years before work began, but he acknowledges that the design of the present eastern arm 'would be out of context before the later years of the eleventh

A

B

C

D

87 (a) St John's Chapel. Capital 11, from the north-west. (b) Capital 12, from the north-east. (c) Canterbury Cathedral. Double cushion capital in the late eleventh-century extension to the crypt, beneath the 'Glorious Choir'. (d) Winchester Cathedral. Surviving double cushion capital on the north side of the nave (east side of Bay 3 from tower).

century and early years of the twelfth century',[62] and he is compelled to postulate that the eastern arm was either built at a late stage in the works or was a re-build. Certainly, the form of the Chichester nave capitals, with an incipient leaf-like motif between the two scallops, seems closer to the post-1107 examples in those parts of the transepts of Winchester Cathedral that were rebuilt after the collapse of the tower than to the well-dated single cushions of 1079–93 in the unreconstructed portions of the Winchester Cathedral transepts.

Another single example of a proto-scallop is found in the nave of Winchester Cathedral (fig. 87d). It occurs on the western face of the second free-standing pier of the north nave arcade and was preserved because a chantry chapel abutted it at the time of Bishop Wykeham's remodelling of the nave in the 1390s. Although this capital might conceivably pre-date the consecration of 1093, it is perhaps more likely that it formed part of the works of extending the nave westwards after the demolition of Old Minster in 1093–4. Possibly the other nave arcade capitals from this point westwards were also of scalloped type, in contrast to the normal cushion capitals seen in the transepts and surviving in part in the first two nave bays to be constructed.

On balance it seems probable, therefore, that the double cushion capitals of St John's Chapel should be assigned to *circa* 1090 at the earliest.

Capital Design and the Chronology of the Building Break

We have already noted that the Taynton stone bases of the western responds were certainly built into the west wall of the chapel before the building break; those of the free-standing piers were probably also set in place then (with the possible exception of Piers 11 and 12). All these elements, together with the capitals, are of the same Taynton stone. It is improbable that this stone arrived in two separate consignments, before and after the break.[63] To argue that a small amount of Taynton arrived on site at the end of Phase 1, and that a repeat order was sent to the quarry at the start of Phase 2, introduces a complexity not justified by the evidence. Furthermore, the Phase 2 capitals could just as well have been made from Caen stone.

Yet, although they are all of the same stone, the capitals in St John's Chapel appear on the basis of style to fall into two groups. In the first group, the chamfered block capitals in particular are characteristic of the earliest Anglo-Norman architecture, and seem best assigned to the later 1070s. There are adequate parallels at that date for the free-standing volute capital, though the type persisted thereafter. The single cushion capital cannot be precisely dated, though Canterbury parallels date from the early 1070s. The second group possesses more diagnostic features for dating purposes, and comprises the two western responds and the two double cushion capitals; both pairs are of a form best dated to the 1090s. This duality of capital type may now be understood as a consequence of the major building break, which seems to have occurred at precisely the moment in construction when the capitals were being prepared. I suggest that work had begun on the creation of the earlier group of capitals (i.e., the chamfered block capitals and the single free-standing volute capital) *before* the building break, even though they were not set in position but stockpiled. When work resumed, only about two-thirds of the necessary capitals had been made, but the Taynton stone for this project was on site, and the extra Taynton capitals, and all the abaci, could be produced; although the stock of Taynton stone seems barely to have proved sufficient, necessitating the piecing together of a number of pieces of stone for the capital of Pier 5.

The Phase 1 date proposed for the chamfered block capitals receives further support from the fact that when the anomalous piers at the apex of the apse were built or rebuilt, the capitals set on top of them were of the standard dimension rather than specially adapted to the smaller diameter of the anomalous pier shafts. A change in stylistic parentage appears to have occurred during the building break. The earlier group of capitals (chamfered blocks and volute capital) looks back to Jumièges and Caen; the second group turns towards the Canterbury of Archbishop Anselm. This second phase perhaps represents the new assurance of a developing indigenous sculptural style.

Intended Original Layout of the Capitals

The interpretation of the capitals as being of two groups—the earlier being stockpiled rather than set in place before the building break—permits some speculation as to the intended original scheme. There are eight chamfered blocks capitals from Phase 1, enough for all the capitals in the straight bays. Also of Phase 1 is the single volute capital. It seems possible, therefore, that the original scheme was for four volute capitals in the apse hemicycle, but that the building break occurred before more than one of these had been produced. When work resumed, there may have been an initial intention to create a volute capital for Pier 5, as a counterpart to Pier 8, but two of the eight chamfered block capitals were set on the narrower Piers 6 and 7. When capitals were produced for Piers 11 and 12, possibly the last piers to be built, the latest double cushion types were made; the capital for Pier 5 was presumably the last to be made, by which time the supply of large Taynton blocks had run out, and the simplest form of cushion capital with mitred corners was assembled out of such fragments as remained.

The Respond Impost Mouldings (fig. 88)

The detail of the respond impost mouldings also provides a key to the probable date of Phase 2. All these imposts occur well after the building break. Some of them are evident replacements, notably on the north side, where the originals were presumably removed to enable presses to lie flat against the pilaster buttresses during the use of the chapel as a record office.[64]

The original impost mouldings are of two types. Some are of a simple hollow chamfer and quirk; this is an early Romanesque form and of little help for dating purposes. These mouldings might have been prepared before the break, but equally could have been the work of a mason working in the traditional idiom after the break. But a second group shows a more advanced form, employing the ogee curves that would become a commonplace in the following century. Very similar mouldings are found at Canterbury Cathedral in the surviving abaci on the capitals of the blind arcading on the aisle walls of Archbishop Anselm's choir (figs 89, 90), and the similarity again seems to point to mutual influences between Canterbury and the White Tower in Phase 2 of the works.

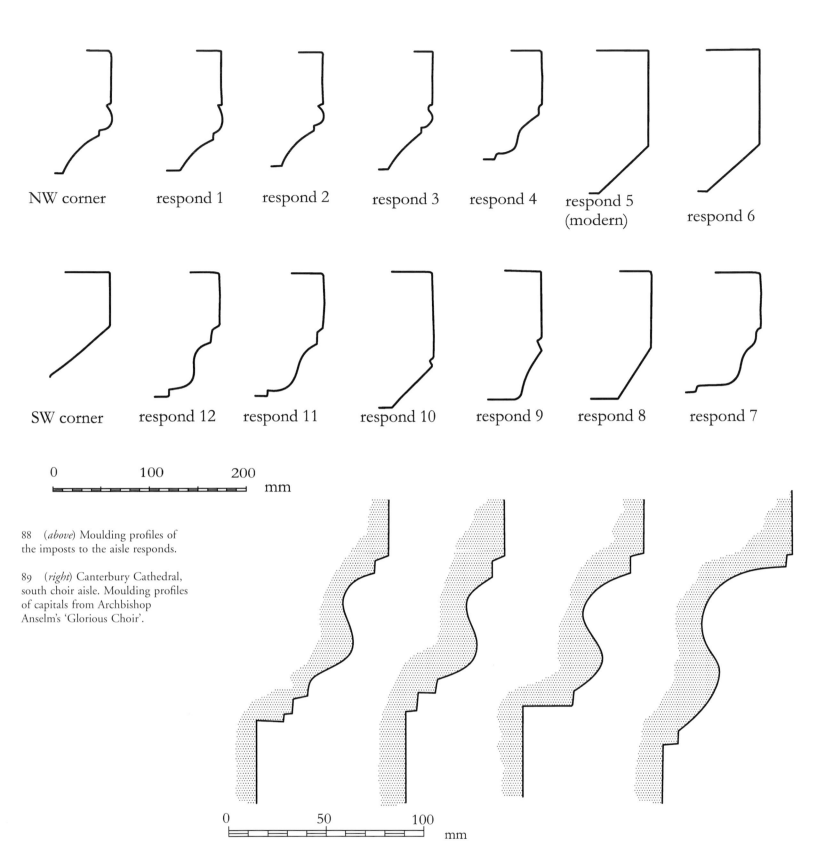

NW corner respond 1 respond 2 respond 3 respond 4 respond 5 (modern) respond 6

SW corner respond 12 respond 11 respond 10 respond 9 respond 8 respond 7

0   100   200 mm

88 (*above*) Moulding profiles of the imposts to the aisle responds.

89 (*right*) Canterbury Cathedral, south choir aisle. Moulding profiles of capitals from Archbishop Anselm's 'Glorious Choir'.

0   50   100 mm

Summary: The Date of the Building Break on Sculptural Evidence

Let us summarise the state of the chapel at the time of the major building break. The outer walls had reached a level between approximately 1.40 m (south wall) and 1.70 m (north wall). The half-shafts of the western responds had been inserted into the wall, and the free-standing piers had reached a similar height,

with the possible exception of Piers 11 and 12. The consignment of Taynton stone had arrived on site sometime previously, enabling the bases of the western responds and the free-standing piers to be set in position; nine capitals had been carved (eight chamfered block capitals and one volute capital).

The capitals providing the best dating evidence for Phase 2 are the two double cushions, not only because of their style but also because of their context. A date

121

90 Canterbury Cathedral. Capital and chip-carving in the south aisle of the 'Glorious Choir'.

much before 1090 seems unlikely on grounds of style. As we have already noted, the piers with these two capitals are also exceptional in their almost exclusive use of Caen stone; it is possible that their piers were not started until after the building break.

The date of *circa* 1090 seems to be supported by the similarities we have noted between the capitals of the western responds (undoubtedly inserted in Phase 2 on mortar evidence) and the 'Glorious Choir' capitals from the Canterbury crypt. True, some of the elements seen in the western responds can be identified at an earlier date: the use of a single row of billets in the hollow chamfer of the abacus is found in the crypt of Worcester Cathedral; the use of chip-cut sunk stars is found in Normandy from the 1070s, though it is equally a feature of Archbishop Anselm's choir at Canterbury (fig. 90). Despite these uncertainties, a date in the early 1090s seems appropriate for the resumption of work after the great building break at the White Tower.

To use the stylistic evidence to determine the date at which work might have been interrupted is rather harder. The earliest capital types in the chapel are the chamfered block capitals and the free-standing volute capital, for which the best parallels appear to date from the mid- to late 1070s. The fact that an insufficient number of capitals from the first phase survive suggests that they were being created at the time the break occurred.

CONCLUSIONS

The Chapel in its Wider Architectural Context

In broad terms at least, the general design of St John's Chapel – in plan and elevation – appears to have been determined from the time construction reached the floor level of the chapel at the very latest, and possibly at a much earlier stage in the history of the White Tower. That the aisles were always intended to be groin-vaulted is shown by the sequence of orders of the outer responds, which are integral with the wall from the floor level upwards. The barrel vaults of the gallery and main vessel did not require this sort of advance preparation, but there is no particular reason to doubt that these vaults formed part of the primary design.

The obvious resemblance of St John's Chapel to the choir of a Romanesque church of apse-and-ambulatory design has already been noted. One way in which the chapel parts company with most eastern arms employing this formula is in the inevitable lack of radial chapels leading off the ambulatory.

If we accept Georges Lanfry's interpretation, based on his excavation,[65] the choir of the abbey church at Jumièges was of this same simple form, and this is of particular interest given the other stylistic similarities we have noted with that church in Phase 1 of St John's Chapel. Obviously, radial chapels would have been impossible at the Tower, and the ambulatory serves simply as a processional path. Churches of this plan are infrequent; a further example is the church of Saint-Saturnin (Puy-de-Dôme).[66]

Richard Gem cites St Augustine's, Canterbury, as another parallel for the plan of St John's Chapel. The choir of the former church is known, of course, only from its surviving crypt, which had compound piers; Gem infers from their spacing that the supports at the main level must have been columnar. At the abbey church of Bury St Edmunds, on the other hand, the crypt had cylindrical columns in the straight bays and wedge-shaped compound piers in the apse; but a uniform system of cylindrical columns at the main level is suggested by the possible survival of a base fragment.[67]

Significance and Usage

It is unlikely that the design of St John's Chapel played any significant role in furthering the evolution of Anglo-Norman church architecture; rather it reflected, on a small scale, trends that were evident elsewhere. The chapel is important above all as a little-altered example of late eleventh-century architecture, with features that have been remodelled out of existence in so many other originally Anglo-Norman ecclesiastical buildings.

The influences determining the quasi-sculptural features (capitals and mouldings) of St John's Chapel appear, however, to have been two-fold, with a change in emphasis at the time of the building break. Phase 1 looks backwards towards Jumièges and employs motifs that were already becoming old-fashioned in Anglo-Norman architecture of the late eleventh century. Phase 2 echoes new developments occurring at Canterbury during the construction of Anselm's 'Glorious Choir'.

There are only a few clues in the fabric and design of the chapel as to how it might have been used. The disturbance to the masonry of the central western niche, to a height of 450 mm, might have resulted from the removal of an original dais. One may therefore postulate that when the king was in residence he would have heard Mass seated in a prominent, axial position, with unimpeded visual communication between the sovereign and the altar, an arrangement that ultimately harks back to Carolingian practice. As Jeremy Ashbee has emphasised, a throne dais was later provided at the Capella dei Normanni in Palermo.[68]

The chapel is notable for the absence of features that might have been used for the performance of the liturgy. The deeper recesses in the aisles, at a point level with the altar, might conceivably have provided space for liturgical furniture. But the uncertainties over the way the chapel functioned do not detract from its undoubted importance as a superb survival of ecclesiastical architecture of the late eleventh century.

Acknowledgements

In addition to those individuals whose specific assistance is acknowledged in the endnotes, I would particularly like to thank the White Tower Wardens and all those who provided access both to the chapel and to other buildings used as *comparanda*. I am especially grateful to Dr Roland Harris for many enjoyable hours of lively discussion.

91   The White Tower from the south-west.

CHAPTER FOUR

The Function of the White Tower under the Normans

JEREMY ASHBEE

When transferred to England the still primitive castle had to be adapted to make provision not only to satisfy the requirements of lordship for the lord in his 'donjon', but also to provide protection and shelter for his Norman staff and garrison, surrounded as they were by an alien and quite likely hostile population. The simplest way to do this was to bring hall, solar and other buildings under one roof within a protective envelope.[1]

One of the most durable and contentious debates about castles concerns their function and *raison d'être*. Scholars have long argued both about how their builders intended them to be used and how they were actually used in practice, although it has perhaps not always been recognised that there may have been a difference. The debate about castles has also been played out in miniature on the subject of castle 'keeps' (also referred to as great towers or, anachronistically, in the modern literature as *donjons*[2]), and has concentrated on two types of use: residential and warfare. Even now, these two are sometimes presented as polar opposites in the minds of designers of castles. For the sake of convenience, defence and residence are treated separately in this chapter, but it is acknowledged that the distinction is to some extent an artificial one.

At least until recent years, writers on castle architecture have traditionally stressed the primacy of military considerations over residential ones.[3] They have cited descriptions in chronicle histories of the violence of the late eleventh and twelfth centuries, and have shown how this situation contributed to the design of great towers, making them enormously solid, with complex internal layouts of partition walls, narrow passages and spiral stairs to impede an attacker. These comments remain largely valid today. It is now generally accepted, however, that this is not the whole story, and several recent scholars have placed a greater emphasis on the *non-military* roles of castles, as centres of administration and lordship. In the field of architecture, castles and their great towers are also increasingly perceived as embodiments of a social ideal and as heavily symbolic.[4] Moreover, outside the field of castle studies, historians and archaeologists have reassessed the form, function and development of other, less-fortified types of domestic complex. The meanings of terms such as 'hall' and 'chamber' have been re-evaluated, and there is wider recognition that the rooms mentioned in documents cannot always be equated with physical spaces in surviving buildings, or those recovered by excavation.

Other chapters in this book describe recent discoveries about the original form of the White Tower, some of them with important implications for its function. This archaeological examination has been accompanied by a new survey of the historical source material for the building and its context within the evolution of the castle as a whole. A new debate about

92 Sculpture from the north doorway of Modena Cathedral, *circa* 1120, showing King Arthur and his knights attacking a moated castle with wooden ramparts and a central stone *donjon* (top).

the uses of the White Tower (fig. 91), both as intended by its builders and in actuality, is now possible and timely.

THE INTENDED FUNCTIONS OF THE WHITE TOWER

The White Tower as Stronghold

In common with other castles and towers, the White Tower and the other buildings of the Tower of London have often been interpreted in the context of strategic military planning (fig. 92). According to this view, castle building should always be understood as a response to threats of violence.[5] While this model is obviously simplistic – ignoring, for example, the way in which the construction of a castle may provoke an escalation of violence – the history of the first years after the Norman Conquest certainly gives ample cause for believing that the Tower was intended for an important military purpose, then as later. Most obviously, as has been discussed in Chapter One, the historical circumstances of its establishment and the topographical situation of the castle show that the Normans had a strong interest in confronting those approaching the city from the east, particularly anyone coming from the sea. When set beside castles at the western end of London – Mountfichet's Tower and Baynard's Castle – the Tower of London can be understood not merely as commanding the approaches from the east, but also as part of a deliberate strategy of control and domination over the city itself and the river crossing at its centre (fig.

93). These objectives, no doubt valid throughout the Middle Ages and even beyond, defined the function of the stronghold (to William of Poitiers, a *munitio* or *firmamentum*) within which the White Tower came to be built, and which William Rufus would shortly surround with a wall.

Since the academic study of castles began in earnest in the nineteenth century, the White Tower has been acknowledged as a building of central and seminal importance. In 1867 G. T. Clark, a great pioneer of castle studies, published one of the earliest detailed analyses of its form. Clark believed that the need for security was the critical factor behind the internal layout of the building, and that the White Tower's designers had allowed military considerations to outweigh those of convenience:

> The arrangements within the keep are very peculiar and show a prevision [*sic*] against surprise, carried, if not to excess, yet to a degree fatal to the convenience of the royal personages and great officers of state, for whose deliberation and occasional residence the building was designed.[6]

Clark's stated objective was to identify a particular 'military' rationale underlying castle architecture, and his interpretation of the detailed internal planning of such a building is now a ripe target for re-evaluation, historical revisionism or even satire. To view the planning of the White Tower in these terms requires the student to forget for a moment that even the Normans might have occasionally imagined the building functioning in peace time, and some of his ideas

93 The line of the eastern wall of the city from the north. The ruined Wardrobe Tower in the near distance is constructed on the footings of a Roman bastion, or possibly part of a city gate. The White Tower stands immediately inside the wall, its apse directly behind the Wardrobe Tower.

verge on the fantastical. To Clark, the natural state of the White Tower involved 'a score of resolute men' holding 'the main door and postern against an army'. The presence of narrow passages at various parts of the building struck him not as the natural consequences of circulation within a building of thick masonry walls, but as a prudent contrivance to limit attackers to single file. If by some disaster the defenders should be overwhelmed on the entrance floor, they could still hold the narrow passage from its eastern room into the north-east stairwell without fear of being outflanked. Should this floor be lost or even the first floor above it, the defenders would easily be able to re-group on the battlements, 'whence the enemy could be assailed to most advantage'. Such a situation would leave to the defenders 'only the last and most terrible recourse of firing the place . . . not even this immensely solid masonry would have resisted the conflagration which a torch, flung upon the wooden floors of the building, would be sure to kindle'.[7]

In his second treatment of the White Tower, published in 1884, Clark amended some of his earlier interpretations of the building, correctly identifying the main entrance to the building in the south wall. Nevertheless, the idea of the White Tower's plan as inherently defensible continued at the heart of his interpretation. It is significant that his comment on

the inconvenience of the planning of the White Tower's rooms remained unaltered.[8]

Revisionism aside, there appear to be several defensive features in the architecture of the White Tower. Most obvious of these is its sheer scale: the height of the building (on the south side, 27.5m from the present ground level to the parapet) and the thickness of its walls (up to 4.5m at the base) would have made it a natural refuge from attack. Second, the original entrance to the White Tower was, as Clark suggested in 1867 and had confirmed by 1884, at an upper level,[9] and so more easily defended than one lower down. At an early stage in its history, probably before 1150, the entrance was covered by a stone forebuilding, projecting from the south façade.[10] It gave access into the large western room of the entrance floor, via a narrow lobby with niches in the two flanking walls, probably seats for guards (fig. 98). A similar niche can be seen immediately inside the main door of Colchester Castle in a position exactly comparable. And as Clark correctly observed, circulation around the interior of the White Tower depended entirely on a single stair, located in the round turret at the north-eastern corner of the building. This stair alone connected all the floors of the tower and provided the only means of leaving the entrance floor. Its location at the opposite corner of the White Tower from the entrance might have proved a hindrance to an attacker, who could theoretically have been contained for a time within the west room on the entrance floor. An alternative, less military reason for channelling visitors through both main rooms on the entrance floor will be suggested below. Within the White Tower, the two halves of the building were separated by the spine wall, a far more solid feature at the time of construction than it is now. Originally, the wall on both ground and first floors was blank on the western side, with arched niches opening into the eastern rooms; these were later broken through to create open arcades, but their original form can be reconstructed from the shuttering of the arch soffits and vertical scars in the reveals of the piers. As the later story of the siege of Rochester Castle shows, the spine wall could present a strong line of defence, behind which the defenders of a castle could retreat if the great tower was invaded.[11] In the White Tower, however, any such capacity for defence was compromised by providing doors through the wall at both the north and south ends. Only the doors on the entrance floor were fitted with drawbars: no evidence for this has been found on the first floor.

As has been described in Chapter Two, the most recent archaeological examinations of the White Tower have shown that the passage running around the thickness of the wall at second-floor level was formerly an external rather than an internal feature. The first-floor rooms did not rise through two storeys to a roof at high level: the rafters of the roof were seated slightly below the level of the floor of the mural passage. The roof was therefore in a 'sunken' position behind high external screen walls, and instead of looking down into the body of the building, the inward-facing arches of the mural passage gave a view only onto the outer sides of the roof pitches. The breadth of these open arches must have made the eastern and western passages inhospitable places to be in bad weather. They would also have allowed anyone at the foot of the White Tower to see the sky through the windows, destroying the illusion that the White Tower contained three storeys above the basement rather than two. Even if the screen wall was designed primarily to present a regular skyline level with the chapel parapet (since this must have been at the highest level from the outset), the builders were almost certainly aware that to a distant observer the White Tower became an even more formidable and massive object. Practical military purposes may also have favoured this arrangement: a sunken roof would have been shielded from projectiles by the screen walls. There are numerous other examples of Anglo-Norman or Angevin military buildings containing screen walls giving the false impression of top storeys, but in fact concealing roofs: these include great towers, such as Hedingham Castle (Essex) of *circa* 1140, and the gatehouse of Sherborne Castle (Dorset), of before 1135.[12]

Above the gallery level lay the parapet of the screen walls with a walkway accessible from the turrets. The spine wall also stood above the roofs to this height, similarly pierced by an arcade to lighten the load: this may also have supported a walkway connecting the north and south parapets, in order to improve circulation around the parapet for watchmen.

As Philip Dixon has recently shown, the idea that castle 'keeps' were designed and built to serve as a 'last refuge' is one of several potent mythologies that surround the type, fuelled by the well-known story of the capture of Rochester Castle in 1216, one of the few sieges that was pressed home floor by floor, leading to the deaths of the defenders. In fact, the surrender of castles in their entirety was a more common outcome.[13] The medieval history of the White Tower shows only a few hints that this was ever considered, though it is interesting that such hints exist at all. Fitz Stephen's description of the Tower, however, explicitly states that the castle was seen as 'very strong' (*fortissimam*): it would therefore be wrong simply to dismiss military notions as modern anachronisms. Though Clark's reading of the White Tower's internal layout as a complex trap for attackers now seems overblown, the socio-political circumstances under which the Tower was built must have made an assault on the royal castle seem a real possibility. In this context, the external capacity of the building to impress and overawe, and by so doing to deter any potential belligerents from hostile action, can itself be considered as a military strategy.

The White Tower as a Palace

Running parallel to the military interpretation of the White Tower is a residential one (fig. 94). This model is based on the notion that the White Tower and other stone great towers of the Anglo-Norman tradition were built to serve as palaces. They were strongly fortified in keeping with the violence of their age, but definitely residential in intention.[14] Though their symbolic power as landscape features was also an important factor in their planning and construction, as will be discussed in the final section of this chapter, the owners of the towers, be they the king, a senior prelate or a member of the Norman aristocracy, expected to live inside them.

In order to assess these claims, it is necessary to take an overview of the different types of high-status house in the period, with some consideration of the place of great towers within these general models. The earlier development of palatial architecture on the Continent is touched on elsewhere in this book, and for the insular traditions a brief summary will suffice. In Anglo-Saxon England, most houses of the highest status were planned as sprawling complexes, each containing numerous detached buildings. This type of house site probably evolved soon after the major Ger-

manic migrations from the Continent in the fifth and sixth centuries AD, but the main types of building within them may represent a hybrid of Continental traditions with a pre-existing Romano-British style of building.[15] In essential form, houses in Anglo-Saxon aristocratic and royal residences up to the eve of the Conquest, including royal palaces such as Cheddar (Somerset) and Northampton, were little different from those of the previous centuries. Many of the principal buildings were single-storeyed and open to the roof, although both documentary and archaeological evidence show that the Anglo-Saxons sometimes built houses with more than one level.[16] Although masonry buildings occurred on both secular and ecclesiastical sites, often using recycled Roman building materials, timber construction predominated overwhelmingly. It has even been claimed that little in the way of a stone-quarrying industry existed in Anglo-Saxon England before the Norman Conquest.[17]

Of the main buildings within such complexes, considerable attention has been given in recent years to 'halls' and 'chambers', separate buildings accommodating respectively public/ceremonial and private/domestic residential functions. These two types of building are more distinctive in the literary and documentary record (as Old English *heall* and *bur*, Latin *aula* and *camera*) than in the archaeological, though discussions of both classes of evidence have recently been published by John Blair and Edward Impey. Both writers have argued that the possession of distinct halls and chamber-blocks, usually of more than one storey, was the hallmark of an architectural tradition current in England from the Anglo-Saxon period to the mid-thirteenth century, and which Impey has shown to have been current in parts of continental Europe for a century or so after the 1120s. Although horizontally planned housing complexes were undoubtedly present on the Continent in the eleventh century, it is possible that the appearance of the 'hall

HIC HAROLD MARE NAV

and chamber-block' arrangement in Normandy was the result of its exportation from England.[18]

Despite the abundant presence of multi-storeyed buildings and towers (notably church towers) in Anglo-Saxon England (fig. 95), the large stone *donjon* as a type seems to have been an import from the Continent, and only after 1066. As discussed in Chapter Nine, residential towers were well known in the Île-de-France, Maine, Anjou and Normandy long before the conquest of England. It is clear, however, that the Anglo-Saxon tradition of horizontally planned houses not only survived in England after 1066, but flourished. The rural palace at Cheddar continued to be developed under the Normans and Angevins, as did the urban royal sites of Kingsholm (Gloucester) and Westminster; all of these conformed to the 'hall-and-detached-chamber' model.[19] Whatever the intended use of the White Tower and similar towers, they had to function alongside a still-vigorous and constantly evolving tradition of residential complexes containing open halls at ground level and other buildings of one or two storeys. Sites such as Westminster in the later eleventh century, and in the mid-twelfth Wolvesey (Hampshire) and perhaps the castles at Old Sarum (Wiltshire) and Sherborne – both containing towers, but both planned with low ranges around courtyards – and later Clarendon (Wiltshire) and Windsor (Berkshire), all show a striking endorsement of this mode of living by the Norman and Angevin monarchy, episcopate and aristocracy in the century following the Conquest.[20] If the White Tower and other great towers were palaces, they were unusual ones in the Anglo-Norman architectural context. Their verticality is best understood as some kind of specialised adaptation.

According to most of the previous interpretations, all three essential components of a palace or great house – the 'hall', 'chamber' and 'chapel'[21] – were provided inside the White Tower, in multiple copies and on a gigantic scale. The supposed presence of all of them should confirm that the building was designed as a complete palace compressed under one roof. The 'halls' have been identified as the large rooms in the western half, the 'chambers' as the slightly smaller rectangular rooms lying to the east of the spine wall, and the 'chapels' as the apsidal spaces in the south-eastern corner, facing east in the correct liturgical manner.[22] In several interpretations of the White Tower, a hall, a chamber and a chapel are represented not just once, but on each of the two main floors above the basement, so that the two levels duplicate each other. From this it follows logically that these floors may represent two separate apartments stacked one above the other.[23] In fact, even if one accepts these contentions, several difficulties remain: the White Tower seems not to have provided separate accommodation for children or servants, or, more crucially, a space for the cooking and preparation of food. It is doubtful that the building could have functioned completely in isolation, but it could have formed the main residence, serviced by a number of ancillary structures.

Interpretation is helped by the fact that the fabric of the White Tower is remarkably complete and evidence for its original layout abundant. Several potentially important pieces of evidence for its function, however, are now missing. No fixed furnishings survive, beyond traces indicating the former presence of doors. With the exception of the moulded capitals, bases, abaci and imposts of St John's Chapel and a simple string-course above the western room of the

96 Interior of the 'chapel crypt' facing east. The vault is modern, replacing a nineteenth-century neo-Norman scheme with false ribs and blind arcading. There does not seem to have been any communication between this room and St John's Chapel immediately above.

first floor, the interior is now completely devoid of decoration (particularly an almost-complete absence of painting, even in the chapel): there is no possibility of inferring a hierarchy of rooms from the richness of the interiors, or much potential for art-historical stylistic analysis. Another caveat concerns circulation around the building; this may originally have been very different from the present arrangement, with timber or textile partitions dividing some of the vast rooms into smaller spaces.[24] If these ever existed, they have now left no trace, but, as will be seen below, inferring their former presence would provide a solution of sorts to several difficulties of interpretation, such as the presence on both the ground and first floors of two doors through the spine wall connecting the east and west rooms, where concerns for security might make single doors preferable.

The chapel of St John the Evangelist is the only room in the White Tower that can be identified with complete confidence.[25] In contrast, for example, the apsidal room directly underneath it is extremely hard to interpret: it is considerably smaller than St John's Chapel and less well lit; its relationship to the other rooms on the floor is different (it communicates only with the eastern room); and, unlike St John's, it possesses a small mural chamber on its northern side (fig. 96). The absence of garderobes and fireplaces makes a residential use unlikely, though sixteenth-century graffiti show that this room has at times been used for imprisonment. It has sometimes been suggested that it originally served as a 'lower chapel' for a distinct and inferior sector of the household.[26] If this interpretation is correct, the small side chamber may

have functioned as a sacristy. Certainly, upper and lower chapels do exist in other castles, such as Dover, and may be particularly characteristic of the houses of bishops,[27] but it must be admitted that no unequivocally 'ecclesiastical' features survive in the room at the White Tower, and nor is there any means of communication between the 'chapels' on these two levels. Service as a strongroom or treasury is among the other possibilities for the apsidal room.[28]

The original uses of the basement rooms can be inferred with a fair degree of confidence. Historic plans and surviving fabric show that none of them possessed anything more than rudimentary windows.[29] The western room contained the White Tower's well. No fireplaces or garderobes have been found anywhere in the basement, and although the construction of the brick vaults and piers in the 1730s may have concealed any of these had they existed, there is no evidence for them in any of the earlier plans and cross-section drawings. On present evidence, it is overwhelmingly likely that the main basement rooms were intended for storage.[30]

A problem with this interpretation, however, is posed by the doors between the western and eastern rooms, since they could be barred from the east side. While it is conceivable that the apsidal basement room may have been intended as a prison, to be sealed from outside, this is highly unlikely in the case of the western room in view of its size and the presence of the well. An alternative explanation might be that the western room had an independent external entrance: although this would fly in the face of long-held assumptions about the inaccessibility of great tower basements, such doorways are known elsewhere,[31] and fourteenth-century accounts do suggest that there was at least one and possibly two, linking the basement to an external kitchen and the constable's hall, standing adjacent;[32] certainly, this would have made it easier to use the space for storage, although access through a hatch in the floor above is an obvious alternative. Alternatively, barred access from the western basement may have been a defensive feature, because forced entry by an aggressor would have been easy enough once the western half of the building had been occupied. There is, therefore, no reason to assume that this room was intended for anything other than storage.

A modern visitor to the entrance and first floors is left in little doubt that the Normans expected that the White Tower would be used on a regular basis and probably inhabited. This is indicated by the ample provision of fireplaces and garderobes to the rooms on both the entrance and first floors. The two largest rooms on each floor contained a fireplace apiece, set in an outer wall with a short flue running through the thickness of a buttress to paired outlets. There were two garderobes in the western room of the entrance floor but none in the eastern: on the first floor, there were four garderobes, two in each half of the White Tower. With one exception, all the garderobes discharged through the north wall.

In most recent interpretations of the White Tower, the first floor is held to have contained the apartments of the king himself.[33] Undeniably, it has numerous features suggesting a high-status function, especially the chapel of St John, but also windows of two lights rather than one, a more generous provision of garderobes and, by virtue of being reached only via the north-eastern vice, a location in 'less accessible space' within the building. Externally also, this floor was given architectural emphasis by setting its paired windows in recessed panels under distinctive round super-arches: it has been plausibly suggested that the form of these may derive directly or indirectly from imperial Roman structures on the Continent, such as the Constantinian basilica at Trier.[34] However, the previously accepted reconstruction of the rooms on this floor as open through two storeys has now been shown to be false: though they were indeed open to the roof, this was set at a low level, and its tie-beams, if it had any, were close to the level of the present upper floor, so that the rooms may have appeared little higher than those on the entrance floor. This notwithstanding, it has become conventional to see a hierarchy between the entrance and the first floor of the building; since it lies beneath the 'royal apartments', the entrance floor has been assigned by historians variously to the keeper of the Tower, the garrison or some other figure or body of less than royal rank.[35]

Such an interpretation intersects with a vigorous debate among architectural historians over the function of the different floors within multi-storeyed buildings, a debate that has perhaps become unnecessarily polarised between 'believers' and 'sceptics' in the existence or prevalence of 'first-floor halls'.[36] Much of this debate in England is a reaction to an influential paper of 1958 by Patrick Faulkner. He proposed that where the layouts of two floors duplicated each other in a medieval house, the upper floor was to be understood as the exclusive province of the 'family', the lower as a subordinate apartment for the use of the 'household'.[37] Certainly, there is explicit evidence from the Continent that the use of different floors could sometimes be arranged for social segregation of this kind: an example of this is the twelfth-century upper hall (*Salle Synodale*) of the Bishop's Palace at Angers, which contains an inscription: 'the priest and knight may come in, but the lower orders must go elsewhere, for this fine room is suitable for the former and the humble downstairs room for the latter'.[38] It would be wrong, however, to assume that this was a standard arrangement: an early twelfth-century description of a tower at Ardres in Flanders shows the opposite arrangement, with the junior members of a household living on the highest floor (beside the chapel) and the more important people below them.[39] In the keep at Dover Castle, the forebuilding gave access directly into the highest floor, and the more private apartments could be reached only by descending a spiral staircase to the floor below. Other examples, such as Norwich and Castle Rising in Norfolk, may have been arranged with segregation running horizontally across their first floors rather than vertically up and down the buildings. There is such variety in the configuration of great towers that it would be rash to generalise about the use of the spaces inside them.[40]

In the present interpretation of the White Tower, it is proposed that social segregation was not the principal factor differentiating the uses of the entrance and first floors. In the new model, it is believed that the rooms on the two floors were intended for distinct but complementary functions, serving not two different groups but one single household. That is to say, the building may have contained not two separate suites of 'hall, chamber and chapel', but a single, six-roomed apartment (above storage rooms in the basement) that conformed to a more elaborate pattern and which was spread across both of the two main floors of the building. This interpretation has been adopted as a result of an examination of the morphology of the building, and some discussion of significant architectural features is now necessary.

The entrance floor, into which the visitor gained access from outside (eventually via the forebuilding), has several shortcomings as a self-contained residential apartment (fig. 97). In particular, the White Tower's sole entrance and the only stair to the other floors lay at opposite corners of the building, requiring visitors to cross both of the main rooms in order to move up or down, surely a major inconvenience to anyone living on this floor. Moreover, the eastern room, even if the route from the western room to the stair was screened off by a partition, does not commend itself as a 'chamber' since it has no garderobes. It also contains one interesting architectural feature that suggests a less private function – the deep recess under a broad arch in its south wall, containing a doorway into the room under the chapel. The presence of the arched recess, the absence of garderobes and the location on the only route of circulation around the building all accord with some kind of ceremonial function for the eastern room of the entrance floor. An attractive possibility is that the room was intended for the formal reception of visitors, with the arch perhaps framing something akin to a dais. Immediately adjacent to the arched recess is one of the two doorways through the spine wall. This door may have been intended only for the use of the king or figures of the highest rank, in contrast to the other door at the far end of the room, for those of lower status. No

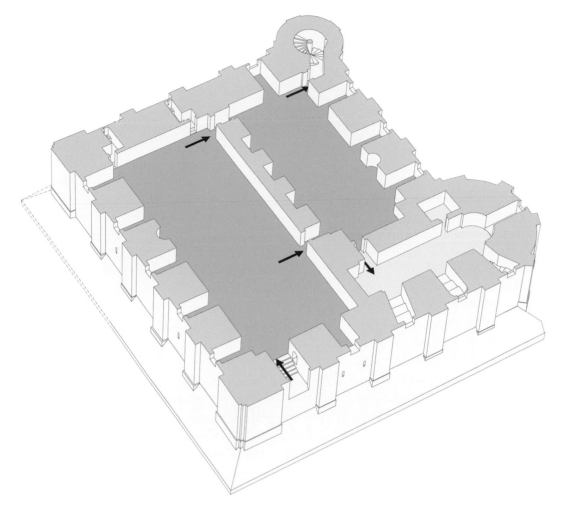

98 One of the two arched recesses flanking the main entrance door at the south-west corner of the building. The White Tower also contains several larger niches, interpreted as architectural settings for seats or tables.

documents of the period explicitly mention a 'Presence Chamber', but the room would have been well suited to a ceremonial role of this kind. Comparable arched recesses can be seen at Castle Rising (*circa* 1138), one now blocked, and others have been inferred at Norwich (possibly as early as the 1090s), perhaps performing a similar function. That at Castle Rising contains sinkings in the voussoirs and beam slots in the surrounding walling, possibly for a curtain or even for some form of canopy (fig. 99).[41]

The White Tower contains several other possible 'throne niches'. Another arched recess, though considerably shallower, occupies much of the west wall of the central vessel in the chapel of St John. The capitals of the responds to either side of it are among the most ornate in the building, with angle volutes obviously derived from Roman Corinthian prototypes, and it may not be fanciful to imagine that a throne could have been set here for the king, facing the altar: as has been pointed out in Chapter Three, the west wall of this recess also shows signs of disruption at floor level, consistent with a dais having stood here and later been cut away. The *locus classicus* for a throne facing the altar is, of course, the palace chapel of Charlemagne at Aachen, now the cathedral, in which the throne is set at tribune level. There are, however, closer parallels, in which the throne stood at ground level. For example, a western arch very similar to that

at St John's Chapel can be seen in the west wall of the forebuilding chapel at Portchester Castle.[42] The most appealing comparative example is the dais against the west wall of Roger II's chapel in the Palazzo dei Normanni at Palermo in Sicily; the dais is an original

feature of the mid-twelfth century, though it has recently been argued that its antecedents are Islamic rather than Western in origin.[43] Occasionally, chronicle histories mention a similar arrangement: in the late twelfth century, Richard the Lionheart's chapel at Château Gaillard (Eure) contained 'a royal throne beside the door', in which King Richard was physically assaulted by Bishop Hugh of Lincoln for failing to show him sufficient respect.[44] The White Tower's eastern chambers on both entrance and first floors also contain lines of three niches in the spine wall; though this interpretation is highly conjectural, these may likewise have been designed to accommodate the seats of other senior members of the court.[45]

The western entrance-floor room, as the first space to be entered by the visitor, would therefore be an ideal place for guards and visitors to congregate and wait to be admitted into the more exclusive space of the eastern room, in which they might expect to meet the king. From here, if they were deemed acceptable, they could be allowed into the other storeys of the White Tower. This is close to the interpretation provided for Continental *donjons* by Jean Mesqui, in which the entrance levels contained a series of public reception rooms, contrasted with the more private domestic accommodation and the household chapels at the higher levels of the buildings.[46]

The rooms on the first floor could be reached only by the spiral staircase in the north-eastern turret. From here a door now opens directly into the eastern

room on the upper floor, but this may not have been the original arrangement. It is possible that a screen formerly existed across the northern end of this room, creating a narrow passage along which visitors were channelled westwards, past a garderobe in the north wall, to a door leading through the spine wall into the western room. Such a screen would help to explain the unique location of a second garderobe within the body of the eastern room, accessible by a door in the northern reveal of the first window embrasure: this is the only garderobe not set in the north wall of the White Tower. Moreover, the spine-wall doorway from the 'passage' into the western room contained its door at the eastern end, to face an approach from this direction, where all other doors in the wall faced west. Most pertinently, the other spine-wall doorway at this level faced west, regulating entry from the western room back into the eastern half. These features, taken in conjunction, suggest that there was a route of circulation from the spiral stair across into the west room and, only from there, back though the spine wall into the eastern room by the other door. Worshippers wishing to enter the chapel were also able to do so directly from the western room by means of a narrow passage at its southern end, leading into the south aisle: there was no requirement to pass through the eastern room. If the hypothesis about a screen is correct, it seems that the layout of this floor was contrived to isolate the eastern room as much as possible; in comparison, the larger western room was very accessible (fig. 100). It is on this floor, if anywhere in the building, that there may be said to have existed a western 'hall' and an eastern 'chamber'.

This interpretation, however, does not explain several peculiarities of the first floor. These include the puzzling evidence for a drawbar socket in the doorway leading from the north aisle of the chapel into the east room; this is the only drawbar identified on this floor. Clearly, it was felt desirable to seal the chapel against entry from the eastern room, although why this should have been a requirement, or how it could have prevented anyone from simply walking round and entering the chapel by its other door, remain a mystery. This may possibly have been related to the liturgy of the royal chapel, a subject on which very little is known. But liturgical texts such as the *Laudes regiae* show that the ritual of Norman court worship could be very elaborate,[47] and it is attractive, if fanciful, to imagine that the entry of the king into the chapel could be dramatised, with some form of spoken or sung exchange accompanying the opening of the door from the royal chamber, like a bishop gaining admittance to his cathedral church at his enthronement.

Another strange feature on this level is the presence of eight small square niches, with wooden lintels, in the reveals of the window embrasures (fig. 101). The

100 Cut-away reconstruction of the first floor as originally configured, showing the effect on access arrangements of introducing a timber screen across the north end of the eastern room, directing visitors first into the western 'hall' and from there back into the eastern 'chamber' or to the chapel.

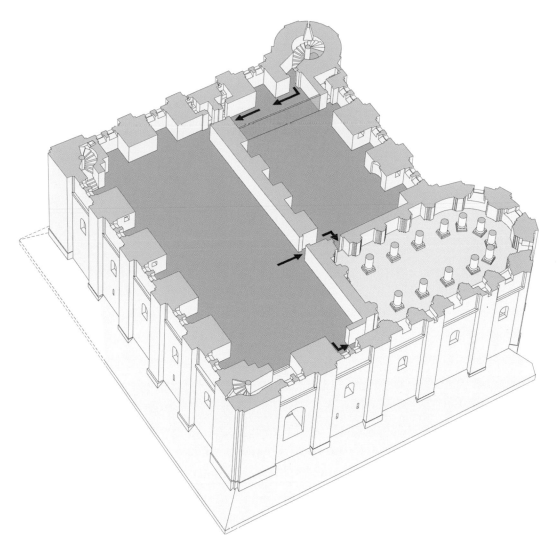

101 Wall cupboard in a window embrasure on the first floor. These cupboards exist in both east and west rooms, but only in the embrasures immediately flanking the fireplaces. Their function is uncertain, but is likely to be connected either with maintaining the fire or with keeping some commodity warm and dry.

complete absence of smoke blackening to the lintels rules out their use for lamps,[48] although the fact that they are found only in the embrasures flanking the fireplaces may suggest that they were intended to hold kindling or salt. But such details serve only to remind us of how little we can say for certain about the function of individual rooms and buildings in this period.

Since the rooms of the first floor lay directly beneath the roof trusses of the building, they may have been free of posts; the rooms on the entrance floor presumably contained posts supporting the upper level.[49] As on the entrance floor, the eastern room contained a fireplace in the east wall and three tall arched niches in the spine wall, though no recess in the south wall. Unlike the eastern room of the floor below, it also contained its own garderobe, in addition to another at the north end, which may have lain beyond a screen, as discussed above. The larger western room contained a fireplace and access to two garderobes, one partially concealed in the thickness of the northern passage through the spine wall and the other a few steps up inside the north-west turret. The latter was perhaps intended for the use of guards in the mural passages and on the parapets above.

It has been argued above that the rooms on this floor may have accommodated functions of a more

domestic character than the more 'public' rooms beneath them. Beyond such generalities, it is difficult to interpret the functions of the two rooms. To the modern visitor, it must be admitted that their enormous volumes make them unappealing as domestic spaces, although we have no means of knowing whether the Normans would have shared these misgivings: cer-

tainly, anecdotes about the construction of Westminster Hall suggest that William Rufus liked his rooms to be immense. Though their elevated position and restricted access may have made them more suited to 'private residence' than those on the floor below, a 'public' function, perhaps for banqueting or receptions, seems equally likely. For all this, as will be discussed below, high-ranking prisoners were probably lodged in the White Tower very early in its history – a residential function of a kind.

ACTUAL USES OF THE ANGLO–NORMAN *DONJON*

Much of the above assumes that the model of the *donjon* as a residential palace compressed into a single building is correct. It is possible, however, to take a reductionist line and argue that any such consideration of a building's intended function is irrelevant if there is no evidence that the building was ever actually used in this way. In fact, there is surprisingly little evidence, either from England or the Continent, that *donjons* were inhabited by the people for whom they were built. One of these rare examples is a late eleventh-century account of the wooden tower at Le Cour Marigny (Loiret), which states that the building contained 'an upper floor in which Seguinus and his household lived, conversed, dined and slept at night'.[50] Another, roughly contemporary, reference, this time from a collection of miracle stories, describes the tower at Castelpers (Aveyron) with three storeys: a dark basement room, sometimes used as a prison; a central floor with a series of reception rooms (*exedrae*); and, at the top of the building, further rooms, one serving as the lord's chamber (*herilis camera*), in which he and his intimates slept, and another in which, on this occasion, a prisoner was detained.[51] The third text, a remarkably detailed and well-known description of a timber house at Ardres (Pas de Calais), coming from around 1120, likewise gives the impression of a building configured in much the same way as the White Tower:

> [The carpenter] crowned the whole house with a chapel in a fitting place at the top on its eastern side. He built three floors in the house and set the roof so high above the floor that it seemed to hang in the air. The lowest floor was at ground level and contained the cellars and granary and also great chests with barrels and casks and all the other domestic things. On the next floor were apartments and a common meeting-room for the inhabitants; here were store-rooms, the pantry, the buttery and a large chamber in which the lord and his wife slept, with a closet adjoining it, which served as the chamber and bedroom of the handmaids and children. In a more secluded part of the great chamber, a private room led off, where they used to make a fire in the evening, or when there was illness or for

blood-letting; this was where the maidservants or the weaned children used to go for warmth. This floor also led to the lord's kitchen, itself containing two floors . . . On the upper floor of the house were made several chambers, in one of which the sons of the master of the house slept when they wished, and in another, the daughters as they had to: here also the watchmen and the servants set to keep watch over the house slept whenever they could.

> Stairways and passages led from one floor to another, from the house into the kitchen, from chamber to chamber and from the house into the *logium*, which derived its name by good and consequent reasoning from *logos* meaning 'speech', since it was the place where they were accustomed to relax and talk: from the *logium* they could go into the oratory or chapel, made like the Temple of Solomon in its paintings and its ceiling.[52]

This passage is obviously written in a florid literary style and its meanings are not always entirely clear. Certainly, three floors are described in the main house, the lowest used for storage, the middle floor for both accommodation and public functions, and the uppermost for the domestic quarters of certain (lower-status) members of the household, together with a chapel. There were also independent structures, a *logium* communicating with its own oratory, and a kitchen, apparently detached. Given the detail with which the author describes the disposition and functions of rooms within the *domus*, it is frustrating that he says so little about the layout of the *logium* and its functional relationship to the main building. This could have been informative about the uses of *donjons* as distinct from those of the ground-level buildings beside them. What is clear from this text is that, at least as far as the author was concerned, individual rooms were allotted very specific functions.

Remarkably few English texts conclusively refer to residential functions of rooms within *donjons* and fail to make it clear whether this use should be regarded as the norm. They also tend to be far removed in time from the construction of the buildings. To take two examples, Henry III's instructions for works at Winchester Castle in 1266 include repairs to 'our lodging in our Great Tower'.[53] In the reign of Edward I, accounts again suggest that the king himself retained a chamber in the keep at Corfe (Dorset), though again whether this was ever used as such must be questionable.[54] As will be discussed in this and the following chapter, all of the explicit documentary references to habitation inside the White Tower are connected with imprisonment. No conclusive evidence has yet been found to indicate that anyone ever lived there of his own volition.

Much of the construction of the White Tower probably took place in the reign of William Rufus.

102 Conjectural reconstruction of the Palace of Westminster *circa* 1100, showing the Great Hall constructed by William Rufus. Much of the palace is exactly contemporary with the White Tower, though its elegant sculpted capitals suggest a far greater attention to architectural detailing. Although it is uncertain that this was intended, Westminster became the central locus of royal government and residence in the London area, increasingly relegating the Tower to roles connected with security and storage.

Rufus's own tastes in architecture, however, tended towards the sophisticated and exotic, perhaps making him more anxious about the comforts of his palace at Westminster, also under construction at this time (fig. 102).[55] Certainly, for most of his successors it was usual practice, when staying in London, to live at Westminster and to move the court to the Tower only in extraordinary or dangerous circumstances. In this context, it is interesting that there is a very early documentary reference to use of the Tower, almost certainly the White Tower, by someone other than the king. The account refers to the years 1100 and 1101, when the White Tower was newly complete. Immediately on his accession, Henry I had committed the unpopular Rannulf Flambard, Bishop of Durham, to the fortress as a prisoner. According to Orderic, however:

> It was the king's order that he should have food to the value of 2 shillings sterling every day, and thus he lived the high life in prison, with help from his friends. Every day he would order a marvellous feast for himself and his guards. One day, a rope was smuggled to him in a cask of wine. The generous bishop then laid on a lavish banquet at which the guards ate and drank with him and, in due course, became intoxicated with all the wine they had consumed. When they were all completely drunk and snoring soundly, the bishop fastened his rope to a column between two lights of a window in the

tower, and still clutching his pastoral staff, he began to let himself down. But he had forgotten to put on gloves to protect his hands and they were cut to the bone by the roughness of the rope. The rope itself was too short to reach the ground, and the fat bishop had to fall heavily to the ground: the drop nearly flattened him and he howled miserably with the pain. His faithful friends and trusted supporters were waiting in great fear at the foot of the Tower, with the fastest horses ready for him.[56]

As Bishop of Durham and Justiciar of England, Rannulf was a figure whose political importance approached that of the king, and it should perhaps come as no surprise that a prisoner of his rank was allowed to use the White Tower, especially as an expedient short-term measure. Presumably, Rannulf was required to live in the White Tower as well as to hold banquets there, although this story incidentally provides a useful early confirmation that the building, explicitly named as *turris*, was suitable for a grand occasion, a lavish feast ('copiosus convivii apparatus'). Whatever the apocryphal details of the tale, it does imply that, from very early in the White Tower's history, kings were prepared to use it as a prison rather than their own lodging. The threatened imprisonment of Flemish hostages in the Tower of London in 1101 and the confinement of the Count of Mortain from 1106 suggest that this may not have been a unique occurrence.[57]

An important question on which there is frustratingly little information is the layout of the fortress as a whole, especially the presence or absence of residential buildings other than the White Tower. Unfortunately, as discussed in Chapter Five, administrative records, which provide the principal source for building works, do not exist in any quantity until the second half of the twelfth century; by this time several other royal houses already existed in the castle. It is likely that some were built at the outset, although whether this is true or what they were have yet to be established. With the exception of the fact that the Tower was surrounded by a wall dating to the reign of William Rufus, few concrete statements can be made about the buildings of the castle before the 1160s or 1170s.[58] From the single surviving Pipe Roll of the reign of Henry I, dating to 1129–30, it is clear that a chapel was being refitted and that works were carried out to the houses of Othuer, the late keeper of the Tower.[59] Until 1190 the castle enceinte was, according to most interpretations, extremely small, with a substantial portion being taken up by the footprint of the White Tower itself.[60] The question of whether the castle possessed an additional large outer bailey before the thirteenth century is considered in Chapter One.[61]

In a recent article, Philip Dixon and Pamela Marshall have proposed that several Anglo-Norman great towers were built not to be inhabited, but for the occasional performance of ceremonies associated with lordly rank.[62] Their close examination of the tower at Hedingham Castle in Essex has revealed several important design features. As at the White Tower, the uppermost floor can be shown to have been originally a 'false storey', in which screen walls with elaborately moulded windows concealed a sunken roof. Both the high 'upper hall', with its mezzanine gallery, and the 'lower hall' at entrance level consist of single rooms occupying the entire area of the floor, spanned by massive diaphragm arches rather than two spaces divided by a spine wall. The building contains numerous small rooms within the thickness of the walls, but none of these is large enough to have functioned as a chamber: they seem little more than cupboards. Nor is there a chapel. This impracticality, together with the ostentation of a false top storey, suggest that the entire keep may have been built explicitly for display and celebration, possibly even for a single occasion, and that it was never intended to function routinely as accommodation: when staying at Hedingham, the lord and his family perhaps lived in a conventional hall and chamber somewhere beside the tower. This concept of the *donjon* as a building of overt symbolism and theatricality may find several resonances in the architecture of the White Tower.

One of the few documented occasions for royal occupation of the Tower of London in the twelfth century may likewise have been highly dramatic, or was at least intended to be. This was Whitsun 1140, when King Stephen was forced to establish himself at the Tower, rather than Westminster, the traditional place for the festival.[63] With the exception of the Bishop of Sées, most magnates and bishops stayed aloof or were afraid to follow him there. Stephen, however, presumably made some attempt to observe the occasion with the traditional splendour and, particularly, he would have been expected to wear his crown. Like Christmas and Easter, Whitsun was to be marked with feasts, councils and religious services in which the crowned king would be acclaimed in a recital of the *Laudes regiae*, an elaborate antiphon on the subject of earthly and heavenly kingship. Though William of Malmesbury's account of this occasion does not mention the White Tower, its enormous rooms and magnificent chapel would have made it an ideal setting.

CONCLUSION: THE WHITE TOWER AS A SYMBOL (fig. 103)

One of the earliest and best-known statements about the function of the Tower of London comes to us from William Fitz Stephen in the late twelfth century. He has been widely quoted for his description of the Tower as '*arx palatina*', usually translated as 'fortified palace', 'palatine Tower', 'fortress-palace' or other variants.[64] To cite only these two Latin words, however, is to take them out of their original context in a far longer sentence ('Habet ab oriente arcem palatinam maximam et fortissimam'), which could legitimately be translated with a very different emphasis. An alternative translation might read: 'the city has at its eastern part a huge and very strong palatine citadel'. A century after the castle was founded, the Tower was seen primarily as a place of military strength, and its capacity for palatial residence was in some sense incidental. The notion of a strongly defended fortress imposed on a captive city accords well with modern views of the Normans as a warlike race, and there is ample evidence from contemporary sources that they liked to think of themselves in the same way.[65] Fitz Stephen's implication that the military strength of the Tower lay in its immense size seems equally plausible to modern observers of the White Tower. With the exception of the keep at Colchester Castle, whose ground plan occupies a larger area, the White Tower is by a considerable margin the most substantial surviving Norman castle building in England, and in features such as the thickness of its walls and the height of its parapet, it is easy to appreciate its potential as a refuge in war.

Its credentials as a palace are less easy to evaluate. The building as it survives may have grandeur, but with the possible exception of St John's Chapel, all its interiors now appear crude, stark and somewhat forbidding, particularly in their vast scale. Nor is the elaborate

architectural decoration, which characterises other exceptional castles such as Norwich, Castle Rising and Sherborne, to be seen on the outside. The aesthetic of the White Tower, as far we can understand it, is one of simple massive forms executed with weight and solidity. The fact that fireplaces and garderobes were provided at all suggests that the building was intended for regular use or habitation, but its form is in essence so different from that of horizontally planned palaces such as Westminster that it seems inescapable that its use was intended to take a different character as well. Whether or not this was a result of compromises forced on the designers by military necessity, as G. T. Clark maintained, cannot be resolved conclusively. Within decades of the White Tower's completion, however, some Norman builders had managed to contrive more expansive types of palace within fortified castles, as at Caen, Old Sarum and Sherborne, all of which conform more completely to the 'horizontal' mainstream of architecture.[66] All through this period, towers were also still being built in castles. For this reason, it is preferable to suppose that the tower was chosen as an alternative architectural form primarily because it was eloquent of some other virtue.

The White Tower can be most readily appreciated as a symbol of the Norman monarchy and an embodiment of its power. While its location seems to have been chosen with some strategic considerations in mind, in order to 'guard' London's approaches from the sea, the technology of the time would have allowed it to function only as a vantage point and a base from which soldiers could be deployed. Its sym-

bolic function, however, as a permanent and intrusive reminder of the presence of the Normans, must have been highly effective, as photographs taken before the rise of modern buildings behind it so clearly show.[67] That this was the intention is shown by the care lavished on the elevations facing the city and the river, and in the extra height provided by the 'false' top storey. As such, it was a structure to be seen from a distance as much as a building to be used.

Inside the White Tower, some of the functions of the individual rooms still evade us, and other essential services, such as kitchens, have not been found. Nevertheless, a 'hall', 'chamber' and 'chapel' all appear to be present. The tower was capable of functioning as a residence, and the occasional confinement of important prisoners there may be taken to confirm this. The White Tower, however, was built for something grander; it provided spaces not merely for living but also for impressing. Inside and outside, it was intended to underline the authority of the Norman kings. More than merely sheltering them in times of crisis, its imposing characteristics were emphasised precisely in order to subdue their opponents and to prevent opposition from transforming itself into action. On occasions, it may have been intended to provide the kings and their households with state rooms for ceremonies, hospitality and perhaps even accommodation on a suitably huge scale. There is frustratingly little evidence that the building was ever actually used in these ways, but this may be an accident of history, rather than proof that such was never the intention.

CHAPTER FIVE

The Structure and Function of the White Tower, 1150–1485

JEREMY ASHBEE

Facing page: 104 The earliest-known image of the White Tower to represent the building's actual appearance, from a late fifteenth-century collection of poems by Charles, Duke of Orléans. The White Tower is painted white with turrets capped by conical roofs, surmounted by gilded weathervanes with the royal arms and gold crowns. The forebuilding is shown with a two-light window and a chimney. Inside the White Tower, the imprisoned duke is shown writing at a table and (left) at a window awaiting his ransom from France. The details of the building's interior, shown in the cut-away, are entirely invented: some, such as the fireplace behind the table, may suggest that the artist was French.

In the previous chapter, there was discussion of the use of the White Tower during the first seven decades of its existence (fig. 104). This is presumably the period in which its functions resembled most closely the intention of its builders and the patrons who ordered its construction. This period is also almost completely without surviving documentation; the Tower of London (and sometimes specifically its *donjon*) are mentioned in occasional chronicle entries, but references in the very few government records are almost non-existent. For this reason, the statements and hypotheses made about the function of the building are based principally on the evidence of the standing building and of other comparable sites. They assume that the patrons and builders of the White Tower collaborated closely on its design, and that, at least in these earliest years, the building functioned as they planned. As the evidence of the present chapter will show, these assumptions of a simple correlation between form and actual function may well be unjustified, but in the absence of other contemporary evidence, extrapolation from the standing building is the only method available.

This chapter, by contrast, will describe the operation of the White Tower, and more generally the Tower of London, in a period for which documentation exists, and at times gives a good idea of what was genuinely taking place. For most of the Middle Ages, it would be fair to claim, the Tower of London was among the most intensively documented historic sites in England. Since the time of its foundation, the

Tower has been a royal castle; its operations have been ordered and recorded by the sometimes powerful and often diligent royal bureaucracy of the Chancery, Exchequer, Wardrobe and Household, succeeded in later periods by the Ordnance and the Office of Works. Unfortunately, it is hard to identify material specifically concerned with the White Tower from the extensive corpus of information that these departments produced. In part, this may reflect the generally good condition of the White Tower during the Middle Ages. Before the remodellings of the seventeenth, eighteenth and nineteenth centuries, works to the building were confined, with a few very significant exceptions, to regular maintenance of a few perishable elements, particularly the timberwork of floors and roofs and the leading of roofs and gutters. The documentary sources mention little else and the building shows only a few traces of other major alterations.

Alternatively, it could be the case that the documentary record, as modern historians have interpreted it, is misleadingly under-representative of the White Tower's history. If so, this is partly the result of its celebrity and prominence. This single building was perceived through almost the whole of the Middle Ages and beyond as the embodiment of the whole castle, and was effectively synonymous with it. Almost from the beginning, the proper name for the fortress was *Turris Londoniarum*, that is, the Tower of London – or a variant on the same wording. At other castles containing keeps, *turris* usually denotes the keep alone: here, along with Rouen[1] but perhaps nowhere else, the word was normally used with reference to the entire fortress. The context of a reference may sometimes clarify the matter, but this is certainly not always the case. For this chapter, most medieval references to *Turris Londoniarum* are taken to signify the whole castle, rather than the White Tower. More specific terms, including 'Great Tower' (*magna turris*) and 'Tall Tower' (*alta turris*) appear in documents from the thirteenth and fourteenth centuries, with *dongeoun* appearing in the early fifteenth century; for the purposes of this discussion, it is assumed that they always denote the White Tower. These are unlikely to have been the only terms used for the building in the Middle Ages. It is possible that some references to the keep by another name may have escaped notice here, as previously.

This chapter contains a narrative of developments in the castle, both building works that altered its layout and the changing functions that accompanied and sometimes caused them to be carried out. Where possible, this discussion is focused on the White Tower, though for long periods the record is silent about the building, and the only possible statements are inferences based on what we know of events elsewhere in the fortress. In a site as large as the Tower of London, with a history so long and complex, no search of the documents can be comprehensive. The chapter is based on a survey of several classes of document: Close, Patent and *Liberate* Rolls, particularly for the thirteenth century, and Exchequer Accounts, either appended to the main series of Pipe Rolls or enrolled separately as Particulars of Account.

It is worth noting at the outset that several archaeologically obvious alterations to the White Tower's fabric have not been found during this search of the documents: these include the raising of the roof from its original low position to its current setting at the top of the building. It is to be hoped that this and other problems may be resolved in the future.

THE TOWER OF LONDON FROM HENRY II (1154–89) TO JOHN (1199–1216)

During the twelfth century, if not before, some form of residential accommodation in addition to the White Tower was constructed in the castle. Unfortunately, the archaeological and documentary evidence for this early development is extremely scarce. The first references to other buildings occur in 1129–30, with a mention of houses formerly belonging to Othuer Fitz Earl, a custodian then deceased,[2] but this is followed by a hiatus until the 1160s, when orders were issued for works to 'the King's houses at the Tower of London'.[3] This general formula was used throughout the remainder of the twelfth century and the first decades of the thirteenth. The very fact that the buildings required repairs in the 1170s (if this is the import

of *reparationes*) suggests either that they had been present for some considerable time or that they were timber-framed.[4] In the 1180s there appear documentary references to a kitchen,[5] a gaol[6] and a bakery,[7] some of which may also have lain outside the White Tower. In 1211 there is a reference to 'the King's wardrobe at the Tower of London'.[8] These give some sense of a busy castle, but for most of the eleventh and twelfth centuries the internal layout of the royal lodgings or ancillary buildings within the castle cannot be reconstructed in detail.

During excavations in the Inmost Ward in the 1950s and 1970s, one masonry feature was discovered that could have originated in this period: a large foundation running approximately north–south, possibly incorporating a pilaster buttress on its western side.[9] The structure could not be closely dated, but its position and alignment are now thought not to have conformed to the layout of the palace as it was reconstructed by Henry III. This suggests that the building was demolished by the 1220s or early 1230s, when documentary sources record that Henry III's building works in this area began in earnest. Recent discoveries at Windsor Castle have provided further support for St John Hope's hypothesis that, during the reign of Henry II or even before, a sophisticated lodging was constructed there, planned around regular courtyards.[10] The medieval footing in the Inmost Ward of the Tower runs at approximately a right angle to the south wall of the White Tower, perhaps significant in the context of an enigmatic reference in the Pipe Roll of 1185–6 to 'the cloister (*claustrum*) between the chambers'.[11] Perhaps like Windsor Castle, Everswell (Oxfordshire) and a documented palace built by the same king at Saumur (Maine-et-Loire), Henry II's lodgings at the Tower exhibited some form of regular planning.[12]

The form of the defences in this period is equally mysterious. Chronicle histories mention that the fortress saw military action during the wars of Stephen and Matilda. In the summer of 1141 the Londoners apparently laid siege to the Tower, which Geoffrey II de Mandeville was holding for the empress: the *Flores Historiarum* states that he had previously strengthened its defences.[13] Whether Henry II later undertook any work to the defences is unclear. Possibly the Wardrobe Tower, formerly linked to the apse of the White Tower by a wall with pilaster buttresses of plausibly twelfth-century date, may be a work of his reign, enhancing the partly Roman defences of the Tower's eastern side. It is more certain, however, that in the late 1180s and 1190s the Tower was the scene of intense building work, associated with an expansion of the fortress westwards and the attempt of Justiciar William Longchamp, Bishop of Ely, to create a water-filled moat around it.[14] This marks the first securely recorded act in the extension and upgrading of the defences around

105 The Bell Tower, built in the late twelfth century, is the most substantial survival left by the Angevins in the Tower of London. It contains rooms on two storeys, a guardroom with arrow-loops below and a residential chamber with a fireplace, garderobe and two-light windows above.

the fortress's perimeter, on which the security of the Tower was now largely to depend. One major survival almost certainly from this campaign of works is the Bell Tower, which then formed the new salient south-western angle of the castle. Though a formidable defensive work in its own right, it is also notable that the tower contains elaborate chambers on both storeys. The upper chamber was provided with elegant two-light windows set in deep arched embrasures, a garderobe and a fireplace, while the lower chamber is roofed with a rib vault of some sophistication, springing from moulded corbels. In common with near-contemporary structures such as the Butavant Tower at Corfe in Dorset, the polygonal Bell Tower represents a significant advance on the simple rectangular timber-backed mural towers of other late twelfth-century English castles, such as Framlingham in Suffolk and the Inner Ward at Dover in Kent.[15] It might be excessive to describe the Bell Tower as a second *donjon*, but it would certainly be fair to see in this building a reflection of contemporary developments in Continental architecture, combining potential residence and defence in a single structure (fig. 105).[16]

Regardless of its architectural quality, the Tower of London was by no means impregnable as a fortress. In 1191, while his building works were in full spate, Longchamp was forced to retreat inside the fortress by a besieging mob under the leadership of King Richard's brother, Prince John: after a single night, the intolerable overcrowding within the castle forced him to sue for peace.[17] In the invasion of 1216 by the French under Prince Louis, while Dover and Windsor successfully withstood a French siege, the Tower was

handed over without a struggle by rebels, and was only returned to the English in the following year.[18]

THE REIGN OF HENRY III (1216–72)

Building Works at the Tower of London

While works at the Tower during the reign of King John had been largely confined to repairs, it was his son Henry III who was to order the most radical campaigns of new building at the Tower of London. During the early years of his minority, these works generally took the form of *reparationes*, that is to say, the repair or completion of existing buildings, including 'the King's hall and chamber'.[19] At some time early in the 1220s, however, the young king's regents set in motion a programme of works that over the next two decades would create a sophisticated residential complex along the southern side of the fortress, while enlarging and modernising the curtain defences in line with the most recent Continental precedent. After the construction of these new lodgings in the bailey, it became even less likely that the White Tower would be used routinely for royal accommodation.

The form of Henry III's new royal lodgings has been the subject of considerable attention among architectural historians in the *History of the King's Works*,[20] but also in publications by Peter Curnow[21] and most recently by Simon Thurley.[22] The extent of the complex and the functions of individual buildings can be reconstructed only tentatively, but it is clear from the wording of writs recorded in the Close and *Liberate* Rolls that the residential buildings of the Inmost Ward were large and extensive. When complete, they included a Great Hall, Great Kitchen with attendant services, sets of chambers for the king and queen, numerous chapels and some accommodation for the royal wardrobe. Attention was paid to their appearance, both internal and external: important buildings such as a 'Great Chamber' of the king were whitewashed externally and provided with heraldically painted window shutters, while there are documentary references to internal adornments, such as a wooden screen at the entrance to a domestic chapel, a glazed chapel window, painting inside the king's Great Chamber, and a pattern of red masonry outline with flowers in the Queen's Chamber.[23] Of Henry III's buildings, the circular Wakefield Tower still survives, containing a spacious upper chamber and chapel over an unheated lower room probably intended for guards (fig. 106). Clearly, some of the royal accommodation at the Tower was located in defensible turrets such as this, although the conventional interpretation of the upper room as Henry III's principal chamber is open to question.[24]

Despite the attention and resources spent on the royal apartments, the Tower did not become a major royal residence during the reign of Henry III. His itin-

106 Photograph of the upper chamber of the Wakefield Tower in 1978. Although heavily altered in the nineteenth century by Anthony Salvin during conversion into the Treasury of the Crown jewels, this room is one of the best-preserved royal domestic buildings of Henry III's reign. It was constructed in the 1220s and '30s, probably as part of the king's own accommodation within the fortress: it contained a fireplace and private oratory and communicated with a new Great Hall close by on its eastern side. The White Tower had long since ceased to be considered as a royal residence except during the direst emergency.

erary shows long absences punctuated by stays that were generally of short duration and invariably forced on him by political or military adversity. Westminster remained the principal royal residence for London, and insomuch as the Tower retained any significance for the king, it was as a fortress rather than a palace.[25] Concern for security can be seen clearly in Henry III's new stretches of curtain wall along the north and east sides of the fortress, each containing several D-shaped mural towers (fig. 107). Efforts were made to present a bold and martial face to the city of London, with an elaborate gateway planned for the western side, complete with barbicans or other outworks, although this gate collapsed soon after construction and efforts to rebuild it proved fruitless.[26] Within the enceinte, the buildings of the royal lodgings may have been in some ways architecturally second-rate, probably as a result of established royal practice not to use the Tower voluntarily, but also perhaps a reinforcement of this reluctance. Even if the king was not regularly present in person, however, the spectacle of royal chamber blocks fronting onto the river, with the Great Hall between them, backed up by the massive White Tower, may have been intended as a permanent symbol of royalty to visitors sailing up the Thames. This point seems not to have escaped the artist of the famous 'Orléans' manuscript illustration of *circa* 1480.[27]

The White Tower

As well as ordering works to the royal lodgings in the Inmost Ward, Henry III's writs contain several instructions regarding the White Tower. Most of these concern routine maintenance on the lead and tim-

berwork of the roof[28] or repairs to the windows.[29] Perhaps more significant is the instruction that has given the building its name: the king's command to have the whole of the exterior whitened. The first known order to this effect appeared in March 1240, with an instruction to Richard de Freslingfield, keeper of the works at the Tower of London, to have the 'Great Tower' whitened (*dealbari*) both inside and out.[30] This was followed in December of the same year with a more detailed injunction that the leaden gutters of the 'Great Tower' should be lengthened to run down to the ground, so that 'the wall of the said tower, which has just been whitened, may not perish at all or suddenly spall away through the action of the rain'.[31] This suggests that this was the first time that the building had been whitened, although Henry's initiative could have been a continuation of, or a revival of, a much earlier tradition. Thereafter, however, the practice of whitening the White Tower – or at least the expectation that it should be whitened – continued throughout the Middle Ages (though no actual account paying for a later re-painting in the Middle Ages has yet been found[32]). It is shown as shining white in the 'Orléans' manuscript illustration, while in the 1530s it was being routinely described as 'the White Tower',[33] and as late as 1598 John Stow wrote of the building as 'the high White Tower of London'.[34] While the reason for whitening the keep has never been explicitly stated, it was almost certainly governed at least partly by an intention to maximise the visual impact of the building on an onlooker outside the fortress. This action also concealed some of the uneven character of the White Tower's facing stonework. In this last objec-

107 The curtain wall constructed by Henry III in the late 1230s and early 1240s. With its regularly spaced mural towers, the new fortification reflected fashions in castle design from the Continent. Contemporary accounts make it clear that Londoners interpreted these new walls as a direct challenge to their liberties by the king.

tive, it was plainly successful: two Irish friars passing through London in 1324 commented that the White Tower was built 'with immeasurable solidity from cut and dressed stone'.[35]

It has already been noted that the White Tower was not the only building in the Tower of London that was made white in the reign of Henry III. This fact probably contributed to the confusing later ascription of the name 'White Tower' to another building within the fortress. Thus in a dilapidation survey of 1335, 'la Blanchetour' is mentioned in contexts that preclude an identification with the present White Tower, mentioned in the same document as the 'high tower' (*alta turris*),[36] while in 1339 an enrolled account for repairs makes reference to 'the white turret next to the lord King's exchange', almost certainly the building now known as the Bell Tower.[37] The keeps of other castles were also whitened: in 1240 Henry III commanded the constable of Rochester Castle to whiten 'the said [great] tower in those places which are not already whitened',[38] and in 1244 a order was issued to whiten the keep at Corfe, notwithstanding that the building was already faced with fine ashlar masonry.[39] The fact that of the numerous possible white towers, it was the *donjon* at the Tower of London that was eventually immortalised as 'The White Tower' could be either the product of its whitening over a longer period or a testament to the visual impact of its size and setting.

Within the keep, the chapel of St John the Evangelist continued in regular use during this period, even though the expansion of the enclosed area had by now brought the larger chapel of St Peter ad Vincula into the fortress,[40] while the royal lodgings contained several other oratories and chapels.[41] The *Liberate* writ of December 1240, containing the instruction to whiten the keep, also makes provisions for the internal decoration of the chapel of St John, including stained-glass windows showing the Virgin and Child on the north side and St John the Evangelist and the Holy Trinity on the south. A rood beam was to be mounted above the altar, and there was to be a representation of St Edward the Confessor giving his ring to the Evangelist in the guise of a beggar (fig. 108).[42] Writs of 1241 and 1242 order payments to chaplains of both 'St Peter within the bailey' and 'St John in the Tower': each of these chaplaincies was worth 50 shillings per annum.[43] In 1244 the Close Rolls record an instruction to find a chaplain for St John's Chapel and to provide him with a chalice and vestments.[44] In 1261 an arrangement was made with the Hospital of St Katherine immediately to the east of the fortress, whereby the hospital would provide a chaplain to say a daily commemorative Mass in St John's Chapel for the soul of the late Sanchia of Cornwall, the king's sister-in-law.[45] This was not a unique occurrence in the history of the chapel, for among the items listed in an inventory of the castle in 1327 was a charter of *la chauntrie en la tour*, conceivably St John's Chapel.[46]

During the 1240s there also occur documentary references to other possible uses of the White Tower. The first of these, a continuation of the same writ of December 1240, also contains the provision that

great galleries of good strong timber, well-leaded all over, are to be made at the top of the great tower

108 Mid-thirteenth-century manuscript illustration showing the tomb of St Edward the Confessor in Westminster Abbey. Note that the shrine is flanked by two sculptures, one showing St Edward holding out his ring, the other of St John the Evangelist in the guise of a pilgrim. In December 1240 Henry III commissioned figures of the same images for St John's Chapel in the White Tower, to be set up 'in the most fitting location there'.

on the south side facing south, so that if need arises, people may go up and see down to the foot of the tower to defend it better.[47]

These covered galleries (*aluras*) presumably covered only the eastern bays of the south elevation and did not run over the forebuilding (fig. 109). The most likely explanation of this order is that Henry III was conscious of the White Tower's potential defensive function as a building of last resort. At this date, his works to upgrade the curtain defences of the Tower of London were in full spate, despite a setback earlier in the year, when his 'noble gateway' had collapsed.[48] Should these defences be breached, his lodgings in the Inmost Ward were only protected by single walls along the east and west sides of the palace area and by the Coldharbour Gate beside the south-west corner of the *donjon*. It might therefore be prudent for him to remove himself and his household to the White Tower. In addition to its obvious size and strength, the building contained a well and ample storage space in the basement. It is also clear from a reference in a *Liberate* writ of 1240 that there was a kitchen specifically for the White Tower.[49] The smoke louvre on the apex of its roof needed repairing, which indicates that it was open to the sky: either it was mounted on the roof or in one of the turrets, as at Orford Castle in Suffolk, or stood at ground level adjacent to the keep itself, as accounts from the fourteenth century suggest was then the case. With these services and new defensive works such as the *hourds* around the parapets, the building was adapted to withstand, at least temporarily, a siege.

The upgrading of the defences of the White Tower in 1240 may have been a response to immediate political circumstances, making the king particularly sen-

sitive about his security. In 1238 he had narrowly survived an attempted assassination within his house at Woodstock by an agent of the rebel William de Marisco,[50] and there had been widespread outrage among the nobility and clergy at his sister's clandestine marriage to Simon de Montfort in the same year.[51] The expansion of the fortress was meeting with vocal resistance from the citizens of London, and relations with the Church were equally poor, as a result of royal interference in elections.[52] The collapse of the new gateway at the Tower in April 1240 may have made the king particularly aware of how ill prepared the Tower was against an assault that was beginning to seem increasingly likely. These difficulties, however, eventually passed without serious incident and Henry III was not to make a prolonged stay at the Tower for another twenty-one years. In the meantime, the White Tower could be put to other uses, not least the imprisonment of important hostages (fig. 110).

During the 1240s the Close Rolls and chronicle histories make reference to the detention of prisoners in the White Tower. Most famous of these was the Welsh prince Gruffudd ap Llywelyn, whose fatal fall from an improvised rope, while attempting to emulate the escape of Rannulf Flambard 143 years earlier, was graphically described and illustrated by Matthew Paris.[53] Gruffudd was held in the same room as his son, who, after his father's abortive escape, was kept under closer supervision than before. Gruffudd's custody, almost certainly within the White Tower, had been entrusted not to the constable's men, but to royal serjeants answerable to the king himself.[54] The Chancery documentation also provides some information as to where and how other prisoners were kept within the building. In November 1245 two other Welsh prisoners were held on the middle floor of the

tion by the Jews of London and a naval blockade by a Gascon fleet on the Thames.[60] The role of the White Tower in these military operations is not stated: very probably, it played no part in them at all. The wording of royal communications in 1240 suggests that the White Tower was perceived as a possible refuge in the direst emergency. For more peaceful times, however, an alternative pattern for its use was already set.

EDWARD I (1272–1307) TO EDWARD III (1327–77)

Building Works at the Tower of London

The death of Henry III represents a watershed in the documentation of royal building works. Henry's often attested interest in architectural matters and his frequent personal involvement in their procurement and design had been expressed by a readiness to use the form of writ known as *Liberate*. By this writ the clerks of the Exchequer were instructed on the king's authority to release the necessary sum of money (sometimes, in projects of greatest importance, potentially infinite) for building works on which the king had set his mind.[61] The reign of Edward I was markedly different in the character of royal administration from that of his father, and saw an increase in the use of the Privy Seal to authorise actions on the royal initiative, with the result that detailed personal instructions, if they were ever made, are now largely unknown.[62] The

109 Wooden fighting platforms projecting in front of the battlements of a castle enabled defenders to drop projectiles directly onto attackers below: the photograph shows a modern replica at Caerphilly Castle. Henry III commissioned similar galleries on the south front of the White Tower, overlooking the area of his royal lodgings in the Inmost Ward.

Tower ('in medio stadio eiusdem turris').[55] Four years later, two contemporary writs, of 25 and 27 November 1249, made provision for the confinement of Gascons suspected of treason.[56] Two hostages were to be guarded securely on the top floor of the tower ('in superiori stadio'), but otherwise they were to live lives of relative freedom at the constable's discretion and were not to be fettered ('sine ferro et modo quo voluerit vivant de proprio'). The remaining traitors were to be kept on the middle floor, immediately below them: the conditions of their confinement were not stated. The prisoners were eventually returned to Gascony for trial.[57] These references provide evidence only of occasional use of the White Tower as a prison, and in all these instances for individuals or groups of political importance. Whether the building contained prisoners at other times in Henry III's reign is unknown.

During the 1240s and most of the 1250s the political situation did not deteriorate to the extent that the king was forced to take refuge in the Tower of London. The documentary sources describe embellishments and improvements to the royal apartments, but make few detailed recommendations specifically concerned with the defences, although it is likely that works to the curtain wall continued. The Tower once again became an important centre of military operations for Henry III in 1261, with initial successes in his conflict against Simon de Montfort.[58] Two years later, however, the garrison was forced to come to terms with de Montfort, and it was from Windsor rather than the Tower that the king was to rally support for his cause.[59] In 1267 violence flared up again when the city of London rose against the king in support of the disaffected Gilbert de Clare, Earl of Gloucester. The Tower came under siege again and was saved from capitulation only by strenuous efforts from the king's party, including the defence of part of the fortifica-

110 Matthew Paris's marginal illustration showing the fatal fall of the Welsh prince Gruffudd ap Llywelyn while escaping from the Tower of London on 1 March 1244. Gruffudd's rope was improvised from tablecloths and bed linen, and broke before he reached the ground. Gruffudd's arms are depicted below, inverted to show his death.

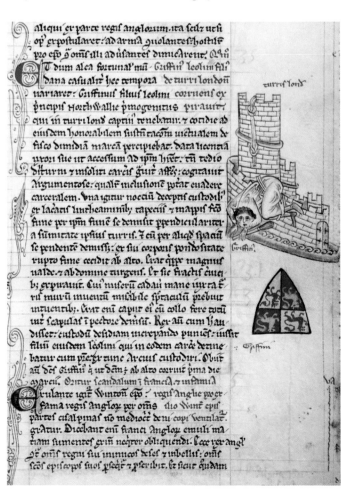

architectural historian of this later period must place a greater emphasis on surviving audited accounts submitted by keepers and clerks of works, detailing payments to individual craftsmen and labourers for carrying out particular tasks or providing materials, as well as the series of Exchequer Pipe Rolls, which continues uninterrupted. In addition, the Close Rolls contain some evidence for the uses of the buildings during the reigns of Edward I and his successors.

In the later thirteenth and early fourteenth centuries the evidence of building works to the White Tower itself is decidedly sparse and suggests small-scale alterations rather than substantial repairs. Most of the references are to repairing the lead of the roof and turrets, and the only entry of any specificity is an order for a housing for a bell mounted on the top of the 'Great Tower'.[63] During the reign of Edward I and his son, the emphasis in the Tower of London was firmly on building works associated with the castle's perimeter defences. Around 1275 Edward I set in motion the construction of a second curtain wall, running concentrically outside Henry III's inner curtain, and the excavation of a new moat outside this. These works entailed building an elaborate and well-defended landward entrance at the south-western corner of the fortress, incorporating two twin-towered gatehouses and a semicircular barbican, all of them protected with a series of drawbridges, gates and portcullises, and further covered by numerous loops for archers. The completion of the circuit of the outer curtain also involved the reclamation of land from the Thames, creating a new shoreline to the south. Henry III's royal lodgings, which had formerly stood on the foreshore, were separated from the river by a strip of land, now known as Water Lane. In the late 1270s Edward I's masons also built a new and elaborate water gate, projecting southwards into the river, enclosing a fortified basin in which boats could dock: imaginative post-medieval commentators later named this 'Traitors' Gate'. Above the water gate were a hall and chamber that may have been for the king's personal use, a right that Edward I was evidently loath to exercise.[64] The accounts show that these rooms were architecturally sophisticated, with tiled floors, figural stained-glass windows and painted statues above the rooms, perhaps mounted on the battlements, as at Marten's Tower at Chepstow and the Eagle Tower at Caernarfon.[65]

In general, as throughout the Middle Ages, there is nothing to suggest that the fabric of the White Tower was in disrepair: references are almost entirely restricted to routine maintenance. Mention is made in the accounts of the repair of various defects of the leadwork of the roof in 1315–16.[66] Three years previously, carpenters had been ordered to fix swinging hatches ('heckas cadentes') between the merlons of the battlements on the eastern side of the White Tower;

this would have afforded protection to soldiers positioned there, but given the position and height of the White Tower, an element of broadcasting that the Tower's defences were being maintained and enhanced may also have been intended.[67] The fortification of the Tower of London, however, was more than merely cosmetic: the account unusually mentions that the works had an unfortunate consequence, 'that by virtue of this command [to enhance the Tower's defences], all hopes of peace between the King and the Earl [of Lancaster] were dashed'.[68] Chronicle histories also tell of violent conflicts between the constable and the city in September 1312,[69] which may lie behind some of the other documented works to the castle, such as the widening of the crenellations over the water gate to make room for 'springalds' (mounted crossbows).

Unfortunately, no evidence has yet been found for the date of some of the more substantial alterations that the White Tower is thought to have undergone during the later Middle Ages. These include the construction of a large stone building on its eastern side and the insertion of a spiral stair in the thickness of the south wall, leading directly to the western entrance to St John's Chapel, both of which have conventionally been dated to the fourteenth century.[70] The documents, however, do give some idea of the changing character of the fortress. In visual terms, one of the most striking features is the presence of numerous other buildings clustered around the White Tower, which would have compromised its defensive capacity and suggest that the role of the *donjon* as a refuge was losing importance. The garderobe outlets on the White Tower's north side made building at the foot of this wall undesirable, but documents show that the east, west and south sides of the keep were encumbered with buildings. For example, in 1306 an order was issued to rebuild a ruined 'stable next to the Great Tower'.[71] The 'small hall', part of the royal lodgings, was described in 1321 as standing 'on the eastern side at the end of the Great Tower' or 'on the eastern side below the Tower'.[72] An account of 1313 mentions a kitchen specifically dedicated to the White Tower: the wording ('quoquina in magna turri') would normally be taken to mean that this was located somewhere within the White Tower itself. A list of timbers needing repairs, however – braces, laths, posts, roof timbers (*punsonis*) and gutters – suggest, particularly the last-mentioned, a building open to the roof.[73] In 1334 there is a reference to a stone-built 'Great Kitchen on the western side of the Tall Tower' ('magna coquina alte turris ex parte occidentale'), and to a 'long building below the Tall Tower'.[74] A survey of dilapidations, made in 1336, identifies the need for repair of the timber of 'unius aeriae coquinae' of the 'Tall Tower', probably a wooden floor.[75] It is unclear how access was provided from a kitchen on the west side of the keep into the building itself, though most probably it communicated with the basement, whose western room was known as the 'Black Hall' (see below): there is a reference from the 1350s to 'a great kitchen in the Black Hall'.[76] No fireplace has ever been found inside the room formerly called the 'Black Hall', and it may be that the doorway through the west wall into the southern end of the basement, shown in eighteenth-century plans (perhaps the same as the opening 'broken' into the basement in 1729), may have originated as a medieval entrance into the White Tower from a kitchen just inside Coldharbour Gate.[77]

There is also a suggestion in such accounts that the area to the south of the White Tower, between the keep and the Great Hall of the royal lodgings, was occupied by buildings for the constable. Certainly, within the fortress there was an area or areas variously known as the *constabularia* or the *liberatio constabularii*, the latter described in 1316 as situated 'inside the gate [Coldharbour Gate] of the Tall Tower'. This area contained a hall and chambers for the constable 'next to the Great Tower'.[78] In the 1320s the house of the constable's *familia* was described as 'below' the White Tower and probably abutting it, so that there was a gutter between the two buildings.[79] In the 1330s the White Tower and the constable's kitchen were separated by a partition (*interclausum*),[80] and in the late 1340s there existed a door from the Constable's Hall into the White Tower's western basement ('Black Hall').[81] A different site, on the south-west corner of Tower Green, has traditionally been seen as the site of the medieval constable's house and now known as the 'Queen's House'; this may have been assigned to the constable's deputy at this time.[82]

A dilapidation survey of 1336 also listed defects to the 'Tall Tower' in the stonework of the walls, crenellations and stairs, the timber in two rooms at the top, a turret, windows, doors and, in the room next to the doorway, the leadwork of the gutters, the glass in St John's Chapel and generally to the ironwork of doors and windows. The sheriffs of London were commanded in the following year to allocate £40 for repairs to the building.[83]

The Tower as a Prison and Arms Manufactory

From the reign of Edward I onwards, there was an increasing specialisation of function among the numerous royal palaces and castles in London and the south of England. The enrolled accounts of the late thirteenth and early fourteenth centuries show that the Tower was taking on an industrial character, and was used more and more for the manufacture and maintenance of armour, weaponry and siege engines. Documents increasingly referred to places such as 'the house in which the King's spears are made', the 'chamber of the lance-maker', 'the long stable where the *springalds* used to be made' and the 'chambers

where the crossbows and quarrels . . . are placed'.[84] From the 1330s at the latest, these types of weapon were joined by gunpowder and the first in the Tower's battery of firearms, some of which were manufactured within the Tower of London as well as kept there in readiness for deployment in France and Scotland.[85] The Tower served as a base for the king's master mason, smith and carpenter, responsible for the whole of England south of the Trent.[86] Accounts also show that a large stock of lead, the king's *plumbaria*, was held in the Tower.[87] More famously, from the 1270s at the latest, until 1810, the Tower was one of the locations of the Royal Mint, established probably from the outset in the outer ward of the fortress between the inner and outer curtain walls on the western side, an area still known as Mint Street.[88] The Tower also served as the home of the king's menagerie and as the site of extensive gardens both inside and outside the castle enceinte. The detention of prisoners likewise continued.

The implication of these references is that, during the late thirteenth and early fourteenth centuries, the Tower of London's role as a royal residence was systematically downgraded and the site increasingly given over to other specialised functions, including industrial working. The court did occasionally visit, as attested to by the birth of a daughter of Edward II there in 1321, known forever as Joan of the Tower.[89] It is noticeable, however, that there is a common strand linking all the activities and offices listed above: they were all by definition sedentary, and unable to follow the itinerant royal household around the country and abroad. During the frequent long absences of the sovereign, the pressure of space at the Tower from the Prison and the Wardrobe may have been acute: certainly, when one traces the history of some of the residential buildings of the royal 'palace' during the fourteenth century, it is clear that they were often given up for other functions. For example, during the reign of Edward II, the Wakefield Tower's fine upper chamber housed part of the royal wardrobe (probably the Great Wardrobe, responsible for storage of royal property in bulk),[90] while under Edward III the lodgings that his grandfather had built over the water gate were fitted out with shelves for armour and rails from which to hang crossbows.[91] When members of the royal family did stay at the Tower, they appear to have changed rooms with some frequency.

Imprisonment specifically within the White Tower may well have continued throughout this period. This is very rarely specified in the documents, and it should certainly not be assumed that any prisoner committed to the Tower of London would necessarily have been confined in the *donjon*. Some prisoners, particularly those of high rank, were held in other parts of the fortress. For example, accounts for the first half of the fourteenth century identify the present Salt Tower

III Detail of the north face of the White Tower showing the outlets of the Norman latrines. Originally, the north face of the White Tower overlooked the castle's boundary ditch, but expansion of the fortress during the thirteenth and fourteenth centuries made this one of the central areas of the fortress. In the early fourteenth century an order was issued for the construction of a stone wall to hide the filth dropping from the White Tower's latrines: clearly, the building remained in heavy use or even full-time occupation.

as 'turellum Balliols' or 'Balliolstour', a memorial of the enforced stay there of King John Balliol of Scotland between 1296 and 1299; and in 1330 Roger Mortimer was walled up for security in a turret in the king's lodgings.[92] As the fourteenth century progressed, it may even be possible to see prisons gaining prominence in the nomenclature of the Tower, after English victories in wars against the Scots and the French. For example, the list of buildings in a works account of the early 1350s contains a large number of entries such as 'cleaning out various turrets to hold prisoners . . . the tower in which Walden is imprisoned . . . the tower in which William Douglas was imprisoned, a small chamber in the tower where John Pikard was confined, a tower in the corner next to the crossbow-maker, where Roger Holme is imprisoned'.[93] In the fourteenth century the Close Rolls indicate that towers within the fortress were sometimes even used for the confinement of prisoners other than the king's. For example, in the 1370s the constable was ordered to prepare a tower for the keeping of the Comte de Saint-Pol, a prisoner of the lord chamberlain, who provided guards from his own retinue.[94] Should it have been necessary to confine a large number at once, however, the White Tower may in all probability have served as the prison. For example, it has been claimed that large numbers of the Jewish community were held in the basement of the White Tower during the reign of Edward I;[95] whatever the location, in the late 1270s there is record evidence for the confinement of 600 Jews over a period of 140 days, in connection with allegations of coin clipping.[96] In 1309 the Tower was used as the collection point for all the arrested Templars from southern England and East Anglia.[97] From details such as an order of 1313 to build a stone wall beneath the 'turret of the garderobes of the Great Tower' in order to contain the filth, it is clear that the upper floors of the White Tower were in occupation or regular use (fig. 111).[98] It would

be tempting to assume that this waste was generated by a complement of prisoners were there not evidence that the principal rooms of the White Tower were sometimes used for other purposes in the early fourteenth century. The 1350s account mentioned above also contains an entry for cleaning out the White and Black Halls, probably two rooms in the *donjon*, to receive prisoners from various turrets of the castle: doubtless the number of Scottish prisoners was becoming unmanageable.[99]

The White Tower as Repository for State Documents and Treasure (fig. 112)

It is known that some state documents had been deposited somewhere at the Tower of London from at least the reign of Edward I.[100] In 1312 Thomas of Sandal, Edward II's acting treasurer and chamberlain, ordered improvements in the storage of records, with the construction of wooden presses (*almaria*) in the 'Treasury of the Tower' to contain them.[101] This development may well be connected with the final suppression in 1312 of the Knights Templar: the New Temple in London had hitherto been used extensively for the storage of the treasury and archives, and the dissolution of the house left Edward II in need of a new repository.[102] It has been claimed that at this time the principal treasury of the Exchequer was located in St John's Chapel.[103] Further reforms were necessary, however, and in 1320 Edward II demanded a thorough reorganisation of documents, which had not been securely stored or properly ordered. Many documents were transported in large canvas sacks from Westminster to the Tower, where much of the reordering and deposition took place inside the White Tower. In particular, more presses were made in this year for the 'chapel in the said King's Tower of London', which V. H. Galbraith identified with St John's Chapel:[104] in view of a nearly contemporary reference to the assembling of rolls in 'the lord King's chapel at the top of his Tower of London', this interpretation seems very plausible.[105] Some documents remained in the chapel for some time after the reorganisation: a description of the contents of the treasury in the early 1330s makes reference to 'the muniments, fines, rolls and other things being in the chapel in the Tower of London'.[106] For some of the records, however, St John's Chapel provided only a temporary home, and soon after 1320 they were removed into storage elsewhere in the fortress; others, such as the Exchequer records, were returned to Westminster. Other rooms at the Tower are mentioned by name in connection with the reordering and storage of records in the fourteenth century. These include the 'Black Hall' (*aula nigra*) in which certain documents relating to Gascony were to be stored awaiting attention, and the 'Black Chamber' (*Nigra camera*). Other terms such as the 'inner chamber' adjacent to the Black Hall or alternatively

the 'outer chamber', likewise close by, may refer to the same room.[107]

In an essay written in 1925, Galbraith proposed that these rooms all lay within the White Tower. His paper contained an assumption that the phrase 'The Tower of London' was generally used to denote the White Tower, a usage that in fact was comparatively rare. It is, however, theoretically possible to reconcile the documentary clues with the layout of the White Tower, although not exactly as Galbraith intended. One of the medieval names, 'Black Hall' (*aula nigra*) can be conclusively identified as the west room of the White Tower's basement, on account of its containing the well: a résumé of works carried out in 1353–4 includes 'cleaning out the well in the Black Hall'.[108] It was in this Black Hall that diplomatic documents were held temporarily, before being moved wholesale into St John's Chapel, their final repository. Adjacent to the Black Hall were an outer chamber, containing the treasury of the Wardrobe – clearly the east base-

ment – and, most evocatively, the secret jewel chamber in the apsidal basement room under the chapel, into which it led.[109] Some idea of the security in these rooms is provided in a memorandum of 1323 concerning the possession of keys:

> Memorandum that the venerable Father Roger de Northburgh, now Bishop of Coventry and Lichfield, visited on the 17th November and took from Roger de Waltham, keeper of the king's wardrobe 49 keys relating to the office of the said wardrobe which he had had since the time when the said bishop had been keeper of the wardrobe before Roger de Waltham, namely four large keys of which two were the bigger and two the smaller keys of the outer chamber next to the Black Hall in the Tower of London, and forty-five small keys which were the keys of the chests containing the muniments and other memoranda of the Lord King in the same chamber . . .[110]

113 Reconstructed medieval plan
of the White Tower basement,
showing the uses of individual
rooms for storage in the 1320s.
These are (1) the 'Black Hall', a
repository for records concerning
Gascony, (2) the outer chamber,
housing part of the Treasury of the
Wardrobe and (3) the king's private
jewel chamber. These identifications
are described in detail in several
contemporary inventories.

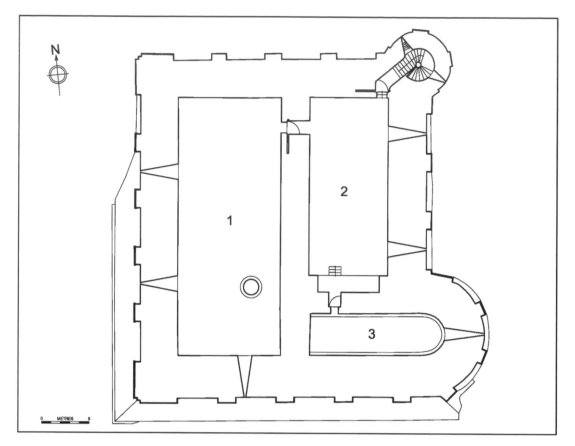

The documentary sources provide other evidence that the White Tower was used to house some elements of the Royal Treasury in the fourteenth century (fig. 113). An inventory of the treasury made early in the reign of Edward III lists the contents of several coffers or chests, each of them labelled with a letter. Several of these are described as lying 'in an upper chamber of the Tower', and containing both vessels and jewels. One of these coffers, mentioned among the contents of this upper chamber, was specifically dedicated to materials belonging to the chapel, and many of the items within it appear to have been for liturgical use.[111] From later in Edward's reign come references to 'les joialx et vesselements . . . en la Blaunche Tour deinz la Tour de Londres' and to the storage of coronation vestments 'en la Tresorie deinz la haute Toure de Londres'.[112]

The use of the White Tower as a repository for state documents certainly continued until the second half of the century, when political circumstances made it necessary to review the arrangements. The English victory at Poitiers in 1356, among other gains, brought a particularly valuable hostage, King Jean II of France. For most of his captivity in England, he lived in comfort at a variety of locations, including Windsor, Somerton in Lincolnshire and the Savoy Palace.[113] Shortly before negotiations for his ransom began at Brétigny, however, preparations were made to transfer the prisoner to the Tower of London, and specifically to the White Tower: this entailed the removal of a number of state documents to make room for him. Possibly, the relocation of the prisoner to a famous or

even infamous fortress was intended to overawe the French and persuade them to concede more generous terms, but this is unlikely, since the records for Jean's stay show his regime to have been remarkably permissive, with frequent excursions outside the castle and royal banquets both at Westminster and at the Tower (with himself as the host).[114] Alternatively, an idea of the White Tower as a building of especial antiquity or suitable for lavish ceremonial may not have been entirely forgotten, although in order to make the rooms fit for habitation, a carpenter was required to make four wooden window frames filled with oil cloth. In any event, on 28 April 1360 payment was ordered to the serjeant Jordan de Barton for

> his expenses incurred by the Council's command for the removal of the rolls and memoranda of chancery as well of the times of former kings as of the present out of the King's Great Tower of London, wherein the King, by assent of the Council, has ordered the dwelling of his adversary of France, and for placing them elsewhere, for repair of the chests and for making new aumbries for keeping the said rolls and memoranda . . . [fig. 114][115]

The new repository for these Chancery records lay in a 'certain house within the Tower': but its dilapidated condition, particularly the poor repair of its roof, gave Edward III cause for concern.[116] Two years later, some of the Chancery documents had been moved again; they now lay within a tower in the fortress, usually interpreted as the Wakefield Tower.[117] The lodging of

114 Contemporary portrait of Jean II of France (1319–64), held in comfortable captivity inside the White Tower for several months in 1360.

such an important personage as the King of France in part of the former record office would suggest that the rolls and jewels had spread by 1360 onto the first floor of the White Tower beside the chapel, probably the most prestigious accommodation afforded by the building. It is not known whether, after their removal in 1360, the White Tower was again used for the storage of records in any quantity until the sixteenth century.

The Royal Wardrobe at the Tower of London

During the fourteenth century English involvement in wars with the Scots and in the Hundred Years War placed an increasingly heavy logistical burden on several branches of the royal wardrobe, responsible for supplying and arming the king's forces. In particular, this task fell to the organisation known as the Privy Wardrobe, a permanent storehouse for arms and weaponry based inside the Tower of London.[118] Though the Tower had been used as an arsenal and arms factory throughout the Middle Ages, the emergence of a formalised department seems to have occurred in the mid-fourteenth century. At around this time, a separate organisation (the Great Wardrobe) responsible for the bulk storage of durable goods began to move out of the Tower into premises in the western part of the city near Baynard's Castle, presumably making more room available inside the fortress for military stores and records.

It is tempting to see the construction of the enormous eastern annexe to the White Tower as an attempt to provide even more storage at the Tower for these military supplies at some time in the mid-fourteenth century. This building is not explicitly mentioned in the works accounts, but a tradition of long standing attributes its construction to Edward III.[119] In the light of extensive research into Edward III's Exchequer accounts, which survive as an almost complete sequence through his reign, this dating seems less certain than it did in the nineteenth century when it was first suggested, and, most recently, Randall Storey has questioned the assumption that the medieval Privy Wardrobe in the Tower was large enough to have needed such an enormous storehouse.[120] Archaeological excavations in 1954 showed that the foundation of this building cut through a deposit containing pottery 'of the 14th century', and even suggested that the Roman city wall may have remained standing until then, the most likely context for its demolition being the construction of the new building.[121] The function and construction date of this building therefore remain mysterious. Certainly, in later periods this sector of the castle was the location of Wardrobe buildings, a usage commemorated in the name 'Wardrobe Tower', still given to the ruins of the medieval turret that formed the south-eastern corner of the eastern annexe. In the late fourteenth century some arms were undoubtedly kept in the White Tower, of which the eastern annexe was certainly later considered a component,[122] though other buildings are equally prominent in Wardrobe documents, not least the royal chambers themselves, and the rooms in St Thomas's Tower 'hanging over the water'.[123] A convenient (presently unprovable) hypothesis is that the eastern annexe was constructed during the fifteenth century, for which the documentation of the Tower is extremely sparse (fig. 115).

Inside the White Tower itself, there is architectural evidence for alteration in the fourteenth century, particularly the remodelling of doorways in the basement. Although reference has been made above to documented work on the doors of the White Tower, it is not possible to match the archaeological and documentary evidence precisely. In particular, dendrochronological analysis of the door between the eastern basement chamber and chapel basement has shown that the boards dated to some time after 1346, probably soon after.[124] Both this doorway and the door at the north end of the basement spine wall were altered, presumably at this time, although it is interesting that the new doorway openings were round-arched, with no attempt to introduce Gothic motifs into the building. The latter alteration involved the hanging of a door at the eastern end of the spine-wall passage, partially in-filling the eastern entrance where formerly the passage had opened directly from the

115 Nineteenth-century engraving of the annexe on the eastern side of the White Tower. This has conventionally been interpreted as a building connected with one of the branches of the Wardrobe.

eastern chamber. Clearly, some consideration was being given to matters of security, and circulation around the building became even more restricted, though whether this was caused by the detention of prisoners or the storage of valuables cannot be ascertained on present evidence (fig. 116).

THE TOWER IN THE LATE MIDDLE AGES

The routine use of the Tower of London and the White Tower differed little in the late fourteenth and early fifteenth centuries from that in earlier periods. The fortress remained an armoury, arsenal and store, as well as a mint, a prison and a military fortress for times of emergency. Few accounts survive for building works in this period and none gives details of alterations to the White Tower, although a reference in 1442–3 to the carriage of timber from the wharf to 'le dongeon' may indicate that works were being carried out there.[125]

116 Eastern end of the door in the spine wall connecting the east and west rooms of the basement. The present doorway is set in a blocking of a taller Norman archway. The timber door in another doorway with an identical rebate was dated by dendrochronology to the mid-fourteenth century, and it is likely that this alteration was carried out at a similar time.

The growing independence of the Privy Wardrobe as an institution, the emergence of an embryonic office of Ordnance and an ever-increasing use of artillery placed still greater emphasis on the fortress's role as an armoury and arsenal: the space allotted to these functions inside the fortress grew more extensive. Official posts were created, such as *Meistre et gardein de votre arterie deinz votre Tour de Londres*.[126] During the early fifteenth century the Patent Rolls frequently refer to the grants of houses within the Tower to officers such as the royal bowyer, the keeper of the king's armour and the royal fletcher.[127] In the middle of the century, the Ordnance was formally granted the

use of all of the eastern part of the wharf, extended in the late fourteenth century across the castle's whole river frontage.[128] In the outer ward, the Royal Mint remained a constant presence and was the subject of occasional building works throughout the period, as was the menagerie in the barbican at the south-western entrance.[129] The storage of records within the Tower likewise continued, although no evidence has yet been found to suggest that they were returned to the White Tower after the release of Jean of France. The occasional references to record storage in the fifteenth-century Patent Rolls are generally unspecific about the location and suggest that more than one building was used. For example, during the reign of Henry VI, there are mentions of 'the tower within which the rolls of the King's chancery are contained',[130] but also of the storage of records in a 'house'.[131]

Within the castle, imprisonment continued under varying conditions. Foreign hostages such as Charles, Duke of Orléans and King James I of Scotland probably lived in relative comfort.[132] At the other end of the scale, confinement could be more spartan. For example, in the reign of Richard II, orders were issued that a traitor, John Carpenter, be held in irons, a situation in which he survived for only four months.[133] In 1421 Lady Mortimer appealed to Henry V to ease her husband John's imprisonment in the Tower. She complained that he was held below ground in a chamber completely devoid of light, conditions that he was plainly finding impossible to endure.[134]

At the end of the fourteenth century there is evidence that parts of the White Tower were used for the storage of weaponry, something that is assumed for previous periods but which cannot be proven. Specifically, accounts of the Privy Wardrobe in 1382 mention the frantic clearance of chests containing armour from the Great Hall and the Queen's Chamber before the arrival of Anne of Bohemia: the armour was to be placed either in the 'tower over the water gate' or 'the Great Tower'.[135]

The Knights of the Bath

As the fourteenth century progressed, the Tower of London was perceived ever more clearly not as a royal palace but as a storehouse, armoury and arsenal, and as a prison. The royal lodgings were in most circumstances given over to ancillary functions, and the royal court usually preferred to stay at Windsor, Eltham, Langley or Westminster. It is therefore all the more remarkable and unexpected that, from the end of the fourteenth century, the Tower was chosen as a setting for an elaborate ritual to mark one of the central rites of passage in the life of a monarch: the initiation of Knights of the Bath, as a prelude to the procession to Westminster for the coronation.[136]

The origins of this ritual are admittedly obscure. The earliest firm references have generally been taken to date its inception at the Tower to the coronation of Henry IV in 1399.[137] Entries for items such as baths and beds in connection with knighting rituals, however, can be found in the Royal Wardrobe accounts from at least the thirteenth century and imply that parts of the ceremony are older.[138] It has been suggested in a recent study that the ceremony of the Bath is not peculiar to England and that it follows conventions identifiable in romance literature of the earlier Middle Ages.[139] For example, there is an allusion to making someone a 'Bathed Knight' (*cavalier bagnato*) in the Ninth Tale on the Eighth Day of Boccaccio's *Decameron*, written several decades before Henry IV's accession.[140] Whatever its origins, the ceremony was certainly not peculiar to the Tower and was often held elsewhere, as in the investiture of the future Henry VIII in the Palace of Westminster.[141] Henry V even initiated new knights at Caen while on campaign in Normandy.[142] However, it became a feature of all coronations from that of Henry IV to Elizabeth I that an investiture took place at the Tower of London two days before the ceremony, when the royal party stayed in the fortress before processing on horseback through the city to Westminster.[143]

The ritual is described in several treatises, most of which survive only in manuscripts from the sixteenth century or later. The assumption is that these late sources preserve some of the character of the ritual in its earliest manifestations, but since the period they document most compellingly is post-medieval, detailed treatment of these descriptions will be given in Chapter Six.[144] Two essential points need to be made here. The evidence is unequivocal that some form of ceremony was carried out at the Tower for the coronation of Henry IV and his successors down to Richard III in 1483. Second, there is circumstantial evidence as to the form of the ritual, and that one stage in particular took place in the White Tower. A detailed description of the coronation of Henry VII in 1485 contains the following entry, concerning the first evening of the ritual, in which the initiates took a bath and were instructed in the duties and responsibilities of knighthood:

> After that the esquires governors were assignid them and there baynes were prepared in a great chamber in the downgeon as of old tyme hath ben accustomed. And when it was night the king himself of his benigne goodnis nobly accompanyed with the Duke of Bedford, the Erle of Oxenford, the Erle of Darbie, the Erle of Devonshire with many other noble Lordes, knyghtes and Esquiers first [gave] them in the baynes the advertisement of the order of knighthode and after him other Lordes and Estatis.[145]

The words 'as of old tyme hath ben accustomed' are evidence of the most circumstantial kind: that in 1485

a chronicler wished to state that the new Tudor king was scrupulous to observe the same forms of ritual as his Yorkist opponents, and presumably the Lancastrians whose heir he claimed to be. Nevertheless, the description suggests, quite plausibly, that in the fifteenth century as in the sixteenth, the bathing took place in the White Tower.

The reasons for locating substantial elements of this ritual within the White Tower can only be guessed at. Practical details such as the huge size of the rooms, their darkness and cold, must have made the ceremony even more of an ordeal for the initiates. (The setting may even have enhanced some of the heady symbolism of light/darkness, finery/simplicity, comfort/asceticism and exaltation/humility that characterised the ritual.) Abigail Wheatley, however, has shown that the White Tower's construction was attributed by some late fourteenth-century writers to Julius Caesar: the building had plainly become associated with an impossibly remote antiquity and its origins were relegated to the stuff of mythology.[146] This ancient building may have been chosen as the setting for the royal ceremony (with its connotations of regenerating the monarchy and its knightly power base) as a deliberate attempt to harness these antique associations to the service of the monarch in the present; in short, the king was aiming to contrive a sense of continuity.

Military Engagements, Political Crises and the White Tower

The perception that the Tower of London should serve as a refuge for the royal party in times of crisis continued. For example, in the 'Appellant' crisis of 1387 disturbances against Richard II's unpopular councillors forced him unexpectedly to keep Christmas in the Tower rather than at Windsor; this change of plan obliged the Privy Wardrobe to have stone cannonballs and two *springalds* removed from the Great Hall of the royal lodgings, a striking image of the conditions in the Tower during the long royal absences.[147] The reign of Richard II also witnessed two of the most dramatic incidents in medieval English history, and in both of them the White Tower is said to have been closely involved.

The Peasants' Revolt of 1381 remains the most humiliating episode in the fairly undistinguished military history of the Tower during the Middle Ages. Soon after unrest in Kent was detected, the king and his councillors retreated to the safety of the Tower of London, where they were joined by the king's mother, Joan of Kent. Repeated attempts by Richard II to parley with the rebels failed until Friday, 14 June, when he and his entourage deemed it safe to ride out to Mile End to meet them. The events that followed their departure from the Tower are notoriously unclear. Whether through incompetence or, as seems very likely, some form of collusion between the garrison and the protestors, a party of rebels was able to penetrate the Tower's defences, almost certainly unopposed.[148] The results were disastrous. The rebels were able to enter all parts of the castle, including the royal apartments in which the king's mother had taken refuge, and, according to Froissart's later version, tearing her bed to pieces. They also took the opportunity to settle scores with Simon Sudbury, Archbishop of Canterbury, whom they found in one of the chapels of the Tower, where he had just finished Mass;[149] by tradition, this was the chapel of St John in the White Tower. Sudbury and four others were dragged from the Tower to a summary beheading outside. If all the details of this incident are true, it represents the only known occasion when the defensive capability of the White Tower was put to the test. As a refuge from attack, it proved the most dismal failure (fig. 117).

While it cannot be established with complete certainty how destructive the peasants had been inside the Tower, it has been suggested that the years immediately afterwards witnessed a series of building works to make good the damage caused by the rebels and to improve security.[150] Certainly, the works accounts mention the construction of a substantial stone house adjoining the Privy Wardrobe for John Lydwyk, keeper of the king's wardrobe, possibly to protect the keeper and some of the property in his charge against any recurrence of unrest.[151] It is also tempting to interpret the remains of the elaborate decorative painted scheme surviving in the upper chamber of the Byward Tower, and likely to date from the 1390s, as a redecoration of a room damaged by the rebels in 1381.[152]

The White Tower may also have provided a setting for events surrounding the end of Richard II's trou-

118 Manuscript illustration showing the abdication of Richard II in favour of Henry of Bolingbroke, later Henry IV. Of the many chronicles that describe this scene, only that of the Frenchman Jean Froissart places it in the White Tower, the very building in which Richard's grandfather had imprisoned the King of France in 1360.

bled reign. Having crossed into Wales from Ireland in July 1399 to deal with an invasion by the exiled Henry Bolingbroke, the king advanced slowly through Wales, his support rapidly ebbing away. Though the exact timing of the events is uncertain, it is clear that around 20 August the king was in the power of Bolingbroke and was transferred to London. By 2 September Richard was confined in the Tower.[153] Most of the accounts are unspecific about the location of the king's quarters within the fortress, merely stating that he was securely guarded. The exception is Jean Froissart, who places Richard in the White Tower, noting how apposite it was that the king should be confined in the same building in which his grandfather had imprisoned King Jean of France thirty-nine years earlier.[154] This episode may well be more of a literary interpolation than a factual account: for example, Froissart describes an entirely inaccurate or fictional scene in which the king's captors were able to intimidate him by parading his accomplices in the yard of the Tower below his window before dragging them off to execution.[155] While several accounts make extensive reference to meetings in the Tower between Richard and Bolingbroke, Froissart alone locates one of them in a 'chambre' in the 'grosse tour'.[156] Perhaps in the surroundings of the White Tower, the king's resistance broke and he became aware that his abdication in favour of Bolingbroke was a fait accompli, though the official Lancastrian account disguises his reluctance by reporting that he abdicated cheerfully and almost without hesitation (fig. 118).[157]

The fifteenth century began with characteristic violence in the 'Epiphany Rising' against the new king, Henry IV: faced with active opposition, the king followed historical precedent and retreated to the Tower with his family.[158] Throughout this turbulent century, the Tower continued to serve as a royal refuge, a prison and, on account of its stores and armoury, an important element in military strategy and action. The control of the Tower was perceived as a major advantage for any party over an opponent and, in the absence of a powerful royal authority to check the ambition of magnates, the possession of the fortress became on occasion a divisive issue. As in previous centuries, it is never specifically stated whether a military engagement at the Tower involved the White Tower, but in the context of an increasing use of artillery for assault, the *donjon*, being set well behind the curtain walls, would have provided some of the most secure lodgings (or prisons) within the fortress, while the outer buildings were more open to attack. It is known, for example, that in the summer of 1460 the Lancastrian defenders of the Tower, under the command of Lord Scales, were subjected to an artillery bombardment from the forces of the Yorkist Salisbury, positioned in Southwark on the opposite bank of the Thames; the walls of the fortress were damaged in several places.[159]

In 1471 the Tower was again seen as strategically important for the political control of London. In the previous year Edward IV had been deposed in a rapid coup by his former ally, Warwick, and replaced on the throne by the Lancastrian Henry VI. In March 1471 Edward returned to England from Burgundy and, within a month, was able to recover control of London and recapture King Henry, then staying in the Bishop of London's palace. Edward proceeded to defeat those Lancastrians still at large in battles at Barnet and Tewkesbury, killing both Warwick and Henry VI's only son, thereby extinguishing the direct succession of the Lancastrian dynasty. Following the battle of Barnet, Henry was returned as a prisoner to the Tower.[160] A third Lancastrian force remained at large, however, under the command of the Bastard of Fauconberg. In May 1471 Fauconberg attempted first to gain entry to the city, and, when this was resisted, came down the Thames from Richmond, setting fire to London Bridge and turning his guns on the city from the south bank. Part of his strategy may have been an attempt to rescue King Henry from the Tower. Edward IV's Household Accounts mention the hurried stockpiling of weapons and gunpowder in the Tower and works to the defences, including the dismantling of a wall on the eastern side and the digging of 'bulwarkes' on the riverbank, strengthened with casks filled with sand to deaden the impact of artillery.[161] Edward IV's brother-in-law, Earl Rivers, then besieged in the Tower with the queen and other members of the royal family, was able to make a sortie from a postern with a small force of Yorkists and launch a counter-attack: Fauconberg was compelled to withdraw.[162]

The death of Henry VI in the Tower on the night of Edward IV's triumphant return to London is famously unexplained. The official Yorkist account related that the king had died through 'sheer displeasure and melancholy' on hearing that his cause was lost and his son killed at Tewkesbury, although an examination of his bones in 1910 showed signs of trauma consistent with a violent death.[163] An enduring legend has it that the king's body was laid in state in St John's Chapel before being taken from the Tower and publicly displayed in St Paul's Cathedral.[164] To manhandle a corpse into St John's Chapel from outside the White Tower would inevitably be an undignified business: it would be more credible if Henry had been already imprisoned there. In view of the fact that the defenders evidently expected to be attacked from the river, it seems unlikely that such an important prisoner would be kept in the vulnerable royal lodgings beside the Thames, and a room in the White Tower is as likely a place as any. Whatever the location, payments are recorded to a clerk for officiating at the king's 'ultimum vale' in the Tower, torchbearers for accompanying his body from the castle to the cathedral and a military escort for taking it by barge to Chertsey, where he was buried.[165]

The experience of 1471 seems not to have precipitated any immediate strengthening of the Tower's defences, but around 1480 Edward IV ordered the construction of a permanent fortification in brick around the western entrance to the Tower, known as the 'Bulwark'. This represents one of the earliest adaptations of the Tower for artillery warfare, with bastions covering the two main approaches to the enclosure from Tower Hill and Great Tower Street. Whether or not the fortifications hurriedly prepared on the river bank to resist Fauconberg were retained after 1471, it is clear that the new bulwark was intended to defend the entrance of the fortress against assault from land rather than from the Thames.[166] In the following century, the poet John Skelton wrote that Edward IV had 'made the Tower strong', but in the absence of a large body of surviving buildings or documentary evidence, it is unclear exactly what this meant.[167]

Edward IV's second reign was characterised by jockeying for position at court between rival factions, with only the king himself able to maintain a political balance between the faction of his wife, Queen Elizabeth Woodville, and others suspicious of their influence. Immediately after the king's death on 9 April 1483, conflict began. The Woodville family, already in command of the young Edward V and of the Tower of London (in the person of the Marquess of Dorset, deputy constable), persuaded the Royal Council to send a fleet to sea, in the process decimating the Royal Treasury.[168] Chronicle histories suggest that the late king's brother, Richard, Duke of Gloucester, and his supporters were able to present the seizure of the Tower and the Woodvilles' unilateral dispatch of a fleet to sea as an unjustified and provocative action; this was portrayed as a pre-emptive strike against the peaceful continuity from Edward IV's reign and as the beginning of a Woodville *coup d'état*.

Believing correctly that the actions of the queen's family had alienated many, Gloucester and his ally Buckingham intercepted the group escorting the young Edward V from Ludlow and arrested his maternal uncle, Rivers, together with his stepbrother and his chamberlain. Once in control of the boy, Gloucester proceeded to the capital, presumably initiating the letter that the king wrote ahead entrusting the Tower of London and its treasury to the Archbishop of Canterbury. On arrival in London, the young Edward was first lodged in the Bishop of London's palace while preparations were made for his coronation. All the while, Gloucester made efforts to portray himself as the rescuer of the new king from the unnatural violence and ambition of his mother's affinity: he also stressed the danger that she and her allies posed to the smooth transition of rule and to his own person as Protector. In the context of a very fragile peace in the city and of preparations for a coronation, Edward V moved to the Tower at a date around 19 May. On 16 June the queen was persuaded to allow her younger son, Richard, Duke of York, to leave sanctuary in Westminster Abbey and join his brother in the Tower.

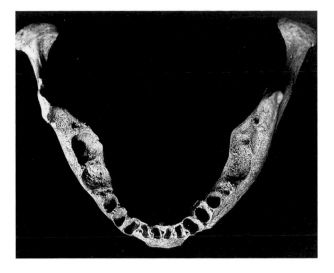

119 (*right*) Photograph showing the lower jaw of one of the supposed 'Princes in the Tower', discovered in 1674 during building works beside the White Tower and re-examined in 1933.

120 (*far right*) The modern stair against the south front of the White Tower replaces a stair demolished in 1674, during the course of which the bones of the 'Princes' were discovered. This burial place concurred with Sir Thomas More's story that the bodies of the murdered children were hidden 'at the stair-foot meetly deep in the ground under a great heap of stones', though More later added that their bodies were moved to a secret location elsewhere in the castle.

Meanwhile, Gloucester perceived what he characterised as a plot against his protectorate by the faction around the queen, leading him to appeal for help to his northern allies. In an unexpected development, during a meeting of the Royal Council in the Tower, Gloucester accused his former supporter, William, Lord Hastings, of conspiring with the queen against him, and had him summarily executed. The tradition that this meeting took place in the uppermost storey of the White Tower is certainly false; it is presently believed that no floor existed at this point before the reign of Henry VII and there is documentary evidence from earlier in the fifteenth century that the Council met 'in the King's inner chamber within his Tower of London', presumably a room within the royal lodgings to the south of the White Tower.[169] In an atmosphere of suspicion and uncertainty, rumours circulated that the sons of Edward IV were illegitimate. On 26 June the lords and commons petitioned Gloucester to accept the crown; he was immediately enthroned in the Court of King's Bench in Westminster Hall, and declared this the first day of his reign. On 4 July he and his wife, Anne, moved to the Tower of London for the preparations for their own coronation, including the investiture of new Knights of the Bath.[170] Two days later, Gloucester was crowned at Westminster as King Richard III.

The fate of the two 'Princes in the Tower' has been debated for centuries, hotly and inconclusively. In view of the activity at the Tower in preparing for Richard III's coronation, the location of their confinement is likewise uncertain. The 'Bloody Tower', the traditional site of their deaths, may have acquired its name only in the 1560s; it is not certain that the tower was associated with the story before this date.[171] Contemporary chroniclers, all of them to some extent ill informed, partial or subjective, were generally imprecise about the whereabouts of the Princes' lodging, although Dominic Mancini recounted how they were withdrawn into the inner apartments of the Tower itself ('in penitiores ipsius turris edes reducti'), where they were briefly seen behind the window bars, before they disappeared altogether.[172] This could be taken to refer to the White Tower, although such an occupation would probably have been impossible during Richard III's coronation preparations, when much of the *donjon* would have been required for the Knights of the Bath. As will be discussed in Chapter Seven, the discovery of some bones in 1674, later claimed as those of the 'Princes in the Tower', has been taken to strengthen the association of this infamous episode with the White Tower (figs 119, 120). But, as ever at the Tower of London, the body of tradition and legend on the one hand, and revisionist history on the other, have ensured that there is no shortage of alternative storylines and locations.

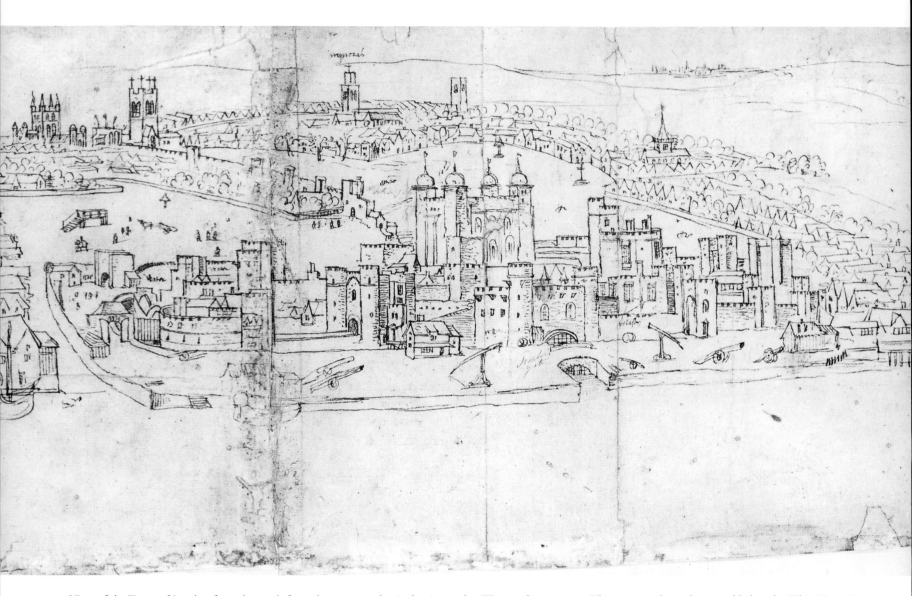

121   View of the Tower of London from the south from the panorama by Anthonis van den Wyngaerde, *circa* 1544. The ogee cupolas and vanes added to the White Tower in 1532–3 can be seen clearly, as can the rectangular form of the twelfth-century forebuilding.

CHAPTER SIX

The White Tower, 1485–1642

ANNA KEAY AND ROLAND B. HARRIS

In the period 1485–1642 the Ordnance and Armoury offices dominated the White Tower. Given that the building continued to function as a repository for highly valuable, and often flammable, commodities including regalia and state records, its growing use as a gunpowder store is remarkable. Tellingly, the Tudor monarchs continued to use the keep for royal ceremonial events, uncomfortable and inconvenient as this must have been. Structurally, this period is delimited by major works – the insertion of a second floor and the raising of the roof *circa* 1490, and, in 1638, the first and most extensive replacement of medieval ashlar with Portland stone.

THE REBUILDING OF *CIRCA* 1490

Today, the roofs of the east and west rooms of the White Tower are a storey higher than they were when it was first built.[1] The earliest evidence of the creation of a new, higher, roof is provided by the surviving roof structure (fig. 122). Dendrochronological analysis has established that the timbers for a ridge piece, tie-beam, purlin and rafter were felled between spring 1489 and spring 1490.[2] The roofs of both east and west rooms and the chapel are of entirely consistent form and technique, and their construction can therefore be placed within a year or two of 1490.[3] Documentary accounts for this period are sporadic and no reference has so far been found to these works. There is structural evidence, however, to show that the rebuilding of the roofs was accompanied by the insertion of new floors at the level of the mural passages, thereby creating second floors in the east and west rooms for the first time.

A crucial piece of evidence for such flooring was preserved in the spine wall at this second-floor level, for, despite the successive rebuildings of the floors of the east and west rooms in the seventeenth and eighteenth centuries, an area of earlier floorboards remains under the southernmost arch. These boards produced a felling date of spring 1488, consistent with that of the roof timbers.[4] Moreover, excavation of the floor surfaces under these boards and in the east and west mural passages in 1996–7 revealed joist sockets.[5] These sockets were located in a band of mortar that was sharply differentiated from the eleventh-century fabric, and which matches the mortar used in the thickening of the west wall of the chapel roof space necessary to carry the roof of *circa* 1490. In the absence of any evidence for an earlier roof at the higher level or for an earlier second floor, it is probable that these joist sockets formed part of the works of that time.[6]

While the analysis of the surviving fabric provides sufficient grounds for dating the creation of the second floor to *circa* 1490, the absence of direct documentary evidence is unfortunate, for it deprives us of any certain historical context for the remodelling. The new floor to the White Tower increased the amount of space within the keep by about a third. The two great rooms that were created were not equipped with fireplaces or garderobes, and there is no evidence that they were ever domestic in function. The likelihood must be that they were intended from the outset to

serve for military storage, as they certainly did from the mid-sixteenth century. It is not surprising, perhaps, that the greatest alteration the White Tower ever saw was, like its creation, the work of a king who had seized the throne by force and was in the process of consolidating a new dynasty. In the years after he took the English throne in 1485, Henry VII was to have frequent reason to call the military infrastructure of his new country into action. Two years after Bosworth, he fought the battle of Stoke against a sizeable army of Irishmen and foreign mercenaries, funded partly from Burgundy by the powerful Margaret of York. In April 1489, in honour of his pledge to help the dukes of Brittany maintain independence from France, the king dispatched an army of 6,000 men to the Continent. Three years later he would ride out himself at the head of a much greater force and audaciously assert English sovereignty over France. Though a serious campaign never came to pass, it was perhaps in these circumstances that a massive increase in the capacity of the White Tower was considered necessary, and the building's status as Tudor England's greatest arsenal confirmed.[7]

HENRY VIII AND THE TOWER OF LONDON

The next campaign of work at the White Tower was carried out in the 1530s. A detailed estimate for com-

prehensive works to nearly all the Tower of London's mural towers and defensive walls had been prepared sometime before 1532.[8] If acted upon, those works would have seen the outer defences brought into a really good overall state of repair for perhaps the first time since their construction, but nothing was planned for the White Tower itself. The works actually commissioned in the early summer of 1532, however, were rather different in nature. Instead of amounting to a campaign of general repair, they centred around the royal lodgings, and the queen's apartments in particular. The likely reason seems clear: in the summer of 1532 it was reported that arrangements were to begin for the king's marriage to Anne Boleyn and for her coronation; and on the eve of a coronation the royal party always lodged at the Tower of London.[9]

During the autumn and winter of 1532 the Tower was seething with activity: in October Thomas Cromwell was pressing for news on progress and was assured that a workforce of some four hundred men was employed there. The king himself visited at least twice to view the works: on 5 December he came with the French ambassador and four days later he brought Anne Boleyn herself to see what was being done.[10] The main focus of all this activity was the royal lodgings, but there were also two strands of works at the White Tower. These involved repairs to the structure's exte-

rior, perhaps to make it a suitable backdrop to the pre-coronation celebrations, and fitting-up for the creation of Knights of the Bath (below). Masonry repairs at this time concentrated on the upper parts of the building and involved the replacement of the battlements and some quoins.[11] During the repair programme of 1997–8, a high concentration of Caen stone was identified in the quoins and battlements of the south elevation. These blocks had apparently first been cut and set as coping stones, probably as part of the improvements to the White Tower during the 1530s. They were later reset in their current positions as plain facings, presumably when the battlements were again rebuilt, this time in Portland stone, in 1638–9.[12] Similarly, the prevalence of reset Caen stone in the upper parts of the two eastern buttresses of this elevation could represent reuse of sixteenth-century material rather than that of the eleventh century: the Caen stone of the lower parts of the buttresses is largely identifiable as part of the primary construction of the White Tower and would have been obscured in 1532 by the fore-building and the Jewel House (below). It was also during these works that the four turrets acquired their distinctive ogee cupolas,[13] of which the original carpentry survives: timbers in the north-east turret, which include ogee braces, produced felling dates ranging from spring 1532 to spring 1533.[14] Top-floor joists in the south-east turret probably also belong to this work, since two sampled timbers show that they were felled in the years 1503–35 and after 1515. That the works of 1532 included floors in the turrets is confirmed by the reference to the framing of a floor for the north-east

turret.[15] The new cupolas were then surmounted by 'great' weather vanes, supplied and gilded by the Italian royal painter Ellys Carmyan (figs 121, 123).[16]

Despite all this, the building work was by no means finished by the time of Anne Boleyn's coronation. In particular, the worrying state of the roof of the White Tower remained to be addressed, and on 26 July 1534 the Surveyor of the King's Works, James Nedeham, reported to Thomas Cromwell that 'the Rof of the White Tower as yo[r] maistership knowith well ynough must nede have great rep[er]acions'.[17] This does not appear to reflect general deterioration of the roof of *circa* 1490, but rather localised structural failure. In 1536 substantial works to the roof were undertaken, apparently concentrating on the northern part of the structure and probably the western room in particular. A massive beam had been felled and fetched from Stratford, to the east of London, in 1532, apparently in preparation for this work.[18] If so, it reveals a relaxed timescale for the repairs and makes the decision in 1534 to mount guns on the roof, which if carried out would have exacerbated any structural failure, rather surprising.[19] In 1535 a gin was built in readiness for hauling the beam up to the roof and set into the side walls ready to support posts and brackets to strengthen the roof trusses.[20] This suggests failure of a single tie-beam, with all trusses reinforced to prevent similar problems occurring elsewhere. In 1536 work on the masonry for the brackets was completed, the roof raised into place using jacks or 'screwes' and the brackets installed; the great beam was framed, raised and fitted at the north end, and the planking and lead there were made good.[21] In 1536 Cromwell was able to record among his list of 'things done by the King's highness sythyn I came to his service': 'he hath repaired the Tower of London'.[22]

THE CORONATION AND THE KNIGHTS OF THE BATH

The rituals associated with the creation of the Knights of the Bath were the only royal ceremonies that continued to take place within the White Tower after the Middle Ages. Knights of the Bath were created sporadically, normally on the eve of primary royal occasions, such as marriages and coronations. In the case of coronations, the knights were usually created at the Tower of London, where the monarch normally lodged before the magnificent procession to Westminster (fig. 124). The ceremonies that surrounded their investiture consisted of an evening dinner, bathing and instruction, a nocturnal vigil in a chapel and the investiture itself, and finished with a meal.[23] Knights of the Bath were created at the Tower immediately before the coronation processions of Henry VII,[24] Elizabeth of York,[25] Henry VIII,[26] Anne Boleyn,[27] Mary I[28] and Elizabeth I.[29] The White Tower was usually, and perhaps always, used for the bathing of the Knights

of the Bath in the Tudor period, and the account of Henry VII's coronation clearly indicates that it was considered the historic location for the event.[30] Elizabeth I was the last English monarch to spend the eve of her coronation at the Tower of London, and therefore this was the last occasion on which Knights of the Bath were created there. James I's coronation was to be preceded by the creation of Knights of the Bath at the Tower, but the ferocity of the plague then raging in London caused the cancellation of both the visit to the Tower and the coronation procession with only a fortnight to go. The knights were instead created at St James's Palace.[31] Some preparations were made at the Tower for the coronation of his son in 1625–6, but in the event Charles I went to the abbey directly from Whitehall, and those created Knights of the Bath were ordered to present themselves at Westminster, not the Tower, on 30 January.[32] At the Restoration, the monarch's pre-coronation sojourn at the Tower, which had not taken place for a century, was abandoned completely. By this time the poor state of what remained of the royal lodgings would have been a real deterrent to royal residence of any kind, and in 1661 the Knights of the Bath were instead created at Westminster.[33]

Several versions, in early Tudor script, survive of the instructions for the creation of the Knights of the Bath, and describe how the bathing ceremony was to be conducted. Baths, 'wrapped with lynen cloth clene and whyte and covered with thycke carpettes or mantelles for the colde of the nyght', were to be set up; alongside each was a bed 'withoute celour or courteyns' (fig. 125).[34] The White Tower itself was decorated with textiles for the creation of the knights, as was much of the Tower of London, and indeed the entire route of the coronation procession from the

Tower to Westminster.[35] While a proportion of the vast quantity of rich fabric provided for the coronation of Henry VII was certainly used to decorate the Tower,[36] it is with regard to the ceremony at the coronations of Anne Boleyn and Elizabeth I that details survive of how this was used in the White Tower. In 1533 a chamber there was provided with eighteen baths and equipped with rails 'to be hangid for the knyghts of the bathe', while in 1559 eleven baths were set up, covered in white fabric and shaded by canopies bearing the knights' arms. Alongside each, contrary to the rubric, stood a bed hung with curtains of silk and gold.[37] In 2005 a series of features was identified on the timber roof beams of the White Tower that may be the remnants of such decorative arrangements (fig. 126). The preparations for the creation of sixty-two knights at the coronation of James I in 1603 had only just started before plague aborted the occasion, with plasterers preparing 'Casars hall' in the White Tower and new planks being laid over its broken floors.[38]

Contemporary accounts make it clear that the ceremonies of the creation of the Knights of the Bath took place largely within the White Tower; furthermore, they also make it possible to identify where within the building they took place. The evidence for the bathing of the Knights of the Bath at Anne Boleyn's coronation indicates that it happened on the top floor (the works to the roof in 1536 were 'over' the room in question), and the description of a 'long' chamber suggests that it was the west room.[39] The west room on the top floor was certainly that, called 'Caesar's Hall', prepared for use by the Knights of the Bath in 1603. Accounts for the replacement of the western uppermost floor in 1604–5 show that the planks that were used had been

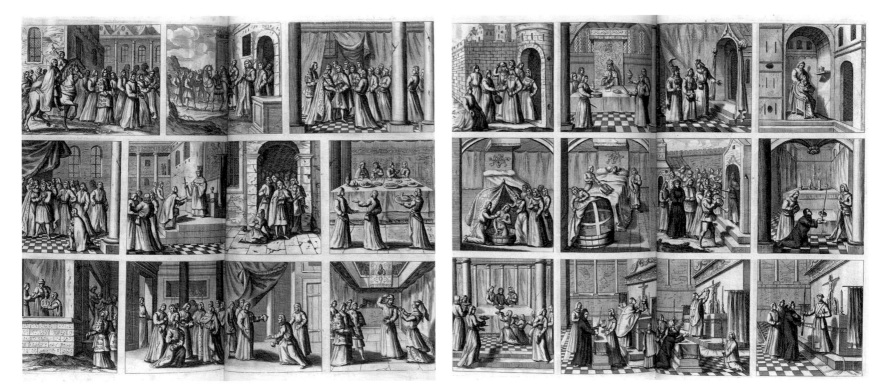

125 (*left and right*) The ceremonies of the creation of the Knights of the Bath, engraved for Edward Bysshe's edition of Nicholas Upton's military treatise, published as *Nicholai Uptoni in studio militaris* in 1654. The illustrations derive from the early Tudor 'Garter book' of the herald John Writhe (died 1504). Although it does not represent the Tower of London naturalistically, the series clearly shows the events happening in a medieval castle.

sawn two years previously and laid there temporarily for the benefit of the Knights of the Bath (see below), while a reference to the new floor stretching all the length of the White Tower indicates that it is the western room that is being referred to.[40] The knights created on the eve of Queen Elizabeth's coronation had their baths laid out in a 'hall', which may also describe this room.[41] Interestingly, in 1559 the banquet for the knights elect, usually held in the buildings of a royal palace, was also held in the White Tower; this was probably because the great hall was, at this date, unusable, being 'in very great decaye so as it is lyke to fall'.[42]

In using a second floor that had probably been inserted only as recently as *circa* 1490, the Tudor ceremony of the Knights of the Bath must have differed in this detail at least from what went before. Knights of the Bath, however, had long been created in a great variety of places, so such a minor change is not especially significant in the history of the ceremony.[43] More interesting are any implications of changes in the use of the White Tower, for it may be that the top floor was used in the sixteenth century because the lower storeys were no longer available or suitable for such sporadic yet splendid occasions. This is further suggested by the fact that at least by 1559 the chapel to which the knights repaired was not the chapel of St John, but the free-standing chapel of St Peter ad Vincula in the Middle Ward. The detailed account of the creation of the knights in January 1559 describes them leaving the White Tower for prayers in 'the Church'; after hearing mass the knights, accompanied by heralds and musicians, returned 'to the White Tower . . . daunsinge and leaping'.[44] It is possible that the chapel of St Peter was also used in 1533 and that

the swift construction of a new timber staircase at that date was to allow the knights to process to St Peter's from the top floor of the keep.[45] Although there is no definite evidence that the chapel of St John had ever been used by the knights, it seems likely that it had been at some point; this is also suggested by the magnificent illustration in Writhe's 'Garter book' showing the vigil of the Knights of the Bath taking place in the chapel of a great keep (see fig. 125). It may be that by 1559 the chapel of St John was otherwise employed, or simply that since its reconstruction in 1519–20 the chapel of St Peter was thought a grander and more appropriate location for this solemn ceremony.[46]

THE WARDROBE

Nearly all the departments that used the White Tower in this period had grown out of the medieval Wardrobe; the records, the arms and armour, and the jewels of the crown had all once been within its fold. By the sixteenth century a variety of specialist household and state departments had evolved that had responsibility for distinct types of royal equipment. The Great Wardrobe, part of the Lord Chamberlain's department, with its own headquarters outside the court on the western side of the city, near Baynard's Castle, was responsible for the supply, transport, storage and maintenance of the monarch's furniture, and the Wardrobe of the Robes for the clothes of the sovereign and royal family and all household liveries.[47] Both had major storehouses at the Tower of London. Though technically two separate departments, the two Wardrobes shared staff and suppliers and certainly had adjacent if not shared accommodation at the Tower.[48]

Although the evidence is not complete, it seems likely that in the sixteenth century the eastern annexe

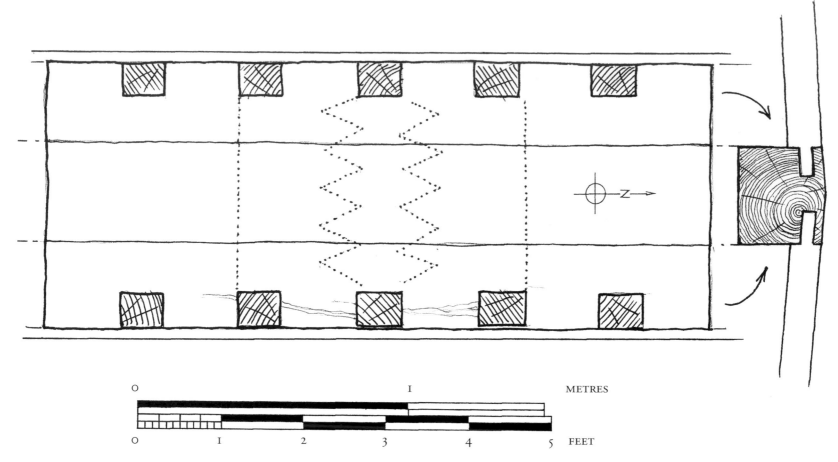

O   I   METRES

O   I   2   3   4   5   FEET

126 The roof of *circa* 1490 at the southern end of the western room. This shows primary mortices in the soffit of the tie-beam, and the chevron pattern of tacks on the soffit and sides of the adjacent ridge: both appear to relate to a decorative treatment at this end of the room, evidently more complex than a transverse screen and which combined timber and a cloth hanging.

of the White Tower was part of the complex of buildings used by the Royal Wardrobes.[49] This is suggested for a number of reasons. The area to the east of the keep was clearly dominated by Wardrobe accommodation: the tower at the south-east corner of the annexe was called the 'Warderoap Tower', and in 1532–3 a substantial new building for the Wardrobe was erected, running east–west between the eastern annexe of the White Tower and the Broad Arrow Tower (fig. 127).[50] This new building probably replaced an earlier Wardrobe building in the same location, since in the estimate that preceded these works the Broad Arrow Tower is already described as being at the 'east end' of the Wardrobe, and both may have been extensions of Wardrobe accommodation in the eastern annexe.[51] Further evidence for the eastern annexe functioning as a Wardrobe repository is to be found in the 1650s, when it was adapted to serve for gunpowder storage and proofing, discussed in pages 181–2 below.

What evidence there is suggests that both the Great Wardrobe and the Wardrobe of the Robes had rooms in the eastern annexe of the White Tower and its adjoining buildings.[52] The inventory made of Henry VIII's goods on his death in 1547 demonstrates just how valuable the contents of these buildings were. In addition to the numerous beds, carpets, cushions and canopies, the Tower was home to many of the great Tudor suites of tapestry, including sets depicting the

Life of David, the *Deeds of Hercules* and the *Seven Deadly Sins*—some of the most spectacular and valuable pieces of decorative art anywhere in the kingdom (fig. 128).[53] Foreign visitors to the Tower who were shown the collections recognised them as being among the wonders of the land, and the surviving written accounts invariably include breathless descriptions of the magnificent tapestries, cloth of gold hangings, state beds and jewel-encrusted fabrics.[54] Because these fragile items were stored for months, even years, on end at the Tower, a careful regime was maintained to keep them from decay. The clothes and furniture were stored in an assortment of presses, coffers, bags, baskets and custom-made cases.[55] Garments and tapestries were hung on rails or ropes operated by pulleys, to allow airing, and a special supply of coal was maintained to the Wardrobes at the Tower to burn fires in the stores.[56]

THE JEWEL HOUSE

As has been discussed in Chapter Five, the White Tower was certainly home to jewels and plate belonging to the monarch in the reign of Edward III, and quite probably well before then.[57] By the reign of Edward IV, the office of the Jewel House, which was responsible for the king's jewels and plate, was staffed by a keeper, a clerk, a yeoman and a groom.[58] The post of keeper was held in tandem with that of treasurer of the chamber in the fifteenth century, but had

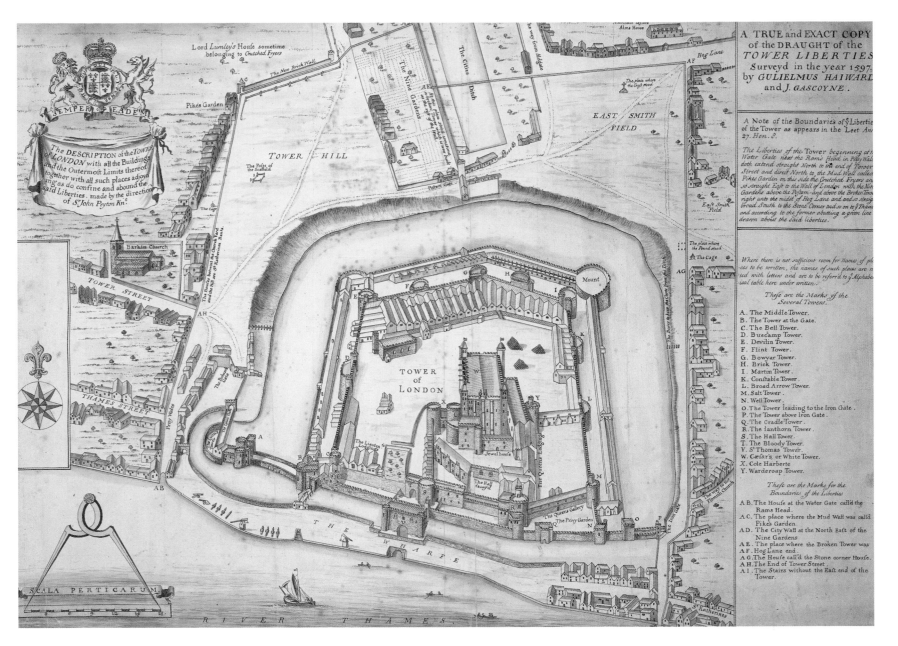

127 The Tower of London in 1597 by William Haiward and John Gascoyne, a copy of the lost original made in 1741. This combined measured plan and bird's-eye view is the best visual source for several of the clusters of structures that grew up to the south and east of the keep in the later Middle Ages. Shown clearly are the Coldharbour Gate (x), the forebuilding, the standing jewel house, the eastern annexe, the Wardrobe Tower (y) and the Tudor Wardrobe range.

apparently become separated from that position, and was a distinct department, by the reign of Henry VIII.[59] The department was responsible for the storage and transport of the regalia and plate belonging to the king, and had repositories (jewel houses) in the larger of the palaces (fig. 129).

By the early sixteenth century these items were no longer stored within the main structure of the White Tower, but in dedicated buildings that stood very close to it. The evidence for these buildings is complex, and begins with the construction of a jewel house by Henry VII: money was paid to John Henry in 1508 for 'the making of the Juellhouse wtin the to[we]r of london'.[60] There is nothing in this reference to link this building with the White Tower, but this can be deduced from later developments. A plan to have the office of the Jewel House in the Tower of London 'newe made', which was recorded in the estimate preceding the works of 1532, was not fully executed until 1535, and only minor works were carried out in the intervening years.[61] No doubt the fact that Thomas

Cromwell himself was Keeper of the Jewel House ensured that the buildings of that office received the attention they required.[62] In 1535 the Tower was already equipped with two jewel-house buildings: one abutting the White Tower, which was re-roofed in the early months of 1535, and another very near by, described as adjoining the king's great buttery, which was entirely rebuilt in the summer of 1535.[63] The latter was 'old' in early 1535,[64] so it was presumably the former, adjoining the south face of the White Tower, that was built by Henry VII in 1508.[65] This jewel house to the south of the White Tower was demolished in 1669,[66] but it is shown in Haiward and Gascoyne's survey of 1597 (fig. 127). While evident inaccuracies in minor details of the White Tower urge caution in the use of the survey, it is reliable in its depiction of the position, scale and general form of the various buildings at the Tower.[67] Therefore, it can be safely assumed that, by the end of the sixteenth century, the Jewel House adjoining the White Tower was a long, low structure extending along most of the south front,

167

128 *The Labours of Hercules,* woven for Henry VIII in Brussels in the early 1540s and among the tapestries listed in the Great Wardrobe store at the Tower of London in 1547.

abutting the forebuilding to the west and projecting southwards by a comparable distance. The Jewel House is shown with a central doorway, windows for two floors, a low mono-pitch roof and battlements.[68] A turret, round in the view of 1597 but polygonal in Hollar's drawing of *circa* 1640–60 (see fig. 59) marks the junction of the Jewel House and forebuilding and, in view of its exterior doorway, could have provided access to either building.[69] The height of the Jewel House is less certain, since Haiward and Gascoyne's survey is the only source and is ambiguous in its depiction of the main bands of fenestration on the White Tower. That the Jewel House comprised, at the most, two storeys, however, is indicated by the fact that it is shown as half the height of the forebuilding. This suggests that the Jewel House abutted the south elevation just below the entrance-floor windows. The sills of these windows are approximately 8.5 m (28 ft) above modern ground level, thus leaving ample height for

two floors. Some further evidence for this is provided by a description of 1535 of 'the stayres goyng upe to the old juellhouse of the whyte towre'.[70]

Inevitably, the internal arrangements of the Jewel House against the White Tower are more difficult to reconstruct. There are no detailed accounts for construction, and the only information about the interior given in those for the roof repairs of 1535 is that there was a wainscot ceiling immediately below the roof.[71] Although little is known of the layout of the Jewel House other than that it most probably comprised two storeys, it is clear that the construction of this building, whether in 1508 or earlier, marked, or followed, the end of the use of the main entrance: it occupied the space where the main stair to the White Tower formerly stood, and possibly where the Constable's Hall was located from the early fourteenth century.[72] Certainly, from 1508 there could not have been a great entrance stair across the south face,

168

129 Detail of *Charles I* by Sir Anthony Van Dyck, 1636. In the sixteenth and early seventeenth centuries the state regalia, including the king's state crown, was kept at the Tower of London, while the coronation regalia was housed at Westminster.

though it may be that the Jewel House did not abut the forebuilding and so left room for a modified stair to the forebuilding in this area. The independent access to the first floor via the intramural spiral staircase, created some time after 1350, starts 4.3 m above modern ground level, and must always have required an external stair to reach it. By 1663 the stairs were within an adjoining brick tower, but how access to it worked before the Restoration is unclear. The height of the doorway to the stair is consistent with the eleventh- and twelfth-century arrangement, with the stair across the south front, a modified stair to the forebuilding (either after the construction of the Jewel House or the earlier Constable's Hall), or even with access from the first floor of the Jewel House (should it have abutted the forebuilding).

The two jewel houses had different functions: that adjoining the buttery contained the removing plate, while the other, adjoining the White Tower, was the standing Jewel House.[73] That is to say, the former was home to a changing assortment of precious objects, and the latter had constant charge of a collection of items.[74] Whereas the removing Jewel House of plate seems to have contained the administrative part of the office, the Jewel House adjoining the White Tower may have been little more than a strongroom for the storage of precious objects called on infrequently.[75] The contents of the latter building were stored in 'cases' (for the jewels), chests (for the plate) and presses.[76] These receptacles, and the doors, were provided with locks, and the glass windows with iron casements.[77] Assuming that no great change occurred in the use of these buildings in the next century, the 'upper' and 'lower' jewel houses described in 1649 would seem to equate to the 'White Tower' and 'buttery' jewel houses of 1535–6, respectively.[78] By the 1640s, at least, the upper Jewel House was in the charge of the Keeper of the Jewel House, the lower of the

groom of that office.[79] The collections of the jewel houses were shown to visitors to the Tower providing they were wealthy enough to pay or important enough not to, though in this period the jewel houses were less shown, it seems, than the Wardrobes or Armoury. James I personally took Christian IV of Denmark into the Jewel House in 1606, where 'were presented the more rare and richest jewels and beawtifull plate'.[80]

RECORD REPOSITORY

As has been discussed above, the records of institutions of state had been housed within the Tower since the fourteenth century at least, and the castle became associated particularly with the storage of the records of Chancery.[81] The estimate that preceded the works of 1532–3 describes the Wakefield Tower on the inner curtain wall as the 'tower where the kyngs records lyeth', as they may well have done since their removal from the White Tower to allow the imprisonment there of King Jean of France in 1360.[82] Thereafter the White Tower is not known to have been used for record storage again until the 1560s.[83]

The squalor of the conditions in which the Tower records were kept came to the fore in the early years of Elizabeth I's reign. In 1564 a dispute had broken out between Edward, Lord Stafford, an Exchequer chamberlain, and William Bowyer, Keeper of the Tower Records. The argument principally concerned administrative jurisdiction over the records at the Tower, but it also brought to light the worrying state of the Tower records. In particular, complaint was made that the records had been dispersed within the Tower and that some had recently been happened upon lying forgotten and fast disintegrating; in this manner, 'for lacke of good keping', many of the records had been 'ymbecillid awaie'.[84] The case was settled in Bowyer's favour, and in 1567 it was decided that all the Chancery records from 1483 to 1553 should be transferred into his care and that new records accommodation should be provided.[85]

In May 1567 the warrant for moving the Chancery records of the preceding five reigns to the Tower was drawn up.[86] It stated that the records had not been moved before because of the absence of an appropriate place in the Tower to store them, but that the transfer could now take place because the Lord Treasurer, William Paulet, Marquis of Winchester, had found such a place. The chosen 'convenyent place' was 'the great Tower in the Tower of London', and it remained only for some repairs to be done there for the transfer to go ahead.[87] The Elizabethan accounts do not indicate which room in the White Tower was to be used for the records, but it seems likely that it was the chapel of St John. This room was certainly being used for the storage of records in the mid-seventeenth century, while in the early years of the eighteenth century the Wakefield Tower and the chapel of St John were still the only repositories and there is no evidence of any movements of records in the interim:[88] as has been discussed above, by 1559 the ceremonies associated with the creation of Knights of the Bath no longer made any use of the chapel of St John, and there is in fact no firm evidence of its use for any sort of worship in the sixteenth century. After some delay to the necessary work in May 1569, Cecil was prompted to re-start it and it was completed in 1570.[89] In the event, the expected Chancery records were never transferred, but the Keeper of the Tower Records presumably made use of the new accommodation that had been provided for them.[90]

In the early seventeenth century the Record Office in the Tower was staffed by two clerks. They were charged with making searches among the records for others and with care of the collection; and also, increasingly, were engaged in organising and calendaring the documents.[91] In 1602 William Lambarde, Keeper of the Tower Records, proudly presented Elizabeth I with his six-volume calendar, of which she remarked that nothing had given her such pleasure since the start of her reign.[92] The records were frequently used by all sorts of individuals and institutions as sources of evidence and precedents with which to settle legal disputes.[93] A fee was charged for searching the documents in the Tower, which was at this time levied per day.[94] Many records, however, remained unavailable to private searchers.[95] The administrative part of the Tower Record Office was housed in the Wakefield Tower, close to which was the lodging assigned to the Clerk or Keeper of the Tower Records, known as 'Bowyer's House', doubtless after the tenacious William Bowyer. The White Tower functioned as the stacks for less-used parts of the collection.[96] Despite the considerable efforts of various individuals in collating and calendaring the records, and the provision of presses and cupboards for their storage, the records at the Tower seem to have been in a fairly chaotic state in this period.[97]

MILITARY USE

The offices of the Ordnance and Armoury were set up on very much the same terms in the fifteenth century, both emerging from the department of the Privy Wardrobe that had had charge of all weapons and armour at the Tower until that time.[98] Both offices were concerned with military supply. As their names suggest, the Armoury was responsible for protective armour of all descriptions, including helmets, shields and mail, while the Ordnance dealt with the supply of artillery, gunpowder and the endless accoutrements necessary for the use of firearms at this date. Although they were in theory two quite separate institutions, each with its own staff and premises, in reality the two overlapped considerably in terms of personnel,[99] buildings,[100] and what they supplied.[101]

The fate of these two institutions in this period was to be dictated by the changing nature of warfare. During the period covered by this chapter, the old missile weapons of bow and arrow were permanently eclipsed by firearms. As the Ordnance Office expanded rapidly to provide for this, the Armoury Office became gradually less important. Armour had ceased to play a real part in modern warfare by the end of the seventeenth century. It has been noted that the Armoury issue books show only eighty-eight issues of armour to have been made in the course of thirty-two years from 1682.[102] The Armoury Office was to be incorporated into the Ordnance Office in 1671, but their merger was proposed as early as 1630, on the basis that the informal 'mixture of the offices' had already taken place and was causing 'much confusion and error in the accompts'.[103]

Armoury

Before the Civil War the Armoury used the Tower largely for the storage and maintenance of its equipment. Unlike the Ordnance Office, the Armoury did not have its headquarters at the Tower, and its most conspicuous presence was at Greenwich Palace, where highly skilled foreign armourers had been installed by Henry VIII to make elaborate armour for the monarch and his family.[104] Although much of the Armoury's work revolved around producing pieces of the highest quality, it also supplied armour to ordinary troops, though it usually did not manufacture these itself. As was explained in a report of 1630:

> At the tower . . . no armours have been made: neither doth the office of the Armorie make provision of armes for service against an enimie. But in effect is imploied only in reparing decaied armours and making clean the armer in store.[105]

Apart from the Tower, armour was also kept at Hampton Court, Windsor and Westminster.[106] The first evidence of the Armoury using the White Tower as a repository occurs in 1567 when an account was rendered for 'making framing and finyshing twoe newe Armouries in the white Tower'.[107] This work seems to have been carried out at the same time as that for the Record Office (see above). As with the Record Office, work paused in spring 1569, but was completed by 1570.[108]

The armouries provided in 1570 do not appear to have sufficed for long. On 1 July 1580 commissioners for the office of the Armoury appointed a group of men to inspect the armouries in the Tower of London, and to consider the state of the stores and the cost of putting them in order. The report of 26 August included an estimate for making rooms in the White Tower for 'placeing and hanging upp of all the armoure',[109] but there is no evidence that the work was carried out. Indeed, if the subsequent condition of the armour is anything to go by, it seems unlikely that any improvements were made in 1580. In 1588 the helmets being supplied from the Tower were in such bad condition that men were refusing to wear them, and the Earl of Leicester demanded that 'hir ma[ts] Armoury be better looked to'.[110] Sir Henry Lee's examination of the state of the armour and weapons throughout the realm of 1589 showed the Tower armouries to be in a sorry state, although he argued that this was simply the result of many of its charges being recently used in service.[111]

The growing obsolescence of the office is visible in the early seventeenth century. A report of 1628 found that 'the Armorers did litle or no woorke for want of an overseer or surveigher', and recommended that two surveyors could be appointed without employing more staff, 'because Brigandines [a form of body armour] were now out of use', and the Brigander's post could be dissolved.[112] By 1630 the Armoury had ceased even importing armour itself, the Ordnance having taken over that task,[113] and this was symptomatic of a transfer of responsibilities for a whole range of items formerly the Armoury's concern.[114] The report of 1630 suggested that the armoury at Greenwich be disbanded because 'their are now no armes at Greenwich w[ch] are serviceable for the warres', although this disbanding had been largely achieved, since most business had transferred previously to the Tower. The dominance of the Ordnance Office was fully recognised, and the report suggested that the Armoury be 'reduced to a subalternal relation to the office of the ordinance'.

Ordnance

As the Armoury declined in this period, so the Ordnance Office prospered. By 1580 the Ordnance Office had a salaried staff of seventeen, besides more than a hundred gunners and 'cannonneers', while the Armoury had only five officers in addition to the twenty armourers employed at Greenwich.[115] The expansion of the Ordnance Office meant that it was constantly in need of more room; like the Armoury, it did not manufacture the goods that it supplied, but it did store and repair them, and this required considerable space. The Ordnance Office was given premises within the Tower of London in the mid-fifteenth century, and by the early sixteenth century had extensive buildings to the north of the White Tower against the inner curtain wall, which were rebuilt in 1514 and again in the years 1545–7.[116] These buildings provided accommodation for both Ordnance and Armoury stores, but were not big enough to contain all their charges. Certainly from the mid-sixteenth century, but very likely from much earlier, the White Tower was used to store military equipment. This became the predominant function of the building to the extent that in 1623 the White Tower was described as 'y[e] battery and Storehouse for y[e] Magazen', and by 1641 was considered to 'belong' to the Ordnance Office.[117]

One of the stores with which the Ordnance Office had to be particularly careful was gunpowder, and the saltpetre that was its main constituent. Although gunpowder was not manufactured within the Tower, both saltpetre and gunpowder were stored there. A 'powder house' within the Tower is mentioned in 1461, and powder was certainly kept within the White Tower by the end of the sixteenth century, when efforts were made to improve its storage there.[118] This work, in 1594 and 1595, involved setting up wooden doors and windows in the White Tower powder room 'for defence of lightringe and other like dangers'.[119] Again, it is unclear exactly where in the White Tower the powder was kept: the three new wainscot doors made in December 1595 were for 'the estend of the powder lofte in the Whitte Tower'.[120] It is possible that these were trapdoors, as has been suggested,[121] this being consistent with the use of the term 'loft', which indicates that powder was kept at an upper level. The choice of an upper room would have been sensible, given that gunpowder was vulnerable to damp.[122] Although the basement of the building was occasionally used for storing powder, such use was greatly disapproved of: partly because of the damp conditions but, more importantly, because the darkness of such underground rooms caused candles to be lit there.[123]

Despite the work of the mid-1590s, the provisions made for the storage of powder in the White Tower were considered insufficient, and powder 'which was wont to be stowed in vaults or in the White Tower' was being kept in other buildings, including, it appears, the Ordnance Office itself, to the north of the chapel of St Peter ad Vincula.[124] This situation had not been resolved by 1598, when a full-scale inquiry into the state of the Ordnance Office deplored the practice.[125] The risks presented by inadequate provision for powder storage had been pointed out by William Partheriche four years before, when he had written to Sir Robert Cecil asking him to consider the high risk of an explosion in the Tower.[126] Although more than 2,000 barrels of gunpowder were already being stored in the White Tower, the report of 1598 considered that the space there was too restricted; as a consequence, gunpowder was being stored in unsuitable places elsewhere in the castle, while in the keep, 'for lack of convenient roome wee are constrained to heape and pile the new powder uppon the olde'. The solution was to convert more of the building to ordered gunpowder storage, and works were ordered to begin immediately.[127]

In the event, the creation of the powder house did not occur until 1604–5, when a new floor was laid for that reason 'all the length of the great white tower'.[128] It seems likely that the delay was due, in part, to the

ADVERSA DEDERVNT
DECVSQVE

INCARCERATVSSEPT.1645
LIBERATVSAPR.1648

130 Medal designed by Jan
Roettier for Charles II, one of a
projected series commemorating the
trials of royalists during the Civil
War. This is the earliest source to
show the north face of the keep,
and it clearly depicts the doors into
the entrance and first-floor rooms
on the west side of the keep (right).
The purpose of the large features
shown in the easternmost bay is
unclear.

death of Queen Elizabeth and anticipation of the use
of the White Tower by those to be created Knights of
the Bath on the eve of her successor's coronation. The
accounts for 1604–5 show that the works extended to
a complete reframing of the floor, with some works to
the floor frame below.[129] The floorboards for the
powder house had been cut two years earlier and were
laid temporarily in 'Caesar's Hall' for the initiation of
the Knights of the Bath before being put down properly in 1604–5.[130] The accounts indicate that the room
prepared for the knights and that which was to function as the new powder house were the same. The
room in question was the western chamber on the
second, or uppermost, floor: the reference to the
length of the room implies that it was on the western
side of the White Tower; and that it was the upper
floor is implied by the fact that the floor below is
called the middle floor, and that the work included
replacement of posts supporting the roof.[131] Dendrochronological analysis of the arcade posts, plates
and joists confirmed that this was the case, since
precise felling dates were produced for the period
summer 1602 to spring 1603.[132]

Ordnance Office debentures dated 1606–8 record
further work on the White Tower in 'fitting & fur-

nishinge of a convenient powder roome'.[133] It is unlikely that this represents a delayed fitting out of the
powder house of 1604–5, since the accounts give
details of the laying of a new floor of Norway deals,
and we know that the earlier powder house was
boarded. Moreover, the room fitted up in 1608 was
provided with nine double windows, each with
'double leaves', which can apply only to the first-floor
western chamber, significantly a room called the 'oulde flower' in 1604.[134] The accounts of the work of 1608
refer to the new room variously as storehouse, match
room (match being the cord or rope used in igniting
cannons) and powder house, so it is likely, therefore,
that this room had a more varied use than that
above.[135] This may explain the absence of such substantial work to floor frames and posts as had been
necessary in creating the second-floor powder room,
but more probably this could simply reflect the fact
that the earlier rebuilding of the second floor had
required substantial works to the first floor as well.[136]
Again, dendrochronology has confirmed that this
took place, for one of the arcade posts supporting the
first floor was felled in summer 1602.[137]

The height at which gunpowder was stored meant
that specialised lifting equipment was necessary to
hoist it up and down, and a reference was made in
1611 to 'a Crane to drawe up powder to the topp of
the White Tower'; a pulley and special white rope were
also supplied for this purpose.[138] Since there were no
exterior doorways to the first or second floors at this
date, it must be supposed that the crane was internal.[139] This would be consistent with an interpretation of the three new doors of 1595 as trapdoors, and
with the later graphic evidence.[140] Given the absence
of direct external access to the powder rooms in the
early seventeenth century, it is interesting to note that
the earliest added doorway at the White Tower is that
in the north wall to the entrance-floor western room.
Both this and the doorway above are shown on a
remarkably detailed view of the north elevation on a
medal of 1660–85 (fig. 130). The lower entrance appears
earlier on architectural grounds: the segmental form
of the barrel vault of the passage combined with an
external relieving arch suggest an early post-medieval
date. The passage to the rear of this doorway has a
splay on the east side only, and this cuts through an
eleventh-century garderobe (fig. 131). This eccentric-
ity suggests access to the north-east corner of the western room, while its width indicates that the doorway
was for stores. Since the main entrance via the Romanesque south forebuilding is likely to have ceased
to provide straightforward access to the White Tower
following the construction of the Jewel House against
the south wall in 1508, this northern entrance would
have been the obvious point of access from that time.
The surviving north doorway could date from the
construction of the Jewel House, from Cromwell's

Right-hand internal jamb of the doorway in the north wall of the western room of the entrance floor. The splay of the probably sixteenth-century doorway cuts through the adjacent eleventh-century garderobe.

ily for Wyatt, the shots had little effect, all seven or eight missing their targets 'somtymes shoting over and somtymes shoting short'.[147] In reality, though, the guns were seldom used, but were nevertheless one of the highlights of a visit to the Tower, not least for Christian IV of Denmark, who in 1606 was given the honour of letting one off himself.[148]

PRISONERS

One of the functions that the White Tower performed in the sixteenth century, but which leaves little trace in the building accounts, was to serve as 'a prison of state for the most dangerous offenders'.[149] The housing of prisoners required little in the way of preparation, save a lock or two, and many of the buildings in the Tower served this purpose when not otherwise in use.[150] In 1535 at least seven prisoners were being held within the White Tower for illegal coining, while the room below St John's Chapel held some of those imprisoned after Wyatt's rebellion.[151] Many more prisoners must have been kept here, of whose sojourn we know nothing.

It also seems clear that the White Tower was used for the torture of prisoners. The description given by the Jesuit priest John Gerard of the site of his torture in the Tower in April 1597 is the White Tower basement:

> the chamber was underground and dark, particularly near the entrance. It was a vast place and every instrument of human torture was there . . . they took me to a big upright pillar, one of the wooden posts which held the roof of this huge underground chamber. Driven into the top of it were iron staples for supporting heavy weights. Then they put my wrists into iron gauntlets and ordered me to climb two or three wicker steps. My arms were then lifted up and an iron bar passed through the rings of one gauntlet, then through the staple and rings of the second gauntlet. Then, removing the wicker steps, they left me hanging by my hands and arms.[152]

works of the 1530s or from the first usage of the White Tower as a gunpowder store. It is possible that this doorway and passage are the subject of a reference in 1637 in which the carpenter Mathew Banks provided deal boards 'in the passage where the Powder is taken upp to keepe ye Barrells of Gonn Powder from the wall':[141] more probably, given the coincidence of dates this may refer to another new doorway, created in 1636,[142] which appears to be the wide-splayed doorway of the first-floor eastern room and which has been related to the creation of an additional powder house in the same year (fig. 132).[143] It is clear, then, that during the 1590s and 1610s there was a dramatic expansion in the space devoted to gunpowder and other Ordnance storage in the White Tower, hastening a process that was to continue into the 1630s and the troubled years beyond.[144]

As well as being a store for powder, the White Tower carried a battery of guns. These had been mounted on the roof since Henry VIII's reign and probably before. They are shown on the view of 1597 and numbered sixteen early in the seventeenth century, mounted permanently on platforms on the leads.[145] As threats to London were more likely to come from insurrection than invasion, the guns were deliberately trained on the city.[146] That they were not simply for show was discovered by Thomas Wyatt and his supporters when they marched on the capital on 26 February 1554. Luck-

While specific rooms were fitted up for the storage of gunpowder and armour in the White Tower in the sixteenth century, it seems that the basement was not used as a permanent repository for any equipment in particular, and this may account for its occasional use as a prison.[153] In 1609 the Lieutenant of the Tower wrote to the Earl of Salisbury of the 'vile words uttered against His Majesty by a traitorous Jesuit' and reported that he had 'clapped' this 'lymme of the Devyll' in 'the Dongeon under the White Tower to good a prison for so fylthy a varlet'.[154]

The prisoners known to be held within the White Tower during this period were of considerably humbler origins than most of those held elsewhere in the Tower. Very high-status prisoners such as Sir Thomas More, Lady Jane Grey, Thomas Cranmer, Princess Elizabeth, the dukes of Northumberland and Sir Walter

132 The wide-splayed doorway of the north wall of the first-floor eastern room. This replaced a Romanesque window and probably represents a remodelling of 1636 necessary to allow access to the new powder house.

Ralegh and were never kept in the White Tower.[155] For whereas in 1360, when it held the King of France, the principal floors of the White Tower could still pass for royal lodgings,[156] by the sixteenth century the best lodgings were to be found elsewhere in the Tower. As a prison it served only as an occasional overflow, and its use after Wyatt's rebellion was probably caused by the sheer numbers rather than normal practice.[157] The fact that no part of the White Tower is described as a prison in a list of lodgings of 1641 suggests that by then its use as such, at least on a regular basis, had ceased.[158]

Although prisoners were the responsibility of the Lieutenant of the Tower, while the gunpowder stores belonged to the Ordnance Office, the two jurisdictions seem to have managed to operate alongside one another in the White Tower when necessary.

MAJOR REPAIRS OF 1620–40

In July 1620 the distinguished lawyer Sir Edward Coke reported to the Privy Council 'abuses' that were occurring in the management of state affairs within the Tower of London. As a result, as well as countering these abuses, the Council ordered 'the loopholes and battlements [to be] put in order, and the gunpowder removed further from the records and the crown jewels'.[159] The proximity of a gunpowder store to the priceless contents of the Jewel House and the record repository was to be a matter of concern to

numerous others in the course of the next two hundred years, though it had, surprisingly, raised little comment during the expansion of gunpowder storage in the keep in the 1590s and 1610s. When it was asked in 1623 what had been done about moving the gunpowder, the answer was clearly nothing, and the rather lacklustre order was issued that 'some place be thought uppon for the disposeinge of the said Magazen with safety and les danger'.[160] The report of 1620 called for a detailed survey of the Tower, which was undertaken by a committee including the Lieutenant of the Tower, Sir Allan Apsley, and the Lieutenant of the Ordnance, Sir Richard Morrisson. Their findings were presented on 31 December 1623 and, in their consideration of the White Tower, were largely restricted to the upper parts of the exterior. The south-west and south-east turrets were in good condition and roughcast, whereas the northern turrets were 'much ruynd': repairs and roughcasting were proposed. The battlements were in reasonable repair, and minor works only were deemed necessary. The leads were considerably damaged, especially around the gun platform, and recasting was suggested.[161] It is not clear whether all the recommended works were undertaken, but the platform and leads were certainly repaired in the years 1624–8.[162]

That the repairs required in 1623 were inadequate is apparent from the programme of major works of only a few years later, between 1638 and 1640. The

decision to undertake substantial repairs to the Tower of London had been made by mid-June 1636, and may have been a result of the inspection of the Ordnance stores in the Tower that had taken place shortly before then.[163] The works to the White Tower were put in the hands of the mason William Mills and included the first and most substantial programme to replace decayed Caen ashlar with Portland stone.[164] On the west side, in particular, the work is carefully itemised; it comprised the replacement of quoins, window and door architraves on the north-west turret, and dressings and facings to the buttresses, the blind arcading and the battlements, along with the cornice of the south-west turret. Also listed in 1638 is the replacement of quoins to the buttresses, blind arcading and the inserted fourteenth-century doorway on the south front, and similar work round to the middle of the east side.[165] In 1639 further work was undertaken on the west side, while anticlockwise progress was resumed with work to the buttresses, window architraves and blind arcading of the remainder of the east side, the north-east turret and the north side.[166] The absence of details other than for the west side makes it difficult to identify the extent of Mills's repairs, and

the subsequent use of Portland stone from the later seventeenth to the nineteenth centuries has exacerbated this.[167] Taken at face value, the works account for replacement of all the battlements, and most of the quoining and windows that were visible above the various abutting buildings. Possibly, however, the reduction in detail in the accounts as they follow the masons' progress reflects a diminution in the work. While it is difficult to differentiate plain ashlar or quoins of this date from later Portland stone repairs, the windows of 1638 were distinctive, and are represented by survivors on the second floor on the east elevation and in the two western bays of the south elevation. These windows are distinguished by understated key stones flanked by long, single and rather thin voussoirs (figs 133, 134); they survived as late as 1784 on the first and second floors of the west elevation and on the south side of the north-west turret.[168] In addition to the replacement of stonework, the works of 1638–40 included the addition of three great downpipes with hopper heads from the main roof, the re-fixing of a vane on the north-east turret, the joisting and boarding of the central valley and side gutters of the main roofs, repairs to the timbers of the chapel

roof and the re-leading of the gun platform on the roof. At the end of it all the building was white-washed.[169]

It is worth giving some thought to the significance of this two-year campaign of works to the White Tower. Given the political context of the late 1630s, it is not surprising that major repairs should have been undertaken to one of the country's most important military storehouses. However, though the years 1638–40 saw the outbreak of the Bishops' Wars in Scotland and storm clouds gathering in Westminster, the work to the keep had been agreed in less troubled times several years earlier. Furthermore, the repairs that were undertaken were far from utilitarian in form: the windows, buttresses and battlements could have been repaired functionally in brick or some other cheaper building material (as had happened on earlier occasions), but instead expensive Portland stone was used.[170] The effect must have been dazzling: newly painted walls with their Romanesque features sharply edged with white Portland stone and all surmounted by the great weather vanes, their royal arms and imperial crowns freshly gilded.[171] Charles I had visited the Tower at some point in the 1630s and had personally approved the conversion of the half-collapsed Great Hall into a military store. It is possible that he had discussed the repair of the White Tower at the same time.[172] It is tempting to see the

treatment of the White Tower in the 1630s, like the provision of a vast new British flag to be flown over it 'upon all solempnities [sic] or triumphs', as part of a renewed recognition of its potency as a symbol of ancient English monarchy.[173] The keep was a highly prominent part of the scenery of public and state occasions, and in its repaired and retouched state must have loomed spectacular in the background of such events – as Wenceslaus Hollar's engraving of the execution of the Earl of Strafford on 12 May 1641 demonstrates vividly (fig. 135). Although there is little to suggest that the work was done for this reason, the two great royal entries into London that took place in these years (that of Marie de' Medici in November 1638 and of her son-in-law Charles I three years later) would also have benefited from the improvements to the White Tower's appearance.[174] Whatever the motivation, the work saw the basic language of the Romanesque architecture respected, notably in the case of the windows, where the round arches and the double- or single-light arrangements were retained. While the repairs to the roof in the 1620s had been carried out by the Ordnance Office, this work was done by the Office of Works. This was, of course, during the Surveyorship of Inigo Jones, and there is every reason to suppose that Jones would have been personally involved in the decisions about the treatment of the White Tower.[175] The other major com-

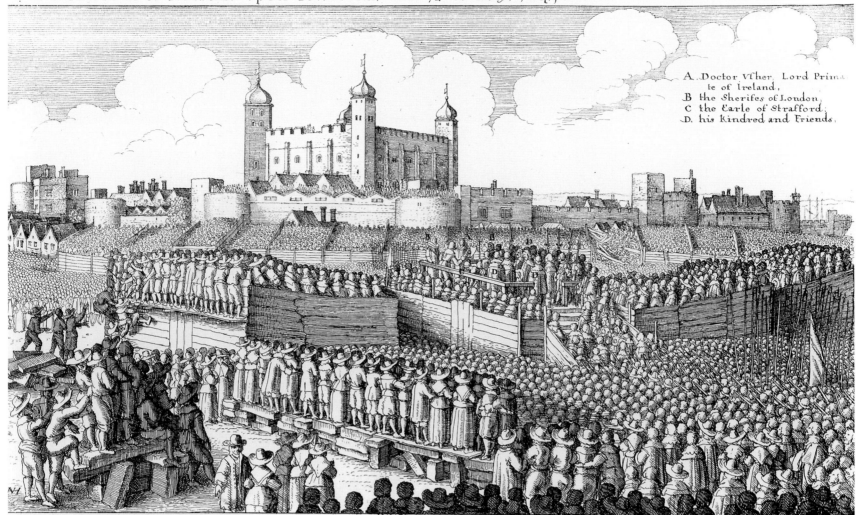

THE TRUE MANER OF THE EXECUTION OF THOMAS EARLE OF STRAFFORD, LORD
Lieutenant of Ireland, vpon Tower-hill, the 12ᵗʰ of May, 1641.

A. Doctor Vsher, Lord Prima
te of Ireland.
B the Sherifes of London.
C the Earle of Strafford.
D. his kindred and friends.

Execution des Grafen Thomæ von Stafford Statthalters in Irland auf dē Tawers platz in Londen 12 Maj 1641.
A. Doct. Vsher Primat in Irland.   C. Der Graf von Stafford.
B. Rahts Herzen von Londen.   D. Seine anverwanten vnd freunde.

135 The execution of Thomas Wentworth, Earl of Strafford in 1641, by Wenceslaus Hollar.

mission on which he was working at this date was the repair of St Paul's Cathedral, where Portland stone was also used, though here Norman round-headed arches were actually refashioned as round-headed classical arches.[176] The approach taken at the White Tower was to prove highly influential for the Tower of London, and in the eighteenth century the use of Portland stone round-headed windows was to be extended throughout the castle.[177]

Acknowledgements

Elizabeth Hallam Smith, Monika Hauth, Gordon Higgott, the late Giles Worsley, Simon Thurley, Geoffrey Parnell, Jonathan Coad, Tom Campbell.

136   *Sir John Robinson, Mayor of London and Lieutenant of the Tower of London*, by John Michael Wright, *circa* 1662. The view of the White Tower behind Robinson shows one of the crumbling drums of the Coldharbour Gate and the forebuilding, two of the structures which were thought to pose a threat to the safety of the keep, and would soon be demolished.

CHAPTER SEVEN

The White Tower, 1642–1855

ANNA KEAY WITH ROLAND B. HARRIS

During the two centuries after the Civil War the White Tower functioned as a storehouse for two very different types of material—military equipment, particularly powder and small arms, and historic manuscripts. In the first part of the period, the dangers and conflicts inherent in keeping such different collections in the same building caused great concern to the institutions responsible. The reduction of risk in the Restoration period, however, by clearing adjacent buildings and the consolidation of the roles and respective jurisdictions of the Master of the Ordnance and the Keeper of the Tower Records, allowed for a relatively peaceful coexistence during the eighteenth century. This period, interestingly, saw a temporary lapse in the White Tower's place on the itinerary of visitors to the Tower of London, but in the early nineteenth century public interest in the building and its historical associations took off dramatically. Thanks to this and a range of administrative reforms, the White Tower's use for large-scale storage of records and service arms was called into question, with fundamental consequences for its future use.

THE COMMONWEALTH TOWER OF LONDON

In February 1642 Charles I relinquished the Tower of London. He had removed from Whitehall and the capital in January, and, playing for time to dispatch his wife and daughter safely to the Continent, conceded to Parliament's request that the lieutenancy of the Tower should be taken from the royalist Sir John Byron and put into the hands of Sir John Conyers.

The military and symbolic significance of this concession was huge; Lord Clarendon later mused that 'from that time they [Parliament] thought themselves even possessed of the whole militia of the kingdom'.[1] So it would prove to be, and when Charles I next saw London it was as a prisoner awaiting trial. Interestingly, when he did return, the king was held at St James's Palace, not the Tower and, unlike Anne Boleyn, Lady Jane Grey and the Elizabethan Earl of Essex, he was not executed there but instead before the Banqueting House at Whitehall Palace. Whitehall was perhaps preferred to the Tower for being an open location where the king's sentence could be seen to be publicly and legitimately carried out. It may also be, however, that while it was one thing to execute the king against the backdrop of the Italianate hall that was so characteristic a creation of the dilettanti Stuarts, it was quite another to do so before the great White Tower, construction of the Conqueror or maybe even of Caesar himself, and a defining symbol of the longevity and legitimacy of English kingship.

The fates of the various departments of state that used the White Tower will be considered below. It is perhaps worth remarking, in general, that while the abolition of the monarchy did not close down the royal household altogether, it did see many of its departments dramatically reduced in scale and some dispensed with completely. This was to have a significant impact on the Tower of London, where several of these departments still had substantial accommodation in the early seventeenth century. The jewel

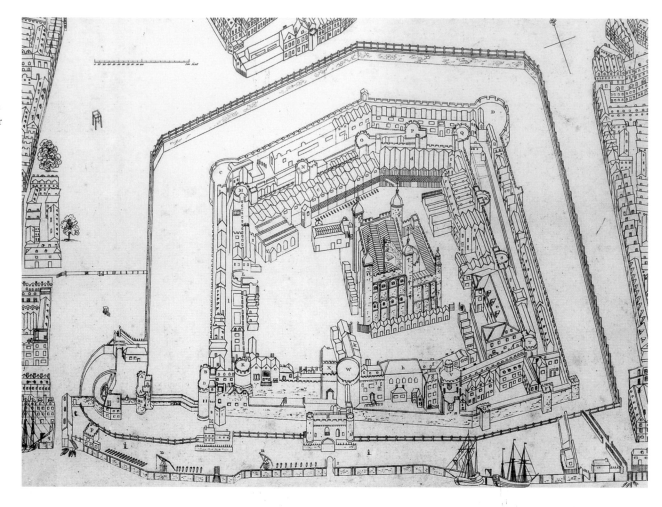

137 The Tower of London, by Holcroft Blood, 1688. The last of the demolitions of the 1670s saw the destruction of the thirteenth-century Coldharbour Gate, which was replaced with a simple palisade gate. Along the east and south faces of the keep are the sheds erected for Ordnance storage in 1686, while at the south-east corner of the annexe can be seen the turret erected in 1674 after the destruction of the long east–west Wardrobe range in 1670.

houses and the Wardrobe buildings were stripped out given over to military control, and although both institutions were to have a presence in the Tower after the Restoration, they were never again to function there in the way they had before 1642.[2] The Interregnum effectively removed the last real remnants of the royal palace from the Tower of London's identity. Never again was the Tower to house the monarch on the eve of the coronation, or to host to the initiation rites of the Knights of the Bath. Indeed, no sovereign ever spent the night there again and, come the Restoration, the centrepiece of the royal lodgings, the Great Hall, was known simply as 'the mortar piece storehouse' (fig. 137).[3]

The Great Wardrobe

Once the Tower came under the control of Parliament in 1642, the Great Wardrobe's position there went into a swift, terminal decline.[4] On 4 July 1649 the Commons passed an act declaring that all the goods and possessions of the king, queen and Prince of Wales were forfeit and should be examined, inventoried and disposed of for the good of the state.[5] John Pidgeon provided the meticulous inventory of the contents of his charges in the Great Wardrobe at the Tower, which gives a sense of the riches that visitors viewed with such awe. No fewer than fifty-seven individual tapestries were here, including Henry VIII's great set of 'Antiques' reserved for Oliver Cromwell's own use at

Whitehall, and the nine-piece set of the *Acts of the Apostles* sold to Robert Houghton for a massive £4,429 on 11 October 1650. As well as the tapestries, Pidgeon recorded seventy-one further hangings, six cloths of estate, eighteen Turkish carpets, twenty-eight embroidered cushions, two beds and the great gold and calico pavilion given to James I by a Russian ambassador.[6]

The goods were duly sold, many of them in December 1649, and the Wardrobe buildings, almost certainly including the eastern annexe of the White Tower (see above, p. 166), were left empty of their precious contents. On 9 January 1650 the Council of State issued an order that 'the Wardrobe in the Tower bee prepared for keepeing the powder yᵗ is to be prooved, being a place fitt for that purpose' (this work is considered below, on pp. 181–2).[7] A decade later, at the Restoration, the Tower of London was the first building for which a standing Wardrobe keeper was appointed, but there is no evidence that a Wardrobe storehouse was ever re-established there.[8] Indeed, the post itself lasted only one reign: the household reforms of 1685 recorded as 'Wardrobe Keeper att the Tower' one 'Daniell Dewes . . . Dead' and declared the post 'supprest'.[9]

The Jewel House

Like the contents of the Wardrobe buildings, the precious objects held by the Jewel House came under swift scrutiny by the new parliamentary regime. The Clerk of the Jewel House, Carew Hervey Mildmay, continued to man it until 1649, and in August of that year he produced the inventory of his charges required by the Parliamentary commissioners.[10] The contents of the 'lower' Jewel House, that described as adjoining the buttery in 1535 and containing the removing plate and the department's offices, was valued at some £6,500. The 'upper' Jewel House adjoining the south front of the White Tower contained the more personal royal items, including Charles I's and Henrietta Maria's crowns of state, the former alone valued at more than £1,000 (see fig. 129), and unicorns' horns to the value of £600. In addition to all of this, the coronation regalia from Westminster had now also been brought to the Tower. Although Mildmay participated in the process of cataloguing the collection, he refused finally to relinquish the keys. On 20 September the commissioners still did not have possession of the jewel houses, something that was causing mounting anxiety, because the sale of the plate, which was to make up the first lots, had already been advertised, but still nothing could be done to prepare the material for sale or for viewings to take place. Sir Henry Mildmay, the pro-Parliament Master, sent orders to Carew to give up the keys, but without success and on 29 September Carew was dragged off to the Fleet prison and the doors of the Jewel Houses broken down.[11] By the end of December most of the collection had been disposed of; the vast majority of objects were sold as individual pieces to private buyers, but the few items most emblematic of monarchy, including the crowns, were to be 'totallie Broken and defaced', their gems sold and the gold sent to the Mint to be struck into coinage. A Bible, encased in silver-gilt, was saved for the use of the Council of State.[12] Even the furniture of the Tower jewel houses fetched a price: in May 1650 a Mr Tennant bought the bric-a-brac that remained, everything from the chests and coffers down to the carpet from the jewel-house floor.[13]

The Armoury

In 1644, two years after Charles I had lost control of London, most of the armour at Greenwich was moved to the Tower; from this time on the Tower was the main repository for armour of all kinds and the Greenwich Armoury was abandoned. This is reflected in a report of October 1660, which describes the Tower as home to 'sundry complete armors, and others whereof some of them were standing formerly at Greenwich, in the Green Gallerie there'.[14] Of the pieces that came to the Tower from Greenwich, those that were to form the basis of the 'Line of Kings', soon to become one of the capital's great tourist attractions, were housed in the hall of the lieutenant's lodgings in the Tower in 1660.[15] An inventory of the charges of the Armoury made in April 1650 records a large quantity of armour, including a number of high-status gilt pieces that may have come from Greenwich, stored in great trunks in the 'Lower Roome' in the White Tower, and nearly 3,000 swords and 1,000 belts in the 'Upper Roome'.[16]

At the Restoration, though Colonel William Legge was appointed Master of the Armoury, the department was not to last long. The combination of the seriously depleted duties of the office and the financial pressures of the Restoration years saw, first, the office's budget reduced to a mere £400 a year, and then, in 1671, the complete abolition of the Armoury Office and the transfer of its duties and charges to the Ordnance Office.[17]

The Ordnance Office

On 28 January 1642, only weeks before the Tower and the capital were to be permanently lost to Charles I, Sir John Byron, the Lieutenant of the Tower, warned that soon 'there will be little cause to stand in awe of the Tower for almost all the arms are already issued out for Ireland and . . . the powder likewise decreases apace', military stores of all descriptions having been heavily depleted by expeditions dispatched to Scotland and Ireland in the years 1639–41.[18] The outbreak of the Civil War that summer saw two separate ordnance institutions come into being: the Tower of London became the headquarters of a parliamentarian ordnance office, while the royalists' ordnance supplies were managed from Oxford.[19] The importance of a good supply of gunpowder and artillery to the Parliamentary army ensured that the dwindling stores at the Tower were soon bolstered. In 1644 it was ordered that all the gunpowder anywhere in London should be moved into the Tower; and, in contrast to an initiative of 1640 to empty it of powder, the White Tower became home to an increasing quantity of ordnance stores in the course of the 1650s.[20]

On 5 January 1650 the Council of State ordered the Armoury Office to allow the storage of powder that had not yet been proofed in 'ye roome next to the powder room in ye white Tower, now belonging to your office'.[21] The room in question must have been the east chamber on either the first or the second floor, and may have been that set up with racking for armour in 1567 (see p. 170 above). This was a temporary solution to the endemic problem of housing powder that was waiting to be proofed, and a week later the order was issued by the Council of State for the Wardrobe buildings to be converted for this purpose.[22] Both the long building, or gallery, running from the Wardrobe Tower to the Broad Arrow Tower (shown on the Haiward and Gascoyne plan (see fig. 127)), and the eastern annexe of the White Tower seem to have been adapted for this purpose.[23] Work immediately commenced and was complete within six months; it involved extensive brickwork (some 53,000 bricks were used), which was then rendered, and the cutting out of new doors and windows.[24] The work completed, the unproofed powder could be held in the annexe and gallery, and once it had passed proof taken up to the rooms on the top floors of the White Tower, where it was stored until required for service.[25] Many thousands of barrels of gunpowder were stored in the White Tower, to which access was carefully guarded; the existing rooms in which it was stored (the west rooms on the top two floors and one of the east rooms) were soon considered insufficient and in 1657 yet another room in the keep was racked out for this purpose.[26] Although the White Tower was turned over substantially to the storage of gunpowder, it was also used for various other military purposes, including, on an apparently haphazard basis, for housing troops.[27]

Also in 1650 the Ordnance officers were asked to consider the dangers posed by chimneys in the vicinity of the White Tower and 'whether itt bee necessary to have those Chymnies pulled downe yt are in or neare ye White Tower'.[28] There is no evidence that any demolition took place, but the safety of the magazine certainly remained a matter of concern: in April 1651 the Council of State sent a committee to the Tower to view the proof houses after a paper had been presented to the Council 'alleging the danger of using those houses'.[29]

By 1651 the royal arms had been taken down from the great weather vanes on the cupolas of the White Tower and replaced with the arms of the Commonwealth. All remnants of the Tower of London's royal domestic character were now gone, completely overwhelmed by the martial, the bureaucratic and, for a time, the republican, character of the age.

THE ORDNANCE OFFICE AND THE GUNPOWDER MAGAZINE IN THE LATER SEVENTEENTH CENTURY

Plans to Clear Coldharbour, 1660–9

At the Restoration the Ordnance Office was revived in its pre-1642 form. As early as January 1661 the Privy Council dispatched a committee of its members to the Tower of London to inspect the magazine there, 'the safety thereof being in all respects of so important Consequence'. Two specific questions were to be answered: whether part of the powder stored in the Tower ought to be moved somewhere else and whether the buildings that adjoined the White Tower represented a danger to the powder magazine there (fig. 136).[30] The committee reported back on 4 March; it did not propose moving the magazine and so confirmed the White Tower's pre-Restoration role as the primary national powder store. On the question of the adjacent buildings, the Privy Council agreed that the buildings adjoining the keep 'at ye two corners of

ColeHarbour' (presumably the south-east and south-west corners) should be demolished to create a 20 ft buffer area between the keep and other buildings. In addition, though the Jewel House was not to be demolished, its chimneys were to be taken down and no fires were to be lit there again.[31] This was the first step in the process of making the White Tower function as a powder magazine in a safe and efficient manner, which was to be pursued for the following three decades.[32] The proximity of buildings that were not in the control of the Ordnance Office to a building that housed the country's principal gunpowder stores had long been a cause of concern to all parties.[33] The explosion of a store of gunpowder on Tower Street in 1649, which had killed dozens and destroyed completely fifteen houses, can only have alerted those at the Tower even more keenly to the potential there was for explosion.[34] There was, however, no action on the Council's recommendations on this occasion, and it was to be another five years before the issue was raised again.

In February 1665 Charles II declared war on the United Provinces and the condition of the country's military infrastructure became a matter of the utmost importance. The following March a committee was once again appointed to view the Tower to consider whether there was another place that would be better suited to the storage of Ordnance material, particularly powder, and also to see if there was a better way of bringing it into the fortress.[35] The committee made several recommendations: first, that the place where the powder was 'received in' and proofed was unsuitable for such a purpose because it was too close to the 'Grand Magazine of Powder' in the White Tower. The commissioners suggested that instead the powder should be proofed on the wharf and then brought into Coldharbour, the area immediately south of the White Tower, by means of a 'passage' that could be created by knocking through the inner and outer curtain walls. It was further recommended that the upper rooms of the White Tower should continue to serve as a gunpowder store, and that they could securely store some 10,000 barrels of gunpowder, providing 'some lodgings and houses near and around ye White Tower' were pulled down.[36] These were buildings 'part belonging to our L[ieutenan]t of our saide Tower part to ye office of our Jewell house and ye rest to other offices'.[37] Thus the decision was taken to continue to use the White Tower for the powder magazine, but to make changes to the way in which the powder was handled and to make it to some degree a free-standing structure; the commissioners were told to put their recommendations into action right away. The summer passed without any movement on this, however, and it was not until the dramatic events of September 1666 that the Ordnance officers were spurred into action.

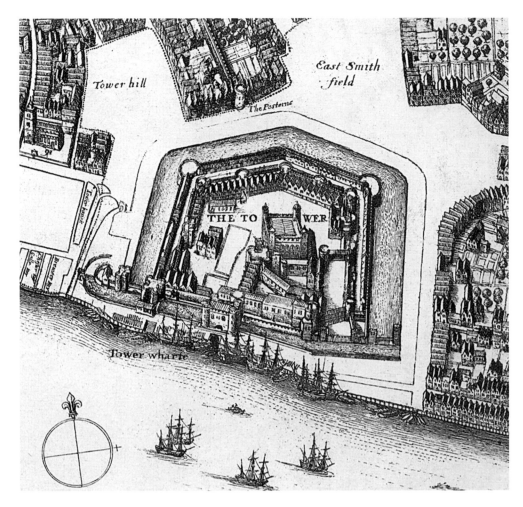

the warrant ordered that the whole of the Inmost Ward south of the keep, was now to be at the disposal of the Ordnance Office. The actual demolitions around the White Tower were therefore to be limited, but strict instructions about the removal of all chimneys from those buildings that stood close to the White Tower were issued. These comprised the Surveyor of the Works' house on the west of the White Tower, the lodging in Coldharbour Gate, that part of the Jewel House that was to remain, the house of a warder – one Mr Masters – and 'the White Tower adjoining to the stair case going up to the Chapel', presumably the medieval forebuilding.[40] The absence of a functioning principal access into the White Tower on the south face of the building at this date, and the description of what appears to be the eastern annexe as the place for proving 'and receiving in' the powder, suggest that it was to the annexe that the access from the wharf was to be made, and that it was from here that the powder then passed on into the White Tower itself. It may be, therefore, that the part of the Jewel House that was to be demolished to facilitate this access was not the building that lay against the south face of the White Tower itself, but the other Jewel House, which, it has been suggested (see previous chapter, p. 167), ran south from the south face of the eastern annexe (see fig. 127).

By 22 April 1667 the orders had 'already in some measure been put in execution', but the scope of the works was now extended and 'all that grownde and ould buildings in the Tower called Cold Harboure' were to be demolished, altered and rebuilt.[41] This encompassed the whole area south of the White Tower; the only structure excepted was 'one pile or Tower neare to Coldharbour Gate, with the stair case so reserved for the Jewel House' (again, probably the forebuilding and adjoining staircase tower). Despite the relative clarity of the order, works proceeded in a remarkably piecemeal fashion. This was probably because, although the whole of the ground to the south of the keep was supposedly now in the hands of the Ordnance Office, in reality the buildings there were occupied by a whole range of other state offices, among them the Office of Works and the Lord Chamberlain's department, over which the Ordnance had no jurisdiction.

In the works carried out in the course of the summer of 1667 those buildings directly adjoining the White Tower were quietly omitted from the demolitions.[42] In November the Privy Council committee issued the specific order that all the buildings and houses with chimneys that they considered to be dangerously near the White Tower were to be demolished.[43] This shows that the order of the previous year for the chimneys of the buildings adjoining the White Tower to be taken down had not been carried out. A further report from the committee of April 1668 again

138 Detail of the map of London by Wenceslaus Hollar showing the city after the Great Fire of 1666. The blank plots of land immediately to the west of the Tower of London indicate just how close the Tower, and the magazine of gunpowder in the keep, came to being consumed by the flames.

The Tower of London was thought, at first, to be safe from the flames of the Great Fire of London, which began on 1 September 1666. The goldsmiths had even moved their money there for safety, but, as the fire spread, the horrific prospect of the White Tower catching alight became very real. The lieutenant ordered the powder magazine to be emptied and the king went to the Tower to oversee the demolition of buildings about the moat, since, in John Evelyn's words, 'had they taken fire, & attaq'd the white Towre, where the Magazine of Powder lay . . . demolition beyond all expression' would have resulted. Dozens of houses to the west of the Tower were torn down to create a fire break and this, combined with the luck of a counter wind, saw the fire halted at 'the very gates' of the castle (fig. 138). All Hallows, Barking, was singed, but the Tower of London, remarkably, was saved.[38] On 15 November 1666 the warrant for the demolitions specified eight months earlier was at last issued.[39]

Work on the creation of the passage from the wharf to the Inmost Ward was to start, to detailed plans by the great Ordnance Office engineer Sir Bernard de Gomme, but the scheme to carry out all gunpowder proofing on the wharf seems to have been rejected. Instead, part of the Jewel House was to be demolished to facilitate the carrying up of the powder into the White Tower and to open a clear passage to the ordinary proof house (the eastern annexe). In addition, detailed the demolitions that it considered were still necessary.[44] The Surveyor of the Works' house on the west of the White Tower was to be taken down; the rooms in Coldharbour Gate were to have all their chimneys and hearths 'filled up'; the house and tower belonging to the warder Mr Masters was to have all its windows, chimneys and doors filled up, as was part of the Jewel House; while another part of the Jewel House, where the keeper lived and which adjoined the White Tower, was to be pulled down. The 'Square Tower' in Coldharbour, again perhaps the forebuilding, was to be retained but to have its chimneys filled up. In 1669 it was reiterated that as soon as the Keeper of the Jewel House could be moved, his house was to be 'stopped up', Coldharbour Gate was to be shut and general access to the inmost ward was to cease.[45]

The Jewel Office Leaves the White Tower

The orders of the late 1660s therefore saw the end of the White Tower's long-standing function as a repository for royal plate and jewels. As is discussed in Chapter Six, the jewel houses had been emptied and their contents sold in 1649–50. At the Restoration, Sir Henry Mildmay forfeited the post of Master of the Jewel House and Sir Gilbert Talbot was appointed in his place. Since only three swords and the coronation spoon remained of the old regalia, the crown jewels had to be completely remade. The office re-established itself to the south of the White Tower, certainly in the building adjoining its south face, and quite likely in the other Jewel House building close by. Although schemes for demolishing all or part of the Jewel House's buildings at the Tower were mooted throughout the 1660s, it was only in 1668 that Talbot felt sufficiently threatened by these to petition the Council for some other place to house the jewels.[46] While the Martin Tower in the north-east corner of the inner ward was being prepared for this purpose, the jewels and their keeper were temporarily housed in a room in one of the condemned jewel houses.[47] Despite the temporary nature of this arrangement, in spring 1669 visitors could still view the regalia here, kept in a chest and secured with a strong grate.[48] In June 1669 the works to the Martin Tower were being hurried to completion. Real urgency seems now to have been felt about removing this last obstacle to the creation of the buffer around the White Tower. The contents of the Jewel House were moved to the Martin Tower that autumn, and the White Tower's association with the safe keeping of royal plate and regalia, at least 300 years old, finally ceased.

The Demolitions of the 1670s

While works to clear the area to the south and west of the White Tower were afoot, changes were also being made to the buildings to the east of the White Tower, where gunpowder was actually received and dispatched. In the spring of 1670 the 'long powder house', the 100 ft-long building erected for the Great Wardrobe in 1532–3, was dismantled.[49] The demolition had not been specified by the Privy Council committee, but was nonetheless carried out by the Ordnance Office, perhaps to facilitate the movement of stores to and from the new storehouse (today known as the New Armouries) erected in 1663–4. The demolition of the long powder house was followed over the next year by works to the eastern annexe to the White Tower, 'the powder house', which remained.[50] These included the laying of deal flooring and the construction of an external staircase.[51] Finally, works were finished off with the construction of a slim turret on its south-east corner. Tall and square in form and capped with a cupola roof, this structure closely echoed the turrets of the White Tower itself; its construction was certainly complete by 1674, when the 'extraordinary' clock designed by Thomas Tompion was mounted on its south face (fig. 137).[52]

It was only in 1674 that the demolitions to clear the White Tower of encumbrances were finally completed.[53] The forebuilding,[54] Coldharbour Gate[55] and some part of the Jewel House[56] certainly remained standing alongside the White Tower until 1674. In March 1674 one Mr Couren was engaged by the Ordnance Office to perform the task of 'pullinge down yᵉ Tower against yᵉ White Tower'.[57] Mr Couren was lent a 'Great Screw' for 'throweinge down yᵉ Ruinous Walls next yᵉ White Tower', and it seems that these walls probably included all the remaining structures on the south face of the building, which had all been empty since 1669 (fig. 139).[58]

During these operations a remarkable discovery was made. As the historian Francis Sandford wrote three years later:

> Upon Friday the [17th] day of July An 1674 . . . in order to the rebuilding of the several Offices in the Tower and to clear the white Tower from all contiguous buildings, digging down the stairs which led from the King's Lodgings to the Chappel in the said Tower, about ten foot in the ground, were found the Bones of two striplings in (as it seemed) a wooden Chest . . .[59]

It was almost immediately claimed that these were the remains of Edward v and his younger brother, the Duke of York, the infamous 'Princes in the Tower', and on Charles ii's command the bones were placed in Westminster Abbey.[60] The implication of the contemporary descriptions is that the bones were found beneath, or at the foot of, the structure adjacent to the forebuilding that housed the stairs leading up to the first-floor entrance to the keep.[61] This would seem to be the building described as the Brick Tower, which was provided with a window in 1663, and which must have stood immediately to the east of the forebuilding.[62] If the

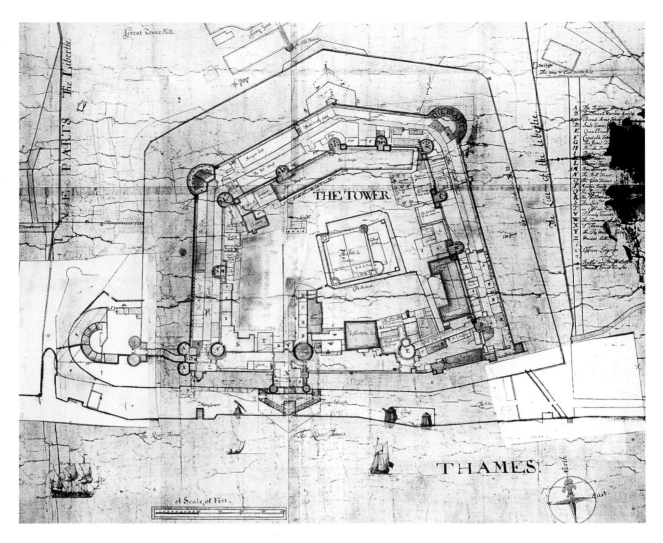

139 Plan of the Tower of London made in 1681–2. The plan was made to accompany a report on the condition of the Tower of London presented to the Privy Council on 8 February 1682. It shows the White Tower after the campaign of demolition of the 1660s and '70s, which left it standing free of adjoining structures—other than the great east annexe, which would remain for another 200 years. It was to stand solitary in this manner for barely a decade before buildings began to spring up around it again from the mid-1680s.

bones unearthed in 1674 were indeed buried in the 1480s then they could well have been trapped beneath a building erected in the sixteenth century.

Whatever remained of the Jewel House must have been removed at this time as well. In November of the following year the order was issued for Coldharbour Gate to be demolished, and the work was carried out in January and February 1676.[63] The great thirteenth-century gatehouse was replaced by a wooden gate in a spur to the palisade fence, which, with the forebuilding removed, could now be extended across the south face of the White Tower, so completing its encirclement.[64] The stone from Coldharbour Gate was not to be wasted, though, being taken downriver to be used in the construction of the new observatory on Greenwich Hill. While this building was being erected, the holder of the new Ordnance Office post of Astronomer Royal, John Flamsteed, lodged with Sir Jonas Moore at the Tower of London. Here he set up his instruments, and over the summer of 1675 made a series of astronomical observations. Although there is no contemporary evidence that he did so from the roof of the White Tower, it seems likely that he would have made some use of by far the tallest building in the castle. One of the turrets of the Tower was described as an 'observatory' in the mid-eighteenth century, though without any explicit link to Flamsteed.[65]

In the mid-1680s ranges of sheds were built along the south, east and west faces of the White Tower to house various Ordnance stores. Though these stood within the 'corridor' that the demolitions of the 1660s and 70s had been designed to create, they were under the Ordnance Office's command and not domestic in character, and so posed nothing like the threat of their predecessors.[66] The sheds were built in the early months of 1686 and were painted.[67] Those on the south of the White Tower were intended for the storage of wagons, while in 1688 those on the east were fitted up for the reception of small arms (fig. 137).[68]

Finally, therefore, by the mid-1670s, the great powder magazine of the White Tower was freed from the dangers of the numerous adjacent buildings. The powder rooms were re-floored and various other repairs and improvements were made.[69] Less than twenty years later, however, disaster struck: on 9 July 1691 part of one of the upper floors in the White Tower collapsed and some 2,000 barrels of gunpowder were sent crashing to the floor below. Queen Mary recorded the news in her diary, remarking that though no great explosion had happened, 'yet the consequences of it might have been terrible, had it taken fire'.[70] The incident was discussed at the Privy Council meeting that same day, and it was concluded that 'the keeping of so great a quantity of Powder at present is extreamly dangerous to the

Tower, and City of London' and the officers of the Ordnance were to 'consider of a fitt place or places where the stores of Powder may be conveniently lodged, aswell for the security thereof, as of the Tower and City of London'.[71] So the White Tower's role as England's principal powder magazine ended. Shortly before the collapse nearly 3,700 barrels of gunpowder were stored in the Tower of London, but by mid-1695 it had already been reduced to a quarter of that number.[72]

THE RECORD OFFICE TO THE CRIMEAN WAR

The events of the mid-seventeenth century saw the records held at the Tower of London take on new significance. In the summer of 1647 Oliver Cromwell and Sir Thomas Fairfax entered London, fresh from the bloody victories of the first Civil War. Fairfax rode into the Tower, where he inspected the stocks of ammunition, marvelled at 'the strength of the White Tower' and visited the Record Office. Sensing an unmissable public relations opportunity, he called for Magna Carta, which he said he longed to see. When the document was brought to him he removed his hat in respect, and remarked gravely: 'this is that . . . which we have fought for, and by Gods help we must maintain'.[73]

On 27 October 1643 the Tower of London Record Office had been taken out of the hands of the royalist keeper, Sir John Borough, and put under the keepership of the great antiquary and opponent of the Divine Right of Kings, John Selden. With the abolition of feudal tenures in 1645 and the subsequent demise of the Court of Wards and Liveries, which had made frequent use of the Tower records, the Record Office had lost much of its trade. Since 'the profitable part of that office' had consequently been 'taken away', Selden's ability to employ clerks and keep the office open was called into question. The danger of the records being 'rendered useless, or lost, or disordered' was considered worrying, and evidence given at the Restoration of the presses in the chapel of St John being broken down and burnt by soldiers garrisoned at the Tower further indicates that the records had suffered during the Civil War.[74] In 1650, therefore, the Council of State asked for a report on the 'usefulness of the office of Records in the Tower' to be drawn up. The importance of the office was firmly upheld by the report, and it was consequently recommended that the clerk be paid a salary, in lieu of fees, by Parliament directly and, furthermore, that a calendar of the records be compiled for parliamentary use.[75] The officers of the Records were to have their work cut out: for after Cromwell had finally pacified Scotland in 1651, it was decreed that the Scottish records of state should be taken from Stirling Castle (to which they had been removed from Edinburgh Castle) and sent to London.[76] The records were brought to the Tower of London by sea in 1651, and the long-

serving clerk William Ryley was paid an extra £50 to cover the costs of installing them in the Tower; the following year another £100 was allowed to him for 'the clerks to be employed about the Scotch Records in the Tower and the charge of paper & parchment &c for methodising and ordering the said records for public use'.[77] Although some documents were returned in the 1650s, most of the Scottish records were to remain in the Tower until the Restoration.[78] Unfortunately, there is no evidence of where in the Tower the Scottish records were kept, but it seems likely that some, at least, were housed in St John's Chapel in the White Tower.

The Tower records continued to be accessible to private researchers during the Interregnum. Elias Ashmole, for instance, undertook much work on his history of the Order of the Garter there in the late 1650s.[79] At the Restoration, William Prynne was appointed keeper and William Ryley was confirmed in his post as clerk; much of the later months of 1660 were spent preparing the remaining Scottish records to be handed to Sir Archibald Primrose, registrar of Scotland, and returned to Edinburgh.[80] Though there were disputes between the staff of the Record Office and those of the Ordnance about the lodging attached to the Wakefield Tower, the records continued to occupy St John's Chapel in the White Tower and the Wakefield Tower, apparently without challenge.[81]

After the Restoration, as very probably was the case before, the White Tower was a storehouse for records, not an office or a reading room. When Anthony Wood visited the Tower in 1667 he was shown 'a place where he should sit and write . . . the Repertorium', introduced to a Mr Jennings, the reacher of records, and saw William Dugdale at work on his *Monasticon Anglicanum*, but all these were in the rooms in and around the Wakefield Tower. Wood was then taken to see the White Tower, 'where he was strangely surprised to see such a vast number of charters and rolls that were there reposed'.[82] Those who came to consult the records went to the Wakefield Tower, where they would find the office open from 7 a.m. to 11 a.m. and from 1 p.m. to 5 p.m., except in November, December, January and February, when the shortness of the days curtailed the hours.[83] It seems that, as a result of its peripheral status, the record room in the White Tower suffered from considerable neglect. The Council inquired into the condition of the records in the Tower in 1676[84] and again in 1681.[85] The investigation of 1681 escalated into a survey of the condition of the Tower of London as a whole, but in the recommendations that were made regarding improving the operation of the Record Office at the Tower, no mention was made of the White Tower (fig. 139).[86] In their critique of the current state of affairs, though, both inquiries revealed the records in the chapel in the White Tower to be in a sad condition, not least because the presses had broken down and burnt by soldiers 'in y[e] late Tymes' and had never been replaced.[87]

Because the demolitions of 1674 had destroyed the external access to the staircase that led to the chapel, in the autumn of 1676 a new access was provided. The mason John Thompson repaired the buttresses on the west end of the south face of the White Tower and 'made a pa[r] of stone staires going up to the Record office', comprising twenty-five steps. At the same time the internal stairway seems also to have been replaced: the carpenter William Cozens submitted a bill for making 'the staires goeing up to the Record Office', which consisted of forty-seven steps, a newell and 20 ft of flooring, which presumably ran from the top of the external stairs up into the chapel.[88] Ten years later the external stair was replaced by the bricklayers John Downes and Robert Fitch, who dug new foundations for stone stairs. The stairs seem to be those that ran from the south-west corner of the building, across its south face, up to the doorway between ground and entrance level, and which were later hidden from view by the carriage storehouse of 1717.[89] It is likely that they were installed at this time to make possible the construction of the wagon shed.[90] So it was that the records kept in the White Tower continued to have their own, quite separate, access from the Ordnance stores that occupied the rest of the building. Perhaps due in part to this simple arrangement, the two functions were to continue to coexist reasonably happily within the White Tower for the following century and a half.

Despite the many reports and recommendations, it was not until 1704 that the condition of the records in St John's Chapel was given any serious attention. A committee of the House of Lords, led by Charles Montagu, 1st Lord Halifax, inspected the records in the Tower in March of that year, and reported that while those in the office, the Wakefield Tower, were in good condition and carefully kept, in 'Caesar's Chapel, under the leads in the White Tower, multitudes of records . . . lie in confused heaps, and if Care not speedily taken of them, are in great danger of utter perishing'. In order to put this right, the Lords recommended the appointment of extra clerks, and suggested that if the records were cleaned and put into order, they might all fit into the office – the implication being that the White Tower repository might be abandoned.[91] In May 1704 a committee of informed and interested individuals, including the Keeper of the Tower Records, William Petyt, and Sir Christopher Wren, were charged with producing a detailed scheme for improving the state of the records, based on the Lords' suggestions.[92] They reported on 6 September: they too considered the records in the chapel of St John to be in a parlous state, and recommended that 'drawers, shelves and presses' be provided for their storage, and detailed the way in which the cleaning and sorting of the records should be carried out.[93]

By November 1704 new clerks had been appointed, and were busily sorting the records into baskets in the office, and collecting occasional batches from the White Tower. The records in the chapel were still in a terrible condition, though: wagonloads lying in heaps on the floor, and under piles of dust and rubbish, all 'in the most Dirty and perishing condition imagineable'.[94] In September it was also suggested that two first-floor rooms next to the Wakefield Tower, over the Treasurer of the Ordnance's office, might be appropriated for the housing of the records from the chapel of St John.[95] The Treasurer of the Ordnance objected to the scheme, suggesting that the Record Office should make better use of the buildings it already occupied, the chapel in particular.[96] In August 1705 estimates were prepared both for making the necessary alterations to the two rooms and for carrying out works to improve the two existing repositories. The Office of Works submitted the substantial estimate of £752 4 s. 8 d, of which more than half was for repairs and improvements to the White Tower record room. The works proposed included the provision of sixteen window frames with glass and iron bars; presses and wainscot doors; some £180 worth of deal shelves, partitions, chests and covers for the records; three tables and two ladders.[97] Mending the 'old Terras ffloor', which was estimated at £20, must have been omitted at some point, because ten years later it was recommended that the floor of the chapel be boarded, since it was 'much broken'.[98] The account also refers to fourteen stone steps, 4 ft in length. Too few and of the wrong material to have been intended for a stair between the chapel floor and the gallery, these were clearly used to link the chapel roof space to the south-east turret, since the existing stair in that position has fourteen steps, of which the lowest are the right material and dimensions.[99] The provision of a lead cistern and 42 ft of stone coping confirms that the works extended beyond the main interior of the chapel, and it may be that this stair, if the identification is correct, represents nothing more than replacement of the previous means of access to the roof space. Given the context of these repairs, however, it could suggest that the roof space formed part of the Record Office, perhaps even before this date: certainly, the room is large enough to be useful and accessible, if not to the general public, and a reference of 1704 to records 'under the Leads in *The White Tower*' would seem to support this. Whatever the case, it is clear that the scheme of 1705 was for the chapel to become a proper record repository, rather than a dumping ground for neglected manuscripts.

The estimate was approved, and work was under way in the White Tower and Wakefield Tower by mid-November 1705; by late December the chapel was furnished with boxes and shelves, and the decision had been taken that it would be home to all the docu-

ments relating to Chancery, while the Wakefield Tower would house the older and most valuable records, a distinction that was to remain until the Tower was emptied of records in 1858.[100] When the Lords visited some years later, they reported that the records that had been in so sorry a state in the chapel 'were most of them sorted and put into Order of Time, in an excellent manner' (fig. 140).[101]

Despite all these works, the problem of space had not been entirely solved. The Six Clerks' Office on Chancery Lane was keen to transfer some of the mounting piles of Chancery records that they had accumulated to the Tower. In 1714 the transfer had been approved, and all that remained was to decide where in the Tower the 2,200 bundles of records, each more than 3 ft long, were to be stored. Christopher Wren recommended that the eastern chamber on the top floor of the White Tower, 'a large Vacant Room', should be used for this purpose, remarking that the Board of Ordnance had no objections to this.[102] The room had probably been used for gunpowder storage from sometime in the seventeenth century, with changes after the collapse of 1691 presumably causing it to be empty in 1714.[103] An estimate of £330 was submitted for fitting the room up for the reception of records.[104] But Wren's confidence about the amenability of the Ordnance Office seems to have been misplaced. In March 1716 the Board reported that the room had now been fitted up to house stores and was not available;[105] the Works Office suggested that these stores would be better placed in a 'plainer' building,[106] but the Board of Ordnance pointed out that since they had recently spent some £5,000 repairing 'this

ancient large building', they expected some reimbursement before they vacated any of its rooms.[107] By this time both the principal rooms on the upper storey were being discussed. An impasse seems to have been reached. In 1722 the Six Clerks raised the question again, but to no avail,[108] and it was not until 1736 that the Board of Ordnance finally agreed to 'lend' the eastern chamber on the top floor of the White Tower for the keeping of records until a better place could be found.[109] A contemporary plan of the top floor of the building records the Master-General of the Ordnance's assent to the scheme, and which room was intended, although it is quite likely that the plan itself dates from earlier in the negotiations (fig. 141).[110] In March 1737 the Office of Works submitted an estimate of £265 for the necessary work, including the erection of shelves and presses. The Records officials' request, however, that a vault be inserted into their new top-floor room as a precaution against fire was refused because the rooms on the first and entrance floors were not vaulted.[111] In 1739, the work being finished, the documents from the Six Clerks' Office were finally transferred.[112] After this no more records were sent to the Tower from the Six Clerks of Chancery for forty years. The transfer that occurred in 1779 was not a major operation involving new classes of documents, but comprised only those records dating to before 1714 that had been omitted from the transfer of 1739 – fewer than a hundred bundles.[113] The condition of these records was considerably improved in the late eighteenth century by the efforts of the keeper, Thomas Astle, and his clerk Robert Lemon, but it was still the contents of the chapel in the White Tower that were afforded the least attention, being 'supposed not to be important' (fig. 142).[114]

The White Tower was clearly an imperfect record repository: at the end of the eighteenth century the floors were suffering from the weight of the records, and the leaking of the roof was doing terrible damage to the vulnerable manuscripts.[115] In the first fifteen years of the nineteenth century the Tower Record Office acquired significantly more room in the White Tower. In 1808 the two rooms in the north-east turret were equipped with doors, partitions, shelves and presses for the records,[116] while in 1811 the western room on the second floor was transferred from the Ordnance Office for the storage of records.[117] The possibility of using the north-west and south-west turrets for the same purpose was investigated.[118] This great expansion was necessitated by the transfer to the Tower of the Admiralty Records, which the Treasury had ordered to be transferred from the Doctors' Commons (where the Admiralty courts were housed).[119] In order to accommodate the new classes, Samuel Lysons drew up plans for fitting out the western room and the two west turrets with bookcases. As well as involving the con-

141 Plan of the second floor (here titled 'Third Floor') of the White Tower, 1736. In this year the Board of Ordnance finally agreed to lend the east room on the top floor (B) of the keep to the Record Office for the storage of manuscripts, some fifteen years after this had been proposed by Sir Christopher Wren. The chapel (A) was already being used for this purpose

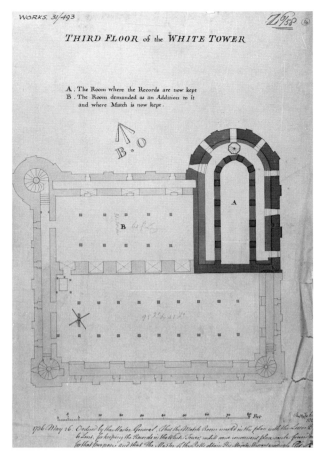

THIRD FLOOR of the WHITE TOWER

A . The Room where the Records are now kept
B . The Room demanded as an Addition to it
and where Match is now kept.

142 Records stored on the top floor of the White Tower, by Charles Tomkins, 1805. This view apparently shows the east room on the top floor, but with the central presses and the timber uprights that supported the roof omitted. Despite its inaccuracies, it does correctly show the recesses in the central arcade filled with manuscripts, and is the only known view of the top floor when occupied by the record office.

struction of numerous presses, the works of 1812 saw the creation of a gallery around the west room and a 'bridge' across the middle connecting the east and west sides. It is clearly to these works that the present second-floor windows of the western room belong: they are much larger than the Romanesque originals or the replacements of 1638 (recorded in a view as late as 1784, fig. 143), and the accounts for 1812 refer to opening of windows in the 'west end' and making Portland stone window sills and jambs.[120] Four new skylights were created in the roof to allow more light into the room, while the gallery was to have a sloping wooden roof over the bookcases 'so as to throw off any wet that may come from the cracks in the lead'. In the south-east room, occupied by the upper level of the two-storey chapel, a similar 'bridge' was built connecting the two west ends of the gallery.[121]

In July 1800 the Select Committee appointed the previous year to inquire into the state of the records of the nation had made its report.[122] The committee recommended that the numerous buildings that housed the records of state be repaired; that proper inventories be prepared of all their contents; and that a central repository should be established to house the contents of all the record offices. The recommendations of the commission were finally implemented when the records in the chapter house of Westminster Abbey narrowly avoided destruction by the Palace of Westminster fire in 1834, and in 1838 the Record Act instituted the combined Public Record Office.[123] On 10 July 1840 the Keeper of the Tower Record Office

was asked formally to hand over custody of the records to Francis Palgrave, one-time Keeper of the Records in the chapter house and the first keeper of the new Public Record Office; the Tower then became a 'branch' record office.[124] While the central repository was being planned and built, the intention was to reduce the number of small record repositories and to rationalise the contents of the remainder. As a result, the Tower was to receive a variety of records from other institutions. In 1841 naval records from Deptford were transferred, and were housed in the north-east turret.[125] It was proposed that when the first phase of the new repository at Chancery Lane was completed, all the records in the custody of the Master of the Rolls would be transferred there, except the Admiralty records in the White Tower; these were to remain at the Tower until the second phase of building was completed, not being very much in demand. The outbreak of the Crimean War in 1854, however, led to a massive escalation in the activities of the Board of Ordnance, and on the urgent request of the Storekeeper of the Ordnance, and the provision of temporary accommodation on the Rolls Estate, the last records in the White Tower were finally removed in the summer of 1858.[126]

THE ORDNANCE OFFICE AFTER 1691

Saltpetre and Gunpowder

After the collapse in the White Tower of 1691, it was never again to be country's main gunpowder store. The Board of Ordnance maintained its headquarters at the Tower, however, and the White Tower continued to serve as one of its stores, housing a wide variety of its supplies, including a much-reduced quantity of saltpetre and gunpowder, small arms, swords, match rope and other ordnance equipment.

The way the building was used during the eighteenth century is considered in detail below by the different uses to which the building was put. It is worth saying in summary, however, that there were two

143 The White Tower from the west, Samuel Hooper, 1784. The top-floor windows were given the form shown here in the Mills work of 1638, and would be enlarged to their current size as part of the programme of works to the record office in 1812. In 1784 the windows on the first floor were still of the Norman two-light form; these were almost certainly turned into very large single-light windows in 1805.

periods when the building as a whole underwent change. In the years 1715–19 the sheds to the south of the keep were demolished and various alterations were made throughout the building, including fitting out the basement for saltpetre, fitting out the entrance and first floors for arms storage – including enlarging the windows – and the establishment of the Ordnance Office's own record repository and drawing room in the eastern annexe. The second phase of change was in the 1730s. In 1729 the eastern annexe was partly rebuilt; three years later work began to create the existing brick vaults in the basement; and, though the initial proposal to introduce vaults throughout the building was not executed, all the other three floors were fitted out with purpose-made structures and receptacles for the proper storage of their various charges. In the course of this work the windows on the top floor were given new casements and the floors there replaced.

As the Council had declared after the collapse in the White Tower in 1691, other places were to be found for the storage of powder, both for the security of the stores and of the Tower and the city. In 1694–5 the Ordnance Office constructed a new powder house at Greenwich, specifically to solve the storage problem created by the Council's reluctance to permit substantial quantities of powder to be housed in the Tower.[127] By 1702 nearly 5,000 barrels of gunpowder were housed at Greenwich, and in 1716–17 two new powder magazines were constructed at Tilbury Fort on the north side of the Thames estuary. As a member of the Ordnance establishment reported of the eastern chamber on the top floor in 1716, 'a Great Quantity of Gunn Powder was lodged in that romme untill

upon the Citys applycation to Her late Majesty it was removed to Greenwich . . . since that time the same has been fitted up & made use of to lodge stores in, wᶜʰ was very much wanted before'.[128]

Nevertheless, the White Tower continued to house a limited stock of gunpowder throughout the eighteenth century, along with quantities of its principal constituent, saltpetre.[129] By 1705 saltpetre was being stored in the basement of the White Tower, in 'vaults' – presumably a reference to the use of the vaulted south-east chamber.[130] It seems quite likely that at this time the basement was being used only in a haphazard fashion, as it had been for the storage of a great variety of stores throughout the previous century, and it was not until 1715 that work was carried out there to create a dedicated repository – a 'salt petre warehouse'.[131] In 1714 superficial works were done to 'a new salt petre room', largely involving the provision of doors, but the following year much more substantial renovations were carried out in the whole basement.[132] At this time the ground in the eastern room was lowered and levelled,[133] and both the east and west basement rooms were laid with deal boarding on the walls and floors.[134] The west room was fitted up specifically to receive the load of saltpetre recently purchased from the East India Company.[135] The east room, presumably to be used for saltpetre as well, was provided with platforms.[136]

The vaulted south-east room was apparently not to be used for saltpetre once these works had been completed,[137] but may have housed the remaining stock of gunpowder, of which no more than sixty or seventy barrels were being stored in the basement in 1719.[138] Various minor works were carried out in the follow-

144 The basement of the White Tower today, showing the brick vaults inserted during the years 1732–4 to improve the conditions for the storage of gunpowder and saltpetre.

ing years, including repairs to the floor, the provision of doors and the stopping-up of the well – presumably to prevent damp, for which reason it was blocked again in 1734.[139] An account for 'breaking a doorway into the Salt Petre Room' of 1729 may refer to the external doorway in the south end of the western wall, which features on a plan of that year, and which must have provided useful ground-level access to the basement.[140]

The security of the saltpetre was doubtless the reason the decision was taken to vault the whole of the basement of the building in 1732. A plan and section of 1729 show that the insertion of vaults into all but the top level of the rooms in the western half of the building had been considered, and rejected, presumably on grounds of cost.[141] The works of 1732–4 were therefore limited to the construction of the brick vaults in the east and west basement rooms, which survive today, but nevertheless constituted the first major structural change to the main body of the White Tower since the construction of the existing roof *circa* 1490 (fig. 144). The three arcades of timber posts in each room were replaced by groin vaults springing from spur walls rather than piers or responds (fig. 145, cf. fig. 146).[142] This has the effect of providing clearly de-

fined bays to either side of the central aisle. In both east and west rooms, a narrow passage was created to allow access around the inside of the outer wall of the building. By 1754, and very possibly from the outset, this passage and the bays were further separated by timber partitions, leaving only small openings or doorways necessary for access (fig. 151). With the exception of the partly preserved window in the south wall of the western room (no doubt then invisible), the surviving eleventh-century basement windows in the west room were destroyed by the large squared recesses cut into the outer side walls in each bay: these now provided more substantial natural lighting and ventilation, albeit indirectly from the embrasures of the windows on the entrance floor.[143] The basement windows/vents were provided with grilles and trapdoors flush with the floor above. These details, and the absence of decorative work other than the plainest of stone plinths and imposts, emphasise the strict functionality of the new basement arrangements.

In 1753 the east room and most of the west room were being used to house saltpetre, while the southeast room, two floors below the chapel, held gunpowder, and the southern section of the west room, partitioned off from the rest, was used for cooperage.

145 Plan of the basement (here titled 'Vault Floor') of the White Tower made for the Board of Ordnance, 1729. On the plan are marked the piers of the vault that would be inserted into the building during the years 1732–4.

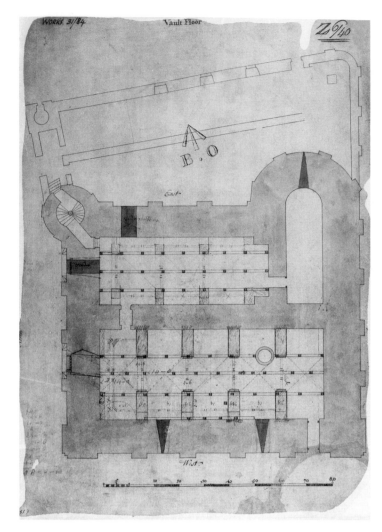

146 North–south section of the White Tower by Clement Lemprière, 1729. The section shows the basement before the insertion of the brick vault, and the timber structures inserted into the entrance and first floor for storage. The building to the south (right) of the keep is the Carriage Storehouse built in 1717.

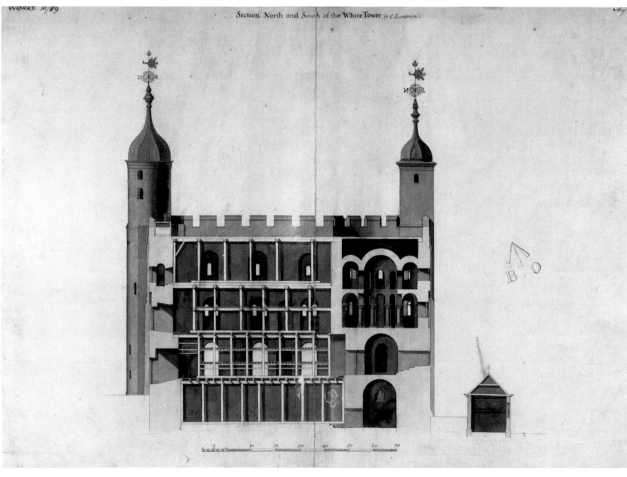

It was in that year that a doorway and a window 'in the party wall between the saltpetre vaults and the powder magazine' (i.e., the eleventh-century doorway into the chapel sub-basement) had been filled in by bricklayers, leaving only air holes with copper grates for ventilation.[144] It must also have been then, at the latest, that the existing opening at the west end of the room was punched through the medieval wall.

The result was that two distinct and completely separate areas were created in the basement with no internal access between them. The northern two-thirds were occupied by saltpetre and could be reached only from the north-east stair; the southern third of the basement housed cooperage and gunpowder stores and was entered from an external doorway at the south end of the west wall. Saltpetre, which does not naturally occur on any scale in northern Europe, was imported in huge quantities by the East India Company, who sold it on to the Crown.[145] By the 1760s an arrangement had evolved whereby the Company stored saltpetre in the basement of the White Tower, for which the Board of Ordnance paid only as it was removed for service. As a result the saltpetre stores in the basement of the White Tower were not actually in the Board's control, and the Company was allowed to place its own locks on the magazine doors.[146] Saltpetre was kept in bags, some 16,000 of which the East India Company proposed to store in the basement in 1763, while gunpowder was stored on great racks in wooden barrels piled ten or so high (fig. 156).[147]

Saltpetre continued to be stored in the basement of the White Tower well into the nineteenth century. Complaints about the danger the ordnance stores posed to the increasing numbers of records on the upper floor were dismissed by the Board of Ordnance in 1832 as of secondary importance to the need to keep in the White Tower 'a store of powder necessary for the defence of that Place'.[148] The Record officers were even more concerned when they learnt of the Board of Ordnance's plan to construct a railway between the wharf and the White Tower to facilitate the transport of stores into the building in 1834–5.[149] This was to run on the surface from the wharf to a storehouse north of Water Lane, and then to continue under ground to the basement of the White Tower. Work started in 1834 and involved breaching the westernmost bay of the south wall of the White Tower with a brick-built tunnel 12 ft 9 in. (3.88 m) wide and with a vault approximately at modern ground level: a drawing of 1850 appears to show the proposed removal of the vault of the tunnel,[150] but nonetheless a short length survives as a sub-basement within the White Tower, still penetrating the wall and projecting 940 mm beyond the plinth, and complete with rails.[151] The construction of the railway necessitated the removal of the saltpetre from the west basement room into a more secure space, so in 1834–5 the vaulted floor under the eastern annexe was converted into a magazine to compensate for this loss.[152]

Small Arms and Other Stores

With the diminution of its role as a powder store after 1691, the White Tower was to become home to a different and less combustible assortment of stores. Adequate provision for these required quite different fitting out and access requirements than had hitherto been the case, and as a consequence this period is marked by modification to the carpentry – in itself substantially altered by the insertion of the basement vaults in the years 1732–4 – a reduction in hatches and an increase in staircases. The present form of the interior of the east and west rooms of the first floor of the White Tower was largely achieved during this period, although with the loss of the innumerable racks, bins and the stores themselves; only the redundant mortices in the supporting posts now bear witness to the density and complexity of their contents.

In the early summer of 1698 rooms in the White Tower were fitted up for the storage of small arms, rather than heavy ordnance.[153] That most of the work was concentrated on the western chamber on the first floor is evident from the reference to '12 windows being single lights w[i]th hance heads 5 fo[o]t 4 inches high & 2 f[oo]t 8 inches broad from out to out' and the enumeration of 108 posts with musket racks, of which 36 were larger since they also had a structural purpose: these details uniquely match this room as recorded in a plan of 1729 (fig. 149)[154] This work included construction of a staircase, which, its thirty-seven steps indicate,[155] was probably that from the entrance to the first floor rather than that for the shorter distance from the first to the second floor: indeed, the latter appears to have been the stair of thirty steps built in 1716 and shown in a plan of 1729 (fig. 148).[156] The eastern room on the first floor, known as the 'Scotch' storehouse,[157] received further attention in 1716, when it was provided with a new mezzanine floor shown on a plan and section of 1721 (fig. 157).[158] In 1729 the 'binns floors and partitions' were pulled down,[159] for in 1732, in the wake of the creation of vaults in the basement, 'proper conveniencies for the Reception of stores' were provided.[160] The arms kept in the small armoury on the entrance floor were stored in a variety of ways: racks, or stalls, ranged between the posts seem to have been common.[161] Bins were also used: those that were provided for the White Tower store in 1718 can be seen on the plan of 1729,[162] while smaller stores were provided with presses with shelves and drawers (fig. 149).[163]

Small arms were also stored in the eastern annexe of the White Tower from at least 1715, and quite possibly before then.[164] The small gun office inhabited the area that had been used for the storage of powder,[165] and its firm establishment in the annexe followed the end

147 East–west section of the
White Tower by Clement
Lemprière, 1729. The section shows
the eastern annexe after the internal
reconstruction of that year.

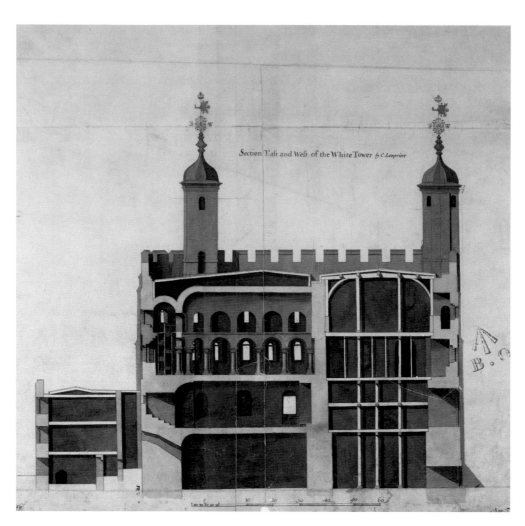

of that building's connection with powder-proving.[166]
The sheds that had been built along the east side of
the White Tower in the 1680s for the storage of small
arms were finally demolished in 1716, and their contents were moved into the ground floor of the eastern
annexe.[167] The office remained in that location after
the reconstruction of the eastern annexe in 1729–30.
The guns were stored in racks running across the
room, and smaller pieces in presses (fig. 151).[168]

By the mid-eighteenth century a repository for 'sea
service', that is, naval, arms had been established in
the western room on the entrance floor of the White
Tower,[169] and it seems likely that room was already
being used for this purpose in 1718 (fig. 152).[170] It was
almost certainly for this room that five new 'semicircular sashes' on the west front were provided by the
carpenter, William Ogbourne, in 1716, presumably for
the five windows enlarged by the mason Robert
Churchill in the previous year.[171] The western chamber on the entrance floor was, like the two floors above
it, furnished anew in the wake of the works connected
with the insertion of the basement vault. The scheme
to equip the room as a proper repository for sea-service
arms, submitted and approved in June 1734,[172] would
seem to have been completed in 1736.[173] These works
included the enlargement of the external window of
the western garderobe in the north wall, and the insertion of the surviving borrowed light in the wall of its

dog-legged passage.[174] It was probably around this time
that the staircase through the building in the centre of
the north end of the western chambers was replaced
by less intrusive stairs in the north-west corner of the
same rooms.[175] Swords also specified as for sea service
and stored on the top floor of the eastern annexe of
the White Tower were moved to the eastern room on
the top floor of the White Tower itself in 1715,[176] filling
a chamber that had apparently been empty in the years
before that date.[177] The swords were also specified as
part of the sea-service stores, but had been removed
from the building by 1736, when the room was lent by
the Board of Ordnance for the storage of Chancery
records (discussed above). The racks (fig. 158) and
presses in which the swords were kept were also moved
from the annexe into the White Tower in 1715.[178]
Storage arrangements here seem to have been similar to
those in the general small arms rooms: the walls were
lined with presses and chests,[179] and racks constructed
between the upright posts, while other receptacles,
such as 'a bench with drawers' supplied in 1739, held
the smaller items.[180]

In 1718 Christopher Wren and the officers of the
Works described the White Tower as being home to
'divers Course Stores and Utensills',[181] and to some
extent they were right, for tools, match rope, wheelbarrows and spades were all kept in the White Tower
in the eighteenth century. In 1737 a carpenter's bill was

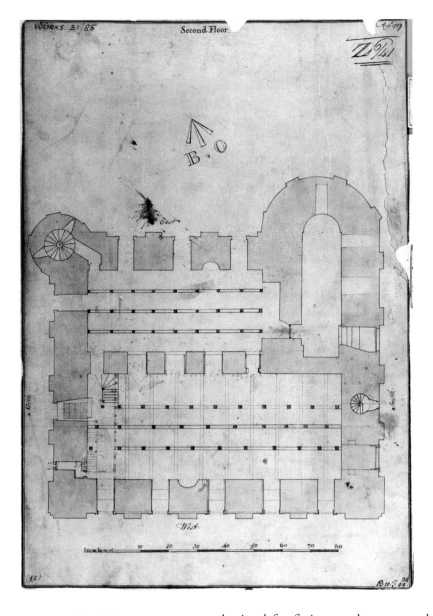

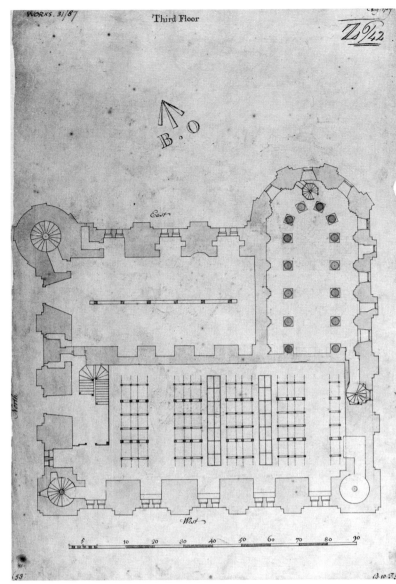

148 (*left*) Plan of the entrance floor (here titled 'Second Floor') of the White Tower made for the Board of Ordnance, 1729.

149 (*right*) Plan of the first floor (here titled 'Third Floor') of the White Tower made for the Board of Ordnance, 1729.

submitted for fitting up the eastern chamber on the entrance floor with 'conveniences to stow pick-axe, spaids, pole axes etc'.[182] These were no mere tool-boxes, but 'a multitude of fine closets, presses and lockers, all filled with an almost incredible number of tools for the war service'.[183] The western chamber on the top floor was also to be used for storing a variety of miscellaneous stores, among them match rope, shovels, wheelbarrows, sheep skins and tanned hides.[184] These rather less valuable stores do not appear to have been afforded the elaborate storage conditions given to the tools, and it seems probable that until they were established in the western chamber on the top floor they were housed wherever there was room within the building.[185] The storage of these miscellaneous stores on the top floor was apparently formalised in the 1710s, and in 1719 it was reported that of the two main rooms on the top floor 'One . . . is the Sword Office for sea service and the other for match'.[186] The sword and match rooms on the top floor, like much of the rest of the building, were revamped in the early 1730s: they were provided with new leaded casements,[187] with various equipment for 'the Reception of stores',[188]

and re-floored.[189] While the eastern sword room pass-ed out of Ordnance control to be used for record storage in 1736 (see above), the western match room remained an Ordnance storeroom (fig. 154). Supplies could be raised and lowered by means of the capstan at the north end of the room, partitioned off in 1750,[190] which could lift goods up through a trapdoor from the entrance floor. It is unclear whether the internal capstan ceased to function after a crane was attached to the north face of the White Tower in 1778.[191]

The Ordnance Storerooms in the Early Nineteenth Century

The armouries in the White Tower, which had been used in much the same way since the 1730s, under-went subtle but highly significant changes in the early decades of the nineteenth century. Since the end of the seventeenth century the building had operated principally as a functional military storehouse for a variety of arms and artillery-related supplies, with the Record Office as a quiet cohabitant. From the early nineteenth century, though, its formerly exclusive

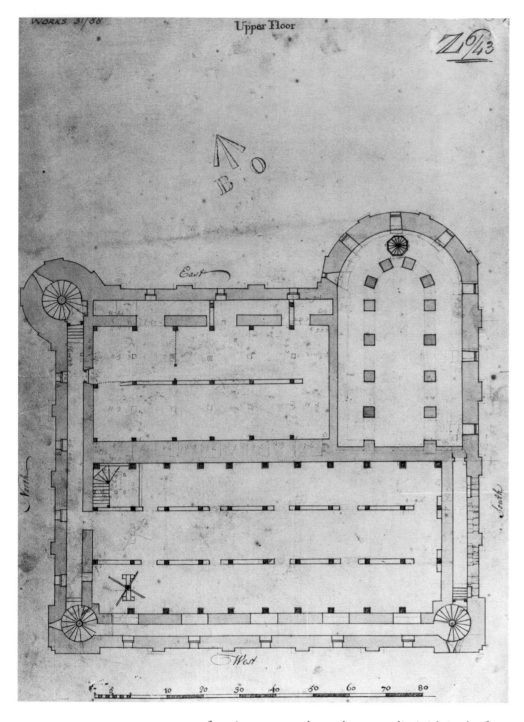

150 Plan of the second floor (here titled 'Upper Floor') of the White Tower made for the Board of Ordnance, 1729.

function as a storehouse began to diminish in the face, in particular, of its growing status as a tourist attraction. The subject of tourism is discussed in detail below, but the main changes that it brought to the storage of service arms are covered here. In 1800 works were done to the 'new sword room' in the White Tower. Possibly this was the room under the chapel, which would have become available if its early eighteenth-century function as a store for Ordnance record had ceased with their transfer to the new top storey of the eastern annexe, completed in that year.[192] In 1805 rather more substantial changes were made to the armouries in the White Tower. From September 1804 to March 1805 the Volunteer Armoury in the White Tower was set up, for which the carpenter's bill amounted to more than £3,000.[193] Immediately thereafter, in the spring of 1805, £1,300 was spent on refit-

ting the Sea Armoury.[194] At the same time work was done to the windows of the White Tower, which necessitated 'cutting out walls', possibly involving the replacement of surviving double windows.[195] The earliest detailed description of the contents of the White Tower after this rearrangement (in 1815) shows the sea arms to have been moved to the west room on the first floor, and the Volunteer Armoury set up in the west room on the entrance floor below.[196] Significantly, these Volunteer and Sea armouries could now be viewed by the public (below, p. 204), and it seems likely that the rearrangement and the opening of these two rooms were closely connected. Certainly, the rooms now combined the storage of a great number of service arms with the ornamental display of obsolete ordnance and armour; and the erection, in early 1810, of a staircase in the Volunteer Armoury would have made public access much easier.[197] In 1812 works were carried out in the White Tower, fitting up yet another armoury, this time the new sword room.[198] Coming seven years after the sword room of 1805 was established, this was presumably a different room, perhaps the eastern chamber on the first floor, which by 1815 was home to the swords and pistols of the Cavalry Armoury.[199] Further rearrangement in the White Tower took place in the wake of the relocation of the Horse Armoury to the new purpose-built structure on the south face of the building in 1825 (below, p. 205). In 1834 arms racks and fitments for tools were taken down in the White Tower; shelves were then fitted up in the New Armouries building, recently vacated by the Horse Armoury, to receive the tools from the White Tower.[200] Clearly at this time the tool room, the east room on the entrance level, was dismantled and its contents removed from the White Tower.[201] The clearing away of arms racks at this time was specifically to allow the fitting up of 'intermediate floors' to increase storage space.[202] It is not clear which rooms were provided with these mezzanine floors at this time, though of the surviving posts (entrance and first floors) only those of the first floor have what appears to be evidence for this. Here, sloping mortices indicate that two intermediate floors (or just conceivably heavy racking) were inserted. The arms racks were described as being taken down in, variously, the 'cells' in the White Tower, and the '3 large Rooms' of the White Tower.[203] In 1837 the south-east room on the entrance floor was fitted up to house 'Queen Elizabeth's Armoury', and ceased to function as a repository of service arms. The bill for 'rebuilding part of the cavalry armory' submitted in early 1837 presumably related to this room;[204] the chamber may even have been cleared of its stores earlier, perhaps as one of the 'cells' in which storage racks were dismantled in 1834. Although this room was lost as a repository of service arms, the Board of Ordnance gained a chamber in 1843, when Sir Francis Palgrave agreed to relinquish the 'anti chamber' in the

151 Plan of the basement (here titled 'Ground Floor') of the White Tower by Peter Campbell, 1754.

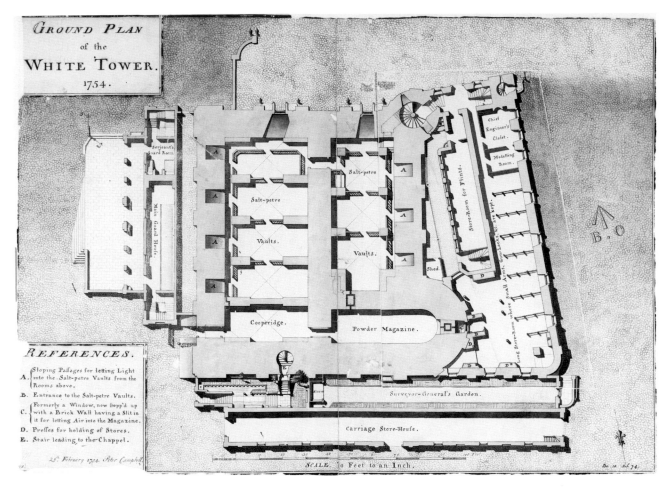

152 Plan of the entrance floor (here titled 'First Floor') of the White Tower by William James, 1754.

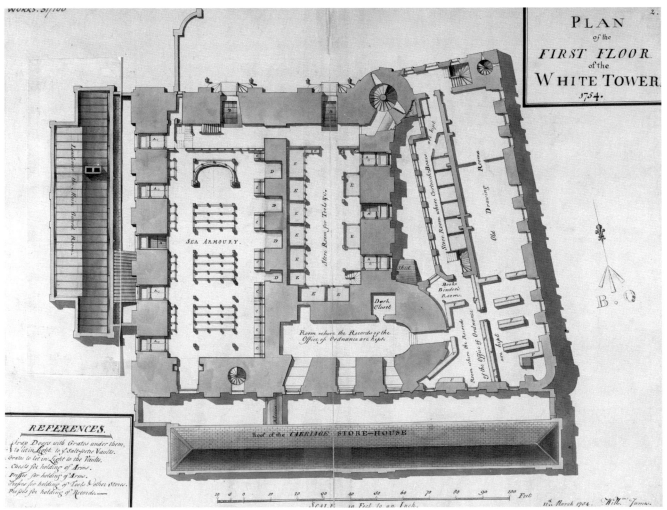

153 Plan of the first floor (here titled 'Second Floor') of the White Tower by Peter Campbell, 1754.

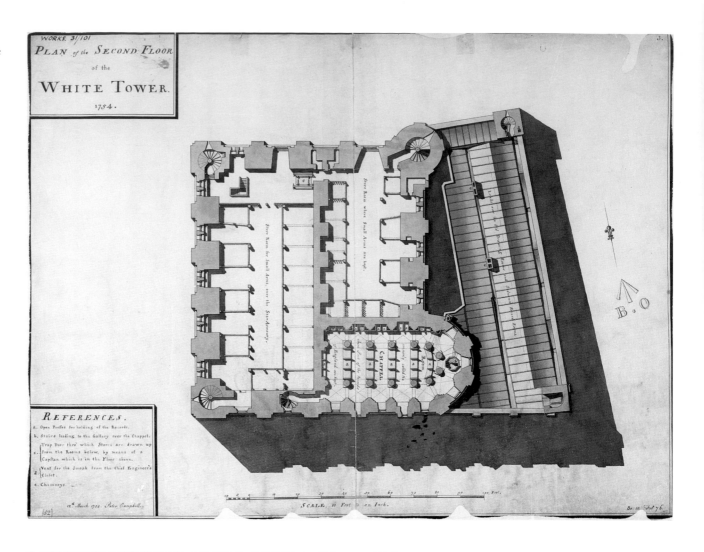

154 Plan of the second floor (here titled 'Third or Upper Floor') of the White Tower by William James, 1754.

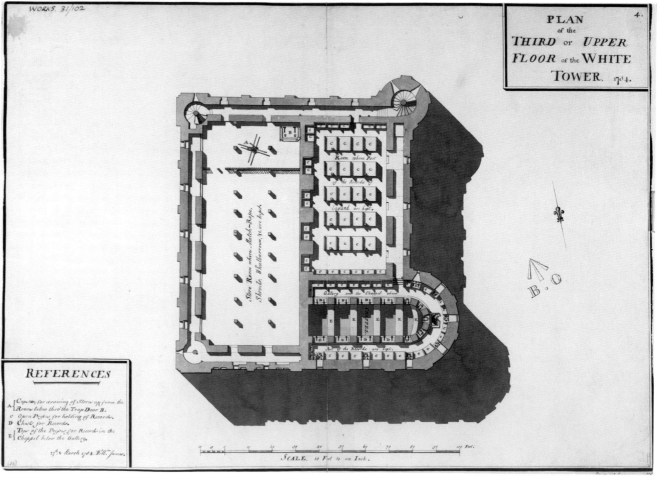

155   Plan of the roof of the White Tower by Peter Campbell, 1754.

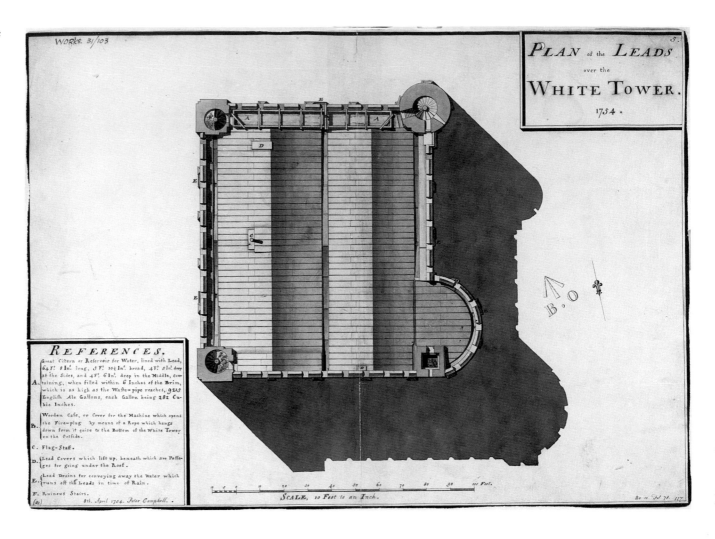

156   Plan and section of the southern part of the White Tower by Douglas Campbell, 1754. The drawing shows a proposal for new wooden racks for gunpowder that would have made it possible to store some 800 barrels in the south-east room alone.

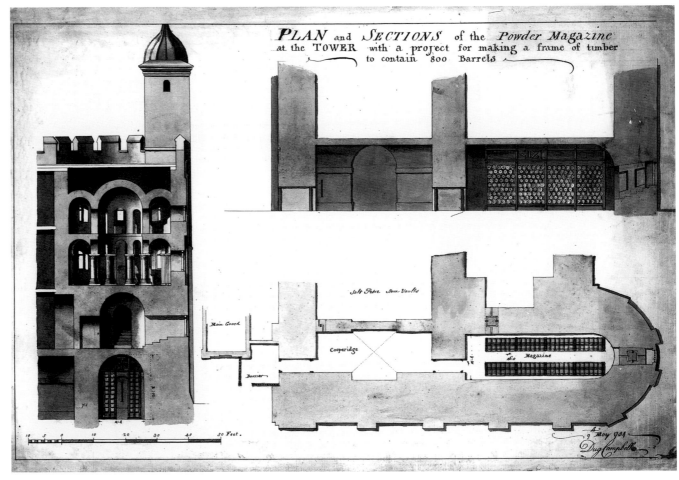

157 Plan and sections of the 'Scotch Storehouse' in the eastern room on the first floor by Clement Lemprière, 1721. The drawing shows the 'new floor' inserted here in 1716 to increase the capacity for storage, and the remaining two-light windows in the east wall, which seem to have remained until 1805.

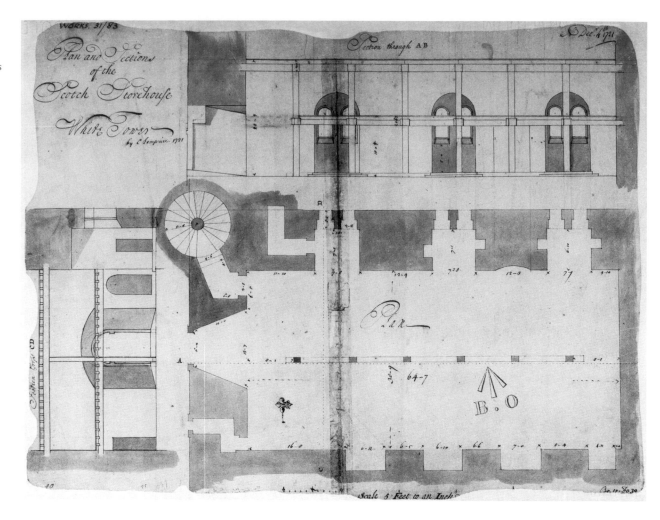

White Tower to the Ordnance Office.[205] This was presumably one of the rooms on the top floor.

The Record and Drawing Rooms

In May 1715 an estimate was requested by the Board of Ordnance for making the necessary receptacles in the White Tower for the storage of the office's records.[206] In early 1716 the Board ordered that the top floor of the eastern annexe, recently vacated by the removal of the swords to the White Tower itself, should be 'fitted up for a Repository for all Draughts, Plann, & Projects belonging to the Office', as well as for 'the Old Books and Records of the Office'.[207] This work saw the eastern annexe converted to form the first permanent accommodation for the newly created Ordnance Drawing Room. This institution, which had come into existence in the early 1710s with the appointment of Robert Whitehand as the first Ordnance Office Draughtsman, would soon be famous across the globe as the Ordnance Survey. For its new role the annexe was provided with shelves, presses and glass windows, some of which can be seen on a plan and section of 1717 (fig. 159), and supplied periodically with necessary equipment, including pencils and weights for the drawings.[208]

In 1729-30 the eastern annexe saw major works, which included the creation of a vaulted basement.[209] The internal walls were wholly rebuilt where the annexe joined the apsidal projection of the White Tower. The single-storey lean-to structure built up against the west wall of the body of the annexe was also rebuilt as a more substantial building within the same shell (fig. 159, cf. fig. 147).[210] The roof and presses of the drawing room were taken down in the summer of 1729.[211] The new heightened western building was to contain a new modelling room (see below), while the Drawing Room, reinstalled in 1730, continued to occupy most of two large rooms looking eastwards.[212] By 1754, though, the Drawing Room had vacated the eastern annexe for new spacious rooms elsewhere in the Tower, while a modest closet on the ground floor had become home to the modelling room, and cartouches boxes (wooden cases for storing and transporting fabric- or paper-wrapped charges) were being kept in the upper storey of the western building.

The records that occupied the southern end of the eastern annexe were only those of the Ordnance Office itself, and were quite separate from the records that were kept in the Wakefield Tower and the White Tower proper. The officials of the Tower Record Office, however, advised on the appointment of one Sebastian Smith to keep the Ordnance records in 1717, and all the Ordnance books to 1702 were to be sent to the new repository.[213] The reconstruction of 1729-30 slightly increased the space available for the Ordnance records,[214] but it was with the creation of a passage into the south-east apsidal room on the

158 'Light and Heavy Dragons [Cavalry] Swords' from a late eighteenth-century drawing, showing how the swords in the White Tower would have been stored.

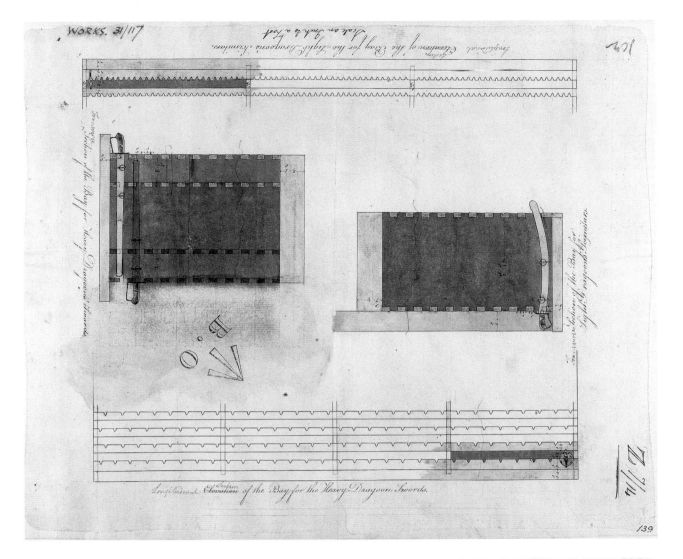

159 Plan and section of the eastern annexe to the White Tower by Clement Lemprière, 1717. This drawing shows the internal structure of the annexe before its reconstruction in 1729–30. In 1716 the top floor had been fitted up with racks and shelves for the plans administered by the newly created Ordnance Drawing Room, the forerunner to the Ordnance Survey.

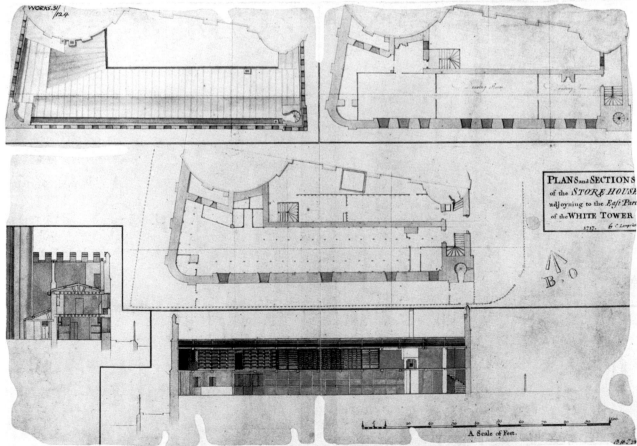

160 The White Tower from the north-east by Thomas Malton, 1799. The eastern annexe was to be substantially enlarged with the addition of an extra storey the following year.

entrance floor (adapting the Romanesque window embrasure), probably in 1734, and the acquisition of that room for the Ordnance records that their space was substantially increased.[215] The record rooms were provided with shelves and presses for the documents, and by 1737 a bookbinder was established there.[216]

The Ordnance modelling room, responsible for ensuring that English weaponry was produced to standard designs (and for the models of these agreed designs), had operated from the annexe since its reconstruction in 1729–30. It had for a short time occupied only a small chamber on the ground floor of the annexe, but, in 1758, expanded into the rooms on the top floor vacated by the drawing office in the early 1750s.[217] In 1800 an additional storey was added to the eastern annexe, described as a 'new room over the Modelling room', though it is unclear whether this was to provide accommodation for that department, or for some other purpose.[218] This largely replicated the eastern elevation of the first and second floors (with their triplets of three windows), but did not extend west from the Wardrobe Tower, because this would have blocked the windows of the apse of St John's Chapel (figs 160 and 162).

The Ordnance records continued to be stored in the eastern annexe of the White Tower during the early nineteenth century, and indeed seem to have required ever more space.[219] The removal of Ordnance papers from the room beneath the chapel, perhaps in 1800 (see above), suggests that the additional storey to

the eastern annexe completed in the same year may have been for the storage of those displaced Ordnance records.[220] By 1870 the records had gone and the annexe was occupied by carpenters' shops.[221]

The Carriage Storehouse and the Main Guard

Two buildings were constructed alongside the White Tower in 1717. Since neither of these had any internal access to the White Tower, and neither actually abutted the main body of the White Tower, they will be mentioned only briefly. While the small arms stored in the sheds on the east side of the White Tower were moved into the eastern annexe in 1716, the contents of the sheds that had run along the south face of the White Tower – principally gun carriages – were provided with a new permanent building in place of the sheds. Work began on the foundations of the new building in early 1717,[222] and a drawing of the structure of that date shows the end result.[223] The storehouse, which consisted of two storeys with fifteen bays, remained on the site until it was replaced by the New Horse Armoury in 1825.

The second structure, on the west side of the Tower, was the Main Guard. The estimate of £983 14s. 6d for the building was approved in March 1717, and work was carried out throughout that year.[224] The building seems to have been constructed quickly, and by September bills for internal works, including flooring and wainscoting, were being submitted.[225] It comprised two storeys, the first floor containing guard

beds, and the ground floor the guardrooms; a staircase filled each end of the structure.[226] The building seems always to have been rather unsatisfactory,[227] and, despite various alterations,[228] it was finally replaced by a new Main Guard, to the south of the old structure, in 1846.[229]

The End of the Ordnance Office

The Ordnance Office's failure to arm British forces efficiently during the Crimean campaign, with tragic results, led directly to its abolition in May 1855 and the subsuming of its responsibilities within the War Office.[230] The combination of the passing of the White Tower into the control of the War Office, far less closely connected to the Tower of London than the Board of Ordnance had been, and increasing interest in the White Tower as a historic building, was permanently to alter the use and perception of the White Tower.

THE WHITE TOWER AND TOURISM

As has been discussed in the previous chapter, the White Tower and the collections stored there and in adjacent buildings were among the great sights of the city of London before the Civil War. Descriptions of visits to the building are to be found in a clutch of memoirs written by visiting foreign dignitaries towards the end of Elizabeth I's reign. The principal attractions were the impressive collections, military and civil, of the Armoury, Ordnance, Wardrobe and Jewel House. As well as being celebrated for its contents, the White Tower was itself an attraction, chiefly because it was widely believed to have been built by Julius Caesar. So Paul Hentzner commented on 'that very ancient and very strong tower, enclosed with four others, which in the opinion of some was built by Julius Caesar', while the Duke of Stettin Pomerania was shown 'what is held to be Julius Caesar's dining-rooms'.[231] Visits such as these were either laid on for a dignitary by the sovereign, as was the case with the visit of the King of Denmark in 1606, or a guided tour could be arranged privately with Yeoman Warders for a fee.[232] The White Tower continued to be an attraction during the seventeenth century, though the fact that it was the work of William the Conqueror rather than Caesar was becoming gradually more widely known.[233] This realisation, combined with the reorganisation of Ordnance and Records storage in the early years of the eighteenth century, saw the White Tower gradually dropped from the tourist itinerary of the castle. Though the keep was pointed out to visitors of the early eighteenth century, they seldom saw inside it.[234] In 1740 it was noted that 'the inside of this grand Tower is not publickly shewn', and when the first visitors' guide was published, with a list of the fees to see various parts of the castle, entrance to the White Tower was not among them.[235]

The White Tower was not, therefore, one of the great tourist attractions of the eighteenth century, but this

was to change at the beginning of the nineteenth. In
1805 the stores in the western rooms on the entrance
and first floors were rearranged (above, p. 196), and by
1807 access to these rooms was part of the visitor tour
of the Tower of London.[236] A payment of 2 shillings
gave the visitor entry to the Grand Storehouse, Spanish Armoury and these two chambers in the White
Tower.[237] The rooms still contained vast numbers of
contemporary operational arms, 'fit for service at five
minutes notice', but among them were now sprinkled
objects of historic interest, such as the armour of

Charles Brandon, Duke of Suffolk, and ordnance tak-
en by General Wolfe at the capture of Quebec in 1759.

One of the greatest attractions at the Tower of
London in the eighteenth and nineteenth centuries
remained the Line of Kings, a series of life-size
mounted figures of the kings of England, carved in
wood and dressed in armour, which had been displayed at the Tower from 1660 and since 1688 in the
New Armouries.[238] Despite the display's popularity,
Samuel Meyrick, the pioneering scholar of arms and
armour, observed that the collections at the Tower

163 The vestibule at the east end of the New Horse Armoury, *circa* 1870. The doorway shown to the right of the slide led visitors from this building up into the eastern annexe and on into the White Tower.

were shown with extraordinary ignorance of their original use, and that such 'false representations' were seriously deceiving visitors.[239] After consultations with the Duke of Wellington, Meyrick offered to oversee their reorganisation, pending the provision of 'a proper receptacle' for their display,[240] and by July 1825 work was under way on a new building along the south front of the White Tower,[241] fitted out in spring 1826.[242] The building stood on the site of the Carriage Storehouse of 1717 and, like its precursor, was separated by several feet from the south wall of the White Tower to leave access to the stair to the chapel.[243] Stylistically, it was designed to blend in with the White Tower and eastern annexe, with a flat roof, crenellated parapet and round-headed doors with Portland keystones and voussoirs. (fig. 162) The interior also echoed the White Tower, with piers in the vestibules at either end imitating those of St John's Chapel, albeit anachronistically combined with chevron-decorated arcades. (fig. 163). The display, duly reordered in the course of 1826 under Meyrick's direction, opened to the public in the spring of 1827; in his view, it was 'the only collection in Europe truly and historically arranged'.[244]

In 1825 Meyrick also advised on alterations to the 'Spanish Armoury'. This much-visited collection was composed of arms, armour and other objects supposedly carried aboard the ships of the Spanish Armada, among them a range of gruesome torture instruments that the Spanish were planning to use in pacifying English Protestants. Meyrick's suggestion that this eclectic collection be renamed 'Queen Elizabeth's Armoury' (because much of it clearly had nothing to do with the Armada) was not taken up until 1831.[245] This display, which had been housed in a building to the south-west of the White Tower, was moved into the room beneath the chapel on the entrance floor in 1837. Three contemporary drawings illustrate the proposal to decorate the room with assorted Norman architectural details, several deriving from twelfth-century forms. This entailed covering the wall surface and barrel vault with shafts and ribs, creating five bays of quadripartite vaulting. In one design the two primary doorways in the northern wall were incorporated within a continuous band of interlaced blind arcading (fig. 164).[246] Work done in 'rebuilding part of the cavalry armoury' in the early months of that year presumably related to the fitting up of this room.[247] The

entrance was from the eastern annexe, through the primary window embrasure at the east end of the room, while the figure of Queen Elizabeth and her page, which had been refurbished in 1825, formed the focus of the room at the western end. Visitors approached 'Queen Elizabeth's Armoury' from the New Horse Armoury via a staircase in the eastern annexe;[248] this staircase was replaced in 1851, at which time two rooms, one above the other, at the south-east corner of the annexe were acquired for the display of more historic armour.[249]

Popular interest in the Tower of London, to which these displays responded, was spurred on by a number of important publications on the castle in the 1820s and decades following. The first great work on the Tower was written by John Bayley, intimately familiar with the keep through his work as a clerk of the Tower Record Office. His two-volume *History and Antiquities of the Tower of London*, published between 1821 and 1825, contained the first scholarly work on the building. As well as being firmly based on documentary evidence, the book included detailed accounts of the many famous figures imprisoned at the Tower, an aspect of the castle's history that, surprisingly, had gone largely unexploited until this time.[250] Bayley's work captured imaginations and was swiftly followed by a number of other publications on the Tower: John Britton and Edward Brayley's one-volume *Memoirs of the Tower of London* appeared in 1830, and in 1836 the antiquary and publisher Charles Knight took the contents of these works to a wider audience by devoting two editions of his *Penny Magazine* to the Tower. These works all saw the White Tower given new attention, for two principal reasons: first as the oldest part of the fortress and second as the supposed location of some memorable incidents in English history, including the incarceration of Sir Walter Ralegh and Richard III's dispatch of Lord Hastings to the scaffold. This new fame brought, in turn, dismay that the entire keep was 'not open to the inspection of the general visitor' and criticism of the arrangements for visiting the Tower as a whole.[251] Knight remarked that 'the necessity of being attended by a warder, and the sum paid for a sight of the armouries, is an effectual barrier' to proper enjoyment of the visit.[252]

Disquiet about the visiting arrangements to the Tower combined with increasing political interest in the improving qualities of museums and art galleries. In 1838 Hampton Court Palace was opened to the public free of charge, bringing increased pressure on the officials of the Tower to reduce or abolish the charges, which could total more than 4 shillings per person.[253] Though the Constable of the Tower of London, the Duke of Wellington, was adamant in his opposition on the basis that the safety of the arsenal could not be maintained if the numbers coming in were to increase, the entrance fee for all but the Crown Jewels was dropped to 1 shilling in 1838 and then to sixpence the following year. Visitor numbers exploded, rising from 10,000 per year in 1837 to almost 100,000 in 1840. One of the buildings belonging to

165 *Queen Jane's First Night in the Tower* by George Cruickshank for Harrison Ainsworth's best-selling *The Tower of London: A Historical Romance* (1840). Ainsworth located Lady Jane Grey's spine-chilling encounter with a headsman's axe, the augury of the fate that was to befall her, in the chapel of St John.

the menagerie was converted to a ticket office, one of the first of its kind at a historic building, and a waiting room for visitors was established.[254]

In 1841 a Select Committee was appointed to inquire into the fees and entrance arrangements at a number of national monuments, including the Tower.[255] Among the witnesses called before the committee was John Britton, who reported that because of its use for storage, the most interesting building, the keep, was 'not easily to be examined'. Robert Porrett, Chief Clerk to the Principal Storekeeper of the Ordnance, was pressed on whether more of the keep could be opened to the public, but was very reluctant to allow it, arguing that the stairs would pose difficulties for older visitors, and that though the chapel was thought 'amongst the connoisseurs of ancient architecture' to be 'a very pure specimen of the Norman style . . . to a general visitor it would not be of interest'.[256] All the Tower officials were quick to argue that while allowing visitors to wander freely might be appropriate at the National Gallery or the British Museum, the

Tower attracted a different sort of visitor from these institutions of high culture, and thus it was essential that all visitors continued to see the castle as part of a guided group.

In the event, the Select Committee did not effect any significant changes to the visiting regime at the Tower. Whole areas of the castle, however, were to be opened to the public for the first time over the following decade or so, thanks almost entirely to the publication of William Harrison Ainsworth's wildly successful novel, *The Tower of London*. Ainsworth first decided to write a book set at the Tower after visiting the castle in 1824. Interestingly, he deliberately conceived the novel, which took as its subject events surrounding the brief reign of Lady Jane Grey, 'to contrive such a series of incidents as should naturally introduce every relic of the old pile'. It was another of Ainsworth's stated purposes that his book would cause more of the Tower to be opened to the public

> There seems no reason why admission should not be given, under certain restrictions, to that unequalled specimen of Norman architecture, Saint John's Chapel in the White Tower, – to the arched galleries above it, – to the noble council-chamber teeming with historical recollections, – to the vaulted passages – and to the winding staircases within the turrets – so perfect, and so interesting to the antiquary.[257]

The book was published in monthly instalments throughout 1840 and was immediately a hit; it was in its sixth edition within five years and was swiftly translated into French, Spanish, German and Dutch.[258] Ainsworth made the White Tower, and particularly the chapel of St John, the setting for a number of the novel's most dramatic and memorable moments, including Lady Jane Grey's terrifying nocturnal vision, the betrothal of Mary I to Philip of Spain and the Duke of Northumberland's conversion to Catholicism (fig. 165). As a result, the fame of the building would soon eclipse that of the arsenal it contained, and its days of functioning principally as a storehouse were coming to an end.

166 'Sketch for the proposed Restoration of the South Side of the White Tower', Anthony Salvin, 1857. Salvin's scheme for the wholesale 'restoration' of the keep was not adopted, and his work was instead restricted to the interior of the top floor and St John's Chapel.

CHAPTER EIGHT

The White Tower, 1855–2000

ANNA KEAY WITH ROLAND B. HARRIS

Since the mid-nineteenth century the White Tower has functioned first and foremost as a visitor attraction. The records of state were removed in the 1850s and by the end of the First World War the entire building was open to visitors. Since that time, public interest has extended beyond its contents to a much greater recognition of the importance of the building itself. This shift contributed to the decisions of the 1980s and '90s that resulted in removal from the Tower of the vast majority of the historic arms and armour to a new museum in Leeds. In terms of the structure of the keep, this period saw few significant changes. The end to large-scale alterations was caused by a move from building works aimed at adaptation and reuse to those seeking to conserve, and even enhance, the building as a medieval monument. Although enthusiasm for the Tower of London's medieval past was enormous, the White Tower fared lightly at the hands of the Victorians and the only permanent imprints of revivalism are the sixteen chapel windows refashioned by Anthony Salvin in 1864, and the four similarly styled windows of the apsidal room below, which date from *circa* 1880–2.

RESTORATION AND RE-MEDIEVALISATION

The removal of the records from the Tower of London in the 1850s coincided with increasing interest in the antiquity of the fortress, and in the White Tower in particular. In 1842 the publisher and antiquary Charles Knight had lamented:

> What is the White Tower now? Its walls remain; but modern doors and windows have taken the place of the old Gothic openings; and within, the fine ancient apartments are divided and subdivided into various offices. The chapel . . . is fitted up as a depository for records; – and the vaulted rooms in the basement are filled with military stores and gunpowder. To none of these places are the public admitted; nor if they were could they form any notion of the ancient uses of the building. It would be a wise thing in the Government to sweep away all that encumbers and destroys the interior of the edifice; and to restore it as far as possible to the condition in which it was at some given period of our history . . .[1]

Many of the works of the later nineteenth and early twentieth centuries addressed, by degrees, Knight's complaint.

The removal of the records from the top floor of the White Tower was completed by mid-August 1856, in the process of which the openings in the spine wall between those rooms were emptied and those still containing records were ordered to be bricked up.[2] The Crimean War, which had so increased the work of the Board of Ordnance that the top floor of the White Tower was cleared of records before the scheduled time, ended in April of the same year. This, combined with the radical reshaping of military supply that followed the end of the war, prevented the rooms from being pressed into immediate military service.[3]

The feeling that the Tower of London was not well served as a historic castle by its principal occupants, the staff of the Board of Ordnance, had been growing

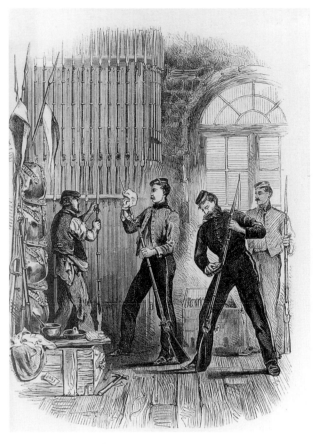

in the late 1840s. An anonymous letter to *The Times* of July 1851 asked just who was in charge of maintaining the architectural and historic integrity of the great fortress, and counselled that rather than relying on 'the military clerk of works or whoever the leading official might be', 'some architect such as Salvin, Scott, Hardwick or Barry be called upon for advice, for ancient architecture is evidently not part of a sapper's education'.[4] It was Prince Albert himself who was to respond to such cries, by declaring that nothing within the Tower of London should 'be built, altered or restored until the plans and elevations should have been officially submitted for her Majesty's personal approval'. Furthermore, Anthony Salvin was engaged to oversee the restoration of the Salt and Beauchamp towers during the 1850s.[5] When the top floor of the White Tower was relinquished by the Record Office, the War Office, backed by the Treasury, tried to retain it for military use, but was thwarted because the Constable of the Tower had already obtained 'her Majesty's sanction' to his proposal that it should be restored by Salvin and opened to the public. After some heated discussion (during which the War Office officials threatened to force their way into the rooms through a 'loophole'), it was 'the Prince's suggestion' that brought about the compromise arrangement whereby the 'exhibition' of the rooms themselves would be combined with their use as an armoury by the new Military Stores Department.[6]

On 13 December 1856 Anthony Salvin was asked to prepare an estimate for restoring the top storey of the keep 'exactly to its original appearance'.[7] Salvin sub-

mitted his report on 31 January 1857, outlining his scheme for the Council Chamber (the western room of the second floor) – though the size of his estimate meant that works could not begin for a year at least, when the money had been approved by Parliament.[8] Salvin proposed strengthening the roof (which he misidentified as chestnut) with iron, thus allowing the removal of the free-standing posts.

The new roof was to have false 'hammer beams' or braces, which in the first (rejected) proposal would have required heightening the walls to enable the braces to clear the crowns of the (asymmetrically opposed) window embrasures and spine-wall openings. Although the repaired roof was to retain its late medieval form, the skylights introduced in 1812 were to be substantially enlarged.[9] Lack of light in the rooms below was to be addressed by light-wells in the floors of the second-floor and first-floor rooms, although in the event only the roof lights and wells in the second-floor rooms were installed.[10] As Salvin acknowledged, however, the benefits would have been reduced had his suggested replacement of the large post-medieval windows with smaller Romanesque-style openings framed in Bath stone been taken up.

While his estimate was principally concerned with the top floor, Salvin took the opportunity to provide a price for the restoration of the rest of the exterior of the White Tower, and the interior of the chapel of St John. His vision for re-medievalising the keep can be seen in his elevations of 1857, which show the addition of string-courses and arrow slits, and a wholesale replacement of windows (fig. 166).[11] The proposed restorations deviate considerably from what we now know of the original form of the White Tower.[12] For example, the design of the south elevation omitted restoration of features for which good evidence survives, such as the double windows of the east and west rooms of the first floor, windows in the buttresses of the chapel and the main entrance in the westernmost bay. The heightening of the walls, the introduction of wide crenellations with arrow slits and the removal of the turret roofs would have been more radical, and it is unclear how seriously such proposals were presented or received. With hindsight, it is perhaps fortunate that restoration at this stage was limited to reinforcing the roof (with corbels and bolsters and without raising the wall-heads), removing the posts and creating second-floor light-wells.

In the early months of 1862 the White Tower was a hive of activity, as arms racks were installed both in the top floor and in the floor below to carry thousands of rifles (fig. 167).[13] Though these were fully functioning service weapons, they were arranged with a view to providing an attractive sight for the visitor. The scheme was for the apartment to be 'divided into several narrow aisles, which, when occupied by the multitude of arms, will, by their long perspective, make a good

show'.[14] In addition to the smartly ranged arms, the passages, ceilings and window embrasures of the rooms were covered with elaborate displays of weaponry, and their component parts, 'in various groups and devices, so as to resemble flowers &c'.[15] The arrangement of arms to form such symbols and patterns had long been practised at the Tower, most notably by John Harris, who had designed the displays for the Small Armoury in the 1690s,[16] while in the early part of the nineteenth century the Spanish Armoury had 'been ornamented with fanciful devices, formed from the blades of swords, &c by Mr Stacey, in a manner highly creditable to his taste and ingenuity'.[17] The displays in the White Tower were finally completed and the rooms opened to the public by the end of May 1863 (figs 168, 169).[18]

By June 1858 the last of the records had been moved out of St John's Chapel.[19] According to the memoirs of the Lieutenant-General of the Tower, Lord De Ros, it was only because of the change of government and appointment of Jonathan Peel as Secretary of State for War in February 1858 that a plan to make the chapel one of the new Directorate of Clothing stores was avoided.[20] This possibility rejected, the chapel, considered one of the 'royal palace' parts of the castle, was duly handed over to the Office of Works. Although the chapel was empty from 1858, it was not until 1864 that Anthony Salvin was again engaged by the Office of Works to prepare a specification for its restora-

tion.[21] This commission gave Salvin the opportunity to implement, at least partially, his plan for re-medievalising the exterior, and he introduced Bath stone windows with nook shafts similar to those he had proposed throughout the building seven years earlier. The good preservation of the eleventh-century window embrasures to within 300 mm of the exterior face ensured that Salvin's new windows were of the approximate dimensions of the originals, even if the refenestration of 1638 had removed anything on which he could base the detail of his designs (fig. 170). His restoration evidently included the discovery and re-opening of the blocked buttress window in the south wall of the chapel gallery.[22] From structural evidence it is clear that works to the chapel interior at this time extended to the removal of the spiral stair in the ambulatory, the making good of the vault above, scraping clean and repairing the ashlar, and repointing much of the rubble walling.[23]

It is interesting to note that although a date of *circa* 1078 for the construction of the White Tower was accepted in the mid-nineteenth century, Salvin's new chapel windows used angle-roll mouldings on the arches, first known in England *circa* 1093 at the cathedrals of Chichester, Canterbury and Durham, and from the later 1090s at Norwich Cathedral, reflecting the imperfect understanding of stylistic chronology of the time.[24] The latter is most significant because Salvin undertook the remodelling of the exterior of

By 1866 Salvin's work was complete, and both the chapel and the top two floors were open to the public (fig. 171). Having viewed the New Horse Armoury, visitors in their guided parties were conducted up the spiral staircase in the south wall of the White Tower, into the chapel, and then round the armouries.[29] Three years later the displays in the New Horse Armoury were reordered, with a greater emphasis on chronology, by the dramatist and antiquary James Robinson Planché. Although Planché told anyone who would listen that the collection needed a curator rather than the occasional services of an interested antiquarian, the War Office was not yet sympathetic to such a view.[30]

The chapel of St John was restored in the mid-1860s but seems not to have been used for formal worship until some years later (something for which there had been no clear evidence for at least 350 years). In December 1877 the Office of Works included in its bid to the Treasury £50 to provide a communion table for the chapel of St John, suggesting its use for services by that date, if not before.[31] Since the chapel of St Peter ad Vincula functions as the principal church of the Tower, the use of St John's Chapel since its restoration has always been on an occasional basis.[32] In the 1880s the rehabilitated chapel provided a place of worship within the castle for its non-conformist inhabitants.[33]

DEMOLITION OF THE EASTERN ANNEXE AND REARRANGEMENT

Alongside the growing numbers of visitors to the armouries – some 151,281 in 1875 – the collections themselves

170 One of sixteen windows that formed part of Anthony Salvin's re-medievalisation of the chapel of St John in 1864. Portland stone architraves from the remodelling of 1638 were replaced with Bath stone windows with nook shafts in a conjectural reconstruction of the Romanesque originals.

171 The interior of St John's Chapel by John Crowther, 1883. The chapel was opened to the public for the first time after Anthony Salvin's restoration of 1864. The tile floor laid at this time was removed from the body of the chapel in 1967.

the south transept and work in the choir at Norwich Cathedral in the years 1830–34.[25] The replacement of the windows was the only major change to the White Tower's exterior appearance in this period. This is perhaps remarkable, given its iconic status and that the post-medieval aspects of its appearance were universally disliked.[26] This can, in part, be put down to the fact that, unlike many medieval buildings, the White Tower had remained in continuous use since its construction. As a result, it had neither become ruinous nor been extensively modernised in a way that would warrant dramatic restoration.[27] The long-standing division of responsibility for the White Tower's administration between two bodies, until the War Office relinquished it in the early twentieth century, also prevented quick and firm decision-making on such matters. In 1865 the Lieutenant-General of the Tower wrote apologetically of the lack of restoration, giving as an explanation for what he feared would be considered negligence that 'the authorities of the Tower have, of themselves, no power to order the most common repairs; and it is only by persevering application to different Government offices that the most trifling restorations can be effected'.[28]

172 'Queen Elizabeth's Armoury' in the south-east room, immediately beneath the chapel, on the entrance floor. From 1837 to 1880 this room housed the collection of instruments of torture once known as the 'Spanish Armoury'. A Yeoman Warder can be seen showing the visitors the infamous block and axe.

were expanding, and further space was desperately needed for their display.[34] Part of the south end of the eastern annexe had already been converted to house armoury items in 1851 (see Chapter Seven), but increased pressure by the mid-1870s prompted a scheme to increase its use still further, and in 1876 expenditure of £1,000 was approved to extend the displays of historic armour over all floors of the building.[35] The work, however, would never be undertaken. In December 1876, presumably in the course of preparing for the proposed renovation, the disastrous structural condition of the annexe was fully realised. The western wall was found to be in 'a very dangerous state' and it was considered absolutely necessary that this be dismantled.[36] The eastern wall, still largely the original, was not thought to be immediately dangerous, but the Board of Works decided that, since it would need to be replaced in the near future, the whole building should be demolished.[37] Following further examination of the annexe in the spring of 1878, the Board of Works architect, John Taylor, recommended once again that it be removed, considering this an opportunity to return the White Tower to 'its original condition'.[38] The partial demolition of the annexe appears to have taken place in the first half of

1879 and Taylor was firm in his view that, regardless of its great age, the whole building 'ought to be pulled down'. That summer the 79-year-old Anthony Salvin was called in to view the parts of the White Tower that had been exposed by the demolition. Twenty years earlier Salvin had remarked on the antiquity of the annexe and recommended that it be restored. In the event, however, its demolition seems not to have worried him, and he was, instead, much more anxious that nothing should be allowed to rise up in its place, 'so that the noble & most interesting building (the White Tower) may be fully developed clear of any modern building'.[39] In the course of the demolition the remains of the medieval Wardrobe Tower were exposed, along with traces of the Roman city wall onto which it had been built.[40]

With St John's Chapel now restored, widely admired and in periodic use, the sight of the room beneath it – generally considered to have been the chapel crypt – adorned with early nineteenth-century mock-Norman decorations and crammed with horrific torture instruments, must have seemed singularly inappropriate (fig. 172). The removal of the plaster decoration was proposed in 1877 and accepted by all concerned as absolutely necessary.[41] In 1878 the room still contained 'Queen Elizabeth's Armoury', installed there in 1837. By September 1880 this display had been cleared away in preparation for the stripping of the interior, and five years later was to be seen in the western room on the second floor.[42] Work in the 'crypt' was under way by 1881, and the sum of £300 was requested from the Treasury to 'continue' the restoration in 1881–2.[43] It was almost certainly during this restoration and the making good following the removal of the eastern annexe, that the four Romanesque-style windows of the entrance floor apsidal room were added. These match the detail of Salvin's chapel windows above and are also of Bath stone.

Although the number of visitors to the Tower was continually growing, no changes had been made in the arrangements for viewing the armouries. As a guidebook of 1858 explained, 'the warders . . . conduct the visitors through both collections, as soon as a party of twelve are collected, or otherwise every half hour from 10 to 4'.[44] These rules had been in place since 1838 (although visitors to the Tower had been accompanied round the fortress in groups by Yeoman Warders since at least the sixteenth century) in spite of many calls for a free-flow system to be introduced to prevent delays.[45] The result was that by 1880 visitors were regularly waiting for several hours to gain access to the building. Following a protest on Tower Hill in April 1880, the Secretary of State for War himself, Hugh Childers, visited the Tower incognito to investigate and was appalled at the delays he met.[46] In that year, nearly five decades after the inquiries of the Select Committee on National Monuments (see

173 'Scene of the explosion in the Tower of London', from *The Illustrated London News*, 31 January 1885. The bomb, placed in this the west room on the first floor, did substantial damage to the thousands of rifles stored in the keep, but left the building intact.

House of Commons and Westminster Hall, and the resulting fire spread upwards through the light-wells, and a hole caused by the blast, to the room above (fig. 173). Fortunately, the fire was swiftly extinguished, the presence of fire hydrants and trained men, introduced after the burning of the Grand Storehouse in 1841, proving invaluable.[51] The bomb – placed by the Fenian Brotherhood – did surprisingly little serious damage: no one was killed, though several were injured, and the only harm done to the main fabric of the building that Taylor could identify consisted of a few cracks in the masonry, which he thought might well have existed before.[52]

The general desire to clear the White Tower of later accretions contributed to the decision to demolish the New Horse Armoury, on the south face of the building. Its removal was part of an ambitious scheme by Taylor to reconstruct the essentials of the inner curtain wall and 'restore' the Tower to its medieval appearance.[53] The architecture of the New Horse Armoury had never been greatly admired, and must have become even less so as regard increased for the White Tower itself. As one commentator put it, 'the old keep that seems to look down with such ineffable contempt on these romantic battlements, belongs to a period long before buildings, or any feature of them, had begun to pretend to be aught else than they were'.[54] Another described the demolition of the building as merciful.[55]

The War Office accounts do not record the destruction of this building; while the second curator of the Tower Armouries, Charles ffoulkes, gives two different dates – 1883 and 1885 – for the demolition in different publications.[56] A watercolour by John Crowther dated 1883 shows that at that time the eastern half of the building had been removed and the eastern end of the remaining section walled off, though the rest was still standing firm (fig. 174).[57] In November 1884 *The Builder* carried a report of a discussion of works at the Tower that mentioned that the 'sham Gothic horse armoury' had 'still to be cleared away', while *The Times* reported in September 1885 that the Horse Armoury building was 'about to be taken down'.[58] Therefore, though the building was not completely demolished until the later months of 1885, the eastern half had already gone. It may be that the latter had been demolished in 1883, or even perhaps in connection with the tearing down of the eastern annexe, to which it was linked, in the years 1879–81;[59] or it may even have been that 'part' of a building on the east side of the Horse Armoury that had been removed as unsafe as early as June 1877.[60] Whatever the precise chronology, by August 1885 the contents of the Horse Armoury had been moved into the western room on the second floor of the White Tower, known as the 'Council Chamber', and the building of 1825 was shortly to be no more.[61]

Chapter Seven) had recommended it, a scheme was finally put in place to allow visitors to see the Tower unaccompanied, albeit on an experimental basis.[47] As a result, changes were necessary to the warding arrangements and the routes of access from room to room; in September 1880 the Office of Works was asked to create a doorway from the basement floor of the White Tower to the parade ground on the north side, and to provide a staircase in place of 'the existing window & incline' specifically 'to facilitate the convenience of the visiting public'.[48] All this was done in the face of enormous opposition from the Yeomen Warders, who greatly resented losing the complete responsibility for visitors they had long held. Much as had been the case in the 1840s, many of the Tower staff felt that such changes would allow uncontrolled access to the sort of working-class visitors whose presence they felt was most undesirable; an embittered letter to the Constable complained that the changes were introduced by the War Office, which was 'in favour of the working man, and of the curiously dressed class from the East of London'.[49]

The new regime started on 11 October of that year and was found to work well.[50] However, it was apparently the freedom this arrangement permitted that made it possible for a bomb to be placed in the western room on the first floor, known as the 'Banqueting Hall', on 24 January 1885. The bomb exploded at 2 p.m., at the same time as others planted in the

174   View of the White Tower
from the south, by John Crowther,
1883. The great east annexe was
taken down in the years 1879–81,
and the New Horse Armoury, of
which the eastern end had already
been demolished, was probably
removed completely in late 1885.

Immediately following the bombing of 1885 the White Tower had been closed to the public, and when it reopened a far stricter regime was enforced and public access curtailed. Although, after much discussion, the old regime of obligatory guided tours was not re-established, the movement of visitors within the galleries was to be very closely overseen and many more barriers and screens were introduced.[62] While the New Horse Armoury and the eastern annexe were still standing, visitors had seen the displays in those buildings and the south-east room on the entrance floor before exiting the White Tower and re-entering it to visit the upper floors of the keep separately, by the spiral stair in the south wall.[63] When the White Tower reopened to the public after the bomb, however, the New Horse Armoury and annexe were no longer attractions, and though visitors continued to enter the building by the southern spiral staircase, they could not enter St John's Chapel and were able properly to view only the second-floor rooms of the building. They were then shepherded down the north-eastern staircase to the first floor, where a new staircase took them from the western room down to the entrance floor below, leaving through the door at the north of the east room onto the parade.[64] The contents of the New Horse Armoury, the eastern annexe and 'Queen Elizabeth's Armoury' were all installed in the west room on the second floor of the White Tower (fig. 175).[65] The transfer of the contents of these buildings to the second floor of the White Tower was made

possible by the gradual removal from the Tower of its remaining War Office stores. In 1869 a great mass of stores had been moved to Woolwich, and by 1885 the decision had been taken to remove the vast majority of the 'whole of the large store of arms which have been kept at the Tower' to the central depot at Weedon in Northamptonshire.[66] In January that year, when the bomb exploded, most of the small arms had already been cleared from the entrance floor, and as a result the damage was far less than it might have been.[67]

REORGANISATION OF THE COLLECTION, 1892–1916

The removal of much of the service weaponry from the Tower of London made the management of what was increasingly a collection of historic arms and armour by a War Office storekeeper all the more anomalous, and in February 1886 a committee was appointed to consider how things might be improved. The pressing need for a catalogue of the collections, and someone sufficiently qualified to compile it, was identified, and would result, after the usual delays, in two commissions for the distinguished historian of armour and military dress, Harold Arthur Lee (from 1892 Viscount Dillon). On the recommendation of the Society of Antiquaries, Lee was commissioned to write a catalogue and, on the death of the Head Armoury Keeper, he was appointed the first Curator of the Tower Armouries.[68] In the first two years of Dillon's tenure, the scheme to empty the

first floor of the modern small arms and to allow the contents of the armoury on the second floor to be spread out was executed.[69] The contents of the Horse Armoury remained on the second floor, but the arms of more recent date, many of the oriental pieces, the contents of 'Queen Elizabeth's Armoury' and 'various personal relics' were moved to the floor below.[70] The visitor to the Tower now entered on the south face, passed up the small spiral staircase to the first floor, there saw the chapel and the east and west rooms before passing up the south-west staircase, viewing the second floor, and then descending to exit the building.[71] Lord Dillon's arrival saw the beginning of a formal, museological approach to the collection, which for the first time was displayed according to function and date, rather than for overall visual effect or the association of individual items with historical events and personalities. All the arms and armour were inventoried and labelled, and the regular practice of dispatching items to Drury Lane to enliven theatrical productions was brought to an end (fig. 176).[72]

The changes to circulation in the White Tower, described above, were in practice delayed by the removal, shortly before February 1893, of the external stair leading to the doorway at the foot of the spiral stair in its south wall. Plans were immediately drawn up for its replacement, but were delayed by the need to repair the roof covering the tramway of 1834 in the same area, made unsafe by the demolition of the New Horse Armoury.[73] After much wrangling between the Office of Works and the War Office over who should pay for the repairs, funds were finally released for both pieces of work to be carried out in the financial year 1894–5.[74]

THE WAR OFFICE BOWS OUT

The extraordinary situation whereby the War Office was responsible for the care of one of the country's most important historic buildings and most popular tourist attractions was finally and formally addressed in 1902. In November of that year a conference was held in Whitehall to discuss the proposal to transfer the Tower of London and Edinburgh Castle to the Office of Works.[75] The proposal won support all round, and it was decided that all the relevant Tower staff, including the Curator of the Tower Armouries, should become the employees of the Office of Works.[76] With the War Office withdrawing ever further from the Tower, and the number of visitors to the armouries now approaching half a million a year,[77] proposals were soon made to dedicate more of the White Tower to public display.[78] In 1910 the scheme to open the basement of the building was first mooted, the accepted view that these rooms were dungeons and torture chambers making them the most obvious part of the building to display next.[79] This gained approval, and in November the logistics of opening the rooms – removing the rifles stored there and the racking that supported them, and taking up the boarding on the floor – were being considered. Though the scheme could not be carried out immediately, due to lack of funds,[80] the Office of Works promised that the plan would 'not be lost sight of', and indeed a year later enquiries were being made by that office into the cost of opening both the basement and the entrance floor.[81] The issue continued to be discussed for several years. Small arms were still stored in great numbers on the entrance floor,[82] and a new

216

176   The post of Curator of the Tower Armouries was created in 1895, and saw the displays in the White Tower become increasingly orderly, with the grouping together of objects in a more didactic fashion and the introduction of glass cases and labels.

home for them had to be found, the War Office considering it imperative that a substantial number of service rifles should remain at the Tower.[83] Brass Mount, one of the mural towers on the outer curtain wall of the Tower, was eventually fixed upon as the best location for the rifles, and the hydraulic lift that had moved them between floors in the White Tower was to be moved there also.[84]

By early 1914 the public were clamouring in vain for entry to the 'dungeons' of the White Tower.[85] Although work was finally nearing completion in November 1914, the opening of the basement was postponed because the advent of the First World War necessitated its use for stores, including military bicycles and the most valuable items from the armouries above.[86] Once the Brass Mount small arms store was ready, however, the pressure of the war on space in the White Tower apparently eased, and by the end of August 1915 the entrance floor was empty and on 25 November it was handed over to the Tower Armouries.[87] This spurred on the pre-war plans to open both floors, and work continued throughout the winter of 1915–16, and on 10 April 1916 both the basement and entrance floors were opened to the public (fig. 177).[88] Despite the start of Zeppelin raids in 1915 and the detention and execution of eleven enemy spies within the castle between 1914 and 1916, the Tower, and the armouries in the White Tower, remained open to the public, though in 1914 the most valuable items in the collec-

tion were packed in cases and stored in the south-east room of the basement.[89]

The route that the public were now to take saw the north-east stair, which in recent years had been used only by members of the Tower staff, come into its own as the main vertical access route.[90] The new routing necessitated several structural alterations to the building: the wooden staircase of 1885 between the entrance and first floors was removed, and a 'thirteenth-century' doorway was opened out of the spiral staircase in the south wall into the entrance floor. Since the southern access to the building was no longer to be used, the lower part of the internal stair was filled in, and the external staircase on the south front of the building removed. The basement rooms were provided with new flagstones, and oak stairs leading to the parade ground were created at the north end of the principal rooms. The office of the Curator of the Tower Armouries was moved from the section of the passage at the south end of the west room on the second floor into the top of the north-east turret and the light-wells between the first and second floors were filled in.[91] Finally, the north-west turret was used as a repairing shop for the Armouries, allowing the removal of the partition in the east room on the second floor, which had contained the workshops until this time.[92]

Owing to the gradual transformation of the Armouries' collection from an arsenal into a museum, the exact range of objects it considered worthy of acquisi-

177 Visitors to the south-east
room in the basement of the White
Tower. The association between the
basement and the incarceration and
torture of prisoners made these
rooms especially popular.

tion and display lacked clear delineation. The galleries
in the White Tower were increasingly used to display
objects that had little or no connection with the building or its principal collections. In 1907 Edward VII's
and Queen Alexandra's coronation robes were displayed on the first floor of the building, with their
place taken, in 1912, by the field gun used to carry the
body of Edward VII at his funeral. The coronation
robes were then taken on by Sir Guy Laking, first
curator of the London Museum, and it was with
Laking, and Sir Hercules Reed of the British Museum,
that Dillon's successor as curator, Charles ffoulkes,
attempted to rationalise the collections of arms and
armour in London's museums.[93] As a result of their
deliberations, the specific range of objects that each
museum would collect was fixed upon and the Tower
Armouries were recognised as the proper home for
arms and armour from 1066 onwards and ordnance
to 1700. As a direct result in 1914 many of the Tower's
oriental, Greek and Roman exhibits were transferred
to the British Museum, and various other objects to
the London Museum and Royal United Services Institute.[94]

The transfer of the entrance floor and basement to
the Armouries gave ffoulkes further scope to rearrange
the collections. He disapproved of the decorative patterns created from broken-up pieces of weaponry and
armour with which the walls of the building had long
been adorned, remarking that it seemed to him
'incongruous to cover the walls of an eleventh-century
fortress with these ornaments, however ingenious they
might be',[95] although their removal left the walls largely bare. In the years 1913–16 ffoulkes masterminded
the redistribution of the Armouries' collections over
the newly acquired floors of the White Tower, the

extra space enabling him to continue Lord Dillon's
work in classifying the collection into typological and
chronological categories and displaying them accordingly. The basement was to be used to show the guns
from the gun-park; the entrance-floor west room was
named the 'small-arms room' and contained firearms
and small cannon; the east room was designated the
'record room', and housed the collection of personal
effects of historic figures accumulated by the Armouries. The east room on the first floor housed
swords and daggers, and the western crossbows and
staff weapons. On the second floor the essentials of
the Horse Armoury remained in the west room, with
the equestrian figures ranged down the centre of the
room – the light-wells having been filled in – while the
east room housed the grandest of the Tudor items in
the collection. The block and axe and instruments of
torture were once again moved to the room beneath
the chapel on the entrance floor.[96] This arrangement,
effected in the years 1913–16, was to remain un-
changed in essentials until the 1960s.[97]

THE SECOND WORLD WAR

The Second World War had a more far-reaching effect
on life at the Tower than the war of 1914–18. The
fortress was completely closed to the public and, in
August 1939, both the Crown Jewels and the more
valuable of the Armouries' exhibits were removed for
safe keeping. Soon afterwards, the stained glass from
the windows of St John's Chapel was also carefully
taken down and stored in the basement of the Wakefield Tower.[98] Photographs of that year show the
rooms with some objects remaining, secured in cases
or racks, taped up to prevent shattering and with numerous fire extinguishers and buckets of sand standing

178 The east room on the top fitted up as a bar during the Second World War. In 1939 the castle closed its doors to visitors, and by 1941 the top floor of the keep was being used for soldiers' entertainment, with a bar in this room and a theatre and badminton court in the west room.

ready. By 1941 the great rooms, with their exhibition cases pushed against the walls, had become appropriated for the use of soldiers at the Tower. The east and west rooms on the second floor served as a bar and theatre and badminton court, respectively, the east room on the entrance floor as a canteen and library, and the basement – provided with bunk beds – as an air-raid shelter (fig. 178).[99]

Despite the fact that fifteen bombs fell on the Tower in the course of the war – one reportedly missing the keep by just 7 yards – the White Tower remained undamaged. The Victorian Main Guard, however, immediately to the south-west, was hit and burnt out on 29 December 1940. This building had obscured the view of the White Tower from the south-west, and the demolition of its ruins in the autumn of 1943 led the Chief Inspector of Ancient Monuments to recommend that the chance should be taken to improve the area around the White Tower. A programme of work was suggested that included the excavation and exposure of both the foundations of Coldharbour Gate and the plinth of the White Tower itself, as well as the excavation of the place where the forebuilding was thought to have stood, with a view of reinstating the original entrance to the building.[100]

POST–WAR PRESENTATION

Since the Second World War, the conservation of the White Tower has followed the fashion of the times, in that it has been focused on maintaining the historic fabric, even in the face of structural failure, and each programme of works has been taken as an opportunity for archaeological investigation. Works on the heating system in the vicinity of the White Tower were taken as an opportunity to investigate Coldharbour

179 Children inspecting exhibits in the White Tower shortly after it reopened following the Second World War.

Gate, and the foundations of the twin drum towers of the thirteenth-century entrance to the Inmost Ward were duly located in 1953, and consolidated for public display the following year.[101] The end of these works overlapped with the start of works to the plinth of the White Tower, beginning with the newly exposed and rough-looking west side (see fig. 35),[102] which ultimately provided important evidence that the executed plan of the eleventh-century building had been intended from the start.[103] Nothing was revealed of the eleventh-century finish of the plinth, however, and it was given a smooth batter in the manner of that surviving at Colchester. Works to the plinth continued into 1957 and were followed by the landscaping and grassing over of the adjacent areas.[104]

In 1952 an examination of the roofs of *circa* 1490 over the east and west rooms was undertaken, and revealed a death-watch beetle infestation in the chapel roof.[105] Overhaul and repair were envisaged rather than large-scale replacement of timber, although one of the beams in the east room required immediate propping.[106] By 1954 a second beam was identified as failing and timber was located for the replacement of the two failed tie-beams in 1955.[107] When the leads and boards were lifted, however, much more extensive beetle damage was apparent.[108] Nothing more than the replacement of the two tie-beams and immediately adjacent decayed timber was undertaken, so that an examination of the deteriorating roofs was required again in 1958.[109] This showed that more substantial

repairs were necessary, to the extent that its entire replacement in pre-stressed concrete was considered.[110] Eventually, in 1961, it was decided that an effective solution would be one in which the timbers were freed of their nineteenth-century ironwork, repaired as necessary and then suspended from light steel trusses placed immediately above the timber roof, also carrying the weight of the lead covering.[111] The roof of the White Tower today is, therefore, something of an illusion, but one that has kept the fabric of the late medieval roof substantially intact (fig. 180). Repairs to the roof on the west side were completed by the summer of 1963, and on 8 December the following year the great west room, complete with newly arranged exhibits, was opened to the public.[112] The east room on that floor was not ready to be handed back to the Armouries until 1966, and even then further disruption to the public came over the following four years as works were undertaken to remove several centuries' soot and grime from the exterior masonry (fig. 181).[113] In reinstating the collections after the work to the roof, the Master of the Armouries, W. A. Dufty, made various changes to the displays, including installing glass showcases to protect many of the main Tudor and Stuart armours. Rather than grouping the British collections largely by object type (small arms, staff weapons, etc.), the new displays broke them up by context or period, so that the Sporting and Tournament galleries were created on the entrance floor, while the main rooms of the two floors above displayed the high-

181 The White Tower during
cleaning in 1968. Between 1966 and
1968 all four faces of the White
Tower were cleaned of soot and
grime, which had accumulated
since it was last whitewashed in the
late 1630s.

lights of the collection by period: medieval, Renais-
sance, Tudor and Stuart.[114]

The opportunity was taken during the works to the
chapel roof in 1965 to review the presentation of the
chapel itself. Following correspondence with repre-
sentatives of the Council for the Care of Churches and
the Historic Churches Preservation Trust in December of that year, proposals were put forward for
improving its appearance.[115] As a result, the Victorian
altar, now considered 'out of place', was to be removed
and a new altar to be covered with a cloth in the
colours of the Order of the Bath was commissioned
to replace it.[116] In the course of preparing estimates
for replacing the altar, the Chief Inspector of Ancient
Monuments recommended that the Victorian tile
floor should be replaced by a stone floor, and the work
was agreed, although the tiles in the gallery remained
(fig. 182).[117] In the autumn of 1967 the chapel was
closed to the public for the work to be carried out,
and by June of the following year the works had been
completed and the chapel reopened.[118] This mod-
ernist approach to the furnishing of the chapel was
not to last long. In the mid-1990s the dismantled altar
was identified in the English Heritage store at Fort
Brockhurst in Gosport, and reinstated in 1998.[119]

As early as 1913 the desirability of bringing people
into the building by the original entrance had been
recognised.[120] In 1943 the reopening of the south
doorway on the entrance floor was proposed and rejected in the same document, since the visual impact
of the necessary external staircase was considered
detrimental to the appearance of the building.[121] In
1963 the suggestion was made again, this time meeting
general approval, and an external stair was designed
and an adapted visitor route devised. As ever, lack of
funds meant that the scheme was postponed, but
finally, ten years later, the existing timber staircase was
constructed across the south elevation of the White
Tower and its original entrance reinstated (fig. 183).[122]
Details of the eleventh-century doorway were discovered during the lowering of the threshold to its original level, and these are discussed in Chapter Two.[123]

182 The floor of St John's Chapel during repaving works in 1967. This involved replacing the small earthenware tiles introduced by Salvin in 1865, which survive in the gallery, with the present limestone slabs. The exposed primary sub-floor make-up and the height of the pier plinths indicate that the eleventh-century floor was at approximately the same level as the floor today.

183 The new timber stair to the south door under construction, 1973. The creation of the external timber stair to the south entrance of the keep saw this primary door brought back into use for the first time since, perhaps, the reign of Henry VII.

184 An inspection of the damage caused by the IRA bomb that exploded in the basement of the White Tower on 17 July 1974.

In a strange echo of the events of 1885, only months after new access and circulation arrangements were put in place, the building was damaged by a bomb laid by Irish republican terrorists. On 17 July 1974, a busy summer day on which the Tower received 9,000 visitors, an incendiary device was placed under a gun barrel in the eastern room of the basement. It exploded with enough force to blow out the door and windows at the top of the north-east turret and lifted the floors of the room above (fig. 184). One visitor, Dorothy Household, was killed and thirty-seven others were hurt. The IRA claimed responsibility, and many feared that this event would mark the beginning of a new phase of terrorism directed at historic buildings.[124] The works to repair the building began immediately, and just over six months later it reopened.[125] The decision to celebrate the supposed 900th anniversary of the White Tower's construction in 1978 was perhaps partly inspired by a determination to stand firm in the face of such aggression (fig. 185).[126]

In November 1970 the Ministry of Public Building and Works, the dominant administrative body responsible for the Tower of London, was abolished and its duties vested in the newly created Department of the Environment. In 1989 the Historic Royal Palaces Agency was created and given responsibility for running the

185 The 'novo-centenary goblet' created to commemorate the 900th anniversary of the building of the White Tower, which was celebrated in 1978.

186 The 'Line of Kings' in the White Tower, a re-creation of one of the most famous historic armour displays at the Tower of London, installed as part of the redisplay of the keep in 1998.

Tower of London, with four other major royal sites in Greater London.[127] The reorganisation of the responsibilities of the Department of the Environment, set out in the National Heritage Act of 1993, saw the Tower Armouries become the Royal Armouries, and the board of trustees established to run it came into being on 1 April 1984.[128] The focus that followed on the long-term future of the Armouries' collections saw the development of a plan to increase the size of the galleries substantially, which, in turn, led to the momentous decision to move to a new site. In 1991 it was announced that the bulk of the collections were to transfer to a new purpose-built museum in Leeds, while the 'historic and Tower-related' objects would remain and be shown in the White Tower.[129] The dismantling of the displays in 1995, the removal of the collections and associated reservicing, provided the opportunity for a study of the building on which this book is based. The development of the new displays, opened by Queen Elizabeth II in November 1998, was master-minded by Peter Hammond, the Deputy Master of the Armouries, and Geoff Parnell, Keeper of Tower History – a post created in 1992 to ensure a continued link between the institution and the castle (fig. 186).[130] The White Tower was now shown in a new and different way, with an emphasis on the display of the collection, the history of its display in the building and, for the first time, of the building itself.[131]

PART III

Context and Significance of the White Tower

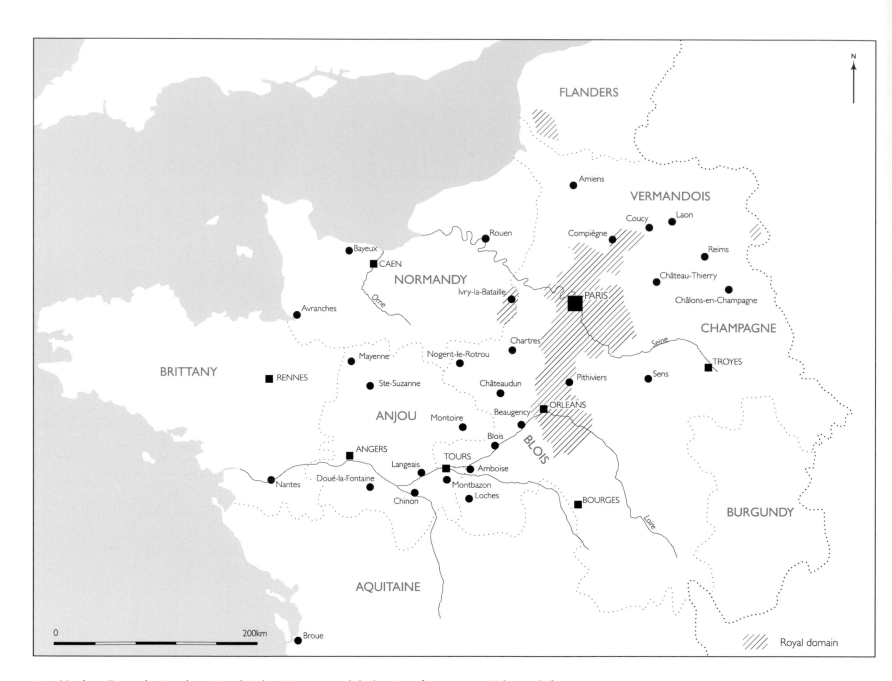

187 Northern France showing the main political entities *c.*950, and the location of great towers (•) known before *c.*1050.

CHAPTER NINE

The Ancestry of the White Tower

EDWARD IMPEY

The White Tower, as established elsewhere in this book, is the supreme example of the 'keep', *donjon*, *tour maîtresse* or 'great tower', terms applied to buildings of differing form but which combined residential, defensive and symbolic functions within a turriform structure. This chapter sets out to re-examine both the origins and development of the great tower as a structural and functional type, and the more immediate inspiration and ancestry of the White Tower itself. It provides a summary of what is known of the origins, date and form of the earliest buildings plausibly identifiable from their physical remains or written sources as 'great towers'. It then examines the functions of these buildings and whether they may, on the basis of common characteristics, be considered as belonging to the same tradition as the White Tower and its immediate precursors. Consideration is then given to why and where the type seems to have emerged, the processes and chronology of its proliferation, and the structural developments that accompanied and encouraged its adoption. The sources for the design of the White Tower itself are then addressed in detail, in the light, in particular, of recent work on closely related great towers of before *circa* 1050 in Normandy itself.

GREAT TOWERS BEFORE 1050: IDENTIFICATION AND STRUCTURAL FORM

The Earliest Examples

That the immediate ancestry of the White Tower and the post-Conquest great tower in England lay in northern and eastern France, assumed since the mid-nineteenth century,[1] is confirmed below. Nevertheless, we cannot be equally certain that the tradition itself had its origins in this area: towers are part of the common currency of architecture the world over, and were going up, certainly in an ecclesiastical context, in other areas of France and western Europe from at least the mid-ninth century. Furthermore, by the early twelfth century towers that shared important functional characteristics of the great tower tradition as defined above, such as the spectacular *Bergfrieden* of Germany and the celebrated towers of the north Italian cities, were being built in other areas of the Continent. Although there are no hints of this in the existing literature, further research may reveal pre-eleventh-century traditions, akin or 'typologically' linked to that discussed here, elsewhere in continental Europe. This study, however, concentrates on France, and for three reasons. First, this is where the model for the White Tower itself quite clearly came from. Second, the great tower tradition as it existed in this area on the eve of the Conquest was—whatever else may have existed in parallel—the product of an evolutionary process *observable in this area*. Third, there is, as will be shown, much to suggest that it was here that the process originated (fig. 187).

Before circa 950

While the existence of the great tower tradition after *circa* 1000 is demonstrated by surviving buildings, its identification in the previous century relies largely on the occurrence in literary sources of *turres*. This carries obvious risks, for the word may not necessarily have been used to denote 'tower' in an entirely literal sense by tenth- and eleventh-century authors, but 'stronghold' or 'fortification', without any consistent distinction from widely used terms such as *castrum*, *castellum*, *munitio* and *oppidum*. There are, however, important safeguards. First, a study of terminology in Flodoard's *Annales* (covering the period 919–66) and Richer's *Historia* of 995–8, two of the most important sources, has shown that *turris* was at least not used as a synonym for the words listed above.[2] Second, and more importantly, however, incidental information not only unquestionably identifies certain *turres* as towers, but also does so frequently enough for this meaning to be inferred in other cases where allowed for by other information.

The known sequence of relevant tenth-century buildings nevertheless begins with two that substantially survive – Doué-la-Fontaine (Maine-et-Loire), firmly implicated in the study of castles and the *donjon rectangulaire* since the 1960s, and the more recently studied structure at Mayenne. The remains at Doué consist of a block measuring 16.5 by 23.5 m externally, with walls surviving up to about 5 m, with at least one small annexe. According to its excavator, Michel De Boüard, the original structure, of *circa* 900, was single-storeyed and contained one room, with a central hearth, two doors and at least one window,[3] subsequently divided by a cross-wall.[4] This he assumed to have functioned as a hall or 'salle d'apparat'.[5] Following a fire *circa* 930–40,[6] however, it was heightened to house at least one more storey,[7] creating what De Boüard interpreted not only as an early 'donjon rectangulaire' but probably the first. Subsequently, in the eleventh century, the lower openings were blocked and the edifice partially buried within a motte. Nevertheless, the structure in its present form, admittedly weathered and damaged since the 1960s, reveals no discernible break between the original build and its supposed heightening,[8] and could therefore have been a plausibly turriform structure as early as *circa* 900. Whether it was intended for defence or was simply a two-storey domestic building is unclear: but if the former, Doué might indeed be identified as a great tower and be the earliest known example, if for rather different reasons and from a different period from that identified by De Boüard.

The rather more complete building in the castle at Mayenne has been dated on the basis of finds analysis and radiocarbon dating to *circa* 900 and loosely attributed to Charles III, great-grandson of Charlemagne and uneasy heir to part of his empire (see fig. 191). How the building was used is unclear, but it was, whatever else, quite clearly a tower: the building consisted in plan of a main block containing a basement with at least two levels above, with interior dimensions of 10.7 by 7.6 m, and an attached turret rising above it.[9] As with Doué, however, what it may have contributed or may tell us of the development of the great tower remains open to debate.

In the order at least of the dates given by near-contemporaries to the contexts in which they first appear, the successors to Doué and Mayenne form a group centred on the Île-de-France. The existence of an early tower at Compiègne (Oise) is revealed by an account in Helgaud de Fleury's *Life of Robert the Pious*, of an incident there at the beginning of the eleventh century, associated with the 'oratory' in the 'tower of Charles':[10] whether the name current in Helgaud's time commemorated Charles II (the Bald), Charlemagne's grandson (840–70) or Charles III is unclear,[11] and the name in any case may have been attached to a more recent building with no real associations with either. Nevertheless, an attribution to Charles III is perfectly believable, and if so would date the tower's construction to one of his two periods of power, 893–7 or 898–922. Known along with other important examples from Flodoard, writing from an informed position in the period and area under discussion, is a tower at Château-Thierry (Aisne); here, according to his Annal for 924, 'the tower of the fortress above the river Marne, where Herbert [Herbert II of Vermandois, 873–943] had imprisoned Charles the Simple was suddenly destroyed by fire'.[12] Flodoard also tells us that when, in 949, Charles the Simple's son, Louis IV 'd'Outremer' (936–54), retook the city of Laon (Aisne) by surprise, he overpowered the guards 'with the exception of those who had taken refuge in the tower of the royal palace, which he himself had built at the gate of the town'.[13] Whether Flodoard was attributing the 'tower' or the 'palace' to Louis IV is unclear, but if the latter the tower may perhaps be identified with the 'new stronghold' that the same author tells us had been put up by Herbert of Vermandois,[14] with whom Louis was contesting the throne, and thus necessarily when he was in possession of the city in 928;[15] alternatively, if Louis IV was its builder, it must have been completed in 936 or 937, before his parting with Hugh the Great, initially his protector, and his first loss of the city. The tower and house can be placed adjacent to the Porte Ardon, on the south side of the early enceinte, on the basis that the 'palace of Laon' is placed in a document of 954 'at the monastery of St John', known to have been in that position.[16] The tower may have been in some sense outside or projecting from the gate, which it is described by Flodoard as having been 'before' (*ante*).[17] The same tower occurs again in the context of the war in the 980s between Hugh Capet and the last Carolingian claimant, Charles of Lorraine, in which the city played a crucial part: Richer relates that, following its capture in 988,[18] Charles set about strengthening the town's defences to resist an imminent Capetian attack, in the process of which 'he built up the tower which so far had low walls, with projecting battlements and surrounded it with extensive ditches'.[19] In August of the same year, having repulsed the attack, he also 'enlarged and fortified the tower with better buildings and extended it and strengthened it both inside and out'.[20]

The same writer reveals the existence by 958 of a tower at Coucy (Aisne), better known as the site, from the thirteenth century to its destruction in 1918, of perhaps the most magnificent great tower ever built. In an account of the surprise attack by which Artaud, Archbishop of Reims, attempted to regain the town from Theobald the Trickster, Count of Blois and Chartres, we are told that

> Hardouin, a subject of Theobald, and to whom Theobald had entrusted the castle, seeing that the town had fallen, retreated with his supporters into the citadel. This was a very strong tower.[21]

The tower may well have been an adjunct to the town's first defences, put up in 922 by Archbishop Hervé, but, if not, it was perhaps more probably the work of one of several owners over the next two decades, or of Theobald himself, clearly in possession by 948.[22]

By the mid-tenth century a tower also existed at Sens (Yonne), inherited by Count Rainard of Sens (circa 951–96) and described in the early twelfth-century Chronique de Saint-Pierre le Vif as 'the tower of the city of Sens', while he himself constructed a 'very great tower . . . in a corner of the city'.[23]

Meanwhile, three possible great towers occur rather further afield. To the south-west, at Nantes (Loire-Atlantique), Alan Barbetorte (Count of Nantes, 937–52), once in possession of Brittany in 937, reoccupied the abandoned capital, had an earth rampart thrown up around the ruined church, restored its 'main tower' and 'made it into his house'.[24] To the north-east of the Île-de-France, the existence of two towers by 950 is signalled by Flodoard at Amiens (Somme). In the context of the campaign by Hugh the Great (died 956) and the Bishop of Amiens, Raimbaud, to oust Count Arnulf I of Flanders (count 918–65), he tells us that Hugh

> led an army to Amiens, and was received there in the tower which Raimbaud held. He then laid siege to the other tower (turris), which was garrisoned by Count Arnulf's men.[25]

Raimbaud's tower can be assumed to have been within or associated with the episcopal palace, adjacent to what then still remained a 'groupe épiscopale', in the north-eastern corner of the late Roman enceinte; Arnulf's tower can be identified with the Roman amphitheatre, converted into a fortress in the early Middle Ages.[26]

Circa 950–1000

Both chronologically and geographically, the next significant group of towers are those of the mid- and later tenth century attributed to Theobald I 'le Tricheur' or 'Trickster' (died circa 976), Count of Blois (936), Châteaudun (936–40) and Chartres (circa 950), and possessor, through his wife, of the greater part of Champagne. From the mid-eleventh-century Chronicle of Nantes we learn that, following the death of his brother-in-law Count Alan, and in receipt of additional income as regent, Theobald 'created towers at Chinon, Blois and Chartres'.[27]

Theobald's tower at Chartres (Eure-et-Loir) is also referred to in the late eleventh-century Liber Hagani, part chronicle, part cartulary, in which the monk Paul describes the properties received by or returned to St Père de Chartres under Bishop Aganon (died 941). The text also shows that it stood within the Gallo-Roman enceinte, and probably on a strip of land against the eastern rampart and to the south of the cathedral.[28] Its site may therefore lie within that of the modern Place Billard, and it may be that the massive tower that stood there until the early nineteenth century, known from views, descriptions and mid-eighteenth-century plans,[29] was, or may have incorporated, his work.[30]

Further reference to Theobald's tower at Chartres and the building of another at Châteaudun (Eure-et-Loir) is given in a poem incorporated in the eleventh-century Historia Sancti Florentii Salmuriensis ('History of St-Florent de Saumur'): 'Theobald', it explains, 'in his lifetime built high towers and dwelling places—one at Chinon, another at Châteaudun; nor did he ignore his own [i.e., Blois], providing the town with a tower'.[31] The construction of the towers at Blois (Loir-et-Cher) and Chinon (Indre-et-Loire) can be placed between Alan of Nantes' death in 952 and Theobald's, in or around 976; Châteaudun can have received his attention only after its acquisition in the late 930s, and Chartres between his seizure of the county in 950 and of the necessary plot in or shortly before 954. The sites of the towers at Chinon or Blois are unknown, although they probably underlie those of the later castles.

Outside Theobald's orbit but within this period lies the tower at Châlons-en-Champagne (formerly Châlons-sur-Marne), mentioned by Flodoard in his account of the events of 963 in which the episcopal town, held for Bishop Giboin (947–98), was captured and burnt by Herbert 'the Old' of Vermandois and his brother Robert of Troyes, 'sparing only the soldiers who had taken refuge in the tower of that place'.[32] The site of the building is unknown, but it was probably associated with the episcopal palace and cathedral towards the western end of the Carolingian enceinte.[33] In the same region, a tower occurs at Reims (Marne)

229

in the context of events in 990, when, according to Richer, Bishop Arnulf took refuge in it from Charles of Lorraine.[34]

Meanwhile, in Normandy, now gathering strength under Richard I (Count of Rouen, 942–96), Robert of Torigny tells us that a tower was put up at Rouen within the comital palace,[35] situated in the south-east angle of the Roman walls.[36] Robert conveniently adds that Henry I of England also built 'a tower no less tall in the castle of Caen',[37] of interest because the latter, certainly familiar to him, survived into the nineteenth century and has since been excavated. As a result, it is known to have measured 24.0 by 27.4 m in plan and at least 25 m in height.[38] The conspicuous height of Richard's tower is also clear, not only from its early reputation (below), but from William of Malmesbury's account of the death of the traitor Conan in 1090, hurled from the battlements after a witty invitation to admire the 'wide view'.[39] Along with sheer scale, the comparison with Caen also suggests a sophisticated plan and functional capacity, and it may be that the 'hall of the tower' (*aula turris*) in which a charter was sealed in 1074[40] was within it, a possibility perhaps reinforced by Henry I's subsequent construction of a separate house (*mansio*) alongside it. A text of 1119 refers to the 'Duke's chamber', which may also have been within the building, as may, conceivably, the 'chapel of the tower' (*capella de turre*) mentioned in the twelfth century.[41] The *arx* that a twelfth-century source tells us that Count Richard built or possessed in association with his palace at Bayeux may also have been, or have included, a tower, although no traces of such a building can be identified from records made at the time of the castle's demolition.[42] A tower may conceivably also have existed at Evreux in the ducal period.[43]

The Early Eleventh Century

A group of three great towers, two of which partially survive (and are the earliest to do so apart from Doué-la-Fontaine and Mayenne), date from the years around and shortly after 1000. Chronologically, the first of these is the well-known example at Langeais (Indre-et-Loire), probably built for Fulk Nerra, Count of Anjou (987–1040), but conceivably for Odo II, Count of Blois and Champagne (996–1037), with whom this territory was hotly disputed.[44] In its original form it consisted of a main block containing a vast room, equipped with fireplace, windows and probably an external gallery, raised over a deep, ill-lit basement, with two tower-like annexes projecting from its east side (see fig. 191).[45]

The second is the tower at Pithiviers (Loiret) mentioned by Orderic Vitalis in the same context as his references to Ivry-la-Bataille (below), and of which, he tells us, Lanfred, *architectus* of the Ivry building, had been the 'master of the works' on behalf of Aubrée, wife of Raoul, Count of Ivry.[46] Whether a tower really existed there in the period of which Orderic was writing, still less its attribution, is uncertain. Nevertheless, his credibility is increased by the certain existence of a great tower at Pithiviers in the twelfth century, its description in a *chanson de geste* as 'la riche tor',[47] and the fact that by then it had acquired sufficient status and antiquity to be attributed to Heloïse, daughter of Odo I of Blois (died 996), and wife of Rainard, a member of the circle of Hugh Capet.[48] Some authors have assumed that this was the building –certainly a great tower–known from seventeenth- and nineteenth-century views[49] that stood until *circa* 1810 on the site of the Place du Grande Cloître.[50]

More significant, however, is Ivry-la-Bataille (Eure) itself, described as a 'famous, huge and very strong tower' by Orderic Vitalis in the 1120s (see figs 191, 192).[51] Standing on a crag above the town are the ruins of a block measuring 25.0 by 32.0 m externally, divided into unequal parts by a spine wall and with an apsidal projection at the north end of its east side. Most of what survives is original (Period Ia), but the south wall and the south-east corner are marginally later, or conceivably the result of a change in plan during construction (Period Ib). The number of upper levels and the functions of its rooms are unknown, although it is clear that there was at least one upper floor and that the main room had a fireplace, and very probable that the east-facing apsidal projection contained a chapel.[52]

The most magnificent of the surviving pre-1050 great towers, prefiguring the White Tower in scale and sophistication, is that at Loches (Indre-et-Loire: see figs 189, 190, 191), studied by Jean Mesqui[53] and convincingly re-dated by dendrochronology to 1013–35,[54] placing it in the reign of Fulk Nerra (figs 188, 189) This consists in plan of two blocks – what Mesqui has called the *grand donjon*, measuring 25.2 by 13.7 m and originally up to 32.3 m in height, and the *petit donjon* (13.2 x 9.1 m), attached to its northern side. The former contained a deep basement with three well-lit floors above, all equipped with fireplaces and latrines and linked by a vice (between the top and middle floors) and straight stairs in the thickness of the east wall. The *petit donjon*, originally the same height, contained a stair linking the main external entrance (between basement and first-floor level) to the first floor of the *grand donjon*, with a chapel and further chamber above.[55]

Equally important but less well known is the 'Tour de César' at Beaugency (Loiret), long assigned to *circa* 1100, but which has now been shown to date largely from *circa* 1015–30 (Period I),[56] and therefore under the ultimate suzerainty either of Fulk Nerra or his bitter rival, Odo II, Count of Blois (figs 188, 191). As originally constructed, the building consisted of a single block measuring 22.4 by 17.6 m externally and up to 30 m in height, containing a deep, vaulted base-

188 (*above left*) The 'Tour de César' at Beaugency (Loiret), viewed from the east. The early eleventh-century structure, containing a deep vaulted basement and with two floors above, rose to just below the row of rectangular windows and was crowned with battlements (traces survive at the level of the window sills). The rectangular windows were created with the heightening of the building in the twelfth century, and the storey and corner turrets above early in the next.

189 (*above right*) The *donjon* at Loches (Indre-et-Loire), viewed from the south-west. The large opening towards the top of the main (south) front opened onto a gallery, carried by beams for which the slots are visible on both elevations. The other openings at this level were reduced to slits in the late twelfth century, and those below altered in the fourteenth or fifteenth century. In the foreground is part of the earliest curtain wall associated with the *donjon*, dating from the twelfth century and subsequently heightened.

ment with two well-lit floors above, crowned by a crenellated wall-walk. The width of the tower must have required a spine of timber supports on the long axis to carry the second floor (and perhaps the roof), and which may, given that there were Period 1 fireplaces in both side walls at both upper levels, have formed a partition, in effect creating a 'double-pile' plan. Together with the presence of latrines at each level, an oratory in the embrasure of an east-facing window (second floor, north end) and traces of further north–south partitions, this would have allowed for a complicated and sophisticated arrangement. The external entrance to the building was in the upper part of the north basement wall, and led to ground level via a short vice and a timber stair, and to the room above by a straight stair in the wall thickness, the top floor being reached by a second straight stair in the same wall. The early twelfth century saw the addition of a third floor and the early fourteenth century a fourth, accompanied by corner turrets, the existing mullion and transomed windows, and three tiers of stone arcades in place of the timber spine.[57]

On a comparable scale but still less well known is the great tower at Nogent-le-Rotrou (Eure-et-Loir), where the three lower levels, including the basement, pre-date the extensive twelfth-century remodelling that gave the building its present appearance (fig. 191).[58] As originally built, it consisted of a main block measuring 15.00 by 21.10 m externally, probably with a fore-building to the north,[59] and with a cross-wall towards the south end at all levels. Constructional details, and

in particular the similarities of the narrow conical-hooded fireplaces and high-set flanking windows that existed at both first- and second-floor levels to internal elevations at Langeais and Loches, suggest a date no later than *circa* 1050. Possibly, on the basis of the quoining to its east-facing windows, which extends laterally just below the springing in typically 'pre-Roman' style, the topmost storey may also date from this period. At least the main part of the building is therefore attributable to Geoffrey I of Nogent, Viscount of Châteaudun (1020s–*circa* 1040) and vassal of Odo II of Blois, or possibly to his ultimate successor, Rotrou I.[60]

By 1027 a great tower evidently existed at Amboise (Indre-et-Loire), then also in the hands of the Count of Blois. The *Cronica de gestis consulum Andegavorum* ('Chronicle of the Deeds of the Counts of the Angevins') tells us that, by 1002–3,[61] two important noblemen, Sulpice 'The Treasurer' and his brother Archambaud de Buzançais, jointly possessed a 'defendable house' (*domus defensabilem*),[62] subsequently described in the *Gesta Ambaziensium dominorum* ('Deeds of the Lords of Amboise') as having been a 'wooden house' (*domus . . . lignea*).[63] But the *Gesta* then also tells us that, following Archambaud's death, Sulpicius replaced the building with a 'stone stronghold' and presented it to his niece,[64] at some stage before his death in 1027.[65] Although its remains survived into the eighteenth century,[66] the clearest indication of its form is to be found in the fifteenth-century *Recouvrement de Normendie* ('Recovery of Normandy'), which, in describing the siege of Caen

ment, a habitable floor with large windows and an uppermost stage with intramural galleries. Dating evidence is provided by *opus spicatum* and *petit appareil* walling and, more importantly, the decorative use of alternating brick and stone voussoirs (fig. 191).[71]

The dramatically sited tower at Broue (Charente-Maritime) can now also be attributed, thanks to dendrochronology, to around 1050,[72] consistent with its structural detail and architectural similarities to Loches and Langeais and supporting an attribution to Geoffrey Martel, Fulk Nerra's son and successor as Count of Anjou. Consisting of a single tower measuring 15 by 28 m, this would appear to have contained a single habitable room, with fireplace and windows, over a deep basement.

Finally, mention must be made of the magnificent tower at Montbazon (Indre-et-Loire), since, although not firmly dated, the crudeness of its construction in comparison to that of its near-neighbour at Loches points to an origin at least before about 1050.[73] Nearly 30 m tall and measuring 19.65 by 13.75 m in plan, the building contained a deep basement, entered from well above external ground level, surmounted by an upper storey with large windows and latrines, and above that either a further floor or an enclosed wall passage surrounding a 'sunken' roof. Modifications attributed to the later eleventh century saw the heightening of the tower and the addition of a forebuilding.[74] The tower is positioned, as at Loches and Langeais, to command the approach to the rest of the castle, which extends over the tip of a long rocky promontory overlooking the Indre.[75]

These examples, clearly, were not the only ones extant in the period before 1050. Other buildings, no doubt, were never mentioned by any early author, or remain to be identified either from texts or from physical remains. Furthermore, as the house mentioned *circa* 1000 'built very solidly from stone' at Sault (Bas Berry),[76] the 'defendable house' at Amboise,[77] and the 'stone hall which served as a citadel' at Brionne (Eure) in 1047[78] so clearly show, any number of buildings described in early sources simply as 'house' (*domus*) or 'hall' (*aula*) may have been as tower-like as some described as *turres*. In addition, not least since the now-established dates of Loches, Broue and Beaugency are all earlier than previously thought, a number of other surviving towers may eventually prove to have been built before 1050. Amongst these is the well-preserved three-floored example at Sainte-Suzanne (Mayenne), assumed to post-date 1083 by its omission from Orderic's account of the Conqueror's siege, but which may well, judging by its construction, be considerably earlier.[79] Less well known, but equally viable a candidate for an early date, is the fascinating *donjon* at Montoire (Loir-et-Cher), in its original form significantly similar to Langeais in plan, proportion and scale (Table 1).[80]

190 The interior of the *donjon* at Loches, showing the south and west walls to the left and right respectively. At the lowest level is the deep basement, entered via the small door in the angle of the two walls. Above that were three levels of well-lit rooms, equipped with fireplaces and latrines, and linked at all three upper levels to the forebuilding or *petit donjon* to the north. The view shows at a glance the level of sophistication achievable in the design of such buildings more than a generation before the setting out of the White Tower.

in 1448, mentions 'a very strong donjon (*dongon*) . . . consisting of a square tower, like that in London or that at Amboise, were it to remain complete'.[67] Assuming, therefore, that the one described is the one known to have existed in the early eleventh century and not a later creation, comparisons with the White Tower and Henry I's building at Caen suggest a very impressive structure indeed. At least by the middle of the century Amboise may have possessed a second tower, described in the twelfth century as 'the very strong house in the place which still today is known as Fulk's Motte';[68] this appeared under the rule of Geoffrey Martel (Count of Anjou, 1040 and 1060), but probably dated from the early 1040s.[69]

By the middle of the eleventh century at the latest Normandy had acquired, at Avranches (Manche), another great tower in addition to Ivry, known since the late nineteenth century[70] but fully appreciated only in the last few years. Situated at the rounded south-eastern angle of the late Roman ramparts, it was oriented north–south and divided internally by cross-walls in both directions, with external dimensions of approximately 37 by 27 m. It contained a deep base-

Table 1. Pre-1050 towers in approximate date order. In the case of the wider date ranges, a mid-point date (in brackets) has been used for ordering purposes. Sites with surviving remains are identified by an asterisk in the final column. The two phases of Doué-la-Fontaine are those identified by De Boüard.

Date range	Location	Builder / owner	*Département*	
*c.*900 ('Period 1')	Doué-la-Fontaine	Charles II	Maine-et-Loire	*
*c.*900	Mayenne	Charles II?	Mayenne	*
892–922 (907)	Compiègne	Charles III?	Oise	
924	Château-Thierry	Herbert II of Vermandois?	Aisne	
*c.*930 ('Period 2')	Doué-la-Fontaine		Maine-et-Loire	*
922–48 (935)	Coucy	Hervé, Archbishop of Reims?		
		Theobald I, Count of Blois?	Aisne	
937	Nantes	Alan, Count of Nantes	Loire-Atlantique	
before 938	Laon	Charles III	Aisne	
before 950	Amiens	Bishops of Amiens	Somme	
before 950	Amiens	Counts of Amiens?	Somme	
before 951	Sens		Yonne	
950–54	Chartres	Theobald I, Count of Blois	Eure-et-Loir	
936–74 (955)	Blois	Theobald I, Count of Blois	Loir-et-Cher	
938–74 (956)	Châteaudun	Theobald I, Count of Blois	Eure-et-Loir	
943–74 (958)	Chinon	Theobald I, Count of Blois	Indre-et-Loire	
before 962	Châlons-en-Champagne	Bishop Giboin of Châlons?	Marne	
942–96 (965)	Rouen	Richard I, Count of Rouen	Seine-Maritime	
951–996 (973)	Sens	Rainard, Count of Sens	Yonne	
988	Laon	Charles of Lorraine	Aisne	
before 990	Reims	Archbishop of Reims?	Marne	
before 1000	Pithiviers	Heloïse and/or Rainard of Pithiviers	Loiret	
*c.*1000	Langeais	Fulk Nerra, Count of Anjou?	Indre-et-Loire	*
*c.*1000	Ivry-la-Bataille (Period 1a)	Ralph and/or Aubrée, Count and Countess of Ivry	Eure	*
early 11th century	Ivry-la-Bataille (Period 1b)			*
1013–39	Beaugency	Count of Blois or Anjou	Loiret	*
1013–35	Loches	Fulk Nerra, Count of Anjou	Indre-et-Loire	*
before 1027	Amboise	Sulpicius the Treasurer	Indre-et-Loire	
before 1050	Broue	Geoffrey Martel, Count of Anjou	Charente-Maritime	*
before 1050	Avranches	Robert, Count of Avranches	Manche	*
before 1050?	Montbazon	Fulk Nerra, Count of Anjou?	Indre-et-Loire	*
*c.*1050?	Sainte-Suzanne	Hubert, Viscount of Maine	Mayenne	
before 1050	Nogent-le-Rotrou	Geoffrey I or Rotrou I of Nogent	Eure-et-Loir	*
*c.*1050?	Montoire		Loir-et-Cher	*
before 1060	Amboise	Geoffrey Martel, Count of Anjou	Indre-et-Loire	

THE FUNCTIONS OF THE EARLY TOWERS

The evidence presented above identifies thirty-one plausibly turriform secular buildings, used or created in a high-status context. However, the extent to which it can be claimed that they represented a coherent tradition, and thus in any real sense ancestral to the White Tower, depends as much on what can be said of their function as of their structural form. In particular, the extent to which they can be shown to have served or been capable of residential, defensive and symbolic functions needs to be examined in more detail.

Residential Functions

An examination of the residential role and capacity of the early towers can be approached through three separate but related questions. First, to what extent did they or could they have served as entire residences? Second, what was the residential function of such buildings when providing only part of a residence? Third, how did the use and development relate to that of high-status domestic architecture in general?

Of the standing buildings that are at least large enough to be readily considered as 'whole houses', Loches is the most obvious candidate: not only on the basis of its sheer size and complexity, but also because as originally built it stood alone, without a walled enclosure surrounding it.[81] Jean Mesqui's new description and analysis of the building both amply demonstrate its sophistication and offer an interpretation of how it functioned.[82] According to this, the deep basement of the main block served as storage space, and the main room at first-floor level (level 1), measuring 9 by 20 m, as the 'Grande Salle publique' – a 'palatial space, admittedly simple in its decoration, but extremely luxurious in intention'. Mesqui identifies the west end, with its fireplace, as the 'upper' end, with the lower end, served by the entrances, to the east. The adjoining room in the *petit donjon* or forebuilding he identifies as a 'chambre d'apparat', for councils or for receiving particularly important guests. On the basis of its 'depth' within the building, its smaller fireplace and the placing of the chapel at this level, he considers the floor above (level 2) a more private space; level

233

3, accessible only via a spiral staircase, he sees as more private still, although not necessarily, given its defensive role, of higher status. Mesqui therefore sees the building as providing spaces with different functions for a single household, as Ashbee sees the White Tower.[83] The alternative view, prompted by what we know of French high-status houses from the twelfth century onwards, would be that it was designed to provide near-identical accommodation for different sections of the household, differentiated by status, but it is not in this case supported by the building, notably the position of the chapel. Beaugency may also have been designed to contain at least a full set of high-status living spaces, particularly if each floor was divided by longitudinal (and other) partitions, which would have allowed for subtleties of functional demarcation and circulation almost on a par with Loches. Depending on the number of floors, a similar interpretation could be put forward for Ivry-la-Bataille, in both its Period 1a and Period 1b forms.

None of those towers known only from documentary evidence can be proven to have provided an entire residence in their own right, although this is certainly suggested in the case of the tower 'made into his house' by Alan of Nantes.[84] Nevertheless, there are indications that specific functions were allocated to particular spaces within buildings, and that they were therefore components of a complicated layout. Possession of an integral chapel or oratory (*oratorium*), and at least a 'reception' capacity, was clearly a feature of the tower at Compiègne, where the robbery described by Helgaud de Fleury took place while Louis the Pious and 'some of the more intimate members of his household' were 'gathered together in the oratory of the Tower of Charles'.[85] The reference in 1074 to the 'hall of the tower' (*aula turris*)[86] at Rouen, and the indications that it contained an integral chamber and chapel, leave little doubt that it could at least have provided the essential private, 'public' and liturgical accommodation associated with the seigneurial residence. At Amboise the tower that had been built by Sulpice the Treasurer in the early eleventh century contained, at least as described *circa* 1100, a cellar below the 'chamber of the tower', clearly implying that the building had some residential function and perhaps, since 'chamber' is specified, other rooms. Of the surviving sample that might be interpreted as only parts of houses, Doué and Mayenne are too little understood to add much to the debate, leaving Langeais as the earliest candidate. In this case, however, the supposition that it might not be a whole house relies not on topographical or archaeological grounds, but simply on its size,[87] and subjective doubts as to whether the entire accommodation of a high-status house could have consisted of no more than one large room. By the standards of the late eleventh century and later this is certainly unlikely, and it is

certain in several instances that 'single-room' towers after 1100 contained a part only – and not necessarily a particularly important part – of a larger domestic complex.[88] But to assume that this was the case in the preceding century and earlier may be a mistake. Certainly, this is suggested by the celebrated description of *circa* 1080 of the tower at Le Cour Marigny (Loiret), where the room that seems to have taken up the top part of the tower served Seguinus and his household as a place to 'stay', converse, eat and drink in company and to pass the night;[89] both the description – which refers also to the floor below as a storeroom – and the function could fit the *donjon* at Langeais very neatly. Thus, whereas we can argue that Loches was a whole house on the basis that it clearly could have accommodated a whole household, we cannot argue that Langeais was not: we can imagine a situation whereby the relatively minor *seigneur* was content to live in a small tower in one room. If this is the case, it would have much to say about the perceived advantages of a tower over some more convenient arrangement.

Nevertheless, there are at least some hints that a few of the early towers known from written sources provided only a part of the domestic accommodation within a larger complex. At Laon, for example, Louis IV's *turris* is described not as the 'royal house' but as its tower, while that at Château-Thierry was described by Flodoard as the tower 'of the *praesidium*'; Duke Richard's tower at Rouen had been built, according to Robert of Torigny, *within* rather than to contain his palace, and at Bayeux, although again only in the twelfth century, the duke was credited with both an *arx* and a *palatium*.[90] Precisely what part was played by the accommodation offered by towers accompanied by other domestic buildings – whether there was a fairly standard arrangement – and the extent to which their presence set them apart from the provision and arrangement that would be found at a 'normal' site are difficult to assess: we are hindered by ignorance as to what the *domus* at Laon, the *praesidium* at Château-Thierry or the *palatium* at Bayeux actually consisted of, and the planning of grand domestic architecture in this period in general. Textual sources provide plenty of references to high-status residences and their constituent *camerae* and *aulae* and other components, but, *capella* and *oratorium* apart, the particular functions that these structures or apartments may have served at individual sites are never clear.[91] Surviving non-turriform buildings of the period in question are of little help, since the only substantial survival is the early eleventh-century 'Salle Comtale' in the castle at Angers.[92] But in all probability, in the years around 1000, as throughout the *floruit* of the great tower afterwards, the residential uses of such towers, and their residential function in relation to other domestic buildings at the same site, followed no particular formulae: some towers contained all accommodation in one room, some in many; while others under normal circumstances provided only part of the available high-status living space. Finally, it is worth underlining that, in spite of the high number of early survivals relative to other forms of pre-1050 domestic building, towers were always a rarity: most great men did not own, still less live in, great towers.

Defensive Functions

The contexts in which they are mentioned make it clear that the early towers known from texts alone were implicated in conflict. Several of these instances clearly also indicate that such buildings were perceived as viable refuges and fortresses in their own right. This is illustrated, for example, by the success of the 'very strong tower' at Coucy to which the garrison retreated on the fall of the town in 958, and where it successfully held out until the arrival of a relieving army.[93] Similarly, although the nature of the building is unclear, the 'tower' at Châlons-en-Champagne and its garrison survived the destruction of the town in 963 by Herbert II of Vermandois' sons, just as Count Arnulf's tower at Amiens successfully 'held out' against Hugh the Great (although whether this was the fortified amphitheatre as a whole, or a tower within or attached to it, is not clear). At Sens, what can be assumed to have been Count Rainard 'the Old's' tenth-century tower was held against Robert the Pious by Rainard's grandson 'for many days',[94] and when 'at last' it was captured, the king 'piously spared the lives of the defendants'. Illustrative at least of the perception of towers as places of security is the use of the 'tower (turris) of the city of Sens' by Count Rainard as a place of safe deposit for the relics of the church of Our Saviour, seized after his capture of the bandit Boso.[95] Flodoard also tells us that in 949 Louis IV was able to reduce the 'tower of the royal palace' only by 'building a wall around it, cutting it off from the city', indicating a structure deemed to be impregnable, at least in the short term, and presumably a threat to its assailants.[96] But alongside the impression of strength is one of vulnerability, as illustrated by Richer's description of the events at Reims in 990. According to this Bishop Arnulf,

> pretending to be moved by the cries [of the townsfolk], and feigning fear, headed for the tower and climbed up it; his companions followed and barred the door behind them. Charles, who was looking for Arnulf and failing to find him, looked everywhere to find his hiding-place. As soon as he saw them at the top of the tower, he immediately put a guard on the door. Arnulf and his companions, who were without either arms or provisions, surrendered to Charles and emerged from the tower.[97]

A similarly varied picture is borne out by the design and features of the surviving examples. At the top end of the scale there can be no doubt of either the defensive capacity or the intended defensive purpose of the gigantic donjon at Loches, fitted from the beginning for hourds, and with its two original entrances at first- and second-floor levels.[98] Loches was also clearly conceived as an entire fortress – as it was as an entire house – as is indicated by the absence, as built, of a chemise or bailey, its sheer size and the provision of vast storage spaces and a well. The tower at Langeais, as originally built, with no truly ground-floor access, was also quite clearly a defensible structure.[99] Not enough is known of the donjon at Avranches, but its massive construction suggests that it too was independently defensible. The presence of ground-floor doorways in both early structural phases of the great tower at Ivry-la-Bataille (one unbarred) might suggest that defensive considerations were not very serious, but we should be careful in judging the defensive capacity of early buildings by the more familiar standards of the later eleventh or twelfth centuries: the difference is underlined by the improvements that we know to have been made to early buildings at that stage, not least at Ivry itself in the 1180s,[100] and what can be seen as an upgrading of the tenth-century tower at Rouen with the addition of 'outworks' (or possibly battlements) in the early twelfth century.

From this material it is clear that security and defensive capacity can be shown to have been a function, and an intended function, of a significant sample of the early 'great towers', both before and after 1000.

Symbol and Ostentation

Although recent work on the more familiar 'great towers' of the later eleventh and twelfth centuries, and on the White Tower itself, has stressed the importance of display amongst their functions, it would be dangerous to assume that this was of equal importance to their pre-1050 precursors.[101] That the early buildings could be physically impressive enough, however, to perform a symbolic role is suggested, for example, by the inclusion of his 'high towers' among the achievements of Theobald the Trickster,[102] and – equally significantly – his vilification for their creation by other early chroniclers.[103] Similarly, the impact of the tower at Ivry may be illustrated – unless referring more to its historical associations – by Orderic's description of it as 'famous'. In the case of Rouen, the twelfth-century byword 'Pèser comme la Tour de Rouen' reflects the scale of Count Richard's creation, and its commemoration in the historic name of the 'Place de la haute vieille tour' expresses its legendary stature.[104] From at least the early eleventh century, the scale that such buildings could achieve is left in no doubt by the standing structures at Loches, Beaugency and Nogent. Although inextricably linked with considerations of physical security, it is significant as well that great towers were in some instances also closely associated with the act and consolidation of conquest. It was, for example, the first act of Alan of Nantes on the retaking of his capital to improvise a great tower, while at Sens, in the context of the struggle between the Carolingian and Capetian parties in the mid-tenth century, Count Rainard's seizure of the town was followed by the building of a great tower within it. Similarly, Theobald the Trickster's successive acquisition of Chartres and Châteaudun were followed, once his finances allowed, by the construction of great towers in their midst: in the case of Chartres, it is tempting to see the planting of his tower on land seized from the bishop and the monks of St Père as a quite deliberate assertion of authority over the monks and the bishop, whose quasi-comital authority he was usurping.[105]

A similar picture emerges if we look at the other circumstances in which some towers functioned or had been created. It has been suggested, for example, that the siting and construction of Richard I's tower at Rouen beside the cathedral, then still a relatively 'low-rise' *groupe épiscopale*, deliberately exploited the symbolic and psychological advantages of association with the Church and his authority over it.[106] At Amiens (admittedly with the proviso that one of them may not have included a tower), it is easy to imagine that the fortresses of the bishop and the count, at opposite corners of the town, functioned as highly effective visual expressions of their rivalry. Towers put up by the great nobility may also have played a symbolic role in offsetting the dominance, at least on the skyline, not just of ecclesiastical fortresses but also of churches and their towers. When the siting of a town was particularly elevated or dramatic, as at Laon, the visual impact of one tower, and thus the incentive to match it with another, must have been particularly marked. Although belonging to a later period and operating at a lower social level, a rivalry of similar type, expressed through the possession of towers, is offered by the situation at Amboise in the early twelfth century:

> There were then in Amboise three noblemen, of whom none believed themselves inferior to any other, and owed no service one to the other, and who each had defensible houses. Sulpice, Lord of the stone tower, and Fulk de Torigny, who had inherited [his] from the first Count 'Martel' [d. 1060?], and who was Lord of the house known as 'Fulk's motte'; the third was Arnoulf, son of Leo of Magdunum, guardian of the Count's house known as the 'little house', to which the greater part of the town of Amboise belonged.[107]

There is at least no reason, therefore, to assume that the symbolic value of the early great towers was any less important to their builders before *circa* 1050 than it clearly was to those of the later eleventh and twelfth centuries.

THE GENESIS, PROLIFERATION AND STRUCTURAL DEVELOPMENT OF THE GREAT TOWER, 900–1050

Genesis

The origin of the great tower has attracted as much scholarly attention as (and has frequently been confused with) the origins of the castle. Particularly since De Boüard's work at Doué-la-Fontaine, this has focused on the development of a structural type—essentially on how the form that enabled a set of functional characteristics to be combined within a single structure was first arrived at. Interpreting what he found as a ground-floor hall converted into a storeyed building, he asked: 'need we look further for the origins of the rectangular donjon, masterpiece of the military architecture of the 11th and 12th centuries?';[108] and that we do not has been widely and enthusiastically accepted. R. Allen Brown, for example, speculating on the process by which both the stone castle and the 'keep' first emerged, suggested that at Doué we find ourselves in 'the very presence of the events we seek'.[109] Problems with De Boüard's interpretation of the building, as discussed above, however, suggest that its real significance is not as the site of an almost accidental invention of a new structural type, but as an example of a plausible great tower dating from as early as *circa* 900. Such a reassessment of Doué-la-Fontaine is a reminder that to look for the origins of the great tower tradition in technological development, let alone a breakthrough at a single site, is probably a mistake. The idea of living in a tower is, after all, both obvious and structurally simple, and even masonry tower building was in any case well developed, at least in an ecclesiastical context, by the end of the ninth century.[110] In fact, the origins of the tradition must—if necessarily backed up by technical capacity—lie in the combination of the set of functional needs that the known great towers performed, and which sustained their continued creation for several centuries. These factors were not all of equal importance, for, as suggested by the evidence given above and shown by the experience of the later eleventh and twelfth centuries, great towers were neither conspicuously successful fortresses nor convenient residences: while the combination of these functions led to the development of the castle, it cannot explain the origin of the great tower. This suggests that the crucial motivation to build a tower *rather than something else* lay in its third defining function—the tower's outstanding potential as a statement of status and authority.

Acknowledgment that, from a technical point of view, the great tower could perfectly well have existed before *circa* 900, and that Doué was not in fact a crucial prototype, leaves open the possibility that the type emerged well before *circa* 900. If so, an origin might be suggested in the most flourishing decades of the Carolingian period, and the *Granusturm*, still standing at the west end of the great audience hall of the imperial palace at Aachen, dating from shortly before 800 (although showing little adaptation to a residential function), might be suggested as an example.[111] Nevertheless, the earliest buildings that can be shown to be ancestral in a functional sense to the White Tower date from the tenth century. That this was also the period of origin is in keeping with the political circumstances of the time, which saw the disintegration of Carolingian authority and incessant internecine struggle, which, although begun after the reign of Louis the Pious (814–40), took off in the last decades of the ninth century and dominated the next. This connection partly lies in the association, at least demonstrated in the later eleventh and twelfth centuries, of great towers with conflict rather than stability, and in particular the affirmation of conquest and possession (above). But in addition, the builders of the early towers were the main protagonists in these conflicts, such as the Carolingian kings Charles III and Louis IV and their supporters, Herbert II of Vermandois and Theobald I, Count of Blois – great men with great resources, carving out or defending their lands and authority, and contesting prizes as important as the crown of France. Under such circumstances it is easy to imagine that the links between visible and actual power, real authority and its trappings and symbols – of which the great tower was such a successful example – were unusually close. It can be suggested, therefore, that the origin of the great tower lay not in, or simply in, a technological advance, but in response to a set of functional requirements, amongst which the demonstration of authority was paramount.

Proliferation

The received understanding is that, even if De Boüard's interpretation of Doué-la-Fontaine is upheld, the origin of the great tower as more than a one-off example lay in the Loire valley and Anjou: Michel Bur, for example, hazarded that 'the Loire valley seems to have been the region of origin of these residential donjons, which in turn scattered themselves over Normandy and England'.[112] Pierre Héliot, in one of his two important articles on the subject, asserted that the tradition, if foreshadowed by developments in Capetian France, had its true origins on the middle reaches of the Loire in the mid-eleventh century.[113] But, as shown above, the earliest known towers likely to date from the first half of the tenth century were not in Anjou, but broadly within 75 miles and largely to the east of Paris – at Compiègne, Coucy, Château-Thierry, Laon, Reims and Sens (see fig. 187). Nevertheless, it is thanks to the continuation of tower building in other

areas and under other rulers that the tradition that produced the White Tower and its successors was consolidated and developed. Although the exact chronology of this process and the relative importance of various individuals and dynasties in sustaining the tradition and prompting imitation are impossible to identify in any detail, some tentative observations can be made. Although the sample is very small, the creations of Theobald the Trickster to the south-west of the Paris region, at Blois, Chartres, Chinon and Châteaudun, may be identified, after those in the Paris area, as the second major group. Although only three early towers are known in Normandy, these post-date those of Theobald the Trickster and can be seen as a third group. A fourth group, even if overlapping with the third in date, is formed by the celebrated examples at Langeais and Loches, along with Beaugency and Nogent-le-Rotrou and (possibly) Montbazon, in the domains either of the counts of Anjou or the counts of Blois and Chartres.

Meanwhile, by the mid-tenth century at the latest, great towers had also been appearing further to the east, such as Bishop Bruno of Cologne's (963–5) tower at Xanten (Westphalia),[114] or the one that may have existed Soest (Hesse) by the same period.[115]

Broadly speaking, the impetus for tower building, once the tradition was established, must have been that of imitation, and an understanding that great men built great towers. Clearly identifiable instances of imitation and rivalry, either between individual magnates or particular buildings are rare, but there is evidence that Duke Richard I's construction of a tower at Rouen, supplanting his earlier palace at the other end of the town, was in imitation of the same operation carried out by the Count of Blois at Chartres about 955: certainly, in other respects the lead of Richard's greatest rival and most feared neighbour was followed in Normandy, not least in the development of ecclesiastical architecture.[116] Although it may never be established which was begun first, it is easy to imagine that the building in the same decades of the great towers at Loches and Beaugency, respectively by Fulk Nerra and Odo II of Blois, was the result of one of these notorious rivals' anxiety not to be outdone by the other. Similarly, as seems likely for chronological reasons, Geoffrey I of Nogent's construction there of a gigantic tower rivalling Loches or Beaugency could have been a deliberate statement of his new-found riches and authority on inheriting the viscounty of Châteaudun, and establishing a dynasty later to assume the county of Perche.[117]

Structural Development

What is known of the towers dating from before 1000 suggests, certainly in the case of those that appear to have contained a multiplicity of rooms, a high degree of technical competence in their construction and

191 Plans of the buildings at
1. Avranches; 2. Beaugency;
3. Doué-la-Fontaine; 4. Ivry-la-
Bataille (Period 1a); 5. Ivry-la-
Bataille (Period 1b); 6. Langeais;
7. Mayenne; 8. Montbazon;
9. Montoire; 10. Loches and
11. Nogent-le-Rotrou, shown at
basement level and reproduced to
the same scale. In plan, the crucial
development is from the simple
rectangle, via the adjunction of a
small rectangle, to the 'double-pile'
plan, forerunner of the four-square
donjon rectangulaire, of which the
White Tower is an example (for
plans of great towers of the next
generations, see Chapter Ten).

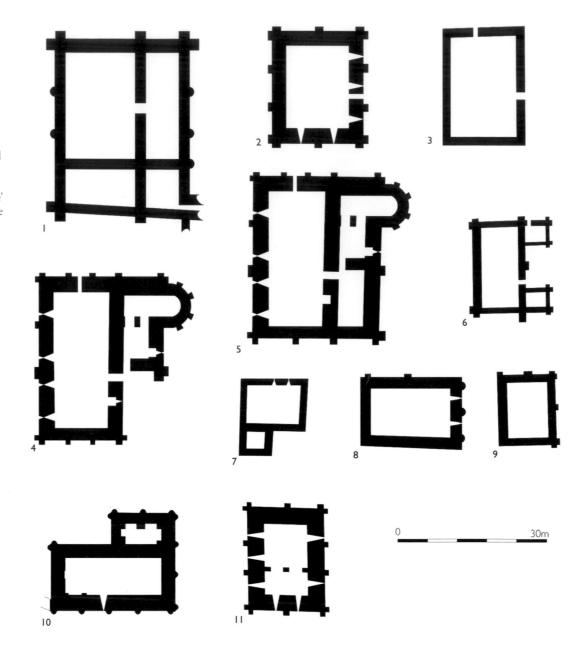

complexity in their design (fig. 191). Although this cannot be said of the earliest known survival, at Doué-la-Fontaine, it can of Mayenne, with its attached stair turret and splendid range of brick-arched windows.[118] Nevertheless, the dearth of surviving buildings means that little can be said of developments in design and technology during this period. After *circa* 1000, however, important advances can be identified both in construction and the developments in design that this allowed.

In constructional terms the underlying development is the progression from the sub-Roman *petit appareil* tradition of Langeais, through the frankly 'experimental' construction of Ivry-la-Bataille and Doué, to the confident, highly developed ashlar construction of Loches, all within one or two generations.[119] With the resultant thickening of walls and accompanying developments, probably pioneered largely in the more active milieu of ecclesiastical building, came the possibilities for mural passages and spiral stairs—neither of which are known to occur at

Langeais or Ivry, but both of which were used at Loches and Beaugency.

In design, three main developments and additions to the repertoire of basic forms can be identified. The first is the addition of an annexe or turret to the simple rectangular block as found at Doué-la-Fontaine and (the substantially later) buildings at Montoire and Beaugency: these are present in a variety of forms at Mayenne, Langeais, Loches, Ivry in its 'Period 1a' form and at Nogent-le-Rotrou.

The second is the adoption of the 'double-pile' plan, in which two blocks are built side by side to create a single rectangle divided by a spine wall, of which (Period 1b) Ivry-la-Bataille, Avranches (and Beaugency in a planning if not a structural sense) are the only early examples, but which was an essential prerequisite for the emergence of the mature four-square Anglo-Norman *donjon*; its appearance therefore can be seen as a crucial moment in the ancestry of the White Tower. The detailed affinity and possible relationship between Ivry-la-Bataille and the

White Tower is discussed below, but Ivry may also be of significance in the development of the double-pile plan itself, for it can be argued that it was there, in the conversion or change of plan that produced its Period 1b form, that the conceptual leap between a variation of the single-pile plan of Loches to the fully integrated four-square plan was first made. If so, it would identify Ivry not just as an early example, but also as the prototype for the mature *donjon quadrangulaire* itself. In either case, however, it is of interest that the two fully developed examples are both in Normandy, hinting that the duchy was particularly important in the emergence of the type.[120]

The third development, illustrated by Loches, Beaugency, Nogent-le-Rotrou and Montbazon, and which was clearly a feature of the tower at Rouen, is the tremendous height that such buildings could attain, permitting as many as three habitable floors within the same block, with highly sophisticated interconnections, and in which rooms could have served clearly distinct functions. Conceivably, the towers at Ivry and Avranches combined both great height and a double-pile plan, but their relatively thin walls suggest that they may have been lower, and at least as wide as they were tall.

The occurrence of these developments, however, should not be taken to indicate that the design of the great tower followed a simple linear progression from simple to complicated, and that any particular pattern therefore prevailed at any period. Rather, the developments simply increased the repertoire of designs available, for, as is suggested both by the pre-1050 evidence and the known variety of later buildings, the very simplest forms continued to be built alongside more complicated ones. Thus the simplicity of Langeais, for example, should not therefore be taken to indicate that earlier ones were simpler. In addition, great towers could be converted or upgraded from one form to another, as at Ivry, or created by the fortification of previously domestic buildings, as may have occurred Laon in 988, and in the post-Conquest period at Castle Rising and Norham.[121]

THE DESIGN OF THE WHITE TOWER

It has now been shown that the great tower had existed on the Continent for almost two centuries before the Conquest. It is also clear from what is known of these buildings that the White Tower was not an innovation in scale, or in its double-pile plan, or in possessing an externally expressed apse. The view once held by scholars such as Pierre Héliot, who considered that the mature *donjon quadrangulaire* was an innovation on English soil after the Conquest,[122] then exported back to post-Conquest Normandy, is clearly no longer tenable. It remains, however, to examine where the immediate inspiration may have come from and by what route.

In searching for this there is a theoretical possibility that it was arrived at entirely independently. Certainly, it would be in the context of a major royal building at the greatest city of a newly conquered kingdom that significant developments in design and sophistication might be expected. The plan of the White Tower is so significantly similar, not only to Ivry-la-Bataille, but also to the keep at Colchester, however, that any quest for a prototype must concentrate on an examination of its relationship to these two buildings.

Colchester

The distinguishing similarities in the plans of the great tower at Colchester to the White Tower, first pointed out in print by George Clark in 1884,[123] have long been noted and are not in doubt, although Dixon (below, Chapter Ten) stresses important differences in internal layout and functioning. Colchester's significance for present purposes, however, depends on its date. The evidence for this has been well rehearsed by Paul Drury in two major articles, more recently reviewed by Eric Fernie, and needs only summary treatment here. The main literary source is the thirteenth-century *Colchester Chronicle*,[124] which states that the town was handed over to Eudo the Steward in 1072, following the Danish raid of the previous year, and that in 1076 'he built the castle on the foundations of the palace of Ceol, formerly king'. There is no reason to doubt either the act or the date,[125] and the detail concerning the reuse of an ancient site, suspected since the nineteenth century,[126] has been proved by excavation. In any case, Henry I's grant of the 'city of Colchester *et turrim et castellum*' by a charter of 1101, and the date of *circa* 1100 that has been attributed to the capitals flanking the keep's main entrance,[127] show that it existed, up to a certain height a least, by the end of the eleventh century. Since the White Tower is known to have been under way only by the late 1070s, it would follow that the design of the London building *could*, in theory at least, have been based on that of Colchester.[128] The argument for this would be very strong if it could be shown that a crucial feature of their common design, the apse, had indeed been 'imposed by circumstances' – the uncovering of a fourth-century round-ended addition to the temple platform during the tower's construction.[129] The evidence for the platform's existence has not stood up to detailed scrutiny, however, and Drury has now modified his interpretation.[130] More important in evaluating the nature of any 'typological' relationship between Colchester and the White Tower is the known employment of the double-pile plan and externally expressed apse at Ivry several generations before the Conquest, and the certainty of its familiarity to the Conqueror and his associates. While in theory this would still have allowed for Colchester to be modelled on Ivry, and London on it, the much closer similarities between the Norman building and the White Tower make this highly unlikely.

Ivry-la-Bataille

The basic implications of Ivry for the ancestry of the White Tower, as has been explained above, derive from their astonishing similarity in plan (fig. 192). At the crudest level these similarities lie in their overall scale and proportions – the main external dimensions of the White Tower being 30.0 by 35.5 m and those of Ivry 25.0 by 32.0 m, and more importantly that both are split into unequal parts by a north–south spine wall and possess an east-facing apsidal projection. Closer inspection, however, reveals some striking similarities in detail too: the dimensions of the western rooms at the Tower and at Ivry, at 27.0 by 10.8 m, and 26.70 by 10.75 m respectively, are almost identical, and the basement spaces under their apsidal cells, at 4.40 and 4.20 m, are almost exactly the same width.

Whether Ivry itself was the model for the White Tower is another question. On the face of it, a better candidate might be the tower at Rouen, as suggested long ago by R. Allen Brown.[131] The Rouen building, however, was the work of Richard i, and thus more than a century old by 1066. If so, it would not be surprising that the builders of the White Tower turned to what may have been the most recent, and thus perhaps the most advanced, building of its type to be found in the duchy. That Aubrée's tower had some special status, retained even in the twelfth century, is also implied by Orderic's description of it as 'famous':[132] in addition, the story that Orderic relates about the execution of the architect, so that he could never produce another building to equal it, is certainly the kind to have grown up about an extraordinary structure. But the most important indication of a direct link between Ivry and the White Tower lies in the similarity of their internal dimensions, which surely suggests a direct reference from one building to the other. In support of the case for a direct link are the number of individuals who could have been both familiar with Ivry and in a position to influence the design of the new building. A prime candidate is William Fitz Osbern, the Conqueror's friend, steward,[133] one-time viceroy and a well-known builder of castles. He had very strong connections with Ivry, as a grandson of its builders and a nephew of Hugh of Bayeux, who held the castle during William's own lifetime; his father, Osbern de Crepon, held Breteuil, 30 miles to the west.[134] William's death at Cassel in 1071 is not necessarily a disqualification, since the decision to build the White Tower might already have been made and its general specification agreed. A second candidate is Roger of Ivry, the king's butler after 1068 and probably assistant to the master butler, Hugh d'Ivry (who was either his brother or his uncle).[135] Although the exact nature of his connection with Ivry and his relationship to the family of Raoul,

Count of Ivry, is unclear,[136] Roger was the founder of the abbey at Ivry, and so both familiar with the castle and, close to the king, in a position to influence events in London. The third is Gundulf of Rochester, the only individual whose involvement in the White Tower's construction is actually documented,[137] and who, as a former resident of Rouen and a monk of Bec Hellouin, must have known Ivry by reputation, if not personally.

Last but not least is the Conqueror himself, if only on the grounds that he must have been familiar with the Norman building: during his youth it was held by his great-uncle, Hugh of Bayeux – a connection perhaps reinforced during his minority by the marriage of his guardian, Osbern de Crepon, to Hugh's sister Emma – while as an adult he controlled the castle himself through a series of custodians.[138]

The Contribution of the White Tower

This chapter concentrates on the White Tower's precursors, and Chapter Ten on the impact of its creation and its design on the use and development of its successors. But the innovative character of the White Tower itself, however, was very marked and very important. First of all, as is discussed in chapters One and Ten, no such building seems to have been built in Normandy after the first decades of the eleventh century, and its construction marked a re-endorsement of the tradition that was to ensure its persistence and development for another century. But its own design incorporates elements that put it far in advance of Loches, Ivry or Avranches. The most obvious of these is that on the Continent the 'tall tower', as represented, for example, by Loches, Beaugency, Nogent-le-Rotrou and Broue, is likely to have been an alternative to the 'squat' tower, represented by Ivry and Avranches. But in London the two forms are combined to produce a structure with a tower as broad as Ivry and as tall as Loches, a pattern then followed in England alongside a continuation of the 'squat' tower form, as manifested at Castle Rising and probably at Colchester. But important advances were also made at a more detailed level, thanks to the undoubted ingenuity of the White Tower's designer, but also to general advances in the sophistication of construction evident from ecclesiastical buildings put up in the previous half-century. Most conspicuous among these is the gigantic spiral staircase communicating between all floors and expressed architecturally on the building's exterior. Most impressive is the design of the chapel, which, with its ambulatory, was a radical departure from the much simpler arrangement that existed at Loches and is implied at Ivry. Whether the 'sunken' roof had pre-Conquest Continental precedents in any context remains unclear, but numerous other details, including the corner turrets, arcaded spine wall and lavish fenestration, routinely included in its successors, make their first known

192 Reconstructed plans of the great towers at the White Tower (*right*) and Ivry-la-Bataille (*far right*), taken at basement level and reproduced to the same scale.

0   20m

appearance in this building. In spite of the length and complexity of its pre-Conquest ancestry, the White Tower therefore occupies a uniquely important position in the perpetuation and development of the great tower in its own right.

CONCLUSIONS

In conclusion, it can now be said that what can for convenience be called the great tower existed as a cohesive functional and structural type on the Continent for nearly two centuries before the Conquest. It would appear to have emerged in the milieu of the last Carolingians and the early Capetians, and their powerful neighbours, and that the crucial factor in its emergence and sustained use – the one that made great men build a tower and not something else – was its symbolic capacity: its birthplace seems not to have been Anjou or the Loire valley, but the environs of Paris, from which it spread through adoption by rival magnates, including, by 996, the Count of Normandy. With regard to the ancestry of the White Tower's particular design, a number of survivals, particularly Loches (1013–35), show that the scale and structural sophistication of the White Tower had also been anticipated well before the Conquest (although simpler forms continued to be built throughout the pre-Conquest period

and the later *floruit* of the great tower). The crucial structural development in the ancestry of the White Tower, however, was the double-pile plan, exhibited first at Ivry, where peculiarities of the structure suggest it may first have been arrived at. Since the only other pre-Conquest building known to exhibit this, at Avranches, is also in Normandy, the design of the White Tower can be claimed to be based on a specifically Norman precedent: similarities in detail between the White Tower and Ivry, still a celebrated building in the twelfth century, in fact suggest that it was on this particular quasi-ducal building of the early eleventh century that the London building was based.

Acknowledgements

I am very grateful to a large number of people for help with the research, fieldwork, and access to buildings and documents on which preparing this chapter has depended, and for commenting on it in draft. Among them are, Frederic Aubanton, Robert Baudet, Dr John Blair, Jacques Charles, Christian Corvisier, Dr John Crook, Professor Philip Dixon, Pauline de Ayala, Paul Drury, Professor Eric Fernie, Professor Michael Jones, Francoise Lecuyer, Elisabeth Lorans, Karen Lundgren, Claude Perron, Aline Pouget, David Stockton, Dr Kathleen Thompson and Bernard Vella.

CHAPTER TEN

The Influence of the White Tower on the Great Towers of the Twelfth Century

PHILIP DIXON

The White Tower is among the best preserved of Romanesque great towers, and one of the few that presents the viewer with that combination of solidarity and grandeur that was part of the builder's intention. Its extraordinary survival makes detailed comparison with its contemporaries and its immediate successors the more difficult in that almost none is so well preserved. The resultant unconformity has led students of their architecture into one of two positions: either to classify by broad-brush groups, such as the well-known division between tower-keeps (higher than broad) and hall-keeps (broader than high),[1] or to describe the type as a series of individual examples, with little attempt to form clusters.[2] With some reason Thompson asked for more subtle classifications,[3] though the response to his plea is still awaited, and the analysis has tended to be towards wholly separate studies of individual structures.[4] This is not altogether surprising: between the Norman Conquest and the early years of the thirteenth century approximately 200 keeps are known to have been built in Britain. Of these nearly half have left some physical traces, but no more than some thirty or forty have been well-enough preserved to allow discussion of more than their ground plans or of the details of crags of masonry. Very few of these survivors fall obviously into groups or classes. In a very real sense each is a unique design, apparently a response to different requirements, and even studies of the whole group tend to concentrate on the details of date or layout of individual examples.[5]

This chapter seeks to examine a small group of towers that by date and patron seem linked to the White Tower, to provide a framework for the understanding of the function of their internal arrangements, and to try to explain the development of these massive buildings at the end of the eleventh century and the beginning of the twelfth, and to show how their creation inspired a later generation to imitate them, and to add to the early design fresh elements to suit the changing needs of their time. The display and ceremony that is so obvious an element of this study is but one of the purposes of the great tower: its functions as a storehouse, especially for military munitions, as a defence and as a dwelling perhaps need no emphasis. But in an age that saw wholesale revolutions in the machinery of both fortification and government it is the great tower that remained remarkably constant, so that the builder, for example, of the extraordinary and showy building at Coucy-le-Château (Aisne) may well have empathised with the purpose of the White Tower, a century and a half before.

In the following sections it will be argued that the primary role of the White Tower was to provide a series of rooms suitable for display, entertainment and receptions, and that this was the function also of the great tower at Colchester, with the addition of a residential suite below, perhaps for the steward, Eudo. It will be suggested that the tower of Canterbury had a slightly different purpose and provided a living suite with guest rooms attached to the hall. It will be shown that the great tower at Norwich (at least as it was mod-

Facing page: 193 Entrance front showing the original squat tower at Portchester, Hampshire, of *circa* 1120 doubled in height in the second half of the twelfth century.

194 Diagram of the accommodation in the wooden donjon at Ardres, *circa* 1120, showing the three floor levels with the names given. The greater the seclusion of the room, the darker the hatching in the diagram. Although one must assume internal staircases, their position is not described in the text.

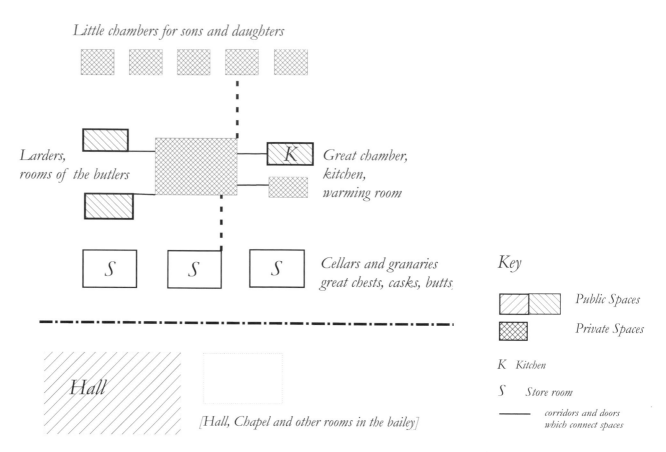

Little chambers for sons and daughters

Larders, rooms of the butlers

K *Great chamber, kitchen, warming room*

S S S *Cellars and granaries great chests, casks, butts*

Hall

[*Hall, Chapel and other rooms in the bailey*]

Key

Public Spaces

Private Spaces

K *Kitchen*

S *Store room*

corridors and doors which connect spaces

ified in the early twelfth century) was of yet another design, with spacious living and reception areas for the king, and with no purpose-built guest accommodation. Norwich proved a significant step, and its design led to the building of a small group of royal towers that extended this ancient palatial design towards the middle of the twelfth century, long after its heyday. With few exceptions, even the greatest of the barons did not construct great towers until the end of the reign of Henry I. Imitation of these earlier royal works began largely during the reign of Stephen.

It will be suggested that a quite separate tradition of tall towers, some intended for accommodation, existed in the late tenth and eleventh centuries, contemporary with the palatial towers. They appear to have been largely royal or ducal. These buildings too seem to be more rarely constructed after the middle of the eleventh century. Starting from the early twelfth century they were adopted into the symbolism of castle building, and the type developed, with complex patterns of construction, into the common twelfth- and thirteenth-century great towers. It will be suggested that this was due to the interpersonal striving for power within the members of a small group of royals, and the imitation of their works by their magnates, whose means were better adapted to the building of the smaller towers, and whose aspirations were best served by lofty structures.

The following account concentrates on the apparent original usage of the rooms, based largely on the degree of seclusion of each space, its relationship with

its neighbouring chambers and, where they survive, the built-in fittings of the room. It attempts to place the White Tower among comparable structures elsewhere. It shows that the particular characteristics of the Tower were to be found among other Norman great towers only rarely, and suggests that the White Tower and its immediate relatives were among the last of a particular type rarely required by the patrons of succeeding generations.

Within these towers the least-private space is generally called an 'entrance hall', or if small an 'ante-room'. More secluded, and generally smaller, rooms are called 'chambers'.[6] A hall, normally larger than the adjacent spaces, is taken to be a room of several functions, including ceremonial and business; these rooms share the characteristic of easier access to them than to any adjacent chamber. *Aula* (hall) and *camera* (chamber) are terms found in the written accounts of the period, but it is not assumed that these relate directly to the hall and chamber of the following account. It must not be forgotten how little we know of the use of these interiors during the eleventh or twelfth century: most of our knowledge derives from the accounts and depictions of the later Middle Ages, and even these by their very nature tend to focus on the spectacular or the unusual, rather than on the daily usage of the buildings. One important document survives from the twelfth century, the eulogistic recollection of the *domus lignea* of Arnold Fitz Arnold of Ardres, at Ardres (Pas-de-Calais) beside Calais (fig. 194).[7] This wooden tower was built about 1120; the

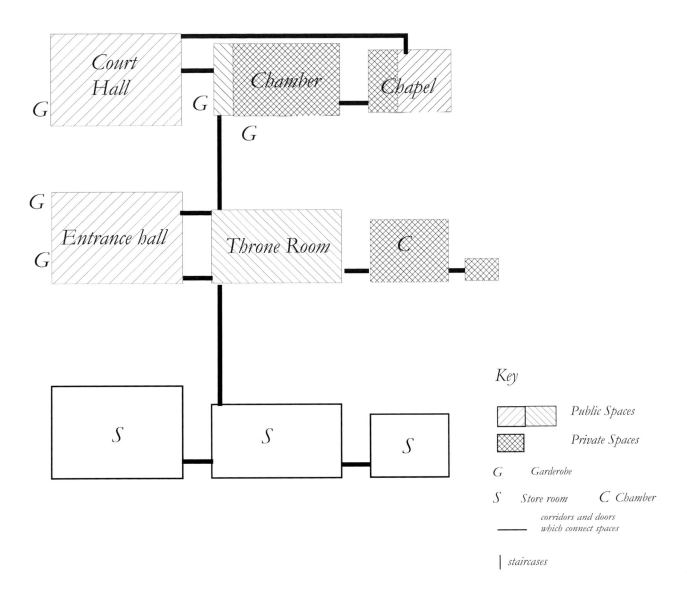

Key

Public Spaces

Private Spaces

G Garderobe

S Store room   C Chamber

corridors and doors which connect spaces

| staircases

description of it was written at the end of the twelfth century and probably relates to a real structure. Stripped of its repetitions, it describes a building on a motte (*dunjo*), a building that was laid out not for ceremony, but as a private house, which probably contained three storeys: the ground floor contained cellars and granaries (with chests, casks, butts); the first-floor living quarters consisted of the great chamber (used for sleeping by the lord and lady) with a maidservants' and children's room beside it, and a small private room with a fire; the kitchen (sounding perhaps larger in the description than in fact) was adjacent. On the top floor were small chambers for the sons and daughters, and others for attendants and guards. What are missing from this account are the rooms for public ceremony, which were to be found outside the *domus lignea*, but a nearby loggia or parlour is mentioned, with an adjacent chapel, which may have been on, or on the slope of, the motte. A hall and other buildings stood in the bailey. These additional buildings provided the framework for the proper and ceremonial use of the castle of Ardres.

THE PALATIAL TOWERS

Colchester

To investigate its influence, the starting point must be an understanding of the design and functioning of the White Tower itself. Much advanced by the present study, this is set out above, and needs no repetition here (fig. 195).[8]

The analysis, therefore, begins with Colchester, closely related to the White Tower, as has frequently been observed, both in its external plan and size.[9] The internal differences are at first sight considerable.[10] Because of the massive Roman podium on which the tower was built, the entrance floor at Colchester was at a substantially raised first-storey level, and was treated very simply: it lacked fireplaces or garderobes, unlike the complex arrangements at the White Tower. It appears, furthermore, always to have been low, not much more than 5 m high. Access to the upper floor was provided by a massive newel stair opening off an anteroom immediately beside the entrance, allowing a progression to the upper rooms without entering the main rooms on the entrance floor. At the White Tower, however, the staircase to the upper floor is from the further end of the inner room, permitting a quite different control of access.

It is the first floor at Colchester that has a little more in common with the layout of the entrance floor at the White Tower. It contained a hall lit by no fewer than nine loops and had two fireplaces, and, in its early phase two garderobes. What now appears as a separate central chamber may have been divided from the hall by an arcade, and so have been effectively part of the hall; and the inner eastern room, like that at the White Tower, was entered through a door that was closed against the hall. Drury very reasonably regards this hall as rising through two storeys, in distinction to the eastern chambers, both of which may have been floored at second-floor level, the present level of the much-reduced wall-head.[11] Vestiges of a mural passageway at this point survive on three of the four sides of the building. On the side of the hall, therefore, this would have looked down on the floor of the hall below. On the side of the eastern chamber the passage would have equated with the level of the floor of the chamber.[12] If this interpretation were accepted, however, the access to these chambers would be very problematic. Unless there were internal steps arranged inside the first-floor chamber, the only way to reach these second-floor rooms in the eastern half of the keep would have been from the main stair (or the small newel stair at this period inserted into one of the hall garderobes), in both cases at the western side of the keep, and on the other side of the tall open hall. The route to the private chambers would therefore have been solely along the galleries over the hall and the mural passages. A more likely supposition is perhaps that the whole tower was floored at the upper level, and that the two floors had similar arrangements, with the access to the upper eastern chamber via a door through the now-demolished cross wall from the proposed upper hall, which would be reached directly from either of the western stairs. Both upper hall and upper chamber would then have had their own approaches to the floor of the chapel, with now-lost doors leading into the mural passages. It seems generally supposed that the chapel arrangements at Colchester provided a superimposed pair of single-storeyed rooms, barrel-vaulted, appearing from the outside as a variant of the corner towers: these need not have risen far above the roofs of the adjacent apartments, particularly if the original wall-head at Colchester was as high above the mural passages as those at the White Tower.[13]

Because of the loss of so much fabric, the functional analysis of Colchester remains uncertain. Perhaps a starting point is to consider the ground-floor entrance, anteroom and great staircase as a separate element, an access that is functionally really part of the first floor

(fig. 196). The use for storage of the remainder of the ground floor would then equate with that of the whole basement at the White Tower. The difference between the layout of the two buildings at this point would then be due to the need to separate the storage rooms from the access to the upper floor, the anteroom providing an area of separation. An identical scheme was adopted at the much later tower of Warkworth in Northumberland, which, like Colchester is entered at the level of a raised ground floor, which is largely given over to storage.[14] The large hall would then equate with the large entrance hall at the White Tower, and the inner chamber with that identified as a throne room. But at Colchester the differences are very apparent. In the first place, the inner chamber seems to have been isolated, with no further access beyond it except to a small chamber in the north-east corner; it remains uncertain whether an original door led from the chamber into the basement of the chapel (the 'sub-crypt'): both the present openings seem to have been inserted, and both are in any case very irregularly set out, and are unlikely to be original. The most likely position for an entrance to this sub-crypt is at the western end, where major post-medieval alterations have made investigation difficult, but where the symmetry of the vaulting suggests it. In this case the sub-crypt would be associated with the western anteroom at the entrance to the hall (or with an approach from the southern end of the arcaded hall itself), rather than with the inner chamber to its north. Secondly, the private door, which in other keeps[15] opens into the privy chamber or similar room, at Colchester gave access to the more public upper 'entrance' hall. This latter room lacks obvious social orientation. Its lower end is presumably to the south, next to the entrance from the great stair. Its fireplaces heated the centre of the hall, and the northern end contained not only the staircase, but also the surviving garderobe. Logically, then, the upper end of the hall should be against the eastern side, facing the fireplaces and backing against the eastern chamber. The hall should thus be seen as orientated not along its longer axis, but against its shorter side, with its superior end perhaps behind an arcade to hold the upper part of the keep at the position of the first spine wall. The still-extant doorway in the second spine wall would in that case flank the dais. Assuming that the whole of the building was floored to produce a second hall, chapel and chamber on the missing floor above, the access to this suite would then be achieved either by bypassing this 'entrance' floor altogether (by continuing up the great staircase) or by crossing the lower end of the hall to the small inserted newel stair in the north-western corner. This stair could also be reached directly from the outside by entering the postern door at the north-western corner. This latter stair lacks the quality of the great staircase. It opens from the in-go of the private door, and shared

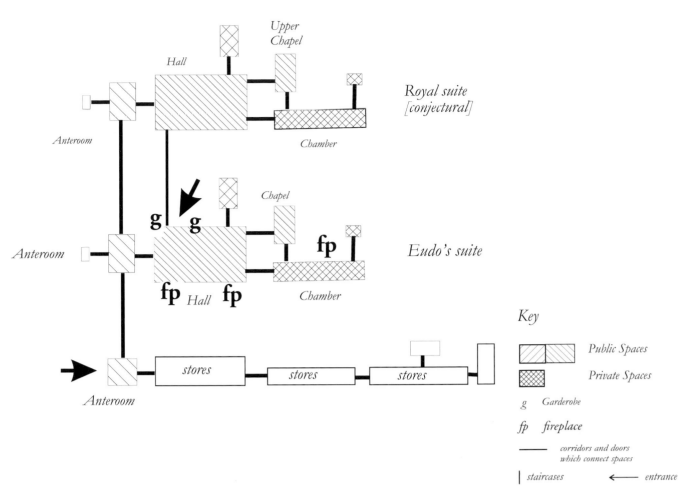

196 The arrangements at Colchester probably were intended to provide a hall and chamber with a chapel reached from either room, on two floor levels, for Eudo and for the king. Notice that the backstair gave access to the hall, and not as commonly to the chamber: this suggests that it was seen as providing an entrance to the royal apartments above, and less to the lower hall.

its passage with the only garderobe in the hall, but it was possible to go from this door to the stair without entering the hall at all.

To discuss the arrangements of the top floor is to speculate with little evidence, but if it be assumed that they resembled those of the floor below, the accommodation in the keep consisted of a pair of double apartments, each with a hall and chamber, and each reached almost separately by the great newel stair, directly linked only by the inserted privy stair.

Described in this fashion, the great tower at Colchester differs significantly from the White Tower, and appears to have contained a lower hall linked only slightly (via the privy stair) with the upper hall, and a lower chamber built as a cul-de-sac. The upper chamber perhaps opened from the upper hall, and both these rooms seem to have had access into the chapel. This arrangement suits the accommodation for a pair of households, and it is therefore significant that the early history of the castle exactly matches this situation. It may be suggested that the reason for the difference between what are otherwise buildings of similar appearance is that while William the Conqueror began the works at Colchester, the second period of construction, which included most of the significant details discussed above, was constructed by the steward Eudo, after 1101.[16] In his building, on this

view, he constructed a hall (the 'entrance hall') for regular public use, with a chamber suite opening to the east (and perhaps a small withdrawing chamber or muniment room at its north-east corner) for his own apartments, while the upper floor, separately reached by a grand stair, or by the private back stair, was provided for his master.[17] It cannot now be demonstrated, however, that this grand combination of state apartment and royal residence (perhaps made the more plausible because the king lacked at Colchester the palace that was available for his residence in London) was in fact completed as planned, since we do not know the extent and nature of the upper storey removed in the seventeenth century.

Norwich

As at Colchester, the great tower at Norwich has been considerably damaged by neglect and by rebuildings, making reconstruction of the original interior arrangements hazardous. Attempts to explain the structure have been made by Drury and by Heslop,[18] whose restored plans show anomalously shaped rooms at the western end of the building. The loss of the interior walls without record has made it unlikely that the full development of the building will ever be demonstrated, but the recent surveys and discussions provide the basis for an appreciation of the design of the build-

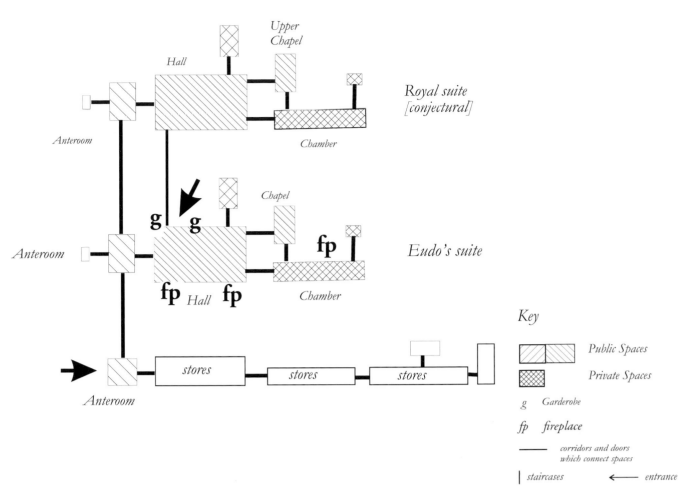

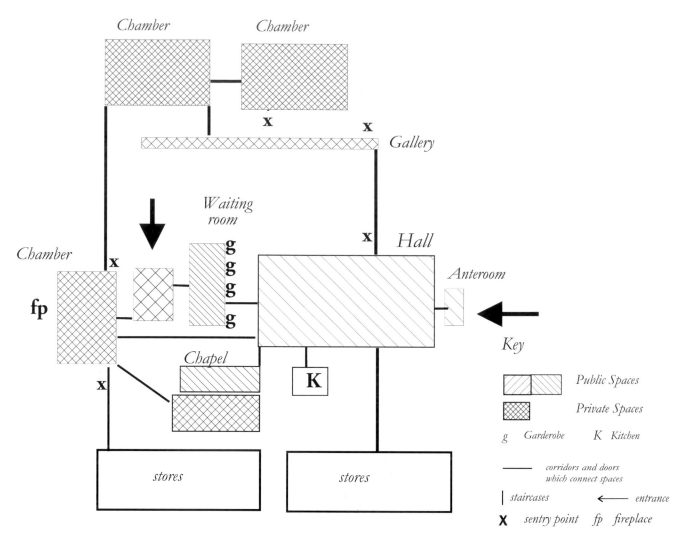

197 The complex planning at Norwich provided a sequence of rooms from the hall through a waiting area (provided with latrines) to the great chamber. From here access was provided to the upper chambers, which were also reached by the gallery that ran around the upper part of the first floor. Seclusion, however, was gained by a series of sentry posts in the corridors and at the junctions of stairs.

Chamber   *Chamber*

Gallery

Waiting room

Chamber   **fp**

g g g g g

Hall

Anteroom

Chapel

K

stores   *stores*

Key

Public Spaces

Private Spaces

g   *Garderobe*   *K*   *Kitchen*

—— *corridors and doors which connect spaces*

| *staircases*   ← *entrance*

X *sentry point*   *fp*   *fireplace*

ing at the time of its completion in or before 1120.[19] The original design, of about 1095, involved a multi-storeyed building of square plan divided into two sections by a spine wall, and with a newel stair in three of the four external corners. The internal angles of the ground floor were bridged by elegant triangular vaults, perhaps as an attempt to reinforce the corners of this heavy building set on the top of a recent mound. It is likely that this scheme was left incomplete at the eastern side of the building, where an internal wall, which later served to support the chapel, was inserted as a subdivision into the southern basement room. The original design for the upper floor or floors is not known. What was eventually constructed involved some changes from the initial plan at any rate, since the north-western stair was left unfinished and was replaced by the kitchen fireplace.

At the time of its completion, *circa* 1120, the access to the first floor was via a largely open external stair to a holding area outside the elaborately carved portal. Beyond this lay the hall, extending over much of the northern side of the building and open to the roof. The suggestion that the missing southern wall of this room may have framed a pair of dais arches is very reasonable,[20] given that the social orientation of the room, like that at Colchester, has its upper end on the

long southern side, with the long northern side of the hall serving as the lower end, since it contained both the entrance door at the east and a kitchen at the west of the room. A doorway on the dais side of the hall gave access directly to a tall heated room to its south; this is very reasonably regarded as a state chamber, with a chapel at its eastern side. At the western end of the hall, the position of the kitchen is clear. Beside it to the south is a massive array of latrines, arranged in two groups of eight on either side of a window. Further to the south are the remains of the vaulting of a small chamber, into which a private door formerly led, presumably from a timber external stair. The plan shows a possible reconstruction of the first floor: this differs from that already published only in the treatment of the western side of the tower.[21]

This reconstructed plan suggests the following arrangement of accommodation. The hall was served by a small kitchen, beside which was a door that led to a long chamber; this was decorated with blind arcading. This long room was provided with suites of garderobes, and is interpreted as a waiting room, which had all the characteristics of such spaces (fig. 197):[22] it had its access from the hall controlled by a door; it was itself closed off against an audience chamber or inner room; it was architecturally the most elaborately decorated part of the interior;[23] it gave access to latrines; and it was shaped to allow lateral benching for those waiting for admittance to the suite beyond. The small tapering room to the south was vaulted. It may have served as an anteroom or inner waiting area to the great chamber beside it; it certainly provided an entrance hall for the privy stair. It formed part of a sequence of rooms leading towards the great or state chamber itself. This room rose to the roof; it was heated and well lit, and had a wash basin beside the 'public' entrance door. Both this door and the private door from the side of the dais seem to have lain within a single-storey section, formed by the extension of the structure of the second floor as a jetty into the western side of the room.

Two further doors led from the great chamber. In the first place, a door in the eastern wall presumably led into the west end of the adjacent chapel (the wall itself, like almost all the other internal divisions, is now represented only by a scar on the inner face of the keep); the chapel was also entered directly from the hall by a long passageway against the eastern face of the keep, in a fashion similar to that into St John's Chapel at the White Tower.[24] Secondly, a door in the window jamb at the south-western corner, beside the 'public' door from the antechamber, gave access to a mural passageway. This was well lit; it contained a tall wall niche, perhaps serving as a sentry box for an attendant, and led to a newel stair, which rose to the third storey.[25] This upper floor spanned only the eastern third of the keep, and contained two large chambers, well lit by two tiers of large windows; these may be identified as the royal apartments. They were also accessible from the mural passageways at the level of the third storey. These passed along the long sides of hall, chamber and chapel at a high level, and contained a series of openings looking down into these rooms. In addition to the approach from the royal chambers, the passageway was entered by a newel at the north-eastern corner of the keep, immediately inside the main entrance. At first sight this represents a surprising lack of seclusion for the royal occupants. However, a pair of what seem to be sentry boxes with seats was provided for attendants to command the approaches along these passages, which in terms of royal life in the early twelfth century may well have seemed adequate privacy. Furthermore, the northern mural passage leading to the north-eastern stair enabled the occupants of the third storey to reach the entrance to the keep without passing through the rooms on the first floor, while that in the southern wall allowed inspection of the chapel from above, in a similar fashion to that provided by the gallery in St John's Chapel. It may thus be suggested that the mural passageway, or rather gallery, actually was conceived of as an extension of the royal apartments, rather than an intrusion into it.[26]

Canterbury

The fourth example in this group is the great tower at Canterbury (fig. 198), almost exactly contemporary with Norwich, and seemingly identical in scale to Henry I's tower at Domfront in Normandy (Orne). Following the loss of its upper portion, and the stripping off of some of the ashlars and detail, any analysis of the accommodation is speculative.[27] Early drawings show the keep with three rows of windows below a ruined wall-head, and there seems every reason to suppose that the building was three storeys high. The interior was divided by substantial walls into three unequal parts. The entrance was at first-floor level into the centre of the western side, reached from an added forebuilding whose plan recalls that of Norwich, and like that one may have had a holding or waiting area immediately outside the portal.[28] The entrance door led directly into the largest room in the keep, which was lit only by windows at its further end. The internal subdividing walls are preserved only to the top of the ground storey, but the scars on the inner face of the keep show that these partition walls were continued at least to the level of the second floor. Two staircases survive, one in the north-eastern corner, which rose throughout the building, and another in the centre of the southern side, which linked the basement with the first floor. A third stair, right beside the entrance, started at first-floor level and rose upwards to the second floor. This is known from early accounts, but the wall that contained it has now collapsed.[29]

These staircases provide a clue from which a tentative reconstruction of the internal arrangements can be suggested. The central first-floor room forms an entrance hall. The room immediately to the south of the entrance contains a well shaft; it was connected by its staircase directly to the basement stores, and has the remains of a large corner fireplace. This is almost certainly the kitchen, a notably large room in comparison with examples in the keeps at Norwich or Castle Rising (fig. 199), and its door was presumably close to the well shaft at the lower end of the hall. Flanking the upper, eastern, end of the hall lay two rectangular chambers. The smaller, to the south, seems to have been unheated, but was well lit, and probably contained a garderobe in its south-eastern corner. The larger northern chamber was similarly lit with three windows, one set in a massive window embrasure. It was heated towards its centre and was connected by the staircase at its north-eastern corner with the basement and the second floor above. A cranked mural passage at the north-western corner of the room led to a small chamber at the western side of the keep, close to, and linked with, the now-lost spiral stair beside the main entrance door. The function of these two large northern and southern rooms has been ingeniously suggested as summer and winter

249

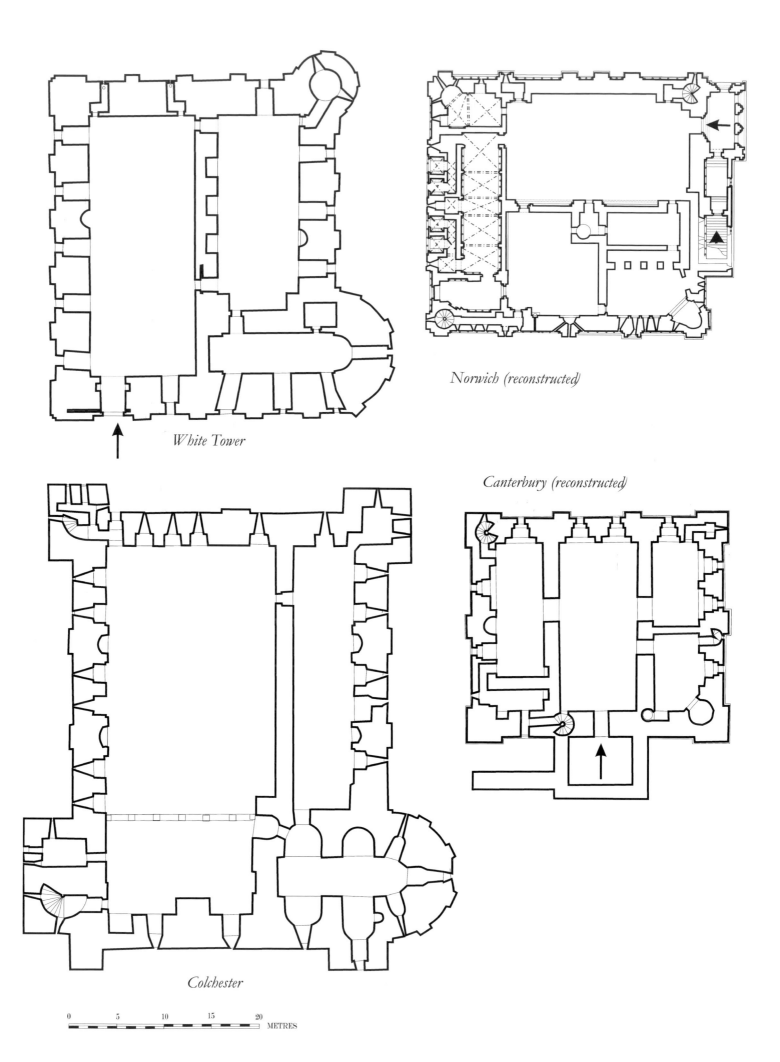

Norwich (reconstructed)

White Tower

Canterbury (reconstructed)

Colchester

0   5   10   15   20
METRES

199 Suggested use of the rooms in the ruined great tower at Canterbury. The first-floor entrance led into a hall in the centre of the building, flanked by a kitchen and service area, with an independent chamber beside it on one side and a more complex array of chambers on the other. Newel stairs enabled servicing from the basement. At the upper end of the more complex chamber a stair (also probably reached from the entrance) led upwards to a gallery that overlooked the hall and gave access to the upper chambers in the wings, thus allowing the hall to rise through two storeys.

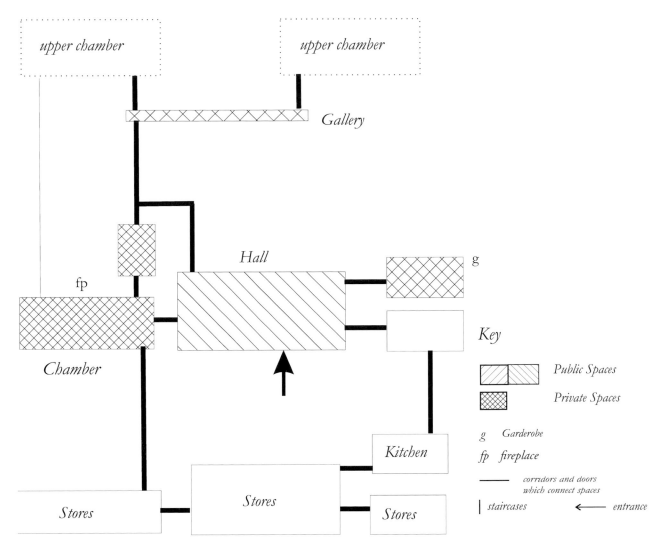

chambers.[30] The staircases, however, suggest a different function for them: the smaller room to the south is unconnected with the rest of the keep. That to the north, however, is central to the distribution of accommodation. This it may be suggested was the great chamber, and it was itself perhaps orientated: its doorway should have been at the dais end of the hall, and the eastern side of the chamber then forms the lower end, which the north-eastern stair links to the stores below and the rooms above. On this argument, the upper end of the chamber lay to the west (a dais or bench against the west wall, flanked by the cranked passage), with a more private room beyond; from this a passage led to a stair to the second floor. This was also accessible for those entering the keep without having to cross any of the first-floor rooms. The more private rooms were thus on the top floor, approached by stairs linked with the great chamber, but the arrangement of this missing third storey is even harder to guess: it appears to have replicated in general outline that of the first floor. It is possible that the first-floor hall was a double-height space, which rose to the roof like those at the White Tower, Norwich and elsewhere. In this case the access to the southern chambers (above the kitchen and the 'summer chamber') must have been solely along the gallery that linked the western stair with the chamber. The great height of the first floor (about 8.6 m) and the position of windows shown in early drawings, however, suggest that a double-height room here would be extraordinarily lofty, and that there was a second hall above the first. In this case, the provision of two staircases would allow a flexible entry to the upper hall, since those permitted into it could pass up one, while the other provided a separate and more private access. The keep at Canterbury may thus be seen to have contained many of the elements that are found at the White Tower and perhaps at Colchester, particularly the provision of a hierarchy of halls and chambers, but the quite different arrangement in detail of the layout of the apartments, and the unique placing of the main hall in the centre of the building, mark it out as a quite distinct design within this group.

The Chronology of this Group

The date range for the building of the White Tower has been established fairly closely, above. It belongs to the last quarter of the eleventh century, with a starting date of about 1075–9, and a completion of the main structure not later than the early years of the

Facing page: 198 Early palatial towers before 1120.

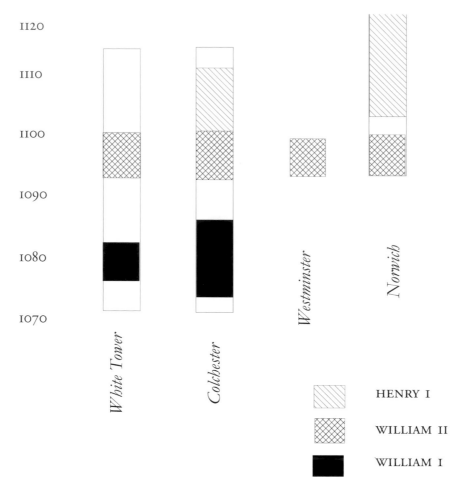

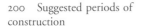

1120

1110

1100

1090

1080

1070

White Tower

Colchester

Westminster

Norwich

HENRY I

WILLIAM II

WILLIAM I

twelfth century. This phasing involves a clear break around the middle of the building programme, after which the White Tower was completed probably to the original plan, but with a restriction in the use of ashlar and the modification and cheapening of some other details. It is interesting to see the same sequence in two other great towers of this period, Colchester and Norwich, both of them royal works. In each of these a clear division can be seen a little below halfway up the walls. In the case of Colchester, the first building period ended with the provision of battlements. This has been linked to the threat of Scandinavian attack,[31] but, given the slowness of the setting of lime mortar, this interpretation of the break as an immediate response to a sudden need is not convincing. Examination of the internal walls has not been decisive in solving this matter, but the horizontal building break above which the temporary battlements were constructed occurs about 1 m above the first-floor joists, and shows that the openings, fireplaces and similar elements that we find on the first floor were all below the break and so were part of an original design. Work was then stopped: the building of battlements suggests that this was anticipated to be a long pause.[32] The attribution of the main newel staircase (which begins below the building break) to the second phase of building suggests quite strongly that the resumed work involved some rethinking about the accommodation.[33] The stopping of work at Colchester, then, may have in-

volved rearrangement of the main access, and may have been a lengthy pause, but in other respects it was like that at the White Tower, whose first phase ended in an unlooked-for interruption to work in progress, leaving carved capitals for the chapel waiting to be put in place, but with only very minor changes to the work in the second phase.[34] The changes to the stairs at Colchester suggest a rather greater alteration of the design of the upper part, and this redesign is more clearly demonstrated at Norwich, where the work stopped at the top of the lower storey. Here the unique vaulting system was probably unfinished, and may not have been completed on the eastern side;[35] the resumption of building involved a change of staircase and perhaps of other significant elements.[36] The chronological link between these buildings is indicated in the diagram above, which suggests that the White Tower and Colchester were begun together under the Conqueror; after half a dozen seasons work at the former stopped about the years 1079–83 and at the latter at about the same time. The building of the White Tower was probably resumed *circa* 1090, but Colchester may have waited longer (fig. 200). A completely new keep was then begun by William Rufus at Norwich, perhaps about 1095,[37] coinciding with the new great hall of the palace of Westminster,[38] and the stopping of work at the keep of Norwich was perhaps due to the king's death in August 1100. The resumption of building at Norwich, with an altered design, was undertaken by

201 View of the interior of the tower of Falaise, Normandy, before the recent rebuilding, showing the hall in the foreground, with the chamber behind on the left, and the waiting room and other smaller chambers on the right.

Henry I, and was finished by about 1120, by which date the White Tower and Colchester were presumably both already complete.[39] The extent to which the original scheme for Colchester was fully implemented remains uncertain, though it is clear that an additional upper storey, with battlements and towers, remained until its demolition in the seventeenth century, and it is possible that the completion of this upper floor was undertaken by Eudo Dapifer after the grant in 1101 by Henry I to him of the city of Colchester 'et turrim et castellum'.[40] A fourth royal great tower, at Canterbury, may belong to the same period. Though once attributed to Henry II, and dated to the 1170s,[41] this was probably begun either by William Rufus or early in Henry I's reign, and completed before *circa* 1120.[42] At some point close to this date, Henry I added a great tower to the buildings of the ducal castle at Falaise, discussed below.[43] Henry I was also responsible for several other great towers that should form part of this group, but their fragmentary remains, or total loss, makes comparison unhelpful.[44] In view of the habit of the Norman kings of wearing their crowns at Christmas at Gloucester, the loss of the early twelfth-century keep there is particularly unfortunate.[45]

The Family of Norwich

Falaise

Two further great towers, belonging probably to the next generation, one built for Henry I, perhaps in his later years, and one for his widow, Queen Adeliza, by her second husband, have layouts that closely resemble that suggested for Norwich, and may be considered here. At Falaise in Normandy (Calvados) the great tower, conventionally dated *circa* 1120, now lacks much of the evidence for its internal arrangements.[46]

The main entrance, reached by an apparently secondary stone forebuilding, opened directly into the end of the largest space in the building (figs 201, 202). Two staircases opened immediately from within the door, a newel to the roof from the in-go, and a straight mural stair to the basement from the corner of the room. This hall was lit by a pair of two-light windows in large embrasures. No other details of the hall are known, but it too seems to have been socially orientated so that the lower end was the southern, long side; and the possible former existence of a kitchen in the north-western angle turret adds some confirmation to this impression. On this western side of the building scars formerly visible on the face of the tower suggest that there were at least two separate rooms, one adjacent to the kitchen and provided with probably two garderobes, and the other, at the south-western corner, with access to what may have been a private door or postern.[47] The southern side of the tower was largely taken up by a single large chamber, heated by the only fireplace, and lit by a large two-light window. To the south-east, and reached from this chamber, an elegant chapel occupies a small wing or jamb projecting from the south-eastern angle. A newel stair in the western corner of the chapel gave access to a sub-chapel or crypt at ground-floor level, but with this exception all the accommodation seems to have been provided on one level, and all apartments seem to have opened to the roof, with comparatively low wall-heads. The first storey was lofty, but lacked architectural detail. Despite its scale, it seems to have consisted only of spaces for storage, a conclusion reinforced by the simple access to it, which lay immediately inside the external entrance to the tower.

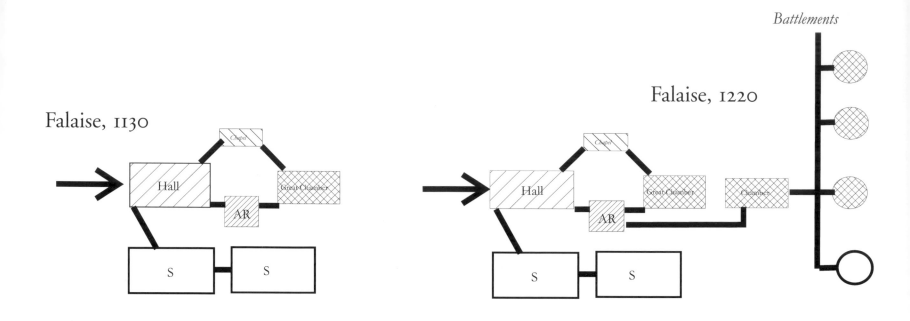

Falaise, 1130

Falaise, 1220

Battlements

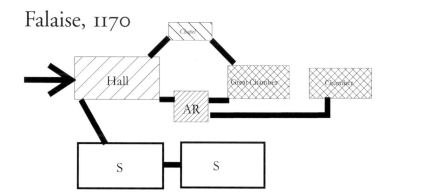

Falaise, 1170

Key

Public Spaces

Private Spaces

S   Store room   AR Anteroom

corridors and doors
which connect spaces

| staircases   ← entrance

202 The original arrangement at Falaise, with access through the hall to the chapel and the chamber anteroom, was a simplified version of Norwich. During Henry II's reign this was modified by the addition of a new chamber block to provide more private accommodation. After the fall of Normandy the building of a *tour philippiene* about 1210 added a group of private chambers further to extend the amount of secluded rooms. The original chamber survived these changes as part of the ceremonial suite.

The arrangement of accommodation in the eastern half of the building is comparatively straightforward. The upper end of the hall lay on the long southern wall, and from it access was presumably provided by a door beside the dais to the chamber. The spine wall is thick, and may have contained a passage down to a narrow door commanding the stair in the forebuilding, which is shown in a nineteenth-century plan by Doranlo. There may have been a complex provision of both public and private access to the chapel, such as we have seen at the White Tower, Colchester and Norwich, but on the whole the position of the single chapel door rather close to the chamber fireplace suggests fairly strongly that the only approach to the chapel was through the chamber itself, and that therefore the chapel was intended for private devotions. This is a significant consideration when assessing the intended use of the tower as a whole. The arrangements at the western side of the building are more open to doubt. Fragments of vaulting were formerly visible on the inside between the southern garderobe and the private door, and this implies the former existence of internal walls to support the other sides of the vault. The function of these rooms is even less

certain, but comparison with the buildings discussed above suggests that they may have consisted of a waiting room (with garderobes) and an antechamber (with a privy door, and a small storage or muniment chamber in the angle), from which a separate access to the chamber was provided.

These similarities with elements of the plan of the earlier great towers serve also to heighten the differences between them and Henry I's great tower at Falaise. Though the storage available is very large, and though an additional storey could have been added in the fashion of Colchester or Norwich, the domestic accommodation actually provided is of large size and high quality, but of very limited extent. This tower may well therefore have been conceived as a set of apartments for the king's private use, a private hall, a great chamber and a grand oratory, with a separate waiting area and antechamber for such business as might be done in this place, and no provision for the grander ceremonies such as might be provided for by the halls of the White Tower and Norwich. It entails, of course, the existence of such halls and facilities outside the great tower: in this it is merely following the normal arrangements, since all the examples dis-

203 View of Castle Rising, Norfolk, from the south-west, showing the garderobe outlets and the external access to the chamber that forms an element in almost all the early great towers.

cussed above were accompanied by blocks of buildings in their courtyards, but among the royal great towers so far examined Falaise stands out as an early example of the type sometimes described as a 'solar keep'. The changes to this early design during the next generation are described below.

Castle Rising

A great tower that seems closely imitative of the work at Falaise, and echoing Norwich, was constructed from the later 1130s at Rising in Norfolk by William de Albini, who had married Henry i's widow, Adeliza of Louvain. In view of the excellent accounts of the building available, the discussion here need only be short.[48] The approach to the entrance is by an elaborately decorated staircase leading to a large waiting area outside the main door.[49] The hall, reached by a short flight of steps, presumably to heighten the grandeur of the entrance, is once again orientated along its long side, and, like Norwich and perhaps Falaise, had a kitchen at its further end. Two niches were set in the spine wall, behind the dais end, and a door to the chamber lay beside this high table. At the eastern side of the hall, to the north of the main entrance, a spiral stair gave access both to the basement and the upper part of the building. To the south of the entrance, a cranked passageway was extended to command the adjacent forebuilding, in a similar fashion to that which probably once existed at Falaise. Beside it a door led through a small chamber formed against the spine wall, and on into the nave of

the chapel in the south-eastern angle. At the western end of the hall a corridor led to a pair of garderobes, and a door opened into a small unlit chamber, which may have been divided into two storeys. The chamber, entered by a door beside the dais, was provided with two garderobes in its western wall, one of which was probably designed as a private door (fig. 203). It was heated by a fireplace and had its own staircase in the south-western angle. From its eastern side a door led into the western end of the adjacent chapel.

The analysis of the accommodation suggests a close similarity to the design of both Falaise and Norwich. Once again, the differences between them are instructive. At Rising there are no suites of rooms suitable for audience or crown wearing, and the chamber in the position taken elsewhere by anterooms was a storeroom (fig. 204). The layout of the main entrance shows that though ceremony was an element in the design, the waiting area was confined to the space at the head of the forebuilding, and the chief element of segregation and separate access was provided by the distinguishing of approaches to the chapel (fig. 205). The overall design suggests, like Falaise, that the concept was of a lord's private house, with a level of ceremony appropriate for de Albini, who did not require the more elaborate sequence of approach suitable for the king. It is extremely interesting to note that the great tower at Rising was almost certainly abandoned unfinished, perhaps roughly roofed over below its parapet, nearly 4 m below

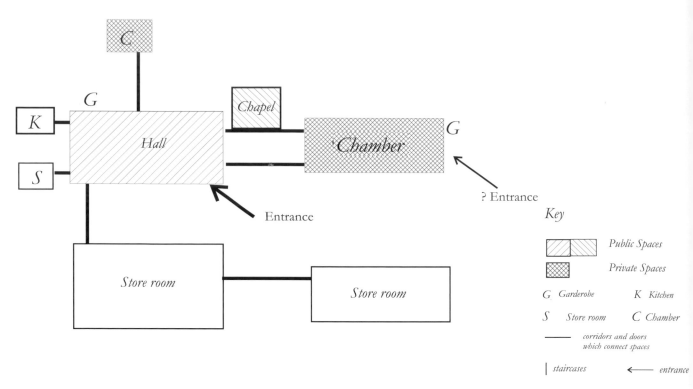

Facing page 205 Great towers of Henry 1.

their present height, and was probably never used by its builders. It was finally completed in the middle of the thirteenth century, probably at the time of a change of ownership. Even then occupation (judged on the nature of its garderobe pits) was infrequent: it may have been refurbished as a home for the disgraced Queen Isabella after 1329. The reason for this interruption of the building is not at all certain. The de Albinis may have found the site remote; the noble world was soon to fall apart in the Anarchy, and their place in that society may have fallen short of what was expected of a queen dowager in 1138. William de Albini was created Earl of Sussex in 1141, was already lord of Arundel by virtue of his marriage, and seems to have moved close to the court. Adeliza herself died in 1151, after which William required no stately palace in northern Norfolk.[50]

The Palatial Towers: Their Purpose and Decline

Towers are so obvious a vehicle for display and prestige that it is hard to envisage a world without them. But, as Crouch points out, it was halls rather than castles of any sort that at least at first were the *mise en scène* for grand display.[51] This is borne out by the Bayeux Tapestry: whenever fighting takes place, the tapestry displays motte and bailey earthworks. Whenever justice or decision is displayed, the frame displays a hall.[52] It is perhaps for this reason that the new great towers, cube-shaped or even squat, such as Ivry and the White Tower, laid emphasis in their interior planning on the presence of a hall. This is clear in the case of the largest surviving great tower in Britain not obviously built by royalty, that at Chepstow, which consists of a single large room, which was heated in the centre of its long side, lit largely from the side looking down on the river, and surrounded by mural niches like sedilia on three of the four sides. Like the White Tower, this hall was reached through a door placed well below the floor, to allow a stately entrance. Within the building only ceremony was possible, as is clear by the later developments here: the hall was floored over and the chambers missing from the original design were inserted. Though normally attributed to William's companion, Fitz Osbern, the great tower displays horizontal building breaks at about 3 m intervals, and was clearly built over several seasons, perhaps seven or eight. Since Fitz Osbern died as early as 1071, if the building is his it is unlikely to have been finished by then, and the date of its completion is not known. Recent arguments point to the second rather than the first generation after the Conquest.[53] The White Tower, with its two large halls and audience hall, fits well into this pattern.

There is clearly a further element in the design of the White Tower for display and prestige, and that is the use of the vocabulary of the architecture of the Roman past, a past that in the eleventh century was even more obvious than it is to us, since so many more of the buildings were then still standing. The new cathedral of Lincoln, an exact contemporary of the White Tower, shows the use of this vocabulary. In 1072 William 1 appointed Remigius as bishop to the ancient see of Dorchester on Thames, re-establishing its centre at the north of the diocese, at Lincoln. From then until his death in 1092 Remigius created a new cathedral beside the existing Anglo-Saxon church of St Mary of Lincoln. What now survives is a western block of late eleventh-century masonry, conceived as a probably free-standing gate into the western end of the old church. This has been shown to have con-

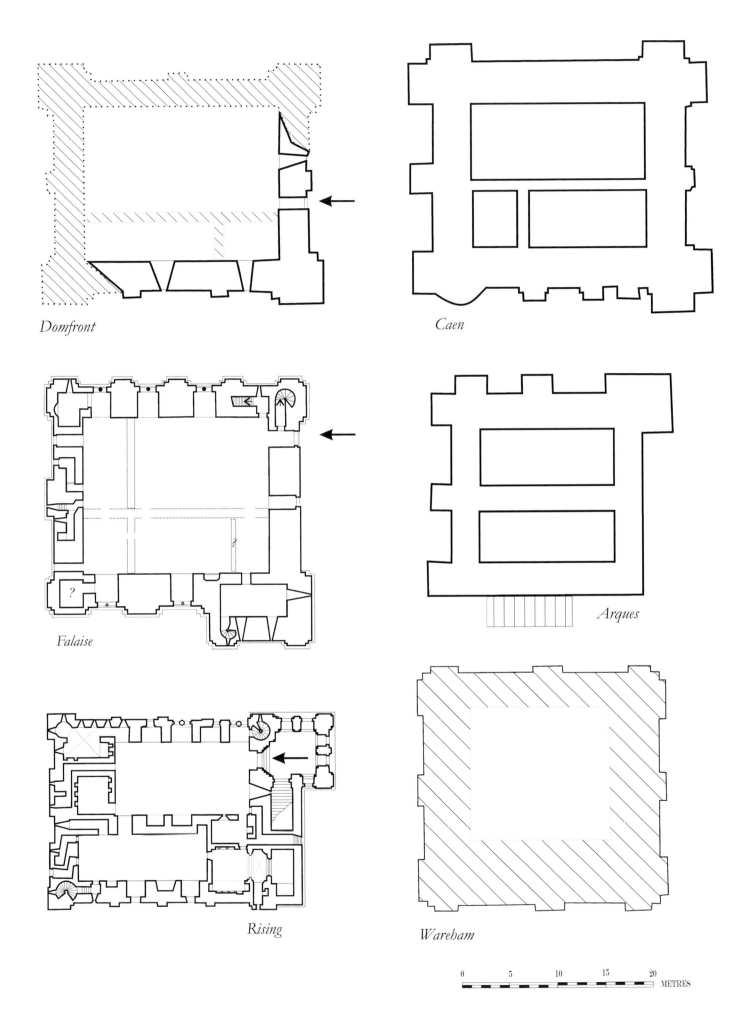

Domfront

Caen

Falaise

Arques

Rising

Wareham

0   5   10   15   20
METRES

tained the bishop's palace above the entrance,[54] and has been interpreted as an independent great tower ostentatiously placed at the cliff edge in the centre of the old Roman city.[55] Stripped of its Gothic over-building, this remarkable structure, with its three huge arches and (probably) an inscribed frieze above them, is clearly derived from the triumphal arches of ancient Rome, already imitated in the abbey gate at Lorsch (Hessen) in Germany (circa 780) and in Carolingian reliquaries,[56] and visible in Roman gates at the time, some of which still survive.[57] In this context the blind arcading that so distinguishes the elevation of the White Tower is a plain reference to the majesty of the Roman world. Like Charlemagne before him, William himself was clearly aware of these undercurrents. He encouraged the rapid construction of major churches: the huge new cathedral that was begun and very quickly finished, beside his palace at Winchester, was designed to resemble the massive regularity of Roman buildings, and, significantly, to exceed in scale the huge imperial cathedral of Speyer (Rhineland-Palatinate), the burial place of the Ottonian emperors.[58] The Roman past demonstrated power, authority and stability.

Work on the great towers, once they had been begun in the 1070s, proceeded slowly, and it has been shown above that in each case, except perhaps Canterbury, the towers display a clear building break after the first few years of construction. In some cases (Colchester, Norwich) this was followed by a reworking of the design. It seems that the patrons of these great towers were losing interest in their designed purpose: at the least their priorities were elsewhere. The date of this pause at Norwich was perhaps during the last years of the eleventh century, and the resumption of the building programme here seems due to the direct interest of Henry I, who was responsible for the completion of the earlier works and the building of new towers, which are discussed below. But these new towers increasingly turned away from the 'hall in a fortress' concept that we find in the earlier buildings, and introduced a degree of subdivision and domestic accommodation. This is perhaps the point at which the direct line of the White Tower and its relatives died out, in the unfinished hulks of these great buildings at the end of the eleventh century. But what they symbolised, their massive authority, remained an important reference point for the builders of the next generation, and so formed a potent element in the expression of power in the twelfth century.

THE SMALLER TOWERS

Malling, Bramber and Rochester Cathedral

All the towers so far discussed have characteristics in common, to the extent that it is reasonable to see them as part of the same family. A quite different group of great towers is represented by the tall, often relatively slender, structures that are often taken to be typical 'keeps'. These have a long ancestry, stretching back on the Continent to the tall towers of the early eleventh century. The grandest of these, Loches in Indre-et-Loire, has recently been shown to belong to the decades from circa 1013 to 1035.[59] Others, such as Loudun (Vienne) and Montbazon (Indre-et-Loire), probably belong to the same period.[60]

In England three towers in this category stand out – West Malling, Bramber and the tower to the north of Rochester Cathedral. The tower of West Malling in Kent is most complete, but its function is very hard to establish: each of the four storeys is of great height, no less than 7 or 8 m, and each lacks features suitable for accommodation, such as garderobes, fireplaces and mural chambers. Each storey is lit by narrow windows high above the floor, reached by stepped splays. The arrangement most resembles that of the German Bergfrieden, or the French beffrois (fig. 206), and perhaps like them the tower was intended to be a refuge or watchtower beside the adjacent monastery. Both monastery and tower are attributed to Gundulf, Bishop of Rochester from 1077 until his death in 1108.[61] The only detail on the tower, the blind arcading around its central storey, most closely resembles that in the late eleventh-century hall at Chepstow and at the top of the great tower at Corfe, probably of the beginning of the twelfth century, and so it can reasonably be dated to circa 1100 (fig. 207). Gundulf was perhaps also the builder of the tower whose remains are attached to the slightly earlier northern transept at Rochester Cathedral in Kent. Only the lower part of this remains, but it seems to have been a simple building containing a small room on each floor, perhaps a little more elaborately furnished than West Malling. The tower at Bramber in West Sussex, of which only a single wall still stands to anything like full height, was probably similar in its appearance to West Malling, with a small square room on each of the four floors. It differs from the other two in that it stood beside the gate to the castle, and formed the main part of the entrance defence. In this it is linked with some earlier towers of perhaps the later eleventh century, St Michael at the North Gate of Oxford and St George, now a tower inside Oxford Castle, which before the building of the castle around it may have stood at the former West Gate of the town. Oxford's eastern gate may have had a similar tower. These buildings are clearly different in form and purpose from the great towers already discussed, and should presumably be described in terms of elements of the defence of the gate.[62]

Two Squat, Square Towers: Bridgnorth and Portchester

This positioning, however, links the slim gate towers with a more obvious great tower, the keep at Bridg-

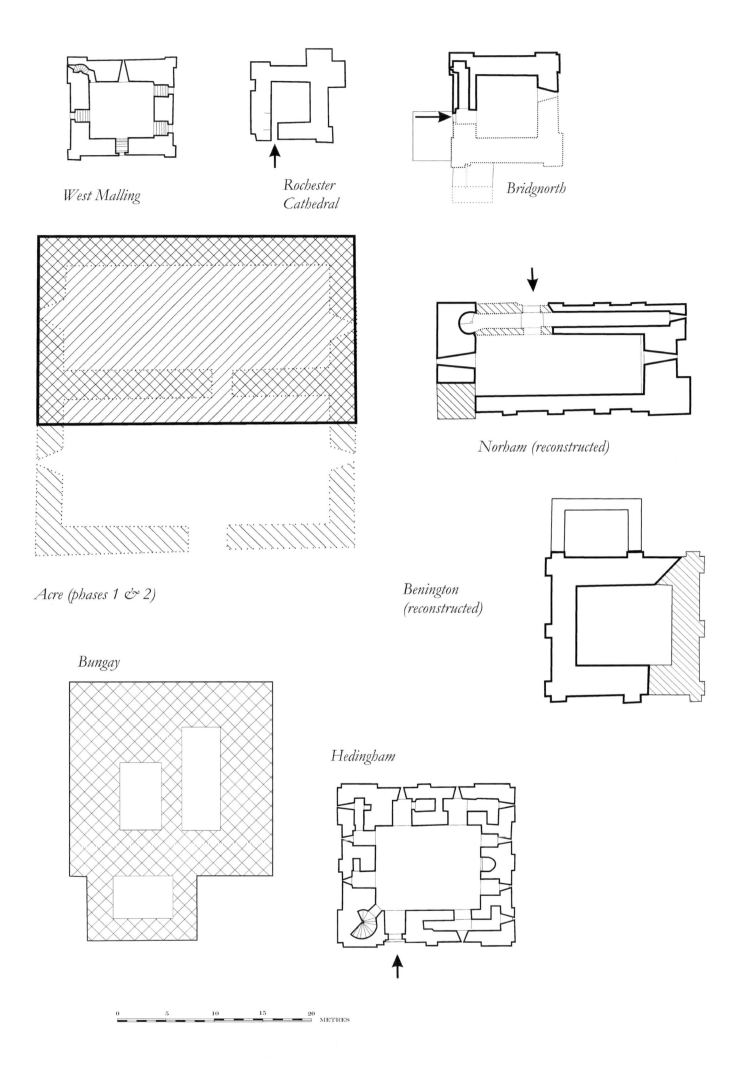

West Malling

Rochester
Cathedral

Bridgnorth

Acre (phases 1 & 2)

Norham (reconstructed)

Benington
(reconstructed)

Bungay

Hedingham

0   5   10   15   20
METRES

207 General view of the late
eleventh-century tower at West
Malling, Kent, showing the external
plain blind arcades that resemble
the arcading at Corfe and
Chepstow.

north Castle, Shropshire, which stands immediately
to the east of the former gate into the middle bailey,
at first on the bank that divided the middle and inner
wards from the outer courtyards of the castle and later
protruding from the stone curtain wall that replaced
the earthworks. This great tower was contrived to
contain on its southern side another gatehouse,
between the middle and inner courtyard. It is a squat
building, a little taller than it is square, and contained
a single large room at first-floor level, above a storeroom. This room was provided with a garderobe,
discharging northwards into the ditch, and large
windows looking into the baileys; it was entered not
from the inner, but from the outer ward. It had a
chamber at second-floor level, with a newel stair in
the south-east corner linking basement and roof. The
keep was capped by a roof in the shape of the letter
v, with the drainage in the centre, well below the wall-
heads. The placing of the (added) forebuilding and
external staircase to the first-floor entrance on the
western side (the middle ward) is significant, since one
might expect it to be sited instead in the inner bailey.
It seems, therefore, that the keep at Bridgnorth was
laid out to control access from and to the controlling
point of the inner castle, the main gate, and to provide
an entrance into the inner ward, with its royal hall and
apartments. The date of this tower is not yet certain.
It is traditionally attributed to the Earl of Shrewsbury,
Robert de Bellême, who moved his castle from its old
site a mile away downstream at Quatford to command
the crossing of the River Severn at the site of an
Æthelrædan burh in 1100 or 1101.[63] Despite his vast

resources,[64] it is unlikely that he would have made any
progress on the building before the king besieged and
captured this new castle in 1102, and thereafter it
remained in royal hands until the seventeenth century.
On the whole, although it is possible that de Bellême
began the tower (a change in stone coursing just below
the first floor suggests two phases), it is likely that it
was at least completed by Henry I after the earl's dis-
grace, perhaps during the king's consolidation of his
kingdom during the 1110s.[65]

The details of the Bridgnorth keep link it with the
first phase of another royal castle, Portchester in
Hampshire. Here the great tower was initially completed exactly as at Bridgnorth with a main floor above
a basement, and a low chamber or loft above this (fig.
193). Like Bridgnorth, too, the roof was constructed
with a v-section, the drains being in the centre; but
here the building was larger, and built as a double pile
with two rooms separated by a spine wall. Each room
contained a garderobe, and the inner room was heated.
It is difficult not to see these two towers as designed
by the same hand. Portchester became royal in 1120,
after the death of its Domesday owner, and if Henry I
constructed the tower at Bridgnorth it is likely that his
masons then worked on the one at Portchester. Despite
their close structural affinities, the arrangements of
Bridgnorth and Portchester are not alike. The limited
though superior accommodation at the former, and
the provision of its access from the middle bailey, while
protecting with its gate the inner bailey, shows that the
tower was built to house an official with control over
the traffic into the royal lodgings. At Portchester, on
the other hand, the great tower is remote from the
entrance, probably placed beside an earlier hall, and
presents a more conventional picture of a reception
hall and withdrawing chamber on one level.[66] Both
rooms are large: the hall was well lit, and contains a
well, a staircase giving access to the ground-floor stores
and a garderobe with its entrance close to the chamber
door. The chamber, slightly smaller, was lit only by
four high and narrow loops, but contained its own
garderobe and was heated by the only fireplace in the
building at this period.

Castles without Great Towers

A great number of castles were constructed during the
second half of the eleventh century in England. Most
of these were earthworks, their type either motte and
bailey, with a high hill of earth, or ringworks, both
with earthen banks, ditches and timber defences and
accommodation.[67] It is worth noting how few of these
new castles contained great towers.[68] These include
some strategically important royal castles, such as
Bamburgh (Anglo-Saxon), Dover (1063), Winchester
(*circa* 1070), Newcastle upon Tyne (1080), Rochester
(1089) and Carlisle (1092), at which great towers were
first added up to a century or more after the castles

Interior of the great tower at Domfront, Normandy, showing the first-floor entrance into the hall on the left. This was a tall room extending to the roof. On the right lay paired chambers on two floor levels above the basement.

themselves were built. Baronial castles too lacked great towers in the two generations after the Conquest. Some of the greatest of them, such as Castle Acre (Norfolk), Barnard Castle (Durham), Norham, Elsdon and Prudhoe (all in Northumberland) were built at first as ringworks containing unfortified domestic buildings, though most of them were to receive great towers during the course of the twelfth century; others, like Eynsford in Kent, remained stone enclosures with halls and chambers inside them. The change in this pattern seems to have begun during the early years of Henry I, and at first it seems to have involved solely royal castles.

THE CASTLES OF HENRY I

Domfront, Corfe, Wareham, Gloucester, Bamburgh and Carlisle

Henry I's interest in castle building on the Continent was well known to his contemporaries.[69] Examination of the design and detail of surviving buildings suggests that his work in England was equally extensive.[70] The crucial site is perhaps Domfront, where Henry, as Count of the Cotentin,[71] seized the old de Bellême castle in 1092 (fig. 208), and began an extensive restoration, including the building of the great tower whose fragmentary remains survive.[72] It was a tall build-

ing on a generous floor plan, containing, it is suggested, three storeys above a basement.[73] The first-floor entrance led into a large hall, which may have risen through two storeys. Beyond this lay a narrower chamber, which may have been subdivided, and which was floored across to produce a mezzanine level (if the hall was two storeys high). The floor above was supported on a scarcement ledge on both surviving sides, and was reasonably tall below the wall-head, but has preserved no other features at all.[74] The layout of this building cannot be discussed with confidence, but it seems to have contained a storage basement, a large hall and two superimposed chambers that had windows but no signs of other features. Above this there seems to have lain a tall featureless room, with no traces on the walls of the subdivision that we see below. On the whole it seems more likely that this was a roof space below the wall-heads, rather than a room. From the ground one cannot trace any leading at this level, but the roof may have been a pyramid, similar to that at Hedingham (Essex) and Carrickfergus (Co. Antrim, Northern Ireland), which would leave no evidence of gables on the walls. If this is true, the accommodation provided at Domfront was relatively small, a hall and two (or possibly four small) chambers, a little larger than Portchester, but on a comparable scale.

In 1100 Henry became king, and in 1106 Duke of Normandy in addition. It is presumably to this period that one should attribute the building of at least three of the great towers that belong to his reign, Corfe,[75] Wareham (both in Dorset) and Caen (Calvados). In terms of their scale these form with Domfront a group, sharing a plan nearly square, with walls of 3 to 4 m thick, shallow but prominent buttresses, and the internal space subdivided into unequal parts. None is well preserved. Corfe is reduced to three fragmentary walls, Caen to the basement and ground floor, and Wareham to a fragmentary plan based on small-scale excavations.

A little can be said about the arrangements at Corfe: the great tower consisted of a basement with probably two storeys above. These are likely to have been subdivided: a jamb survives from the cross-wall door on the southern side at both first- and second-floor levels (fig. 209). The tower was arranged for accommodation, and a small annexe, to contain a suite of rooms including garderobes serving the top storey, was added on its southern side, probably during its construction (fig. 210). Since the entry to the great tower was into the southern half at first-floor level,

this implies a sequence of rooms as follows. A fore-building led to the door of a first-floor entrance hall, from which access was obtained to a withdrawing chamber or chambers at the same level. There was a spiral staircase at the top of the missing south-east corner that presumably led from the second floor; otherwise, it would be necessary to reach this upper floor by a stair in the forebuilding.[76] This topmost floor contained a large chamber on the south, with a door leading into the chapel at the top of the annexe. The tower was presumably placed beside an earlier hall or halls within the inner ward: what it seems to provide is a reception room, perhaps a smaller audience chamber and a full domestic suite (perhaps separately reached), including latrines and a chapel on the floor above. For more extensive receptions the halls in the inner or the middle ward would be available. It is interesting to note that after no more than 100 years it was clearly felt that the accommodation in the building was inadequate, and so it was supplemented, or superseded, by the creation of a large courtyard house, containing a full range of hall, chapel and chambers, and known thereafter as the king's houses, or the 'gloriette'.[77] A royal great tower of

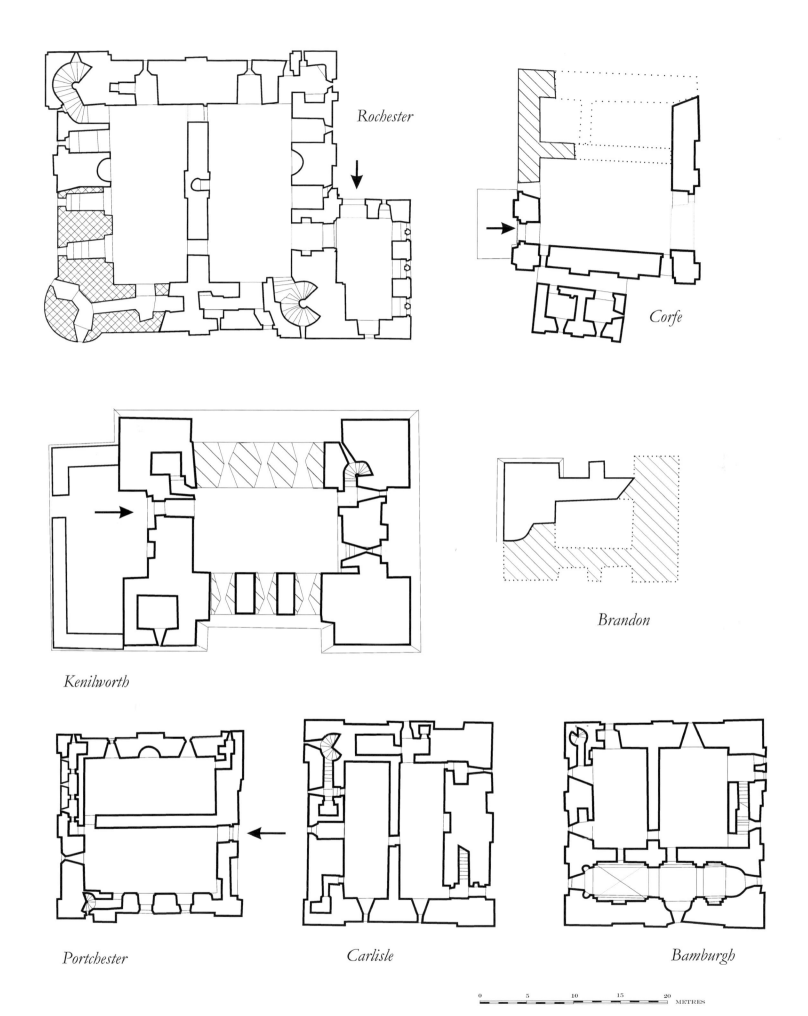

Rochester

Corfe

Kenilworth

Brandon

Portchester

Carlisle

Bamburgh

0   5   10   15   20
METRES

similar size was built at Old Sarum in Wiltshire in the late eleventh century or early in the twelfth, and should be considered here.[78] This seems to have consisted of a large square tower subdivided into two rooms on each floor, with annexes at either end containing on the one side the forebuilding and on the other a postern-gate tower. The suggested reconstruction provides a quite elegant classical façade, with a solid cube mass in the centre flanked by a pair of balanced turrets. The tower is likely to have contained two storeys, set high above a filled-in basement.

One further great tower should belong to this phase of building: that at Kenilworth in Warwickshire.[79] This is usually dated to the last quarter of the twelfth century, and it is likely enough that the top of the building, with its splay-footed loops, belongs to a period after about 1190. A clear building break below the top distinguishes the phases, however, and it is very likely that the tower was begun by Geoffrey de Clinton between 1124 and 1130. At this time de Clinton, as sheriff, was being promoted by Henry I to overweigh the suspect power of the Earl of Warwick, and the great tower that was probably then built was effectively another in the series of royal keeps of this period (fig. 211). It contained a large hall raised above a solid basement, with bold projecting corner towers. Its design is a novelty,[80] but the function of the structure was clearly to provide, like Chepstow, a prestigious hall raised in a massive building.

A contemporary building highlights the contrast between royal and baronial aspirations. At Norham (Northumberland) in the 1120s Bishop Flambard of Durham constructed a castle whose central feature was a large room raised on a vaulted basement, almost certainly battlemented above the first floor. Its function was probably to serve as a private hall, facing the more conventional ground-floor hall across a courtyard. Though comparable to Chepstow, the first phase at Norham was neither large nor strong, and had little of the obvious massiveness of the royal towers. Later in the century this raised hall was doubled in width to provide a withdrawing chamber, and it acquired a further chamber in a prominent tower, by now resembling, for example, the bishops' castles at Sarum and Sherborne, both of which were contemporary with Norham Phase I, but from the first incorporated a small but prominent tower intended to contain a private chamber. By now the hall at Norham gave the appearance of a rather irregular great tower, but it was not until the 1420s, with yet another rebuilding of the structure, that it assumed the shape of a 'typical' example.[81]

Two further great towers extend Henry's buildings northwards, Bamburgh and Carlisle. Both castles were built originally without great towers; Bamburgh, indeed, had been fortified since the sixth century AD, and Carlisle seems to have been constructed in 1092 as a simple small ringwork, which presumably contained the necessary hall and chamber inside its earthworks. Neither of the great towers subsequently added is accurately dated: that at Bamburgh has been dated as late as 1164,[82] and that at Carlisle to the time of any king between William Rufus and Henry II.[83] The *History of the King's Works* is inclined to attribute the building to David of Scotland (who held Cumberland

264

212 The extreme complexity of the accommodation at Rochester provides three linked suites of hall and chamber, with withdrawing rooms. This suggests that the apartments were intended for separate households, perhaps for the constable, the archbishop and the king.

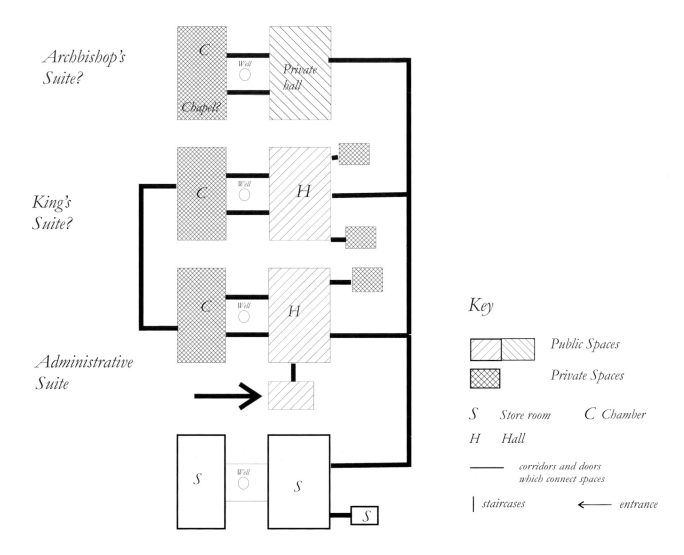

Archbishop's Suite?

King's Suite?

Administrative Suite

Key

Public Spaces

Private Spaces

S   Store room   C   Chamber

H   Hall

——— corridors and doors which connect spaces

| staircases   ←——— entrance

between 1136 and 1157).[84] More recent work suggests that the great tower was built after Henry I's visit to Carlisle in 1121, though it may well still have been under construction in David's time.[85] This makes it most likely that the two towers were the result of a single design, perhaps from the later 1110s at Bamburgh and during the 1120s at Carlisle, and makes more reasonable the use of early-looking squared ashlars with wide joints, particularly obvious at Carlisle. In size, these towers are almost identical, measuring respectively about 20 by 18 m and 20.7 by 18.3 m. Considering their plan dimensions neither is tall, though Bamburgh is slightly squatter (16.5 m as against 20 m for Carlisle). In this they have some similarity to the early squat keeps at Bridgnorth and Portchester, though each of the northern buildings contained one additional storey. Each tower is divided into two cells by a cross wall, and at present their ground floors are extremely similar, though in detail this is certainly in part the result of later alterations. Bamburgh is interesting because it contained a quite large chapel in a position comparable to that at the White Tower (thus suggesting use of the interior for

ceremony), but on the first rather than the uppermost floor, and, very significantly, both contained an internal straight staircase in the thickened entrance wall, a sort of internal forebuilding.[86]

Our examination of the surviving towers attributable to Henry I has revealed several distinct groups: in Normandy there are large towers (Domfront, Caen), with fairly simple internal design, usually with cross-walls dividing the interior into two unequal parts. In England, probably immediately after his accession, Henry built similar towers, on a slightly smaller scale (Corfe, Wareham, perhaps Old Sarum and probably Gloucester). After a few years, perhaps in the 1110s and '20s, he is found building smaller and squatter towers (Bridgnorth, Portchester, Bamburgh, Carlisle).

Rochester

One further great tower belongs to the workshop of the royal court, constructed in Rochester Castle by the Archbishop of Canterbury, William de Corbeil, who held it from 1127 until his death in 1136.[87] The building therefore falls into precisely the same period as those just described (fig. 212). The castle remained in the hands of the archbishops until 1215, with a series of royal officials holding the office of constable, and subsequently was entirely taken over by the Crown, and it was maintained at royal expense until the seventeenth century.[88] The clearest and most thorough account of the building is provided by R. Allen Brown, and the present discussion varies from his interpretation in only a few details.[89]

In plan, the great tower resembles Carlisle, and is the same length, though a little wider. But it is in its height that Rochester is outstanding: nearly 38 m high, more than twice the height of Bamburgh. The building consists of three large superimposed rooms ('halls') set beside three very slightly smaller rooms ('chambers'), above a large and comparatively complex basement storey, the apartments on each floor separated by a substantial spine wall. In addition to the normal large storerooms, this lowest storey contained small mural chambers at the corners, and may have had an unlit private chamber with a garderobe in the basement of the adjacent forebuilding. The access to the great tower was provided by a large staircase that passed into a large and very well-lit anteroom at the head of the stair, a waiting room such as that suggested for the very similar position at Castle Rising, and one that, like that at Rising, provided a suitable view of the main door, decorated with chevron and nook shafts. The door led to the eastern side of the larger room on the first floor. This was perhaps the lower end of this room, since it contained also a garderobe, set in a mural passage next to a small private door, perhaps leading to a bridge from the adjacent curtain wall. The fireplace is set towards the upper end of this hall, which is rather better lit than the lower end, and has at its western corner a heated private mural chamber, which Brown suggests may have been the privy apartment of the constable.[90] A door in the spine wall at this north-western end (with its rebate against the hall) led from the hall into the adjacent chamber. This room had a garderobe in its western wall, a spiral stair leading upwards in the corner and a fireplace matching that in the hall.

Understanding the layout of this room (and indeed all the apartments on this half of the building) is obscured by the loss of about one third of the side of each of these rooms, due to rebuilding after the destruction of the corner during the siege of 1215, when King John's miners tunnelled beneath the angle of the tower and brought it down. It now contains a second garderobe in the window embrasure next to the fireplace, and may have had a mural chamber in the now-rebuilt southern corner. This suggests that the chamber was orientated with its more important end towards the south. A further problem in any interpretation of this and the other chambers, however, is the second door in the spine wall, which led directly from the lower end of the hall into this southern end of the

chamber, and therefore suggests that it was the other end of the chamber that was the more significant.[91] The three pairs of 'hall and chamber' are each arranged in a similar fashion, but that on the second floor, in which the spine wall is perforated by an arcade, preserves traces of only the north-western doorway.

The internal design of these rooms thus remains problematic. Some conclusions may be guided by the position of the staircases and of the galleries. The north-eastern staircase, beside the entrance door, permits access to all floor levels, including the storage basement, and should perhaps therefore be seen as a service or more functional stair. The south-western stair connects the inner rooms, but not the storage basement, and is therefore a more private access, solely linking the chambers. The third storey contained a pair of tall rooms, separated by an arcade, and linked at an upper level by a mural gallery. This provided a clerestory with large double lights to both apartments, and produced a walkway around the whole building. This gallery has no apparent checks to free passage, and effectively would reduce the privacy of the apartments on the third storey. Circulation of this floor would therefore be from the north-eastern stair towards the western end of the hall, which is provided with a garderobe, and then through the sole doorway in the arcade into the western end of the chamber (the door shows that the arcade was partly closed by an apparently low screen). The chamber was similarly provided with a garderobe or garderobes. Brown calls this pair the 'state apartments and the grandest residential suite'.[92] They are clearly the largest and most impressive in the keep, but perhaps it may be better to regard them as a single large room divided by an arcade, around which the circulation is anticlockwise, and in which the focal point, seat or dais, was perhaps at the south-eastern corner. This would be visible from most points of the upper gallery, and would make the third storey into a grand reception room, from which access to the chapel would be possible by continuing the anticlockwise direction, processing from the south-eastern corner through the arcade and across the lower end of the 'hall'.

If this is the proper function of the third storey, the initial difficulty of having no fewer than three superimposed hall-and-chamber blocks is much diminished. What on this interpretation we can now see is that the keep consists of two distinct apartments, each consisting of a hall with an adjacent and linked chamber, these suites separated by a single large state or reception room attached to a chapel. The ownership of these two apartments is in doubt. It may be that the fragment of a great blind arch in the south-eastern gable of the top-floor chamber suggests the use of this room as a state bedroom or throne room, and that the top suite would therefore

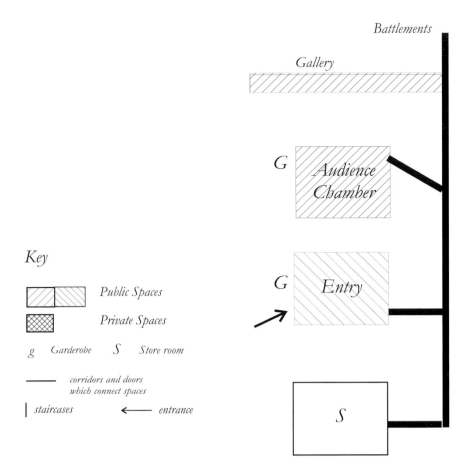

Battlements

Gallery

G   *Audience*
    Chamber

Key

///	Public Spaces
###	Private Spaces

g   *Garderobe*   S   *Store room*

———   corridors and doors
      which connect spaces

| *staircases*   ←   *entrance*

G   *Entry*

S

213   The accommodation at Hedingham was simple: two superimposed halls provided identical features, with an upper end by the fire and a lower end with a garderobe. The upper hall was reached from the newel that linked all floors by an additional stair of a dozen steps inside the room, to increase its grandeur. There were no private apartments or service rooms in the building.

be for royal use, and the first-floor chamber for the use of the archbishop, but our evidence does not take us this far. The discussion above, however, has tended to emphasise the north-western end of the halls as being superior. It is quite possible, on the other hand, that the intended orientation was (as in the case of Norwich, Castle Rising and Falaise) along the spine wall, and that the north-eastern, long side of the hall (containing the entrance, the stair and the private corner room – or perhaps kitchen?) was the lower end. The presence of a well at the upper end in this case corresponds remarkably with the arrangements at Norwich.

Castle Hedingham

Often linked in the literature with Rochester is the tall tower at Hedingham in Essex, which was placed at the centre of an older ringwork castle. This *donjon* has been described as a hall and chamber, upended in the interests of defence.[93] Earlier studies of this building had identified a simple sequence involving the superimposition of an entrance hall, a great hall with its high-level mural gallery and a suite of chambers below battlement level (fig. 213).[94] A recent study of this building, however, showed that the top floor was of more recent origin, and had been formed above the original sunken roof, whose internal gutters and roof crease had been preserved in the fabric.[95] In consequence, the keep contained neither chapel nor private apartments: it consisted solely of two reception rooms (an entrance hall and a state hall) above the basement,

and the mural chambers shown clearly on the plans were in fact too small to use as private rooms, being less than 1 m wide and with a large part of their floor area taken up by the swing of their closing doors. The approach to the building was by a simple low staircase, the forebuilding being a later addition. The conclusion of this analysis is that this great tower was intended with little attention to defence, with few of the necessities for residence, and contained two halls and no private chambers – it was in fact solely for receptions: a suitable context may be the ennoblement of its owner, Aubrey de Vere III, who in 1142 was created Earl of Oxford, and who in the third generation of loyal royal service was now displaying his new status. The great tower at Hedingham is thus doubly significant, in the first place as perhaps the earliest surviving of our great *donjons* that was built by one of the barons, and in the second place since so many details of its layout and decoration show that de Vere intended to construct a grand framework in which he could display himself.[96]

Castle Acre

In this connection the works that were carried out at about this very period at Castle Acre in Norfolk provide an interesting correlation. This important de Warenne castle was built as a large double-pile house enclosed in a simple ringwork, probably in the 1070s or 1080s. In the early 1140s the upper part of the house was removed, and a thick-walled keep was begun on the lower walls. During construction this tower was reduced in size, and eventually occupied only half the area of the original house. It is suggested that the new works were abandoned when William III, second Earl of Surrey, died without male heirs on Crusade in 1147.[97]

It seems likely that the emphasis on display that motivated de Vere at Hedingham is here being shown: this is made more obvious by the excavators' observation that, during this phase of building, the stone curtain wall in front of the new great tower was actually reduced to half its height.[98] The only reasonable explanation is that this was intended to make the new building more visible to visitors approaching along the road from London. This recognition of the importance of ceremony is clear enough, and was soon afterwards matched at Lincoln, where Henry II ordered a small royal palace to be constructed in the suburbs, to enable him to wear his crown in a suitable building at the ceremony in December 1157.[99]

THE CASTLES OF HENRY II AND THE REVIVAL OF THE GREAT TOWER

Scarborough

The extent of Henry II's castle building and repairs has been set out by Brown.[100] In the context of the influence of the White Tower we need concentrate on only four major works, ignoring the great expenditure in repairs and alteration to nearly ninety other castles. These four are the great towers of Scarborough, Orford, Newcastle upon Tyne and Dover (fig. 214).

During the manoeuvres for power after the death of Stephen and the accession of Henry, the new king recovered the northern counties from King Malcolm. Almost his first act here was to appropriate the Yorkshire castle of Scarborough from its builder, William, Count of Aumale. At this point the castle consisted of a wall and a new but partially collapsed tower cutting off the access to the headland:[101] this sounds a similar arrangement to the towers beside gates discussed above. Henry demolished this work, and replaced it with a great tower placed forward over the gate, in a similar position to Aumale's.[102] The positioning of the building beside the entrance is strikingly similar to the earlier work at Bridgnorth, and the new tower was protected by the thickening of its exposed wall, and perhaps by the provision of garderobes discharging beside the passage. The dramatic siting of the tower was remarked on by Clark, who was surprised by its proximity to the approach, and infelicitously described it as 'not a citadel but the mere gateway'.[103] The primary intention was perhaps to place the tower on the highest ground dominating the town: to put it further back would have lessened the impact of the new work, since it would have vanished behind the shoulder of the hill. As it is, the castle was clearly regarded as occupying merely the nearer tip of the hill, with the *donjon* and its inner courtyard reached only by passing around the northern side of the tower to reach a gate on the east.

It is reasonable to suppose that the reason for the demolition (rather than repair) was not that the existing tower was dilapidated (as Newburgh was to say, some fifty years later),[104] but that it did not satisfy Henry's plans for his castle. The probability, considering the surviving remains, is that the king's intention was to add accommodation to the more obvious military functions that the earlier tower presumably displayed. Henry's tower was partially demolished during the siege of 1645, but much of the detail of its interior can be reconstructed. It was taller than many of its predecessors, and contained three storeys above a basement, linked by a newel stair set in the centre of the thickest of the walls. The first floor contained a large heated room, spanned, like Hedingham, by a diaphragm arch. It was probably served by a garderobe in its north-western corner, where there are traces of chutes. Above the forebuilding there may have been a chapel, reached by a door on the southern side. The upper end of the hall, against the eastern wall, bristled with small chambers, no fewer than four in this half of the hall. Three are small enough to be cupboards, similar to those at Hedingham. The last, measuring about 1.5 by 4.5 m, may be a small *studium* or with-

drawing chamber. Access to the upper floor and the basement was via the newel stair, beside the garderobe door. This led to a pair of chambers. The outer of these probably contained a garderobe, and may have been heated: the wall here has now completely collapsed. A door in the eastern corner led to a stair and perhaps to the roof of the forebuilding. The inner chamber was reached through the outer one. It contained a fireplace and two small mural chambers, and a garderobe reached by a long passage in the northern wall. The third floor was probably also reached from the newel stair. It may have been subdivided, but all one can now see is that the inner chamber, at any rate, was lit by four double openings. It is the extent of accommodation that is most striking here: the hall is of good size, a little less than 10 by 8.5 m, with a chamber and a chapel adjoining. The upper floors contained perhaps four chambers, each approximately 10 by 4 m; these seem to have formed two self-contained suites, well provided with garderobes.

Orford

If Scarborough shows an increase in the amount of private accommodation in proportion to the whole, and a degree of sophistication in the subdivision of rooms greater than most of the buildings before the Anarchy, Henry's next tower took the notion much further. As the Scarborough tower was being completed Henry commissioned a new castle at Orford in Suffolk, apparently to overawe the local baronage.[105] This consisted of halls, chambers and other offices, and in the centre a great tower that contained two self-contained apartments, identified as being intended for the king and for his castellan (fig. 215).[106] Within a comparatively small footprint the tower managed to include not only two superimposed private halls, with attached chambers, garderobes and closets, but also two kitchens, a chapel and a room for a priest, and a oubliette prison with its own garderobe. The complexity of these arrangements is shown in the planning diagram. The design, however, goes much further than this, and much further than that of the round or polygonal great towers that are often cited as its origin.[107] The decorative use of local and imported limestones on the façades could be matched at Castle Rising, but it is the detail of the mason work that is so unusual: the entrance door is triangular-headed with joggled voussoirs; the windows are two-light, but square-headed under round arches, and with broad flat mullions; and the capitals in the chapel are the contemporary trumpet style, but with the centres hollowed out to form an inverted omega. In short, it is not only the overall design that is unique,[108] but also the fine detail of the building. It is unfortunate that we do not know the identity of the builder, but it is clear that he was reinventing many of the contemporary conventions of castle building.

Facing page 214   Great towers of Henry II.

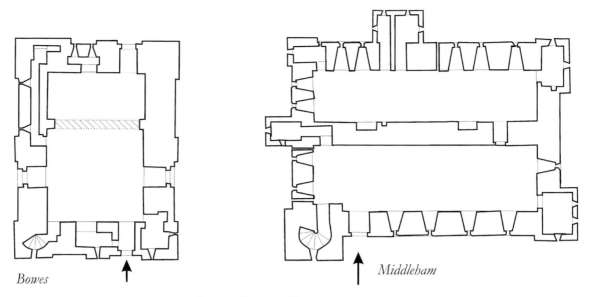

Bowes

Middleham

Late Great Towers

Scarborough

Dover

Orford

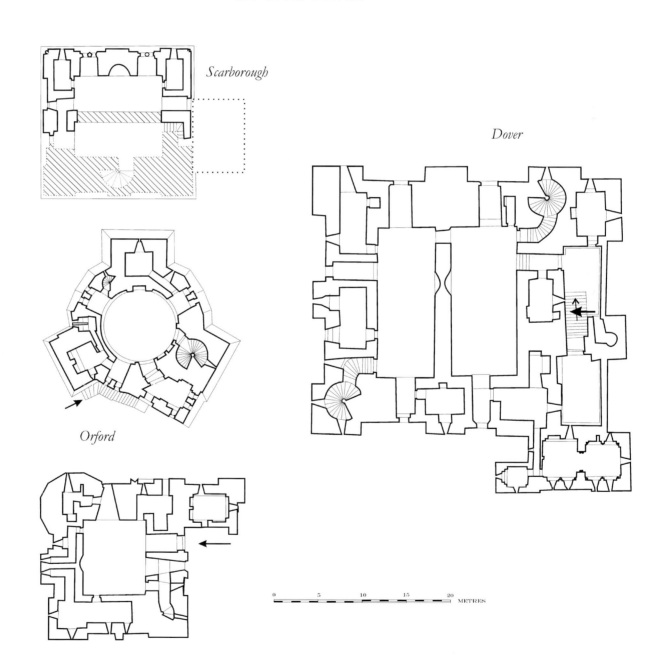

0 5 10 15 20
METRES

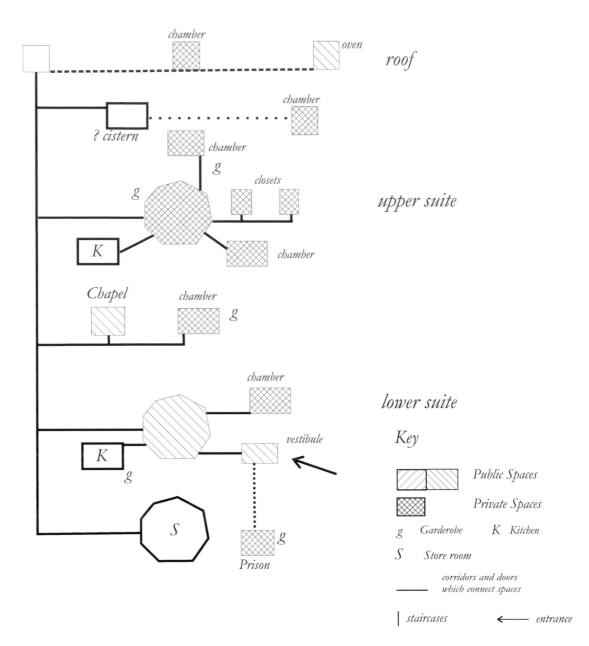

215 The complex plan of Orford provides a hall with chambers, and two private suites on the upper floors, probably for the constable and for the king.

chamber   oven   *roof*

? cistern   chamber

chamber

upper suite

g   closets   g

K   chamber

Chapel   chamber   g

chamber

lower suite

K   vestibule   Key

g

S

Prison   g

Public Spaces

Private Spaces

g   Garderobe   K   Kitchen

S   Store room

corridors and doors
which connect spaces

| staircases   ⟵ entrance

Newcastle

Before the great tower at Orford was complete, Henry II commissioned another great tower, in the old royal castle at Newcastle upon Tyne. Here for nearly a century a hall and chamber blocks had stood inside an earthen ringwork, protected on its rock by small square mural towers.[109] Henry's tower stood in the centre of this courtyard (in a fashion similar to Hedingham) and rivalled in size the works of his grandfather, Henry I. It clearly contained private apartments, but Newcastle takes up a different and more ceremonial design than the heavily domestic Scarborough. Work began in 1168. At least after the year-long pause that was the result of the Scottish war of 1174, it was under the control of Mauritius *cementarius* (mason), one of the very few castle builders of the early Middle Ages whose identity is known (figs 216, 217).[110]

The new tower consisted of only three floors, and was approached by a forebuilding designed integrally

with the building. On the ground floor of this lay the chapel, probably to be reached solely from outside: the present communicating door is an insertion. The position of this chapel is rather anomalous, since it is inconvenient to reach both from the tower and from the bailey, whose occupants it was presumably serving, and its altar must have lain below the staircase and guard-chamber. The stair led up two storeys to enter the *donjon* at the topmost floor. This was a large, almost square room, rather higher than long, which contained garderobes, a kitchen in a mural chamber at its lower end, a fireplace and a withdrawing chamber in its upper side. This last is well fitted, with a fireplace and its own garderobe, and was lit by elegant windows looking southwards. A newel stair gives access to a mural gallery high above the hall, above the original pitch of the roof, and a second staircase from this level provides an alternative route to the battlements. From the hall the first staircase runs down to a second hall, the same plan as the hall above, but very low in com-

216 (*above left*) View of the nave of the basement chapel at Newcastle, reached originally only from the courtyard outside the keep.

217 (*above right*) Interior of the Withdrawing or King's Chamber at Newcastle; this chamber with a fireplace is at the level of the entrance hall.

parison. The withdrawing chamber on this floor is on the northern side of the keep and is dimly lit by lancets, but like that on the floor above it is well fitted with garderobe and fireplace. A separate chamber, at the opposite side of the keep, is separate from the apartment proper, since it is directly entered from the stair, and seems to have controlled the staircase and an adjacent postern gate. The stair continues down to an attractively vaulted ground floor, which has two mural chambers, one apparently a prison, but has neither heating nor garderobes.

The accommodation diagram shows the oddity of the planning. The grandest of the rooms in the building is the entrance hall: everything else is more secluded. It seems most probable that the second-floor room was intended as the king's reception hall and that this was placed at the top of the building to emphasise its significance. If so, there is no anteroom, and in a real sense the approach to royalty was the extended staircase (fig. 218), and the 'guardroom' at its top served as a porters' lodge to hold those approaching until the proper time, rather than as a military point for soldiers to hold off an assault: the 'guardroom' allows no retreat. The floor below this entrance hall is arranged for convenient accommodation, and presumably was intended as the great chamber with withdrawing chambers off. This makes greater sense of the postern gate, which would serve the first floor's occupants as a private staircase, such as we have seen at the White Tower, Colchester (both

inserted) and Norwich (original). This analysis of Newcastle shows that Maurice's intention was to provide a grand reception room, with suitable accommodation beneath. The grand withdrawing chamber at the top level, however, leaves open the possibility that the design was intended to provide the king with a suitably grand suite on the second floor, but one not made complex with additional private rooms because of the shortness and infrequency of likely visits, and a less elaborate lower level (but with more separated rooms) for a more permanent royal official, such as the constable.

Dover

To a large extent the layout of Newcastle is repeated in Maurice's second great tower, at Dover in Kent.[111] This was begun in 1180 or 1181, two years after work at Newcastle was finished, and Maurice, by now termed *Ingeniator* (engineer), was in charge throughout. The staircase, arranged to run around two sides of the building, led up to a small chapel, where it turned and climbed up to a platform in front of the entrance, like Newcastle arranged to give access to the top storey, and controlled by a small guardroom. Dover has more than twice the floor area of Newcastle, and is divided into two almost equal halves, both probably heated by fireplaces in the spine wall.[112] The entrance hall was provided with a well room, and from the hall a door in the in-go of the south window led to the private chapel, immediately above the stairs and the lower

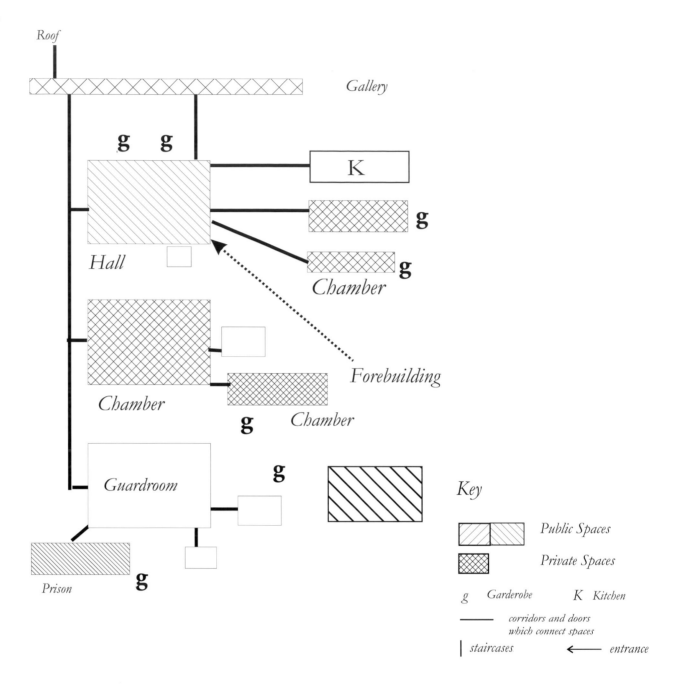

218 The plan of Newcastle provided an entrance hall at the top of the building, from which well-appointed chambers and a service room could be reached. On the floor below was a smaller complex of more private chambers, thus providing accommodation for two separate households. At ground-floor level lay storerooms and a prison with some small chambers for staff. The chapel served the whole of the bailey, and was reached by an external door.

chapel. Most unusually, from the entrance doorway steps lead *down* into the hall, clearly to make a royal show for an audience waiting in the hall, and a great arch at the dais end, reached originally by steps, allowed a similar performance on the way to the chapel. A door in the spine wall at the opposite corner of the hall led to the inner room, which contained three large mural chambers, two of which, at least, contained fireplaces and garderobes. It seems reasonable to see this as the great chamber, with royal withdrawing chambers in the mural rooms. But both the entrance hall and the great chamber are provided with spiral staircases, each rising from the basement to the roof. Each stair accordingly provides unimpeded access to its half of the building, while the doors in the spine wall permit entry between the halves at all levels.[113] This flexibility must have allowed the build-

ing to be put to a large variety of uses, but it makes it hard to be certain how the room usage was envisaged. The first floor almost exactly replicates that above, differing in its mouldings and its much lower headroom, but not different in any meaningful way in its layout, except the provision of additional mural chambers in the lower hall. Thus we have two superimposed blocks of hall-and-chamber with mural rooms, each with free communication with the other. Though this recalls the layout of the archbishop's tower at Rochester, the communication is freer here, and there is little suggestion at Dover that the king was to share his accommodation with another. Nonetheless, it seems better to see the plan as the provision of multiple apartments for two households.

Maurice the Engineer was clearly in touch with the current changes in decorative detail: at Newcastle his

ing chambers on a grand scale, it is clear that only the older rectangular form was possible.[114]

This was not the end of the great tower. For almost every decade during the next three centuries a new great tower was founded in some part of England or France, and the late examples had the same architectural vocabulary of dominance and irresistible power that we have seen in the buildings of the eleventh and twelfth centuries. But the reign of Henry II is a suitable place to finish this account of the slow development of the designs derived from the White Tower, since by the end of his reign the form had become widely established well beyond the narrow circle of royal court, archbishops and the greatest magnates, which is where in the eleventh century it had begun.[115]

CONCLUSIONS

Dover was among the last of the great rectangular great towers: by now baronial castles were being ennobled with examples, such as Richmond (figs 219, 220) (*circa* 1170) and the huge Middleham (both North Yorkshire), which of them all has the most resemblance to the ideas of the White Tower, with a hall and chamber on two floor levels (*circa* 1180). Within this period of a little more than a century the great tower had spread from its original position as the product of the highest ranks of monarchy or aristocracy to be the symbol of a much wider baronage. This was not a steady progress, and the discussion has identified three successive stages in the development of the great tower.

In the first wave, the rectangular great towers of the eleventh century were introduced as part of a policy of the Conqueror, a policy that linked size, Roman authority and the essential of statecraft, the ceremonial hall. The ultimate origin of this design may well lie in the palaces of the Carolingian world, and more immediately the great towers of the tenth and early eleventh centuries in the Île-de-France, Normandy and Anjou, and William's use of it may even have been a revival of a style that was reaching its end early in the eleventh century.[116]

The location of his great towers is instructive here: London, which in 1066 William treated with the utmost respect, advancing on the city only after first marching about it for a quarter of a year,[117] and Colchester, which faced a Scandinavian threat that continued throughout the 1170s, since it provided secure harbours and a swift passage to London along the old Roman road from Essex. These are clearly places in which the king's standard needed to be shown, in the context of the aftermath of the Conquest, and were supplemented by the new works at Lincoln (at that point effectively on a northern border) and Winchester, where (like Durham in the next reign) the ostentation and conspicuous show of the church emphasised the king's position.

219 The exterior of the great tower at Richmond, North Yorkshire, showing the three huge openings overlooking the town, which were probably intended to give access to a balcony for presentation or display.

mouldings are the latest styles, and the capitals of the windows of the upper part are the waterleaf fashion that was then being introduced to England. At Dover he took this further, and used primitive stiff-leaf carving on his capitals, a new style, significantly enough, which linked the keep at Dover with the new building at the pilgrimage centre of Canterbury Cathedral. His use of the rectangular form, however, has been taken to be old-fashioned in contrast to the circular designs used on the Continent, and he has been compared unfavourably with the builder of Conisbrough in South Yorkshire (*circa* 1190), the buttressed cylindrical tower built for Henry's half-brother. But Conisbrough is arranged as a private tower, with chamber and private chamber arranged above one another. Unlike Orford, Conisbrough has a more limited function, without the need for the accommodation of multiple households, and so it has few mural chambers in its massive walls. This reticence is appropriate for such private towers, as one can see at Etampes near Paris (Seine-et-Oise). But for the combination of reception halls and withdraw-

But once begun the work on the first of these great towers proceeded slowly, and eventually came to a stop. Since all but one of these massive buildings showed a major building break, it is likely that both William I and William Rufus downgraded their programme of great tower building as the kingdom settled into order. Rufus, who had founded strategic castles on the new northern frontiers at Newcastle (1080) and Carlisle (1092), was clearly alert to the utility of castles, but chose only one site for a great tower, the new castle at Norwich. Here he was probably emphasising the royal presence in the new city, as it developed at the expense of the ancient centre at Thetford.[118] Work here probably stopped at his death, and by this time he had presumably completed the building of the White Tower, at least to the stage when it was possible to incarcerate Rufus's chancellor, Rannulf Flambard, Bishop of Durham, though one must note that he managed to escape.[119]

It seems that at this point the great tower was becoming no more than a curiosity. If so, it was revived by another man with a reputation to enhance. During William Rufus's reign his younger brother, Henry, had been making his way with difficulty, and for a time lost even the lordship that he had bought from his eldest brother, Robert.[120] His capture of Domfront in 1092, and the subsequent building there of a massive tower, must be seen in this context: with his hall inside the tower he expressed his authority, and like his father, the Conqueror, at Caen, he expanded the town of Domfront, including the founding of at least one abbey beside his castle.[121] Once he succeeded to the English kingdom, with his newly acquired wealth he followed the same programme, and used his new re-

sources in founding great towers within older castles at strategic positions that were at positions of potential threat from Normandy, Wales and Scotland: Corfe, Wareham, and then Gloucester, Bridgnorth, Portchester, Bamburgh and Carlisle. He completed Rufus's tower at Norwich in the most elaborate style, and in the castles of two of the principal towns of his duchy he planted great towers, at Caen and Falaise.

During the 1130s there appears to be a decline in the undertaking of new royal works, though it is clear that Henry I continued to repair the many older royal castles. Perhaps due to the effect of the mass of royal works of the first quarter of the twelfth century, it seems that the symbolism of the tower was being adopted at least by the greatest of the barons, perhaps at Bridgnorth by Earl Robert de Bellême or Pevensey by the Count of Mortain.[122] The small scale of these two towers, despite the great wealth of these magnates, by far the richest in the realm, underlines the difference between the abilities of the barons and the king in the provision of resources for tower building. The confusion of control and the release of large parts of the royal demesnes that was introduced by the usurpation of Stephen and the conflict with Matilda seems to have encouraged a new aspiration for display, since the competing barons used their growing wealth to construct not only new castles, mostly earthworks like Burwell near Cambridge,[123] but also new towers in their older seats, as we see at Hedingham and Castle Acre.

In the 1140s, during the Anarchy – in a phase of the struggle that Bradbury has termed 'The Castle War'[124] – the young Henry (later Henry II) learnt both statecraft and warfare. In 1147 he had had the ultimate discomfiture of lacking the funds to pay his troops, being forced to apply to his uncle, King Stephen, for funds to pay them off, even though he had brought his army to England to unseat Stephen.[125] When he became king in 1154 the relevance of castles and the importance of restoring his prestige seem to have been combined in his immediate crown-wearing around his kingdom and his founding of new great towers, most clearly at Scarborough (1158), where he emphasised his control over the castle of the Count of Aumale; at Orford (1163–7), where he set the royal authority against the power of the local lords, particularly Bigod; at Newcastle (1168–78), where he set his flag against William the Lion, King of Scotland, who was to invade before the new tower was finished; and at Dover, where his great new castle controlled access to the kingdom from northern Burgundy and the Low Countries, in a military context, set ready for French attack at a period when King Louis and his son Philippe were testing the Norman frontiers; but, more immediately significant, Dover was the gateway for foreign lords to enter the kingdom on their journey to the new pilgrimage centre of Canterbury, and here Henry II created his largest and most expensive castle.

These, then, are the three waves of the building of great towers that a study of the influence of the White Tower has identified. Each was, it is suggested, the product of a complex of the needs of ceremony and display, as succeeding generations redefined the architectural frame through which the original purpose was expressed. It is probably no coincidence that the beginning of each of these three waves may be attributed to a monarch whose earlier career was uncertain, and whose claim to his rank was achieved only after a struggle: William I, whose legitimacy in title was gained by conquest; Henry I, who took England and later Normandy by imprisoning his eldest brother; and Henry II, whose claim to power was long threatened, and who gained rank only by outshining his uncle, Stephen.

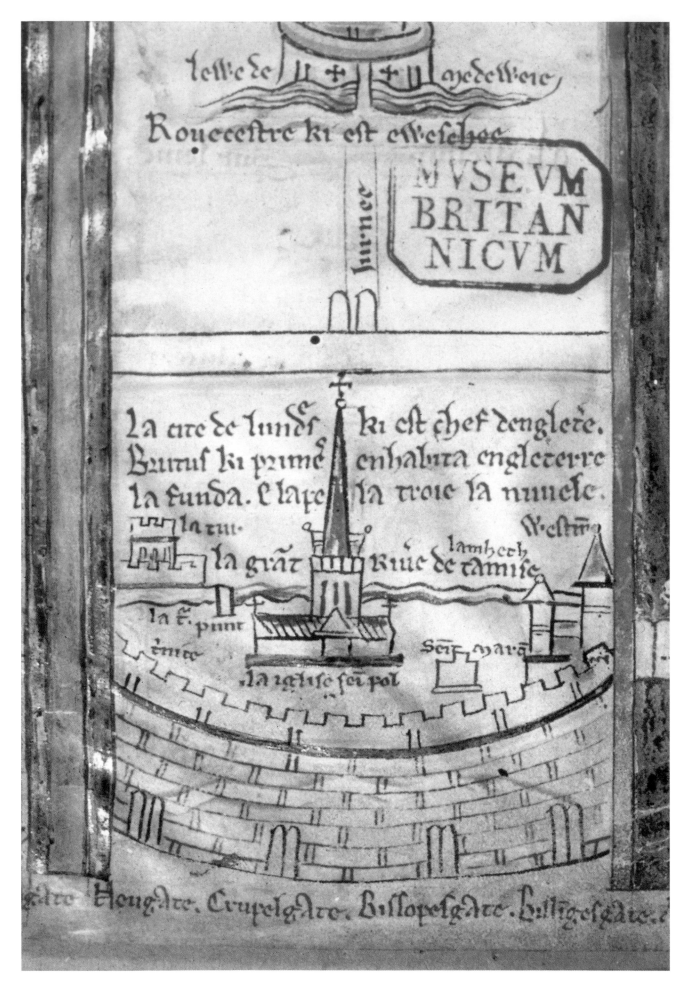

221 Plan of London by Matthew Paris from his 'Itinerary from London to the Holy Land', 1253–9. London, British Library.

CHAPTER ELEVEN

The White Tower in Medieval Myth and Legend

ABIGAIL WHEATLEY

Other chapters in this book address the dating, design and functions of the White Tower. They are concerned with establishing the facts of the building's design and subsequent adaptation through the Middle Ages. The subject matter of this chapter, by contrast, is entirely fictional, in that it deals with the legendary histories associated with the building. While these legends are often at odds with the known circumstances of the White Tower's history, their study can add to our understanding of how its builders intended it to be perceived – a question examined both here and elsewhere in this volume. The central aim of this chapter, however, is to examine how the building was actually perceived in the Middle Ages, a question that most architectural and documentary evidence is less able to answer.

The principal material comprises a number of medieval legends associated with the White Tower. Three are foundation myths that suggest that Julius Caesar, or Brutus (the legendary Trojan founder of Britain) or Belinus (a legendary early British king) built the White Tower. The third is not concerned specifically with foundation, but cites the Tower of London as one of King Arthur's key strongholds. All these legends seem to suggest a much earlier date for the White Tower than its actual foundation; they also indicate that certain patterns of interpretation can be identified for the building.

At first sight it may seem surprising that educated medieval observers could maintain, not long after the White Tower's construction, that it was a building from the remote past: after all, it shared obvious archi-

tectural characteristics with other structures of its period. Nevertheless, medieval observers often misjudged the actual age of buildings; indeed, even in 1818, by which time the essentials of stylistic development were approximately understood, the White Tower could still be attributed to the Romans.[1]

Before proceeding any further, it is worth pointing out that the authors of the legendary material, in common with others, used the terms 'Tower' and 'Tower of London' to describe both the White Tower and the castle as a whole. In what follows, the present author follows the prompting of the texts, using 'White Tower' only where the context suggests that this is what is meant. But the very fact that the White Tower gave its name to the whole castle is relevant to the theme of this chapter, since it so clearly demonstrates and preserves a medieval recognition of the structure's status and importance.

PRELIMINARIES

Geoffrey of Monmouth seems to have been the first to create a written mythology for the White Tower. In 1138 he completed a work known as the *History of the Kings of Britain* (*Historia regum Britannie*), an immensely popular and controversial 'history' of Britain's legendary past, partly adapted from earlier sources and partly invented.[2] In this work Geoffrey dwells at length on the legendary origins and early history of London, suggesting founding figures for many of the capital's historic structures. He tells us that the ancient British king, Belinus, then returned to Britain and led out the remaining days of his life in peace in his native land . . . In the town of Trinovantum he created an amazingly built gate on the bank of the Thames, which the citizens in his time called Belinesgate [Billingsgate] after his name. Above this he built a tower of great height and beneath, at its foot, a harbour suitable for the berthing of ships.[3]

There can be little doubt, as scholarly opinion has accepted, that the 'tower of great height' is a reference to the White Tower.[4] Its supposed builder, according to Geoffrey's own chronology, lived after King David, the prophets Elijah and Isaiah and the foundation of Rome by Romulus and Remus,[5] but before Julius Caesar and the birth of Christ.[6] Precisely why Geoffrey backdated the foundation of the White Tower to this remote period may never be clear. Did he expect that the foundation legend would simply be accepted as a metaphorical acknowledgement of the building's importance, or accepted as fact? Did he believe it himself? The likeliest motive, perhaps, is broadly speaking political. As his name suggests, Geoffrey of Monmouth was probably Welsh,[7] but his multiple dedications of the *History* to powerful members of the ruling Anglo-Norman aristocracy show a desire to provide a work that would be palatable to them.[8] Possibly, then, the ancient and venerable legendary foundation for the White Tower provided a convenient way of flattering its Norman occupants and creators.[9]

Geoffrey's attribution of the White Tower to Belinus certainly seems to have found favour for a while, since it was perpetuated in later adaptations of the *History*. In 1155 the poet Wace adapted Geoffrey's work for the court of Henry II, translating it into Anglo-Norman French as the *Roman de Brut*, and at some point between 1189 and the mid-thirteenth century, Wace's work was turned into an English poem, now known as the *Brut*, by Layaman.[10] Wace tells us that Belinus 'made in London, his best city where he dwelt most, a marvellous gate, by the river carrying ships . . . Above the gate he made a tower, very large in height and breadth.'[11] Again, it seems likely that this is a reference to the White Tower. Through his travels in England and intimacy with the court, Wace may have been aware of the building himself.[12] This may also have been true of Layaman, as his version suggests:

He wende riht to Lundene – the burh he
   lovede swithe.
He bigon ther ane ture, the strengeste of al the
   tune,
and, mid muchele ginne, a gaet therunder
   makede.
Theo clupede men hit Belyaesgate[13]

The emphasis on the White Tower is perhaps particularly marked in Layaman's text, in so far as it uses the word 'ture' in close proximity to 'Lundene', evoking the standard term 'Tower of London'.

The White Tower's physical dominance provides one explanation for its repeated attribution to legendary founders. There may also, however, have been more concrete reasons for medieval observers to relate such buildings to the antique past, through the frequent physical associations between Norman castles and antique remains. Castle builders in post-Conquest England displayed a marked preference for placing their creations on Roman sites. N. J. G. Pounds calculates that, of the thirty-seven royal castles established before 1100, twelve were built in towns of Roman origins, where impressive Roman remains were often still visible.[14] Other early castles were associated with a variety of surviving Roman structures. At Pevensey in Sussex, the campaign castle of 1066 may have been contrived within the corner of the Roman fort, while great towers were subsequently planted within the Roman walls at Portchester in Hampshire (*circa* 1120), Brough in Cumbria (*circa* 1100) and Bowes in County Durham (1170s onwards).[15] The Tower of London, sited within the south-east corner of the Roman city walls, is itself an example. This frequent association may have led observers to overestimate the age of Norman buildings located with Roman ones, or, as in the case of Geoffrey of Monmouth, to invent or elaborate foundation legends.[16]

Geoffrey, and writers after him such as Wace, also found that the association between medieval and ancient defences could be turned to good use in flattering the Norman rulers of Britain. In doing so they were prompted, once again, by associations with the ancient world made by the Normans themselves – this time not in architecture but in contemporary language. The Latin word *castellum*, meaning, in classical usage, an outpost or a defended town or village,[17] was a standard medieval word for a castle, and the origin of the English word 'castle'.[18] The word, however, also occurs in various ancient texts that were highly important for medieval readers: in classical authors, including Caesar and Vegetius, and even in the Vulgate Bible.[19]

The Norman regime was obviously very much aware of classical precedents and was also instrumental in introducing the word 'castle' into English at the time of the Conquest.[20] It may be that, for its Norman and English users, the term evoked its ancient origins much more readily than it does now. It is quite possible that this may have contributed to the idea that buildings very like, or identical to, medieval castles had existed in antique cultures. The Norman propensity for building castles close to Roman remains can only have helped to reinforce these classical resonances.[21]

The Belinus foundation legend, then, provides the White Tower with classical associations that fit neatly into this cultural context. Belinus is the British king whom Geoffrey of Monmouth credits with the conquest of Rome.[22] The idea that Belinus built the White Tower in his capital city associates the building with the legendary achievements of the British past. It transforms the White Tower's role in the history of the Norman conquest and domination of Britain, making it into a building of which the Britons can be proud, but which the Normans too can be happy to own in full knowledge of its legendary pedigree.

Geoffrey's legendary history caught on in a big way. The translations by Wace and Layaman, as well as the large number of Latin manuscripts of the work, and countless adaptations of Geoffrey's material, attest to its huge popularity.[23] It was adopted with such alacrity and so widely repeated that it seems soon to have been accepted as Britain's official history. Nevertheless, the idea that Belinus had built the Tower was not perpetuated by Wace's and Layaman's successors. Perhaps it was obscured by the rather elliptical phrasing of Geoffrey's description, or perhaps Belinus seemed too minor a character to have founded such an important building. Subsequent developments in the White Tower's legendary history, however, show that Geoffrey had created a formula that worked. The Tower had been established as an ancient structure, built by a hero of the past with strong associations with the Roman Empire. Later legendary histories relied heavily on Geoffrey's pattern, possibly even using his text for inspiration in attributing ever more illustrious founders to the White Tower.

THE WHITE TOWER'S TROJAN LEGENDS

The legend of the Trojan founders of Britain was one of Geoffrey of Monmouth's favourite themes. He did not invent this legend, but adapted it from earlier sources. One of these sources,[24] 'Nennius' (probably a ninth-century Welsh author, although this is disputed),[25] names one Brutus as the founder of Britain;[26] Brutus was, according to one of Nennius' explanations, a relative of Aeneas, born into the community of refugees who had fled from Troy at the end of the Trojan war. After many travels and adventures, Brutus founded Britain, while Aeneas founded the dynasty of the kings of Rome.[27]

Geoffrey's main innovation in all this was to supply a name for Brutus' capital city, the New Troy, and to identify it with London. This was probably not pure fabrication on Geoffrey's part. He picked up the name 'Trinovantum', which is linked with Julius Caesar's British campaign in Nennius and other sources. Geoffrey, making something of a leap, decided that 'Trinovantum' was equivalent to 'Troia Nova', or 'New Troy', the name used for Brutus' capital city in Geoffrey's sources.[28] Once again, Geoffrey's precise inten-

tions in making this identification are not clear, but medieval readers took such links seriously, believing the Trojan legends to be reliable historical sources.[29] Geoffrey's version of these events was well received, and thereafter became the accepted account of the capital's origins.[30] This meant that claims for Britain's pre-eminence as a nation, and for its imperial ambitions, could now be articulated through the city of London and its landmarks.[31]

William Fitz Stephen's description of London, written around 1173, demonstrates that he had studied Geoffrey's *History* and appreciated its symbolic potential.[32] He makes Brutus' foundation of London central to his glowing portrait of the city's venerable traditions. He also implicates the White Tower in this imperial heritage. The terms of his description demonstrate how well the Trojan foundation legend fitted the existing convention of associating medieval and classical defences:

In its eastern part, the city contains a fortress – palatine, massive and very strong, its walls and its floors rising from very deep foundations.[33]

The description is brief, but in it Fitz Stephen's imperial claims for London are succinctly expressed through the city's most important castle. The meaning of the term *arx palatina* (palatine fortress) is discussed elsewhere in this book, but for present purposes its significance lies in its deliberate linking, through the use of the adjective *palatina*, of London's *arx* (fortress or citadel) to the Roman Palatine, the landmark and eponymous monument from which the word's architectural and political sense derives.[34]

Fitz Stephen's description of London prefaces a *Life* of Thomas Becket, since the saint was a Londoner by birth. This context aligns it consciously with the classical literary genre of city description,[35] an allusion emphasised by Fitz Stephen's liberal use of classical quotations. He also compares London favourably with Rome on several occasions. London's claims rest on its supposed founder, Brutus, whose legend is used to match Rome's illustrious Trojan heritage, through Aeneas.[36] Fitz Stephen's description of the Tower thus implies an ancient and imperial context for the citadel as well as for the city.

The combination of an ancient founder and a medieval city proved a powerful one for all these authors. It was perhaps to be expected, therefore, that Brutus' foundation of London would eventually be traced more directly onto the fabric of the medieval city. Gervase of Tilbury, writing in 1216, made the connection in his work *Recreation for an Emperor* (*Otia imperialia*):

Brutus founded a very strong city called Trinovantum to keep alive the memory of the old Troy, placing within it a citadel like Ilium, containing a

palace enclosed by mighty fortifications, on the eastern side of the city, where the Tower of London is, with the water of the river Thames flowing around it, which is replenished daily when the sea pours in at high tide. On the western side of the city he built a new Pergamum, namely, two castles constructed with magnificent ramparts, one being Baynard's Castle, while the other belongs by right of succession to the Barons of Monfiquit.[37]

This description seems to echo Fitz Stephen's wording, which similarly combines implications of strength with imperial grandeur, contained this time within the word *palatium* (palace). Like Fitz Stephen's *palatinam*, this carries a direct reference to the Roman Palatine.[38] Once again, the White Tower seems to be singled out for special attention – it, surely, is the *palatium* that is surrounded by the mighty fortifications of the outer defences.[39] The specific reference to Ilium – a name associated with the city of Troy, but often used more specifically of its main tower or citadel – further reinforces the spatial correspondences between the defences of the two cities. Gervase's most significant suggestion, however, is that Brutus founded London's citadel, as well as Baynard's and Mountfichet's castles, the two other London strongholds extant in his own time.

Gervase's wording implies that Brutus chose the layout of these defences deliberately in order to re-create the plan of Troy on the site of London, the New Troy. This makes London the New Troy not only conceptually, but also in its appearance and geographical layout. It also confirms the central importance of the White Tower in the mythography of the city. With Brutus as its founder, the building becomes a relic of the original foundation of London.

Gervase's motivation may well have been similar to that of the other authors who ascribed foundation legends to the Tower. Gervase spent much of his later life in Europe, where he is thought to have completed *Recreation for an Emperor* around 1214–18. He probably came from Tilbury (Essex), however, as his name suggests, and in earlier life he had a close association with the court of Henry II.[40] It was this court circle that produced not only Wace's *Roman de Brut*, but also Benoît de Sainte-Maure's *Roman de Troie*, both texts that employ British foundation legends, and especially the Troy legend, to celebrate the illustrious ancestry of the English monarchy. It seems likely that Gervase's version of the foundation legend was either learned, or invented, within this context.

Gervase's particular version of events seems not to be repeated elsewhere in the literature of London's history. In visual representations of medieval London, however, the White Tower does seem to feature as a symbol of the city's Trojan origins. A remarkable seal of the 'barons' of London, thought to date from the late twelfth or the early thirteenth century, gives the first hint of this iconography. It depicts a large figure of St Paul on the obverse, and of St Thomas of Canterbury on the reverse, each above a small cityscape of London (fig. 222).[41] The city seems to be viewed from the south on the larger, obverse depiction. A wavy line in the foreground suggests the river, with a river wall and gate, St Paul's Cathedral in the centre and castles at either end of the city.

John Cherry suggests that the castle structure at the right of this depiction represents the White Tower, which he identifies as the squarish central element, surrounded by tall outer walls. The castle at the other end of the cityscape suggests either Baynard's Castle or Mountfichet Castle.[42] Cherry also proposes that the depiction of a river wall on the obverse view is based on the Roman river wall mentioned in Fitz Stephen's description of London, since the wall itself had ceased to exist by the end of the twelfth century.[43] The London shown on the seal therefore represents not a contemporary portrait of the city, but an imaginative reconstruction, showing legendary landmarks alongside ones familiar to medieval observers. The depiction of the White Tower can be seen in a comparable light. Although it clearly existed in medieval London, it seems that it, too, was identified as a relic of the city's ancient past.

The seal also shows other, more political, similarities to the legendary history texts. The surviving seal was engraved around 1219, but the inscription suggests that its design may date from the brief period in 1191 when the citizens of London were recognised as a commune.[44] The inscription reads 'Seal of the barons of London' ('Sigillum baronum Londoniarum'); these 'barons' were not aristocrats in the conventional sense, but the proud citizens of the independent city.[45] The seal's emphasis on those London landmarks credited with ancient origins can be understood as a concise way of asserting this claim to special status. This suggests political motives similar to those seen in Fitz Stephen's and Geoffrey's works.[46]

The very unusual attempt in the barons' seal to represent London's topography can be interpreted in a similar light. Uncertainties as to the seal's dating make it difficult to put forward a specific relationship with the passage in Gervase of Tilbury. Both sources, however, make great play on the topography of the city in articulating its legendary past. The Tower and the other London castles, one of which also appears on the seal, are crucial to Gervase's argument, in relation to each other, to the river and to the city walls. All these elements appear on the seal, and seem to be arranged in some attempt to portray their actual topographical relationships. If this is the case, the seal is a remarkable piece of iconography, combining complex literary allusion and innovative representation to create a kind of palimpsest city, onto which succeeding ages have overlaid successive sets of buildings and mythological connections.

Several later images seem to reflect the iconography of the barons' seal, and confirm this interpretation of its imagery. A schematic diagram of London in one of Matthew Paris's mid-thirteenth-century itineraries bears a close formal resemblance to the smaller view of London on the reverse of the barons' seal (fig. 221). Seen from the north with the city wall and four gates in the foreground, St Paul's is again in the centre, with the Tower (la tur) to the left, at the edge of the river that forms the far boundary of the city.[47] The White Tower is the focus of this depiction, as on the seal, and is similarly portrayed as a tall, square structure enclosed by lower walls. While Matthew Paris provides a sparer, more diagrammatic representation than that of the seal, he makes an explicit link with the city's legendary past in an inscription over the design:

> The city of London which is capital of England. Brutus who first colonized England founded it. And called it the New Troy.[48]

Matthew Paris's other itineraries contain comparable images, but they are not the only place where similar imagery occurs. A late thirteenth- to early fourteenth-century copy of Geoffrey of Monmouth's *History*[49] contains several small sketches of various British cities in the lower margins of the manuscript. These correspond to passages of the text that mention each place's legendary foundation. In many of these sketches, the cityscape can also be identified by the accurate depictions of important landmarks the artist has included. Laid alongside Geoffrey's text, the juxtaposition of contemporary landmarks and legendary history in these pictures is striking.

One of the sketches illustrates the passage describing Brutus' foundation of the New Troy, and shows some marked similarities to the cityscape on the barons' seal (fig. 223).[50] It seems to be a picture of the city of London, with the White Tower shown as a squarish block surrounded by an outer wall, its placing at the far right of the picture corresponding to that of the seal. As in the seal, churches feature centre and left, with St Paul's Cathedral in the middle; tall, thin banners stick up into the city's skyline, resembling the flag held by St Paul on the seal. All these details suggest a connection between the sketches of the *History* and the barons' seal. The juxtaposition of specific, identifiable cityscapes with passages describing the cities' foundations is clear and consistent in the manuscript. It underlines the connections between medieval cities and their legendary past, focusing on landmark buildings as sites of local identity through time. Once again, the White Tower features as a physical reminder of the capital's ancient past, present in the medieval city but bridging the gap between the legendary past and the medieval present.

JULIUS CAESAR AND THE WHITE TOWER

The tradition that Julius Caesar built the Tower of London is still perhaps the most famous of the Tower's legendary associations.[51] This is mainly by virtue of its appearance in the works of Shakespeare. An American scholar, Homer Nearing, examined the origins of this legend at some length in the late 1940s.[52] Although some of the dating he cites has been modified by later literary scholarship, his articles still provide a thorough survey of most of the relevant material. Nearing traces the first documented occurrence of the legend to Nicholas Trivet's Anglo-Norman Chronicles, written probably between 1328 and 1335.[53] It then appears in Gray's *Scalacronica* (begun in 1355), and in the slightly later poem, *The Parlement of the Thre Ages* (1370).[54] In the fifteenth century it was cited by Lydgate in his prose life of Caesar, *The Serpent of Division* (between 1400 and 1423), which was quoted in several volumes to which Shakespeare may have had access, including Grafton's sixteenth-century *Chronicle at Large*.[55]

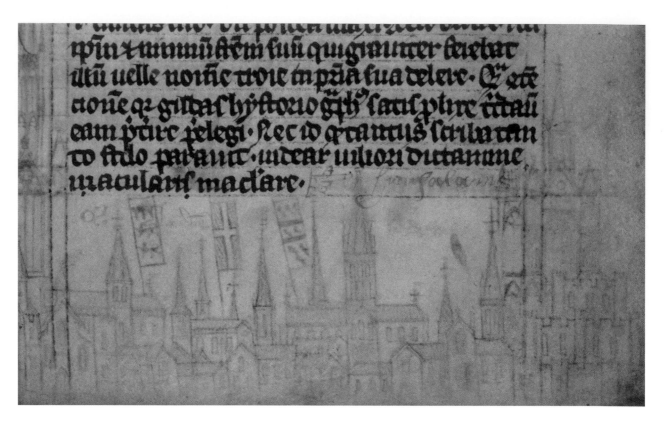

The legend seems to have arisen in circumstances rather similar to the Brutus connection: that is, in a combination of mistaken identity and location. Homer Nearing points to a passage in Geoffrey's *History*, in which both Caesar and the walls and towers of London are mentioned:[56]

> And after Lud, the brother of Cassibellanus who fought with Julius Caesar, had acceded to the government of the kingdom, he girdled [the capital] not only with the most noble walls but also with towers constructed with wonderful skill.[57]

As Nearing suggests, a hasty reader of this passage might well conclude that Julius Caesar had acceded to the government of the kingdom, and carried out the relevant building works. The lack of punctuation in the original text would have made mistakes of this kind more likely. Moreover, for a reader vaguely familiar with the sources Geoffrey adapts here (Caesar and/or Orosius), this might well seem plausible. Both texts state that Julius Caesar overcame Trinovantum (or the Trinovantes) during his British campaign. Of course, thanks to Geoffrey, Trinovantum was from the twelfth century equated with London, the New Troy, as discussed above. Within this context, the reference in Geoffrey's passage to the towers of the capital might well be taken as a reference to the Tower and London's other castles.

Nearing suggests that the victory implied in Caesar's conquest of 'Trinovantum' was crucial to the development of the British Caesar legends, since it was taken as evidence of the success of Caesar's invasion. Increasing numbers of buildings were attributed to Caesar's British campaigns, even as far afield as Scotland.[58] This development must also have increased the credibility of the claim that Caesar had founded the Tower of London. This proliferation of Caesar-related foundation legends, however, can be accompanied by rather vague architectural terminology. For example, Trivet attributes several castles to Caesar very casually:

> Julius Caesar . . . in demonstration of the Conquest made of the realm of Britain, as England was called, built the castle of Dover and of Canterbury and of Rochester and of London . . .[59]

By contrast, other versions of similar lists do seem to refer more specifically to the White Tower. The fourteenth-century alliterative poem *The Parlement of the Thre Ages* is one inheritor of Trivet's material:

> Thane sir Sezere himselven, that Julius was hatten,
> Alle Inglande he aughte at his awnn will,
> When the Bruyte in his booke Bretaine it callede.
> The trewe toure of Londone in his time he makede,
> And craftely the condite he compaste thereaftire,
> And then he droghe hym to Dovire, and dwellyde there a while,
> And closede ther a castelle with cornells full heghe . . .[60]

Lydgate's work, *The Serpent of Division*, written at some point between 1420 and 1423, reverts to the list once more:

Julius Cesar edefied in this londe dyverse Castelis & Citees, for a perpetuell memorye to putte his name in remembrance, that is for to seyne the Castelles of Dovir, of Cantorbury, Rowchestire, and the towre of London . . .[61]

Both these later versions take care to use the phrase 'Tower of London'. This is especially pointed in Lydgate's version, where the economy of phrasing and the rhythm of the list are broken to specify the 'towre', as distinct from the other numerous 'castelles'. Particular recognition of the White Tower is implied through this phrasing, which emphasises the presence of the great tower at the centre of London's fortress. The Caesar foundation legends of medieval Britain, however, were not supported only by these textual references. Several of Nearing's literary examples seem to have been bolstered by archaeological evidence of Roman remains.[62] Dover is one of these cases: its *pharos* or signal-station is described in a local monastic chronicle as having been built as Caesar's treasury:[63]

> Julius Caesar built a tower in the place where the Castle of Dover now is, to place his treasury in. This very same tower now stands in Dover Castle next to the church . . .[64]

The identification was approximately correct, because the structure is certainly Roman and displays its characteristically Roman banded masonry to this day. Although this reference dates from a fifteenth-century text, it provides a good explanation for the origins of the idea that Caesar built the whole of Dover Castle: possibly the chronicle records a long-standing local legend that started the tradition.[65]

The Tower of London may well have been involved in a similar mythographic process. The proximity of the Tower to London's Roman city wall has been noted above. Part of this wall still stands near Tower Hill Underground station, displaying its characteristically Roman banded masonry. The wall once formed a much larger section of the Tower's defences, and legendary developments may hint that its banding helped to identify the whole castle, or specific parts of it, as Roman for medieval observers.

Recent evidence suggests that a banded effect was also applied to certain medieval structures on the Tower's perimeter. Excavations in the Tower's western moat from 1995 to 1997 uncovered the footings of a gate faced with alternating bands of Purbeck marble and Reigate stone.[66] Dendrochronological evidence from associated timberwork dates the structure to around 1240, when Henry III was engaged on building new defences at the Tower. This structure at the Tower can be seen in the context of Henry's other architectural projects, which often invoked Roman architectural precedents through the use of multi-coloured marbles, including Purbeck. Henry had been present at Canterbury Cathedral in 1220, when St Thomas' remains were translated; the king presumably saw the marble Cosmati shrine pavement and Purbeck marble columns there.[67] The style of these works is echoed in Henry's own later projects at Westminster, including the Cosmati shrine pavement of around 1268, made of multicoloured marble inlaid in a Purbeck marble matrix. The multicoloured banding and marble of the Tower gate may well have been intended to evoke Roman imperial architecture in a similar way, echoing the rather rougher tile and masonry banding of London's Roman wall, but outdoing it in the quality of the materials and their finish.

It may be significant that the year 1240, in which the banded gate was constructed, also provides the first evidence for the whitewashing of the White Tower. It seems from the documents that other parts of the Tower were also whitewashed at this time, possibly including the Roman wall.[68] At first glance, this may seem to defeat the argument that the Roman work was accorded any special significance at this period. Both the whitewashing and the Purbeck banding do indicate a particular sensitivity at this time to the surface finishes of the Tower's buildings, however, and it may be that these improved and luxurious finishes were intended to reinforce the Roman connotations of the castle by outdoing the Romans themselves. The Roman wall, and the White Tower, were, after all, both old structures by this time, and their materials – rubble and tile on the one hand, and irregularly shaped Kentish Ragstone on the other (if with high-quality ashlar dressings)[69] – do not match the opulence that Henry demanded of his own architectural improvements. Elsewhere, he had been known to use paint effects to create faux marble: at Ludgershall in 1245 and on the hall arcades at Guildford ten years later.[70] It is possible that the whitewash had a similar purpose. Michael Greenhalgh stresses that 'The Middle Ages appreciated the equation between whiteness and purity . . . but they were also fascinated by the idea of the finish which they found in antique sculptures and buildings.'[71] By disguising the shabbier surfaces of the Tower beneath layers of gleaming whitewash, Henry may have sought to create the effect of a smooth and opulent material. A description of the White Tower recorded by a visitor in 1324 confirms that the paint effect was entirely successful in creating the impression of beautifully cut and squared masonry:

> And at the edge of the same city in the direction of the sea is a most famous and impregnable castle, encircled with two walls, very deep ditches filled with water and every device of warfare. In its centre is that most famous tower which is called 'The Tower of London', built with immeasurable solidity of cut and dressed stone and raised to a wondrous height.[72]

It is informative to compare this description with that given by Fitz Stephen: the connotations of impressive strength are still present, but with a new emphasis on expensive and skilled craftsmanship. If this was Henry's intention, it is entirely in keeping with his use of multicoloured banding of unprecedented luxury on the prominent water gate at the Tower, and with the opulent *Romanitas* of his other projects.

This imperial luxury at the Tower of London, however, was not perceived to have entirely positive connotations. The banded gate of 1240 was almost certainly part of the new work, which (as an account by Matthew Paris shows) provoked hostility from Londoners, perhaps exacerbated by an understanding of its imperial and despotic connotations.[73]

Foundation legends, deployed for the purposes of empowerment and legitimisation, may create a unifying local identity,[74] but they can also, as in this case, foster social divisions.[75] This duality can be discerned in medieval literary attitudes towards Britain's Roman past, in the recurrent motif of a British reconquest of Rome, be it by Belinus or Arthur.[76] Both heroes were associated with the White Tower, balancing the building's imperial associations somewhat by their nationalist agendas. It is King Arthur's connection with the White Tower to which we now need to turn.

THE TOWER OF LONDON IN ARTHURIAN MYTH

If the connection between London, the Tower and Brutus was a logical outcome of the mythographic process, then association with King Arthur was also, perhaps, inevitable. A beginning can be seen early on in the development of the Welsh Arthurian legend, in a brief reference in *The Triads of the Islands of Britain* (*Trioedd Ynys Prydein*) and in the collection of tales known as the *Mabinogion*. In 'Branwen Daughter of Llyr' (in the *Mabinogion*) it is related that the great Welsh hero Bendigeidvran (Brân the Blessed), king of all the islands of Britain, is mortally wounded. He orders his companions to carry his head to London, and to bury it there on the White Hill, facing towards France, where it will protect Britain from invasion.[77] The *Mabinogion* makes reference at this point to the *Triads*, and it is only in the shorter version recorded there that Arthur's part is explained:

> The Head of Brân the Blessed, son of Llyr, which was concealed in the White Hill in London, with its face towards France. And as long as it was in the position in which it was put there, no Saxon oppression would ever come to this Island . . .
>
> And Arthur disclosed the head of Brân the Blessed from the White Hill, because it did not seem right to him that this Island should be defended by the strength of anyone, but by his own.[78]

Of course, given that Britain had already been invaded successfully by the time this was written, the brief reference implies Arthur's fatal arrogance, as well as his greatness – a contrast that is also emphasised in other Arthurian legends, including Geoffrey of Monmouth's.

The connection with the Tower of London is through location. Rachel Bromwich notes that by the 'White Hill', 'probably Tower Hill is intended, though I[for] W[illiams] suggests as an alternative the hill on which St Paul's now stands'.[79] The identification is therefore not certain: the use of the same epithet, 'white', for both the hill and the tower is probably mere coincidence, and there seems to be no further reference to this particular legend in the medieval literature of the Tower of London. It is notable, however, that this story fits well with the legendary histories provided for London by Geoffrey and his followers. By the time this particular version of the Triad was written, Geoffrey's work had become an accepted part of the Welsh legendary material,[80] and it is possible that the tendency to connect the capital with the most important figures of national legend was reinforced by this contact.

Later Arthurian legends include much more positive identifications of the Tower of London. Although the Tower is not one of the castles most famously associated with Arthur, such as Camelot and Carlisle, it features as the setting for a climactic episode in the French Vulgate Arthurian cycle, and subsequently in the English *Stanzaic Morte Arthur* (*circa* 1350) and Sir Thomas Malory's work, the *Morte Darthur* (1460–62).[81] When Arthur is engaged abroad towards the end of the final tale of the destruction of the Round Table, Guenevere is threatened with a forced marriage to Arthur's illegitimate son, Mordred. The queen takes refuge in the Tower of London, stocks it with provisions and men, and manages to hold out against Mordred's siege. Finally, she escapes from the Tower to become a nun.

It is consistent with the French origins of this episode that the sexual motivation of this siege, and the gender of besieger and besieged, are reminiscent of the Castle of Love, attacked by knights and defended by ladies. This motif appeared in pageants on the Continent from at least the early thirteenth century, and steadily made its way into poems, manuscript illustrations and ivory carvings in England and continental Europe over the next century.[82] In many versions of the Castle of Love, the besieged ladies capitulate cheerfully, and welcome their attackers into the castle with kisses, a symbolic surrender of both the castle and themselves to male desires. Guenevere's successful escape to a celibate life, however, expresses the sincerity of her defence of both the castle and her body. The *Stanzaic Morte Arthur* is economical in its phrasing, but creates dramatic tension by its emotive characterisation of the protagonists:

> The queen, white as lily flowr,
> With knightes fele of her kin,
> She went to London to the towr

224 Mordred's troops besiege the
Tower of London, *circa* 1300.
London, British Library.

vant il ont fait le sai

And sperred the gates and dwelled therein.
Mordred changed all his colour;
Thider he went and wolde not blinne;
There-to he made many a showr,
But the walles might he never win.[83]

The contrast between Guenevere's purity and Mordred's anger emerges forcefully here, creating a strongly gendered image of the siege. Malory's version is longer, but creates a similar effect, dwelling on the stalemate of the siege, and again emphasising the treachery of the besieger and the steadfast innocence of the besieged:

> Than sir Mordred soughte uppon quene Gwenyver by lettirs and sondis, and by faire meanis and foule meanis, to have her to com oute of the Towre of London; but all this availed nought, for she anwerd him shortely, openly and privayly, that she had levr sle herselff than be maried with him.[84]

It is notable that neither of these texts (nor, indeed, the French Vulgate version) includes a description of any part of the Tower, even though it is clearly identified by name.[85] Perhaps this is because the castle is treated here in terms reminiscent of the Castle of Love, which is significant for its conventional defensive symbolism rather than the particulars of its architecture. An illustration (fig. 224) accompanying the description of the incident in the French Vulgate text *Le Mort le Roi Artu* (from about 1300) confirms this visually.[86] The castle depicted bears no particular resemblance to the Tower of London, and the arrangement of the action and the activities of the individual combatants are similar to those found in depictions of the siege of the Castle of Love (fig. 225). This is despite the specific mention on the same folio of the 'tor de logres', a phrase clearly indicating the Tower of London. This is in marked contrast to the other legends of the Tower discussed above, which can provide remarkably accurate verbal or visual depictions of the structure.

In common with the Brutus and Caesar myths, however, the legend of Arthur harks back to a distant past in which Britain was an imperial power, led by a forceful and charismatic monarch. The anachronism of this Arthurian chronology may not be so obvious to the modern reader. The idea that Caesar built the White Tower is clearly implausible to anyone with a basic understanding of British history and architecture, but it is somehow easier to accept the appearance of castles in Arthurian legends, without realising the chronological implications. King Arthur, by Geoffrey of Monmouth's calculations, died in AD 542.[87] This dating was still broadly relevant by the time that Malory came to tackle the material: he sets the start of the Grail Quest 454 years after Christ's death, pro-

viding a dated mid-point for Arthur's reign.[88] Once again, this pushes back the notional date of the Tower long before the Middle Ages. Despite the lack of detail in the architectural description of the Tower in the Arthurian legends, this chronological framework anchors the building firmly in Britain's pre-medieval, legendary history. Medieval visitors to London, including Malory himself, could imagine, or believe, that the Tower that they saw had also been looked on by Arthur and Guenevere, and so represented a continuity between past and present London.

In his *Morte Darthur* Malory provides a powerful demonstration of this perceived continuity, structuring the Arthurian legend to reflect, and even provide commentary on, much more recent events in English history.[89] This tendency takes on a particular significance in the Tower episode. Malory includes a rare passage of authorial comment, in which he bemoans the fickleness of the population, who have treacherously joined Mordred's army in the siege of the Tower and in the subsequent battle against Arthur.[90] Here he implicates all 'Englysshemen' in harbouring treacherous intentions against their kings, a sentiment that would have had many contemporary resonances in the context of the Wars of the Roses, under way at the time of writing. It could indeed be read as an ironic or apologetic reference to Malory himself, whose loyalties changed during the conflict.[91] Like Guenevere, Malory had experienced imprisonment in the Tower – in his case for his supposed involvement with the Yorkists. He may even have been a captive during the Yorkist siege of July 1460. If so, his description of the Arthurian siege has intense personal relevance,[92] combining the Tower's supposedly ancient pedigree

with an acute appreciation of its contemporary use as a stronghold in times of political crisis. Here, once again, a duality can be discerned in the depiction of the Tower, emphasising Britain's national greatness, but also its ultimate weakness and division, both in the contemporary world and in legendary times.

POSTSCRIPTS AND CONCLUSIONS

This chapter is chiefly concerned with the medieval legends surrounding the White Tower. The final section, however, traces the transmission of these legends through to later tradition. The Caesar legend seems to have been the only survivor into the immediate post-medieval period, thanks largely to Shakespeare, who mentions it in both *King Richard III* (1591) and *King Richard II* (1595).[93] Homer Nearing plausibly suggests as Shakespeare's sources Grafton's *Chronicle*, the *Anonymi chronicon* of the reign of Henry VI and the *Cronycullys of Englonde* of the reign of Edward IV.[94] Shakespeare, then, received this tradition straight from medieval sources, but his emphasis is quite different. Shakespeare's characters are anxious to establish the evidence for the Tower's ancient origins. Questions are asked about the truth of the story, and a distinction is implied between the reliability of oral and written evidence:

PRINCE   I do not like the Tower of any place.
            Did Julius Caesar build that place, my lord?
BUCKINGHAM He did, my gracious lord, begin that place,
            Which since, succeeding ages have re-edified.

226 W. Stukeley, 'Londinium Augusta', in his *Itinerarium curiosum; or, An Account of the Antiquitys and Remarkable Curiositys in Nature or Art, Observ'd in Travels thro' Great Britain* (London, 1724), plate 57.

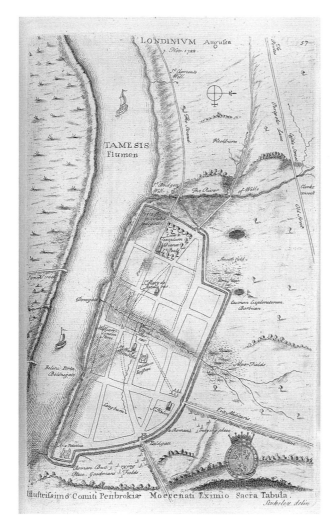

PRINCE	Is it upon record, or else reported
	Successively from age to age, he
	built it?
BUCKINGHAM	Upon record, my gracious lord.[95]

It is interesting that Shakespeare puts such questions into the mouths of his medieval characters, suggesting that they were critical receivers of legendary accounts. Such concerns were certainly reflected by Shakespeare's contemporaries in their assessments of the Tower's origins.[96] John Stow, for example, in his *Survey of London*, first published in 1598, dismissed the 'common opinion . . . that *Iulius Caesar*, the first conqueror of the Brytains, was the originall Author and founder aswell thereof . . . but (as I have alreadie before noted) *Caesar* remained not here so long, nor had hee in his head any such matter'.[97]

In addition to refuting Caesar's involvement, Stow was also aware of the *Textus Roffensis*, which associates work on the White Tower with Gundulf of Rochester under William the Conqueror, and on this basis attributed the building to 'about the year 1078'.[98] Nevertheless, Stow's arguments did little to stem the tide of legendary history. While obviously preferring documentary material that he saw as reliable to legendary histories, he himself resorts to quoting Geoffrey of Monmouth and William Fitz Stephen where he has no better evidence,[99] and their texts continued to be cited

in histories of London for years afterwards. The enduring appeal of these texts lay in the way that, unlike administrative documents, they attempted to explain the unique appearance of the building, which was still hard for observers to reconcile with its medieval origins. Succeeding antiquarians could not let go of the idea that the building was Roman, even though Caesar himself could no longer be claimed as its founder. John Bagford's insistence in 1715 on the Tower's Roman origins, in a letter published in Hearne's edition of Leland, takes on a decided circularity:

> The Architecture of this White Tower is perhaps as ancient as any Building now remaining amongst us. It is built like one of the Roman Rotundas, and exactly corresponds therewith . . . It is commonly reported to have been built by Julius Caesar, which I look upon as a good argument to shew that it is of the Roman Times.[100]

Here again, it is clear that the White Tower's unique appearance was the motivating factor behind successive attempts to explain its origins. Accordingly, medieval literary accounts resurfaced briefly in the mythography of the Tower.[101] A reconstructed plan of Roman London made in 1724 by William Stukeley draws on both Fitz Stephen and Geoffrey of Monmouth (fig. 226).[102] The reconstructed riverside wall and *Arx Palatina*, depicted as a square, turreted construction clearly representing the White Tower, derive from Fitz Stephen, and the high-arched *Belini Porta / Belinsgate* from Geoffrey. Other conjectured features of Roman London include the Temple of Diana, supposed to have occupied the site of St Paul's Cathedral.[103]

The Roman archaeology of the capital continued to colour contemporary literary understanding of the city for some time after this. Henry Hart Milman (1791–1868), Dean of St Paul's and a distinguished historian, had a lifelong fascination with the archaeology and legends of London.[104] Milman's epic poem, *Samor, Lord of the Bright City*, set in the period of the British struggle with the Saxons, synthesised an impressive quantity of legendary history. The Tower of London receives the benefit of Milman's compilatory powers: his model is broadly historical, but he weaves in elements from the legendary traditions. The action of the poem begins in Troynovant, the ancient London, whose walls have been built up from their Roman ruins:

> Upon the azure bosom of the Thames
> Reclining, with its ponderous mass of shade,
> Arose the royal Citadel, the work
> Of the great Caesar.[105]

Such pedantic constructions could not be taken altogether seriously by Milman's contemporaries. The juxtaposition of serious archaeological enquiry with legend, of the kind demonstrated by Milman, is mocked by Richard Harris Barham in 'A Strand Eclogue', in which one of the humorously obscure and tortuous papers announced to 'The Antiquarian Society' discusses the correct identification of Caesar's London tower.[106] A similarly sceptical view is taken by John Moultrie (1799–1874): *Sir Launfal*, a parodic epic in the style of Spenser's *Faerie Queen*, mocks the archaeological fantasies of his contemporaries:

> But to proceed – the Anglo-Fairy kings
> From Elfe to Oberon, their horde's migrations,
> And how they did a thousand wondrous things,
> And rein'd in peace for many generations,
> Built Windsor Castle, (all except the wings)
> And London Bridge, the Tower, and other stations –
> In short, their actions, whether great or mean,
> Are they not written in the Faerie Queen?[107]

Whether in the weighty Miltonics of Milman or the lighter offerings of his critics, the Tower's medieval legendary paraphernalia was very much alive well into the nineteenth century. But after this period of renewed vitality, the legendary founders of the Tower were once again condemned to obscurity. With the building's medieval origins now firmly established, the impetus to search for more ancient associations went, although the process of mythologising the castle – if not solely the White Tower – has continued unabated, with tales of ravens, executions and torture taking the place of Brutus and Caesar.

Such associations do not always have a direct bearing on the interpretation of the archaeological record. All the specific legends discussed here grew up after the White Tower's foundation, and are therefore secondary to the original building. Nevertheless, such traditions can provide invaluable evidence of people's understanding of the building, even very soon after its construction. Later building projects can also be materially affected by legendary connotations that seem relevant at the time. The legendary associations of buildings such as the White Tower in the end provide their own justification. They take on their own cultural life, inspired by, but not dependent on, the building itself. To acknowledge this is to accept the building as a cultural artefact, constructed in the imagination as well as in reality.

Acknowledgements

In writing this chapter, the author has received generous advice and assistance from many scholars spanning several different disciplines, not least from Jane Grenville, Christopher Norton and Felicity Riddy. While extending many thanks to these and other scholars during the course of this chapter, the author nevertheless accepts full responsibility for any errors. Some parts of this chapter reiterate material first published by the author in Wheatley 2004a.

PART IV

Methodological and Technical Appendices

APPENDIX I

Measured Survey

ROLAND B. HARRIS

The White Tower Recording and Research Project (WTRRP) draws heavily on metric, or measured, survey data. This comprises surveys undertaken before, during and after the emptying of the White Tower for representation of the building and the Royal Armouries collections (1996–8), and repairs to the south external elevation (1997–8).[1] Much of the metric survey undertaken during this period was acquired for Historic Royal Palaces through the Surveyor of the Fabric's Department and its consultant, Ross Dallas, and made available to the project with the help of Bridget Litchfield. Measured survey of a more archaeological nature was obtained directly through the Curatorial Department of Historic Royal Palaces, through the contracts with the Oxford Archaeological Unit, and the Historic Buildings Recording Unit (HBRU) of the University of Reading: in the case of the last, specifically for the purposes of the WTRRP.

STEREO–PHOTOGRAMMETRY

Photogrammetric survey – derived from scaled stereoscopic photographs – represents one of the main and most useful measured survey products used in this study. A wealth of such material was produced by the Downland Partnership at the time of the representation of the White Tower, much of which remains as archived negatives as yet not plotted to produce scale drawings. Examples of this include the uncontrolled semi-metric photography of the soffits of the window embrasure arches. More immediately useful to archaeological study has been photography

acquired with a metric camera (i.e., large-format, calibrated and equipped with a plate providing fiducial – or reference – marks on each plate), controlled by a network of temporary targets measured by EDM (Electromagnetic Distance Measurement), and plotted to produce CAD (Computer Aided Drafting) elevational drawings for all exterior faces of the White Tower and a few of the interior walls. The external elevations of the north, east and west faces were almost complete, with stone-by-stone line detail plotted to a scale of 1:50. The south elevation was only partly finished due to the presence of the external timber stair and temporary protective hoarding, both reducing photographic coverage. The three-dimensionality of the CAD plots has proved particularly useful for the study – and orthogonal projection – of the major curved elements of the White Tower: the apsidal projection of the chapel and the circular north-east turret.

RECTIFIED PHOTOGRAPHY

Rectified photography comprises the rectification of single photographs to produce two-dimensional scaled images of planar subjects (which can then be combined, or 'mosaiced'). It has been used extensively in this project as a means of deriving accurate scaled elevations for the internal walls. This proved a cost-effective means of using the archived negatives deriving from stereo-photogrammetric coverage of the internal walls of the east and west rooms, recorded (but not plotted to CAD line drawings) as the representation works exposed them. Digital rectification of high-resolution scans was undertaken by HBRU using the program ARCHIS. Where no metric photography had been taken (e.g., the chapel and, most importantly, parts of the south elevation), non-metric medium-format photography was acquired and rectified (HBRU), using control established with an EDM tacheometer and reflective temporary targets.

EDM AND REDM SURVEY

Sixteen measured plans of the White Tower at 1:50 were prepared from an EDM survey of 1994 by Sterling Surveys, and were used in this project, albeit partly redrafted (e.g., removing the stylised rendition of rubble walling) and updated by HBRU (using an REDM – reflectorless EDM). These CAD plans show the building at all levels from the sub-basement remains of the blocked tunnel to the turrets, and include separate roof and ceiling plans. Sterling Surveys established a site grid for the White Tower and installed semi-permanent survey markers defining an external EDM traverse, with an OSBM (Ordnance Survey benchmark) vertical datum: this control was used for the WTRRP, although for the purposes of publication plans have been rotated to sit squarely on the page.

HAND–DRAWN SURVEY

Hand-drawn survey (typically at 1:20 scale, and achieved using steel tapes) was undertaken where no metric survey existed or where this needed enhancement or completion. An example of the former is the archaeological investigation carried out by Oxford Archaeological Unit in the second-floor mural passages and spine wall.[2] Other hand-drawn survey includes the addition of detail to photogrammetric plots (most notably the south elevation, where the photogrammetry and infill non-metric rectified photography still required considerable additions, especially under and behind the external stair, but also where scaffolding of this elevation permitted fine detail to be added) and to the measured plans (especially with observations allowing the preparation of the reconstructed plans of the primary building in this book).

CAD LAYERING

The use of CAD for all line-drawings derived from measured survey – bar the Oxford Archaeological Unit archaeological records – means that different elements of the drawings can be assigned to layers (virtual overlays), allowing selective display or the application of different line colours, styles or other different graphical treatment. The original needs of several of the metric surveys used here (such as the photogrammetrically derived elevations) frequently differed from those of archaeological analysis, and thus most such base surveys have been restructured by HBRU. For example, the south elevation data was structured to permit selective viewing of the different stone types and mortar types, possible as a result of access provided by scaffolding and the petrographic analysis undertaken by Bernard Worssam and Robin Sanderson (see Appendix III).

CAD SOLID MODEL

Although not strictly part of the measured survey of the White Tower, the metric survey data from the various surveys was used to produce three-dimensional solid models of the building in its primary form and with the forebuilding. This was undertaken as an integral part of the analysis of the structural history of the White Tower, the three-dimensionality enforcing more rigour in the reconstruction of the primary form of the building. Examples of details where such modelling permitted more reliable interpretation of the architectural features include the spiral stairs and the basement window in the south wall (which were found to interfere and thus could not have coexisted, as previously considered), the potential drain outlet at the second-floor level on the west face of the south-west turret (where it was discovered that a drain linking this to the western gutter would have passed neatly through the vaulting of the spiral stairs), and the south-east turret (where its irregularity was explained as a means of locating its supporting arches in the chapel roof space above the chapel piers, rather than on unsupported vaulting between).[3] The modelling was undertaken by Helen Jones of HBRU, drawing on an earlier three-dimensional wireframe CAD 'as is' model undertaken by Sterling Surveys for the Surveyor of the Fabric's Department. The HBRU reconstruction was created in AutoCAD (versions 14 to 2004), though final colouring of the figures in this book was undertaken in Corel-DRAW (version 12) in preference to AutoCAD renders. Particular challenges comprise the spiral stairs and, especially, St John's Chapel with its apsidal projection, irregular window embrasures, quadripartite groin vaults, barrel vaults and arcades.

White Tower Dendrochronology Programme

DANIEL MILES

During 1997 and 1998 the re-presentation works to the White Tower resulted in the process of lifting floors and opening up later finishes for updating services and effecting needed repairs. This once-in-a-lifetime opportunity gave access to timbers that would not be exposed again for the foreseeable future. Given these circumstances, Edward Impey, then Curator of Historic Royal Palaces, commissioned a thorough programme of dendrochronology through the Oxford Archaeological Unit. The project brief was designed with Julian Munby, who supervised the work on behalf of the OAU. Michael Worthington of the Oxford Dendrochronology Laboratory assisted both the sampling on site, as well as in the Laboratory. Colleagues Dr Martin Bridge and Cathy and Ian Tyers provided invaluable assistance at various stages, and in providing reference chronologies.

Dendrochronology, or tree-ring dating, is the process of comparing ring-width sequences of unknown date with a variety of local and regional chronologies that have been dated absolutely in time. By comparing the annual variations in ring-width patterns in timbers used in the construction of the floors, roof and doors, precise dates can be ascribed to each growth ring.

METHODOLOGY

To effect this, samples need to be taken from what appeared to be primary first-use oak (*Quercus* spp.) timbers with reasonably long ring sequences, or with some indication of sapwood. Most of the *in situ* timbers were sampled using a 16 mm hollow coring bit. However, a number of early doors and boards making up drawbar socket linings were required to be dated, and these would be destroyed by extracting cores of this size. In addition, the surface of the timber was too damaged to allow the rings to show clearly enough to be accurately measured. To have resurfaced the timber to enable the rings to be visible would have caused unacceptable surface damage and was therefore not an option. Therefore a system of drilling with micro-bores was developed. This uses a drill almost 1 m long that gives a core about 5 mm in diameter. The secret is in the use of compressed air, which is fed through the centre of the drill to clear the dust and keep the bit cool. By mounting the door on a sliding press, and carefully aligning it with the surface of the boards, it was possible to obtain a succession of cores from one board through into another. These were then mounted and prepared in the same manner as the larger samples.

Some elements, however, such as the lintels to the niches in the embrasures on the first floor, were so delicate that it was not possible to sample them physically, even with the microborer. Another technique developed with English Heritage was the photographing of the tangential surface of a timber and measuring the rings from a high-quality print, here produced by John Crook.

The dry samples were sanded on a linisher using 60 to 1200 grit abrasive paper, and were cleaned with compressed air, to allow the ring boundaries to be clearly distinguished. They were then measured under a ×10/×30 microscope using a travelling stage electronically displaying displacement to a precision of 0.001 mm, rounded to the nearest 0.01 mm.

After measurement, the ring-width series for each sample was plotted as a graph of width against year on log-linear graph paper. The graphs of each of the samples in the phase under study were then compared visually at the positions indicated by the computer matching and, if found satisfactory and consistent, were averaged to form a mean curve for the site or phase. These mean curves, together with the individual ring sequences, were then compared against dated reference chronologies to obtain an absolute calendar date for each sequence.

In comparing one sequence or mean curve against another, *t*-values over 3.5 are considered significant, although in reality it is common to find *t*-values of 4 and 5, which are demonstrably spurious because more than one matching position is indicated. For this reason, dendrochronologists prefer to see some *t*-values of 5, 6 and higher, and for these to be well replicated from different, independent chronologies with local and regional chronologies well represented. Where two individual sequences match with a *t*-value of 10 or above, and visually exhibit exceptionally close ring patterns, they most likely come from the same parent tree. Same-tree matches can also sometimes be identified through the external characteristics of the timber itself, such as knots and shake patterns. For shorter ring sequences from the same tree, lower *t*-values are often encountered.[1]

Here dating was accomplished by using a combination of both visual matching and a process of qualified statistical comparison by computer. The tree-ring curves were first matched visually, and then independently matched by computer. The ring-width series were compared on an IBM-compatible computer for statistical cross-matching using a variant of the Belfast CROS program.[2] A version of this and other programs were written in GW-BASIC by D. Haddon-Reece, and latterly rewritten in Microsoft Visual Basic by M. R. Allwright and P. A. Parker.

A methodical approach is taken in dealing with the individual samples. Occasionally, samples from duplicate radii from a single timber are taken to maximise sapwood or length of ring sequences. These are first cross-matched and compared, and, if the matches are satisfactory, combined to form a single-timber mean. These multiple radii are generally identified by using an 'a', 'b', etc., after the timber sample number. Cores that have broken into one or more segments are further identified by a '1', '2', etc., after the radii prefix. Once a single mean sequence for each timber has been produced, then the next step in the analysis is to check for same-tree matches. Again, all samples clearly identified as having originated from the same parent tree are combined to form a mean sequence for each tree. It is not until this preliminary analysis stage is completed that individual samples/trees are then compared with others from the site and combined into larger site masters.

All individual sequences and components of same-timber means and same-tree means are presented in table 1. Because this is the primary summary of all material on which the dendrochronological analysis has been based, both actual samples and averaged sequences are presented here. The means of individual radii, as well as same-tree means, are differentiated in the table by the use of italic text. To avoid unnecessary confusion, felling seasons and dates, or date ranges, are not presented in the final column for individual radii comprising a single timber; instead, these are presented only for the mean of these individual sequences. Where two or more timbers have been found to originate from the same parent tree, each timber has been given a felling date or date range, but this would be the same as the mean sequence for the tree. Where one of the components making up a same-tree mean has complete sapwood, and another with only partial or no sapwood, then the latter would be given the precise date in brackets, even though it would have produced only a *terminus post quem* (*tpq*), or at best a felling date range, on its own. Where all the individual same-tree components have incomplete sapwood, then a felling date range for the mean is produced by taking the average heartwood/sapwood boundary date, from which the appropriate 95 per cent sapwood estimate is used to work out the felling date range.

INTERPRETATION

Once a tree-ring sequence has been firmly dated, a felling date, or date range, is ascribed where possible. With samples that have sapwood complete to the underside of, or including bark, this process is relatively straightforward and a *precise felling date and season* can be given. The latter depends on the completeness of the final ring, and whether it has only the spring vessels or early wood formed, or also includes the latewood or summer growth. If the sapwood is partially missing, or if only a heartwood/sapwood boundary survives, then only an *estimated felling date range* can be given for each sample. The number of sapwood rings can be estimated by using an empirically derived sapwood estimate with a given confidence limit. If no sapwood or heartwood/sapwood boundary survives, then the minimum number of sapwood rings from the appropriate regional sapwood estimate is added to the last measured ring to give a *tpq* or *felled after* date.

An accepted sapwood estimate for British and Irish oaks on the basis of statistics is between 10 and 55 rings with a 95 per cent confidence range.[3] A recent review of the geographical distribution of dated sapwood data from historic building timbers has shown that a 95 per cent range of 9–41 rings is more appropriate for the southern part of England,[4] and 8–24 rings for Baltic timber imports.[5]

It must be emphasised that dendrochronology can only date when a tree was felled, not when the timber was used to construct the structure under study. It was common practice in the Middle Ages to build timber-framed structures with green or unseasoned timber, however, and construction usually took place within twelve months or so of felling.[6] Given the protracted nature of high-status building campaigns, more caution must be shown in interpreting construction dates, especially in subsequent phases of work.

Interim summaries of results have been published in the journal *Vernacular Architecture*[7] and presented at the European Dendrochronology Conference.[8] Detailed results of the dating are included in the English Heritage Research Department Report Series.[9]

RESULTS

A total of 243 samples were taken from 155 individual timbers representing ten principal building phases or elements from the White Tower. The earliest of these is the primary Norman construction phase, of which no primary timber was initially thought to have survived. However, sections of boards still *in situ* in a basement drawbar socket, and dislocated fragments in a drawbar socket in the south entrance, provided some material to work from. Then a perfectly preserved timber socket lining in the spine wall of the ground floor was discovered. These timbers produced a latest *tpq* or felled-after date of 1068 for the basement drawbar socket lining, and a felling date range of 1049–81 for one of the boards from the ground-floor drawbar socket lining.

The lintels to the niches to the embrasures on the first floor were studied, and a combination of micro-bores and photographs enabled a number of these to be dated, two giving felling date ranges of 1055–87 and 1072–1104 respectively. The final element of what was thought to be primary phase material was that discovered under the east and west mural passages on the top floor, interpreted as the rainwater drains to the original roof. On the west side, the lead was laid over u-shaped oak linings, one giving a *tpq* of 1014, while on the east side a board was found giving a last-measured ring date of 1092. Since there was no evidence of sapwood, only a *tpq* of 1102 could be given. Clearly, this sample was not of the same phase as the lower drawbar socket linings, and although it was not possible to say just how much heartwood and sapwood had been removed, experience has shown that often it was kept to a minimum. Nevertheless, it is possible that this board represents an early modification after the traditional completion of *circa* 1100.

The final area of potentially primary Norman work to be investigated was found not at the top of the building, but in the well deep below the basement floor. Five beech samples were dated, the best matches being with the London beech chronologies constructed by Ian Tyers. The latest sample produced a last measured ring of 1081, giving a *tpq* date of after 1082. Given that the mortar used in the construction of the associated stonework is typical of the post-1090 construction break, the well is most likely to date from the early 1090s.

Progressing chronologically, the next phase of construction is represented by the door at the south end of the eastern basement room. Here eleven micro-bore samples were dated, and although none of them retained any sapwood, the end dates were all so close together that it is likely that the minimum amount of heartwood was removed. A latest *tpq* of 1345 for the group was determined, with felling probably around the middle of the fourteenth century. The door to the bottom of the great vice in Flamsteed Tower was similarly sampled, and although five boards were dated, the alignment of the last heartwood dates were not as consistent, so one can only suggest that these might have been felled *circa* 1475. The timber used in the construction of both doors was found to be imported from the Baltic.

The main roofs to the whole of the White Tower were found to have been renewed shortly after 1490, as revealed by felling dates of spring 1489 and spring 1490. Although forty samples were taken from the main roofs, only eight precise felling dates were obtained, since virtually all the sapwood had been removed from the timbers when the roofs were repaired in the 1960s. A ninth felling date from a floorboard under the spine-wall arcade on the top floor produced a felling date of spring 1488, and two other floorboards were found to have originated from the same trees as used in the main roofs, demonstrating that the top floor had been constructed at the same time.

Although no surviving timbers relating to the 1530s repairs to the main roofs were found, six samples from the ribs of the Flamsteed Tower were dated, with some precise felling dates ranging from the winter of 1531–2 through to the spring of 1533. Four floor joists and a beam in the south-east turret also dated to this period, with one precise felling date of spring 1532.

The reconstruction of the western half of the White Tower at the transition between the reigns of Elizabeth I and James I is revealed by a good assemblage of precise felling dates ranging from summer 1602 to spring 1603. The eastern half of the building has proved more enigmatic, however, with only one post on the first floor producing a felling date of winter 1565–6, shortly before the first recorded use of the building by the Armoury in 1567.[10] Two other posts from this room produced sequences dating a century earlier. This may simply be because they lost their heartwood/sapwood boundaries along with a large number of heartwood rings, but more likely they may have been reused from an earlier phase that is yet to be identified. Accounts from 1734 suggest that these posts and floors had been taken down and reconstructed, so it is likely that none of these timbers are *in situ*.

Later repair episodes have been identified through the dendrochronology. An unknown phase of strengthening to the south-west turret was revealed by felling dates of winter 1616–17, and a study of contemporary bricklayers' accounts indicated that the walls to the turret were repaired between October 1618 and October 1619. A more major change was the insertion of the brick vaults in the basement. This was confirmed by tree-ring dates of winter 1732–3 and spring 1733 from the east chamber above, and supported by contemporary building accounts.

Finally, the latest sequence of dates related to the reconstruction of the four turrets. Eighteen samples produced thirteen precise felling dates, which showed a progression of repair. This started with the south-west turret, with latest felling dates of winter 1779–80, followed by the north-west and south-east turrets, and finally to the Flamsteed Tower, with latest felling dates of spring 1783. Again, much of this work is supported by contemporary documentary accounts.

In conclusion, the programme of dendrochronology within the White Tower has succeeded in dating all but 22 out of 155 timbers sampled. Of these dated timbers, 43 produced precise felling dates for seven of the ten phases of construction studied. This corpus of dated material has been combined to produce nine reference chronologies, many of them well replicated, covering a period of almost a millennium. These chronologies gave excellent matches with local and regional reference chronologies, suggesting that the timber was all obtained locally to London, with the sole exception of the two medieval doors, which were found to be constructed of boards imported from the Baltic region. Overall, the programme has made a major contribution to this study as a whole and to our understanding of the history of the White Tower.

Table 1. *Summary of tree-ring dating*

Sample number & type		Timber and position	Dates AD spanning	H/S bdry	Sapwood complement	No of rings	Mean width mm	Std devn mm	Mean sens mm	Felling seasons and dates/date ranges (AD)
Norman – Primary Phase										
Well in West Basement										
*WT01	s	Plank 1 from East (beech)	927–1081			155	1.00	0.47	0.366	
*WT02	s	Plank 2 from East *ex situ* (beech)	913–1081			169	1.22	0.68	0.363	
*WT03	s	*Ex situ* plank (beech)	950–1070			121	1.13	0.44	0.351	
*WT04	s	*Ex situ* plank (beech)	909–999			91	1.81	1.34	0.257	
*WT05	s	*Ex situ* plank (beech)	906–1072			167	1.59	1.29	0.330	
★=WHITOWR1		Site master (English Beech)	906–1081			176	1.51	1.20	0.310	After 1082
Basement Spine Wall Drawbar Socket Lining										
WT06A	s	East side board	977–1059			83	1.25	0.33	0.231	
B	s	ditto	1003–1059			57	1.79	0.39	0.210	
C	s	ditto	984–1049			66	1.55	0.37	0.215	
WT06		Mean of WT06A + WT06B + WT06C	977–1059			83	1.25	0.33	0.231	After 1068
WT07	s	Bottom board	886–989			104	1.50	0.47	0.230	After 998
Ground Floor South Entrance Drawbar Socket Lining Fragments										
WT08A	s	Fragment 1	958–1018			61	1.21	0.49	0.299	
B	s	ditto	958–1019			62	1.21	0.49	0.290	
C	s	ditto	940–1010			71	1.36	0.48	0.279	
D	s	ditto	934–1012			79	1.39	0.52	0.281	
WT08		Mean of WT08A + WT08B + WT08C + WT08D	934–1019			86	1.32	0.52	0.262	(1049–81)
WT09A	s	Fragment 2	939–995			57	1.31	0.47	0.323	
B	s	ditto	939–988			50	1.38	0.49	0.317	
WT09		Mean of WT09A + WT09B	939–995			57	1.31	0.48	0.306	(1049–81)
*WT10	s	Fragment 3	940–999			60	1.02	0.36	0.236	After 1008
WT11A	s	Fragment 4	926–985			60	1.21	0.41	0.318	
B	s	ditto	926–980			55	1.23	0.44	0.328	
C	s	ditto	925–969			45	1.18	0.39	0.286	
WT11		Mean of WT11A + WT11B + WT11C	925–985			61	1.22	0.39	0.288	(1049–81)
WT12A	s	Fragment 5	907–992			86	1.23	0.54	0.291	
B	s	ditto	907–989			83	1.28	0.53	0.297	
WT12		Mean of WT12A + WT12B	907–992			86	1.25	0.53	0.273	(1049–81)
WT13A	s	Fragment 6	–			20	1.94	0.60	0.272	
B	s	ditto	–			21	1.83	0.42	0.228	
C	s	ditto	–			26	1.56	0.58	0.347	
WT14A	s	Fragment 7	982–1041			60	0.94	0.32	0.272	
B	s	ditto	982–1041			60	0.95	0.32	0.253	
WT14		Mean of WT14A + WT14B	982–1041			60	0.95	0.32	0.246	(1049–81)
Ground Floor Spine Wall Drawbar Socket Lining										
WT15	mc	Bottom board	945–1028			84	1.35	0.41	0.232	(1049–81)
WT16	mc	Top board	917–1012			96	1.57	0.44	0.256	(1049–81)
WT17	mc	Left-hand board	932–1039	(1040)	+ 1 NM to H/S	108	1.38	0.80	0.236	1049–81
WT18	mc	Right-hand board	927–1043			117	1.41	0.52	0.243	(1049–81)
*WT0818		Same-tree mean of WT08 + WT009 + WT011 + WT012 + WT014–WT018	907–1043			137	1.32	0.52	0.238	1049–81
First Floor Embrasure Lintels										
WT19A	mc	NW embrasure, S lintel, front board	961–1023			63	1.45	0.43	0.234	
B	mc	ditto	985–1045	1046	H/S	61	1.17	0.34	0.177	
C	mc	ditto	1007–1046	1046	H/S	40	1.32	0.43	0.179	
D1	mc	ditto	–			28	1.28	0.45	0.241	
D2	mc	ditto	–			31	1.29	0.27	0.208	
E	mc	ditto	–			39	1.43	0.39	0.217	

Key: * = sample included in site-masters; c = core; s = section; mc = micro-core; p = photo; ¼C, ½C, C = bark edge present, partial or complete ring: ¼C = spring (ring not measured), ½C = summer/autumn, or C = winter felling (ring measured); H/S bdry = heartwood/sapwood boundary – last heartwood ring date; std devn = standard deviation; mean sens = mean sensitivity. Sapwood estimate (95% confidence) of 9–41 used for English timbers (Miles 1997a), 8–24 for Baltic oak boards (Tyers 1998)

Sample number & type	Timber and position	Dates AD spanning	H/s bdry	Sapwood complement	No of rings	Mean width mm	Std devn mm	Mean sens mm	Felling seasons and dates/date ranges (AD)
WT19	Mean of WT19A + WT19B + WT19C	961–1046	1046	H/S	86	1.36	0.45	0.206	1055–87
WT20A	mc NW embrasure, N lintel	–			21	2.07	0.58	0.331	
B	mc ditto	–			15	1.75	0.40	0.236	
C	mc ditto	988–1026			39	1.63	0.39	0.212	(1055–87)
*WT21	p NE embrasure, S lintel, front board	968–1040		(1063) + 22 NM to H/s	73	1.65	0.43	0.227	1072–1104
*WT1920	Same-tree of WT19 + WT20C	961–1046			86	1.43	0.46	0.209	105587

Second Floor Gutter Linings

Sample number & type	Timber and position	Dates AD spanning	H/s bdry	Sapwood complement	No of rings	Mean width mm	Std devn mm	Mean sens mm	Felling seasons and dates/date ranges (AD)
*WT22A	s Drain 1, E passage, 2nd floor	816–918			103	0.86	0.22	0.189	
B	s ditto	955–1081			127	0.81	0.18	0.144	
C	s ditto	–			49	0.75	0.19	0.181	
D	s ditto	970–1092			123	0.76	0.18	0.152	
*WT22	Mean of WT22B + WT22D	955–1092			138	0.78	0.17	0.141	After 1101
WT23A	s Drain 8, W passage, 2nd floor (134)	926–991			66	1.18	0.37	0.223	
B	s ditto	932–989			58	1.14	0.40	0.248	
C	s ditto	957–1005			49	1.34	0.32	0.197	
D	s ditto	945–979			35	1.24	0.47	0.242	
E	s ditto	–			44	1.32	0.41	0.236	
F	s ditto	946–970			25	1.22	0.44	0.274	
G	s ditto	935–969			35	1.15	0.45	0.305	
H	s ditto	974–1003			30	1.38	0.32	0.210	
I	s ditto	958–1004			47	1.32	0.29	0.202	
J	s ditto	–			26	1.34	0.36	0.214	
K	s ditto	–			27	1.56	0.45	0.206	
*WT23	Mean of WT23A–WT023D + WT023F–WT0231	926–1005			80	1.25	0.38	0.229	After 1014
★=WHITOWR2 Site Master (English)		816–1092			277	1.04	0.37	0.181	

Edward III alterations
Door to Basement Apsidal Room

Sample number & type	Timber and position	Dates AD spanning	H/s bdry	Sapwood complement	No of rings	Mean width mm	Std devn mm	Mean sens mm	Felling seasons and dates/date ranges (AD)
WT24A	mc Board 1 from West, North face	1175–1273			99	1.43	0.55	0.240	}
B	ditto	1174–1274			101	1.36	0.54	0.218	}
*WT24	Mean of WT24A + WT24B	1174–1274			101	1.39	0.54	0.221	}
WT25A	mc Board 2 from West, North face	1109–1312			204	0.80	0.20	0.223	}
B	mc ditto	1120–1316			197	0.79	0.19	0.219	}
WT25	Mean of WT25A + WT25B	1109–1316			208	0.80	0.19	0.215	}
WT26A	mc Board 3 from West, North face	1216–1281			66	0.87	0.21	0.170	
B	mc ditto	1161–1301			141	1.15	0.32	0.201	
*WT26	Mean of WT26A + WT26B	1161–1301			141	1.10	0.31	0.190	
*WT27A1	mc Board 4 from West, North face	1166–1186			21	1.51	0.61	0.247	}
* A2	mc ditto	1192–1315			124	1.06	0.32	0.217	}
*WT28	mc Board 5 from West, North face	1160–1322			163	0.81	0.21	0.170	} After 1345
WT29	mc Board 6 from West, North face	1169–1329			161	1.04	0.23	0.185	}
WT30A1	mc Board 7 from West, North face				22	1.70	0.30	0.151	
A2	mc ditto				74	1.30	0.28	0.170	
WT31	mc Board 1 from West, South face	1137–1320			184	0.87	0.28	0.255	}
*WT32A1	mc Board 2 from West, South face	1111–1156			46	0.94	0.18	0.204	
* A2	mc ditto	1169–1321			153	0.87	0.18	0.162	

Key: * = sample included in site-masters; c = core; s = section; mc = micro-core; p = photo; ¼C, ½C, c = bark edge present, partial or complete ring: ¼C = spring (ring not measured), ½C = summer/autumn, or c = winter felling (ring measured); H/s bdry = heartwood/sapwood boundary – last heartwood ring date; std devn = standard deviation; mean sens = mean sensitivity. Sapwood estimate (95% confidence) of 9–41 used for English timbers (Miles 1997a), 8–24 for Baltic oak boards (Tyers 1998)

Sample number & type	Timber and position	Dates AD spanning	H/s bdry	Sapwood complement	No of rings	Mean width mm	Std devn mm	Mean sens mm	Felling seasons and dates/date ranges (AD)
*WT33	mc Board 3 from West, South face	1177–1337			161	0.98	0.24	0.173	}
*WT34	mc Board 4 from West, South face	1198–1319			122	1.27	0.29	0.141	}
*WT35	mc Board 5 from West, South face	1140–1234			95	0.96	0.21	0.177	
*WT36	mc Board 6 from West, South face	1181–1316			136	1.23	0.27	0.178	}
WT37A	mc Board 7 from West, South face	1162–1313			152	1.00	0.21	0.185	
B1	mc ditto	1155–1208			54	1.11	0.22	0.193	
B2	mc ditto	1234–1313			80	0.91	0.15	0.182	
WT37	Mean of WT37A + WT37B1 + WT37B2	1155–1313			159	1.01	0.21	0.178	
WT38A	mc Board 8 from West, South face	1154–1321			168	1.05	0.25	0.180	}
B	mc ditto	1159–1323			165	1.06	0.25	0.161	}
*WT38	Mean of WT38A + WT38B	1154–1323			170	1.06	0.24	0.162	}
*WT2537	Mean of WT25 + WT29 + WT31 + WT37	1109–1329			221	0.91	0.21	0.198	
★=WHITOWR3 Site Master (Baltic)		1109–1337			229	1.01	0.19	0.144	*Circa* 1350

Edward IV Alterations
Door to Bottom of Great Vice, Flamsteed Turret

Sample number & type	Timber and position	Dates AD spanning	H/s bdry	Sapwood complement	No of rings	Mean width mm	Std devn mm	Mean sens mm	Felling seasons and dates/date ranges (AD)
WT39A	mc Board 1	1280–1440			161	1.26	0.27	0.149	
B	mc ditto	1280–1440			161	1.27	0.27	0.149	
*WT39	Mean of WT39A + WT39B	1280–1440			161	1.27	0.27	0.144	After 1448
WT40	mc Board 2	1325–1449			125	1.63	0.50	0.187	After 1457
*WT41	mc Board 3	1284–1432			149	1.34	0.35	0.164	After 1440
*WT42	mc Board 4	1245–1411			167	1.11	0.46	0.234	After 1419
WT43	mc Board 5				86	2.06	0.71	0.162	
★WT44	mc Board 6	1288–1411			124	1.51	0.37	0.237	After 1419
★=WHITOWR4 Site Master (Baltic)		1245–1440			196	1.31	0.37	0.167	*Circa* 1475

Henry VII alterations – Main Roof Reconstruction
West Chamber Roof

Sample number & type	Timber and position	Dates AD spanning	H/s bdry	Sapwood complement	No of rings	Mean width mm	Std devn mm	Mean sens mm	Felling seasons and dates/date ranges (AD)
*WT45	c Tiebeam T2	1297–1462	1461	1	166	1.84	0.98	0.196	1470–1502
*WT46	c Tiebeam T3	1306–1460	1459	1	155	1.67	0.77	0.198	1468–1500
*WT47	c Tiebeam T4	1325–1436			112	1.63	0.52	0.232	After 1445
*WT48	c Firring piece to tiebeam T4	1329–1471	1471	H/s	143	1.36	0.51	0.231	1480–1512
WT49	c East upper purlin bay 4	1291–1468	1456	12	178	1.49	0.64	0.203	(1480–1503)
*WT50	c Tiebeam T5	1324–1403			80	1.97	0.45	0.220	After 1412
*WT51	c 1st rafter south of T5, bay 5, east side	1342–1488	1443	45½C	147	1.04	0.40	0.223	Summer 1489
*WT52	c Tiebeam T6	1286–1460	1454	6	175	1.40	0.60	0.205	1463–95
*WT53	c Tiebeam T7	1357–1489	1467	22¼C	133	1.34	0.71	0.177	Spring 1490
WT54	c West lower wall-plate bay 7	–		3	63	2.57	1.19	0.219	
WT55	c West lower purlin bay 7	1302–1479	1468	11	178	1.91	0.67	0.207	(1480–1503)
WT56A	c Ridge beam bay 7	1338–1470	1469	1	133	1.72	0.58	0.205	
B	c ditto	–		15	15	1.04	0.29	0.242	
C	c ditto	1412–1489	1469	20¼C	78	1.24	0.34	0.224	
D	c ditto			8¼C	8	1.21	0.31	0.198	
*WT56	Mean of WT56A + WT56C	1338–1489	1469	20¼C	152	1.64	0.59	0.208	Spring 1490
WT57A	c Tiebeam T8	1310–1469	1464	5	160	1.77	0.62	0.220	
B	c ditto	1463–1489	1463	26¼C	27	1.25	0.17	0.160	
*WT57	Mean of WT57A + WT57B	1310–1489	1464	25¼C	180	1.71	0.61	0.213	Spring 1490
*WT58	c Tiebeam T9	1370–1470	1464	4	101	1.48	0.35	0.165	1473–1505

Key: * = sample included in site-masters; c = core; s = section; mc = micro-core; p = photo; ¼C, ½C, C = bark edge present, partial or complete ring: ¼C = spring (ring not measured), ½C = summer/autumn, or C = winter felling (ring measured); H/s bdry = heartwood/sapwood boundary – last heartwood ring date; std devn = standard deviation; mean sens = mean sensitivity. Sapwood estimate (95% confidence) of 9–41 used for English timbers (Miles 1997a), 8–24 for Baltic oak boards (Tyers 1998)

Sample number & type		Timber and position	Dates AD spanning	H/S bdry	Sapwood complement	No of rings	Mean width mm	Std devn mm	Mean sens mm	Felling seasons and dates/date ranges (AD)
WT59A	c	Firring piece to tiebeam T9	1386–1465			80	1.38	0.36	0.197	
B1	c	ditto	1374–1436			63	1.41	0.47	0.214	
B2	c	ditto	1439–1486	1467	19	48	1.38	0.23	0.140	
*WT59		Mean of WT59A + WT59B1 + WT59B2	1374–1486	1467	19	113	1.42	0.38	0.179	1487–1508
*WT60	c	Tiebeam T10	1305–1470	1470	H/s	166	1.83	0.64	0.206	1479–1511
WT61A	c	East upper purlin bay 10	1399–1442			44	2.40	0.86	0.212	
B1	c	ditto	1397–1440			44	2.47	0.99	0.196	
B2	c	ditto	–			14	1.42	0.30	0.129	
*WT61		Mean of WT61A + WT61B1	1397–1442			46	2.45	0.92	0.194	After 1461
*WT62	c	Ridge beam bay 10	1383–1476	1464	12	94	2.08	0.81	0.207	1477–1505
*WT63	c	Tiebeam T 11	1321–1470	1470	H/s	150	1.65	0.55	0.206	1479–1511

East Chamber Roof

Sample number & type		Timber and position	Dates AD spanning	H/S bdry	Sapwood complement	No of rings	Mean width mm	Std devn mm	Mean sens mm	Felling seasons and dates/date ranges (AD)
*WT64	c	3rd joist from north, west end of bay 1	1367–1467	1467	H/s	101	1.68	0.73	0.198	1476–1508
WT65	c	E lower purlin bay 2	1304–1457	1457	H/s	154	1.72	0.69	0.221	(1485–1501)
WT66	c	E upper purlin 3rd bay from N, East Chamber	1306–1484	1462	22	179	1.59	0.58	0.223	(1485–1501)
*WT67	c	1st rafter from N, 3rd bay from N, E Chamber	1380–1468	1468	H/s	89	1.48	0.30	0.169	1477–1509
*WT68	c	W lower purlin bay 3	1356–1467	1463	4	112	1.81	0.70	0.183	1472–1504
*WT69	c	Tiebeam T3	1350–1470	1470	H/s	121	1.84	0.51	0.227	1479–1511
WT70	c	Ridge beam bay 4	1320–1478	1472	6	159	1.55	0.56	0.227	(1486–1507)
WT71A1	c	Tiebeam T4				13	2.07	0.48	0.226	
A2	c	ditto	1326–1454	1449	5	129	1.27	0.40	0.212	
A3	c	ditto	1453–1469	1452	17	17	0.86	0.17	0.205	
*WT71		Mean of WT71A2 + WT71A3	1326–1469	1451	18	144	1.22	0.40	0.212	1470–92
*WT72	c	Tiebeam T5	1260–1469	1467	2	210	1.44	0.77	0.216	1476–1508

Chapel Roof

Sample number & type		Timber and position	Dates AD spanning	H/S bdry	Sapwood complement	No of rings	Mean width mm	Std devn mm	Mean sens mm	Felling seasons and dates/date ranges (AD)
WT73A	c	Tiebeam T 1 (East Chamber T6)	1275–1483	1473	10	209	1.53	0.47	0.191	
B	c	ditto	1473–1489		17$\frac{1}{4}$C	17	1.45	0.40	0.224	
C	c	ditto	1473–1489	1474	15$\frac{1}{4}$C	17	1.49	0.47	0.229	
*WT73		Mean of WT73A + WT73B + WT73C	1275–1489	1474	15$\frac{1}{4}$C	215	1.54	0.47	0.191	Spring 1490
WT74A	c	Tiebeam T 11	1301–1467			167	1.35	0.41	0.201	
B	c	ditto	1403–1479	1466	13	77	1.13	0.25	0.193	
C	c	ditto	1470–1488		19$\frac{1}{4}$C	19	1.24	0.19	0.185	
*WT74		Mean of WT74A + WT74B + WT74C	1301–1488	1466	22$\frac{1}{4}$C	188	1.32	0.41	0.202	Spring 1489
WT75	c	Ridge beam bay 2	1303–1485	1469	16	183	1.24	0.66	0.207	(1486–1507)
WT76A	c	Tiebeam T III	1361–1476	1473	3	116	1.28	0.38	0.195	
B	c	ditto	1352–1488	1473	15 + (12C NM)	137	1.41	0.43	0.193	
C	c	ditto			+ 9$\frac{1}{4}$C	9	1.65	0.23	0.181	
*WT76		Mean of WT76A + WT76B	1352–1488	1473	15	137	1.37	0.41	0.186	1489–90
*WT77	c	Ridge beam bay 3	1349–1472	1469	3	124	1.61	0.57	0.212	1478–1510
WT78A1	c	Tiebeam T IIII	1297–1368			72	2.06	0.95	0.214	
A2	c	ditto	1370–1458			89	1.07	0.36	0.217	
B1	c	ditto	1323–1392			70	1.51	0.41	0.228	
B2	c	ditto	1407–1483	1469	14	77	0.93	0.26	0.208	
*WT78		Mean of WT78A1 + B2 + WT78B1 + B2	1297–1483	1469	14	187	1.47	0.81	0.207	1484–1510
*WT79	c	West upper wall-plate bay 4	1370–1489	1457	32C	120	1.72	0.67	0.167	Winter 1489/90
WT80	c	West lower wall-plate bay 4			2	95	2.53	1.44	0.177	
WT81	c	Post east end of T IIII over apse end	1270–1461	1461	H/s	192	2.03	0.83	0.201	(1486–1507)

Key: * = sample included in site-masters; c = core; s = section; mc = micro-core; p = photo; $\frac{1}{4}$C, $\frac{1}{2}$C, C = bark edge present, partial or complete ring: $\frac{1}{4}$C = spring (ring not measured), $\frac{1}{2}$C = summer/autumn, or C = winter felling (ring measured); H/s bdry = heartwood/sapwood boundary – last heartwood ring date; std devn = standard deviation; mean sens = mean sensitivity. Sapwood estimate (95% confidence) of 9–41 used for English timbers (Miles 1997a), 8–24 for Baltic oak boards (Tyers 1998)

Sample number & type		Timber and position	Dates AD spanning	H/s bdry	Sapwood complement	No of rings	Mean width mm	Std devn mm	Mean sens mm	Felling seasons and dates/date ranges (AD)
WT82	c	Wall-plate/beam over apse end	–		H/s	96	1.99	0.69	0.189	
*WT83	c	10th joist from north end of apse end	1358–1489	1467	22¼C	132	1.40	0.43	0.208	Spring 1490
*WT84	c	West centre beam over apse end	1293–1472	1466	6	180	1.51	1.10	0.204	1476–1507

Floor Boards, Second Floor

Sample number & type		Timber and position	Dates AD spanning	H/s bdry	Sapwood complement	No of rings	Mean width mm	Std devn mm	Mean sens mm	Felling seasons and dates/date ranges (AD)
WT85A	s	Floorboard over spine wall 2nd floor IV-47	1336–1405			70	1.18	0.45	0.252	
B	s	ditto	1340–1406			67	1.06	0.33	0.210	
C	s	ditto	1353–1419			67	1.18	0.68	0.217	
D	s	ditto	1361–1472	1462	10	112	0.99	0.34	0.167	
WT85		Mean of WT85A + WT85B + WT85C + WT85D	1336–1472	1462	10	137	1.03	0.35	0.190	(1486–1507)
WT86	c	Floorboard over spine wall 2nd floor IV-47	1322–1425			104	1.22	0.42	0.203	(1486–1507)
*WT87	c	Floorboard over spine wall 2nd floor IV-55	1347–1464	1464	H/s	118	0.90	0.23	0.209	(1473–1505)
WT88A	c	Floorboard over spine wall 2nd floor V-64	1415–1485	1469	16	71	1.37	0.39	0.159	
B	c	ditto	1430–1487	1470	17¼C	58	1.29	0.36	0.162	
*WT88		Mean of WT88A + WT88B	1415–1487	1470	17¼C	73	1.37	0.37	0.161	Spring 1488
*WT4955		Mean of WT49 + WT55	1291–1479	1462 Avg H/S bdy		189	1.74	0.62	0.188	1480–1503
*WT656		Mean of WT65 + WT66	1304–1484	1460 Avg H/S bdy		181	1.67	0.61	0.209	1485–1501
*WT7086		Mean of WT70 + WT75 + WT81 + WT85 + WT86	1303–1485	1461 Avg H/S bdy		183	1.35	0.63	0.196	1486–1509

First Floor East Chamber posts (Re-set)

Sample number & type		Timber and position	Dates AD spanning	H/s bdry	Sapwood complement	No of rings	Mean width mm	Std devn mm	Mean sens mm	Felling seasons and dates/date ranges (AD)
*WT89	c	1st post from N, East arcade	1357–1448			92	2.74	1.01	0.225	After 1457
*WT90	c	2nd post from N, West arcade	1328–1407			80	2.68	0.67	0.200	After 1416
★=WHITOWR5		Site Master	1260–1489			230	1.78	0.60	0.153	

Henry VIII Turret Repairs
Flamsteed Tower Roof

Sample number & type		Timber and position	Dates AD spanning	H/s bdry	Sapwood complement	No of rings	Mean width mm	Std devn mm	Mean sens mm	Felling seasons and dates/date ranges (AD)
*WT91	c	Lower rib	1370–1505	1505	H/s	136	1.05	0.53	0.195	1514–1546
WT92A	c	Ogee brace	1457–1530	1515	16	74	1.65	0.37	0.190	
B	c	ditto	1519–1531		13C	13	1.42	0.30	0.246	
*WT92		Mean of WT92A + WT92B	1457–1531	1515	17C	75	1.65	0.36	0.194	Winter 1531/2
*WT93	c	Ogee brace	1421–1504	1503	1	84	1.50	0.92	0.194	1512–1544
*WT94	c	Upper rib	1415–1532	1509	23¼C	118	1.35	0.40	0.160	Spring 1533
*WT95	c	Upper rib	1423–1531	1510	21¼C	109	1.06	0.23	0.180	Spring 1532
*WT96	c	Ogee brace	1461–1528	1502	26	68	1.85	0.64	0.199	1529–43

South-East Turret Upper Floor Replacement

Sample number & type		Timber and position	Dates AD spanning	H/s bdry	Sapwood complement	No of rings	Mean width mm	Std devn mm	Mean sens mm	Felling seasons and dates/date ranges (AD)
WT97A	c	2nd joist from N, top floor frame	1409–1495	1495	H/s	87	1.34	0.95	0.213	
B	c	ditto	1424–1493	1493	H/s	70	1.09	0.48	0.166	
*WT97		Mean of WT97A + WT97B	1409–1495	1494	1	87	1.38	0.95	0.197	1503–1535
*WT98	c	3rd joist from N, top floor frame	1407–1508			102	2.05	1.80	0.196	After 1515
WT99A1	c	4th joist from N, top floor frame	2–26 (Relative dates)			25	2.83	0.71	0.198	
B1	c	ditto	1–25			25	3.11	0.66	0.202	
WT99AB1		Mean of WT39A1 + WT39B1	1–26			26	2.98	0.65	0.203	
WT99A2	c	4th joist from N, top floor frame	3–42			40	2.98	1.07	0.275	
B2	c	ditto	1–44			44	2.86	1.09	0.298	
WT99AB2		Mean of WT39A2 + WT39B2	1–44			44	2.91	1.06	0.289	

Key: * = sample included in site-masters; c = core; s = section; mc = micro-core; p = photo; ¼C, ½C, C = bark edge present, partial or complete ring: ¼C = spring (ring not measured), ½C = summer/autumn, or C = winter felling (ring measured); H/s bdry = heartwood/sapwood boundary – last heartwood ring date; std devn = standard deviation; mean sens = mean sensitivity. Sapwood estimate (95% confidence) of 9–41 used for English timbers (Miles 1997a), 8–24 for Baltic oak boards (Tyers 1998)

Sample number & type		Timber and position H/S	Dates AD spanning	H/S bdry	Sapwood complement	No of rings	Mean width mm	Std devn mm	Mean sens mm	Felling seasons and dates/date ranges (AD)
South-West Turret Top Floor Joists										
WT100	c	Top floor joist 1st from N	1–60 (Relative dates)	H/S		60	1.59	0.54	0.173	
WT101A	c	Top floor joist 2nd from N	–		2	37	1.91	0.67	0.234	
B	c	ditto	–		1	33	2.75	0.87	0.242	
C	c	ditto	–		3	45	1.51	0.64	0.248	
WT101		Mean of WT102A + WT102B + WT102C	21–65			45	2.04	0.61	0.195	
WT102	c	Top floor joist 3rd from N	9–56		H/S	48	1.88	0.54	0.159	
WT103	c	Top floor joist 4th from N	10–65		H/S	56	1.76	0.81	0.221	
WT104	c	Top floor joist 5th from N	3–61		H/S	59	2.32	0.60	0.182	
WT1004		Mean of WT100–WT104	1–65			65	1.93	0.54	0.139	
South-East Turret Main Roof Level Floor Frame										
*WT105	c	East floor beam, main roof level	1411–1513	1513	H/S	103	1.74	0.69	0.229	1522–1554
*WT106	c	South joist, main roof level	1449–1531	1506	25¼C	83	1.61	0.64	0.260	Spring 1532
★=WHITOWR6 Site Master			1370–1532			163	1.62	0.68	0.156	
Elizabeth I Alterations										
First Floor East Chamber posts										
*WT107	c	6th post from N, West arcade	1483–1565	1545	20C	83	2.28	1.14	0.295	Winter 1565/6
James I Alterations										
Ground Floor West Chamber Posts and Beams										
*WT108	c	1st post from N, East arcade	1497–1578			82	1.75	0.56	0.229	After 1587
*WT109	c	2nd post from N, East arcade	1526–1601	1582	19½C	82	2.45	1.04	0.203	Summer 1602
*WT110	c	E arcade beam 3rd bay from N,	1491–1591	1583	8	101	2.24	0.65	0.227	1592–1624
WT111A	c	Floor beam W Chamber GF between 6/7p	1495–1591	1591	H/S	97	1.80	0.59	0.239	
B	c	ditto	1493–1549			57	0.90	0.24	0.212	
C	c	ditto	1493–1587	1585	2	95	1.38	0.48	0.200	
*WT111		Mean of WT111A + WT111B + WT111C	1493–1591	1588	3	99	1.45	0.36	0.203	1597–1629
*WT112	c	3rd post W arcade w Chamber GF	1521–1600	1588	12	80	2.18	0.77	0.229	160–129
*WT113	c	5th post W arcade w Chamber GF	1504–1602	1583	19C	99	2.18	0.77	0.231	Winter 1602/3
WT114	c	1st joist between posts 3 & 4 W arcade	–		10¼C	47	2.59	1.00	0.221	
WT115	c	4th joist between posts 3 & 4 W arcade	–		14C	31	2.87	0.84	0.175	
*WT116	c	9th post W arcade W Chamber GF	1474–1602	1583	19?C	129	1.53	1.19	0.208	?Winter 1602/3
First Floor West Chamber Posts and Ceiling										
*WT117	c	2nd post from N, West arcade	1516–1602	1584	18C	87	1.69	0.54	0.187	Winter 1602/3
*WT118	c	4th post from N, East arcade	1463–1601	1587	14½C	139	2.00	0.50	0.155	Summer/ autumn 1602
*WT119	c	5th post from N, West arcade	1518–1602	1577	25C	85	1.73	0.63	0.196	Winter 1602/3
WT120	c	6th post from N, West arcade	–		21C	85	1.58	1.22	0.220	

Key: * = sample included in site-masters; c = core; s = section; mc = micro-core; p = photo; ¼C, ½C, C = bark edge present, partial or complete ring: ¼C = spring (ring not measured), ½C = summer/autumn, or C = winter felling (ring measured); H/S bdry = heartwood/sapwood boundary – last heartwood ring date; std devn = standard deviation; mean sens = mean sensitivity. Sapwood estimate (95% confidence) of 9–41 used for English timbers (Miles 1997a), 8–24 for Baltic oak boards (Tyers 1998)

Sample number & type		Timber and position	Dates AD spanning	H/s bdry	Sapwood complement	No of rings	Mean width mm	Std devn mm	Mean sens mm	Felling seasons and dates/date ranges (AD)
*WT121	c	2nd joist from N, West side	1556–1602	1591	11¼C	47	4.42	1.42	0.185	Spring 1603
*WT122	c	3rd joist from N, West side	1520–1602	1591	11C	83	2.11	0.75	0.191	Winter 1602/3
WT123	c	6th joist from N, West side	–		20¼C	164	0.98	0.85	0.221	
WT124A	c	10th joist from N, West side	1480–1594	1578	16	115	1.40	0.30	0.168	
B	c	ditto	1567–1602	1580	22C	36	1.85	0.33	0.139	
*WT124		Mean of WT124A + WT124B	1480–1602	1579	23C	123	1.47	0.33	0.162	Winter 1602/3
*WT125	c	28th joist from N, West side	1472–1602	1580	22¼C	131	1.85	0.82	0.183	Spring 1603
WT126A	c	33rd joist from N, centre	–			58	1.76	0.73	0.227	
B	c	ditto	–		44C	82	0.75	0.42	0.213	
*WT127	c	Main beam, West arcade to S of 6th post	1489–1602	1581	21C	114	1.56	0.38	0.184	Winter 1602/3

South-West Turret Diagonal Ties

*WT128	c	SE–NW diag. beam at head of stairs	1522–1616	1600	16C	95	1.95	0.64	0.232	Winter 1616/7
WT129A	c	NE–SW diag. beam above top floor	1520–1611	1597	14	92	2.16	0.75	0.197	
B	c	ditto	1593–1616	1598	18	14	1.53	0.31	0.186	
*WT129		Mean of WT129A + WT129B	1520–1616	1598	18	97	2.10	0.77	0.189	1617–1639
*WT130	c	SE diag. beam above top floor	1517–1599	1598	1	83	1.64	0.44	0.207	1607–1639
★=WHITOWR7		Site Master	1463–1616			154	2.04	0.52	0.140	

George II Alterations
Insertion of Basement Vaults and Reconstruction of Chambers above

*WT131	c	Floor beam East Chamber GF	1668–1710	1710	H/S	43	2.30	0.65	0.230	1719–1751
*WT132	c	2nd post from NE arcade E Chamber GF	1645–1732	1708	24?C	88	2.34	1.16	0.266	?Winter 1732/3
WT133A	c	Joist E arcade 5th post 3rd joist E Chamber GF	–		14	59	2.09	1.13	0.227	
B	c	ditto	–		20¼C	54	2.00	1.17	0.318	
WT133		Mean of WT133A + WT133B	–		20¼C	65	2.11	1.11	0.257	
*WT134	c	Floor beam East Chamber GF	1667–1732	1713	19C	66	2.22	0.74	0.192	Winter 1732/3
WT135A	c	Floor beam East Chamber GF	1656–1690			35	3.14	0.78	0.188	
B	c	ditto	1656–1714	1714	H/S	59	2.27	0.88	0.231	
*WT135		Mean of WT135A + WT135B	1656–1714	1714	H/S	59	2.27	0.88	0.231	1723–1755
WT136A	c	4th post W arcade West Chamber GF	1668–1732	1718	14¼C	65	2.17	0.98	0.234	
B	c	ditto	1694–1732	1718	14	39	1.56	0.42	0.250	
*WT136		Mean of WT136A + WT136B	1668–1732	1718	14¼C	65	2.17	0.97	0.222	Spring 1733
*WT137	c	6th post E arcade West Chamber GF	1674–1732	1721	11C	59	2.80	0.87	0.188	Winter 1732/3
★=WHITOWR8		Site Master	1645–1732			88	2.30	0.73	0.166	

George III Repairs
South-East Turret

*WT138	c	E–W centre beam to roof	1703–1780	1761	19C	78	3.35	1.67	0.248	Winter 1780/81

Key: * = sample included in site-masters; c = core; s = section; mc = micro-core; p = photo; ¼C, ½C, C = bark edge present, partial or complete ring: ¼C = spring (ring not measured), ½C = summer/autumn, or C = winter felling (ring measured); H/s bdry = heartwood/sapwood boundary – last heartwood ring date; std devn = standard deviation; mean sens = mean sensitivity. Sapwood estimate (95% confidence) of 9–41 used for English timbers (Miles 1997a), 8–24 for Baltic oak boards (Tyers 1998)

Sample number & type		Timber and position	Dates AD spanning	H/s bdry	Sapwood complement	No of rings	Mean width mm	Std devn mm	Mean sens mm	Felling seasons and dates/date ranges (AD)
WT139A	c	West perimeter beam to roof	1696–1773	1756	17	78	2.04	0.76	0.193	
B	c	ditto	1700–1721			22	2.37	0.72	0.181	
C	c	ditto	1735–1780	1758	22¼C	46	1.28	0.64	0.239	
*WT139		Mean of WT139A + WT139B + WT139C	1696–1780	1758	22¼C	85	1.89	0.81	0.199	Spring 1781
WT140	c	North perimeter beam to roof	–		9C	27	2.41	0.59	0.214	

South-West Turret

Sample number & type		Timber and position	Dates AD spanning	H/s bdry	Sapwood complement	No of rings	Mean width mm	Std devn mm	Mean sens mm	Felling seasons and dates/date ranges (AD)
*WT141	c	S brace to centre post	1679–1778	1758	20C	100	1.32	0.83	0.216	Winter 1778/9
*WT142	c	N brace to centre post	1680–1779	1760	19C	100	1.56	0.46	0.232	Winter 1779/80

North-West Turret

Sample number & type		Timber and position	Dates AD spanning	H/s bdry	Sapwood complement	No of rings	Mean width mm	Std devn mm	Mean sens mm	Felling seasons and dates/date ranges (AD)
WT143A1	c	Top floor joist SE corner	–		1	29	1.99	0.78	0.272	
A2	c	ditto	–		31½C	31	1.13	0.43	0.180	
B1	c	ditto	–		2	15	3.19	0.63	0.128	
B2	c	ditto	–		37½C	37	1.13	0.57	0.148	
WT144A1	c	Top floor SE diagonal beam	–			48	0.97	0.61	0.212	
A2	c	ditto	–		19C	67	1.75	1.19	0.240	
WT145A	c	Axial beam, top floor frame	1722–1778	1767	11	57	2.60	0.82	0.237	
B	c	ditto	1767–1780	1766	14C	14	2.38	0.92	0.194	
*WT145		Mean of WT145A + WT145B	1722–1780	1766	14C	59	2.54	0.81	0.226	Winter 1780/81
*WT146	c	NW diagonal beam, top floor frame	1629–1776	1723	53¼C	148	1.20	0.76	0.223	Spring 1777
*WT147	c	East perimeter beam to roof	1688–1770	1756	14	83	1.42	0.58	0.241	1771–1797
WT148A	c	S brace to king post to roof	1700–1779	1762	17C	80	2.09	0.68	0.181	
B	c	ditto	1750–1779	1763	16C	30	1.88	0.41	0.207	
*WT148		Mean of WT148A + WT148B	1700–1779	1763	16C	80	2.06	0.67	0.177	Winter 1779/80
WT149	c	N inner sill beam			29¼C	96	1.42	0.97	0.335	
*WT150	c	Main N–S centre beam to roof	1694–1779	1764	15C	87	2.10	0.61	0.213	Winter 1779/80
*WT151	c	NE beam top frame	1710–1780	1760	20C	71	1.98	0.89	0.198	Winter 1780/81

Flamsteed Tower

Sample number & type		Timber and position	Dates AD spanning	H/s bdry	Sapwood complement	No of rings	Mean width mm	Std devn mm	Mean sens mm	Felling seasons and dates/date ranges (AD)
*WT152	c	Main cross-beam to roof	1690–1782	1768	14C	93	2.12	0.76	0.260	Winter 1782/3
*WT153	c	NE upper principal rib	1731–1782	1769	13¼C	52	3.08	0.74	0.137	Spring 1783
*WT154	c	SE upper principal rib	1726–1782	1764	18¼C	57	2.72	1.10	0.210	Spring 1783
*WT155	c	SW upper principal rib	1731–1782	1767	15¼C	52	2.69	0.75	0.137	Spring 1783
★=WHITOWR9		Site Master	1629–1782			154	1.99	0.58	0.178	

Key: * = sample included in site-masters; c = core; s = section; mc = micro-core; p = photo; ¼C, ½C, C = bark edge present, partial or complete ring: ¼C = spring (ring not measured), ½C = summer/autumn, or C = winter felling (ring measured); H/s bdry = heartwood/sapwood boundary – last heartwood ring date; std devn = standard deviation; mean sens = mean sensitivity. Sapwood estimate (95% confidence) of 9–41 used for English timbers (Miles 1997a), 8–24 for Baltic oak boards (Tyers 1998)

APPENDIX III

Petrography of the South Elevation

BERNARD WORSSAM AND ROBIN SANDERSON

The erection of scaffolding and the availability of photogrammetric stonework drawings of the south face of the White Tower in 1997, for the purposes of a programme of repair of the external stonework, presented a unique opportunity for recording exactly the types of stone present on this normally quite inaccessible face. As mentioned above,[1] the repairs coincided with the duration of the White Tower Recording and Research Project (WTRRP). Previously, no published description of the White Tower had been able to pay more than cursory attention to its stonework. Thus in their detailed guidebook Brown and Curnow could report of the White Tower only that 'The material of the keep was rag-stone rubble (mostly Kentish Rag), though septaria was chiefly used in the plinth; the ashlar dressings were originally Caen stone but are now Portland.'[2]

In carrying out a survey of the stonework, the writers recorded stone identifications on ten large (600 × 840 mm) photogrammetric drawings on the scale of 1.20, showing each stone in outline, which together covered the south face of the White Tower. Each drawing was coloured and provided with a key showing its types of sedimentary rock classified stratigraphically, that is, in order of geological age; an accompanying explanatory report describes the geology of the whole face.[3] Some twenty-eight different types of stone were recognised, although a few of these, including bricks and tiles as one type, were sparingly represented, having been used only for minor repairs. Many types of igneous rock were found to be present, but with a few exceptions the stones of igneous origin appeared to be reused ship's ballast cobbles or paving setts, and separate identification was not attempted. Making use of these results, computerised drawings prepared by the Historic Building Recording Unit (see figs 14, 15, 16) show the individual distributions of each type of stone.

Some findings of the survey are of unusual interest from a geological as well as an archaeological point of view, and also illustrate various points that need consideration in identifying stonework. For instance, by 'septaria' Brown and Curnow[4] would have meant large ovate nodules of a fine-grained argillaceous limestone or 'cementstone' that occur in the London Clay. They would not be unexpected in the White Tower, and while some may possibly be present on its other, as yet unsurveyed sides, there are certainly none in the south elevation. Instead, blocks of stone of ovate outline both in the plinth and scattered at higher levels proved to be of a previously unnoticed pale grey, fine-grained, calcareous glauconitic sandstone. Some of these blocks include fossil shells, among which the bivalve *Arctica morrisi*, taken together with the sandstone lithology, leaves little doubt that the stone is from the Thanet Formation (early Tertiary) of east Kent. In fact, it has only one likely source, the foreshore of the south side of the Thames estuary between Reculver and Herne Bay. Thanet Formation sands there form low cliffs, which include one or two layers composed of massive doggers of the sandstone up to about 300 mm thick; the boulder-like doggers, washed out by erosion, litter the foreshore and could have been simply loaded into flat-bottomed boats aground at low tide. The sandstone was extensively used for rubble walling in east Kent in Roman, Anglo-Saxon and later medieval times,[5] but, so far as is known, the White Tower is the only place where it has been used outside east Kent.

The survey was able to establish that the Kentish Ragstone, the predominant building stone of the White Tower, being of medium grain size, unfossiliferous and including a high proportion of chert, came from the vicinity of Maidstone, Kent. The presence of so much chert indicates the upper part of the Hythe Formation, and tends to suggest newly opened quarries, since deeper layers of the formation are free of chert.[6]

The most unexpected finding concerns the Chalk, which occurs mostly in the lowest stage of the south elevation. Although chalk has been used as a building stone in parts of south-east England and eastern Yorkshire, it is in general too soft for exterior use. The best-known varieties, Totternhoe stone from the Lower Chalk and Beer stone from the Middle Chalk, are both even-textured and free of flints, and it was therefore a surprise, on seeing the White Tower wall close-to, to find that its chalk blocks are nodular and include small flint nodules. This lithology resembles that of the lower part of the Upper Chalk (Upper Turonian to Coniacian stage) of southern England, an inference confirmed by the presence in one block of a thin-shelled fossil sea-urchin identifiable as *Sternotaxis* sp. Examination with a hand-lens revealed pinhole-sized perforations in most if not all of the blocks, some of the perforations, of lozenge-shaped outline, suggesting the mineral dolomite (calcium magnesium carbonate). Study of a thin section under a microscope confirmed that the perforations, measuring 0.15 to 0.2 mm across the long axis, could be interpreted as moulds of lost secondary rhombohedral dolomite crystals. In other words, the Chalk had once been dolomitised, and then under different ground-water conditions dedolomitised, in the process becoming much harder.

Dolomitised Chalk does not occur naturally in England, but this type of chalk, at the same stratigraphic horizon as the White Tower chalk, is widespread in northern France in the western part of the Paris basin.[7] It has been quarried and mined until recent years for use as a building stone along the Seine valley downstream from Vernon. The White Tower is the only known location for its use in England except for one instance, of salvaged French medieval architectural detail reconstructed in the early nineteenth century in Highcliffe Castle, near Christchurch, Hampshire (1830–4). The White Tower chalk was presumably imported by the Normans soon after their arrival, as a stone with which they were familiar in Normandy.

Medieval and Later Carpentry and Woodwork

JULIAN MUNBY AND DANIEL MILES

The carpentry and woodwork of the White Tower are scarcely major parts of its obvious historic interest to the public, and have in general received less attention than the masonry. Nonetheless, much is to be learned from the dating and sequence of the remaining timber features of the White Tower, and recent discoveries have played a crucial part in the research project. The scarcity of surviving medieval carpentry from castles in England and Wales is an obvious result of their being dismantled or abandoned, but it serves as an important reminder of the rarity of the Tower of London as a continuously occupied fortress that has retained many interior fittings. The surviving timber buildings, roofs, partitions, doors and portcullis machinery in the Tower are valuable examples of royal carpentry and London practice, though they have attracted relatively little attention.[1] A number of works undertaken since the mid-1990s have provided opportunities to examine the carpentry of the White Tower,[2] and a programme of tree-ring dating undertaken in 1996–7 (reported separately in Appendix II) provided a series of dates that can be compared with historical records. While the resulting dates are not in themselves surprising, that is not to say that the carpentry of the White Tower could have been easily dated without the benefit of dendrochronology, since it is generally devoid of characteristic features that might permit more precise stylistic dating.

Two contemporary investigations may be mentioned at this point, of general relevance for carpentry in the Tower of London. The extensive archaeological excavations in the west moat of the Tower have revealed the foundations of the bridge on the former western approach to the castle. These included the massive timbers of a collapsed bridge of thirteenth-century date, and the beech piles underlying the causeway that replaced the bridge.[3] A more recent opportunity was provided to examine the carpentry of the Byward Tower portcullis when it was lowered for maintenance in 2001; it was found to have some elements of post-medieval reworking of what may be the original portcullis. More recently (April 2005), the well in the basement was emptied and the base timbers subjected to dendrochronology.

THE PRIMARY NORMAN PHASE

No structural carpentry survives from the Norman White Tower, and it is largely a matter of speculation how it was floored and roofed in its earliest phases. Nonetheless, three most interesting finds of wooden components, directly related to their surrounding masonry, should be mentioned. These are: first, the wooden linings of the drawbar sockets by doorways (e.g., in the spine wall of the first floor); second, the wooden lintels of cupboard recesses on the first floor; and third, the wooden lining of the external drains in the passageway at gallery level, which survived in a form that enabled tree-ring dates to be derived from them, and these showed them to be primary features. Combined with the drawbar sockets, we can gain some clues as to what the original doors may have looked like.

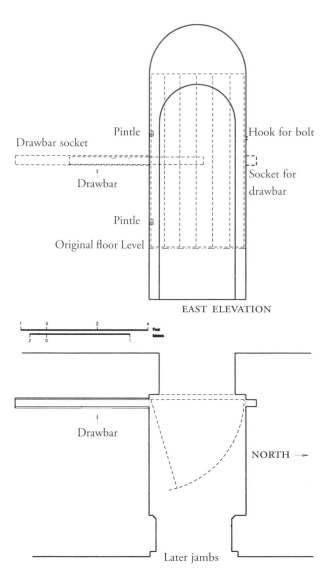

Pintle

Drawbar socket

Hook for bolt

Socket for drawbar

Drawbar

Pintle

Original floor Level

EAST ELEVATION

Drawbar

NORTH →

Later jambs

Basement Doors

In the basement, evidence remains for there having been three doors from the primary Norman phase of construction. The first is at the bottom of the great vice at the north-east corner of the east room; the second is at the west end of the short passage between the east and west rooms at the north end of the spine wall; and the third is at the south end of the east end into the apsidal basement room under the chapel crypt, although the jambs have subsequently been removed.

The door at the bottom of the great vice was replaced about 1475, but it clearly supplanted an earlier Norman door that had a semicircular head, as evidenced by the corresponding recess in the western part of the passage vault. A blocked drawbar socket in the western wall of the passage is evident, with the shallower socket on the east wall to receive the bar.

The second doorway is worth exploring in greater detail, since much of the evidence for the primary door remains. The arrangement of this door is somewhat confusing—the western passage door with the drawbar on the east side would suggest that the door was being defended from access from the west base-

ment. Could this suggest some form of original external access at this level? There is nothing obvious in the surviving masonry of the western basement or the chapel basement.

The door is set back 2 ft (600 mm) from the face of the wall, the jambs protruding 5 in. (150 mm) to form the reveals. A drawbar socket 6 ft 7 in. (2 m) deep is set in the south jamb, the bottom of which is 4 ft 1 in. (1.2 m) above the original floor level. The door would have originally measured up to 4 ft 8 in. (1.4 m) wide and 8 ft 6 in. (2.6 m) high to the spring line of the rear arch. Since the top of the arch to the stone jamb is lower than the spring line of the passage vault, the door itself would have had a square head. The fact that the drawbar socket lining is set 3 in. (75 mm) from the back of the reveal would suggest that this was the thickness of the original door. Truncated remains for two pintles on the south jamb show that it was hung on that side, opening to the east. The two pintles are 4 ft 4 in. (132 cm) apart, with the bottom pintle set 1 ft 7 in. (48 cm) above the original floor level. On the north jamb there is a hole to receive a bolt set 5 ft 4 in. (163 cm) above the original floor level (fig. 227).

The drawbar socket to this door was originally lined with oak, the top board of which still remains *in situ*. This is the only surviving piece of original Norman timberwork on this level of the White Tower. To allow the drawbar to slide smoothly in and out of its socket in the rubble wall fill, a wooden lining was constructed in which it was housed. This took the form of a box made up of four riven-oak boards averaging between ¾ and 1 in. thick that were finished smooth with a plane. The bottom board was set between the side boards, and the top board sat over those, and all were nailed together. The drawbar would have measured slightly less than 4 in. (100 mm) thick and up to 5½ in. (140 mm) high, and it would have to have been placed in the box, and the whole assemblage placed in position, as the walls were being raised, but before they were covered over by subsequent courses (fig. 228). These, therefore, would have

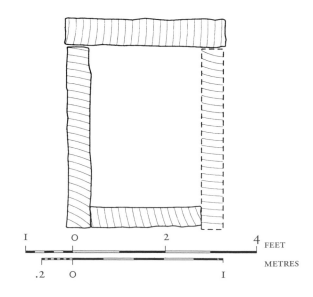

I   O   2   4   FEET

METRES

.2   O   I

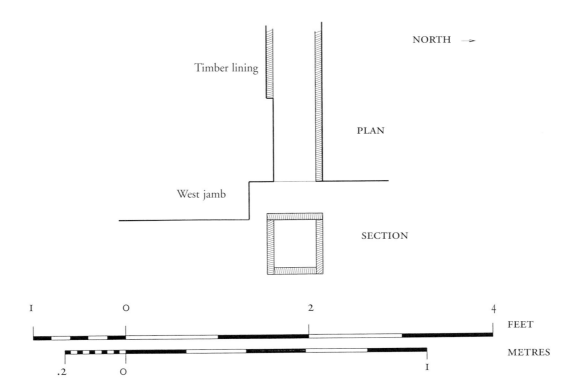

Timber lining

West jamb

NORTH →

PLAN

SECTION

I   0   2   4

FEET

METRES

.2   0   I

been the earliest pieces of timber to be built into the White Tower, in the first season or two of construction, thought to have begun in the 1070s. One of the fragments from the east side of the box had a last measured ring date of 1059; without any sapwood only a *terminus post quem* of after 1068 can be given, which suggests that little heartwood along with the sapwood had been removed during conversion.

Entrance-Floor Doors and Drawbars

On the entrance floor, there remain two doorways that retain their timber-lined drawbar sockets, one in the spine wall cross-passage and the other at the main south entrance. The first is at the western end of the southern cross-passage between the east and west rooms. The drawbar socket was rediscovered during the refitting of the White Tower in 1996–7, having been plastered over with mid-twentieth-century hard cement mortar. Once the blocking was removed, the timber lining was found to be in a perfect state of preservation (fig. 229). It is of the same size and construction as the one described in the basement spine wall, but extends slightly deeper into the wall to a depth of 6 ft 10½ in. (2.1 m). This drawbar was set in the north side of the spine wall, but its receiving socket on the south jamb is missing due to the replacement of some of the masonry. The door was hung on two pintles on the north side of the passage and opened to the east. The hinge bands were set at 2 ft 2 in. and 7 ft 2 in. (660–218 mm) above floor level, and the bottom of the drawbar is 4 ft 10 in. (1.5 m) above floor level. The door would have measured up to 4 ft 9 in. (1.5 m) wide and just over 9 ft (2.8 m) high with a flat head. The west side of the jambs have had a square reveal of 5 in. (125 mm) subsequently cut into the jambs. Evi-

dence for a similar door exists at the north end of the spine wall, although the jambs have been cut back and the drawbar sockets blocked up.

Impressions of the original Norman shuttering boards are clearly evident in the two cross-passages in the spine wall. These measured ½ in. (12 mm) in thickness, 3 to 5 in. (75–125 mm) in width and approximately 4 ft (1.2 m) in length. Two fragments of boards still survive over the southern cross-passage, trapped between the stonework over the jambs and the passage vault.

At the south entrance, there remain two drawbar sockets, 11 ft 6 in. (3.5 m) deep. The lower one is 2 ft 6 in. (760 mm) above floor level and is in the west jamb, with the upper socket built in the east jamb. The original drawbar would have measured 5½ in. (140 mm) wide and 6½ in. (165 mm) high, while the lining boxes were constructed in a similar method to the ones in the internal spine wall, with the exception of the side boards, most of which are cut back about 11 in. (280 mm) from the front; the stonework is similarly cut out to permit the stone to form the actual side jambs of the opening (see fig. 229). What is unusual is that the bottom opening has the stone reveal on the south side only, while the north side has the timber board extending all the way to the wall face, as do the top and bottom boards. Just why the boxes should vary slightly may suggest that coordination between the carpenters and the stone masons was not as good as it should have been, and the facing ashlar had already been laid before the boxes were constructed and the mass walling built around them. The upper pocket on the east side has been blocked with some mortared stones at a depth of 2 ft (600 mm), but the lower pocket on the west was open, and it was possible to remove some fragments of timber still lying in the back of the socket. Among the fragments was a fourteenth-century spearhead, the oldest piece of weaponry actually to be related to the Tower of London.[4] The principal south entrance retains evidence for the thickness of the original doors by comparing the offsets between the edge of the drawbar socket lining and the inside edge of the jamb, which is 3¼ in. (83 mm). Assuming that the greater depth of the socket boxes necessitated a looser fit around the drawbar, it is reasonable to conclude that the main south doors would have measured about 3½ in. (89 mm) in thickness, which is about ½ in. (13 mm) thicker than the internal doors. The overall width of the pair of doors would have been 8 ft 7 in. (2.6 mm), and the total height would have been no more than 12 ft 6 in. (3.8 m) due to the curvature of the vault. It is not known how the tympanum over the doors was configured, for the jambs do not continue in an arch beneath the vault, but instead stop where they intersect it. There is no obvious blocking for a removed timber lintel or beam.

Six fragments of timber recovered from the south entrance socket linings and four cores extracted from the spine-wall linings at the same level could all be dated. One of the cores from the west board in the spine-wall box retained a heartwood/sapwood boundary, thus giving a felling date range of 1049–81, suggesting that construction had advanced quickly to this level.

Norman Doors

Although no Norman doors survive, it is possible to address the question of what they might have looked like. Using the evidence of the offsets from the drawbar sockets, we have been able to determine that the internal doors through the spine wall were about 3 in. (75 mm) thick, whilst the south entrance doors were probably slightly thicker, at least 3½ in. The primary outstanding question is whether the doors consisted of a single covering of planks or boards on a framework, or were built of two or three layers of boards. Only a few English doors survive that are broadly contemporary – the slightly earlier Pyx door from Westminster Abbey (1031–63),[5] the north door at Hadstock in Essex (circa 1066), the Gundulf door at Rochester Cathedral (1075–1108), Durham Cathedral (1099–1134) and the doors at Kempley in Gloucestershire (1114–44).[6] All five of these doors consist of a single layer of boards or planks between 1¼ in. (32 mm) and 2 in. (50 mm) in thickness. The Westminster Abbey example is held together simply by the hinge bands, as possibly might have been the case at Rochester. The Hadstock and Durham doors have rounded ledgers on the back, as that at Kempley may have done. Slightly later are the main gates from Chepstow Castle (1159–89), which consisted of planks

2¼ in. (57 mm) thick on a lattice of 2½ in. (64 mm) thick diagonally set ledges.[7] This is a useful example in that both the gates and the drawbar sockets remain to allow a comparison to be made. The hanging styles at Chepstow measure 5 in. (125 mm) in thickness, whilst the offsets from the inner face of the drawbar socket is 4 in. (100 mm) back from the face of the jamb. It is not obvious whether there was a timber lining to the sockets at Chepstow, but demonstrates that the doors would not be *less* than the distance from the jambs to the drawbar socket reveal.

It is therefore likely that the 3½ in. measurement of the set-back of the socket from the edge of the reveal of the south doors at the White Tower indicates that the doors themselves were unlikely to vary much either side of 4 in. in thickness, with a drawbar of about 5 in. in thickness. Since hanging styles of 4 in. would not really be sufficient for doors of this size, however, a composite door built up of a number of planks is more likely. The best, and most local, parallel would be the basement door of *circa* 1350, where three layers of boards were used. Boarded doors of two layers used externally have a habit of warping when exposed to the weather, but those of three layers balance well any tendency for the timber to warp in relation to moisture and heat. It is likely, therefore, that the door was built up of three layers of boards at least 1¼ in. thick, with the centre boards running horizontally. Such a composite door would have immense strength; indeed, the existing chapel basement door of *circa* 1350 survived a bomb blast set off not more than 25 ft (7.6 m) away in 1974 with hardly a scratch.

The boards used in the doors would have been of good-quality oak, as found in the timber linings to the drawbar socket linings. They would have been riven, and would probably have finished between 6 and 8 in. (150–200 mm) in width. Certainly, edge dowels or pegs would have been used to joint the edges of the boards together, and they may have been rebated, as were all the early examples quoted. Free or slip tenons may also have been used with the iron hinge bands and other decorative ironwork to keep the boards together. The doors would have been manufactured to a high degree of precision, befitting a royal building of the highest importance.

As for the internal doors for which we have evidence, the offset from the reveal to the edge of the drawbar socket lining of 2¾ to 3 in. (70–75 mm) would suggest a door leaf of 3 to 3¼ in. (75–83 mm) in thickness, allowing for a drawbar up to 4 in. (100 mm) in thickness. Again, given the defensive nature of the building, it is likely that these doors would have resembled the door of the chapel basement with a solid 3 in. (75 mm) door. It is possible that the original Norman doors were used as a pattern when the chapel basement door was constructed about 1350.

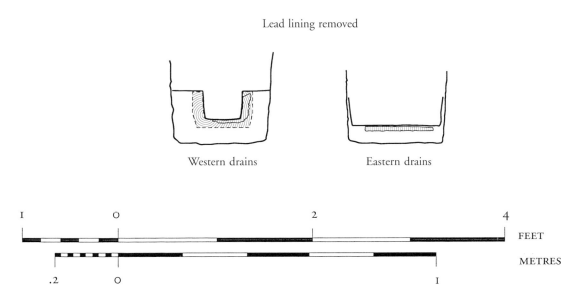

Lead lining removed

Western drains   Eastern drains

1   0   2   4

FEET

METRES

.2   0   1

230 and 231 Cross-section and photograph of timber former for lead drain under west passage.

First Floor

On the first floor is a series of recesses in the window embrasures – four in the southern two alcoves in the east wall and four in the northern two alcoves in the west wall. They were perhaps all cupboards, and are of the primary construction; they are variously just above (east room) or below (west room) the level of the building break. These recesses are noticeably variable both in size and in height above the floor. Four have widths of 21 in. (530 mm), with the other four varying between 22 and 27 in. (560–690 mm). Heights vary between 22 and 29 in. (560–740 mm), and depths between 15 and 20 in. (390–510 mm). All the recesses have timber planks that serve as lintels on which the mass masonry was constructed (see fig. 101). These planks are tangentially converted, but were initially converted through splitting and hewing. Conversely, several planks on the eastern niches are radially split, and at least two planks have redundant peg holes, suggesting reuse (see fig. 21). They average 1½ and 2¾ in. (38–70 mm) in thickness and vary in width between 7 and 15½ in. (180–390 mm). Two lintels in the second embrasure from the north on the west side have rebates for a missing cupboard front. Most of the lintels bear between 2½ and 7 in. (63–78 mm) on either side. Two of these lintels with clear heartwood/sapwood boundaries have been dated, one from the west side to 1055–87, another from the east to 1072–1104.

Second-Floor Wall Drains

The final areas of Norman woodwork to be studied are the timber formers or gutter liners found in the drains under the second-floor mural passages that were observed during the replacement of the floor in 1996.[8]

Western Mural Passage

A series of drains was found crossing under the western passage, some of them with remnants of timber and lead lining. A 2 ft (600 mm) section to

Drain 4 under the west passage was discovered relatively intact, although relatively friable (figs 230, 231). The single piece of wood had been hollowed out to form the drain, 6½ in. (165 mm) wide and 2½ in. (65 mm) high, inside a wider and deeper channel in the stonework. Another was found in Drain 8 on the west side, but was broken up into two dozen small fragments, with a width of ½ in. (13 mm). Both of these seem to be rather small to cope with large amounts of water resulting from a heavy downpour, but the single lead covering that still survives in Drain 3 does extend significantly wider on either side, suggesting that it could cope with excessive rainfall. A number of the fragments from Drain 8 were dated, with a latest ring of 1005. Since there was no heartwood/sapwood boundary, one could say only that it was felled some time after 1014, and was obviously significantly later.

Eastern Mural Passage

Two more fragments were located under the eastern mural passage, quite different in form and date. These were from a single, fractured, board, ½ in. thick and about 9 in. wide (13 by 225 mm), found lying on the bottom of the gutter channel. The outermost ring produced a felling date or *terminus post quem* of after 1101. Again, there was no evidence of a heartwood/sapwood boundary, and whilst fifty years or so might have been lost in the conversion as with the western drains, boards generally tended to have only the minimal number of rings removed during conversion, suggesting a felling date nearer to 1101.

The Norman Roof of the White Tower

With the exception of the chapel, it is now clear that the White Tower was at first roofed at gallery level, although little physical evidence survives for the form of seating that this roof would have had in the walls.[9] There is some evidence in the spine wall for beams for a low-pitched roof dropping to the east over the chapel vaults, but no timber remains of the Norman roof.

The Norman Well

One other feature has the potential to help with dating the Norman phase. In the south-east corner of the west basement room is a circular stone-lined well 40 ft 6 in. deep below present floor level, and measuring internally 5 ft 6 in. in diameter at the bottom and 5 ft 4 in. at the top. The stonework is of diagonally tooled Caen stone, laid in courses varying between 6 and 8 in. (150–200 mm) high and 9 in. (225 mm) thick. The mortar used in the construction of the stone lining is a coarse, gritty light mortar, not dissimilar from that used in the second (upper level) construction phase of the White Tower, dated to after *circa* 1090.[10] The lining is built on a beech timber template, which provided a tree-ring date of some time after 1082, again supporting the second primary phase construction. The shaft passes through gravels down to London Clay. Currently, there is some 28 ft (8.5 m) of water in the well below present floor level (8.4 m OSBD).

The stonework of the well lining sits on a timber base or template that is a fundamental part of the construction process. In sinking a well that is not through a solid substrate such as chalk, the stone or brick lining is constructed at ground level in a shallow excavation in which is laid a timber template or curb. After constructing the lining to a height corresponding to at least the diameter of the well, the earth is dug out evenly from inside the well lining, undermining the timber curb, and thus allowing the entire well lining to settle down into the shaft being excavated. At the White Tower, a pair of cross-timbers measuring 2 by 2½ in. (50 by 65 mm) in cross-section, the broken ends of which are still *in situ*, was built into the stone lining approximately 4 ft (1.2 m) above the timber template. This presumably provided additional temporary support to the incomplete cylinder of stone as it started to descend as the shaft is undermined. As the lining sinks, more courses of stone are constructed on the top at ground level, and every seven or eight courses five or six substantial putlogs 4 to 6 in. (100–150 mm) wide by 7 in. (175 mm) high were built into the stonework, which formed temporary stages to access the bottom of the shaft during excavation. The third course of putlogs from the top consisted of only five timbers, suggesting that the radial putlog timbers were supported on a centre post. Once the water level is reached, the digging process became much more difficult, but no doubt the water was bailed out as much as possible to enable a greater depth to be reached. Once the final depth had been attained and the masonry lining settled to its final position, the stonework would be completed at ground level, and the timber putlogs removed.

Generally, the timber curbs or templates to the well bottoms were of four or more thick timbers jointed together, following the curve of the well lining. Examples recently excavated include the early medieval well at Merton College, Oxford, and a seventeenth-century example at Brockton Farm at Charing in Kent; but the arrangement found at the bottom of the White Tower well is unlike anything previously excavated.[11] Here the curb was constructed of beech (*Fagus sylvatica*), a material generally employed for underwater works, and used as piles under one of the demolished western defences dating to 1241. Beech is not often used above ground since it is prone to beetle attack. Under water, it is even less satisfactory, in that it becomes very weak when submerged for long periods, possibly resulting in structural collapse. The use of beech in structural carpentry seems to have become popular during the Norman period, after which it fell out of favour, most probably due to its poor performance under water.[12] The curb is composed of a series of nine planks varying in width between 8½ and 10¾ in. (215–75 mm), and between 1¼ and 2½ in. (32–65 mm) in thickness. The planks were riven from a large tree of at least 30 in. (750 mm) diameter and finished square-edged. Unusually, the planks were laid parallel running north–south in a single layer, with only a few fastened together by square beech edge-pegs or dowels. What is unusual about this arrangement is the apparent lack of strength in an east–west direction. Here the short lengths of plank are simply butted together, and on at least one dislocated segment there is absolutely no evidence for any edge pegging, or any peg holes on the face suggesting any connections to a second layer of cross-planking. Without any other form of support, the short lengths of plank under the north and south ends of the well would simply fall out.

Unfortunately, only four planks remain *in situ*, with a short length of a fifth plank recovered directly below its original position (fig. 239). Three other sections of plank were recovered from the mud in the centre of the well. The well had been subsequently deepened by about 2 ft, necessitating the shoring up of the curb first by four softwood pit props measuring 4¼ by 5 in. (108 by 126 mm), and secondly by the insertion between these of three courses of reused dressed stonework. Two of these are in the form of narrow piers, allowing the partial underside of the four *in situ* planks to be inspected at least by feel.

So how did the template work whilst the well was being dug? The most likely possibility is that the planks originally extended right across the bottom of the well, with only a small access opening in the centre through which the earth was excavated. If this were so, then there could have been additional east–west planks laid over the surviving north–south planks as

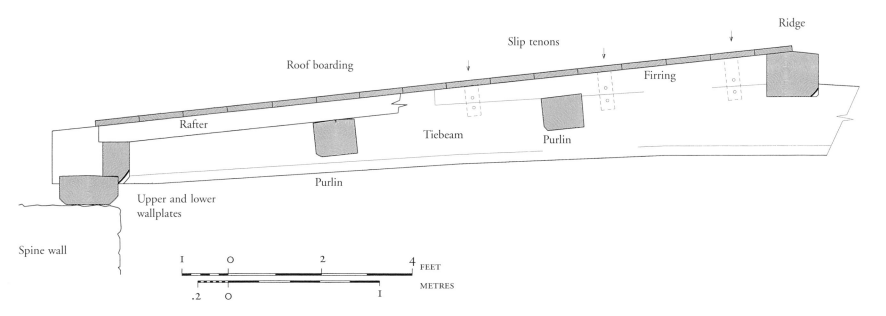

Labels on figure: Ridge, Slip tenons, Roof boarding, Firring, Rafter, Tiebeam, Purlin, Purlin, Upper and lower wallplates, Spine wall

Scale: 1, 0, 2, 4 FEET; METRES; .2, 0, 1

232 Section of west half of typical chapel roof truss

far as the inside of the stone lining. Once the bottom was reached, all the upper-level timberwork from within the shaft lining was removed. The bottom planks would have been cut back to the line of the inside face of the stone lining. Examination of the surviving *ex situ* planks would support this hypothesis in that the outer face of the planks is neatly cut following the line of the outside of the well lining, whereas the internal line is crudely chopped, not unreasonable considering that it would have had to be cut under water. This would have left the short ends of the planks in place, clamped between the stonework of the well above and the London Clay below. It was only on the subsequent deepening of the well by a couple of feet that the shorter planks became undermined and fell down into the mud.

The well was filled up in 1734 to keep the damp from affecting barrels of saltpetre stored in the basement,[13] but was re-excavated in the early twentieth century. When the well was last pumped dry in April 2005 it was found to contain half a dozen cannonballs, bottles, a pair of old boots complete with socks and wheelbarrows full of coppers, none of the coins dating from before about 1900.

LATER MEDIEVAL FLOORS AND ROOF

The Fifteenth Century

Undoubtedly, the most outstanding features of the surviving White Tower carpentry are the low-pitched late medieval roofs. Covering almost a quarter of an acre (almost 1,000 sq. m), the main roofs are the largest surviving examples of medieval carpentry in the Tower. The roofs are divided into three principal sections. One spans the great west room, which covers the entire western half of the building and measures internally about 96 by 41 ft (29.3 by 12.5 m). Another covers the smaller east room, measuring internally 65 by 30.5 ft (19.8 by 9.3 m), and then extending a further

40 ft (12.2 m) southwards to cover the chapel vaults, with an eastern monopitch extension of 25 ft (7.6 m) over the eastern apse. The roofs all run north–south with parapet gutters over the east and west mural passages, and a central gutter supported by the Norman spine wall.

Roofs of this sort were designed for a covering of lead sheets, and are typically of late medieval design, usually found in fifteenth- or sixteenth-century church roofs as described by Howard and Crossley,[14] although an example dating to 1247 has been recorded in Shropshire at Great Oxenbold, Monkhopton.[15] Dendrochronology has shown that all three of the White Tower roofs were constructed using trees felled between spring 1489 and spring 1490, suggesting a construction date of 1490.

Here the roofs employ an enlarged tie-beam known as a 'firred beam', rather than a truss employing collars, struts or rafters. The massive tie-beams run east–west and are supported on double wall plates . 232). The upper wall plate or cornice plate, measuring 11 in. in height and 7 in. in width (280 × 180 mm), acts as a lower purlin and is rebated over the edge of the lower plate, which forms the bed of the gutters and is 8 in. (200 mm) thick (fig. 232). The upper plate is also tenoned into the sides of the tie-beam. The tie-beams are of exceptional size, measuring between 17 and 20 in. (430–510 mm) wide and 27 in. (685 mm) high in the centre, reducing to 16 in. (400 mm) at the ends.

The overall length of these beams is even more exceptional: those over the chapel and eastern room at more than 32 ft (9.8 m) long are outstanding, whereas the western room tie-beams with total lengths in excess of 43 ft (13.1 m) are at a scale quite without precedent in England. Few buildings have clear spans of more than 30 ft (9.2 m), and these are roofed not by single unsupported beams as found in the White Tower, but by trusses incorporating braces and hangers, thus

313

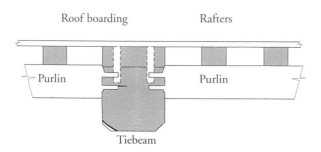

Roof boarding   Rafters

Purlin   Purlin

Tiebeam

reducing the weight supported by the tie-beams, often even removing the tie-beam entirely, as in Westminster Hall and King's College Chapel, Cambridge. The widest broadly contemporary low-pitched roof truss is that of the chapel of St George, Windsor, at 36 ft 6 in. (11.1 m). The importance of these roofs cannot be over-stated in terms of sheer scale, not only in the length of the principal beams, but also of the length of the roof as well. The king's royal forests would have had to be extensively searched to find such exceptional timbers, and after cutting to size, they would have still weighed about 3½ tonnes. The logistics of converting these gigantic trees, transporting them from the forests to the centre of London and hoisting them up into place upon the walls would have been considerable. These efforts were clearly considered worthwhile, however, despite the fact that the Tower was becoming of less importance as a royal palace.

If the Tower was at the span limit for medieval roofs, it was not until the seventeenth century, when Sir Christopher Wren designed engineered trusses for St Paul's Cathedral in London and the Sheldonian Theatre in Oxford, spanning 50 ft (15.3 m) and 68 ft (20.7 m), respectively, that the White Tower roofs would be surpassed.

With many of the tie-beams, it was not possible to obtain the requisite thickness at the centre to maintain the required fall of 2½°; such deficiencies were made up with an added packing or firring piece up to 6½ in. high (165 mm) that is slotted into the top of the tie and secured by under-squinted abutments at each end, square on plan and jointed along the edges with a series of secret, or slip, tenons at about 20 in. (500 mm) centres. Skilfully executed and wedged together at the ridge, these inserts actually pre-stress the beam, giving it more resistance against settlement to the upper face of the beam, which then acts in compression (see fig. 233).

The tie-beams carry a series of butt or tenoned purlins, 9 by 11 in. (225 by 280 mm) in cross-section, two on either side of the ridge piece on the eastern roofs, and three on the western roof. The purlins are tenoned to the ties with the late medieval type of tenon with a diminished haunch (fig. 233).[16] The common rafters measuring 7 by 5 in. (175 by 125 mm) rest on the upper wall plates and purlins, but are jointed into the ridge with central tenons with ½ in. (13 mm) haunches

on either side. There are five rafters to a bay in the west room, and they vary between five and six rafters per bay in the east room and over the chapel.

The large west room is divided into ten bays by eleven tie-beams, including a tie-beam against the north and south walls. The smaller eastern room roof is divided into seven bays, but, unlike the western half of the roof, there is no end tie-beam against the north wall. Similarly, the chapel roof consists of four bays with three tie-beams, but none against the southern wall, although the first tie-beam in the chapel is supported on the stone dividing wall between it and the east room.

There are some differences in the chapel roof, which has to accommodate the eastern apse extending beyond the rest of the roof space. It has a substantial trussed beam 20 in. wide by 11 in. deep (510 by 280 mm), supported at each end on posts 14 in. (360 mm) wide at the base and thickening to 20 in. (510 mm) at the top to align with the wall plate. The plate was further supported by two braces that rise over the stone vault of the chapel ceiling below, and two more from the posts over the aisles. Beyond this plate the apse end is roofed with a gentle monopitch of rafters supported on north–south purlins, each carried on pairs of posts resting on pads or sill-beams. Although these arrangements may appear superficially to be part of some earlier roof, they are clearly contemporary with the remainder, and this is confirmed through the dendrochronology.

Only the upper wall plates/cornice plates and tie-beams are finished with a large chamfer, which varies from 45° to 60° and measures approximately 2¾ in. (70 mm) wide on the plates and 3½ in. (89 mm) wide on the tie-beams. All chamfers on the tie-beams have matching straight-cut stops in line with the plates, forming a mason's mitre in effect. The chamfers on the upper wall plates in the west chamber have a slightly hollow profile.

Despite the defacement of the timbers in the large east and west rooms through the sanding of the surfaces during the 1960s restoration, some of the assembly marks could still be made out. The roof over the chapel was relatively unrestored and could be easily accessed from the stone vaults, and the sequence of assembly marks could be clearly discerned. It would appear that each tie-beam was numbered from I to IIII, starting with the now-missing truss over the stone wall between the chapel and the eastern room. The assembly marks are scribed on the southern face of each truss, adjacent to each purlin, with a corresponding mark on the northern end of the purlin. Those on the west side of the ridge were distinguished from those on the east by the use of a tag, or oblique stroke. Rafters were numbered at the top on their southern face, with a corresponding mark on the side of the ridge, but only at the most northern rafter mortice; it was left to the carpenters assembling the roof to count along the ridge to position the remaining rafters in each bay correctly. Bay I (northernmost bay) and bay IIII have six rafters, whilst the middle two bays have five rafters. In Bay I the eastern Rafter I has replaced Rafter VI, with a new timber inserted in the place of Rafter I. This pair of rafters has been moved further south to accommodate a modern brick wall on the south side of Tie-beam I during the twentieth-century restoration.

The east chamber roof has been very heavily sanded, and therefore only a couple of assembly marks could be made out on the east face of the ridges: a IIII on the fourth bay from the north, and a VI on the sixth bay from the north, which then abuts Tie-beam I over the cross-wall belonging to the chapel roof. This suggests that, as in the chapel roof, the timbers were numbered from the north, but without the northernmost tie-beam, which would have been numbered I. Despite being framed up in two separately numbered frames, these roofs were clearly constructed at the same time, since the ridge in Bay 4 in the east room was cut from the same tree as the ridge from the second bay in the chapel roof.

Further assembly marks were recorded on the large western roof, and the same method of marking was employed, starting at the north end. Although this roof differs from the chapel and east room roofs, which have no end tie-beams, the bay numbering is identical.

Naturally, these extensive alterations to the upper part of the building necessitated the insertion of an upper floor. Some floorboards within the arches in the spine wall were found to date from this phase – one plank felled in the spring of 1488, and two others likely to have originated from one of the same trees as used in the eastern roofs, confirm that this was all part of the campaign of work of *circa* 1490. The floor planks are 2 in. (5 cm) thick, with widths varying between 12 and 15 in. (30–38 cm), tangentially sawn.

The southernmost beam in the west chamber retains evidence for an interesting wall-framing arrangement against the north face of the southern mural passage. Two lines of 4 in. (100 mm) mortices in the soffit, staggered at 8 in. (200 mm), are set at 2 ft (600 mm) centres. These extend across the middle half of the wall and were clearly inserted at the same time as the roof was constructed, for the southern row of studs has been pegged from the south, and the northern line of studs from the north. On the east end they terminate at a substantial spandrel brace and wall-post, about 10 ft (3.1 m) out from the spine wall. Presumably the same arrangement existed at the west end, although the soffit of the beam has subsequently been repaired, removing any evidence.

Related to this is the adjacent ridge beam in the southernmost bay. Here, the soffit and the sides, up to the underside of the ceiling joists/rafters, were decorated with iron tacks forming a series of chevrons. Presumably these tacks were used to fix some coloured material to form part of a decorative scheme. Together with the (presumably) decorative woodwork on the adjacent end wall, this would have formed an impressive backdrop, although just what this would have been used for is open to speculation.

There is no immediately recognisable historical context for this work. It is thought that the upper room of the White Tower was used by the Knights of the Bath for their ritual washing on the night prior to the coronation, but the date of the roof cannot be related to such a ceremony. Henry VII had been crowned in 1485 before he was married, and in fact Elizabeth of York had to wait until after the birth of her first child for her separate coronation in November 1487, on which occasion she travelled by barge to the Tower and returned through the city in a litter, following the protocol used for Richard III's coronation; neither of these can have been the cause.[17]

The Early Sixteenth Century

Although there can be no doubt that the whole of the White Tower was re-roofed from 1490, as demonstrated through the dendrochronology, there exists detailed documentary accounts suggesting extensive repairs to the roofs of both the east and west rooms in the mid-1530s. Perhaps this overly ambitious roof was just one bridge too far. A report in July 1534 stated that the roof of the White Tower required 'great reparacions', and in the following February work had begun on 'the Trussing of the Beames with brases in the Rouffe of the southsyde of the whyte Toure'. The works included replacements of at least one 'great beams' with pendants and braces on the south side of the White Tower, and continued into 1536, with the replacement of a 'great beam' at the north end, and specific reference to 'strengthening' the roof; they were terminated by lead-working and gutter repairs in late 1536.[18] The construction of two 'great scaffolds' on three sets of wheels from which to carry out the work below the roofs would seem to be quite a technical achievement in itself, although entries referring to repairs suggest that the scaffold was not without teething problems. Similarly, the documentation of two windlasses or tread-wheels constructed on the roof illustrated the lengths to which it was necessary to go in order to raise the 43 ft, 3½ tonne 'great beams' from the ground up to the top of the roof. Also, references to at least four pairs of screw-jacks indicate that some of the roof had sagged to the extent that it was necessary to jack up some of the settlement in the tie-beams as the bracing was inserted beneath.

Although the roof was less than fifty years old by the 1530s, the documents suggest that some serious decay was evident in the wall plates under the gutters, and this had affected the ends of the tie-beams, at least one or two of which required complete renewal. This required the lifting of leads, roof boarding, and effecting repairs and replacements to the plates on which the tie-beams rested. Apart from the replacement of a tie-beam or two, the bearing ends of others appeared to be weakened to such an extent that they needed shoring by the insertion of wall posts and braces up to the underside of the tie-beams. These posts extended right down to the floor below, some of these clashing with the openings into the mural passages. Evidence of these posts and braces of the 1530s can be found on Lemprière's section drawing of the Tower of 1729, but the braces had already disappeared when the same room was drawn in 1754, leaving the tie-beams directly supported by two posts in the centre along the line of the lower-floor arcades (see figs 146–52).[19]

A prime objective of the dendrochronology programme was to try to identify these 1530s repairs, and, apart from the northern tie-beam in the west room, and the two northern tie-beams in the east room, all of which were replaced in the mid-twentieth century, all principal beams were found to relate to the 1490s roof, as were all the purlins and rafters sampled. The purlins in the northern bay of both the east and west rooms, however, were markedly different in character, being converted from whole, very fast-grown trees, in contrast to the 1490s purlins, which were from large, very slow-grown trees, cut into quarters. It is also possible that one or two of the three recently replaced tie-beams had actually been 1530s replacements.

So what caused such a roof to last less than fifty years before requiring such a major overhaul? The most likely scenario is that when the roof of 1490 was originally constructed, the gutters had insufficient fall or some other defect in the lead covering that periodically let in water, causing decay in the wall plates and affecting the ends to the tie-beams, through wet rot, or possibly dry rot and/or death-watch beetle infestation. This was no doubt compounded by the inevitable deflection in the western room tie-beams – at more than 40 ft, unseasoned, slow-grown oak will deflect under constant load, and with such a low pitch of $2\frac{1}{2}°$, water would probably have blown up under the laps in the leads during windy conditions.

The later history of the roof can be shortly dealt with. A number of firring pieces were inserted on the rafters (perhaps in the later eighteenth century) to even out the roof slope and to increase the fall, which had been reduced by the sag in the tie-beams. Skylights were enlarged in both halves of the roof in 1858 by Salvin to illuminate the displays beneath (openings in the second floor sent the light down to the first floor). At the same time the tie-beam ends were further supported by brackets or consoles, which were constructed of wrought-iron clad in timber. Further major timber repairs were made to the roof in 1955,

and it is likely that during this period the northern two tie-beams in the east room and the northern beam in the west room were replaced entirely. The extent of the decay in the remaining principal beams, however, was such that finally, between 1960 and 1965, as was then the fashion, an entirely new roof support of steel was built on top of the medieval roof, with the intention of suspending the timbers from above. This was rather a sorry end for a roof that as late as 1600 had been capable of supporting sixteen cannon pointing at the city, but despite these changes the strength of its original form can now be appreciated.[20]

MEDIEVAL FITTINGS

In addition to the door reveals and drawbars described above, there are three surviving medieval doors, as well as medieval timbers at the base of the well.

Door 1, circa 1350

This is the medieval door in the basement of the White Tower, in the round-headed cross-passage between the apsidal basement room and the east basement room (fig. 234). This doorway originally had a jamb at the south end, with evidence for a drawbar socket and hinges on the west wall. The floor level here is thought always to have been at the present level, some 2 ft 6 in. (750 mm) lower than the cross-passage door at the north end of the basement. At some point the jambs at the south end of the passage were removed and a rebate cut in the north end of the cross-passage to receive the present door. This is very well made of three layers of oak boards, 1 in. (25 mm) thick and between 5 and 8 in. (125–200 mm) wide, aligned vertically on the outsides and horizontally in

235 (*above*) Section through fourteenth-century door to basement apsidal room.

236 (*right*) Fifteenth-century door to bottom of 'great vice'.

the middle. The boards are not rebated and have square edges, joined edgewise with ¼ in. (6 mm) square pegs of uncertain length set at 11 to 12 in. (275–300 mm) centres. Clench nails have been driven in a regular 5¼ in. (133 mm) grid from the inside (north) through the layers of boards to the outside (south), where their ends are clenched over (fig. 235). The hinges are doubled, each hinge having a plate on the outer face and another passing between the two inner layers of boarding.

The felling date of the door can be made no closer than 'after 1346', but probably not much beyond 1350, corresponding to a period of busy activity in the Tower at the start of its role as an ordnance store during Edward III's French wars. The character of the carpentry is appropriate for this date, with less of the sophistication that might be expected at an earlier date, while the use of Baltic timber demonstrates the preferred choice of imported boards for quality joinery.[21]

Door II, circa 1475

The door from the basement to the north-east stair turret is a medieval door of less substantial character than the first (fig. 236). It has only two layers of boards, but they are a little thicker at 1¼ in. (32 mm), the outer one of vertical 8 in. (200 mm) oak boards, and an inner face of horizontal 9–10 in. (225–250 mm) elm boards. As in the other, earlier, door at the south end of the east basement, the oak boards are jointed together with ⅜ in. (10 mm) diameter dowels set at 13½ in. (345 mm) centres. The boards are fixed together with clenched nails set at a 4 in. (100 mm) square grid (fig. 237). The door is hung on the west side with three bands sandwiched between the two layers of boards. The use of elm for a door in any situation is unusual, and although it is just possible that these backing boards are a later addition, it is unlikely.

Door III

There remains one early external door on the south side of the White Tower. This is at the bottom of the small vice leading up to the first floor and the chapel entrance passage. This small, round-headed, doorway was a later insertion, perhaps late medieval, and measures 6 ft 7 in. (2 m) high and 2 ft 10 in. (850 mm) wide overall. The front, south face consists of two broad planks, 17 in. (430 mm) wide and 2 in. (50 mm) thick. This is backed by four horizontal planks, the top and bottom planks 17 in. (430 mm) wide, and the middle planks 22 in. (560 mm) wide, all again 2 in. (50 mm) thick, making a substantial door 4 in. (100 mm) thick. The planks are tangentially sawn from a large, fast-grown tree that precluded dendrochronological analysis. The timber was undoubtedly of local origin. The two layers of planks were fixed together with about thirty large, 6 in. (150 mm) nails, the heads measuring between 1 and 1¼ in. (25–32 mm) square and ½ in. (13 mm) deep, set diagonally (fig. 238). The door is hung on two large bands, hinging on the east and opening inwards.

ELIZABETHAN FLOORS

The flooring of the main spaces of the White Tower has been changed once, if not twice. The spans, in excess of 30 ft and as long as 40 ft (9–12 m), could have been covered by large joists, but their strength depended on the condition of their junction with the wall, where rot and insect attack were most likely at a point where the ends of the beams were able to take in moisture. They would undoubtedly have required one or two arcades below to give intermediate support to the beams.

On the second floor the infilled sockets of medieval floor joists were found on the west wall, and these may have belonged to the late fifteenth-century floor indicated by the dating of the planks remaining in the floor of gaps in the spine wall. Whatever remained of the Norman or later medieval flooring was replaced in the sixteenth and early seventeenth centuries, when the present heavy-duty floors were inserted for military stores (and in the eighteenth century by the inser-

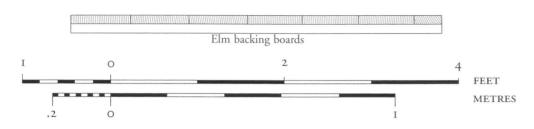

Elm backing boards

I O 2 4 FEET

.2 O I METRES

tion of vaulting in the basement). In order to reduce the span of the rooms intermediate supports were created by the insertion of rows of posts or columns carrying large joists on which the floors could be laid, with a maximum span of between 10 and 16 ft (3.1–4.9 m) for the individual areas of flooring.

Entrance Floor

The Entrance Floor

The floor at the entrance level has been truncated from beneath by the insertion of vaults in the basement in the eighteenth century. Lemprière's section of the White Tower of 1729 shows a row of columns in the basement, and the western half appears now to have the remains of two rows of timber columns (shortened and now resting on the vault) and a north–south run of principal joists. Lemprière's plan of the 'First Floor' shows the arrangement of racks in the western division for the Sea Armoury, and in the eastern division for a tool store, and a number of openings in the floor (especially in window recesses) to allow light into the basement (the chapel basement vault contained the Ordnance Office records). The columns supporting the first floor show some signs of the attachment of racking, and at least one has a regular array of marks indicative of the display of arms.

Entrance-Floor Ceiling (First Floor)

The first floor is supported by two rows of ten columns in the west division (two rows of six in the east). These carry principal joists that are aligned north–south, into which secondary (east–west) softwood joists are lapped at bay intervals. In the western division the secondary joists are staggered so that they do not coincide where they meet the principals, whereas on the east side they are aligned on the columns (and are also within the depth of the principals rather than passing over them). The common joists for the floor rest on the secondary joists and run north–south. The arrangement of the timbers (as seen in the ground-floor ceiling) is obscured by many of the timbers being 'boxed out' to give them a uniform appearance, and the observations on the hole made at the north end of the western division for a new staircase showed that there were several layers of floorboards.[22] The common joists are not visible on

either side: the east division has a pine-boarded ceiling, and the west is plastered.

First Floor

Lemprière's plan of the 'Second Floor' shows the arrangement of storerooms in both east and west divisions for Small Arms, and a trapdoor in the north-east corner of the western division to enable materials to be raised from below (the chapel contained 'Part of the Records of England'). As below, the columns supporting the second floor retain traces of their former attachments, with horizontal slots for three tiers of shelves and in some instances vertical slots into which arms could be fitted for display.

First-Floor Ceiling (Second Floor)

The second floor is supported by an arrangement of columns similar to that of the floor below. The columns carry discontinuous principal joists aligned north–south, on which rest the secondary (east–west) joists. In the western division there is a continuous series of closely spaced secondary joists of irregular scantling, so that a tertiary series of joists was not necessary; whereas on the east side there are three sets of joists as on the floor below. There is a gap in the joists for a possible trapdoor in the north end of the west division, though not exactly as shown by Lemprière.

Second Floor

Lemprière's plan of the upper floor shows an open storeroom on the western division for 'match, ropes, shovels, wheelbarrows, etc.'. The plans shows rows of columns that are no longer there (but not attached to

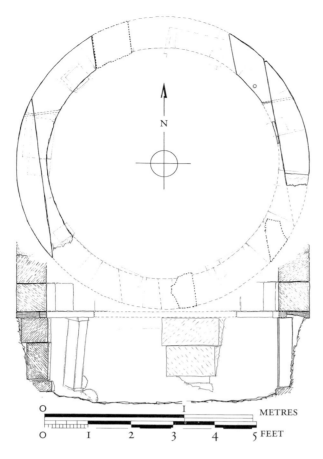

O   I   METRES

O   I   2   3   4   5 FEET

any racking), and towards the north end a 'Capstan for drawing of stores up from the Rooms below thro' a Trap Door' (the trap is immediately above that in the first floor below). The eastern division was connected through to the chapel gallery, and both of these held racks for 'Part of the Records of England'. There are no surviving posts at this level, and the medieval roof has been described above.

Dating of the Floors

The general appearance of these floor structures would suggest a post-medieval date, and that the flooring of the eastern and western divisions was possibly made at different times. The tree-ring dating shows that they were earlier than expected, part being Elizabethan and part Jacobean, and that the east and west parts are indeed distinct.

Phase I

The first-floor columns (i.e., those supporting the second floor) in the eastern division include one felled in winter 1565–6. This fits well with a recorded series of works in the 1560s. The accounts for 1565–7 include 'making a newe office for the recordes, making framing and finyshing twoe newe Armouries in the White Tower'.[23] This was not necessarily the occasion when all the work was done, for in July 1568 there was discussion of how the queen could be persuaded to spend money on the 'great Tower' for the preservation of her armour and records 'which taketh hurte daylie', and what materials would be needed (including 600 trees for this and other work).[24] The following May there

was some delay in obtaining the queen's approval, while 'tymber reddie framed for Westm and the Tower' awaited carriage.[25] In June 1569 the Surveyor Lewes Stockett was ordered to finish the 'works beguon at the Exchequior, the Recordes & other Romes of Tharmory within the Tower of London', though he had still not received full payment in 1570.[26]

Phase II

The columns of the western division of the ground floor (supporting the first floor) and the columns and ceiling joists on the first floor (supporting the second floor) are dated between summer 1602 and spring 1603. Queen Elizabeth died in March 1603, and preparations were made for King James's coronation, and in particular the Knights of the Bath's bathroom in the White Tower (though in the event this took place in St James's Palace and not the Tower of London). The accounts include: 'layinge the newe planckes in Cesars hall in the Tower plaine one by another against the kinges Majestie comeinge for the knights of the Bath all over the olde broken floores . . . Plasterers . . . platforeing the wall of Casars hall for the knights of the Bathe againste the Coronacon'.[27] This has rather a makeshift ring to it, and is hardly consistent with the wholesale refitting that must have happened. There is better evidence for large-scale construction in the following years in association with the new powder house that was being constructed in the basement. In the Works accounts for 1603–4 are more detailed descriptions of the operations:

> framinge of Joystes and Brest Sommers for the newe flower of the powderhouse in the white Tower, liftinge straight of planckes which have been sawen twoe yeares for the same flower, and the next oulde flower under it . . . sommers of the new flower that is making in the white Tower for the new powderhowse helping the Labourers to crane up tymber out of the bardge at the wharf and loading the cartes with it that carried up into the Tower to the Sawpitt, Craning up the framed tymber, framing and raysing of the Carpenters woorke of the postes plates ioystes and breast sommers for the newe flower made in the white tower for the powder house, Craning up the frames tymber framing and leauelling the ioystes upon the walles of either side of the flower, raising the breast sommers and the longe binding ioystes, lifting straight of planckes putting in and leuelling the ioystes for the newe flower, which is making all the length of the great white Tower for the newe powder house[28]

And this continued into the next year of the Works Accounts, for 1604–5:

> joisting and planckinge of the great floore in white Tower for a powder house there puttinge in of sondrie newe joists in the middle floore under the

newe floore Liftinge straighte of planckes and newe
planckinge of the same flower in manie places,
puttinge in of newe plates uppon the walls to beare
the endes of the joists cuttinge out and takeinge
downe some of the uprighte posts in the upper
story of the white Tower which did beare the roofe
and were all rotten and decaied woorkinge and
ymbowinge of newe posts to sett in their place
proppinge and Screwing upp the maine beames
and principall tymber of the roof of white Tower
whilest the olde were taken out to put newe in their
place frameinge in the newe posts and plate into
the beames and braces of the roofe puttinge in of
peces of Tymber on the backside of the other
uprighte postes which stood besides the wall againste the windowes for the strengthininge of them
and boultinge them together with greate yron
boultes puttinge in of some new joiste upon the
toppe of the roofe under the leades and planckinge
the same with newe plancks, puttinge in quarters
under the Recordes offyce and of tymber betwene
the Joists overhead where the spaces were too wyde
to lathe unto frameinge together twoe blocks of
tymber to clippe the foote of the uprighte piller in
the lowe darke sellor under the recordes . . .[29]

If this work does comprise the present flooring of the
western half of the White Tower, as it appears to do,
then the timber must have already been felled.

THE TURRETS

The four stone turrets above the White Tower sur-
mount the spiral stairs in three corners, and the fourth
in the south-east corner rises above the chapel vault.
Three of the turrets are square towers, whereas the
north-east one over the large stair is approximately
round; known as the Flamsteed Tower, its upper room
was briefly used as an astronomical observatory in
1675 by John Flamsteed. With their 'onion'-shaped
roofs, the turrets were the features that made the
Tower a prominent landmark, but their date was
unknown, and it could be speculated only that their
ogival shape was of late fifteenth- or early sixteenth-
century date, when this motif was revived.[30]

The North-East Turret

The most interesting roof is that of the large near-
circular Flamsteed Tower. This is based on a principal
north–south joist 10 by 11 in. (250 by 280 mm) in
cross-section, with four secondary east–west joists, 10
by 6 in. (250 by 150 mm), tenoned into it (with a
double tenon having a shouldered tenon below and a
diminished haunch tenon above) and a central square
formed of two additional timber plates laid on the
secondary joists (some of these timbers in the base
show evidence of reuse). An octagonal central mast is
mounted on the principal joist (now bolted from
below), and a circular plate 6 by 10 in. (150 by 250
mm) is laid on the central square (in six pieces, joined
from below with dovetailed keys), forming a base for
a ring of curved braces rising to the rafters. The rafters
are based on a circular plate around the top of the
wall, and they rise to join the mast, and receive the
braces at or above mid-height. There are eight principal rafters and braces, and four common ones between
them. The remarkable feature of the design is that
the braces curve upwards and outwards in an ogival
(s-shaped) curve, while the rafters curve inwards and
upwards in an ogival curve, making for some extraordinarily shaped spaces (fig. 240). The turret turns out
to be the oldest, with some of the common rafters
dating to spring 1532 and spring 1533, but with extensive reworking of the principals and floor construction with timber felled in spring 1783. The context of
the sixteenth-century work is discussed below.

The North-West Turret

The floor below the roof is formed of a north–south
joist and three common joists (two more in the walls,
and short pieces across the four corners). The joists are
secured with diminished haunch tenons (some with
extended shoulders scribed to the waney edges). The
roof is based on a principal north–south joist and two
east–west joists, with an octagonal central mast (secured
from below with an iron bolt), eight straight braces up
to a ring purlin in eight sections, and downward braces

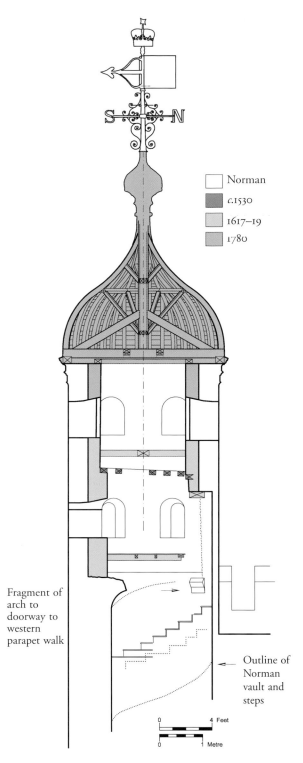

Norman

c.1530

1617–19

1780

Fragment of arch to doorway to western parapet walk

Outline of Norman vault and steps

0   4 Feet

0   1 Metre

to the cross-beams to stabilise the mast. The latest felling dates of the timber are 1780–81, but some stockpiled timbers felled as early as spring 1777 were also used.

The South-East Turret

This turret has a very fine interior of unspoilt medieval masonry, with Reigate stone quoins and ragstone rubble with galleted pointing. The 'ground' floor at the main roof level consists of a series of joists running east–west, which are jointed into edge beams with diminished haunches. Only the two outer joists and the east-edge beam survive, and one of the joists has been dated to spring 1532. There is a floor below the roof, with six east–west joists 5 by 7 in. (125 by 175

mm) in cross-section, resting on bevelled timber plates 4 in. deep (100 mm) let into the walls. At the west side of the floor two of the joists are notched to allow a small opening only 14 by 22 in. (355 by 560 mm) to permit access to the upper level. Another significant feature of this floor is that the joists are not set level, but laid with a fall of approximately 3 in. (75 mm) from one side of the turret to the other internally. Presumably, the floorboards were covered with lead with an outlet drain on the east side of the turret, implying that the openings above were not weatherproof. Two joists were dated, one from 1503–35, and another from after 1517. In view of the precise felling date of 1532 from the lowest floor below, it is likely that these are contemporary with it. The turret roof is based on a cross of two principal joists aligned north–south, with a central octagonal mast holding eight straight braces up to the rafters, and four downward braces to the cross beams. The latest felling dates of the timbers are spring 1781.

The South-West Turret

The upper part of the turret is rebuilt in brick internally, with remains of a floor and two sets of crossbraces below the roof (fig. 241). The upper floor originally comprised six east–west joists, 5½ by 8 in. (140 × 200 mm), set at 16 in. (400 mm) centres on a brick rebate. It looks possibly medieval, but was undated. The fourth of these joists is missing, but evidence in the form of mortices for a lost trimmer on the joists on either side shows that it formed a trap opening against the west wall of the turret. However, from the edge of the missing trimmer there is only a gap of 9 in. (225 mm) to the brick wall. There is evidence that the joists pre-date the insertion of the brickwork lining to the original stone walls, thus making the trap too narrow and necessitating the subsequent removal of the trimmer and joist. And like the southeast turret, this floor also has a fall amounting to approximately 4½ in. (115 mm) from the south to the north. It is almost inconceivable that the joists had decayed to the extent that they had settled this amount by the time the brickwork was inserted without any effort being made to level them. Instead, this raises the question of whether these joists were originally set with a fall to allow for a lead roof above, with a drain on the north side, to protect from wind-driven rain.

At the first landing level seen from the stair below is a pair of diagonally set cross-beams with iron ties dating to winter 1616–17. At a height of 22 in. above the upper floor is another pair of braces, similarly laid corner to corner. Although without sapwood, the upper set of braces was dated to 1607–39, and no doubt felled at the same time as the lower set of braces. This work is probably contemporary with the internal brick lining described above, and which probably relates to an account dating from 1 October 1618 to

30 October 1619, which says: '. . . John Andrrews Bricklayer for bringing up with bricke and paving with bricke an edge with Tarris xxxvi loope holes betwene the battlements on the Toppe of the white Tower . . . xxx s.'.[31] That this work also related to the internal works to the south-west turret is found in a survey of the Tower dated 31 December 1623, which notes: '. . . Two of thos Turrets towards the Thames are roughe case verie Seemely and whereby the walls (formerly Ruyned) are nowe preserved . . .'.[32] This would suggest that the two southern turrets had been repaired by the end of 1623.

The roof is based on a cross-beam (the principal joist runs north–south) with a central mast braced up to a ring purlin, and with downward bracing to the beams. As with the other roofs the mast is secured with a central iron bolt. The latest felling date of the timbers is winter 1779–80.

Dating

The eighteenth-century episode of repair to the Flamsteed Tower is matched in the other turrets, which essentially have modern roofs, with felling dates between 1779 and 1783. The recorded work on the turrets began with the erection of a scaffold in 1780, and various works by masons and plumbers are noted, but not specifically any carpentry.[33] Although a payment was made in December 1782 for gilding the four weathercocks on the White Tower,[34] the felling date of three timbers during the winter of 1782–3 and two more during the spring of 1783 suggests that further carpentry works continued beyond 1782, at least to the Flamsteed Tower.

The context of the 1530s work is interesting, for it again points to a state occasion when the Tower was brought into repair, this time for the coronation of Anne Boleyn in 1533. The Works accounts refer to the carpenters removing 'the olde tymber upon the iiij turretts upon the White Tower', and plumbers covering the four turrets 'being half fynnysshed'.[35] This and the following account have many references to the 'four Types' on the White Tower, which may mean that the turrets were themselves finished with heraldic beasts, though the references to roughcast brickwork suggest that they were set on their own brick piers. There is a separate reference to the north-east turret in the account of works (probably) before January 1533: 'Item a flower made and redy framed for the Rownde Tower on the White Tower whiche is not yet sett up'.[36] Clearly, the roof frame was not quite ready in 1533, since one of the rafters was still growing in the woods that spring.

It must have been at this time that all the turrets achieved their fashionable ogival profile, in what Fletcher noted as the ogival revival around 1500, exemplified by structures such as the bell turret on the Curfew Tower at Windsor Castle, and royal palaces at Richmond, Greenwich and Hampton Court. While the other turrets were repaired in the later eighteenth century, the Flamsteed Tower points to the date of origin as the coronation of Anne Boleyn in 1533.[37] The appearance of the White Tower with four new and decorative turrets, and the four heraldic Types, must have been splendid. The newly repaired battlements were not altogether without purpose, however, and in January 1534 Chapuys reported to the emperor that the king had placed guns on the top of the Tower commanding the city.[38] When required, it could still function as a fortress.

PART V

Selected Texts

Transcripts of Primary Documents: Medieval

SELECTED AND EDITED BY JEREMY ASHBEE

1. Gundulf and the White Tower, after 1077
(*Textus Roffensis*, ed. Hearne, p. 212)

Gundulf was overseeing the building of the Tower, and staying in London. This is dated after 1077, because it was in this year that Gundulf was made a bishop. Traditionally taken to date the beginning of the building and to identify its designer, it actually does neither, merely stating that the bishop had been involved in the works in a supervisory capacity at some stage before the death of the Conqueror.

When this Gundulf was supervising the works of the Great Tower of London on the command of King William the Great, he had been lodged in the house of one Aedmer, who began repeatedly to ask him to admit him into the community of the church of Saint Andrew, of which he was the head.

Dum idem Gundulfus, ex praecepto regis Willelmi magni, præesset operi magnæ turris Londoniæ & hospitatus fuisset apud ipsum ædmerum quadam vice ipse coepit episcopum rogare, ut concedet sibi societatem ecclesiæ quam regebat, videlicet Sancti Andreæ.

2. Rannulf Flambard's imprisonment and escape, 1100–01
(Orderic Vitalis, ed. Chibnall, vol. v, p. 312)

Rannulf Flambard's imprisonment by Henry I and his escape are evoked by Orderic Vitalis. This extract mentions a mullion on the window, and suggests that once out of the *arx*, presumably the White Tower, he could mount a waiting horse and flee; the wall built in 1097 seems not to have been a barrier for him. Rannulf shares the distinction of being the Tower's first known prisoner and escapee.

But then it was God's will that the wind changed: for the many injuries he had done to Henry himself and the other sons of the realm, rich and poor, and the many heartless ways he had brought grievous suffering to others, Rannulf was cast down from the height of his power, and was handed over in chains to William de Mandeville to be held in the Tower of London. But just as Ovid said of Daedalus, 'Misfortunes often stir the intelligence', the cunning bishop was more than capable of getting out from the strictness of his prison, and with the connivance of friends, he fashioned an ingenious escape. He was clever and well spoken though cruel and quick to anger, and he could be generous and jovial, even gracious and affable. It was the king's order that he should have food to the value of 2 shillings sterling every day, and thus he lived the high life in prison, with help from his friends. Every day he would order a marvellous feast for himself and his guards. One day, a rope was smuggled to him in a cask of wine. The generous bishop then laid on a lavish banquet at which the guards ate and drank with him and in due course became intoxicated with all the wine they had consumed. When they were all completely drunk and snoring soundly, the bishop fastened his rope to a column between two lights of a window in the tower, and still clutching his pastoral staff, he began to let himself down. But he had forgotten to put on gloves to protect his hands and they were cut to the bone by the roughness of the rope. The rope itself was too short to reach the ground, and the fat bishop had to fall heavily to the ground: the drop nearly flattened him and he howled miserably with the pain. His faithful friends and trusted supporters were waiting in great fear at the foot of the Tower, with the fastest horses ready for him.

Pro multis enim iniuriis quibus ipsum Henricum aliosque regni filios tam pauperes quam divites uexauerat, multisque modis crebro afflictos irreverentur contristauerat, ex diuino consultu mutato flamine de sullimi culmine potestatis deiectus est: et in arce Lundoniensi Guillelmo de Magnauilla custodiendus in uinculis traditus est. Verum sicut Ouidius dicit de Daedelo canens, 'Ingenium mala sepe mouent'; ingeniosus presul de rigore ergastuli exire sategit, et exitum callide per amicos procurauit. Erat enim sollers et facundus et licet crudelis et iracundus, largus tamen et plerumque iocundus et ab hoc plerisque gratus et amandus. Cotidie ad victum suum duos sterilensium solidos iussu regis habebat, unde cum adiumentis amicorum in carcere tripudiebat, cotidieque splendidum sibi suisque custodibus convivium exhiberi iubebat. Quadam die in lagena uini funis ei delatus est; et copiosus conuiuii apparatus largitione presulis erogatus est. Custodes cum eo comederunt, et Falerno ubertim hausto exhilarati sunt. Quibus admodum inebriatis et secure stertentibus, episcopus funem ad columnam quae in medio fenestrae arcis erat coaptauit, et baculum pastoralem secum sumens per funem descendit. Verum quia manus suas oblitus fuit cirotecis obluere, usque ad eos excoritae sunt restis scabredine et dune ad solum usque non pertingente gravi lapsu compulentus flamen ruit et pene conquassatus flebiliter imgemuit. Fideles amici eius et probati satellites ad pedem turris expectabant, qui non sine timore magno ibidem ei optimos cornipedes preparauerunt.

3. William Fitz Stephen's description, *circa* 1173

(Fitz Stephen, 'Vita Sancti Thomae', ed. Robertson)

William Fitz Stephen describes the Tower of London as a 'fortress–palatine, massive and very strong'. The quotation is more heavily weighted towards the military strength of the site than its potential to serve as a royal palace. The two castles at the western end of the city were Baynard's Castle and Mountfitchet's Tower, both later absorbed into the precinct of the Dominican friars.

In its eastern part, the city contains a fortress–palatine, massive and very strong, its walls and its floors rising from very deep foundations, its mortar tempered with the blood of animals, and at the western end, two most strongly fortified castles . . .

Habet ab oriente arcem palatinam maximam et fortissimam cuius et area et muri a fundamento profundissimo exsurgunt, caemento cum sanguine animalium temperato: ab occidente dua castella munitissima . . .

4. Henry III's works to the White Tower, 10 December 1240

(The National Archives [formerly Public Record Office], hereafter TNA, c62/15 m19)

Henry III orders the manufacture of new gutters to protect the newly whitened walls of the White Tower from rainwater, a fighting platform on the south side and the redecoration of St John's Chapel. The fighting platform overlooked the area of the royal lodgings in the bailey and presumably reflected a worry that the castle might be besieged and the lodgings overrun: it might then prove necessary for the royal household to withdraw into the White Tower. Earlier in the same year, part of Henry III's new curtain defences at the Tower had collapsed, leaving the fortress vulnerable.

The king sends greetings to the keepers of the works of the Tower of London. We command you to make repairs to the granary in the same Tower and improvements all over wherever they are needed. Lengthen down to the ground all the lead gutters of the Great Tower by which rainwater runs down from the top of the same tower, so that the wall of the said tower, which has just been whitened, may not perish at all or suddenly spall away through the action of the rain. On the south side at the top of the same tower you are to make large galleries in good strong timber facing southwards onto which if need arises men can climb and see down to the foot of the tower to defend it better. Paint the whole chapel of Saint John the Evangelist in the same tower white and make three glass windows in the same chapel, one on the north side with a small picture of Mary holding her child, the others on the south side, showing the Trinity and also, on the same side, Saint John the Apostle and Evangelist. Paint the cross and beam over the altar in the same chapel well and in good colours, and make and paint two beautiful figures in the best and most fitting place you can find in the same chapel, one of Saint Edward holding out his ring and giving it to Saint John the Evangelist. Paint all the old wall which runs almost all round our said Tower white . . . Witnessed by the king at Windsor on 10 December.

Rex custodibus operationum Turris Londonie, salutem. Precipimus vobis quod cernerium infra eandem Turrim reparari et bene emendari faciatis per totum ubi necesse fuit. Et omnes gutteras plumbeas magne turris a sumitate eiusdem Turris per quas aqua pluvie descendere debet usque ad terram extendere faciatis et descendere ita quod murus dicte Turris per aquam pluvie distillantem qui de novo est dealbatus nullo modo possit deperire nec de facti prorumpere. Et fieri faciatis super eandem Turrim in parte australi superius versus austrum imas aluras de bono et forte meremio et per totum bene plumbari per quas gentes videre possint usque ad pedem eiusdem Turris et ascendere et melius defendere si necesse fuit. Dealbari etiam faciatis totam capellam Sancti Iohannis Evangelisti in eadem Turri et fieri faciatis in eadem capella tres fenestras vitreas, unam ex parte boreali cum mariola tenente parvum suum, relique in parte australi de trinitate et etiam de Sancto Iohanne Apostolo et Evangelisto in eadem parte australi. Et depingi faciatis patibulum et trabem ultra altarem eiusdem capelle bene et bonis coloribus et fieri faciatis et depingi duas ymagines pulchras ubi melius et decentius fieri possint in eadem capella, unam de Sancto Edwardo tenente anulum et donante et tendente Sancto Iohanni Evangelisto et dealbari faciatis totum veterem murum circa fere dictam turrim nostram. . . . Rex apud Windelsore x die Decembris.

5. Gruffudd ap Llywelyn's attempted escape from the White Tower, 1 March 1244
(Matthew Paris, *Chronica majora*, ed. Luard, vol. IV, p. 295)

Matthew Paris records how Gruffudd ap Llywelyn, Prince of North Wales, falls while escaping from a tower, almost certainly the White Tower, and dies. This version of the story has several similarities to Orderic Vitalis's story of Rannulf Flambard, and while true in outline, some of its details may be apocryphal.

In this world, the state of a man's affairs changes with every roll of Fortune's dice. Gruffudd, eldest son of Llywelyn, prince of North Wales, who was being held prisoner in the Tower of London, daily received more than ample sustenance to the value of half a mark and his wife was allowed to have access to him. Yet the unaccustomed boredom of his daily routine badly bothered him, and so he defiantly hatched a plan to escape from his confinement. One night he slipped away from his guards and using a rope manufactured from cut-up sheets, hangings and tablecloths he let himself straight down from the top of the Tower. But when he had lowered himself a certain distance, the rope snapped through the heavy weight of his body, and he fell from the heights. For he was a very large man, with a round stomach. Thus he broke his neck and died. His wretched body, lying by the wall of the Tower, presented a pitiful spectacle for those who found him early next morning, for his head and neck were forced almost between his shoulder-blades, down in the middle of his chest. When the king heard of his, he punished the laxity of the guards and ordered that Gruffudd's son, who had been kept in the same prison cell as his father, should from then on be guarded more securely. Thus on the first of March died Gruffudd: as the saying goes, 'he reached the heights and fell'.

Et dum alea fortunalis mundana casualiter haec tempora variaret, Griffinus, filius Leolini principis Northwalliae primogenitus, qui in Turri Londoniarum captivus tenebatur, et cotidie ad ejusdem honorabilem sustentationem victualem de fisco dimidiam marcam percipiebat, data licentia uxori suae ut accessum ad ipsum haberet, tamen taedio diuturni et insoliti carceris graviter affectus, cogitavit argumentose, qualiter inclusionem poterat evadere carceralem. Una igitur noctium deceptis custodibus, ex laceratis lintheaminibus tapetiis et mappis facto fune, per ipsum funem se demisit perpendiculariter a sumitate ipsius turris. Et cum per aliquod spatium se pendentem demisisset, ex sui corporis ponderositate rupto fune, cecidit ab alto. Erat quippe magnus valde et abdomine turgens. Et sic fractus cervicibus expiravit. Cujus miserum cadaver, mane juxta Turris murum inventum, miserabile spectaculum praebuit inventibus. Erat enim caput ejus cum collo fere totum inter scapulas in pectore demersum. Rex autem, cum haec audisset, custodum desidiam increpando puniens, jussit filium ejusdem Griffini, qui in eodem carcere detinebatur cum patre, ex tunc arctius custodiri. Obiit autem dictus Griffinus qui ut dictum est, ab alto corruit, prima die Martii.

6. Imprisonment in the 'Black Cellar' of the White Tower, 1295
(Leadam and Baldwin 1918, p. 14)

Matthew of the Exchequer is held prisoner in harsh conditions in the basement of the White Tower on the orders of the Bishop of Bath, after allegedly trying to escape from the Fleet prison. This extract is one of many complaints by Londoners about the bishop's injustices and some of it may be an exaggeration. Polard and Jordan were clearly the names of two prisons in the Tower of London, though they cannot now be identified: the Black Cellar is shown by this and other sources to be the western basement of the White Tower.

The said bishop then falsely ruled that he had broken prison and sentenced him to two years in the Tower of London. Then the said bishop came to the Tower and ordered him to be stripped of this coat, belt and shoes and to be kept without a bed. He ordered him to be placed in *Polard* and to be chained up in *Jordan* with two pairs of fetters. He then had him placed in the Black Cellar, seated on the bare earth floor, and for two years he lived there without any kind of fire or other light. He had no water to drink except from the tower's well with the drowned rats. He lived in this way until our lord king graciously delivered him.

La ly fit le dit Eueke fausement juger quil aveit la prison brusee e ly fit juge a la tour de Londres destre ileuke per ii aunz. E pus vint le dit Eueke a la tour e li fit despoyller destres a la cote, deschauce saunz ceinture, e saunz lit, e ly fit mettre en polard, e enchesner en jordan, en ii peyre de fierges, et pus fu mis el neir celer sur la tere nue, ou il fu per ii aunz saunz nule manere de feu ou autre lumere, ne autre ewe naveit a beyure, fors ke del puz de la tour, ou les raz se neient. E cele vie mena deskes ataunt ke nostre seignour le rey le delivera de sa grace.

7. Fitting out the treasury in the White Tower, 1312
(TNA, E 101/468/20, fol. 2)

Wooden cupboards are made to contain documents, probably in the White Tower: these cupboards reuse wood from a siege engine blown over in a gale.

Payment to the carpenter Thomas Bryedith, engaged on the direction of the then acting treasurer and chamberlain lord Roger de Sandale in making cupboards in the Treasury in which to place and keep rolls, writs, fines, charters, deeds and other memoranda and various other notes and records from various ages, peoples and kingdoms, left in the same Treasury . . . and to Robert of Chester and his fellow-sawyer, engaged in sawing the wood for the same cupboards, out of the timber which came from the smaller engine which the wind blew down . . .

Thome Bryedith carpentario operante circa almaria facienda infra Thesaurum pro ordinatione domini Rogeri de Sandale tunc tenentis loci thesauro et camerario pro rotulis brevibus finibus cartis scriptis et aliis memorandis et aliis diversis minutis recordis gentibus de temporibus pluris regnis in eadem thesauro liberatis et liberandis in eisdem almariis ponendis et salvandis . . . Roberto de Cestre et socio suo sarratoribus operantibus circa maeremium sarrandum ad eadem almaria videlicet de illo maeremio quod fuit de minori ingenio vento prostrato . . .

8. White Tower garderobes, 1313
(TNA, E 101/468/20, fol. 4)

Filth is dropping from the garderobes of the White Tower into the middle of the castle.

Be it recorded that the said William of Norwich, acting treasurer, has ordered the construction of a stone wall to hide the ordures dropping from the garderobe turret of the Great Tower . . .

Memorandum quod dictus Willelmus de Norwico tenens loci thesauro precepit quendam murum petreium fieri pro orduris exeuntibus de turello garderobarum magne turris abscondentibus . . .

9. Description of the White Tower, 1324
(Symeon Semeon, ed. Esposito, p. 26)

Two Irish friars on a pilgrimage describe the Tower of London: although more impressed by the concentric curtain defences of Edward I and Edward II, they also note the high quality of the White Tower's masonry, almost certainly a testament to the effect of whitening the exterior.

And at the edge of the same city in the direction of the sea is a most famous and impregnable castle, encircled with two walls, very deep ditches filled with water and every device of warfare. In its centre is that most famous tower which is called 'The Tower of London', built with immeasurable solidity of cut and dressed stone and raised to a wondrous height.

Et in fine ejusdem civitatis versus mare est castrum famosissimum et inexpugnabile, duplici muro, fossatis amplissimis, aquarum abissis ac aliis bellicis apparatibus circumdatum, in cujus medio est illa turris famosissima, que Turris Londonie nuncupatur, ex lapidibus quadris et sectis mira altitudine erecta et inestimabili firmitate constructa.

10. Condition of the White Tower, 1335
(Original manuscript lost: transcribed in Bayley 1821–5, vol. 1, appendix 1, pp. i–iv)

Extracts relating to the High Tower from the commission for inquiring into the state of the Tower.

. . . we discovered the following defects, namely defects to the walls, crenellations and stairs in the High Tower needing masonry repairs and improvements to a total of 40 pounds.
Item in carpentry defects in the High Tower, in the turrets, two floors of the tower and a floor of the kitchen and in the room hard by the door, in repairs and improvements to the windows and doors, 30 pounds.
Item in leadwork defects to the High Tower and its gutters, 30 pounds.

. . . invenimus defectus subscriptos, videlicet, in defectibus murorum, karnellum et graduum altae turris emendandis et reparandis de opere cimentariorum ad summam xl librarum.
Item in defectibus altae turris de opere carpentariorum in turellis et duobus aeriis turris unius aeriae coquinae et camerae contra hostium, fenestrarum, et hostiorum emendandis et reparandis, xxx. librarum.
Item in defectibus altae turris et gutterarum de opere plumbariorum, xxx. libr.3

11. King Jean II of France held in the White Tower, Monday, 25 May 1360
(TNA, E 101 27/38 m2)

The expenses for the captive Jean II of France on his first day as a prisoner in the White Tower. In order to prepare the rooms for him, it had been necessary to find other space elsewhere in the castle for chancery documents. Jean was later released on the promise of a large ransom, which was never paid: he returned to England voluntarily to resume his captivity, and died there.

On Monday 25 May, the same John de Thorp calculated these expenses: in the office of the pantry, for 74 loaves of bread per hundred 3s 1d, in the office of the buttery for 8 sesters of wine, 16s 6d, 21 gallons of various wines at 2d, 3s 6d, in the office of the wardrobe for 2lb of candles, 4d, 1lb of peppers, 15d, 1lb of ginger, 13d, 10lb of almonds, 2s 6d, 6lb of ric, 9d, in the office of the kitchen, a quart of various goods, 13s 4d, 3 carcasses of mutton 6s, 1 calf 2s 6d, in the office of the poultry for 1 capon 7d, 12 chickens 4s, [illegible] 4d, in the office of the scullery, for 1 bushel of salt, 12d, 17 faggots, 8d, half a quart of coal, 5d, for 14 large *shrids* [?] 6d, for herbs, 3d, in the office of the salsary, half a quart of mustard, 1d, 1 quart of verjuice, 2d, and in the office of the marshal, for the wages of Bartholomew Inworth up to 12d, Risceby Thorp up to 7d, Edward Elmham, William Herny, William of Naples, Thomas Messager and Reginald de Camera, grooms of the King's chamber, 3 pence apiece, to William Wyghman, Walter Scudle, Richard Balle, Thomas Spilman, grooms of the office, 3 pence apiece, and for the wages of 10 watchmen watching each night, each of them receiving 3 pence per night, 7s 9d.

Total 67s 2d

Die lune xxv die maii idem computavit expensas in officio panetrie lxxiiii panes per c iii s i d. In officio butillarie viii sextera vini xvi s vi d xxi lagenas diversas ad ii d iii s vi d. In officio garderobe ii libris candelarum iiii d, I librum pepers xv d i librum ginger xiii d amigdala x libris ii s vi d Rys vi libris ix d. In officio coquine i quart diversorum bonorum xiii s iiii d iii cass multon vi s i vitulum ii s vi d. In officio pulletrie i capon vii d ob xii galla iiii s (illegible) per farma iiii d. In officio scutillarie i bussellum salis xii d xvii fagettos viii d dimiduum quarti carbonis v d xiiii shrid grossiss vi d ob herb iii d. In officio salsarie dimiduum quarti cenapii i d ob i quart vergens ii d. Et in officio marescalli pro vadiis Bartholomei Inworth ad xii d Risceby Thorp usque ad vii d ob Edwardi Elmham, Willelmi Herny, Guillelmi de Naples, Thomasi Messagerii et Reginaldi de Camera vallettorum camere regis quolibet ad iii d, Willelmi Wyghman, Walteri Scudle, Ricardi Ballei, Thome Spilman vallettorum officii quolibet ad iii d. Et pro vadiis decem vigilatoribus quolibet nocte vigilantibus a qualibet capienti de nocte iii d vii s ix d summa lxvii s ii d ob.

12. Richard II in the Tower during the Peasants' Revolt, 1381

(*Anonimalle Chronicle*, ed. Galbraith, pp. 142–5)

During this time, a large number of the commons came up to the Tower of London to talk with the king, but were not able to hear him speak. They therefore laid siege to the Tower, from the direction of St Katherine's on the south side [actually on the south-east] . . .

At this time, the king was inside a turret of the Great Tower of London and saw the manor of the Savoy and Clerkenwell all ablaze. He called all the lords to him in a chamber and asked them their advice of what to do in such a time of need . . .

Then after Thursday, on the feast of Corpus Christi, the king was in the Tower, thoughtful and despondent. He climbed a small tower facing towards St Katherine's, where a large number of the commons were then lying . . .

En qel temps grante partie de les comunes aleront a la Tour de Loundres pur parler ovesque le roy, et ne purront atteindre a son parlance, par qay ils mistrent assege a la toure del part de Seint Katerynes vers la south . . .

En quel temps le roy, estaunt en une turret del graunde Tour de Loundres, vist le manoir de Sawvay et Klerkenwell . . . en feu ardauntz, appelle toutz les seigneurs la entoure luy en une chaumbre et les demanderount conseil qe serroit affair en tiel necessitee . . .

Den apres mesme le ioedy en le dit fest de Corpore Christi, le roy esteaunt en le Tour pensive et trist, ala amount sur une petit tour devers Seint Kateryne ou furont gisauntz graunde nombre des comunes . . .

Afterwards, Richard goes to Mile End; Sudbury tries to escape by river, but is discovered.

Meanwhile, the archbishop was devoutly singing Mass in the Tower. He confessed the prior of the Hospitallers at Clerkenwell and the others, said Mass two or three times, singing the commendation, the *Placebo* and *Dirige*, the Seven Psalms and the Litany, but when he came to *Omnes Sancti, orate pro nobis*, the commons burst in, dragged the Archbishop from his chapel in the Tower, took him and beat him villainously . . . Then they cut off their heads . . . and carried them in procession before them through the city . . . and then brought them back to London Bridge, where they set up the head of the Archbishop above the bridge, and the eight other heads of those they had beheaded, so that everyone crossing the bridge might see them . . .

En quel temps lercevesque chaunta sa messe devotement en la Toure et confessa le priour del Hospitalle de Klerkenwell et autres et puis oia deux messes ou trois et chaunta la comendacione et Placebo et Dirige et les vii salmes et la letanye; et quant il fuist a Omnes

Sancti orate pro nobis, entrerent les comunes et pristrent lercevesque hors de sa chapelle en la Toure et luy ferrent et butent vilaynesment . . . et couperount les testes . . . et les porterount avaunt eux en procesione par tute la citee . . . et retournerount al pount de Loundres et illoeques mistrent le test del ercevesque amount le pount et viii autres testes qe furont decolles, qe toutz purroient veer qe passerount le pount . . .

13. The garrison of the Tower capitulates in the face of the Peasants' Revolt, 1381

(Walsingham, *Historia anglicana*, ed. Riley, vol. I, pp. 458–9)

The mass of peasants then divided into three. Some of them went off on a round of pillage and destruction, as I have already described. Others stayed outside London in the place called 'Mile End'. A third group took to Tower Hill. This group outside the Tower was so insolent and criminal that they looted the provisions which the king had ordered to the Tower. Moreover, they issued an insane order for the King to surrender the Archbishop, the master of St John's hospital and the others sheltering inside the Tower, calling them traitors, intending to put them all to death. In this emergency, the King decided to allow them into the Tower, since he could not safely deny them what they wanted, and they pursued their evil intent into the most inaccessible parts of the castle.

At that time, the Tower contained 600 fighting men, fully armed, brave and experienced, and 600 archers. The strange thing is, all of them completely lost their nerve, so that you would think them more like dead men than living. Certainly all memory of their former deeds of arms died in them, together with any recollection of their previous strength and glory. In short, faced by the whole English peasantry, their courage wilted away. Who could ever believe that these people, not just peasants, but the most wretched peasants, not in a horde but only a few, would fearlessly enter the King's bedchamber or his mother's, brandishing their foul sticks? That they could scare off all of the knights with threats, that they could stroke or pull the beards of the greatest nobles with their uncouth and filthy hands? The nobles spoke to them as if they were close friends, some promising to serve the peasants faithfully, some pledging on oath to join with them in hunting down traitors of the realm, as though they could not see this obvious treason for themselves. They hoisted banners and pennants like a squadron of armed men as mentioned and marched on.

While all this was going on and, as I have said, a few of the peasants had got into the King's chamber, they were insolently sitting or lying on the King's bed, joking: most horrible of all, some of them even asked the King's mother to kiss them.

But strangest of all, out of all those knights or squires, not one dared to come in to stop such intolerable behaviour, to make the peasants take their hands off her, or even refrained from telling them all the secrets of the place. The peasants, formerly servants of the basest sort, now went in and out like Lords: swineherds pretended to be knights, captains of an army not of soldiers but of peasants. I believe that God was teaching the English a lesson: a man's strength lies not in his courage, nor should he trust in his sword or his bow, but in Him who saves us from our oppressors and Who of his mercy and goodness, ever brings those who guard us to confusion.

Erant pro tunc turbae rusticorum in tres partes separatae, de quibus una pars vacabat, ut diximus, destructione praedii supradicti. Alia juxta Londonias exspectavit, in loco 'le Mile Ende' vocato. Tertia vero occupaverat Montem Turris. Ea autem turba quae prope Turrim erat, ita inverecunda et insolens habebatur, ut victualia regis, quae ad Turrim vehebantur, diriperet inverecunde. Et insuper, tanta agitabatur insania, ut regem compelleret ad concedendum eis Archiepiscopum et magistrum Hospitalis Sancti Johannis, aliosque in ipsa Turri occultatos, quos omnes proditores vocabant; alios sciret semetipsum vita privandum. Rex igitur, in arto constitutus, permisit eos in Turrim intrare, et loca secretissima pro sua voluntate nequissima perscrutari, quippe qui nihil negari tute potuit quod petebant.

Erat eo tempore in ipsa Turri ssexcenti viri bellici, armis instructi, viri fortes et expertissimi, et sexcenti sagittarii qui omnes—quod mirum est—animo ita conciderant, ut eos magis similes mortuis quam vivis reputares. Mortua enim erant in eis omnis memoria quondam bene gestae militiae, extincta recordatio antehabiti vigoris et gloriae et, ut concludam breviter, emarcuerat a facie rusticorum pene totius Loegriae omnis audacia militaris. Nam quis unquam credidisset, non solum rusticos, sed rusticorum abjectissimos, non plures sed singulos, audere thalamum Regis, vel matris eius, cum baculis subintrare vilissimis, et ununquemque de militibus deterrere minis, et quorundam nobilissimorum militum barbas suis incultissimis et sordidissimis manibus contrectare, demulcere; et verba modo familiaria serere de socialitate cum eisdem habenda de caetero, modo de fide servanda ipsis ribaldis, modo de juramento praestando, ut communiter cum eis regni quaererent proditores, cum ipsi manifeste proditionis notam devitare non possent, quippe qui vexilla et penicellos erigentes, tali modo cum armata manu pro modulo suo, scilicet modo praetacto, incedere non timebant?

Et cum haec omnia faceret, et, ut diximus, plerique soli in cameram concedissent, et sedendo, iacendo, iocando, super lectum regis insolescerent; et insuper matrem regis ad oscula invitarent quidam; non tamen

—quod mirum dictu est—audebant plures milites et armigeri unum de tam inconvenientibus actibus convenire, non ad impedendum manus injicere, nec verbis secretissimis mussitare. Intrabant et exibant ut domini, qui quondam fuerant vilissimae conditionis servi; et praeferebant se militibus non tam militum sed rusticorum subulci. Quia ut credimus, Deus Anglicis demonstrare voluit, quod non in fortitudine sua roborabitur vir, nec in arcu vel gladio fore sperandum, sed in Eo qui salvat nos de affligentibus nos, et custodientes nos sua misericordia et pietate confundere consuevit.

14. The Knights of the Bath, 1485

(British Library, Egerton MS 595, fols 42r, 43r)

27 October. The White Tower is used for the Initiation ceremony for the Knights of the Bath.

After that the esquires governors were assignid them and there baynes were prepared in a great chamber in the downgeon as of old tyme hath ben accustomed. And when it was night the king himself of his benigne goodnis nobly accompanyed with the Duke of Bedford, the Erle of Oxenford, the Erle of Darbie, the Erle of Devonshire with many other noble Lordes, knyghtes and Esquiers first [gave] them in the baynes the advertisement of the order of knighthode and after him other Lordes and Estatis . . . And then the king departed to his chamber and the newe made knights went to the chapell and offerid as is accustomed. And thei all turned into the hall agayne . . .

15. The Ritual of the Bath prescribed in detail

(British Library, Cotton MS Nero C IX, fols 168v–170v)

This treatise, following earlier French versions, prescribes the ritual of initiation for the Knights of the Bath. No explicit mention is made of the Tower of London: the ritual could be carried out anywhere and was often performed elsewhere. When investitures were carried out for the coronation, however, as mentioned in the title, the Tower was the traditional location, with the bathing and possibly the vigil taking place in the White Tower itself.

The maner of makynge of knyghtes aftyr the Custome of Engelond in tyme of peas and at the Coronatioun, that is knyghtes of the bathe

Whanne a esquyer comyth in to the courte for to receyve the ordre of knyghthode in tyme of peas aftyr the custume of Engelond, he shalbe worshipfully receyved of the officeres of the courte as of the styward or chamberleyn yf they be present and elles of the marshalles and ussheres in the absence of the styward and chamberleyn. And there shalbe ordeyned twoo worshipfull squiers wyse and wele norysshed in curtesy and expert in the deedes of

knyghthod, and they shalbe governours to hym to serve and ordeyne what shall longe to hym for the tyme. And in case that the squyer come before dyner he shall serve the kyng of water of a dysh only of the fyrste course, and that is doo for to take leve of the servyce of squyers.

Thanne his governours shall lede hym in to his chambre withoute anymore to beseyne that day. And at even the governors shall sende aftyr the barbor and he shall make redy a Bathe in the bestwyse that he can. The satte withinne and withoute wrapped with lynen cloth clene and whyte and covered with thycke carpettes or mantelles for colde of the nyght. Thanne shall the squyers berde be shaven and his hede rounded which doone the governours shall goo un to the kynge, and to hym say thus. 'Mooste myghty prince our sovrayn lord, loo hit wexeth more unto the evyn and oure maister is redy unto the bathe when it pleseth unto your royall mageste.'

And upon that the kyng shall comaunde his chamberleyne to goo unto the squyers chambre that is to be made knyght, and to take with hym the mooste worthy and mooste wyse knyghtes that been there present to thentent that they shall the same squyers truly counseyle enforme and teche wysely of the ordre of knyghthod. And soo with that oder yonge squyers of householde mynstrelles fyn synge and dawnsynge shall goo before the chamberleyn and the seyd knyghtes unto the tyme that they come to the chambre dore of the seyd squyer that is to be made knyghte. Whanne the governours heren noyse of mynstrelles, anoon they shall make naked theyr maister and all naked shalbe putt in to the bathe. The menstrallcs before the entre of the chamberlyen and other noble knyghtes shall abyde and be stylle withoute noyse togedyr with the seyd squyers levynge their noyse for the tyme. Whych thyng doon, the chamberleyne with the seide noble knyghtes shall enter prively withoute noyse in to the chambre of the seyd squyere and whan they entre everich to other shall than do reverence and worshipp which of them shalbe the fyrste for to counsell the squyer in the bathe of the ordre and the makynge to perform the kyngs comaundement. And whan they be accorded then shall the fyrste go to the bathe and there he shall knele before the bathe seyenge secretly to the squyer thus

'Right dere brother, grete worshippe be the ordre unto yow, and almighty god yeve yow the [fol. 169r] praisyng of all knyghhod. Loo this is the ordre. Be ye stronge in the feithe of holy cherche and wydows and maydones oppressed releve as right comaundeth, yeve ye to everych his owne. With all thy mynde above all thynge love and drede god. And above all other erthly thynges love the kynge thy sovrayn lord hym and his right defende unto thy powere and be fore all worldly thynges putte hym in worshipp and thyng that be not to be taken, beware to begynne'. In this wyse or better itur.

And whanne the knyghte is thus counselled, the same knyght counseylor shall take in his hande water of the Bathe and shall putte it upon the shulders of the squyer, and take his leve to goon and departe. And the governours at all tymes shall kepe the sydes of the bathe. In this wyse shall all the other knyghtes aforesayd doon everych aftyr other in the best wyse that they can. And this doon the knyghtes without noyse shall goo oute of the chambre for the tyme.

Then shall theyr governours take their maister oute of the bathe and ley hym softly in his bed to drye, and the bed shall not be of grete valewe but withoute celour or courteyns. And when the squyer is wele dryed he shall ryse oute of his bed and shall clothe hym warnid for the wache of nyght. And upon all his clothes he shall have a cape of blak russet with longe sleves and the hode sewed un to the cape in manere of an heremyte. The squyer thus arrayde and made redy the barbor shall put away the bathe and all thyng that is aboute the bathe as wele withinne as withoute. The barbor shall take all for his fee and also he shall have for this shavynge lyke as it folowith heeraftyr. That is to wete yf he be a Duke an Erle an Baron or a Bachelere aftyr the custome of the courte everych shall yeve aftyr his estate and principally yf yeve jugement be requryd it shalbe at the wyll of the kyngs mageste.

Aftyr this the governors shall lede the squier unto the chapell. And when they be in the chapell there shalbe ordeyned spyces and wyne for the knyghtes and squyers, which thyng doone the governors shall lede these knyghtes afore the squyer for to take theyr leve. And he with sylence shall thanke them of theyr labours and worshyppes that they have doone un to hym. In that wyse they shall goo oute of the chapell. The governors shall shutt the dore tyll the dawnynge wex clere and the day come. And there shall abyde in the chapell noon but the squyers governors [officers of arms inserted] and the wayte. In this wyse shall the squyer all nyght tyll it be day enyr in his prayers prayinge and besechyng almighty god and the blyssed vyrgyne marie his moder that thilke passinge temporall dignyte he may receyve to his worshippe and praysinge of god the blyssed vyrgyne marie his moder, holy cherche and the ordre of knyghthod.

And when the dawnynge comyth he shall have a preste and be confessed yf it will lyke him of his synnes and trespasses, which thyng ended he shall have his matens and mass and be comonyd if he wyll. Aftyr his entre to the chapell he shall evermore have a serge or a taper of wex brennynge be

fore hym. And whan masse be gonne oone of the governours shall holde the taper brennynge before hym un to the tyme that the gospell be begonne. And then he shall be take it un to his maister which shall holde it in his hande tyll the gospell be endyd alwey his hede coveryd. And at the ende of the gospell the governour shall receyve the taper agayne and put it before his maister un to the ende of the masse. At the levation of the sacrament oon of the governours [fol. 169v] shall putte of the hoode of his mayster. And aftyr the sight of the sacrament he shall doo it on ayen tyll in principio be begonne. Oon of his governors shall putte of his hoode and make hym stande and holde the sayd taper in his hande havynge in the seide taper styckynge a peny nygh the lyght. And whan the prest seith verbum caro factum est he shall knele down and offre the tapre and the peny. It is to wete the taper to the worshippe of god and the peny to the worship of hym that shall make hym knyght.

These thyngs doon the governors shall lede hym ayen in to his chambre and ley hym ayen in his bed tyll it be forth dayes, and there he shall take the reste that the wache of the nyghte hath made wery, so than the bedde shalbe amended and refreshed before the tyme that his maister wake, that is to wete with coverture of cloth of gold called siglyton, and that shalbe lyned with blewe card.

And whan they see tyms they shall goo to the kyng and sey to hym thus, 'Mooste victorious prynce whan that it lykith unto youre high mageste oure maister shall awake'. And theruppon shall the kyng comaunde the knyghtes squyers and mynstrelles aforesayd that they goo un to the chambre of the squyer to awake hym array hym and clothe hym and brynge hym un to the hall before the kyng hym self. But before the comynge of the knyghtes un to the squiers chambre, the governors shall ordeyne all manere necessaries redy by ordre for to be delyvred un to the knyghtes. And whanne these knyghtes become un to the chambre of the squyere, they shall enter softly withoute noyse and sey to the squyere 'Sir good day, it is tyme to aryse' and with that the governors shall take and arayse hym up by the armes. Thanne the moste worthy and moste wyse shall take unto hym his sherte. Another next worthy his breche, the iiide his dublet, the iiiith shall clothe hym with a gowne of rede tartaryn. Other tweyne shall doon oon his hosyn which shalbe of blac sylke or of blak cloth with soles of ledyr sowed to them. Other tweyn shall boton his sleves. Another shall gyrde hym with a gyrdyll of whyte ledyr withoute harneyse of any metall of the breede of an ynche. An other shall kembe his hede. An other shall yeve him his mantell of the sute of the curtyll of rede tartaryn fastened with alace of whyte sylke with a payre of white gloves hangynge at the ende of the lace. But he shall have of the chaundeler of the householde the corce gyrdyll and the gloves. And on the other syde the chaundelere shall take for his fee all the garmentes and all the array withall the necessaries in the which the squyer was arrayed and clothed the day that he entred in to the courte for to take the ordre togedyr with the bed, in the which he lay furst aftyr the bathe alsowele the cloth of gold called siglaton as other necessaries touchyng the sayd bed.

And this thyng fully doon these wyse knyghtes shall lede the squyer on horsbak un to the kynges halle all tymes the mynstrelles beyng before makyng theyr menstralsye. Theyr horse shal be arrayde in this wyse, he shall have a sadyll covred with blak lether, the arsons of whyte trefoure square and blac styrroped with gilt irons and his sadyll shall have no cropere but a paytrell of blac lether pleyne with large reynes in the gyse of spayne and accrosse plate [?] in the forhede. And there shalbe ordeyned a yonge gentyll squyer for to ryde before the squyer that is to be made knyght. And he shalbe opyn hede. And shall bere the swerd of the squyer the poynt downward with spores hangyng upon the swerd. And the swerd shall have a whyte scabard and fret with the gyrdell and stales with whyte lether withoute any harneyse. And the yonge gentyll squyer shall holde the swerd by the poynte in this wyse.

They shall ryde to the kyngs [fol. 170r] hall all tymes the seyd governors beynge redy to the maister as it is fyttynge to be. And the forseyd noble and wyse knyghtes shall soberly lede this squyer as they owen. And whan the squyer comyth before the hall dore, the marchalles and usshers that be redy afore hym in the most honest wyse that they can seyinge thus 'Cometh down'. And thanne he shall come down. The marchall for his fee shall take the horse or C s.

This thyng thus doon these wyse knyghtes shall lede the squuyere in to the halle or in to the grete chambre un to his table. And forthwith he shall be putte at the begynnynge of the seide table tyll that the kyng come. The seyde knyghtes aboute his persone as on every side and the yonge squyer swerd berer before hym standynge with the swerd betwyx the ii governors.

Whanne the kynge comyth in to the hall and perceyveth the squyer redy to take the ordre in dew wyse, he askyth for the swerd and the spores. The kyngs chambyrleyne shall take the swerd and the spores oute of the handes of the yonge squyere, and shall take and shewe them to the kynge. The kynge shall receyve the right spore and betake it to oon of the moste worthy that standeth aboute comandynge hym that he put it on the right hele of the squyer. And by the kings comaundement that lord

knelynge on the oon kne shall take the squyer by the right leg and putte the foote upon his kne and shall putte the spore upon his hele. And shall make acrosse upon the kne of the squyer and shall kysse it. Thanne shall an other lord put on the other hele an other spore in the same wyse that the other dyd. Than the kynge of the mekenesse of his high myght takyng the swerd in his hands shall gyrde therwith the squyer. Thanne shall the squyere lyft up his armes on high and the king shall put his armes aboute the nekke of the squyer and lyftynge up his right hande he shall smyte the squyer in the nekke seyeng 'Be ye a good knyght' kyssyng hym.

Aftyrwarde these noble and wyse knyghtes aforesayd this newe knyght shall lede in to the chapell with melody as it is to forne seid un to the high awtere. And he shall ungyrthe hym and his swerd with prayers and devotiouns shall offre to god and to holy cherche most devoutly besechyng god that thilke ordre moste worthy dewly he may kepe un to his ende. These thinges so doon he shall take a soppe in wyne and in the goynge oute of the chapell the maister cook shalbe redy and doo of his spores and shall take them to hym for his fee. And the reason is this, that in case be that the knyght do aftyr any thynge that be defawte and reproof un to the ordre of knyghthod, the maister cook thanne with a grete knyf with which he dresseth his messes shall smyte of his spores from his heles. And therefore in remembraunce of this thynge the spores of a newe knyght in order takynge shalbe fee un to the maister cook perteynynge dewly un to his offyce.

Thanne shall these wyse knyghtes aforesayd lede this newe knyght in to the hall ageyn. The which begynnyng the table of knyghtes shall sitte to mete. And the seyd wyse and noble knyghtes shall sitte aboute hym at the table. And the noble knyghtes shalbe served lyke as other been. And as for that tyme he shall not ete nor drynke at the table but yf grete nede be. Nor he shall not meve hym nor loke hedyr nor thedyr more than a wyf newe wedded. And evyrmore oon of his governours shall stonde by hym with a kerchief of the which if any nede come he may serve hym.

And whanne the kyng aryseth from the table and goth in to the chambre the newe knyght shall be lad un to his [fol. 170v] chambre with grete multitude of knyghtes squyers and mynstralles joyinge syngynge and daunsynge un to the entre of his chambre. And there the knyghtes squyers and mynstralles shall take their leve and the newe knyght shall goo to ete, the dore shalbe closed and he shall doo of his array which shalbe yeven to the kyngs other herawdes of armes. And also the sayd kyng of arms and herawdes shall have for the office of arms of any Duke Erle Barown and Bachelere aftyr their estates. And of the lefte xx s for their honours to shewe and to crye them in the kyngs presence and in the sayd court. The grey cope shalbe unto the wayte or a noble for it.

And aftyr this mete this noble newe knyght anoon shalbe arrayde with a robe of blew with strayte sleves and he shall have upon the lyft shuldere a white lace of sylk hanginge. And that lace he shall kepe in that wyse above his clothyng withoute forth from that day forth contynuelly un to that tyme he gete hym som maner of worshippe by defuynge in witnesse of worthy knyghtes and squyers kyngs other herawdes of armes and twelve herawdes clerely theraftyr reported. Which reporte moste entere in to the eares of the worthy prynce which hath made hym knyght or of som noble lady for to take away the lace from the shulder saying thus 'Right dere lord, I have herd so moche of your worshyppes and renown that ye have doon in dyverse partyes un to the grete worshippe of knyghthod to youre self and to hym that made yow knyght that desert and right wyll that this lace be put and take away'.

But after dyner the worshipfull and worthy knyghtes and squyers shall come afore the seyd newe knyght and hym shall lede to the kyngs presence. All tymes beyng before hym the sayd squyers governors. And whanne the newe knyght comyth in to the kyngs presence he shall knele before the kyng and shall sey thus 'Moost drad and moost mighty prynce of an lytill power and of that may I thank yow of all the worshippes curtesies goodnesse which ye have doon un to me'. And this seyd, he shall take leve of the kyng and upon that the governors shall goo and take charyte leve of theyr mayster seyeng thus 'Worshipfull syr by the kyngs comaundement we have served yow. And that comaundement fulfylled and performed to oure powere. And what we have doon in oure servyce ageyn your reverence, we pray yow of your grace to pardon us oure neglygence. Furthermore of the custom of the kyngs courte we aske and requyre yow of robys and fees to the terme of oure lyf convenable to the kyngs squyers felowes to the knyghtes of othyr landes'.

Transcripts of Primary Documents: Post-Medieval

SELECTED AND EDITED BY ANNA KEAY

1. Repairing the keep for Anne Boleyn's coronation; undated, but probably 1532/3
(The National Archives [formerly Public Record Office], hereafter TNA, E 101/474/13)

These extracts are from the Office of Works accounts for repairing the Tower of London before Anne Boleyn's coronation. The precise period of the account is not stated, but the date of January 1533 given towards the end of the document suggests that the account covers the autumn and winter of 1532. The document is mainly concerned with repairs to the royal apartments to the south of the White Tower, but works to the White Tower were also undertaken, among them the construction of the great cupolas (or 'types') and the gilded weathervanes that surmounted them.

[fol. 1r] Carpenters . . . Itm made iiii Types on the top of the white Tower w[i]th their ordenances abowte them that is to sey Joyll peces and boltes to the top of them and a flower levell w[i]th the platt[e]s Joysted & borded

Itm more Joyned to the same Types trymers made Rownde abowte for to defende the water of[f] from the walles And thus the carpentry worke of the seid Types beyng fynysshed was a chargeable pece of worke to doo

[fol. 3r] Carpenters . . . Itm for makyng of a frame for a bell in the white Tower the whiche callith workemen to work and fro work . . . Itm for a great beme that was fett from Stratfordbowe to

set in the white Tower iii carpenters for fellyng and hewyng of the same pece ii dayes

[fol. 3v] Carpenters . . . Itm for ii litle frames made of bourdes for to close in the great faynes that cam from elysys the paynter for hurtyng of the gildyng to ev[e]ry fayne one

Itm a flower made and redy framed for the Rownde Tower on the whyte Tower whiche is not yet sett up

[fol. 4v] Briklayers ffirste the hythenyng of the iiii Types on the white Tower w[i]th bryckeworke every Type a yarde hye

Itm more the batilmentys to the white Tower w[i]th brycke for the masons to Coppe upon and more the Rowgh castyng of those Types and the same Tower . . .

Itm the Juell howse Roughcast rownde aboute and the makyng of bothe the sydes of the stayres goyng up to the Joyell hous w[i]th bryk

[fol. 6r] Plaisterers . . . Itm the iiii Types on the white Tower the playstyng undernethe the batilmentys

[fol. 7v] Plomars firste the takyng downe of the iiii Types upon the great white Tower and castyng and chasyng of the same iiii Types. Itm ii Sesterns on the white Tower westsyde

[fol. 9r] fremasons Itm in the hye whyte Tower the cowpyng of xlviii Coppys on the west syde and so the southsyde the spaces betwene in length vi foot the left and some vii fote and in heyght vi fote and in the estsyde the spaces betwene some vii fote and some vi fote di, ev[e]ry space xxiii fote quynys of cane asheler on the west syde and on the south-syde liiii fote quynys cane asshelar and on the est syde the same Tower lx fote quynys cane ashelar, and on the northsyde the same Tower xl fote quynys in cane ashelar, and more in skew and crestes to the same spacys on the west syde amoun-tith unto iiiC that is to say in ev[e]ry space xxx fote in skew & crest and in ev[e]ry iii fote in heyght of quynys, and more on the south syde in skew and crest iiii Clx fote xv fote, and on the est syde in skew & crest iiii Clx fote, and on the northe syde there is done v spaces havyng in skew and crest iC lxx fote, the west syde and the south syde w[i]t[h] the est syde be alle fynysshed, and the northe syde not alle fynyshed lackyng iii spaces for the same syde the stuffe is wrought save the settyng

[fol. 9v] Itm at the Juell hows doore iii spaces covered w[i]t[h] skew and crest amountyng to xxxvi fote of stone

2. Office of Works accounts for repairing the keep roof, March–December 1536

Despite the fact that the roof was almost certainly completely rebuilt and raised a storey in the late fif-teenth century, it required major repairs within fifty years. These were recorded as necessary in the early 1530s, but were not carried out until 1536. It is pos-sible that the reason the works were set in motion in that year was because of the anticipated coronation of Queen Jane, for which Westminster Hall was cleared and prepared in the summer of 1536, though the event was never staged. The accounts for this are full, but still somewhat confusing, and it seems probable that localised failure of the roof was exacerbated by the mounting of cannon on the leads. The three docu-ments are in two locations today, but represent a con-tinuous run of accounts from March to December 1536.

a. Oxford, Bodleian Library, Rawlinson MS D 778 [Accounts of the Royal Surveyor of Works, 1535–6], fols 109r–110v

12 March–15 April 1536

[fol. 109r] The Toure of london Anno xxvii R. Henr VIII . . . ffrome Soundaye the xiithe daye of Marche Inclusive unto Soundaye the xvthe daye off Apprill Exclusive

Carpyntr[e]s Worckynge aswell upon the fframyng & hewyng of a greate beame w[i]t[h] pen-dannce & Brasses to be leyd in the highe Rouffe of the whyte Toure brode Northe ov[e]r the plasse where the knyghttes of the bathe was mad At the Corronacon of the quenes grace

[fol. 109v] Sawyers Worchyng aswell upon the sawyng of tymb[e]r ffor Brasses Joyestes and Pen-

dannce as ffor Skaffalf Tymb[e]r ffor the Carpyn-ters to stond upon ffor the Rearyng of a greate Beame w[i]t[h] other Nea[cessar]ies to be leyde uppon the Rouff of the said whyte Toure upon the Northend

[fol. 110v] Laborers . . . attendyng to them [the carpenters] ffor carreyng off Tymb[e]r And bourd upe to the said White Toure ffor makyng of Trusses and skaffaldes as laboryng and hewyng into the greate stone walles ffor the settyng in of Corbles of stone w[i]t[h] pendannce and Trusses as ffor the sawyng of stone ffor the Masons

b. Nottingham University Library MS Ne O 1, unfo-liated

7 May–3 June 1536

The Towre of london Anno XXVIII R. H. VIII
ffrome Sondaye the vii[th] daye of May unto Soun-daye the iii[the] daye of June [1536]

Paymentts made and paide by thands of James Nedam Survayor genrall and Clerke of oure Sovreigne lorde the kynges worekes

Carpynters Workynge aswell upon makyng and fframyng off pendannce and brasis ffor the stryn-gthyng of the Rouffe of the whyte Towre . . .

Sawyers Workynge And Sawyng of Tymb[e]r newe off all sortes ffor Joyestes Planckes & others ffor the said Carpynters . . .

Laborers Worckyng and laboring not only upon the brekyng downe & makyng of holis in the wallis of the foresaid Whyte Towre ffor the setting of the said pend[a]nnce butt allso helpyng of the fforsaide carpynters and Sawyers to carry Tymb[e]r and Removyng of the Ronnyng skaffolde ffrom on plasse to an other ffor the assayng of Brassys made for the said pendannce. W[i]t[h]all other na[cessar]ies be them done as theye ar comanndyd to dooe

To [sic] Chambrelayne prest undre Almer to oure sov[e]reigne lorde the kynge / for iii loodds on ffoote of Tymbre of hym boughte and hade ffrome Water [sic] Ockeleye ffor the makyng of brasis for the said work prisse the lod w[i]th the carrage delyv[e]rede At the Towre wherffe viis } xxi^s i^d ob. . . .

To John Mychell of london ffor on C di of Elme borde of hym boughte and spentt in the forsaid worcke w[i]t[h] the carryage of the same At ii^s iiii^d the C } iii^s vi^d

3 June–2 July 1536

The Towre of london Anno xxviii R. H. VIII
ffrom Soundaye the iii[the] daye of June unto son-ndaye the ii^d daye of July . . .

Carpyntrs Worckyng Aswell upon the makyng and fframyng to gether of Brasis and Pendannce for the Rouff of the White Towre . . .

Breckelayers Worckyng Aswell upon the fforsyng of the walls w[i]t[h]in the whyte Towre & stoppyng of dyv[e]rs holles & gutters Above the leades on the Towre syddes w[i]t[h]all other rep[ar]acons neaile be theme doone

27 August–24 September 1536

The Towre of london Anno xxviii R. H.VIII

ffrome Sonndaye the xxvii^th daye of August unto Sonndaye the xxiii^th daye of Septemb[e]r . . .

Masons . . . hewyng off hardston And Reying & settyng upe theme for Corbells in to the walls Aboue in the White great Towre where the knyghtes of the batthes was made to staye And beryng upe of pendannts & brasys of the same as mending of all other crackes & crasys in the same walls and other nea[cessar]ies aboute the said Towre.

Carpyntrs . . . ffor worckyng & makyng of Pendanttes and brasses to be sette upe w[i]t[h]in the greate whighte Towre where the beames of the Rooffe was crased ffor stayinge of thende and mending of the skaffoldes & gyestes to Remove Romnyng to & ffroo upon wheles w[i]t[h] other nea[cessar]ies ther to belongyng . . .

Sawyers . . . sawyng of geystes grols and brassys ffor Rep[er]acons of the skaffold Above the White Towre w[i]t[h]in the same As Allso for the Rep[er]acons of the Tornnyng whelles w[i]t[h] gynnes stonding Aboue the leads of the said White Towre / to and for the kynges use as is affore wrytten to drawe upe the pendannce Tymb[e]r & bordes . . .

Laborers . . . goyng in the Tornnyng whele to howse upe the pendannce brasses & Tymb[e]r for the makyng of skaffoldes and s[er]nyng theme to all mann[e]r of Nea[cessa]ries accordyng to suche comaundementtes as theye ware assigned . . .

To John Crooe of lymehurst ffor di C of lyme of hym boughte had and Rp ffor to make morter ffor leyng in of the Corbles Aboue the White Towre and fforsing & mending of the walls

24 September–22 October 1536

The Towre of london Anno xxviii R.H.VIII

ffrome Soundaye the xxiiii^th daye of Septemb[e]r unto Soundaye the xxii^th daye of Octob[e]r

Masons worckyng not oonly in laying of cor-belles butt allso fforsyng upe the same walles undre the plattes of the greate beames w[i]t[h] mending the walles at the Este end of the whyte Towure . . .

Carpyntrs Worckyng not only upon fframyng of newe Pendannce & brasys for the northendes of thold som[e]r w[i]t[h] laying of newe plattes undre too ends of the same butt allso takyng upe thold bord[e]s lyng undre the leades of the same and

newe bording it Ayen w[i]t[h] lyeke the bording the gutters there . . .

To John Potts off barckyng p[ar]ische for iii ll of Tawllowe candle for the makyng of the darcke holes where the greate soudes & pendannce should be sett in the Roffe of the seid White Towre} iiiid sob

c. Bodleian Library, Rawlinson MS D 780, fols 246r–251r

[Accounts of Royal Surveyor of Works, 1536–7]

22 October 1536–19 November 1536

[fol. 246r] The Towre of london Anno xxviii Henry VIII

[fol. 246v] Masons Worckyng and hewyng of hardstone ffor Corbbes and setting of theme in to the walles above in the White Toure aswell ffor staying of great pendance there comyng ffrom the upper rooffe downe to the staye of the same wall as pynnyng and stoppyng of great holles & fforsyng theme whiche was hewed and brokyn downe of the said walles ffor settyng uppe of the said pendance and ffor the staying of the Beames of the Roff wheras the Knyghttes of the Baathe was made . . .

Laborers to the Masons . . . ffor slackyng of lyme w^t sand and wat[e]r as makyng of morter and s[er]vyng the said Masons in the White Tower / as also for the skoryng of the leddes & makyng clene theme ffor woyding of water.

[fol. 247r] Carpynt[e]rs Worckyng aswell upon the ffraymyng of the newe pendance and brases of the northende of tholde som[e]r w[i]t[h] leyng in of newe plattes under too endes of the same / butt all takyng upe thold bo[u]rdes lying under the leades & newe bo[u]rdyng it Agene w[i]t[h] lyke bo[u]rdyng the gutters there . . .

Sawyers Sawyng of tymb[e]r aswell for pendance ffor the white Towre as plankes goyttes and other nea[cessar]ies ffor the bridge of the Iron gate and for the Rep[air]yng of the gattes of the bulwarke northewest and southe este . . .

[fol. 247v] Plom[e]rs Worckyng aswell for the Coveryng of the leaddds ov[e]r the whyte Towre ov[e]r the northend where as it was Rypped ffor & settyng & leyng in off newe planckes to be cov[e]red as allso for the Coveryng of the great long Som[e]r ov[e]r Chawarthe the Roff ov[e]r the said Northend and aswell ffor the soderyng & stopping of dyv[e]rs holles in the same leaddes whiche holles was mad w[i]th gownes . . .

[fol. 248r] To John Crooe of lymehurst ffor CCC of lyme & di of hym boughte had and Rp aswell to be Imployed upon the leyng in of Corbles as fforsyng and mending of the walles in the whyte Tower . . .

[fol. 248v] Candles To John Thomas of London Tallowe Chaundeler for iiii ll of tallowe Candle of hym boughte at id qa the ll aswell for the Masons to have lighte as ffor the Carpynters to leye in there platts & pendannce under the Rooff of the Whyte Toure

19 November–27 December 1536

[fol. 249r] The Toure of london Anno xxviii R. Henry VIII

19 November 1536–27 December 1536

[fol. 250r] Carpynters . . . ffor the hewyng and nayllyng of great planckes withe great long picked nayeles iiii square heddye dryvyn in to the said lymes & barrowes and more ov[e]r for the strycking And takyng downe of ii greate skaffolddes in the white Tower . . .

[fol. 251r] Skowes Neas[essar]ies borrowed ffor the whyte Tower} To John Beste of London Carpynt[e]r ffor ii peyer of skrowes of hym borrowed ffor bolsteryng upe of the pendannce & Resyng upe of the Roffe of the whyte toure & settyng upe the greate beames at a staye . . .

To Roger Coke Carpynter ffor the borrowyng of ii peyre of lycke skrowes ffor lycke use

3. The creation of the Knights of the Bath, 13 January 1559
(Bodleian Library, Ashmole MS 862, pp. 299–300)

This description of the creation of the Knights of the Bath on the eve of the coronation of Elizabeth I is the fullest surviving account of the White Tower being used for this great rite. On this occasion the knights dined as well as bathed in the keep, but appear to have passed out of the building to the chapel of St Peter ad Vincula for the prayers and vigil.

[p. 299] 'Transcribed from Mr Anthony Anthony's Collect'
The Order of the makeing of Knights of the Bath for the Coronation of Queene Elizabeth the xiiith of January
Item xi knighte videlicet
Item the said Knights haveing a Bankett in the said White Towre before their entering to the Bath.
The said Knights entered into a Hall in the said white Towre and than and there was prepared xi syelde bedes which beddes closed w[i]th Courtyne of silke and golde byfore every sylde bed a Batthe coverid with red say & white Lynnen Cloath And uppon every Batthe the Armes of every Knight.
Item every of the said Knightes sitting byfore their Batthes there being Barbors ready to wash and trymminge them to have shaven the Knights beardes the Queenes Ma[jes]ty pardonyd for their beards And soe being whassed and trymmed enteryd into their bathes nakid and the Musisyons played uppon their instrum[en]ts.

Item immediately the Lord Arundell being Lord Steward of Ingland the Lord William Hauward being Lord Chamberlyn who were brought in by the harrourd at Armes and Sr [sic] Lyeutenant of the Towre Sir Ambrose Kave and Sir William Sackevile The Lord Stuwarde and the Lord Chamberlayn whent with the harrowld at Armys to every knight and gave them their Oathes and so kisses the Booke And that done the Lordes departed and the Knights whent out out of their Batthes and whent to Bed and to every Knight was brought a bolle w[i]th yprocras
Item at iii of the clock in the Morning the said Knightes of the Batthe rose out of their Beddes and were clothed in longe side Gownes of russet cloth w[i]th hoddes over their hedds who were with harrowde at Armes, Gentylmen and the Musysyons playinge and so conducted w[i]th Torche staves to the church in the Towre. And the knights sitting in the Quyer And then & there the parson of the said church knelynge said the procession in Englysshe and all that were there answered the parson.
Item one of the Queenes Chaplaines said Masse And at the consecration hee heavyd not up the osty And whan Masse was done all the said Knightes every of them a perche of wax in their handes w[i]th [p. 300] halfe a grote and so offered the said perche kneeling upon their knees and kissed the patyn and so retorned to their places And immediately the Musicyons played and there the Knightes were served with breade, suckatts, comfetto and yprocras and that done were conducted to the white Tower & there the Knights dausinge and leapeing and after that went to bedd
Mr the xv of January Anno 1558 being upon a Satterday the Queenes Ma[jes]tie was honourably conducted with all the nobles and pyers of the Realme spirituall and temp[or]all from the Towre of London thorough the Citie of London to her Ma[jes]t[y]s palace at Westm[inster] And at her Ma[jes]t[y]s goeing out of the Tower of London there was a great shott of Gunnes and Chambres to the nombre of ix^C shott

4. Creating new armouries in the White Tower, 26 August 1580
(TNA, SP 12/141, no. 42, fol. 100)

On 1 July 1580 a review of the condition of the Armouries in the Tower of London was commissioned, and six weeks later this report was submitted. The intention to extend the use of the White Tower for the storage of arms and armour is revealed by the reference to an estimate for setting up armouries within the White Tower, though in the event this seems not to have been acted upon.

To the right honnorable o[u]r very goyd LL[ord]s and others of her Ma[jes]tis moste honnorable privie councell geve this.

Right honorable o[u]r verye good Lordes, according to yo[u]r honors commdyment by yo[u]r letter bearinge date the fyrst daye of Julye 1580, wee have made a Survey of all the armouries that dothe now remayne in the Tower of London. Wee have also understood what the state, Quantetie, & sortes of the same ware att the tyme of the deathe of S[r] George Howard knight, the decaye wherof, & what chardge maye putt the same in ord[e]r & make it cleane wee have also consythered ~

The chardge of the makinge of romes withe in the greate whytt Tower in the tower of London for the placeinge and hanginge upp of all the armoure wee have throughlye p[er]used and seene by the Judgment of workmen what the chardge maye be, wherof wee do sende yo[u]r honours herew[i]th inclosed an Estymate togeath[e]r w[i]th the chardge of the reformynge & puttinge in ord[e]r of all the armoure, w[hi]ch beinge by yo[u]r honours better consytheryd of maye be p[er]formyd as to yo[u]r good pleasure shall seme most mete, leaveinge yo[u]r hono[u]rs to the kepeing of the Allmyghtie, Wee humbly take o[u]r leave from London the 26 daie of August 1580

Yo[u]r hono[u]rs humbly to comaunde

John Hopton

Kyllygrew

John Hawkyns

Willm holstok

5. Survey of the condition of the Tower of London, 31 December 1623

(TNA, SP 14/156, no. 13, fols 29r–40r)

This detailed survey of the Tower of London was made by Sir Allan Apsley, Lieutenant of the Tower, and Sir Richard Morrisson, Lieutenant of the Ordnance, in 1623. It was commissioned following a damning report submitted to the Council by Sir Edward Coke on 4 July 1620, which highlighted, among other things, the inherent danger of storing gunpowder and the regalia in such close proximity to one another. Transcribed here are the sections relating to the White Tower, concerned principally with the condition of the upper parts of the exterior.

[fol. 29r] The defects of y[e] Towers & Offices and Storehowses belonginge to y[e] Magazen and Artillery w[t]thin y[e] fforte

The Mayne Tower of y[e] fforte called y[e] White Tower nowe in use for y[e] cheife battery and Storehouse for y[e] Magazen hath its dyamiter one ways 6 rod 13 foote and y[e] other way 5 Rod 10 foote the one corner towards y[e] east is p[ro]porconed w[i]th a halfe round Tower whose diamiter is 2 rod 4 foote,

w[i]th in the same half round, And twoe other corners besides are planted in each a square Turrett. In the fowerth corner is a round Turrett wherein is a Staircase goeinge upp to y[e] leads. Twoe of thos Turrettes towards y[e] Thames are roughe cast verie Seemely and whereby the walls (formerly Ruyned) are nowe p[re]served, y[e] other twoe Turrettes are much Ruyned and are in height (viz[t] y[e] Square Turrett) 25 foote highe, and 15 foote square haveinge in y[e] same 12 windowes much ruyned and decaid; The round Turrett or Staircase is 30 foote highe and its dyamiter from oute to out is 25 foote; In y[e] same Turrett alsoe are 12 windowes, much ruyned and decaid All w[hi]ch p[ar]ticulers decayed to be mended from y[e] top to y[e] leads and y[e] walls rounde about rough cast to make them uniforme w[th] yem oth[e]r 2 will cost lxiiii[li] iiii[s]

The parrapett rounde aboute y[e] same Tower; devided in Battlementes is in reasonable good repaire, y[e] Jointes of y[e] ffreestone, and alsoe y[e] lower partes of y[e] loopeholes (w[hi]ch are brick edge wayes) are to be pointed with Tarresse of y[e] whole boddie of y[e] Tower rounde aboute from y[e] topp to y[e] bottom (which contayneth cxiv rodds in measure) There are severall holes and ruyns in y[e] ffreestone windowes and other places of the same to be repaired and round aboute to be roughe cast, which will make it decent, and p[re]serve it from any further Ruyn, All w[hi]ch p[ar]ticulerly estimated will cost cccxlii[li] xvi[s]

[fol. 29v] The said Tower is covered w[i]th lead contayneinge aboute iθ4000[cc] weight, upon y[e] same rounde aboute is a Platforme and Bedd for Ordenannce, where of the foreparte must be supplied and newe made, under y[e] same platforme, the lead in sev[er]all places is decaide and needeth daylie attendaunce to supplie y[e] same w[i]th sodder, beinge it layeth oppen and bare, especially upon such a Battery, where yron Crowes are used aboute Ordenannce, w[hi]ch are throwne out of y[e] hands of Gonners, by which and other suche meanes the leads are Cutt and abused. Some p[ar]te of the Platforme must be remooved and y[e] decayes mended. Butt better it were to be once well donne then often and allways in doeinge.

It may therefore please yo[r] Lo[rdshi]ps that the same be (as aforesaid) newe cast of a lesser weight & covered w[th] boardes, whereby the ov[e]rplus of y[e] lead [fol. 30r] will countervayle towards y[e] charge and soe it will be lesse chargeable and yett a lasting woorke.

Upon the same leads towards the northe from the one Turrett to y[e] other is a wall 7 foote broade, covered w[i]th lead and y[e] same lead covered agayne with brick and stone which lead must be taken upp and putt to better use, and the wall paved w[i]th brick edgways and Tarris w[hi]ch p[ar]ticulers severally estimated will cost xxl[li] xvi[s] [fol. 37r] In answer unto ye latter parte of yo[u]r Lo[rdshi]ps Instruccons delivered unto us the iiii^th of December last Touching the Reporte made by the right honorable ye Lo[rd] Chamberlin ye Earl of Arndell ye Lo[rd] Carew Mr Secrat[ary] Naunton, Mr Chanclo[u]r of ye Excheq[ue]r and Sr Edw. Cooke on the iiii^th of July 1620 to the end that we should not onely certefye what hath bene donne since in the execution of their Lo[rdshi]ps Reporte and the orders of this Boarde Butt alsoe to ad there-unto what may be donne therein wee humbly returne as followeth . . .

[fol. 40r] And lastlye touchinge ye Remooveinge of ye Magazen and Stoare of Powder, lyinge verie neare the Office of Recordes and the Jewells of ye Crowne, Yo^r Lo[rdshi]ps have ordered, that some other place be thought uppon for the disposeinge of the said Magazen with safety and les danger . . .

6. Office of Works' accounts for repairing the White Tower, 1 October 1637–30 September 1639
(TNA, E 351/3271 and 3272)

The annual accounts of the Office of Works record in detail the repairs undertaken to the White Tower between October 1637 and September 1639. This pro-gramme saw the replacement of all the battlements, and most of the visible quoins and windows of the whole building in Portland stone, and represents the first significant use of this material on the White Tower. The keep was also whitewashed (for the last time), so the contrast between Portland and Caen stone that has long been a distinctive characteristic of the White Tower's façades was not visible when the Portland stone was first introduced.

a. TNA, E 351/3271, 1 October 1637–30 December 1638

mending and repairing of the white Tower taking out all the decaied stone and putting in of new, and new gallotting and whiting of it over, mending and peicing of the greate Cornice of the Southeast Turrett and putting in of new ground plate in the Southwest Turrett making of three great Square pipes to carry the water from the Topp of the white Tower and three great Cesternes to them and laying of a new gutter over the Jewellhouse . . .

Taskeworkes Viz to William Mills Mason for working and setting the Coings of Portland stones on the Northwest corner of the white Tower, the iiii^er Butteresses on the inside of the Turrett and the Coings of the Battlem[en]ts on the west side of the said white Tower, working and setting of stone ashler in the foundation of the worke and filling it upp againe behind the ashler, for like working and setting of Portland stone in the five lower windowes the fouer duble windowes and the iiii^er upp[er] win-dowes on the west side of the said Tower and in severall other windowes and Jambes of the doore in the Turrett and on the Northside of the said white Tower, working and setting Portland stone in the fouer arches on the west side, working and setting the skrewes in the fouer Buttresses there and the Turrett and working and setting the facias there and Portland stones in the Vents of the Battlem[en]ts conteyning in all iii^ml vi^C iiii^xx xvi^en foote at x^d the foote . . . More to him the said Wm Mills for taking out the old stones and working and setting of new Coings and ashler of Portland stone on the west and southsides of the said white Tower and the Turrett, and in all the buttresses arches windowes and dores from the second buttresse on the South-side to the second Buttresse on the Eastside of the said Tower, setting of skrewes in the buttresses and Turrett faciaes and the Vents of the Battlem[en]ts all conteyning iiii^ml cccviii^t foote at the like rate of x^d the foote clxxix ^li And more to him for taking out of raggstone and working some p[ar]te of it upp with new, and gallotting and pointing of it and whitewashing all thaforesaid worke by him donne cont vii^ml ix^Cxl foote at ^d ob the foote

Edward Tasker and John Sweat Carpenters for making a Scaffold on the Southside of the white Tower for the Masons to worke on being six foote broad from the wall at the ground iiii^er foote from the wall at the topp conteyning in length x^en rodds the king finding poles bourde and baseropes and they finding Cleates nailes and workmanship . . . And to the said Edward Tasker for making of scaf-foldes from the Southeast Turrett to the East and North Turrett

b. Public Record Office [hereafter PRO], E 351/3272, 1 October 1638–30 September 1639

. . . to William Mills Mason for woorkeinge and setting ccc lxi foote of Coinge stone and ashler on the westside of the white Tower for takeinge downe the old woorke there and fillinge the dore behind, for diginge out the old morter and gallotinge vii^C iiii^xx foote of Raggstone, for workeing and settinge of Coinges and ashler of Portland stone in all the great arches Buttries and windowes from the third buttrisse on the eastside of the white Tower to the north Tirrett in Master Marshes yard, workeinge and settinge of the Skewes and faciaes and the stones betweene the vents of the Battlementes and the Coinge stone of the battlem[en]ts and the Plint in the foundacon of the woorke, takeinge downe the old stone and fillinge it upp againe behind the Coinges and ashler, pointinge and gallotinge all the raggstone woorke there, takeinge out all the old morter and bringeinge upp same p[ar]te of it w[i]th newe stone . . . takeing downe the old worke, and workeinge and settinge of Coinge and ashler of Portland Stone, in all the Buttrisses of the North-east Turrett windowes and dores, and the skewe and facia of the buttresses and the skewe under the Cornice of the Turrett and the facia there, the Coinges on the leades and fillinge upp the dore behind the Coinges and ashler all at the white Tower w[i]th other woorkes done there CCC xxv^{li} ii^s iii^d ob . . .

Edward Tasker Carpenter for makeinge Scaffoldes from the east Buttresse on the east side of the white Tower to the firste on the North side, and scaffoldinge round the north east Turrett to putt upp one of the greate Vanes, and for like makeinge of scaffolds on the Northside for the Masons to woorke on from the ground to the battlem[en]ts

7. William Prynne's account of the Tower records at the Restoration

(British Library, Lansdown MS 504, fols 5r–8r [Notes on Parliamentary Records])

William Prynne, the famous Civil War pamphleteer and lawyer, was given the post of Keeper of Records at the Tower at the Restoration. This account gives a vivid picture of the state of neglect and decay in which he found the records, which Prynne attributed (as Keepers of the Records invariably did) to the negligence of his predecessors. The document indicates that the papers kept in the White Tower (which this document is the earliest to describe as being housed in the chapel of St John) were considered of secondary importance to those in and about the reading room in the Wakefield Tower. In 1661 Prynne described his work to Sir Harbottle Grimston in the following words: 'whilst you are sucking in the fresh country air, I have been almost choked with the dust of neglected records (interred in their own rubbish for sundry years) in the White Tower, their rust eating out the tops of my gloves with their touch, and their dust rendering me, twice a day, as black as a chimney sweeper' (Historical Manuscripts Commission: *Report on the Manuscripts of the Earl of Verulam*, London, 1906, p. 58). The account is undated. The hand is late seventeenth century, and some of the details were recounted to the author by William Petyt, who was initially a clerk of the records and, from 1689, keeper.

[fol. 5r] The Opinion & Judgement of Mr Pryn, who was Keeper of the Records in the Tower of London, how & by what means our ancientest Parliamentary Records have bin consum'd, & utterly lost, soe as never to be retrieved again.

There are no Records at all in the Tower, sayes Mr Pryn (except some few ancient Charters or Exemplifications of them) ancienter then the first year of King John: All the rest, from William the first his Reigne till then, (except some few in the Exchequer, not relating to Parliaments) being utterly lost. . . . [fol. 6r] That he no sooner rec[eive]d his Royall Patent past without Fees, Ano

Dni 1662 for the Custody of his Ma^{tys} ancient Records in the Tower of London even in the middest of his Parliamentary & disbanding Services, then monopolizing all his time, but he designed, endeavour'd the rescue of the greatest part of them from that desolation, corruption, confusion, in w[hi]ch (through the negligence, necsience or sloathfulnesse of the [fol. 6v] former Keepers) they had for many years by past layn buryed together in one confused chaos under corroding putrifying Cobwebbs, Dust, Filth, in the darkest Corners of Caesar's Chapell in the White Tower, as meer useless Reliques, not worthy to be calendar'd or brought down thence into the office amongst other Records of use. In order thereunto he says, He employed some soldiers & Woemen to remove & cleanse them from the filthinesse, who soon growing weary of this noysome worke, left them almost as foul, nasty as they found them.

Whereupon imediately after the Parliament's Adjournment, He & His Clerke (in August & September last) spent many whole days in cleansing and sorting them into distinct confused Heaps in order to their future reducement into Method, the old Clerks of the Office being unwilling to touch them for fear of fouling their Fingers, spoyling their Cloathes endangering their Eye sight & healths by their Cankerous Dust & evill Sent.

[fol. 8r] These Collections I had from Mr William Petyt of the Temple

8. Sir Algernon May's account of the condition of the Tower Records, 14 December 1676 and 3 December 1681

British Library, Stowe MS 541, fols 9v–11v

Algernon May took over the position of Keeper of Tower Records after William Prynne's death in 1669. During his tenure he was asked to contribute to a series of inquiries into the nature and condition of the records in his care. What follows are extracts from his testimonies that relate to the condition of the manuscripts in the White Tower. The accounts reveal, among other things, that the presses within the chapel of St John had been torn down and burned by parliamentary soldiers during the 1640s, and had yet to be replaced.

14 December 1676

[fol. 9v] The humble Answer of Sr Algernoon May Knight Keeper of his Maties Records within the Tower of London which he is required to give to the Rt Hono^{ble} ye Lords Comittees appointed by Order of his Ma^{ty} in Councill to examine and make enquiry into the State and condicon of the said Records to severall particulars contained in their Lo^{pps} Letter to the said Sr Algernoon dated the first of December instant. . . .

[fol. 10r] Great part of the Records viz.ᵗ the Bills answers &c last beforemenconed are kept in the white Tower, the other are in a Tower near Traytors gate where (as in the whole Tower) all imaginable care is taken to defend them against Fire and all other injuries both which said roomes are very dry and with small charge may be made comodious and capeable of receiveing many more Records then we now have. . . . The said Sʳ Algernoon May humbly craves the liberty to propose to yoʳ Loᵖˢ in order to the more safe & convenient keeping of the said Records for the Advancement of his Maᵗⁱᵉˢ service therein the particulars following

1. That an howse may be added to yᵉ sd office
2. That the presses in the White Tower (which were broken down by the Soldiers in yᵉ late Tymes) may be amended and some new ones built
3. That his Salary may be duely paid without which he is not able to sustain the necessery charges of the said office

3 December 1681

[fol. 11r] The state of the office of Records in the Tower of London as it was found & entred by Sʳ Algernoon May and as it is now humbly offered to the consideration of the Lords Comittees by order of Councill 11 August last appointed to inspect the condicon of yᵗ office.

Soon after the Death of Mʳ Prynne I entred upon the charge of keeper of his Majesties Records in the Tower of London by yᵉ bookes and Kalendars I found many Rolls missing out of the office and misplaced scattered in the Chappell of the White Tower and buried in rubbish there in his Lodgings there at the Tower & Lincolns Inne and lent out by him. . . .

In the next place I examined the Rolles & bundells of all the severall Records to see what condicon they lay in and I found the most auncient miserably decayed especially those of King John and Henry the Third were almost totally defaced as may be seen by the Rolls themselves. It is true I have read of a Report to Queene Elizabeth in Councill from some appointed to inspect the office that at those dayes they were much perished especially those two first Kings the words being that they were omnino laceratae but by this tyme the same breaches had broken into the Rolles of all the other Kinges for want of taking care in broken membrana's Rolleing straight and such like neglect rending the edges and soe perishing almost into the middle of the lines in which nothing can be read.

I examined the roomes and found that called Cesars Chappell which is a dry & convenient floored roome for that use quite defaced the presses broke downe & burnt by yᵉ Soldiers [fol. 11v] who did lye there and the Rooles and whatever they were

of several natures thrown into one heap contayneing diverse cart Loads all mingled promiscuously togeather without any possibility to sort them & draw out the usefull from the useless or to put them into any method without great charge and employing many skilful hands Yett out of this vast heap though I could not search exactly to know what all things were I got from thence many Rolles which were ordered into Kings Reignes & placed into their proper Yeares which I believe to be the Reason my Kalendars mentioned Rolles now in the office than any of the former doe they being buried in his heap of unknown things the presses in the Lower office I found in good order & very convenient for those Rolles that bee in them.

9. Privy Council Committee's proposals for clearing the White Tower of adjacent buildings, 3 April 1668

(TNA, PC 2/60, Privy Council Register, p. 254)

At the Tower of London, the reign of Charles II was dominated by a government campaign to demolish the buildings that stood around the White Tower, largely to protect the national gunpowder magazine held there. After some demolition in 1667, this report was presented to the king and Privy Council, setting out in precise detail which buildings it was considered necessary to take down and which needed only to be vacated and put into the control of the Board of Ordnance. Buildings mentioned include the twelfth-century forebuilding, described as the 'square tower' in (no. 8) and Coldharbour Gate, of which both towers were used as prisons (no. 9).

At the Court at Whitehall the 3d of Aprill 1668 . . .

Wheras his Grace the Duke of Albemarle, the Lord Arlington, the Lord Berkeley, Sr John Duncombe, Thomas Chicheley Esqr, Sr John Robinson Leutenant of his Ma[jes]ts Tower of London, & Colonell William Legge Comissioners appointed by Warrant under his Ma[jes]ts Signe Manuall & Privy Signet, bearing date the 21th of March 1665 for Removing & pulling downe such Houses & Lodgings within the Tower of London & making such Alterations as they could conceiue necessary for securing of his Ma[jes]ts Magazine of Power there, Were directed by Order of the Boord of the 27th of Novemb[e]r last to meete with all convenient speed and give Order for pulling down & demolishing all Houses & Buildings within such distance of the White Tower in the Tower of London, as they in their Opinion (upon view thereof) should conceive-may any waies endanger the said Magazine. And wheread their Lo[ordshi]ps did this day represent to yᵉ Boord That in Obedience to the said Order, they have accordingly met and, and upon a serious View of the said Buildings, do humbly offer to this Board, their Opinions as followeth.

1. That ye Coach house & stables adjoining to Major Nicholls his House be quite sleighted & pulled downe.

2. That so much of ye House where Mr Aldrich Wardour lives, as is scituate betwixt the Stone Tower adjoyning the Place where ye Powder is proved and that the East side under the passage of the said House be quite demolished & pulled downe, and ye fface of ye remayning part of that House, that shalbe left, be built up with a good Brick Wall from ye Bottome to the Top.

3. That the Brickwall of ye Gardine which now Captaine Rainsford enjoyeth be continued to meete with the Brickwall that comes from ye Hill, wherein no Door or Passage to be Eastward.

4. That ye Roofe & Chambers of ye Old Hall in Cold Harbour scituate betwixt ye Jewell House & ye rest of ye Kings Lodgings be all demolished to the Bottome, Leaving only ye stone Walls standing, it being the Length of ffourty ffoote.

5. That all ye Windows Chimneys & Doorsteeds of that House & Tower, where Mr Masters ye Wardour dwells be all filled up, and all ye combustible matter in that House remoued & no place left to come at, or enter into it but towards Cold Harbour.

6. The same is to be done to that part of ye Jewell House that comes to ye last menconed Place.

7. The Jewell House where Mr Edwards liveth to be quite demolished, and pulled downe, it joyning to the White Tower.

8. That all Chimneys be filled up, and all Hearthes likewise in the Square Tower in Cold Harbour adjoining to the White Tower, called the Square Tower, nor no Person suffered to dwell there.

9. That all Chimneys & Hearths in the Tower Prison at Cold Harbour Gate on both sides; be filled up and all combustible stuff removed.

10. That the House belonging to the Surveyor of the Workes adjoyning to the West side of the White Tower be quite taken downe.

11. That the Brickwall coming from the Cold Harbour Gate, & leading towards the Hill, be continued all along to the North side of the White Tower, to meete with the Brickwall against Major Nicholls, that the Tower may stand clear from any Persons coming near it.

12. Wee thinke it convenient that of all the Towers & Houses which shalbe left standing within ye Precinct aforesaid, the Possession of them ever hereafter be & remaine within ye office of ye Ordnance.

All which in our opinion tending to the Preservation of his Ma[jes]ts Magazine Wee offer to your Lo[rdshi]ps further consideration.

Albemarle J Duncombe

Which being read at the Boord, And his Ma[jes]tie having taken ye same into Consideration was pleased this day to declare his Pleasure, That the said Com[missioner]s be, and they are hereby authorized & required to cause all ye Particulars abovemenconed to be speedily put on Execution

10. Ordnance Office account for demolishing the forebuilding, March–July 1674

(TNA, WO 47/19B, Ordnance Minutes, fols 39v–53r)

In March to July 1674 the last major structures remaining adjacent to the keep, other than the eastern annexe, which would survive for another two centuries, were demolished. The work was undertaken by the Ordnance Office, and these minutes record the various payments for demolishing the remaining structures, which almost certainly included the surviving Jewel House building, the twelfth-century forebuilding and the thirteenth-century Coldharbour Gate.

10 March 1673/4

[fol. 39v] Ordered . . . That Sr Jonas Moore be called upon for ye heads of ye agreement and contract to be Entered w[i]th Mr Couren for pullinge downe ye Tower against ye White Tower not exceedinge ye Charge of ye summe of 45^li in all

24 March 1673/4

[fol. 42r] Ordered . . . That one Great Screw for throweinge downe ye Ruinous Walls next ye White Tower togeather w[i]th 10 good stronge Ballast Basketts and 5 or 6 Hand Hatchetts be lent to Mr Courens for cleareinge away ye Rubish from ye good Materialls

31 March 1673/4

[fol. 43r] Ordered . . . That 1000^li be Imprested to Mr James Rothwell Clarke to Sir Jonas Moore Kn^t Surveyo[u]r of his Ma[jes]ts Ordnance for ye Carrying on ye workes att Coldharbour by 2 or 300^li att a tyme as ye worke shall require

21 July 1674

[fol. 53r] Ordered That an Estimate be forthw[i]th brought into ye Office of ye Value what ye moste is any person will give for ye stones pulled downe out of ye old Buildinges in Coldharbour and upon y^t they be exposed to sale to his Ma[jes]ts best advantage

11. Privy Council report on the collapse of the gunpowder store, 9 July 1691

(TNA, PC 2/74, p. 204; duplicated in WO 55/339, p. 87)

On 9 July 1691 one of the upper floors of the White Tower collapsed, bringing 2,000 barrels of gunpowder crashing down to the floor below. This dramatic event, noted by Queen Mary in her personal diary, saw the end of the White Tower's role as the nation's biggest and most important gunpowder magazine. The minutes of the Privy Council record their discussion of the event.

At the Court at Whitehall the 9th of July 1691. Her Ma[jes]tys Councill having received an account that by the fall of part of one of the Floores, this morning, in the White Tower, where the Powder was lodged, about two thousand Barrells are falne through, and lye upon the next Floore, And that the keeping of so great a quantity of Powder at present is extreamly dangerous to the Tower, and City of London Her Ma[jes]ty is pleased to Order the Rt Hono[ura]ble Sr Henry Goodriche Kn[igh]t & Bar[one]t Lieuten[an]t Generall, and the rest of the Principall Officers of the Ordnance, to consider of a fitt place or places where the stores of Powder may be conveniently lodged, aswell for the security thereof, as of the Tower and City of London, and make report thereof to this Board.

12. Anthony Salvin's proposals for restoring the White Tower, 31 January 1857
(TNA, WORK 14/2/5, fols 46r–47v)

On 13 December 1856 the distinguished architect Anthony Salvin was asked by the Office of Works to prepare an estimate for restoring the top storey of the keep 'exactly to its original appearance'. His ambitious response proposed, among other things, the replacement of the roof with a new 'hammer beam' construction, which was to entail heightening the building, and the 'restoration' of the windows in Bath stone. Although Salvin was asked only to quote for works to the top storey, he also provided an estimate for the rest of the exterior and for the interior of the chapel of St John. In the event, he was commissioned only to reinforce the roof, remove the timber supporting posts and insert second-floor light-wells.

[fol. 46r] Addressed to 'The Chief Commissioner of Her Majestys Works'

30 Argyll Street, Jan[uar]y 31st 1857

Sir, Agreeable to instructions received I have examined the White Tower with a view to its restoration, and more particularly to the application of that portion, called the Council Chamber, to a store for Small Arms and beg briefly to report.

That I find the Roof weak, though the timber is generally sound, and supported by numerous posts which would interfere with the stands for arms, and that there is a deficiency of light, which would be further decreased when the windows are reduced to their original form and size.

To remedy these defects, I recommend that the roof be taken off, and the present chestnut beams sawn down the middle and wrought iron plate

Girders inserted and bolted together as shewn on drawing No 3 the posts may then be dispensed with as supports, and used in the roof if there should be a deficiency of timber proper to be used again [fol. 46v] The arches over the recesses of the windows and in the division wall and not being opposite each other it becomes necessary to raise the walls that the hammer beams of the roof may be clear of those openings, and the increased height will give additional accommodation for arms, improve the proportions of the rooms and the Elevations of the Exterior which are now depressed by high modern buildings in the vicinity. The bays of the roof to have the same construction of purlins, rafters and boarding and to be of the same material as at present. Skylights to be inserted in a certain number of the bays as shewn in drawing No 1 the lead to be relads on the rest of the roof.

The inside face of the walls to be scraped free from plaster, the jambs, quoins and arches to be restored and the rough walls to have a thin coat of plaster flush with and not covering the wrought stone. The windows to be restored in all their parts with Bath stone from the Coombe Down or Box quarries to their original form and character. Each window to be glazed with strong glass in iron frames and a casement as per drawing No 4.

The floor being supported by posts in a similar manner to the present roof, requires only some additional strength in the centre. But if those posts are ever taken away to clear the rooms below then a new floor of different construction will be necessary to support the great weight of the stands of arms, and I have [fol. 47r] therefore made a seperate estimate of the expence should it be deemed proper to postpone that work. But I beg to recommed that all works in any way connected with the Council Chamber, as the floor, roofs, walls both internally and externally as low as the level A. B. on elevation, the parapetts and four turrets to be executed at the same time, thus avoiding inconvenience and dust after the store of arms are placed in it. The cost of these as per annexed estimate would not exceed £9,947.16.9 and the remainder of the exterior Ashlar Buttresses, windows and base, cleaning and repairing the interior of the Chapel and of rooms below the Council Chamber would not exceed £6,803.17.0

On the east side of the White Tower there was a low building probably of the time of E[d]w[ar]d 3rd and whenever any great change in the occupation of the Tower takes place I should recommend that building to be restored and the building on the South side removed.

The Jewel House formerly stood near this site and must have been a better position than either the Martin Tower which was too small, or the present building which is out side the ballium wall.

Probably at no distant [fol 47v] date the exigences of the service may require more space and a more convenient position for the shipment of stores and then many of the buildings which are now a disight and incumbrance may be removed and other arrangements made for those objects of public interest that may be desirable to keep within the defences of the Tower.

I beg to remain Your ob[edien]t S[erva]nt, A Salvin.

13. Anthony Salvin's specification for restoring St John's Chapel, 11 August 1864

(TNA, WORK 31/527)

After the removal from the White Tower of the last of the records of state, Anthony Salvin was again employed by the Office of Works, this time to restore the chapel of St John. This is his specification for those works (and for works to St Thomas's Tower, not included here), which includes his detailed instructions for the insertion of the new Bath stone windows that he had originally proposed for the whole keep. The drawings for the windows, which were to be 'minutely' followed, accompany the specification.

Specification of Works to be executed in Restoring the Eastern and Southern sides of St Thomas Tower and the Windows of St John's Chapel in the Tower of London for the Commissioners of Her Majesty's Works

Anthony Salvin Architect

4 Adam Street Adelphi

General Instructions

The Stone to be used for the works hereafter specified to be of the best quality. The Bath stone to be from the Coombe Down or Box quarries, and to be wrot on the beds joints and faces to the respective forms shewn by the drawings and left from the Drag.

All stone to be laid with the grain or natural quarry bed horizontal except in arches where the grain is to radiate from the centre.

The Lime to be the best fresh burnt stone lime

The Sand to be River Sand thoroughly cleansed, and free from all loam or other impurities

The Mortar to be composed of Lime and Sand in the proportions directed by the Architect (say one of Lime to two of Sand)

The old stone accumulated during the Works at St Thomas' Tower to be used in building up the gaps and fissures in the walls of that Tower

All rubbish &c to be removed at the conclusion of the works.

The Kentish Rag work to be done in a similar manner to the exterior facing of the Beauchamp Tower . . .

St John's Chapel in the White Tower

The whole of the existing windows on the lower and upper floors to be taken out and the walling around ditto prepared to receive new windows

Insert new windows as per drawings, with jambs, heads sills, caps, columns bases &c of Bath stone wrought on the beds joints and faces and left from the Drag

The Windows to be glazed in Hartley's Glass of an approved tint

Fix wrot iron Saddle bars $\frac{7}{8}^{in} \times \frac{1}{2}^{in}$ (about one foot apart) to each window, on the inside of the outer jambs, the ends to be let into the stonework, dovetailed therein and run with cement

Nos 6 of the windows to have wrot iron swing casements formed between strong wrot iron upright framed between the saddle bars. These Casements will average about $1^{ft} 8^{in} \times 2^{ft} 3^{in}$ and to have strong wrot iron stay bars, centres &c complete.

Make good the walling round windows when same are inserted and made good any damage that may be done to skylights, roofs &c during the works. . . .

This is the Specification referred to in our tender of 11th August Inst. G Myers & Sons. 31 August 1864

Notes

Introduction

1 Bayley 1821–5, passim.
2 RCHM 1930, pp. 70–94. The White Tower is described on pp. 86–92, illustrated with plans, sections and photographs.
3 Davison 1967, 1974.
4 Colvin, Brown and Taylor 1963–82, vol. I, pp. 29–32; vol. II, pp. 706–29.
5 See bibliography, p. 392.
6 Keevill 2004, passim.
7 Geoffrey Parnell, personal communication.
8 Sands 1912, p. 225, n. 2.
9 For example, Parnell 1993, p. 20.
10 Sturdy 1979, pp. 270–72.
11 Renn 1993; R. A. Brown 1978a, pp. 24–6; R. A. Brown 1984; Chatelain 1973; De Boüard 1974.
12 Mesqui 1998; Impey and Lorans 1998.
13 Dixon and Marshall 1993a, 1993b; Drury 1982.
14 Dixon 1996, 2002; Mesqui 1991–3, vol. I, pp. 106–75; Mesqui 1998, pp. 109–15.
15 Stow, ed. Morley, p. 73.
16 See Chapter Eight, p. 224.
17 The repair work began on site on 24 October 1997 and was completed on 21 May 1998. I am grateful to Richard Roberts for these details. A similar programme of work to the east elevation has begun as this book goes to press, to be followed by work to the north and west elevations in 2009–10. The accompanying archaeological recording is being directed by Roland Harris and the petrographic survey by Robin Sanderson and Bernard Worssam. So far as the evidence of the east elevation is relevant, the results yielded so far have confirmed the analysis presented in this volume.
18 HRPA was established in 1989 with responsibility for managing the Tower of London, the Banqueting House at Whitehall, Hampton Court Palace, the State Apartments at Kensington Palace and Kew Palace with Queen Charlotte's Cottage (see Chapter Eight, pp. 223–4). In April 1998 the activities of the Agency were transferred to a Royal Charter Body with charitable status, known as Historic Royal Palaces (HRP), contracted by the Secretary of State for Culture, Media and Sport to manage the palaces on his or her behalf.
19 *The White Tower Recording and Research Project: Brief and Specification for Phase II*, 13 March 1997, p. 1.

Summary History of the Tower of London

1 Davison 1967.
2 Sturdy 1979, pp. 271–3; Parnell 1993, p. 20.
3 W. St J. Hope in Sands 1912, p. 219; Armitage 1912, p. 252; R. A. Brown 1978b, p. 49; R. A. Brown 1984, p. 11 and figs 3 and 4.
4 First observed by Geoffrey Parnell.
5 *Anglo-Saxon Chronicle*, ed. Whitelock, Douglas and Tucker, p. 175.
6 See pp. 5–6.
7 Colvin, Brown and Taylor 1963–82, vol. II, p. 708.
8 Colvin, Brown and Taylor 1963–82, vol. II, p. 708.
9 See Chapter One, p. 22.
10 Roger of Howden, ed. Stubbs, vol. III, p. 33.
11 Matthew Paris, *Chronica majora*, ed. Luard, vol. II, p. 369.
12 Colvin, Brown and Taylor 1963–82, vol. II, pp. 710–11.
13 Colvin, Brown and Taylor 1963–82, vol. II, pp. 712–13.
14 Impey 1998; Keevill 2004, pp. 54–80.
15 See Chapter Five, p. 150.
16 Impey and Parnell 2000, p. 52; see also Chapter Six, pp. 163–4.
17 Bayley 1821–5, passim.
18 It is shown on the Haiward and Gascoigne plan of that year (fig. 127).
19 See Chapter Six, pp. 174–7.
20 Parnell 1981, p. 153.
21 Impey and Parnell 2000, pp. 117–22.
22 See Chapter Eight, p. 224.

Chapter One: London's Early Castles and the Context of their Creation

1 Tacitus, *Annals*, ed. Jackson, vol. XIV, pp. 160 and 162.
2 It has been argued recently that the Latin name *Londinium* derives from the pre-Roman name for the river below a crossing on the site of London Bridge (Coates 1998; Milne 1995, pp. 48–70). Some evidence exists for a bridge in the first century AD (Watson, Brigham and Dyson 2001, p. 30).
3 Parnell et al. 1982, pp. 101–5.
4 Marsden 1980, p. 121. For the political context, see Salway 1981, pp. 219–23.
5 On the historical and political context, see Salway 1981, pp. 273 and 275; Frere 1978, pp. 214–15; Cunliffe 1977b, p. 3.
6 It has been suggested, based on the similarity of their spacing to that of the landward bastions, that the medieval towers on the Tower's southern inner curtain stand on Roman footings (Clapham 1912, p. 35). In addition, William Fitz Stephen's twelfth-cen-

tury 'Description of the Most Noble City of London' describes the city as formerly 'walled and towered to the south' ('similiter ab austro Londonia murata et turrita fuit': Fitz Stephen, 'Descriptio', ed. Robertson, p. 3), although this may have been based on Geoffrey of Monmouth's fanciful *History* of 1138 (Geoffrey of Monmouth, ed. Wright, section 44; see also Chapter Eleven, pp. 277–8).

7   Sankey 1998; Sharpe 2002, p. 123; Keene and Schofield 2004, p. 4.

8   Parnell 1978.

9   For the historical and political context, see Salway 1981, pp. 419–21; Marsden 1980, p. 178; Frere 1978, p. 453; Marsden 1980, p. 179.

10 Parnell 1985b, pp. 30–34; Parnell 1993, p. 15.

11 Whitelock et al. 1966, p. 10.

12 Biddle 1989, pp. 26–9; Cowie et al., forthcoming.

13 Bede, ed. Colgrave and Mynors, p. 152.

14 Bede, ed. Colgrave and Mynors, p. 142: 'et ipsa multorum emporium populorum terra marique venientium'.

15 Biddle 1989, p. 25.

16 Vince 1984; R. Cowie and C. Harding in Museum of London Archaeology Service 2000, pp. 182–3; Bishop and Williams 2004, pp. 56–7.

17 P. Taylor 2004, p. 5.

18 P. Taylor 2004, pp. 5 and 8–9.

19 Kendrick and Radford 1943, pp. 14–18; H. M. Taylor and J. Taylor 1965–78, vol. 1, pp. 399–400; Brooke and Keir 1975, p. 137.

20 Schofield 1994, p. 82.

21 For the reasons for suggesting this, see Wheeler 1935, p. 103; Vince 1990, p. 55; Matthew Paris, *Gesta abbatum monasterii Sancti Albani*, ed. Riley, vol. 1, p. 55. For arguments and evidence to the contrary, see Dyson and Milne 2002; Cowie 2004, p. 203; Blair 2005, p. 273 and n. 124.

22 Keene 2003, pp. 241–2; Keynes 1998, p. 23.

23 Keene 2003, p. 246; see also Hill 1996, p. 218.

24 Watson, Brigham and Dyson 2001, pp. 52–3.

25 Keene 2003, pp. 246–7.

26 This is implied by details in Osbern's account of Cnut's activities following the theft of St Alphege's body from St Paul's (Rumble and Morris 1994, pp. 298–303); Keene, forthcoming.

27 For arguments that a street grid was established, see Biddle 1989, p. 29; Dyson 1978, pp. 200–15; Tatton-Brown 1986, p. 26. Derek Keene suggests that while some streets may have been laid out under Alfred, additions to the grid continued into the twelfth century (personal communication).

28 Haslam 1988, pp. 35–41.

29 Derek Keene, personal communication.

30 Haslam 1988, p. 39.

31 *Cartulary of Holy Trinity Aldgate*, ed. Hodgett, pp. 189–91, nos 960–71; *Regesta regum anglo-normannorum*, ed. Davis and Whitwell, vol. III, p. 189, no. 506.

32 Lincoln (160 houses), York (an entire shire or ward), Shrewsbury (51 houses). Destruction on a smaller scale occurred also at Cambridge, Canterbury, Gloucester, Huntingdon, Stamford, Wallingford and Warwick. For a useful summary, see English 1995, p. 47.

33 Guy of Amiens, ed. Barlow, p. 38.

34 'On the south, London was once walled and towered in a like fashion, but the Thames, that mighty river, teeming with fish . . . has in the course of time washed away those bulwarks, undermined them and cast them down': 'ab austro Londonia murata et turrita fuit; sed fluvius maximus piscosus Thamesis . . . moenia illa tractu temporis abluit, labefactavit, dejecit' (Fitz Stephen, 'Descriptio', ed. Robertson, p. 3).

35 Vince 1990, p. 40 and fig. 23.

36 Vince 1990, p. 40.

37 Butcher 1982, pp. 101–5.

38 Parnell 1983, fig. 17 ('Ditch C'); Parnell 1993, p. 16.

39 Parnell 1993, p. 16, and personal communication. This ditch is not referred to by the original excavator (Davison 1967).

40 Guy of Amiens, ed. Barlow, pp. 38–44.

41 *Gesta Normannorum ducum*, ed. Van Houts, vol. II, pp. 170 and 172.

42 William of Poitiers, ed. Davis and Chibnall.

43 *Anglo-Saxon Chronicle*, ed. Whitelock, Douglas and Tucker.

44 Baring 1909, appendix A, pp. 207–16. On the shortcomings of Baring's methodology and conclusions, see J. J. N. Palmer 1995.

45 Wilson 1985, p. 200; C. Gibbs-Smith in Stenton 1965, p. 176.

46 Guy of Amiens' authorship and the early date of the work have been reaffirmed by Elisabeth Van Houts (1989); Guy of Amiens, ed. Barlow, pp. xl–xlii; and Orlandi 1996, p. 127.

47 See Guy of Amiens, ed. Barlow, p. 39 and n. 4.

48 'Densatis castris a leva menia cinxit, / Et bellis hostes esse dedit vigiles' (*Carmen*, in Guy of Amiens, ed. Barlow, p. 38).

49 'Edificat moles, veruecis cornua ferro / Fabricat et talpas, urbis ad excidium. / Intonat inde minas, penas et bella minatur, / Iurans quod, licitum si sibi sit spacium, / Menia dissoluet, turres equabit harenis, / Elatam turrem destruet aggerie' (*Carmen*, in Guy of Amiens, ed. Barlow, p. 40).

50 'Cernitis oppressos valido certamine muros / Et circumseptos cladibus innumeris. / Molis et erecte transcendit machina turres, / Ictibus et lapidum menia scissa ruunt. / Casibus a multis, ex omni parte ruina / Eminet . . .' (*Carmen*, in Guy of Amiens, ed. Barlow, p. 42).

51 'Inde vero profectus Londoniam est agressus, ubi precursores milites venientes in platea urbis plurimos invenerunt rebelles resistere toto conamine decertantes. Cum quibus protinus congressi non minimum luctum intulerunt urbi ob filiorum ac civium suorum funera plurima. Videntes demum Londonii se diutius contra stare non posse, datis obsidibus se suaque omnia nobilissimo victori suo hereditario domino subposuere' (*Gesta Normannorum ducum*, ed. Van Houts, vol. II, p. 170).

52 *Gesta Normannorum ducum*, ed. Van Houts, vol. I, p. xxxv.

53 R. H. C. Davis 1981, pp. 79–80.

54 *Gesta Normannorum ducum*, ed. Van Houts, vol. I, p. xlviii.

55 William of Poitiers, ed. Davis and Chibnall, pp. xxvii–xxxv.

56 William of Poitiers, ed. Davis and Chibnall, p. xx; R.H.C. Davis 1981, p. 74.

57 William of Poitiers, ed. Davis and Chibnall, p. 147. Baring (1909, p. 27) supports the burning of Southwark.

58 Baring 1909, p. 210. On this see also Stenton 1971, p. 597, n. 1.

59 In William of Poitiers' narrative, this is mentioned *before* the attack on Southwark. But it is clear from the text that the attack had happened well in advance of arrival at the 'position near London', en route to Wallingford, and that no crossing of the river had been made by that stage.

60 I am grateful to Richard Sharpe and Derek Keene for advice on this point. See also R. C. Palmer 1982, pp. 9–10.

61 '. . . praesertim sperans ubi regnare coeperit rebellem quemque minus ausurum in se, facilius conterendum esse. Praemisit ergo Lundoniam qui munitionem in ipsa construerent urbe, et pleraque competentia regiae magnificentiae praepararent, moraturus interim per vicina. Adversitas omnis procul fuit, adeo ut venatui et avium ludo, si forte libuit, secure vacaret' (William of Poitiers, ed. Davis and Chibnall, p. 148).

62 William of Poitiers, ed. Davis and Chibnall, p. 161.

63 'Egressus e Lundonia, dies aliquot in propinquo loco morabatur Bercingis, dum firmamenta quaedem in urbe contra mobilitatem ingentis ac feri populi perficerentur. Vidit enim inprimis necessarium magnopere Lundonienses coerceri' (William of Poitiers, ed. Davis and Chibnall, p. 160).

64 *Anglo-Saxon Chronicle*, ed. Whitelock, Douglas and Tucker, p. 145.

65 *Anglo-Saxon Chronicle*, ed. Whitelock, Douglas and Tucker, p. 144; *Anglo-Saxon Chronicle*, ed. Earle and Plummer, vol. I, p. 200.

66 For the Latin text, see Baudri of Bourgueil, ed. Hilbert. The Conquest is covered in lines 235–558 (pp. 155–63). For a verse translation, see Herren 1988. For other information and comments on the value of the poem as a historical source, see S. A. Brown 1988 and Herren 1988.

67 Baudri of Bourgueil, ed. Hilbert, lines 529 ('Hostis adest' aliqui clamant a turribus altis) and 494 ('Septaque munivit moenia rarus homo').

68 The most enthusiastic advocates of the poem's historical usefulness are C. Morton and H. Muntz (1972, p. xxxv). The strongest critic is R. H. C. Davis (1978, p. 261). A more recent and balanced view is offered by Giovanni Orlandi (1996, p. 118).

69 John of Worcester, ed. Darlington and McGurk, vol. II, p. 606: 'Interea comes Willelmus Suthsaxoniam, Cantiam, Suthamtunensem provinciam, Suthregiam, Middelsaxoniam, Heortfordensem provinciam devastabat et villas cremare hominesque interficere non

cessabat donec ad villam que Beorhchamstede nominatur veniret.'

70 Orderic Vitalis, ed. Chibnall, vol. ii, pp. 194–5.

71 *Brevis relatio de Guillelmo*, ed. Van Houts, p. 33: 'Non diutius vero ibi commoratus versus Lundoniam principalem civitatem Anglie cepit ire et sic ipsam terram Anglorum con-quirere. Deinde ad eum paulatim ceperunt venire Angli plurimi et cum eo pacem facere'; that is, 'not waiting there for long, he began to go towards London, the principal city of England, and in this way to conquer the land of the English itself. Then, shortly after-wards, very many of the English began to come to him and make peace.'

72 William of Malmesbury, *Gesta regum anglo-rum*, ed. Mynors, Thomson and Winterbot-tom, p. 460.

73 Henry of Huntingdon, ed. Greenway, p. 394: 'Willelmus vero tanta potitus victoria, sus-ceptus a Lundoniensibus pacifice'. The first version, of seven books, taking the story up to 1129, was complete by 1130. The final version, of ten books, takes the narrative to 1154 (Henry of Huntingdon, ed. Greenway, pp. lxvi–lxxvii).

74 Eadmer, ed. Rule, p. 182; Gaimar, ed. Bell, p. liii; Simeon of Durham, ed. Arnold, p. 182; Van Houts 1997, p. 106; Wace, ed. Holden, pt 3, p. 288.

75 Stenton 1971, pp. 391–2.

76 Douglas 1964, p. 205.

77 '. . . copioso ac praestantia militari famoso incolatu abundat' (William of Poitiers, ed. Davis and Chibnall, p. 146).

78 'Urbs est ampla nimis, perversis plena col-onis, / Et regni reliquis dicior est opibus' (Guy of Amiens, ed. Barlow, p. 38).

79 William of Poitiers, ed. Davis and Chibnall, p. 165.

80 *Gesta Normannorum ducum*, ed. Van Houts, vol. ii, p. 170.

81 William of Poitiers, ed. Davis and Chibnall, p. 63. See also Gillingham 1989, pp. 148–9.

82 Baring 1909, p. 210.

83 J. J. N. Palmer 1995, pp. 28–9. The fact that no waste is recorded in the environs of Wall-ingford is one of the reasons put forward by Palmer for questioning Baring's methodology.

84 Such as Douglas (1964, pp. 206–7), Brown and Curnow (1984, p. 5), and Rowley (1997, pp. 50–1).

85 Baring 1909, p. 212. Little Berkhamsted would have been approached by a circuitous route through Bedfordshire, Cambridgeshire and eastern Hertfordshire. Baring deduced this from the evidence of waste en route and around the destination, and John of Worces-ter's implication that William had traversed Hertfordshire before getting to *Beorchamst-ede*, which would have been unnecessary had Great Berkhamsted, only 6 miles from the Bedfordshire border, been the destination.

86 See, for example, Barlow 1955, p. 87; H. W. C. Davis 1949, p. 9.

87 J. J. N. Palmer 1995, pp. 33–4. For Great Berkhamsted on the eve of the Conquest, see Clarke 1994, pp. 280–81.

88 Mills 1996, p. 62.

89 William of Jumièges tells us that a Norman advance party penetrated 'in platea urbis' (*Gesta Normannorum ducum*, ed. Van Houts, vol. ii, p. 170), that is, in the 'street' or 'square' 'of the city'. Mills (1996, pp. 61–2) suggests that this may refer to the Folkmoot by St Paul's or Cheapside.

90 Perhaps standing at Ludgate, as Mills (1996, p. 61) implies.

91 Renn 1994a, pp. 180–81; Brian Durham, per-sonal communication.

92 David Stocker, personal communication.

93 But see Guy of Amiens, ed. Barlow, p. 41, n. 4, concerning the possible misreading of the wording here. Direct borrowing from a classical source remains a possibility, although the two words do not appear together any-where in the works of Virgil or Statius, from whom Guy drew most frequently.

94 G. T. Clark (1884, vol. ii, p. 205) seems to have been the first to make this connection.

95 *Regesta regum anglo-normannorum*, ed. Bates, no. 180; Bishop and Chaplais 1957, pl. 14, p. 593

96 Rowley 1997, p. 51. Just conceivably, the 'Barking' incident may reflect real events associated not with the town or abbey, but with its intramural property centred on All Hallows, known as *Berkyncherche* in the mid-twelfth century (Thorpe 1769, p. 10). I am grateful to David Stocker for this suggestion.

97 Wolstenholme 1855, p. 80; Ekwall 1960, p. 39.

98 The possibility of a confusion between Great and Little Berkhamsted has been raised before: Turner 1912, pp. 224–5; Douglas 1964, p. 207; Körner 1964, p. 281; William of Poitiers, ed. Davis and Chibnall, p. 162, n. 2.

99 Orderic Vitalis, interpolation into William of Jumièges (*Gesta Normannorum ducum*, ed. Van Houts, vol. ii, p. 208).

100 Orderic Vitalis, ed. Chibnall, vol. ii, p. 214: 'Locum vero intra moenia ad extruendum castellum delegit'.

101 Braun 1937. Braun's argument was threefold: first, that William of Poitiers' *Bercing* was 'Barking Hill', a name that he says 'seems to have been' attached to 'the hill at this end of the city' (p. 447); second, that if so the Con-queror would have required a fortified base at this point; and third that castles in exactly analagous positions were created at Roc-hester, Canterbury and Winchester (p. 446) – since proved to be incorrect in all cases.

102 See Drage 1987, p. 117; Armitage 1912, pp. 95–6.

103 *Cartulary of Holy Trinity Aldgate*, ed. Hod-gett, p. 168, no. 871. For the area concerned, see also Haslam 1988, p. 36 and fig. 8.

104 Impey 2002a, p. 249; Levalet 1977, pp. 18 and 20–21.

105 The new Jewel Chamber replaced the Wake-field Tower displays in 1967, and was in turn replaced by the existing Jewel House in 1994.

106 See Davison 1967, pp. 40–43; Redknap 1983, pp. 135–49.

107 Davison 1967, p. 40 and fig. 2. For the loca-tion of the trenches, see Parnell 1983, figs 1 and 17.

108 Parnell 1983, pp. 111–13; Parnell 1993, p. 17.

109 Parnell 1983, p. 118; Parnell 1993, p. 17.

110 Davison 1967, pp. 40–41.

111 See Brown and Curnow 1984, p. 5 and fig. 2.

112 King and Alcock 1969; English 1995.

113 Davison 1967, p. 42; Parnell 1983, p. 136 and fig. 17 ('ditch A').

114 *Cartulary of Holy Trinity Aldgate*, ed. Hodgett, p. 190, no. 964; p. 191, no. 966; Neininger 1999, no. 38, pp. 28–9.

115 *Chronicon monasterii de Bello*, ed. Searle, p. 200: 'capella eiusdem Regis iuxta Turrem Londonie sita'.

116 'Anno incarnationis dominice MCLVII anno scilicet III Henrici iunioris tempore Radulfi prioris et Hugonis de Mateni archidiaconi orta est dissensio quedam inter nos et pres-biterum ecclesie Sancti Petri de Ball[ivo] de parte q[uon]dam parochialis ecclesie Sancti Bothulfi foris Algate'; that is, 'In the year of the incarnation of our Lord 1157, [that is,] the third year of Henry the younger, in the time of Ralph prior and Hugh de Mateni archdea-con, there arose a conflict between us and the priest of the church of St Peter's in the Bailey concerning the portion of the former parish church of St Botolph outside Aldgate' (Glasgow University Library, MS Hunter U.2.6, fol. 171v). I am grateful to Hugh Doherty for this transcription of the text.

117 The year 1237: *Calendar of Liberate Rolls: Henry III*, vol. I (1226 40), p. 258. The full text (C 62/11 m12) reads: 'Rex vicecomitibus Lon-donie salutem. Precipimus vobis quod fac-[iatis] habere fratri Willelmo Recluso Sancti Petri in ballio Turris nostre London singulis diebus unum denar[ium] ad sustentacionem quamdiu ibi reclusus fuerit exstiteret et com-putat[is] nobis ad scaccarium. Teste Rege apud Westm[onasterium] xviii die Marc[ii]'; that is, 'The King sends greetings to the Sher-iffs of London. We order you to cause Brother William the recluse of St Peter's in the bailey of the Tower of London to have 1d daily for his maintenance for as long as he shall remain a recluse there. And you shall account to us at the Exchequer. Witnessed by the King at Westminster 18 March [1237].' The hermit in the bailey is also mentioned in a document of two days later, as follows: 'Mandatum est con-stabulario Turris London[ie] quod rex conces-sit fratri Willelmo, presentium latori, quod habeat reclusorium suum in ballio eiusdem Turris quod est in custodia sua, et quod illud reclusorium ei habere faciat'; that is, 'it is made known to the Constable of the Tower of London that the King has granted to Brother William, the present bearer, that he should have a hermitage in the bailey of the Tower which is in his custody, and he should cause this hermitage to be made' (*Calendar of Close Rolls: Henry III*, 1234–7, p. 424).

1239: *Calendar of Liberate Rolls: Henry III*, vol. I (1226–40), p. 396. The original text (C 62/13 m10) refers to the parson of the 'eccle-sie Sancti Petri in balliva Turris'.

1240: *Calendar of Liberate Rolls: Henry III*, vol. I (1226–40), p. 449. The original text (C

62/14 m19) refers to 'Sancti Petri infra ballium Turris nostre'. See also ibid., p. 444.

118 *Cartulary of Holy Trinity Aldgate*, ed. Hodgett, p. 190; Impey and Parnell 2000, p. 16.

119 Ducange 1883–7, vol. x, p. 539; Latham and Howlett 1975–, vol. 1, pp. 175–6.

120 Marshall and Foulds 1997, p. 44; Marshall 2004, p. 55; Drage 1989, fig. 4 and pp. 25, 43.

121 It appears as the 'Boley de Roff' in 1278 and 'le Bole' in 1382 (Wallenberg 1934, pp. 123–4). For the location of 'Le Boley', see also Gomme 1887, p. 183; Flight and Harrison 1978, p. 28, fig. 1. Whether the term is a corruption of 'bailey' or derives from the old French 'la Boleye', 'a place covered with birch trees' (Wallenberg 1934, pp. 123–4), remains unclear. I am grateful to Jeremy Ashbee for advice on these issues.

122 Pounds 1990, p. 211; for Gloverstone's boundaries, see R. Morris, no date, pp. 107–8.

123 Stocker 2004, p. 9 and fig. 1.

124 St Paul's first occurs as 'in ballio' circa 1230 (*Registrum antiquissimum*, ed. Foster, vol. ix, pp. 217–18, no. 2629), St Clement's in 1221 (*Registrum antiquissimum*, ed. Foster, vol. ix, p. 203, no. 2611) and All Saints in 1163. All Saints and St Clement's ceased to exist in the Middle Ages.

125 Popescu 2004, pp. 13–14. St Martin's was demolished in 1562 (Messent 1932, pp. 63–4; Messent 1936, p. 174).

126 The course of the Anglo-Saxon defences in this area is uncertain (Dodd 2003, p. 20), but the north–south ditch discovered in 1982 between Bulwarks Lane and the Wesley Memorial Church Hall (Durham et al. 1983, p. 20) has been identified as marking the western rampart (Blair 1994b, p. 147). If so, in order to have included St Peter's, the postulated bailey would have encroached on the pre-Conquest defended area. Alternatively, if the town's pre-Conquest defences lay almost as far east as New Inn Hall Street, the bailey could simply have covered all the open ground between them and the inner defences of the castle.

127 Drage 1989, p. 28 and fig. 4.

128 Popescu 2004, pp. 209–15; for the Charter of Edward III, see Hudson and Tingley 1906, vol. 1, pp. 23–7.

129 Another example of a vast eleventh-century outer bailey being abandoned, in the twelfth century, in favour of a reinforced nucleus is provided by the castle of Puiset (Eure et Loir: see Fournier 1964).

130 *Regesta regum anglo-normannorum*, ed. Davis and Whitwell, vol. iii, no. 274, p. 99: 'et concedo illi . . . Custodiam turris Londonie cum parvo castello quod fuit Ravengeri'. See also Colvin, Brown and Taylor 1963–82, vol. ii, p. 707.

131 Ravengar is mentioned in Domesday, the only other source from which he is known, only as the former tenant of land then held by others (*VCH Essex*, vol. 1, pp. 448–56, and p. 508, n. 7). All in Essex, it comprised hold-ings of St Mary's monastery in Barking (Bulphan and other property in the Hundred of Barstaple) and of the Bishop of Bayeux (Ramsden, Wickford and Wheatley), also in Barstaple Hundred, and Beckney in the Hundred of Rochford. In three cases (12 hides and property at Wickford, Ramsden and Bulphan in Barstaple Hundred), Ravengar had taken (*tulit*) the land from others.

132 Colvin, Brown and Taylor 1963–82, vol. ii, p. 707.

133 Round 1892, pp. 334–6 and p. 333, n. 4; thus, for example, at Torigny (Manche) a fire destroyed houses up to the 'tower and the small castle around it' ('turrem et parvum castellum circa eam') during the siege of 1151 (Robert of Torigny, ed. Howlett, p. 161).

134 Robert of Torigny, ed. Howlett, p. 106: 'castellum, quod vocatur Archas, turre et moenibus mirabiliter firmavit'; that is, 'he wonderfully strengthened the castle known as Arques with a tower and ramparts'.

135 Robert of Torigny, ed. Howlett, p. 106: 'Turrem nihilominus excelsam fecit in castello Cadomensi, et murum ipsius castelli, quem pater suus fecerat, in altum crevit'; that is, 'he made a tower no less tall in the castle of Caen, and heightened the walls of the same castle, which had been built by his father'.

136 Round 1892, pp. 328–9.

137 *Regesta regum anglo-normannorum*, ed. Davis and Whitwell, vol. iii, p. 149, no. 387; Round 1892, p. 329.

138 Round 1892, p. 328.

139 For these examples and discussion, see Round 1892, pp. 328–46.

140 *Regesta regum anglo-normannorum*, ed. Davis and Whitwell, vol. iii, no. 275, p. 101: 'turrim Lundoniae cum castello quod subtus est'.

141 *Regesta regum anglo-normannorum*, ed. Davis and Whitwell, vol. iii, no. 276, p. 103: 'turris Londonie cum Castello quod ei subest'.

142 Colvin, Brown and Taylor 1963–82, vol. ii, p. 707, n. 3.

143 Robert of Torigny, ed. Howlett, p. 161.

144 The text contains references to individuals known in the late twelfth century, suggesting derivation from an archetype of that period (Derek Keene, personal communication).

145 '. . . a porta de Algate usque ad portam Ballii Turris que nuncupatur Cungata et tota venella vocata Chykenlane versus Berkyngchirche usque ad cimiterium' (*Cartulary of Holy Trinity Aldgate*, ed. Hodgett, p. 228)

146 Lobel 1989, map 4; Derek Keene, personal communication.

147 *Calendar of Close Rolls: Richard II*, vol. ii (1381–5), pp. 178–9.

148 Johns 1989 (map of London *circa* 1270); Bentley 1984.

149 At or after the demise of the bailey, the name seems to have become attached to a gate called the 'Congate', described in 1340 as 'beside the chapel', and thus opening through the Roman wall close to the White Tower chapel, near or beside the Wardrobe Tower (The National Archives [formerly the Public Record Office], e 101 470/8, m2 and m3). I am grateful to Jeremy Ashbee for this information and interpretation.

150 I owe this suggestion to Geoffrey Parnell. For the map and description, see Parnell 1985a, pp. 70–71. Since the gate does not appear on the Haiward and Gascoyne plan (A. Keay 2001), however, it must either have been walled up and abandoned by 1597 – subsequently to be reopened – or have been a post-medieval insertion.

151 De Boüard 1979, pp. 10–11.

152 *Anglo-Saxon Chronicle*, ed. Earle and Plummer, vol. 1, p. 234; *Anglo-Saxon Chronicle*, ed. Whitelock, Douglas and Tucker, p. 75. The 'murus' mentioned in William II's writ of 1094–7 may have been the same wall, although possibly the city wall.

153 *Regesta regum anglo-normannorum*, ed. Bates, p. 593, no. 180; Bishop and Chaplais 1957, pl. 14.

154 Colvin, Brown and Taylor 1963–82, vol. ii, p. 712.

155 *Calendar of Liberate Rolls: Henry III*, vol. 1 (1226–40), pp. 396–7. Land had been acquired from thirty-three private individuals, five monastic foundations and three London hospitals. Where the land lay is not specified, but most or all of it may have been to the east of the city wall.

156 Colvin, Brown and Taylor 1963–82, vol. ii, pp. 711–13.

157 The year 1240: *Calendar of Liberate Rolls: Henry III*, vol. ii (1240–45), pp. 449 and 149.

158 Summarised in Bentley 1987, fig. 1.

159 Bentley 1987, pp. 328–32 and fig. 1. See also Tyler 2000, p. 24; Gaimster and Bradley 2002, p. 163.

160 See *Early Charters of the Cathedral Church of St Paul*, ed. Gibbs, no. 179, pp. 137–8; Moore 1918, vol. 1, p. 213 ('ballio extra lutgate'); Maxwell-Lyte 1890–1915, vol. 4, p. 177 a 7499 ('in ballio'). The church occurs as 'Sancti Sepulchri de Ballio' in 1253, in a confirmation of Roger of Salisbury's grant of the church to St Bartholomew's Priory, and so very probably reproducing a suffix it had had since the twelfth century (*Cartae antiquae*, ed. Conway Davies, no. 340, p. 14). The dedication itself supplanted an earlier one to St Edmund. See Harben 1918, pp. 523–4, for later examples.

161 Maxwell-Lyte 1890–1915, vol. 2, p. 97, a 2581 ('in the bailey without Newgate'). This may have been the 'ballium' mentioned in the writ of 1094–7, work on which was then still required (*Early Charters of the Cathedral Church of St Paul*, ed. Gibbs, no. 190, p. 157). Even if the intramural area of the western castle had by then been abandoned as a royal castle, it would be understandable if the maintenance of a fortified area outside – effectively an extension of the city – was still required.

162 McCann 1993, p. 51 and figs 18, 21 and 22.

163 Derek Keene, personal communication.

164 Based on a fourteenth-century description of boundaries of the Soke of Robert Fitz Walter

('Liber custumarum', in *Munimenta Gildhallae*, ed. Riley, vol. II, part i, p. 150); Keene 2004, p. 18 and fig. 9.

165 *Anglo-Saxon Chronicle*, ed. Whitelock, Douglas and Tucker, p. 163.

166 *Early Charters of the Cathedral Church of St Paul*, ed. Gibbs, no. 13, p. 15.

167 *Early Charters of the Cathedral Church of St Paul*, ed. Gibbs, pp. 23–4: '. . . tantum de fossato mei castelli ex parte Tamesis ad meridiem quantum opus fuerit ad faciendum murum eiusdem ecclesie tantum de eodem fossato quantum sufficiat ad faciendam viam extra murum ex altera parte ecclesie ad aquilonem quantum predictus episcopus de eodem fossato diruit'. See also *Regesta regum anglo-normannorum*, ed. Davis and Whitwell, vol. II, no. 991, p. 102.

168 The *Chronicon* (British Library, MS Cotton Cleopatra C3) is not published, but excerpts are given by Dugdale (ed. Caley, Ellis and Bulkeley Bandinel, vol. VI, p. 147). Little Dunmow was the Essex seat of the Baynards, who had founded the priory in 1106. The chronicle was begun by Nicholas de Brompfield, Canon of Little Dunmow, in 1259 (*VCH Essex*, vol. II, p. 150). William Baynard forfeited it for rebellion (*Anglo-Saxon Chronicle*, ed. Whitelock, Douglas and Tucker, p. 182; Henry of Huntingdon, ed. Greenway, p. 457).

169 Mortimer 1989, p. 252; *Regesta regum anglo-normannorum*, ed. Davis and Whitwell, vol. II, no. 532, p. 10.

170 *Early Charters of the Cathedral Church of St Paul*, ed. Gibbs, no. 198, p. 157; *Regesta regum anglo-normannorum*, ed. Davis and Whitwell, vol. II, no. 749, pp. 52–3.

171 Mortimer 1989, p. 243.

172 *Regesta regum anglo-normannorum*, ed. Bates, no. 128, p. 441.

173 Mortimer 1989, p. 241; Keats-Rohan 1999, p. 327.

174 Derek Keene, personal communication.

175 Stenton 1990, p. 8. The full text is printed in Bateson 1902, pp. 485–6.

176 *Jordan Fantosme's Chronicle*, ed. Johnston: 'Gilebert de Munfichet sun chastel ad fermé / E dit que les Clarreaus vers lui sunt alié.' Gilbert de Munfichet was the cousin of Walter Fitz Robert Fitz Richard of Clare, Lord of Baynard's Castle (Stenton 1990, p. 6). For the date of the *Chronicle*'s composition, see *Jordan Fantosme's Chronicle*, ed. Johnston, p. xxiii.

177 'Habet . . . ab occidente duo castella munitissima' (Fitz Stephen, 'Descriptio', ed. Robertson, p. 3); Stenton 1990, p. 49.

178 Gervase of Tilbury, ed. Banks and Binns, book 2, pp. 398–400. See Chapter Eleven, p. 280.

179 Chibnall 1982, no. 6, pp. 7–8; no. 7, pp. 8–9; no. 8, pp. 9–10.

180 *Calendar of Inquisitions*, vol. I (1219–1307), p. 317, no. 1034.

181 Michel 1840, pp. 118–19: 'Il manda privéement à ses bourgeois de Londres, qui se faisoient apieler baron, ke si chier comme il avoient s'amour à avoir, qu'il abatissent le castiel de Robiert le fill Gautier, que dedens Londres estoit, que on apieloit Castiel-Baignart. Quant li bourgeois oirent che que li rois lor mandoit, il n'oserent trespasser son commandement, ains s'assamblerent et vinrent devant le castiel, si l'abatirent'; that is, 'He secretly ordered his burghers of London, who had got themselves known as "barons", if they wanted to obtain his good favour, that they should demolish the castle of Robert Fitz Walter, which was in London and was called Castle Baignard. When the burghers heard what the king had ordered they dared not disobey their order, and gathered themselves together, came before the castle, and pulled it down.' Although the real extent of 'demolitions' was routinely exaggerated by medieval authors, in this case he was well informed and perhaps an eyewitness (Poole 1955, p. 497). Stow's story of Fitz Walter's rehabilitation and his permit to rebuild is based on a later and spurious source (Stow, ed. Morley, p. 89; Norgate 1902, pp. 289–93).

182 Stenton 1990, p. 7; *Calendar of Letter Books*, C, 71n.

183 Stow, ed. Morley, p. 93. See also Honeybourne 1965, pp. 38–9, and Thurley 1993, p. 36.

184 Guildhall Library, MS 25501, fol. 107r: 'area vocata castra baynardi'.

185 Johns 1989, p. 59; Schofield 1993, p. 38 and fig. 26.

186 Johns 1989, p. 59; Guildhall Library, MS 25121/402: '. . . in Cornerio ex opposito terre decani Sancti Pauli inter terram Davidi Longi Capellani versus aquilonem et vicum australem qui tendit versus murum Civitatis secus fossatum Castri de Munfichet'. I am grateful to Stephen Priestley for transcribing the document and to Derek Keene for advice on its content.

187 Johns 1989, p. 59 and map.

188 Watson 1992, pp. 337–9 and figs 1–4.

189 D. Keene in Keene, Burns and Saint 2004, fig. 9, and personal communication

190 Guildhall Library, MS 25501, fol. 107r: '. . . in area vocata castra baynardi . . . quandam novam ecclesiam et alia edificia eis opportune construere possint . . . ecclesie sue tante longitudinis quante est maius cancellum quod hunc dicti fratres in Anglia erigere possint et ultra cancellum viginti pedum dum cum aquilonarem partem dicti cancelli extra antiquum fundamentum quondam turris de Mounfichet versus portam de Ludgate non erigant'.

191 Watson 1992, p. 337.

192 Thomas and Watson, forthcoming.

193 Johns 1989, p. 59.

194 'Liber custumarum', in *Munimenta Gildhallae*, ed. Riley, vol. II, part i, p. 150.

195 Johns 1989, p. 61, and reconstructed map of *circa* 1270.

196 Schofield 1993, p. 38.

197 Cherry 1990, p. 85.

198 See Chapter Ten, p. 260 et seq.

199 See Chapter Nine, p. 240.

200 Renoux 2003, p. 38; Fleury 1891, p. 146. If Fleury is correct, the tower was square and stood astride the Roman city wall to the north-west of the cathedral.

201 See Chapter Nine, p. 230.

202 Drury 1984, p. 31 and fig. 12.

203 At Rouen, although the precise site of the great tower is unknown, it clearly stood within 20–30 m of the wall (Le Maho 1996, pp. 65–6; Le Maho 2000, p. 74 and n. 3), and at Avranches the tower of *circa* 1000 interrupted the city wall to form its south-west angle (Impey 2002a, p. 249). English examples during the two generations after the Conquest include the keep of *circa* 1130 at Rochester (R. A. Brown 1986, pp. 8 and 22), while at Portchester (admittedly under different circumstances), the outer walls of the keep of *circa* 1140 replaced the upstanding Roman fabric but reused its foundations (Cunliffe and Munby 1985, p. 12).

Chapter Two: The Structural History of the White Tower, 1066–1200

1 For example, see Colvin, Brown and Taylor 1963–82, vol. I, pp. 29–32; Parnell 1993, pp. 19–23.

2 Sturdy 1979.

3 Royal Armouries interpretative panels and models prepared in the course of the White Tower re-presentation project (1997–8).

4 See Chapter One, pp. 17–19.

5 See Chapter One, pp. 19–22.

6 The *Textus Roffensis* is a term used since the sixteenth century for a cartulary of Rochester Cathedral compiled in the 1120s that was bound together with another manuscript, possibly in the thirteenth century and certainly by the fourteenth (Flight 1977, pp. 17–18).

7 *Textus Roffensis*, ed. Hearne, p. 212: 'Gundulfus, ex praecepto regis Willelmi magni, praeesset operi magnae turris Londoniae'.

8 See Introduction, p. xiv.

9 Recently, Colin Flight (1977, p. 32) has suggested that we should be cautious in accepting the evidence of this and several other parts of the *Textus Roffensis*, since they are forgeries: in the case of the agreement between Gundulf and Eadmer it has been rewritten over an earlier erased text, with only the rubric (which fails to mention the Tower) being original. Adding to this, however, Martin Brett (personal communication) considers that the Rochester forgers 'generally worked by interpolation of an extant text, and certainly did not elsewhere invoke pieces of "information" known from other sources to lend their fictions a spurious dignity', and is inclined to trust the link between Gundulf and the Tower, which is incidental to the main theme of the agreement. In the absence of any discernible motive for the fictitious addition of this detail to the agreement, I concur.

10 *Anglo-Saxon Chronicle*, ed. Whitelock, Douglas and Tucker, p. 175; *Anglo-Saxon Chroni-*

cle, ed. Earle and Plummer, vol. 1, p. 234. The building of the wall surrounding the Tower ('turrim Londonie') in 1097 is also mentioned by Henry of Huntingdon, writing in the 1120s (Henry of Huntingdon, ed. Greenway, pp. 444–5).

11 *Early Charters of the Cathedral Church of St Paul*, ed. Gibbs, no. 13, p. 15. The demesne lands of the canons of St Paul's were to be free 'ab omni opere castelli Londonie muri pontis balii'.

12 *Anglo-Saxon Chronicle*, ed. Earle and Plummer, vol. 1, pp. 236–7; *Anglo-Saxon Chronicle*, ed. Whitelock, Douglas and Tucker, p. 177; Orderic Vitalis, ed. Chibnall, vol. v, pp. 310–12.

13 See pp. 50–2.

14 Chaplais 1964, no. 1.

15 OSBM (meaning Ordnance Survey benchmark) is the vertical datum (or height control) used in this project. The suffix OSBM is used in accordance with metric survey (and Ordnance Survey) standard practice for a vertical datum so derived.

16 See Chapter Three, pp. 102–8.

17 The shelly nature of much of the primary mortar at the White Tower was noted as early as 1836: Smirke 1836.

18 See Chapter Eight, p. 211.

19 For a brief account of the main findings of a report on the petrography of the south elevation, see Appendix III, pp. 305–6.

20 Note, however, that by no means all the Caen stone at the White Tower dates from the eleventh century: see Chapter Six, p. 163.

21 See Chapter Three, pp. 104–5.

22 In a square tower this is to be expected, and such clear horizontal banding across the building is seen in near-contemporary buildings elsewhere: for example, at Canterbury Castle (Renn 1982a).

23 This is further confirmed by the banding of ashlar by size across the entire building: see pp. 55–6.

24 See pp. 45–56.

25 See pp. 88–9.

26 For example, at Norwich Castle.

27 See Chapter Three, p. 108.

28 See Chapters Nine and Ten, pp. 239, 244–7.

29 The primary embrasures at Colchester Castle are only approximately 780 mm above the level of the first floor, and the tops of the battlements reach approximately 1.57 m above the floor.

30 For example, Parnell 1993, p. 20.

31 See below, Chapter Nine, pp. 230, 240 and also Impey 2002b.

32 Impey 2002b.

33 Hartmann-Virnich 1996.

34 Canterbury Castle has been dated to 'before 1120 at the latest and possibly around 1100' (Tatton-Brown 1980, p. 214), and as having 'a foundation date of about 1105 ± 20 years' (Renn 1982b, p. 125). The chevron ornament at Canterbury Castle suggests that Renn's dating is too wide.

35 Fernie 2000, pp. 66–7.

36 For example, on the polygonal apse at Wing (Buckinghamshire) and the central tower at Barton-upon-Humber (Lincolnshire).

37 Gem 1981a, p. 60.

38 Lethaby 1906, p. 140.

39 Although begun in 1042, Gem (1981a, p. 54) has demonstrated that the nave of Jumièges dates from after 1052. Given that the church was dedicated in 1067, the lower part of the west end may date from the mid-1050s to early 1060s.

40 Work began at St Etienne in the early 1060s, and was well advanced by 1070. The blind arcading is now restricted to the nave gallery windows, the Romanesque east end having been replaced by a Gothic chevet.

41 Gem 1982, p. 14.

42 Blockley 1997, p. 117 (fig. 49).

43 There is some variation in the spans of the blind arches from elevation to elevation at the White Tower.

44 Given that work at Canterbury Cathedral did not begin until after the enthronement of Lanfranc on 29 August 1070 and the need to demolish what remained of the Anglo-Saxon cathedral (severely damaged by fire in 1067), work on the new building is not likely to have begun until 1071 (Blockley 1997, pp. 22–3 and 30).

45 Although distinctive, the Type 1 mortar itself has no role in the absolute dating of Phase 1: whilst as yet recognised elsewhere only in the Romanesque buildings of Rochester (not even appearing in Lanfranc's cathedral at Canterbury), it is not restricted to the eleventh-century work (where it is used in Gundulf's cathedral crypt and in his curtain wall at the castle), since it was used throughout the *donjon* of *circa* 1127. Of course, if future research is able to confirm that the shelly material is limited to Rochester and the White Tower, this would add an interesting footnote on the supply of building materials and the role of Gundulf, which, fortunately, rests on more substantive grounds (see pp. 43–5).

46 Gem (1981a, p. 60) argues that the general adoption of the smaller regular blocks with wider jointing occurred in 'all the great Anglo-Norman building projects from the '70s onwards', and that the larger blocks and finer jointing of the dormitory at Westminster Abbey pre-date this.

47 Crook 1993, p. 32; Tatton-Brown 1993, pp. 38–9.

48 Tim Tatton-Brown (1980, p. 214) has argued that in east Kent at least Quarr stone was in use for 'about thirty years, fifty years at most (c.1070–1120)'. More recent and wide-ranging research on Quarr stone by Cheryl Bishop confirms that while good-quality Quarr stone was quarried until the late twelfth century, in the later years it was supplied only to areas near the quarry – Hampshire and West Sussex. After *circa* 1120 Quarr stone is not found further afield (Cheryl Bishop, University of Reading, personal communication).

49 Again, while Quarr is used in pre-Conquest eleventh-century buildings, and earlier, the distribution of the stone beyond Hampshire and West Sussex does not occur until after the Conquest (Cheryl Bishop, personal communication).

50 Tatton-Brown 1993, pp. 37–46. The surviving parts of Lanfranc's rebuilding of Canterbury Cathedral (1071–7) show Caen to have been the predominant ashlar, and this provides us with perhaps the earliest well-dated example of large-scale use of the stone in England.

51 See Chapter Three, pp. 110–22.

52 See p. 38.

53 See Appendix II, pp. 293–304.

54 See Appendix II, pp. 295, 297.

55 For discussion of the rate of construction at the White Tower, see pp. 42–3.

56 Unfortunately, this sample has been used elsewhere to date the completion of the White Tower to 1102 (Parnell 1998a, p. 88) and to the reign of Henry I (Fernie 2000, p. 55).

57 See Appendix IV, pp. 312–3.

58 Renn 1959, pp. 1–2.

59 Harvey 1950, p. 17.

60 See Chapter Nine, p. 240; and also Impey 2002b, pp. 189–203.

61 See above, p. 39.

62 *Anglo-Saxon Chronicle*, ed. Earle and Plummer, vol. 1, p. 200.

63 Colvin, Brown and Taylor 1963–82, vol. 1, pp. 21–3.

64 Keene 1985, p. 573.

65 Douglas 1964, pp. 346–63.

66 See Chapter One, p. 23; *Anglo-Saxon Chronicle*, ed. Whitelock, Douglas and Tucker, p. 163.

67 Although this reference is derived from another of the forged parts of the *Textus Roffensis*, there are again no grounds to see the ascription of Rochester Castle to Gundulf as spurious (Flight 1977, pp. 13–14).

68 The following sketch of Gundulf's life is based on Smith 1943 and the most recent edition of the *Vita Gundulfi* (Gundulf, ed. Thomson).

69 Gibson 1978, p. 38.

70 Therefore, it is possible that Gundulf became prior. Recently, it has been suggested that Gundulf was never at St Etienne and that he went directly from Bec to Canterbury in 1070 (Flight 1977, pp. 45–6). Amongst others, Thomson (1977) accepts this detail of the *Vita Gundulfi*, and the grounds for doubting Gundulf's time in Caen are less than wholly convincing. The identification of Gundulf as prior of Caen made in Lanfranc, ed. Clover and Gibson, pp. 176–9, is circumstantial, however, since it is based on a reference in a letter from Lanfranc to his successor at St Etienne suggesting the appointment of Ernost after the imminent departure of the existing prior. It is an assumption that the departing prior is Gundulf, and Cassandra Potts's recent examination of all the Caen *acta* and the unedited Caen cartulary failed to find any charter evidence to substantiate

71   such an identification (Ruud 1989, p. 248, n. 13).

71   For which Lanfranc was responsible (Gibson 1978, pp. 27–8; Vaughn 1987, p. 32).

72   Gem 1982, p. 11.

73   Gem 1982, p. 11.

74   Fernie 1982, p. 27.

75   Woodman 1981, p. 45.

76   Tatton-Brown 1980, p. 214.

77   For example, Douglas 1964, pp. 286, 298, 308 and 359.

78   See Chapter Nine, p. 240, and also Impey 2002b, pp. 189–203.

79   Orderic Vitalis, ed. Chibnall, vol. V, p. 311 and n. 4.

80   Douglas 1964, pp. 231–2. It is interesting to note that it has been argued recently that Gundulf's role in rebuilding his own cathedral at Rochester (1070s) was emphasised only well after the event: initially it was Lanfranc who received the credit (Flight 1977, pp. 61 and 147).

81   See Introduction, p. xiv.

82   Note that the repairs of 1997–8 to the south elevation did not extend to the apse, and thus many of the illustrations accompanying this discussion do not show this projection.

83   In discussion of the exterior elevations, bays and buttresses number from left to right.

84   See pp. 48–53.

85   There is no evidence of any other eleventh-century entrance to the White Tower. The only possible location for a lost entrance at this level is the eastern bay of the north elevation, but the current doorway here reuses an opening that is identical in size and detail to the window embrasures, and this opening is perilously close to the garderobe chutes of the floor above.

86   See Chapter One, pp. 13–26.

87   See pp. 86–90.

88   See Chapter Six, pp. 168–9.

89   See Chapter Seven, p. 184.

90   The doorway is not shown on the drawings of 1729, although it is pencilled onto a plan of this date (The National Archives [formerly the Public Record Office], hereafter TNA, WORK 31/85), along with other details for the fitting-out of the Sea Armoury in 1736.

91   See Chapter Seven, p. 194.

92   See Chapter Eight, pp. 221–2.

93   In the past the southern window has been mistakenly identified as a doorway (Sturdy 1979, p. 272).

94   Their coexistence has been argued (Parnell 1998a).

95   See Chapter Five, note 70.

96   See Chapter Seven, p. 187.

97   See Chapter Eight, p. 213.

98   See Chapter Seven, p. 184.

99   See figs 41, 42.

100   See Chapter Seven, p. 184 and fig. 152.

101   See figs 41, 42, 44, 45.

102   TNA, E 351/3271; see Chapter Six, pp. 175–6.

103   See Chapter Eight, pp. 211–12.

104   See Chapter Six, p. 175.

105   See Chapter Eight, p. 210, fig. 166.

106   See pp. 51–2.

107   See p. 39 and note 48.

108   See pp. 86–90.

109   TNA, WO 52/225, pp. 496–7.

110   Parnell 1998b, p. 172.

111   TNA, E 351/3271, Exchequer Roll.

112   TNA, E 351/3271 and E 351/3272, Exchequer Roll.

113   TNA, WO 49/33, Ordnance Bills and Debentures, fol. 51r.

114   These Romanesque voussoirs show no signs of having been reset.

115   The double windows are recorded in plans of 1729 and 1754, but more useful records are provided by sectional elevations of 1721 (TNA, WORK 31/83) and 1729 (TNA, WORK 31/89 and 31/91) that show the east windows. These drawings are not consistent, since the survey of 1721 places the sills at 23.2 m OSBM, while the surveys of 1729 place them at 22.6 m OSBM. The discrepancy between these and the bottom of the jamb on the south elevation (22.4 m OSBM) is unlikely to reflect poor survey or drawing, since the surviving rear arches of the windows have soffits at 24.67 m OSBM, which is entirely consistent with eighteenth-century surveys. It is more likely that there is a difference between the elevations. Certainly, the chapel windows on the south wall on this floor are, and were always, approximately 100 mm lower than those of the apse bays. Alternatively, it is quite conceivable that rebuilding in Portland stone in 1638 altered the sill levels.

116   Renn 1982a, p. 76 and figs 40–53.

117   This window does not appear in plans, elevations and sections prior to Salvin's restoration of 1864, but the rear arch is bona fide Romanesque masonry: presumably, the blocked window was discovered during the restoration.

118   See Chapter Six, p. 175.

119   Parnell 1998a, p. 88.

120   See Appendix IV, pp. 321–2.

121   See Chapter Six, p. 175.

122   Confirmed during works in 2008.

123   TNA, WORK 14/2418, fol. 25r.

124   For example, Sturdy 1979, p. 270.

125   See below, pp. 63–7.

126   In the course of the recent repairs, several of these coping stones were removed and then replaced.

127   See Chapter Six, p. 163.

128   TNA, E 101 468/20 m3; see Chapter Five, p. 148.

129   See pp. 75–86.

130   An estimate of 750 mm has been used for the depth of the eleventh-century battlements: those today are 780 mm deep.

131   See above, pp. 31–8.

132   See Chapter Six, p. 163.

133   Dolomitised Chalk is not, as it might appear, an especially inferior ashlar type, since the recrystallisation makes for a harder stone than normal Chalk. It is found, for example, in the eleventh-century *donjon* at Ivry-la-Bataille and in the thirteenth-century manor house at Mesnil-sous-Jumièges, near the abbey of Jumièges, and is exposed in the worked cliffs of the Eure and Seine.

134   Reigate was used extensively at Rufus's hall of the 1090s at the Palace of Westminster, and in both the pre-Conquest church and the post-Conquest claustral buildings of Westminster Abbey.

135   Gem 1982, p. 2: 'quadros lapides ad aedificandum'.

136   See Chapter Six, pp. 172–3.

137   The present garderobe window in the western bay probably dates from 1734–6, and was certainly in existence by 1754 (see Chapter Seven, p. 194). It represents a considerable enlargement of the eleventh-century window: this narrow loop appears to have had Portland stone architraves by 1729 (TNA, WORK 31/85). Below this, three courses of ashlar blocking between 14.70 m OSBM and 15.37 m OSBM almost certainly represent the blocking of the garderobe chute.

138   See above, p. 51.

139   TNA, WO 47/70, fol. 73v; TNA, E 351/3269.

140   See fig. 154 for pre-door form.

141   See p. 67.

142   Note, however, that the chute from the garderobe in the north-west turret discharged near, although not directly over, the window of the garderobe in the western bay of the entrance floor.

143   See Chapter Six, p. 175.

144   See above, p. 47.

145   See p. 66.

146   TNA, WO 51/94/37r.

147   See pp. 50–2.

148   Smaller windows are shown in the plans of 1754 (e.g., TNA, WORK 31/98), but the present windows are shown in Nash's plan of 1815. The enlarging of these windows appears to be the subject of accounts in 1812 (TNA, WORK 6/25, fols 154–5; TNA, WORK 5/101, extraordinary account).

149   The (blocked) Romanesque window is recorded in plans and sectional elevations of 1729 (TNA, WORK 31/80, 31/84, 31/86, 31/89 and 31/90), but was gone by 1754 (TNA, WORK 31/95), and probably dates from the works of 1733.

150   See pp. 48–9.

151   TNA, WORK 31/85.

152   Certainly by 1754 (TNA, WORK 31/96). See also Chapter Seven, pp. 200–2.

153   TNA, WORK 31/80, 31/85, 31/86, 31/89 and 31/90.

154   TNA, WORK 31/83.

155   See fig. 62.

156   See p. 68.

157   For example, Parnell 1993, p. 20.

158   See Chapter Nine, pp. 239–40.

159   Parnell et al. 1982.

160   The myth of a plinth extending the whole way around the White Tower is very resilient, repeated most recently in Fernie 2000, p. 55.

161   See pp. 90–3.

162   See pp. 48–9.

163   See Appendix IV, pp. 316–17.

164   In this case the west end: the jambs at the east end of the passage are evidently additions, and are probably of fourteenth-century date.

165 See Appendix II, p. 297.

166 See Appendix II, p. 298.

167 The different heights derive from the south and north sides, respectively.

168 See Appendix II, p. 299.

169 See p. 41.

170 I am grateful to Dan Miles for information regarding the structure of the well noted in the course of his dendrochronological analysis of the template, or curb. For a fuller discussion of the carpentry and its dating, see Appendix IV, pp. 312–13.

171 See Appendix IV, p. 312.

172 See Appendix IV, pp. 317–20.

173 See pp. 47–8.

174 For discussion of originality of the lining planks, see Appendix IV, pp. 308–10.

175 The drawbar socket was unblocked in 1998.

176 The eastern jamb was removed when the corner was given a massive chamfer, prior to 1729, and the quoins and rubble here date from the nineteenth century (the chamfer is visible on TNA, WORK 31/85 – fig. 148).

177 The blocking shown on mid-eighteenth-century plans (e.g., TNA, WORK 31/100, of 1754) is shown as flush with the eastern side, however, and must be later; significantly, no such blocking is seen on an early plan of 1729 (TNA, WORK 31/85): see fig. 148.

178 For example, Parnell 1993, fig. 9.

179 TNA, WORK 31/85: see fig. 148.

180 See Chapter Seven, p. 194.

181 TNA, WORK 31/93 and 31/94.

182 See Chapter Six, pp. 172–3.

183 See Chapter Seven, p. 194.

184 Mesqui 1998.

185 See p. 85.

186 See Chapter Eight, pp. 211–12.

187 See Chapter Four, pp. 134–5.

188 In this case, these are shown as recesses of the correct depth and position on the earliest surviving measured survey (1729: TNA, WORK 31/87). See Chapter Seven, fig. 149.

189 The fireplace was first observed by Geoffrey Parnell.

190 See Chapter Six, p. 175.

191 The width measurements are minimums since the spine wall tapers (see below, p. 86).

192 For example, Armitage 1912, p. 225, n. 2; R. A. Brown 1984, pp. 30–32; Parnell 1993, pp. 20–22.

193 *The Times* (18 June 1996), p. 9. The smoke-blackened outline of a roof was previously noted and recorded in 1966 by the Ministry of Works.

194 Investigations were undertaken by the Oxford Archaeological Unit (OAU) prior to the White Tower Recording and Research Project: the OAU report for this work is TOL64. Another investigation was carried out in the spine wall, and this comprises OAU report TOL72. Copies of these reports and the original archives are held by Historic Royal Palaces.

195 See previous note.

196 The current interpretative material in the White Tower, prepared in 1997–8 by the Royal Armouries. This interpretation has also seen wider publication (Parnell 1998a).

197 See previous note.

198 Geoffrey Parnell, personal communication, 5 June 1998; and Royal Armouries interpretative displays and fly-through reconstruction (1997–8).

199 For further discussion of the spine wall, especially its tapered form, see p. 86.

200 See pp. 73–5.

201 See pp. 31, 36.

202 See pp. 54, 58–9.

203 Oxford Archaeological Unit, TOL64 Report, para. 4.6.

204 See Appendix II, p. 301.

205 Alan Vince, personal communication.

206 See p. 39.

207 Oxford Archaeological Unit, TOL72 Report, 3: layer 7.

208 Oxford Archaeological Unit, TOL72, contexts, 15, 18, 30, 33, 35, 38, 41.

209 As preserved so spectacularly in the heightened walls at Colchester Castle, for example.

210 Oxford Archaeological Unit, TOL64 Report, para. 4.3. The investigators also identified the inner and outer walls of the mural passage as being of different construction and of different dates. While slight differences in the mortar used for the two walls (described in TOL64, para. 4.6) do appear to exist, each of these two mortar types continues seamlessly from the wall into the barrel vault of the mural passage, merging, or meeting, around the apex.

211 Where the quite variable offset is too narrow to support the roof structure entirely, presumably roof timbers were let slightly into the wall face.

212 See pp. 52, 88.

213 See pp. 54–5.

214 See pp. 78, 86.

215 The tacheometric survey of 1994 shows that this doorway formerly opened into the roof space at the junction of the south aisle and the central barrel vaults. Although this is the lowest point in the roof space, the opening on this side would have been approximately 1.05 m from the threshold to the apex of the arch, and, thus, more akin to an access hatch than a 'doorway'.

216 Drury 2002, pp. 227–30.

217 Impey 2000.

218 Cunliffe and Munby 1985, pp. 72–81.

219 Fernie 2000, pp. 68–72.

220 R. A. Brown 1986, pp. 8–10.

221 White and Cook 1986, pp. 3–5.

222 Dixon and Marshall 1993b.

223 Fernie 2000, pp. 60–1.

224 This is the mean value across the offsets and ranges from 11.99 m to 12.09 m.

225 This is the mean value across the offsets and ranges from 9.27 m to 9.33 m.

226 By way of example, late eleventh-century Chepstow Castle has a span of up to 9.40 m, and, from the evidence of its end walls, could hardly have had anything other than a free-spanning roof. Ignoring the ultimately inconclusive evidence for Westminster Hall itself, the adjacent Romanesque Lesser Hall had a free-spanning roof, in this case 11.97 m wide and without the benefit of a massive

false storey (Crook and Harris 2002). More relevant is the case of Norwich Castle (*circa* 1095–1115), where the two roofs were, on the basis of the end-wall details, both free-spanning roofs (that of the northern side approximately 11.6 m), again boxed in (Drury 2002). Most remarkably, however, simple close-set rafter trusses (i.e., without supports or hangers) dating from 1095–1107 survive at the abbey hospice, or Ecuries de Saint-Hugues, at Cluny: here the tie-beams span 10.94 m (Maurice and Salvèque 1992; personal communication, Jean-Denis Salvèque, Centre d'Etudes Clunisiennes).

227 Note, though, that it is possible that the window embrasures had some form of timber infill to seal the mural passage from the weather.

228 The exact date is unknown.

229 The late Martin Caroe, personal communication.

230 See Chapter Seven, pp. 184–5.

231 No remains of the forebuilding were identified during the investigations that revealed details of the White Tower plinth and the foundations of Coldharbour Gate in 1955–6 (TNA, WORK 14/2418 and 14/1497), or the archaeological monitoring of the White Tower electricity cable extension in October 1995 (Hiller and Keevill 1994).

232 A. Keay 2001, pp. 1–5. The copies made directly from the lost original are reproduced as colour plates 1 and 2.

233 Note, however, that the forebuilding at Norwich Castle, Bigod's Tower, encroached into the second bay.

234 Colvin, Brown and Taylor 1963–86, vol. II, p. 728.

235 TNA, WORK 5/13, October and December 1663.

236 Parnell 1993, p. 42.

237 Royal Armouries Collection.

238 See above, p. 53.

239 Hence, its omission from Hollar's ground-level view.

240 See p. 49.

241 For example, Sandford 1677, p. 402.

242 For example, Parnell 1993, pp. 22–3.

243 Mesqui 1998, p. 97.

244 The White Tower has attracted such attention, too, but I am very grateful to Sandy Heslop for sending me his valiant attempts with lamentably inaccurate published plans: although the schemes did not stand up to scrutiny on the larger scale, they greatly encouraged my analysis of the overall plan.

245 Inevitably and regrettably, discussion of angular dimensions has been absent from studies that have attempted to be more rigorous than those based on small-scale drawings, by using direct (but non-tacheometric survey) measurements: a steel tape can hardly be placed at the centre of a pier.

246 For a discussion of Platonic geometry and its application to architecture in the tenth to thirteenth centuries, see Hiscock 1994; for analysis of the use of $\sqrt{2}$ in the study of a single building, see Fernie 1993, pp. 59–105.

247 Inter-pier spaces of western responds and all piers of straight arcade have a mean of 4.337 m (14.23 ft); a standard deviation of 14 mm (0.046 ft); and 95 per cent confidence limits of 4.309–4.365 m (14.14–14.32 ft). For comparison, 20 ft ÷ √2 = 4.31 m (14.14 ft).

248 Inter-pier spaces of the arcade from the north-west respond to Pier 4, and from Pier 9 to the south-west respond have a mean of 2.135 m (7.01 ft); a standard deviation of 43 mm (0.14 ft); and 95 per cent confidence limits = 2.049–2.221 m (6.72–7.29 ft). For comparison, 10 ft ÷ √2 = 2.155 m (7.07 ft).

249 Distances from the faces of the arcade piers to the wall line of Bays II and III, north and south, have a mean of 3.086 m (10.13 ft); a standard deviation of 29 mm (0.10 ft); and 95 per cent confidence limits of 3.028–3.144 m (9.93–10.32 ft).

250 The sixteen angles of 60° between the arcade piers have a mean of 60°19′45″; a standard deviation of 0°22′01″; and 95 per cent confidence limits of 59°35′43″–61°03′47″. This accuracy compares favourably to the setting out of the 90° angles formed by the piers. Since these angles are halved 180° angles along the length of the arcades, they somewhat inevitably have a mean of 90°00′00″: more significantly, they have a standard deviation of the same order of magnitude as for 60° angles at 0°25′59″, giving 95 per cent confidence limits of 89°33′10″–90°26′50″.

251 South-west to north-west corner = 36.47 m; north-west to north-east corner = 36.62 m; north-east to south-east corner = 36.50 m; south-east to south-west corner = 36.62 m; mean side = 36.55 m (119.92 ft; with an overall range of 119.65–120.14 ft).

252 300 mm.

Chapter Three: St John's Chapel

1 See Chapter Eight, pp. 210–12.
2 See Chapter Two, pp. 63–7.
3 Cf. Ivry-la-Bataille (p. 130).
4 See Chapter Four, p. 131.
5 Gem 1990, p. 47.
6 Lemprière's section exaggerates the offsets, particularly on the east side of the wall.
7 See Chapter Two, p. 92.
8 See Chapter Two, pp. 31–6.
9 See Chapter Two, pp. 75–85.
10 These doorways are both original. Daniel Roth (1935, p. 865) wrongly supposed that the north door was a 'new' (i.e., nineteenth-century) opening.
11 See Chapter Two, p. 50.
12 See Chapter Two, pp. 48–53.
13 See Chapter Eight, p. 221.
14 A similar gentle eastward floor slope has been observed at various other churches.
15 Tatton-Brown 1990, p. 72.
16 Worssam 1995, p. 14, claims pre-Conquest use of Caen stone in Sussex at Bosham, Botolphs, Jevington, and Sompting (abundant use); also at Winchester and Romsey (Hampshire), and at St Mary in Castro, Dover (Kent).

17 For Quarr stone, see Anderson and Quirk 1964; Tatton-Brown 1980; Tatton-Brown 1990; Tatton-Brown 1993, pp. 37–9; Worssam 1995, pp. 19–20.
18 Worssam 1995, p. 19.
19 Aldsworth 1990, p. 70.
20 I am grateful to Dr Bernard Worssam and Robin Sanderson for the identification of Reigate stone in St John's Chapel. For a major study of the building use of this stone, see Tatton-Brown 2001.
21 I am grateful to the late Professor Bruce Sellwood, of the Postgraduate Research Institute for Sedimentology at the University of Reading, for confirming and commenting in detail on the use of Taynton stone at St John's Chapel. For Taynton stone, see Sellwood and McKerrow 1974; Worssam 1995, pp. 13–14.
22 See pp. 104, 110, 117.
23 For example, the bases of Piers 7 and 9.
24 See Chapter Two, pp. 90–2.
25 See Chapter Two, p. 31.
26 The blocks of Bembridge stone below the junction in Respond 10 might have been replacements when building resumed.
27 As, for example, in the diaper-patterned blockwork of Westminster Hall.
28 I am grateful to Dr Roland Harris for assistance in the statistical analysis in this paragraph.
29 See Chapter Two, pp. 30–8.
30 See pp. 118–20.
31 *Pace* those scholars who have attempted to make more of these differences. The complete distribution of the various types is as follows:

Piers 1, 4 (corner leaves of four scoops, simple quirk [return rectangular nick] detaching the leaf, base of cross detached from its supporting chamfer).

Piers 6, 7, 10 (corner leaves of four scoops, simple quirk detaching the leaf, base of cross not detached from its supporting chamfer).

Piers 2, 9 (corner leaves of four scoops, double quirk detaching the leaf, base of cross detached from its supporting chamfer [though far less in the case of Pier 9]).

Pier 3 (corner leaves of six scoops, simple quirk detaching the leaf, base of cross detached from its supporting chamfer).

32 Rivoira 1933, vol. I, p. 193. See also Frankl 1926, p. 198. For the best account of the history of the church, see Kingsley Porter 1917, vol. II, pp. 301–12. One of the San Vincenzo capitals is illustrated in Kahn 1991, p. 81 (pl. 125), who, however, dates it to the ninth century (p. 80).
33 Ruprich-Robert 1884–9, vol. I, p. 117: 'la console est même doublée d'une autre console plus petite'.
34 Lethaby 1925, pp. 23–4, fig. 7. This capital was also illustrated by Kahn (1991, p. 81, pl. 125), who attributed it, like the San Vicenzo example, to the ninth century. I am grateful to Mr Tony Platt for showing me the abbey capitals. Two other tau-cross capitals flanking the southernmost window on the west side of the dorter were revealed in the late

nineteenth century when the remains of the rere-dorter, a lower building that returned westwards from the end of the dorter, were demolished. The window in question had survived through being covered by a secondary upper storey over the rere-dorter. Photographs taken during the demolition works were later published by Westlake 1923, vol. I, pls 5B (general view) and 9A (detail of the window). One of this window's capitals appears to be published in Zarnecki 1979, p. 178 (pl. 11); owing to a printer's error the poor image appears on its side.

35 Bilson 1910, p. 401.
36 Gem 1981a, p. 60.
37 Zarnecki 1979, p. 175.
38 For the capitals, see Baylé 1982.
39 Gem 1981a, p. 46.
40 Baylé 1979.
41 Baylé 1988a.
42 Baylé 1974, pp. 261–2.
43 For example, Baylé 1988a, p. 3.
44 Baylé 1988a, pp. 3–4 and pl. 1.
45 This simplification is discussed by Baylé 1988a, pp. 9–10.
46 For the construction of St Nicholas's church, Bramber, by 1073, see Round 1899, p. 405 (notification dated to 1073 of William de Braose's donation to the church of six hides of land and the tithe of his revenues).
47 Gem 1987.
48 Discussed by Kahn 1991, and illustrated on pl. 47.
49 The penultimate pier of the arcade, illustrated in Stoll 1967, pl. 187.
50 Crum and Crum 1933.
51 Kahn 1991, p. 80.
52 Gem 1987, pp. 95–7.
53 For the origins of cushion and scallop capitals, see Fernie 2000, pp. 278–9.
54 Baylé 1988a, p. 11: 'les premiers exemples [des chapiteaux à godrons] connus dans le monde anglo-normand sont les grosses corbeilles de la chapelle Saint-Jean de la Tour de Londres, vers 1080'.
55 See Chapter Two, pp. 43–5.
56 Baylé 1988b, p. 581: 'L'apparition de corbeilles godronnées à côté de formes cubiques à la Tour de Londres (chapelle Saint-Jean) vers 1080 . . . semble confirmer la filiation formelle qui fait du chapiteau à godrons une subdivision des éléments de l'œuvre cubique.'
57 Baylé 1988b, pp. 580–86: 'L'apparition du chapiteau à godrons et le problème de ses origines.'
58 Illustrated in Stoll 1967, pl. 91.
59 William of Malmesbury, *De gestis pontificum anglorum*, ed. Hamilton, p. 206 [ii. 96].
60 *Winchester Annals*, ed. Luard, p. 43 [*s.a.* 1108]: 'Hoc anno Radulfus episcopus Cicestrensem fecit dedicari ecclesiam.'
61 Gem 1981b. Gem's view is endorsed by Tatton-Brown 1994.
62 Gem 1981b, pp. 63–4.
63 A few small fragments of Taynton stone were identified on the external face of the south elevation, all above the level of the chapel floor.

64 See Chapters Six and Eight, pp. 169–70, 210.

65 Lanfry 1928, pp. 116–17 and 'plan restitué' on p. 135. Lanfry kept a careful watch for evidence of radial chapels but found none.

66 Plan and photographs in Aubert et al. 1961, p. 276.

67 Crook 1998, pp. 34–9.

68 See Chapter Four, pp. 133–4.

Chapter Four: The Function of the White Tower under the Normans

1 M. W. Thompson 1995, pp. 81–2.

2 While the word *donjon* seems to have acquired this connotation in England by at least the fifteenth century, there is suggestive evidence that it could previously mean something quite different: a lordly enclave within a castle, such as an inner bailey. To take three examples from England in the thirteenth century, a *Liberate* writ of 1266 for Winchester Castle orders re-roofing both to a royal chamber in the 'Great Tower' and 'the principal chamber in our *donjon*' (The National Archives [formerly the Public Record Office], hereafter TNA, C 62/42 m4); similarly, a works account of *circa* 1280 for Corfe refers to both 'the Great Tower' and a chapel in the 'upper *donjon*', presumably the structure now called *Gloriette* (TNA, E 101 460/27). A survey of 1275 at Carmarthen also mentions both a 'Great Tower' and a '*donjon* made out of 5 small towers', and a similar usage may also have pertained at Deganwy in 1250 (Colvin, Brown and Taylor 1963–82, vol. 2, pp. 601 and 625). In all these instances, *donjon* cannot be synonymous with 'Great Tower', and a reading such as 'inner ward' is to be preferred. A similar imprecision applies to castles in France: see Mesqui 1991–3, vol. 1, p. 89. The standard anachronistic meaning, however, has achieved such wide currency that it would be pedantic to reject it.

3 See Stocker 1992 for a critique of this approach.

4 Heslop 1991, passim.

5 For example, Colvin, Brown and Taylor 1963–82, vol. 1, p. 29; M. W. Thompson 1991, pp. 75–6.

6 G. T. Clark 1867, especially p. 39.

7 G. T. Clark 1867, especially p. 39.

8 G. T. Clark 1884, vol. II, p. 218.

9 For a discussion of the possible entrance into the basement's western room, see Chapters Two and Five, pp. 67–8 and 148–9.

10 See Chapter Two, pp. 86–90.

11 *Barnwell Chronicle*, ed. Stubbs, p. 227. Note that King John's troops would have broken into the keep in the north-east corner at ground level, where the spine wall has only one door. Presumably the defenders found some way to barricade the spiral staircase in the north-west corner, giving access to mural galleries running into the other half of the building. Alternatively, the chronicler may be inventing details.

12 Dixon and Marshall 1993b; White and Cook 1986, p. 3. There are also numerous examples of great towers with sunken roofs but without windows to create the illusion of an additional upper storey. One of the most obvious of these is Portchester Castle (Cunliffe and Munby 1985, pp. 72–81). See also Peveril Castle in Derbyshire, whose roof creases are likewise expressed as projecting stone weatherings.

13 Dixon 2002.

14 For example, R. A. Brown 1979, especially p. 99; Brown and Curnow 1984, p. 9; Renn 1960, p. 20; Thurley 1993, p. 3.

15 James, Marshall and Millett 1984.

16 The *Anglo-Saxon Chronicle* for 978 records that during a meeting of a royal council in a room known as a *solarium* at Calne, the floor collapsed, depositing all but St Dunstan on the floor below (*Anglo-Saxon Chronicle*, ed. Garmondsway, p. 123). Although this interpretation has been contested, Phillip Rahtz (1979, pp. 100, 103–7) interpreted the remains of a timber-framed rectangular building at Cheddar as a two-storeyed structure, and dated it to before the mid-tenth century.

17 Parsons 1991, pp. 6, 17.

18 Blair 1994a; Impey 1996; Impey 1999, pp. 43–73.

19 Colvin, Brown and Taylor 1963–82, vol. 1, pp. 43–7.

20 Biddle 1986, passim; Renn 1994b, pp. 6–10; White and Cook 1986, passim; Brindle and Kerr 1997, p. 33; James and Robinson 1988, pp. 4–5.

21 Mesqui 1996, pp. 53–4.

22 For example, Héliot 1969, pp. 145, 186–7; R. A. Brown 1978a, p. 49; Mesqui 1991–3, vol. 1, pp. 106–61.

23 The author has found only limited documentary evidence for this or other English sites that great towers were divided into separate apartments. A difficult reference of the fourteenth century for the Tower 'pro quodam hostio de novo faciendo ad quandam domum ubi arma regis latent in alta turri', taken literally, would denote the presence of a separate 'house' inside the White Tower, but may alternatively indicate that this house was adjacent or within the close vicinity (TNA, E 101 469/7 m2). See also Corfe Castle in the 1290s ('Item in servicio Iohannis le Bayte pro domibus Turris mundandis contra adventum prisonum xiiid'; TNA, E 101 460/29 rot.2 m1), and a similar usage at Clifford's Tower in York in various documents of the mid-fourteenth century (TNA, C 145/180, no 10, E 101 598/6 and E 101 501/11).

24 The assumption that rooms were internally subdivided underlies much of the interpretation of palaces in Barthélemy 1988, pp. 407, 422.

25 TNA, C 62/15 m19. TNA, C 62/14 m17 refers to the chapel of St John *the Baptist*. This is probably a scribal error, but could possibly denote another chapel within the fortress of which we know nothing.

26 R. A. Brown 1978a, p. 49.

27 See, for example, Crépin-Leblond 1994, pp. 378–88, for a brief review of evidence from bishops' chapels.

28 Parnell 1993, p. 20.

29 A plan of 1729 shows the original positions and form of some of these openings (TNA, WORK 31/84).

30 Mesqui 1991–3, vol. 1, pp. 110–12.

31 For example, at Dover.

32 See Chapter Five, pp. 148–9.

33 For example, R. A. Brown 1978b, p. 25; Parnell 1993, pp. 20–22.

34 Heslop 1994, p. 58. Roland Harris suggests that the feature is more directly a copy of window forms at St Etienne in Caen and Lanfranc's work at Canterbury Cathedral.

35 Parnell 1993, pp. 20–22; Schofield 1993, p. 38. From our knowledge of the structure of the royal household, there were numerous other officers of importance at court, for whom we might expect accommodation to be provided: these include the chancellor, the stewards, the master butler, master chamberlain and the treasurer (White 1948).

36 Blair 1994a, pp. 1–2; for a strenuous refutation of this position, see M. W. Thompson 1998, pp. 125 and 154, n. 1.

37 Faulkner 1958.

38 'Clericus et miles pergant, ad cetera viles / Nam locus hos primus decet, illos vilis et imus' (Mesqui 1991–3, vol. II, p. 85). The fact that this inscription is written in Latin hexameters and in a reversed script reading from right to left must raise at least the suspicion that this is a scholastic joke rather than a genuine and solemn prescription.

39 Mortet and Deschamps 1911–29, vol. 1, pp. 183–5.

40 Impey 1999, pp. 67–8, sets out the counter-argument that, at the time of the White Tower's construction, an arrangement of floors by social status should be expected as the norm.

41 R. A. Brown 1978a, p. 51; Heslop 1994, p. 41. An arched recess in the 'Old Hall' at Pickering Castle in North Yorkshire is a secondary feature and its Norman head is reset, although there may formerly have been such a feature in the original construction (J. Clark 1997).

42 Cunliffe and Munby 1985, p. 85, fig. 41.

43 Tronzo 1997, pp. 68–78, 97–125.

44 'Stabat vero rex ipse secus introitum ostii in solio regali . . .' (*Magna Vita Sancti Hugonis*, ed. Dimock, p. 251).

45 Philip Dixon (personal communication) has suggested that these three recesses on each floor may have been intended for the seats of William the Conqueror's three sons, Robert (born *circa* 1054), William (born 1057) and Henry (born 1068). In 1075 a fourth son, Richard, died in a hunting accident.

46 Mesqui 1991–3, vol. 1, pp. 114–16.

47 Kantorowicz 1946, p. 174.

48 In addition, William Rufus is said to have banished night lamps from his palaces, interpreted by Orderic Vitalis and William of Malmesbury as yet another sign of moral turpitude (Barlow 1983, p. 104).

49 See Chapter Two and Appendix IV, pp. 75–85 and 312.

50 Impey and Lorans 1998, pp. 74–6.

51 Bonassie 1982; the text is partly published in Mortet and Deschamps 1911–29, vol 1, p. 49–50.

52 Mortet and Deschamps 1911–29, vol 1, pp. 183–5 (my translation). There is a discussion of this text in Armitage 1912, pp. 89–91. See also Chapter Ten, pp. 244–5.

53 TNA, C 62/42 m4. See note 2 above.

54 TNA, E 101 460/29 rot.2 m2: 'The wages of John le Mere for heightening the wall of the chapel and the chamber next to the Lord King's chamber, for making a new chimney in the said chamber and making crenellations for the said chapel and chamber.' A marginal note states that these works are located in the 'Turris'. My translation.

55 Heslop 1994, pp. 60–61; Cherry and Stratford 1995, pp. 50–56.

56 Orderic Vitalis, ed. Chibnall, vol. V, pp. 310–12. For confirmation of the essential details that Rannulf was a prisoner and did escape, see Hollister 1973. See also Selected Texts: Transcripts of Primary Documents: Medieval, pp. 325–6.

57 Chaplais 1964, no. 1; Pipe Roll 31 Henry I, p. 143.

58 Anglo-Saxon Chronicle, ed. Earle and Plummer, vol. 1, p. 234.

59 Pipe Roll 31 Henry I, p. 144. The presence of houses formerly belonging to Othuer, almost certainly inside the fortress, supports the notion that the custodian was not intended to live on the entrance floor of the White Tower.

60 Parnell 1993, p. 19. See Chapter One, pp. 19–20.

61 See Chapter One, pp. 19–20.

62 Dixon and Marshall 1993b.

63 William of Malmesbury, Historiae novellae, ed. Stubbs, p. 564.

64 Parnell 1993, p. 19; Stow, ed. Morley, p. 73; Colvin, Brown and Taylor 1963–82, vol. 1, p. 32. I am grateful to Hilary Carslake (personal communication) for discussing this sentence construction, particularly for pointing out that triadic arrangements of adjectives conventionally show rising emphasis from beginning to end. See also Selected Texts: Transcripts of Primary Documents: Medieval, p. 326.

65 R. H. C. Davis 1980, pp. 65–8; Loud 1982; Van Houts 2000, passim.

66 Stalley 1971.

67 Parnell 1998c, p. 6.

Chapter Five: The Structure and Function of the White Tower, 1150–1485

1 See Chapter Nine, p. 230.

2 Pipe Roll 31 Henry I, p. 144.

3 For example, Pipe Roll 13 Henry II, p. 1; Pipe Roll 18 Henry II, p. 144; Pipe Roll 19 Henry II, p. 182.

4 Pipe Roll 18 Henry II, p. 144.

5 Pipe Roll 28 Henry II, p. 159.

6 Pipe Roll 29 Henry II, p. 161.

7 Pipe Roll 30 Henry II, p. 138.

8 Pipe Roll 13 John Michaelmas, p. 109.

9 Parnell 1985b, p. 25, fig. 3 and pl. II.

10 Colvin, Brown and Taylor 1963–82, vol. 2, p. 865; Brindle and Kerr 1997, pp. 32–3.

11 Pipe Roll 32 Henry II, p. 49.

12 See Ashbee 2006a, p. 83.

13 Flores historiarum, ed. Luard, vol. 3, p. 62.

14 Roger of Howden, ed. Stubbs, vol. 3, p. 33.

15 Raby and Baillie Reynolds 1987, p. 11; Cook, Mynard and Rigold 1969, p. 56.

16 Mesqui 1991–3, vol. 1, pp. 162–71, 263–6.

17 Chronicles of Stephen, Henry II and Richard I, ed. Howlett, vol. 1, p. 342.

18 Carpenter 1990, pp. 42, 319 n. 15.

19 Rotuli litterarum clausarum, ed. Hardy, vol. 1, p. 402.

20 Colvin, Brown and Taylor 1963–82, vol. 2, pp. 710–29.

21 Curnow 1977, pp. 155–90.

22 Thurley 1995. For a revision of details of this reconstruction, see also Ashbee 2006b.

23 The National Archives (formerly the Public Record Office) [hereafter TNA], E 372/79 rot.11; TNA, E 372/83 rot.13; Calendar of Liberate Rolls: Henry III, vol. 1 (1226–40), pp. 352, 444.

24 Curnow 1977, pp. 155–90.

25 Carpenter 1996.

26 Matthew Paris, Chronica majora, ed. Luard, vol. 3, pp. 80 and 93–4: 'cum suis antemuralibus et propugnaculis'. A masonry and timber structure, almost certainly a defensive outwork connected to this gateway, was excavated by Oxford Archaeological Unit for the Historic Royal Palaces Agency during 1995 and 1996, in the western arm of the present moat. See Impey 1998.

27 British Library, MS Royal 16r II, fol. 73r. For a discussion of the date of this illustration, see Backhouse 2000.

28 For example, TNA, E 372/70 rot. 13; Calendar of Liberate Rolls: Henry III, vol. 1 (1226–40), pp. 220, 228.

29 TNA, E 372/79 rot. 11.

30 Calendar of Liberate Rolls: Henry III, vol. 1 (1226–40), p. 459.

31 TNA, C 62/15 m19. See also Selected Texts: Transcripts of Primary Documents: Medieval, pp. 326–7.

32 For a seventeenth-century reference to whitewashing, see Chapter Six, p. 176.

33 Oxford, Bodleian Library, Rawlinson MS D 775.

34 Stow, ed. Morley, p. 87.

35 Symeon Semeon, ed. Esposito, p. 26. For a discussion of the reason and effect of whitening the Tower, see Chapter Eleven, pp. 283–4. See also Selected Texts: Transcripts of Primary Documents: Medieval, p. 328.

36 Bayley 1821–5, vol. II: 'alba turella iuxta excambium domini regis'. See also Selected Texts: Transcripts of Primary Documents: Medieval, p. 328.

37 TNA, E 101/470/6 m6. Problematically, other fourteenth-century documents referring to 'la Blaunche Tour' may suggest that the name was used for several buildings, including the White Tower; see Antient Kalendars, ed. Palgrave, vol. 1, pp. 198, 225.

38 TNA, C 62/14 m8.

39 Colvin, Brown and Taylor 1963–82, vol. 2, p. 620, n. 7.

40 See Chapter One, p. 20.

41 These may include a chapel of St Thomas (TNA, E 372/79 rot. 11), of John the Baptist (TNA, C 62/14 m17), the 'chapel of the new turret next to the King's hall' (TNA, E 372/83 rot. 13) and the 'King's chapel' next to the Thames (TNA, C 54/63 m9). In the fourteenth century the king used a chapel dedicated to the Trinity (TNA, SCI 42/106). It is not possible to discount categorically that some of these may refer to the same building, or to identify the surviving oratory in the Wakefield Tower firmly with any of them.

42 TNA, C 62/15 m19.

43 Calendar of Liberate Rolls: Henry III, vol. II (1240–45), pp. 44 and 149.

44 Calendar of Close Rolls: Henry III, vol. V (1242–7), p. 165.

45 Calendar of Patent Rolls: Henry III, vol. V (1258–66), p. 195, although it should be noted that by 1262 the location for this Mass had moved to St Peter ad Vincula in the bailey of the Tower (Calendar of Liberate Rolls: Henry III, vol. VI [1260–67], p. 87). I am grateful to Dr Margaret Howell (personal communication) for bringing this to my attention.

46 TNA, E 101 17/17: see also TNA, E 101 531/17 m2 ('una carta de cantaria in turri') and E 101 531/19 ('una carta de cantaria capelle turris').

47 TNA, C 62/15 m19.

48 Matthew Paris, Chronica majora, ed. Luard, vol. IV, pp. 80 and 93–4.

49 TNA, C 62/14 m17.

50 Howell 1998, p. 22.

51 Carpenter 1996, pp. 202–3; Maddicott 1994, pp. 21–3.

52 Matthew Paris, Life of St Edmund, ed. Lawrence, pp. 86–9, 168–76.

53 Cambridge, Corpus Christi College, MS 16, fol. 170r, reproduced in Matthew Paris, ed. Vaughan, p. 200; Matthew Paris, Chronica majora, ed. Luard, vol. 4, p. 295; Matthew Paris, Historia anglorum, ed. Madden, vol. 2, p. 482. See also Selected Texts: Transcripts of Primary Documents: Medieval, p. 327.

54 Calendar of Patent Rolls: Henry III, vol. III (1232–47), p. 424.

55 Calendar of Close Rolls: Henry III, vol. VI (1242–7), p. 369.

56 Calendar of Close Rolls: Henry III, vol. VII (1247–51), pp. 241, 242–3.

57 Maddicott 1994, p. 111.

58 Carpenter 1996, pp. 205–6.

59 G. A. Williams 1963, p. 222.

60 G. A. Williams 1963, p. 239; Thurley 1995, p. 46.

61 Colvin, Brown and Taylor 1963–82, vol. 1, pp. 53 and 93–8.

62 Colvin, Brown and Taylor 1963–82, vol. 1, p. 163.

63 TNA, E 101 467/9 m3. For the repairs to the leadwork of the roofs and turrets, see TNA, E 372/121 rot. 22 and E 372/151 rot. 16.

64 TNA, E 372/120 rot. 22 mentions the hall and chamber; E 372/125 rot. 2, describing works

to the water-gate tower, states that one of its turrets stands 'prope cameram regis'. For Edward I's reluctance to use the Tower as a residence, see Carpenter 1996, appendix 2.

65 TNA, E 372/120 rot. 22; E 372/121 rot. 22; E 372/125 rot. 2.

66 TNA, E 101 468/20, fol. 8v.

67 TNA, E 101 468/20, fol. 2.

68 TNA, E 101 468/20, fol. 3v

69 *Chronicles of Edward I and Edward II*, ed. Stubbs, vol. I, pp. 215–18.

70 R. A. Brown 1978a, p. 48. Earlier in the twentieth century, the vice was dated to the thirteenth century, though no evidence to support this ascription has yet come to light (TNA, WORK 14/183). The vice cannot have been constructed before the late 1350s: its stairwell partially blocks the Norman window in the south wall of the basement western room ('a certain window in the Black Hall facing the Great Hall') for which *ferramenta* were then ordered (TNA, E 101 471/2 m13). For a contemporary reference identifying this room as the Black Hall (containing the well), see TNA, E 372/201 *rot comp* 37 *in dorso*.

71 TNA, E 372/151 rot. 16.

72 *Munimenta Gildhallae*, ed. Riley, vol. II, part I, pp. 368–9; *Eyre of London*, ed. Cam, vol. I, pp. 60–61.

73 TNA, E 101 468/20 m4.

74 TNA, E 101 469/18 m2 and m3.

75 The original of the survey has now been lost; it is reprinted in Bayley 1821–5, vol. II. The Latin 'unius aeriae coquinae' is difficult to translate with confidence, and the simplest reading is 'a floor of the kitchen', with *aeria* as an alternative to *area*. The alternative reading would indicate that some provision for cooking was provided at the top of one of the turrets. Though there is no evidence for this in the fabric of the building, parallels do exist, as, for example, in a bakery in the turret at Orford.

76 TNA, E 101 471/2 m7.

77 See Chapter Seven, p. 193; TNA, WORK 31/84 and WORK 31/90; WO 51/125, fol. 67r.

78 TNA, E 101 468/20, fols 8 and 9; the latter reference explicitly mentions 'various chambers within the Constable's liberty, namely in the inmost bailey next to the Great Tower'. Among other details, the carpenter John le Rok made a covering for a round smoke louvre above the open hearth of the Constable's Hall (fol. 9v).

79 TNA, E 101 469/7 m2 and m3.

80 TNA, E 101 470/1 m14.

81 TNA, E 101 471/1 m1.

82 TNA, E 101 471/1 m1: 'tegulis pro pavimento emptis pro camera subconstabularii vocata la Blaunchetour'. 'La Blaunchetour' is now thought to be the present Bell Tower, against which the Queen's House and its medieval predecessors were built (Parnell 1993, pp. 49–50).

83 *Calendar of Close Rolls: Edward III*, vol. III (1333–7), p. 584. No itemised accounts have been identified in the Pipe Rolls for the years following the issue of this instruction to the

sheriffs. This may be explained by the more urgent matter of civil defence works against a French invasion (*Calendar of Plea and Memoranda Rolls*, vol. I [1323–64], p. 176).

84 TNA, E 101 470/1 m7 and m8.

85 Tout 1934; Blackmore 1976, pp. 1–3, 251–6.

86 Colvin, Brown and Taylor 1963–82, vol. I, pp. 175–8.

87 TNA, E 101 469/7 m4: 'In cartagia et carriagia xxxvii ponderiorum plumbi de plumbaria regis de Turri usque ad Candelwekestrete ad fundendos.'

88 Barter 1978.

89 For the circumstances of Joan's birth, see *Munimenta Gildhallae*, ed. Riley, vol. 2 part I, p. 409.

90 TNA, E 101 469/7 m4 and elsewhere; for a reference of the 1330s to the Wakefield Tower as 'magna gardaroba', see E 470/1 m14.

91 TNA, E 101 470/1 m2; E 101 471/1 m5. In 1324 Edward II had used the chambers over the water gate to lodge his favourite, the lord Hugh Despenser (TNA, E 101 469/7 m8).

92 For example, TNA, E 101 470/6 m6; Roger Mortimer's imprisonment is documented in TNA, E 372/177 rot. comp 38 and E 101 469/15 m1.

93 TNA, E 101 471/2 m11.

94 *Calendar of Close Rolls: Edward III*, vol. XIV (1374–7), p. 123.

95 Parnell 1993, p. 54. A list of receipts from Jewish prisoners in the Tower in the 1270s makes no mention of the White Tower, though it places them in many other locations, including towers, cellars, stables and the former elephant house (TNA, E 101 249/22 rot.1 m3).

96 TNA, E 352/74 rot.1 m1d, cited in Rokéah 1990.

97 *Calendar of Close Rolls: Edward II*, vol. I (1307–13), p. 177.

98 TNA, E 101 468/20, fol. 4. See also Selected Texts: Transcripts of Primary Documents: Medieval, p. 328.

99 TNA, E 101 471/2 m11.

100 Hallam 1979; TNA, E 101 332/3.

101 Galbraith 1925; TNA, E 101 468/20, fol. 2.

102 Clanchy 1993, pp. 165–6.

103 Galbraith 1925, p. 233.

104 TNA, E 101 469/3; Galbraith 1925, pp. 233–6.

105 Galbraith 1925, appendix 4.

106 TNA, E 101 333/3.

107 Galbraith 1925, p. 239.

108 TNA, E 372/201 *rot comp* 37 *in dorso*: 'mundatione fontis in nigra aula'.

109 Galbraith 1925, pp. 235–6, 237, 239: 'interioris camere iuxta nigram aulam in Turri Londoniarum ubi iocalia thesauri regis privata reponuntur'; that is, 'the inner chamber beside the black hall in the Tower of London in which is the treasury in which the king's private jewels are kept'.

110 Galbraith 1925, p. 247.

111 TNA, E 101 333/3.

112 *Antient Kalendars*, ed. Palgrave, vol. I, pp. 198, 225.

113 For example, TNA, E 101 472/1 m2 records a payment for 'making ironwork for the chamber of the King of France at *Sauvoye*'.

114 *Comptes de l'argenterie*, ed. Douët-D'Arcq, p. 245; Newton 1980, pp. 58–9.

115 *Calendar of Close Rolls: Edward III*, vol. XI (1360–64), p. 24. A detailed account of expenses for King Jean's stay in the Tower, his food, furnishing and guarding, is preserved as TNA, E 101 27/38: this runs from Sunday, 24 May, by which time he had already been in the White Tower for almost two months (*Comptes de l'argenterie*, ed. Douët-D'Arcq, pp. 278–84).

116 *Calendar of Close Rolls: Edward III*, vol. XI (1360–64), p. 64.

117 *Calendar of Close Rolls: Edward III*, vol. XI (1360–64), pp. 64, 336; TNA, E 101 472/9 m2 ('ferramenta . . . pro fenestris . . . cuiusdam turris pro salva custodia rotulorum'); Galbraith 1925, p. 243.

118 Given-Wilson 1986, pp. 80–85; Tout 1920–33, vol. IV, pp. 439–84.

119 Bayley 1821–5, vol. I, p. 117; G. T. Clark 1867, p. 42; Compton 1881.

120 Storey 1998.

121 Parnell et al. 1982, pp. 116–21.

122 TNA, E 101 400/15.

123 TNA, E 101 400/15; E 101 397/19 m1.

124 Dan Miles, personal communication. See pp. 295 and 298–9.

125 TNA, E 101 473/18 m12. Occasional references to repairs to the leadwork may be found: for example, TNA, E 101 502/23 m2. An account for new keys confirms that in the early fifteenth century *dongeon* referred to the White Tower (TNA, E 101 502/26 m5).

126 *Proceedings and Ordinances of the Privy Council*, vol. 2, p. 342.

127 *Calendar of Patent Rolls: Henry VI*, vol. V (1446–52), pp. 314, 523, 556.

128 Bayley 1821–5, vol. I, p. 217.

129 For example, TNA, E 101 473/18 m11, m12; TNA, E 101 473/20.

130 *Calendar of Patent Rolls: Henry VI*, vol. I (1422–9), p. 106; *Calendar of Close Rolls: Henry VI*, vol. III (1435–41), p. 214.

131 *Calendar of Close Rolls: Henry VI*, vol. II (1429–35), pp. 254–6.

132 *James I of Scotland*, ed. Norton-Smith, pp. xxi xxiv. While there would be ample historical precedent for lodging a prisoner as important as Charles d'Orléans in the White Tower, there is regrettably no evidence as yet that the famous illustration of his captivity represents an actual scene (British Library, MS Royal 16F II, fol. 73r). The standard published itinerary for him does not specify how much of his time in London was spent in the Tower (Champion 1911, pp. 667–72). The hypothesis that the two poets, James I and Charles d'Orléans, met while prisoners in the Tower has retained its attractions for modern scholars: for example, Askins 2000, p. 30.

133 *Calendar of Close Rolls: Richard II*, vol. IV (1389–92), pp. 380, 398.

134 *Proceedings and Ordinances of the Privy Council*, vol. 2, p. 311.

135 TNA, E 101 400/15.

136 Pilbrow 2002.

137 Froissart, ed. Brereton, p. 463.

138 Anstis 1725, p. 7 and appendix 7.

139 Lyons 1982.

140 Boccaccio, ed. McWilliam, pp. 627, 856 n. 20.

141 *Letters and Papers of Richard III and Henry VII*, pp. 388–404.

142 Anstis 1725, appendix, p. 27.

143 Anstis 1725, appendix, p. 27.

144 See Chapter Six, pp. 163–5.

145 British Library, Egerton MS 985, fol. 42. See also Selected Texts: Transcripts of Primary Documents: Medieval, pp. 331–4.

146 See Chapter Eleven, pp. 281–4.

147 Given-Wilson 1986, p. 84; Higden, ed. Lumby, vol. IX, p. III; TNA, E 101 400/22 m2.

148 Oman 1906, p. 65; Froissart, ed. Brereton, p. 220.

149 Dobson 1983, p. 173. See also Selected Texts: Transcripts of Primary Documents: Medieval, pp. 330–1.

150 Colvin, Brown and Taylor 1963–82, vol. 2, p. 728 n. 10.

151 TNA, E 101 470/17 m4. This is most likely to have stood not beside the White Tower, as the authors of *History of the King's Works* suggested (Colvin, Brown and Taylor 1963–82, vol. 2, p. 728), but close to the river, beside St Thomas's Tower, then a centre of activity of the Privy Wardrobe.

152 Alexander and Binski 1987, pp. 509–10.

153 Given-Wilson 1993, pp. 32–41.

154 Froissart, ed. Kervyn de Lettenhove, pp. 192–3.

155 Froissart, ed. Kervyn de Lettenhove, p. 195. Sir Bernard Brocas, one of Richard II's knights, was in fact punished only early in 1400 for joining the Holand rebellion to restore King Richard (Given-Wilson 1986, pp. 224–5; Given-Wilson 1993, p. 228).

156 Froissart, ed. Kervyn de Lettenhove, pp. 192–3.

157 Given-Wilson 1993, pp. 161, 163, 168–71.

158 Given-Wilson 1993, pp. 224–8.

159 Gillingham 1981, pp. III–15; Lander 1965, p. 105.

160 Payments for guarding Henry VI in the Tower can be found in TNA, E 403/842 m3 and E 403/844 m7 onwards. TNA, E 403/840 m2 also contains a payment to the chaplain William Kymberley for saying the daily office for 'Henry, lately *de facto* but not *de iure* King of England' during his earlier captivity in the mid-1460s.

161 TNA, E 403/844 m5 and m6.

162 Dockray 1988, pp. 179–84.

163 Hope 1911.

164 For example, Younghusband 1918, p. 235.

165 TNA, E 403/844 m8: Richard Martyn is identified as 'clericus parsone capelle Regis infra Turrim Londoniarum' in TNA, E 403/840 m7.

166 Hutchinson 1997, especially commentaries on the documentary evidence and the construction and function of the Bulwark by Dr Geoffrey Parnell, pp. 109–14.

167 Thurley 1993, p. 18.

168 Ross 1981, p. 65. The events of the spring and summer of 1483 are notoriously among the most controversial in English history. For relatively dispassionate summaries, see *Coronation of Richard III*, ed. Sutton and Hammond, pp. 13–46; Horrox 1989, pp. 89–97.

169 G. T. Clark 1867, p. 32; *Proceedings and Ordinances of the Privy Council*, vol. II, p. 208.

170 *Coronation of Richard III*, ed. Sutton and Hammond, p. 28. The number of new knights invested in 1483 is uncertain and probably greater than the seventeen mentioned.

171 The explicit connection between the name 'Bloody Tower' and the legend of the Princes is stated only in 1602 (Von Bülow 1892, p. 17). I am very grateful to Anna Keay for bringing this reference to my attention.

172 Mancini, ed. Armstrong, pp. 92–3.

Chapter Six: The White Tower, 1485–1642

1 See Chapter Two, pp. 75–86.

2 See Appendix II. The analysis was carried out as part of the White Tower Recording and Research Project (WTRRP).

3 See Appendices II and IV, pp. 299–301 and 313–17.

4 These floorboards are oriented east–west, whereas it could be expected that those of the rooms on either side of the spine wall would have had east–west joists (see below) and north–south boards. If this suggests that these boards have been reset, the evidential value of the dendrochronological analysis is not significantly reduced: they still demonstrate that the raising of the roof coincided with flooring, most probably at this floor level.

5 Oxford Archaeological Unit, TOL64 and TOL72. The conclusions drawn here are different in several aspects from those presented by the excavators in these reports, as a result of re-examination of the western mural passage in 1997 and the wider research of the WTRRP: see pp. 80–1, 315.

6 See Chapter Two, pp. 80–1.

7 The National Archives (formerly the Public Record Office) [hereafter TNA], E 351/3202; Chrimes 1999, pp. 67–89, 226 ff.; P. Williams 1979, p. III; Polydore Vergil, ed. Hay, passim; Wernham 1966, pp. 35–6; Goldingham 1918. In 1620 the Tower of London was recognised as 'the cheefe storehouse and magazine of the warlike p[ro]visions of the realme' (TNA, SP 14/116, no. 5). We are grateful to Jonathan Coad for his views on this.

8 TNA, E 101/474/18. Though John Bayley (1821–5, vol. I, appendix p. viii) assigned this estimate to the 23rd year of Henry VIII's reign, it is, in fact, undated, and his source for such a date has not been identified.

9 *Calendar of State Papers: Spain*, p. 489; TNA, E 101/474/12 and E 101/474/13, passim; *Letters and Papers of Henry VIII*, vol. V (1531–2), p. 563.

10 *Letters and Papers of Henry VIII*, vol. V (1531–2), pp. 618, 626, 679. For details of the work to the lodgings that Anne Boleyn was herself to occupy on the eve of her coronation, see A. Keay 2001, pp. 44–7. See also Selected Texts: Transcripts of Primary Documents: Post-Medieval, pp. 335–6.

11 TNA, E 101/474/12, fol. 4v; E 101/474/13, fol. 9r–v. See also Selected Texts: Transcripts of Primary Documents: Post-Medieval, pp. 335–6.

12 See Selected Texts: Transcripts of Primary Documents: Post-Medieval, p. 340.

13 TNA, E 101/474/12, fol. 4r; E 101/474/13, fols Ir, 3v.

14 It has been argued, on no clear evidence, that the modern form of the cupolas was even earlier: Colvin, Brown and Taylor 1963–82, vol. III, p. 265. The roofs are clearly shown to have rectilineal pyramid-shaped roofs in the 'Orléans' manuscript of *circa* 1500 (pl. 104).

15 TNA, E 101/474/13, fol. 3v.

16 '. . . elysys the paynter', TNA, E 101/474/13, fol. 3v; Auerbach 1954, p. 157.

17 TNA, SP 1/85, fol. 73r.

18 TNA, E 101/474/13, fol. 3r.

19 *Letters and Papers of Henry VIII*, vol. VII (1534), p. 32; Oxford, Bodleian Library, Rawlinson MS D 780, fol. 247v: this account confirms that the guns had at least damaged the lead, referring to 'holls . . . mad wt gownes'.

20 Bodleian Library, Rawlinson MS D 778, fol. 16v.

21 Bodleian Library, Rawlinson MS D 778, fols 109r, 109v, 110v; Rawlinson MS D 780, fols 246v–51v; Nottingham University Library, MS Ne 01. See also Selected Texts: Transcripts of Primary Documents: Post-Medieval, pp. 337–8.

22 *Letters and Papers of Henry VIII*, vol. X (1536), p. 513.

23 For the Knights of the Bath generally, see Anstis 1725; Pilbrow 2002.

24 British Library, Egerton MS 985, fol. 41v; Wickham Legg 1901, pp. 220–2.

25 British Library, Egerton MS 985, fol. 51r; Anglo 1969, p. 50.

26 *Letters and Papers of Henry VIII*, vol. I (1509–14), pp. 37–8; British Library, Cotton MS, Tiberius E VIII, fol. 100.

27 *Letters and Papers of Henry VIII*, vol. VI (1533), pp. 250–51.

28 *Calendar of State Papers, Domestic: Mary I*, pp. 9–10; Anstis 1725, p. 53 (this refers to the knights conducting their vigil in 'the Great Tower whereas the Bath was').

29 Oxford, Bodleian Library, Ashmole MS 862, pp. 299–300; Bayne 1910. In 1559 the knights both dined and bathed in the White Tower: 'the said Knights haveing a Bankett in the said White Towre before their entering to the Bath'. See also Selected Texts: Transcripts of Primary Documents: Post-Medieval, p. 338.

30 '. . . their baynes were prepared in a great chamber in the downgeon as of olde tyme hath ben accustomed' (British Library, Egerton MS 985, fol. 42v).

31 Nichols 1828, vol. I, p 202. The event did in fact take place, almost a year later, on 15 March 1604; James I arrived at the Tower on 12 or 13 March, and on the 15th processed from there to Westminster (ibid, p. 320; Howes 1615, pp. 83–6, 827).

32 The king's lodgings, the Jewel House, the Wardrobe and the White Tower were all

given attention in 1625 (TNA, E 351/3258; SP 16/19, no. 3).

33 *True Relation of the Ceremonies.* It seems likely that, if it had been feasible, Charles II would have stayed at the Tower; in the event he travelled to the Tower in the early morning, in order to start his procession through the City from its gates (British Library, Additional MS 30195, fols 19r ff.).

34 British Library, Cotton MS Nero C. IX, fols 168v–170v; also printed as an appendix to Anstis 1725, p. 53. This seems to have continued to inform the way in which the ceremonies were conducted until 1661, when it was published to coincide with Charles II's coronation. The detailed account of the bathing of the knights in 1559 indicates that this rubric was followed closely (Bodleian Library, Ashmole MS 862, p. 299). See also British Library, Cotton MS Domitian XVIII, pp. 243 ff.; MS Nero D II, pp. 259 ff. See also Selected Texts: Transcripts of Primary Documents: Post-Medieval, pp. 331–2.

35 College of Arms, MS I. 18, fol. 39r.

36 'Item to iiii men laboryng at the towre of london for thapparaylyng thereof by vi dayes at vid the daye', printed in Wickham Legg 1901, p. 199.

37 Bodleian Library, MS Rawlinson D 775, fol. 204r; Bodleian Library, Ashmole MS 862, p. 299, *Letters and Papers of Henry VIII*, vol. VI (1533), pp. 250–1. Sadly, the manuscript in the College of Arms appears to have been lost, so the exact text of this important reference to preparations for the Knights of the Bath is no longer available. The calendar entry reads: 'On Friday, all noblemen &c repaired to Court, and in a long chamber within the Tower were ordained 18 baynes in which were the 18 noblemen all that night, who received the order of knighthood on Saturday'.

38 Howes 1615, p. 827; TNA, E 351/3238.

39 *Letters and Papers of Henry VIII*, vol. VI (1533), pp. 250–1; 'the stayyng of the Beames of the Roff wheras the Knyghtts of the Baathe was made' (Oxford, Bodleian Library, Rawlinson MS D 780, fol. 246v); see also Bodleian Library, Rawlinson MS D 778, fol. 109r.

40 TNA, E 3238, E 3239, 3240. The inclusion of 'The greate roome in the white Towre' in a list of the royal lodgings in the Tower made in 1630 is probably due to this room's use for the bathing of the Knights of the Bath (West Sussex Record Office, Petworth House Archives, 1630, p. 6).

41 Bodleian Library, Ashmole MS 862, p. 299.

42 TNA, SP 12/3, no. 46.

43 For example, the ceremonies for the creation of the knights were conducted at Westminster in 1489, at St James's Palace in 1603, at Whitehall in 1605 and at Durham House in the Strand in 1610.

44 Bodleian Library, Ashmole MS 862, p. 300. This ceremony took place during the tense period following Elizabeth's accession. With the nature of the Elizabeth religious settlement still unclear, great significance was attached to the fact that the celebrant at this

mass in St Peter ad Vincula did not elevate the Host.

45 Bodleian Library, Rawlinson MS D 775, fols 207v, 218v. The fact that this was a timber stair supplied by the carpenters makes it hard to read this account as relating to the spiral stair cut into the south face of the keep at some point before the seventeenth century.

46 Although it has long been assumed that the Knights of the Bath used the chapel of St John, Bodleian Library, MS Ashmole 862 is the only source known to the authors for any period that allows the chapel used by the knights to be identified.

47 See, for example, Aylmer 1974, pp. 26–32; L. B. Ellis 1948; Arnold 1988, pp. 161–75.

48 For instance, John Wynyarde was a page of the Robes as well as a groom of the Beds, and, like numerous others, the coffer maker Thomas Green supplied both offices. One contemporary described the 'Maister of the Wardrobe' as having 'the charge and custody of all former Kings and Queenes auncient Robes, remaining in the Tower of London, and all hangings of Arras, Tapestrie, or the like for his Majesties houses' (Minsheu 1617).

49 See Parnell 1993, pp. 47–8, and Parnell 1998b, p. 173, for other arguments for this function for the eastern annexe.

50 TNA, E 101/474/13: what appears to have been the southern wall of this building was discovered to the east of the Wardrobe Tower in 1993–4 (Hiller and Keevill 1994, pp. 160, 162 and 171–2). The Haiward and Gascoyne survey of 1597 labels the tower at the south-east corner of the annexe the 'Warderoap' tower. That Wardrobe accommodation adjoined the keep is suggested by a number of contemporary references. Thomas Platter, who visited the Tower in 1599, describes how he 'passed through an old armoury into a chamber where there were exceedingly many tapestries' (Platter, ed. Williams, p. 161); building accounts also suggest that the buildings abutted one another, for example, 'stone coaping on the Battlemts on the east and west side of the White Tower & on the wardrobe' (TNA, AO 1/2429/71).

51 TNA, E 101/474/18, mem. 6: 'a new gallery for the quene to be made bytwene the kings gallery and the ende of the kyng Warderobe of his robes'.

52 TNA, E 101/474/13, fol. 2v: 'wardrop next to the kyngys garden where the Robys do lye'.

53 *Inventory of King Henry VIII*, ed. Starkey, pp. 179–95.

54 Von Klarwill 1928, p. 318; Platter, ed. Williams, pp. 161–2; Von Bülow 1892; Hentzner 1894, pp. 37–8.

55 TNA, LC 5/34, fol. 14; LC 5/35, fol. 9; British Library, Egerton MS 2806, fols 57, 159, 167, 191.

56 British Library, Egerton MS 2806, fols 81, 98, 214; British Library, Additional MS 10109, fol. 60v.

57 '. . . les joialx et vesselementz sons ecritz trouvez P les Chamberleyns en la Blaunche Tour deinz la Tour de Londres', printed

in *Antient Kalendars*, ed. Palgrave, vol. III, p. 197.

58 The section of the 'Black Book' of Edward IV relating to the Jewel House is printed in *Household of Edward IV*, ed. Myers, pp. 121–2.

59 For the operation of the Jewel House, see Holmes and Sitwell 1972; Collins 1955; Younghusband 1921.

60 TNA, E 36/214, fol. 151v.

61 TNA, E 101/474/18, mem. 6; TNA, E 101/474/13, fols 4v, 9r–v.

62 Thomas Cromwell was appointed Master of the Jewel House on 14 April 1532 and held the post for almost a decade.

63 Oxford, Bodleian Library, MS Rawlinson D 778, passim.

64 The intention in early spring 1535 was for 'a new Juelhouse to be made for the kyngs plate where as tholde Juellhouse was adjoynyng to the great buttery' (Bodleian Library, MS Rawlinson D 778, fol. 16r). Once work was under way this building was referred to as the 'new' Jewel House, and that adjoining the White Tower started to be described as 'old'.

65 That the roof of this Jewel House was wholly rebuilt in 1535 could indicate that the identification with Henry VII's Jewel House is incorrect, or that the Jewel House of 1508 simply used a pre-existing building.

66 See Chapter Seven, p. 184.

67 A. Keay 2001, passim.

68 The accounts of the rebuilding of the roof in 1535 confirm that it was of lead and that it had battlements (Bodleian Library, MS Rawlinson D 778, fols 7r and 8r), but the other details shown in the survey of 1597 remain questionable (see A. Keay 2001).

69 The drawing is undated, but see Hind 1922, p. 51.

70 Oxford, Bodleian Library, Rawlinson MS D 778, fol. 98v.

71 Bodleian Library, Rawlinson MS D 778, fol. 7r.

72 See Chapter Five, p. 149.

73 That there were two jewel houses with distinct functions in close proximity is shown by the reference to 'the Batilments betwene the stayres foote goyng to the Kings stonding Jewelhouse and the Jewelhouse where the Kings removing plate lyeth' (Bodleian Library, Rawlinson MS D 775, fol. 202).

74 Plate was taken from the Tower to the other palaces for grand occasions; for example, for the state dinner in the Great Chamber at Whitehall on Twelfth Night 1600, there 'came from the Tower of London in seven Carres seven great standardes full of plate' (quoted in Hotson 1954, p. 192).

75 The former included a 'wayting chambre' and a 'counting house' and was provided with 'long settylls wth chests and sellyngs for backs to sytt upon & to laye boks & other records of the Juellhousse' (Bodleian Library, Rawlinson MS D 778, fols 95r, 101v).

76 'Albartt Vauhenes for Ironwork for ii pressyse stondyng in the olde Juelhouse wt in the whyte toure' (Rawlinson MS D 778, fol. 87v). As has been mentioned above, once work was

under way on the rebuilding of the buttery Jewel House, the White Tower Jewel House became known as the 'old' Jewel House.

77 'To Cornelius Johnson . . . for certyn handles and staples for chests occupied for plate & cases for the Juells . . . for an Iron Casse for on of the glasse wyndowes in the said Juell-housse wt in the whyte Toure . . . for men-dyng of certyane locks for doores and chests wtin the same Juellhouse' (Rawlinson MS D 778, fol. 82r).

78 This is suggested not least because the lower Jewel House of 1649 clearly housed most of the plate and large objects used for ban-queting, while the upper contained the most precious and delicate objects, including the state regalia. As A. J. Collins (1955) has shown, the state regalia, as opposed to the monarch's personal regalia, was called on infrequently, and it is in keeping with this that the upper Jewel House should be that designated the standing Jewel House in 1535 (Millar 1972, pp. 1–53). See also Bennett 1885; *Inventory of the Plate in the Lower Jewel House*, ed. Brand.

79 There was a third jewel repository in the Tower, known as the secret Jewel House, which contained the most personal and pre-cious of the sovereign's treasures. In the sev-enteenth century it was the home of fabulous jewels such as the 'Three Brethren' and the 'Mirror of Great Britain'. The contents of this Jewel House were pawned and sold by Charles I, apparently leaving it empty by the outbreak of the Civil War (Collins 1955, p. 178). The whereabouts of this building are not known; it is not mentioned by name in any of the building accounts and it may be that it was housed within one of the other Jewel Houses, or, as was the case with the secret Jewel Houses at Whitehall and Hampton Court, somewhere in the royal palace com-plex itself (Thurley 1995, pp. 75 and 139).

80 Nichols 1828, vol. II, p. 78.

81 *Antient Kalendars*, ed. Palgrave, vol. III, p. 197: 'les fyns roules & totes autres remem-braunces t monimentz' in the Tower. See also Hallam 1979. See Chapter Five, p. 152.

82 TNA, E 101/474/18, mem. 3.

83 TNA, SP 12/47, fols 35–6.

84 TNA, SP 12/33, no. 2.1; British Library, Addi-tional MS 34711, fol. 1r–v. The dispute was sparked when Bowyer would not allow Stafford's lock to be reaffixed on the records. This led Bowyer's servant to assault Staf-ford's, striking 'him one the Heade wythe a Locke, that the Blode rane aboute his Face, and thruste him downe the Staire saying that I [Stafford] had nothinge to do there' (British Library, Stowe MS 543, fol. 60r–v).

85 *Calendar of State Papers, Domestic: Edward VI, Mary, Elizabeth*, vol. I (1547–80), pp. 234, 290, 292. This affair is discussed in Wernham 1956 and in McKisack 1971, pp. 76–7; TNA, SP 12/42, no. 74.

86 TNA, SP 12/42, no. 74.

87 TNA, SP 12/47, fols 35–6; works had taken place the preceding year in 'making a newe office for the recordes' (TNA, E 351/3202).

88 *Journal of the House of Lords*, 17 (1701–4), pp. 555–6.

89 British Library, Lansdowne MS 11, no. 49, fol. 112r; Lansdowne MS 163, fol. 284; TNA, SP 13/H/11, no. 14: 'fynisheing of the works begon at the Exchequior, the Recordes & other Romes of Tharmory within the Tower of London'.

90 British Library, Lansdowne MS 163, fol. 284; British Library, Additional MS 28093, fol. 246.

91 In 1564 William Bowyer proposed that 'a p[er]fit inventory shule be made of all suche bookes and recordes as there dothe remayne'. His own six-volume digest was to form the basis of much later work on calendaring the collection (TNA, SP 12/33, no. 2.1; British Library, Additional MS 34711, fol. 1r–v).

92 British Library, Stowe MS 543, fols 55–8.

93 For example, in 1534 Sir Christopher Willoughby's widowed sister-in-law disap-peared with all the documents relating to his late brother's estate; but he was able to supply this loss in some part by making 'manifold searches in the records in the Tower' (*Letters and Papers of Henry VIII*, vol. VII, 1534, p. 88). The government itself frequently made use of the records to try to find rights and priv-ileges that had lapsed, as in 1556, when it was ordered that 'sum skyful man shulde make searche in the Recordes of the Tower' for information relating to the limits of the English pale in France (*Acts of the Privy Council*, vol. V, p. 296).

94 '. . . in the Tower hee maye search one whole daie for one fee' (British Library, Lansdowne MS 163, fol. 284).

95 One searcher of 1601 knew the letter that he was looking for was most likely among the papers marked 'Francia' in the Tower, but these were 'now most strictly kept and no records to be searched, but such as concern titles of land' (British Library, Additional MS 34711, fol. 1).

96 *Calendar of State Papers, Domestic: Common-wealth*, vol. II (1650), p. 476.

97 Hallam 1979, p. 6; Wernham 1956, passim; TNA, E 351/3255, 3256; British Library, Lans-downe MS 163, fol. 284.

98 For the Tower of London and military supply, see Hogg 1963, vol. I, pp. 78–82; Stewart 1996; Tomlinson 1979, passim. For the history of the Privy Wardrobe at the Tower, nothing has yet superseded T. F. Tout's monumental *Chapters in the Adminis-trative History of Mediaeval England* (Man-chester, 1920–33; revised 1937).

99 For example, Sir Richard Southwell, who was Master of the Armoury and of the Ordnance in the mid-sixteenth century, and William Paynter, who was a clerk of both institutions at the beginning of Elizabeth's reign.

100 For example, the house within the Tower of London built in 1549 for 'all the kinges maiesties store and provision of Artillerie Ordinance and other Municions', which seems to have contained both artillery and armour; when part of it was about to collapse

in 1562, Winchester pointed out: 'what charge Armor Weapons and powder hathe bene this yere to the Quene I nede not to wright to you for it is to you well knowne and therfore it requirith good keping' (TNA, SP 12/22, no. 15).

101 Items such as swords, pikes and halberds seem to have been supplied by both offices on occasion.

102 Tomlinson 1979, p. 105.

103 TNA, SP 16/179, no. 65.

104 For the armoury at Greenwich, see, for example, Hogg 1963, vol. I, pp. 78–106.

105 TNA, SP 16/179, no. 65.

106 Hogg 1963, vol. I, p. 79.

107 TNA, E 351/3202.

108 British Library, Lansdowne MS XI, fols 112, 49; *Calendar of State Papers, Domestic: Ed-ward VI, Mary, Elizabeth*, vol. VII (Addenda, 1566–79), p. 311; TNA, SP 13/H/11, no. 14.

109 TNA, SP 12/141, fol. 100r. See also Selected Texts: Transcripts of Primary Documents: Post-Medieval, pp. 338–9.

110 TNA, SP 12/214, no. 1.

111 TNA, SP 12/227, no. 5; there does not appear to be any sign of action resulting from Lee's report, and in 1594 the need to put the armoury at the Tower in better order was still being remarked upon (*Calendar of State Papers, Domestic: Edward VI, Mary, Elizabeth*, vol. III, 1591–4, p. 408).

112 TNA, SP 16/179, no. 65. Brigandines were composed of overlapping metal scales riveted to and covered by layers of cloth.

113 '. . . al provision for foren service have been bowght of late, by the officers of the Ordi-nance & by them delivered into the Armorie at the tower but at the second hand' (TNA, SP 16/179, no. 65).

114 '. . . the office of the Ordinance is alreadie possessed of a great part of the armes belong-ing to horse & foote, as lances, pike, hal-berds, & of the whole office of musketts, pistols and smale guns; and also of making the provisions of armours, as by the accompt hath appeared' (TNA, SP 16/179, no. 65).

115 *Ordinances for the Royal Household*, p. 254; Stewart 1996, pp. 6–9.

116 Hogg 1963, vol. I, p. 66; Parnell 1998b, p. 171; A. Keay 2001, pp. 39–40.

117 TNA, SP 14/156, no. 13, fol. 29; British Library, Harley MS 1326, fol. 125r. See also Selected Texts: Transcripts of Primary Documents: Post-Medieval, p. 339.

118 *Calendar of Patent Rolls: Edward IV*, vol. I (1461–7), p. 23.

119 TNA, WO 49/18, fol. 114r.

120 TNA, WO 49/19, fol. 142r.

121 Parnell 1998b, p. 172.

122 The Ordnance bill books are littered with references to water spoiling powder, such as this of 1602 to 'so much powder . . . being wracked utterly decaied and eated wth salt water' (TNA, WO 49/29, fol. 111r).

123 In 1637, when 'a dark room under the King's magazine of powder', probably the White Tower basement, was being used for the storage of powder that had yet to pass proof,

the Lords of the Admiralty demanded that the powder be moved immediately for this very reason (TNA, SP 16/353, no. 63).

124 TNA, SP 12/253, fol. 69r.

125 TNA, SP 12/268, no. 13.

126 TNA, SP 12/253, fol. 69r.

127 British Library, Additional MS 34808, fol. 139r; TNA, SP 12/268, no. 13.

128 TNA, E 351/3239.

129 TNA, E 351/3240.

130 '. . . framinge of Joysts and Brest Sommers for the newe flower of the powderhouse in the white tower, lifting straight of planckes wch have been sawen twoe years for the same flower, and the next oulde flower under it' (TNA, E 351/3240).

131 TNA, E 351/3240.

132 Some doubt over the interpretation of these dendrochronological dates must be admitted, since the floor frames of the west side of the White Tower were rebuilt in 1733–4 to permit the insertion of the surviving brick vaults in the basement (TNA, WO 51/128, fol. 73v). However, the western room second floor is unique at the White Tower in that it has north–south principal joists directly carrying closely set common joists of substantial scantling (the other rooms have three orders of joists), of which all six dated examples relate to the rebuild of 1604–5, and may reflect closer replication of the pre-1733–4 ceiling/floor than found elsewhere in the building.

133 TNA, WO 49/33, fol. 51.

134 TNA, WO 49/33, fol. 51; TNA, E 351/3239.

135 Match rope was one of the pieces of ordnance equipment that the Ordnance Office seems to have kept in bulk, and which was equally ineffectual if it was allowed to become damp: in 1601 fifteen tilts of canvas were ordered specifically for keeping dry match that was being sent to Dublin (TNA, WO 49/27, fol. 50v; WO 49/33, fols 87, 97, 120v and 129; WO 49/35, fol. 43v).

136 TNA, E 351/3239.

137 See Appendix IV, p. 319.

138 TNA, WO 49/37, fol. 79; 'ffor Iron and workmanship imployed in mending of a pulley to take up the powder in the white Tower vs vid' (TNA, WO 49/41, fol. 66v); 30 September 1652: 'White Rope for ye Cranes on tower wharfe white Tower & Woolwch' (TNA, WO 49/84, fol. 211).

139 See Appendix IV, p. 313.

140 The earliest plan (1729) of the second-floor western chamber shows a capstan at the north end, although there is no evidence to indicate that it represents the precise arrangement in 1611 (TNA, WORK 31/88).

141 TNA, WO 49/70, fol. 240v.

142 TNA, WO 47/70, fol. 73v; TNA, E 351/3269.

143 TNA, WO 49/70, fol. 178v; Parnell 1998b, p. 172.

144 See Appendix IV, p. 308.

145 In 1534 Charles V's ambassador, Chapuys, wrote to his master that 'guns have been placed on the top of the Tower commanding the city. This has made many persons muse'

(*Letters and Papers of Henry VIII*, vol. VII, 1534, p. 32). The accounts for works to the White Tower roof in August to September 1536 refer to 'gynnes stonding Aboue the leadds of the said White Towre' (Nottingham University Library, MS. Ne. 01).

146 In 1600 Baron Waldstein saw sixteen cannon (Waldstein, ed. Groos, p. 71), as did Thomas Platter in 1599 (Platter, ed. Williams, p. 162). In 1603 James I saw twenty charged off from the roof (Nichols 1828, vol. I, pp. 118–20).

147 *Chronicle of Queen Jane*, ed. Nichols, pp. 42–3.

148 Howes 1615, p. 886. In 1564 all the rooftop artillery in the Tower was overhauled, and many of the platforms replaced; at this date there were seventeen guns on the White Tower roof: six on the west side, five on the south, five on the east and one on the north (TNA, SP 12/33, no. 64).

149 Stow, ed. Kingsford, vol. I, p. 59.

150 British Library, Harley MS 1326, fol. 125r.

151 TNA, SP 1/94, 7; Robert Rudson and Thomas Culpepper were brought to the Tower on 8 February 1554, and their names can still be seen cut into the walls of the room below the chapel.

152 Gerard, ed. Caraman, pp. 108–9; Thomas Platter also describes what may be the basement of the White Tower as being used for torture, and notes there 'the ropes used to rack malefactors' (Platter, ed. Williams, p. 161).

153 The basement was being used to house gunpowder in 1637, while in 1650 cannon were stored there (*Calendar of State Papers, Domestic: Charles I*, vol. XX, 1644–5, p. 490).

154 TNA, SP 14/45, no. 3.

155 It was the lodgings along the south, east and west sides of the inner ward that seem to have been used to lodge such important prisoners in this period, including the Beauchamp, Bloody and Bell towers, as well as the apartments of the royal palace area itself. A. Keay 2001, gazetteer.

156 See Chapter Seven, p. 194.

157 *Chronicle of Queen Jane*, ed. Nichols, passim, for the vast number of prisoners in the Tower at this date, and the amount of shifting around that went on to accommodate everyone.

158 British Library, Harley MS 1326, fol. 125.

159 TNA, SP 14/116, 5. Ironically, after his efforts to improve the fortress, Sir Edward was himself imprisoned in the Tower in 1623.

160 TNA, SP 14/156, 13.

161 TNA, SP 14/156, 13, fols 29 ff.

162 TNA, WO 49/54, fols 67r, 104r, 114r–v; WO 49/57, fol. 63; WO 49/59, fol. 230r; WO 49/60, fol. 16v; E 351/3259.

163 TNA, SP 16/323, pp. 33–4; SP 16/325, no. 77.

164 William Mills carried out work to the Beauchamp and Bloody towers at the same time (TNA, E 351/3272).

165 TNA, E 351/3271. See also Selected Texts: Transcripts of Primary Documents: Post Medieval, p. 340.

166 TNA, E 351/3272. See also Selected Texts: Transcripts of Primary Documents: Post-Medieval, pp. 340–1.

167 See Chapter 7, pp. 184–5, 189.

168 See Fig. 143, p. 190.

169 TNA, E 351/3271; E 351/3272; TNA, AO 1/2429/71.

170 The report of 1623 describes openings on the keep as having 'brick edge wayes' (TNA, SP 14/156, fol. 29).

171 TNA, E 351/3270.

172 TNA, SP 16/425, no. 41.

173 TNA, WO 49/60, fol. 16v. For Charles I's late realisation of the power of the royal progress through London, see Smuts 1989. Several grand architectural projects, which would have brought considerable prestige to the house of Stuart had they been completed, were also embarked upon at this date, including Charles I's ambitious project for rebuilding Whitehall Palace in a more stately fashion to designs by Inigo Jones (see Thurley 1998).

174 We are very grateful to the late Giles Worsley for his generous advice and guidance on these points.

175 Many issues, including, for example, the question of pumping water from the White Tower well, were referred directly to 'Mr Jones' (TNA, SP 16/494, no. 94). The estimate for works to the castle that followed soon after the Council visited in the summer of 1640 was signed by Jones personally, while the evidence from other projects undertaken by the Office of Works confirms that they all 'received the impress of his mind' (Colvin, Brown and Taylor 1963–82, vol. III, p. 138). We are very grateful to Simon Thurley for his guidance on this subject.

176 Higgott 2004. Portland stone for St Paul's was landed on Tower Wharf and the same supply route may have been used for the Tower works. We would like to thank Gordon Higgott for his guidance on this point.

177 Windows following this form can still be seen today on the Middle Tower and the Martin Tower; they were also the models for the fenestration of the Grand Storehouse of 1688–92. See also Parnell 1993, pp. 83–4.

Chapter Seven: The White Tower, 1642–1855

1 Hyde, ed. Dunn Macray, pp. 553–8. Shortly before the castle was relinquished, efforts had been made towards 'making the Tower safe', following the Council visit in the summer of 1640, which included the placing of more than twenty guns on the roof of the White Tower (*Calendar of State Papers, Domestic: Charles I*, vol. XVII, 1640–41, pp. 1, 129, 158, 186; The National Archives [formerly the Public Record Office], hereafter TNA, WO 49/72, fol. 65v).

2 There is still a Jewel House at the Tower of London today, but since 1660 it has been a repository of the state regalia and not of all royal jewellery and plate. Despite the complaints of Sir Gilbert Talbot, Charles II's Master of the Jewel House, that while he was called 'Maister and Treasurer of his Matyes iewells & plate, he is made a stranger to all

but ye Regalia, which alone is in his keeping', this part of his office was never restored (Younghusband 1921, p. 240).

3 The hall was converted for military storage in the 1630s (TNA, SP 16/425, no. 41).

4 In 1644, when the great hangings of the Armada were brought from the Tower to hang in the House of Lords, it was the Lieutenant of the Tower, not the Master of the Great Wardrobe, who was asked to release them (*Journal of the House of Lords*, VI, 1643–4, p. 554).

5 *Journal of the House of Commons* (1648–51), pp. 172, 249.

6 Millar 1972, pp. xi–xxv, 1–19.

7 TNA, SP 25/63, pp. 474, 500, 510; SP 25/64, p. 346; SP 25/100, p. 52; WO 49/86, fols 26–8.

8 *Calendar of State Papers, Domestic: Charles II*, vol. I (1660–61), p. 396.

9 TNA, LC 5/201, pp. 220–21.

10 Millar 1972, pp. xi–xxv, 26–50; *Inventory of the Plate in the Lower Jewel House*, ed. Brand; Mildmay 1897.

11 For Mildmay's papers relating to the fate of the Jewel House in the 1640s, see Bennet 1885; HMC: *Seventh Report*, pp. 594–5.

12 HMC: *Seventh Report*, p. 595.

13 British Library, Harley MS 7352, fol. 105v.

14 HMC: *Fifteenth Report*, pp. 1–2; Hogg 1963, vol. I, pp. 103–5. Edward Annesley, store-keeper and proof-master of the Armoury at the Tower, reported to the committee investigating the dispersal of Charles I's goods on 9 May 1660 that he had 'in his custody all the armour brought from Greenwich to Guildhall and from thence to the magazine in London about the year 1644, except one rich gilt armour delivered by order of the Council to General Cromwell' ('Manuscripts of the House of Lords', HMC: *Seventh Report*, p. 88).

15 Borg 1976, p. 318.

16 Reid 1964, pp. 339–40.

17 Hogg 1963, vol. I, pp. 80–2, 105; Aylmer 2002, p. 43.

18 *Calendar of State Papers, Domestic: Charles I*, vol. XIV (1639), p. 233; vol. XVIII 1641–3), p. 269.

19 Tomlinson 1979, pp. 7–9; Reid 1964.

20 *Calendar of State Papers, Domestic: Charles I*, vol. XIX (1644), p. 154. In 1640 the Council had ordered that the powder that remained in the White Tower was 'to be divided among the other towers in the Tower and none to be left in the White Tower . . .' (*Calendar of State Papers, Domestic: Charles I*, vol. XVII, 1640–41, p. 12). It is unclear whether the intention was for the White Tower to cease functioning as a powder store permanently; if this was the scheme the initiative was clearly overtaken by events, for the White Tower certainly housed powder after it fell into Parliamentary hands.

21 TNA, SP 25/63, p. 474.

22 TNA, SP 25/63, p. 510.

23 For the excavation of the brick-faced remains of the long building, see Hiller and Keevill 1994.

24 TNA, SP 25/64, p. 346; SP 25/100, p. 52.

25 See, for example, TNA, WO 49/89, fol. 57, for powder being taken up and down.

26 *Calendar of State Papers, Domestic: Commonwealth*, vol. VI (1653–4), p. 189; TNA, WO 49/87, fol. 58; WO 49/89, fol. 234v.

27 Soldiers were lodged in the chapel of St John, where they destroyed much of the Record Office furniture (British Library, Stowe MS 541, fols 10r–11v; see also Selected Texts: Transcripts of Primary Documents: Post-Medieval, p. 342), while the Jewel Office rooms were treated as a 'sucklin house for ye souldery at the first coming to London' (HMC: *Seventh Report*, p. 595).

28 TNA, SP 25/63, p. 500.

29 TNA, SP 25/65, p. 206.

30 TNA, PC 2/55, fol. 111r.

31 TNA, PC 2/55, fol. 152r.

32 For a detailed discussion of this, see Parnell 1980b. See also Saunders 2004.

33 See Chapter Six, pp. 171–2.

34 *Death's Master-Peece*.

35 TNA, SP 44/23, pp. 31–2; a draft of the commission also survives: TNA, SP 29/441, no. 6.

36 TNA, WO 47/8, fols 56v–57r.

37 TNA, WO 47/8, fols 66v–67r.

38 Evelyn, ed. De Beer, vol. III, p. 458; Bell 1920, pp. 27, 160, 318, 330–33.

39 TNA, WO 55/332, fols 119–20.

40 TNA, WO 55/332, fols 119–20.

41 TNA, WO 51/8, fol. 35; WO 55/332, fols 140–41.

42 *Calendar of Treasury Books*, vol. II, pp. 97, 161; TNA, WO 51/9, fol. 51r. After the disaster of the Dutch raid on English ships in the Medway in June 1667, works were undertaken to fortify the Thames estuary, and Upnor Castle was converted for the storage of gunpowder, with powder brought here from the Tower (Saunders 1967, p. 15).

43 TNA, PC 2/60, fol. 7; TNA, WO 55/388, fol. 190v; WO 51/9, fol. 51.

44 TNA, PC 2/60, fol. 254. See also Selected Texts: Transcripts of Primary Documents: Post-Medieval, pp. 342, 343.

45 TNA, WO 47/19A, fol. 186.

46 TNA, PC 2/60, fols 254r, 300r.

47 TNA, WO 47/19A, fol. 83v. It is unclear whether this was the 'chamber without a Chimney in the Round Tower' that was suggested as the temporary home in May 1668 (TNA, PC 2/60, fol. 300r).

48 Magalotti 1821, pp. 175–6.

49 TNA, WO 51/12, fols 20, 40v–41r.

50 It has been suggested that the eastern annexe became a powder house only after the demolition of the 'long' powder house in 1669, but the accounts strongly imply that the works done to a powder house in 1670 were to a building already fulfilling that function, and did not represent the adaptation of a building to a new function (Parnell 1998b, pp. 173, 176).

51 TNA, WO 51/12, fols 159v, 163v, 182; WO 51/13, fols 32v–33v. The annexe stood on the sloping ground to the east of the keep and had a basement at its south end.

52 TNA, WO 51/19, fol. 227r. The clock and tower can be seen in an engraving of the Tower

from the river of about 1710, reproduced in Parnell 1993, p. 69.

53 That some demolition had taken place in this area before 1674 is shown by an order of June 1669 for pulling down a house next to the White Tower near Coldharbour Gate (TNA, WO 47/19A, fol. 186r), and the submission in July 1669 of a bill for mending holes in the wall before the White Tower (TNA, WO 51/10, fol. 98v). The house may have been the lodging belonging to the Yeoman Warder, Mr Masters.

54 As Geoff Parnell (1993, p. 67) suggests, this is presumably 'the tower against the white tower' that was to be demolished in 1674.

55 TNA, WORK 5/15, fol. 20r.

56 TNA, WO 47/19A, fol. 186r; in 1672 a door case had been created 'under ye old jewel house in Coldharbour' (TNA, WO 51/14, fol. 61r).

57 TNA, WO 47/19B, fol. 39v. See also Selected Texts: Transcripts of Primary Documents: Post-Medieval, p. 343.

58 TNA, WO 47/19B, fols 42r, 43r, 46r, 49v, 53r. See also Selected Texts: Transcripts of Primary Documents: Post-Medieval, p. 343.

59 Sandford 1677, p. 402; Wren 1750, p. 333; Tanner and Wright 1934.

60 See Chapter Five, p. 159.

61 This is corroborated by the inscription on the urn in which the bones were placed, which translates as '. . . their long-desired and much sought-after bones, after more than 190 years, were found by the most certain signs, deeply buried under the rubble of stairs that led up to the chapel of the White Tower, on 17 July in the Year of Our Lord 1674'.

62 '. . . the brick tower goeing to the Chappell' (TNA, WORK 5/4, fols 10v, 13r, 14r, 17v, 21r).

63 TNA, WO 47/19B, fols 97r, 99v, 105v.

64 TNA, WO 47/19B, fol. 117r. A wall partly encircling the White Tower was built in 1669 (TNA, WO 51/10, fol. 86v). This was extended with palisades along the eastern side of the building once the long proof house had been dismantled (TNA, WO 51/12, fol. 32v).

65 Flamsteed, ed. Baily, pp. 7–105. Among the surviving Flamsteed manuscripts are two volumes of his observations from the Tower of London for dates between April 1675 and July 1675. It was at the Tower that Flamsteed designed his great 6ft 9 in. sextant, which he paid the Tower smiths to construct (Maitland 1756, vol. I, p. 151).

66 The sheds can be seen most clearly on the Holcroft Blood view of the Tower of 1688. The plan of the Tower of 1682 shows the 'corridor' during its brief existence.

67 TNA, WO 51/32, fols 38v, 127v, 178v–179v.

68 TNA, WO 51/37, fol. 217v; WO 51/68, fol. 114v; WO 51/32, fol. 38v.

69 TNA, WO 51/15, fol. 21r; WO 51/17, fols 65r, 170v. The lower floors seem to have been used for various miscellaneous ordnance stores. In 1663 work was carried out in 'ye Lower Match house in the White Tower' (TNA, WO 51/3, fol. 3r); hooks to hang tackles on were provided for a room 'under

ye white tower' in the winter of 1667–8; and in December 1668 the carpenter submitted a bill for mending bedsteads also 'under' the White Tower (TNA, WO 51/9, fols 72r, 196r).

70   Doebner 1886, p. 41.

71   TNA, PC 2/74, p. 204; TNA, WO 55/339, p. 87. See also Selected Texts: Transcripts of Primary Documents: Post-Medieval, pp. 343–4.

72   Tomlinson 1979, p. 126.

73   Sanderson 1658, pp. 1001–2

74   British Library, Stowe MS 541, fols 9r–10r; *Calendar of State Papers, Domestic: Commonwealth*, vol. II (1650), p. 476. See also Selected Texts: Transcripts of Primary Documents: Post-Medieval, p. 341.

75   In an undated paper, which seems likely to have been given to the Council at this time, the clerk, William Ryley, expounded the 'reasons for the pr[e]servacon of the Records in the Tower'. These include that the records contained proof of England's right to sovereignty over France, 'the homage and dependency of England upon Scotland' and the 'tenures of all lands in England'. The records comprised the material 'without which no story of the Nation can be written or proved' (British Library, Additional MS 29547, fol. 62; *Calendar of State Papers, Domestic: Charles I*, vol. XX, 1644–5, p. 399; *Calendar of State Papers, Domestic: Commonwealth*, vol. II, 1650, p. 476; *Calendar of State Papers, Domestic: Commonwealth*, vol. III, 1651, p. 305; TNA, SP 25/89, p. 51). For the growing interest in and respect for records during the Commonwealth period, see Kelsey 1997, pp. 11–19.

76   *Calendar of State Papers, Domestic: Commonwealth*, vol. III (1651), pp. 372, 374, 398.

77   TNA, SP 25/96, p. 48; *Calendar of State Papers, Domestic: Commonwealth*, vol. IV (1651–2), pp. 47, 197.

78   *Calendar of State Papers, Domestic: Commonwealth*, vol. VI (1653–4), pp. 132, 194, 236; Scottish Record Office 1996, pp. x–xi.

79   Ashmole, ed. Josten, vol. II, p. 736; vol. III, p. 847.

80   *Calendar of State Papers, Domestic: Charles II*, vol. I (1660–61), p. 370.

81   *Calendar of State Papers, Domestic: Charles II*, vol. II (1661–2), p. 627.

82   Wood, ed. Clark, vol. II, p. 111.

83   British Library, Stowe MS 541, fol. 9v; Delaune 1681, pp. 14–15.

84   TNA, PC 2/65, fols 123, 131; British Library, Stowe MS 541, fols 9r–10r.

85   TNA, PC 2/69, fols 170r, 209v, 222v, 225v–227v; British Library, Stowe MS 541, fols 11r–12v.

86   TNA, PC 2/69, fols 225v–227v.

87   British Library, Stowe MS 541, fols 10r–11v. See also William Prynne's description of the condition in which he found the records in the White Tower: British Library, Lansdowne MS 504, fols 5r–8r, and Stowe MS 542, fols 74v–75r. See also Selected Texts: Transcripts of Primary Documents: Post-Medieval, pp. 341–2.

88   TNA, WO 51/18, fol. 235r. That the internal spiral staircase was replaced and not a new feature in 1676 is attested to by references to 'ye Staire Case goeing upp to ye Chappell' in November 1666 (TNA, WO 55/332, fols 119r–120r).

89   This is suggested on the basis of the agreement between the measurements given for the stairs constructed in 1685 and those that feature on the plans of the Tower of 1726 (TNA, WORK 31/26) and 1754.

90   TNA, WO 51/32, fol. 45r. The position of the sheds, shown on the Holcroft Blood view of the Tower of 1688, must have required the staircase to be hard against the south face of the building.

91   *Journal of the House of Lords*, 17 (1701–5), pp. 555–6.

92   TNA, T 52/22, pp. 334–5.

93   *Calendar of Treasury Papers*, vol. III (1702–7), pp. 292–3; *Calendar of Treasury Books*, vol. XIX, p. 364.

94   Nicholson, ed. Jones and Holmes, pp. 225–6.

95   TNA, WORK 6/14, p 69; *Calendar of Treasury Books*, vol. XIX, p. 350; *Journal of the House of Lords*, 18 (1705–9), pp. 637–8. The building in question was quite likely the section of the chamber block adjoining the Wakefield Tower on the west, which is marked 'w' on the survey of 1682.

96   TNA, WORK 6/14, pp. 82–3.

97   TNA, WORK 6/14, pp. 99–100.

98   *Journal of the House of Lords*, 21 (1718), p. 135.

99   For example, see TNA, WORK 31/86–9. There had presumably been an internal stair to the gallery for at least as long as the chapel had functioned as a record repository, and it is shown in the earliest detailed plans (e.g., TNA, WORK 31/90).

100 TNA, WORK 6/14, p. 102; *Calendar of Treasury Books*, vol. XX, no. ii, p. 403; Nicholson, ed. Jones and Holmes, pp. 310, 337.

101 *Journal of the House of Lords*, 21 (1718), pp. 134–5.

102 TNA, WORK 6/5, p. 282.

103 TNA, WO 47/29, fol. 66r.

104 *Journal of the House of Lords*, 21 (1718), pp. 134–5.

105 TNA, WO 47/29, fol. 66; WORK 6/7, pp. 60–1.

106 TNA, WORK 6/7, pp. 60–2.

107 TNA, WO 47/32, fol. 14; *Calendar of Treasury Papers*, vol. V (1714–19), p. 437.

108 *Calendar of Treasury Papers*, vol. VI (1720–28), pp. 132–3, 240; TNA, WO 47/20B, fols 108, 13.

109 British Library, Additional MS 34711, fol. 51.

110 It was proposed as early as 1718 that a plan should be made of the rooms in question and it may be that TNA, WORK 31/493 was the outcome (*Calendar of Treasury Papers*, vol. VI, 1720–28, pp. 132–3).

111 TNA, WORK 6/16, p. 56.

112 British Library, Additional MS 34711, fol. 78.

113 British Library, Additional MS 34711, fols 97, 99.

114 British Library, Additional MS 34711, fols 187, 223; *Reports from the Select Committee into the State of the Public Records*, p. 11.

115 British Library, Additional MS 34711, fols 190, 223; British Library, Stowe MS 543, fol. 47r; the leads over the building were made good in 1800 (TNA, WORK 5/89).

116 TNA, WORK 5/97, extraordinary account; WORK 6/24, fol. 49.

117 TNA, WORK 6/25, fols 140–41, 154–5; WORK 4/20, 7 June 1811; WORK 5/101, extraordinary account.

118 TNA, WORK 4/20, 17 January 1812. A plan of the two towers of this date survives, and must have accompanied the proposal (TNA, WORK 31/105).

119 TNA, WORK 6/26, fols 2–3

120 TNA, WORK 6/25, fols 154–5; WORK 5/101, extraordinary account.

121 TNA, WORK 6/26, fols 2–3, 13, 16, 54–5; WORK 6/27, fols 2, 6, 12–13, 24–5, 26; WORK 4/20, 17 January 1812, 14 February 1812; WORK 5/101, extraordinary account; TNA, WO 52/374, p. 100. The accounts are ambiguous but suggest that some sort of gallery existed already, presumably erected to increase storage for the Ordnance Office. See also Bayley 1821–5, vol. I, pp. 15–16.

122 For the commission of 1800 and the immediate results, see Pugh 1966.

123 In preparation for this plans were taken of record offices throughout the country in 1833, including a plan of each of the two floors on which records were housed at the Tower (TNA, MPH 328 [12] & [13]).

124 TNA, PRO 1/4.

125 PRO: *First Report*, pp. 8–10; TNA, PRO 1/5.

126 PRO: *Seventeenth Report*, pp. 20–21; PRO: *Eighteenth Report*, p. 1; PRO: *Twentieth Report*, pp. xxx–xxxi.

127 Hogg 1963, vol. I, pp. 106–7.

128 TNA, WORK 6/7, pp. 60–1.

129 Either potassium nitrate or sodium nitrate. The former, more expensive but more effective, was used for ordnance, the latter largely for mining and engineering works.

130 TNA, WO 51/72, fol. 261.

131 TNA, WO 51/93, fol. 79v. For example, 'Triumph powder', used to create fireworks for public celebrations, was moved from its storage place in the White Tower in 1707, to make room for returning stores (TNA, WO 47/25, fol. 76).

132 TNA, WO 51/92, fols 33v, 113r; WO 51/94, fol. 41v.

133 TNA, WO 47/20A, fol. 48; WO 51/93, fol. 89v.

134 TNA, WO 51/93, fol. 79r–v; WO 47/28, fols 37, 97; WO 47/20A, fol. 25.

135 TNA, WO 47/28, fol. 37.

136 TNA, WO 51/93, fol. 79r.

137 TNA, WO 51/93, fol. 79r refers to the 'old salt petre room' adjoining the east room.

138 TNA, WO 47/32, fol. 14.

139 TNA, WO 51/124, fol. 71r, WO 51/128, fol. 15r; Williamson, ed. Fox, pp. 84–5.

140 TNA, WO 51/126, fol. 96v; WO 51/125, fol. 67r.

141 TNA, WORK 31/86. This was certainly the reason given by the Board of Ordnance to the Office of Works for not vaulting the rooms on the eastern side of the building, in 1737 (TNA, WORK 6/16, p. 56).

142 For the plan of the basement prior to the works, but with the new designs sketched on, see TNA, WORK 31/84.

143 At the end of the seventeenth century Ned Ward described the windows as 'only a slit or two no bigger than the mouth of a Christmas-box in proportion to its vast body' (Ward, ed. Fenwick, p. 238).

144 TNA, WO 51/187, fol. 70v; TNA, WORK 31/104.

145 J. Keay 1991, pp. 126–7, 236.

146 TNA, WO 47/60, fols 355, 373; WO 47/61, fols 78–80.

147 Boreman 1741; TNA, WO 47/61, fols 78–80.

148 TNA, WO 47/1593, fols 10766–9.

149 TNA, WO 47/1647, fol. 5103–9; WO 47/1658, fols 8401–2; WO 47/1671, fols 798–800.

150 TNA, WORK 31/738.

151 TNA, WO 52/661, p. 277; the roof of the tunnel was repaired in 1893 (see below).

152 TNA, WO 47/1647, fols 5103–9; WO 52/661, pp. 158, 202, 320, 239. The scheme is shown in a plan of 26 May 1834 (TNA, WORK 31/735).

153 TNA, WO 51/56, fols 71r, 76v.

154 TNA, WORK 31/87; TNA, WO 51/56, fol. 71r.

155 TNA, WO 51/56, fol. 76v.

156 TNA, WO 51/99/34r; TNA, WORK 31/88.

157 TNA, WORK 31/83.

158 TNA, WO 51/99, fol. 34v; TNA, WORK 31/83; WORK 31/80.

159 TNA, WO 51/128, fol. 16v.

160 TNA, WO 51/134, fol. 30v.

161 TNA, WO 51/56, fol. 71; TNA, WORK 31/97 and WORK 31/101. Stalls were set up in the White Tower for small arms in 1745 (WO 51/160, fol. 37r).

162 TNA, WO 51/102, fol. 99v; TNA, WORK 31/87.

163 TNA, WO 51/144, fol. 51r; WO 51/143, fol. 90v.

164 TNA, WO 51/66, fols 29v ff.; WO 47/20A, fol. 76.

165 TNA, WO 47/28, fol. 47.

166 TNA, WO 47/20A, fols 27–8.

167 TNA, WO 47/28, fol. 47.

168 TNA, WORK 31/99; TNA, WO 47/28, fol. 47.

169 TNA, WORK 31/96; WORK 31/100.

170 TNA, WO 47/30, fol. 308; WO 51/101, fol. 119v.

171 TNA, WO 51/99, fol. 34r; WO 51/94, fol. 37r. The creation of these great windows was apparently part of the process of making the lighting in the White Tower more appropriate to its function as a storehouse, which the Surveyor-General was asked to initiate in March 1715 (TNA, WO 47/20A, fol. 35). For the smallness of the windows in the seventeenth century, see Ward, ed. Fenwick, p. 238.

172 TNA, WORK 31/93; WORK 31/94.

173 TNA, WO 51/133, fol. 96v; WO 51/138, fol. 30v.

174 Although the modification to the outer window and the creation of the inner window are marked on a plan of 1729 (TNA, WORK 31/85), this is a later pencil addition. Most of the pencil work on this drawing depicts modifications made to the west chamber for the new Sea Armoury, but the modifications to the garderobe do not appear on the inked design of 1734 for this work (TNA, WORK 31/93). The work was not carried out until 1736, however, and it is likely that the modification was part of these works: certainly, both windows were shown as they are today by 1754 (TNA, WORK 31/96).

175 TNA, WORK 31/95–103; cf. TNA, WORK 31/85; WORK 5/87; WORK 5/88. The old stair certainly does not feature on the plans of the scheme of 1734 (TNA, WORK 31/93; WORK 31/94). The new stairs may be the four flights of stairs referred to in a carpenter's bill on March 1733 (TNA, WO 51/135, fol. 25v).

176 TNA, WO 47/28, fol. 76.

177 TNA, WORK 6/7, pp. 60–61; Calendar of Treasury Papers, vol. v (1714–19), p. 437.

178 TNA, WO 47/20A, fol. 76.

179 TNA, WORK 31/100 and WORK 31/96.

180 TNA, WO 51/143, fol. 55v.

181 TNA, WORK 6/7, p. 62.

182 TNA, WO 51/138, fol. 94v.

183 Boreman 1741. In 1791 a special counter with drawers was provided for the Corps of Royal Military Artificers' tools to replace the chests that had formerly housed them, which had been found inconvenient (TNA, WO 47/118, fol. 664).

184 TNA, WORK 31/98; WORK 31/102; Anonymous 1754.

185 Work was done in the match room in 1705 (TNA, WO 51/71, fol. 101r; WO 51/73, fol. 33v).

186 Calendar of Treasury Papers, vol. v (1714–19), p. 437. This arrangement is also shown in a plan of that date (TNA, WORK 31/82).

187 TNA, WO 51/126, fol. 89v.

188 TNA, WO 51/132, fol. 42v; WO 51/135, fol. 31v.

189 TNA, WO 51/135, fol. 25r–v.

190 TNA, WO 47/35, fols 471–2.

191 TNA, WO 47/91, fol. 540; WO 47/92, fol. 334; WO 51/289, pp. 39r, 53.

192 Circa 1820 John Bayley (1821–5, vol. I, p. 111) described the south-east room on the entrance floor as having been fitted up for cavalry arms about twenty years previously. Swords certainly featured among the cavalry stores, and it may be that in a building so filled with small arms, the presence of swords was the defining feature of the cavalry stores (Anonymous 1815).

193 TNA, WO 52/218, fols 296–311, including the provision of gun racks for muskets.

194 TNA, WO 52/224, pp. 1–12; the account includes the boring of holes for the storage of pikes and muskets, and work to spear racks.

195 TNA, WO 52/225, pp. 496–7.

196 'Having satisfied your curiosity with the sight of these admirable objects, you will be attended to the White Tower' (Anonymous 1815, p. 27).

197 TNA, WO 52/335, p. 290. This is presumably the substantial staircase shown at the southern end of the west room on the entrance floor on a plan of before 1825 (TNA, WORK 31/752).

198 TNA, WO 52/393, p. 1.

199 See above, note 192. That the 'sword' room housed small guns as well as swords is clear from references to providing hooks, and boring holes for the storage of carbines (TNA, WO 52/393, p. 1; WO 53/377, p. 516).

200 TNA, WO 52/661, pp. 70–2, 74, 75, 105, 201.

201 TNA, WO 52/661, pp. 105, 230.

202 TNA, WO 52/661, pp. 72, 75.

203 TNA, WO 52/661, pp. 105, 200.

204 TNA, WO 52/667, pp. 166, 168.

205 TNA, WO 47/1990, fols 16048–53.

206 TNA, WO 47/28, fol. 118.

207 A. Keay 2001, p. 4; TNA, WO 47/32, fol. 55; WO 51/123, fol. 104v; WO 47/28, fol. 47.

208 TNA, WO 51/98, fol. 59v; TNA, WORK 31/124.

209 TNA, WO 51/126, fols 69r–v, 96v.

210 The 'New Additional Building Adjoining to the Drawing Room & White Tower' (TNA, WO 51/126, fol. 69); two plans of this also survive (TNA, WORK 31/180; WORK 31/181). The completed scheme is shown in two further plans of 1733 (TNA, WORK 31/152; WORK 31/153).

211 TNA, WO 51/128, fol. 16v.

212 TNA, WORK 31/180; TNA, WO 51/126, fol. 69v; TNA, WORK 31/152.

213 TNA, WO 47/30, fol. 183; although ill health prevented Smith from carrying out his work (TNA, WO 47/32, fol. 141; WO 47/30, fol. 220).

214 TNA, WORK 31/152; cf. WORK 31/124.

215 TNA, WO 51/136, fol. 43r. The plans of 1754 clearly show the records to have moved into that room by this time.

216 TNA, WO 47/30, fol. 11; WO 51/140, fol. 15v; the surveys of 1754 show him to have used a room abutting the apse of the White Tower on the top floor of the annexe.

217 TNA, WO 47/52, fol. 412; such as the 'model of the silk engine' that had inadvertently found its way into one of the record rooms in 1755 (TNA, WO 47/45, fol. 45).

218 TNA, WO 52/156, fols 128–9. The building is shown with its new top storey in figs 161 and 162.

219 Lack of space for the storage of Ordnance records, which were also kept in the Office itself, caused the suggestion to be made in 1824 that certain sorts of documents dating to before 1801 should be sold or destroyed (TNA, WO 47/1154, fol. 5845). The records gained some space in 1819 when an office apparently in the eastern annexe was vacated by a member of the Small Gun Office staff (TNA, WO 47/2855, fol. 1821v).

220 The two most authoritative histories of the Tower of the early nineteenth century certainly considered the function of the annexe as a whole to have been the storage of Ordnance records (Bayley 1821–5, vol. I, p. 117; Britton and Brayley 1830, p. 255).

221 Planché 1901, p. 450.

222 TNA, WO 51/98, fol. 138r.

223 TNA, WORK 3/163.

224 TNA, WO 47/30, fols 106, 133, 211; WO 51/100, fol. 53r.

225 TNA, WO 51/99, fol. 53v.

226 TNA, WORK 31/176.

227 Particularly because of the inefficiency of the fireplace and chimney (TNA, WO 47/51, fols 199–100, 262, 293; WO 47/52, fol. 243; WO 47/108, fols 111, 108, 498).

228 Considerable damage to the building, caused by high winds, necessitated work in 1772 (TNA, WO 47/80, fol. 130); alterations were also ordered in 1836 (WO 47/1737, fols 13009–10).

229 TNA, WORK 31/172. An estimate was already being submitted for enlarging the new guard-room in November 1847 (TNA, WO 47/ 2131, fol. 18316).

230 Hogg 1963, vol. II, pp. 1086–9.

231 Hentzner 1894, p. 37; Platter, ed. Williams, pp. 159–63; Von Bülow 1892. See also Waldstein, ed. Groos, pp. 65–71.

232 Howes 1615, p. 886; Nichols 1828, vol. II, p. 78. The fees were not inconsiderable. Thomas Platter made eight separate payments in the course of his visit in 1599, while complaints about the cost were made by visitors in the seventeenth and early eighteenth centuries (Howel 1657; César de Saussure, ed. Van Muyden, p. 91).

233 See, for example, Howel 1657.

234 César de Saussure, ed. Van Muyden; 'Voyage of Don Manoel Gonzales', ed. Pinkerton; Seymour 1734; Anonymous 1740.

235 Boreman 1741; Anonymous 1754.

236 'In the White Tower is shewn: The Volunteer Armory . . . The Sea Armoury' (Anonymous 1807).

237 Anonymous 1815.

238 For the history of the Line of Kings, see Borg 1976, pp. 316–52; TNA, WO 47/1222, fol. 6302–3; WO 52/601, pp. 173–4.

239 Meyrick 1826, vol. III, pp. 132–3.

240 Meyrick 1826, vol. III, pp. 132–3.

241 TNA, WO 47/1222, fols 6302–3.

242 TNA, WO 52/601, pp. 173–4.

243 TNA, WO 47/1222, fols 1302–3.

244 TNA, WO 47/1345, fol. 2443; WO 44/303, letter of 30 June 1826; WO 52/586, pp. 375–7, 381–2, 525; heraldic glass was supplied for the windows by Thomas Willement (TNA, WO 52/601, p. 233).

245 TNA, WO 47/1240, fol. 9038; WO 47/1539, fols 5008–11.

246 TNA, WORK 31/741, 742 and 743.

247 TNA, WO 52/667, pp. 166–8. The room had certainly been home to the Cavalry Armoury in 1820 Bayley 1821–5, vol. I, p. 111).

248 Hewitt 1841.

249 TNA, WO 47/2244, fols 237–40. This space was to be used primarily for the display of oriental arms and armour.

250 Bayley 1821–5. Bayley was advised in writing the sections on the architecture of the White Tower by Henry Petrie and Edward Blore. See also Hammond 1999.

251 Penny Magazine, 272 (May–June 1836), p. 253; Britton and Brayley 1830.

252 Penny Magazine, 272 (May–June 1836), p. 256; Bayley (1821–5, vol. I, pp. 668–9) also complained of the entrance arrangements.

253 Thurley 2003, pp. 317–18.

254 TNA, WO 52/667, pp. 312–13. Robert Porrett described the ticket office as 'built on purpose', though the accounts reveal it was adapted from a menagerie building.

255 Report from the Select Committee on National Monuments.

256 Report from the Select Committee on National Monuments, pp. 138 ff. Porrett pointed out that for very interested visitors, the 'Gentlemen of the Record Office with readiness give admission to persons who wish to see' the chapel of St John (p. 142).

257 Ainsworth 1845, pp. iv–v.

258 S. M. Ellis 1911, vol. I, pp. 406, 412.

Chapter Eight: The White Tower, 1855– 2000

1 Knight 1842, vol. II, p. 214. The hope that the rooms that had housed the records of state would be opened to the public on the removal of the records was expressed by many writers; see, for example, Hewitt 1841, p. 2, and The Times (21 April 1851).

2 The National Archives (formerly the Public Record Office) [hereafter TNA , WORK 14/1/9, fols 7r, 9r–v; by the end of 1856 only the chapel still contained records (PRO: Eighteenth Report, p. 1).

3 PRO: Seventeenth Report, p. 29; Forbes 1929, vol. II, pp. 4 ff.; Allibone 1987, pp. 138–43.

4 The Times (5 July 1851). The creation of four large holes in the masonry of the north-east turret of the White Tower in 1853–4 to allow the insertion of the great four-faced clock that was to remain for the next seventy years caused public dismay at the damage it inflicted on 'that noble and ancient building' (The Times, 20 and 21 January 1854).

5 De Ros 1867, pp. 19–20; TNA, WORK 14/2/5, fol. 58r; Allibone 1987, pp. 138–43.

6 TNA, WORK 14/2/5, fols 1r, 2r, 4r, 6r, 9r, 13r–14v, 20r, 22r–v, 25v–26v, 31v, 32v, 37r; TNA, WO 46/163, p. 150; TNA, WORK 14/1/9, fol. 12r–v.

7 TNA, WORK 14/2/5, fol. 4r.

8 TNA, WORK 14/2/5, fols 46r–47v. See also Selected Texts: Transcripts of Primary Documents: Post-Medieval, pp. 344–5.

9 See Chapter Seven, p. 189.

10 TNA, WORK 31/494, no. 6.

11 TNA, WORK 31/494.

12 See Chapter Two, pp. 45–85.

13 The Times (31 March 1862), p. 9; The Builder (19 April 1862), pp. 275–6; Illustrated London News (Saturday, 30 May 1863), p. 583.

14 The Builder (19 April 1862), p. 276.

15 Harman 1867, p. 8.

16 Parnell 1994.

17 Gentleman's Magazine, 99 (1826), p. 629. This was George Stacey, later Chief Clerk to the Principal Storekeeper of the Ordnance.

18 Illustrated London News (Saturday, 30 May 1863), p. 583.

19 PRO; Twentieth Report, p. xxx.

20 De Ros 1867, p. 21: Peel had been Surveyor General of the Ordnance in the years 1841–6. The Director of Clothing, one of the new posts following the reorganisation of supply during 1856–8, answered directly to the Secretary of State for War and initially had his main clothing repositories at Weedon in Northamptonshire and the Tower. The likelihood of the chapel ever actually being handed over to the clothing department must be doubted, given that Queen Victoria and Prince Albert had planned since September 1856 to have the Duke of Wellington's funeral car placed in the chapel, a scheme still being considered in March 1858 (TNA, WORK 14/1/9, fol. 12v; TNA, LC 1/60, R. Eaton to William Vincent). In the end it was abandoned because the car was too big to get through the outer gates into the Tower of London. The writer of a letter to The Times of 5 July 1851 was appalled to hear that 'the fine early Norman chapel in the White Tower is to be fitted up, not as a place of prayer for which it was consecrated, and for which it might be used by the troops . . . but it is to be desecrated by serving as an armoury, the deed of consecration being supposed to be so old that its sanctity must be worn out'.

21 TNA, WORK 31/527. WORK 31/494

22 See Chapter Three, p. 100.

23 The destructiveness of the cleaning was appreciated as early as 1885: The Builder, 48 (3 January 1885), p. 6.

24 Fernie 2000, p. 274.

25 Cocke 1996, pp. 714–15. By the late 1850s Salvin had built four new 'Norman' churches: St Paul's, North Sunderland (1830–33); Holy Trinity, Sewstern (1840–42); St Andrew's, South Otterington (1844–7); and St Michael's, Cowesby (1846): Allibone 1987, pp. 95–7.

26 Lord de Ros (1867, p. 27) complained that the White Tower had 'been subjected to much modern disfigurement', particularly in the form of the windows, which gave the impression that it dated 'no farther back than the time of Queen Anne or George I'.

27 We are grateful to Dr John Goodall for his advice on the restoration of Norman keeps.

28 De Ros 1867, pp. 16–17.

29 De Ros 1867, pp. 22–3.

30 Planché 1901, pp. 439–50; Barter Bailey 1997.

31 TNA, WORK 14/2/5, fol. 74r–v.

32 'It is now used occasionally for service' (The Graphic, 15 August 1885, p. 190).

33 On 28 April 1880 The Times (p. 7) reported: 'For the first time since the reign of Henry VIII a military mass is now celebrated in the Tower for the benefit of the Roman Catholic officers and men of the guards stationed there'; this seems very likely to have happened in the chapel of St John. See also WORK 14/1493, 21 August 1947.

34 TNA, WORK 14/2/5, fol. 59r; ffoulkes 1916, vol. I, pp. 14–16; Hammond 1999.

35 TNA, WORK 14/2/5, fols 59r–60r, 64v.

36 TNA, WORK 14/2/5, fols 53v–55r.

37 TNA, WORK 14/2/5, fol. 57r–v.

38 TNA, WORK 14/2/5, fols 78v–79v.

39 In January 1857 Salvin had commented: 'On the east side of the White Tower there was a low building probably of the time of Ew^d 3rd and whenever any great change in the occupation of the Tower takes place I should recommend that building to be restored' (TNA, WORK 14/2/5, fol. 47r; WORK 14/3/2, fols 9r–13r, 81r–v; The Times, Thursday, 2 February 1882).

40 In the autumn of 1880 the British Archaeological Association visited the Tower and were

shown what they were informed was 'a reliable piece of the old Roman wall, just uncovered during some excavations near the White Tower. The wall at this point is 7 ft in thickness, and contains layers of the usual flat tiles, alternating with thick layers of fine rubble-mortar or concrete' (*The Builder*, 30 October 1880, p. 525). See also TNA, WORK 31/526; *The Times*, 4 January 1881.

41 TNA, WORK 14/2/5, fols 61v–70r.
42 TNA, WORK 14/3/2, fol. 6r; TNA, WO 94/65, the route that visitors were to take in the new access arrangements of 1880 did not include the old 'Queen Elizabeth's armoury, and was to include only the room beneath the chapel once its restoration was completed. *The Graphic* (15 August 1885, p. 190) describes the block and axe and torture instruments – prominent exhibits of 'Queen Elizabeth's armoury – in the 'Council Chamber'.
43 TNA, WORK 14/3/2, fols 15v, 16r.
44 Weale 1854.
45 Anonymous 1858.
46 *The Times* (Monday, 19 April 1880), p. 6; TNA, WO 94/65, Yorke to Ponsonby.
47 TNA, WO 94/65, Yorke to Childers.
48 TNA, WO 94/65, Milman to First Commissioner of Works. This is illustrated in a section of that year (TNA, WORK 31/495).
49 TNA, WO 94/65, 'The Warders Wail'.
50 TNA, WO 94/65, Lieutenant of the Tower to the Secretary of State for War.
51 *The Times* (26 January 1885), p. 10.
52 *The Builder*, 48 (31 January 1885), p. 160; Gower 1902, vol. II, pp. 145–7; Hearsey 1960, pp. 231–2.
53 For the details of this, see Parnell 1993, p. 106.
54 Weale 1854, p. 777.
55 ffoulkes 1939, p. 49.
56 Charles ffoulkes (1939, p. 49) gives the date of 1885 for the demolition; though in his earlier *Inventory and Survey of the Armouries of the Tower of London* (ffoulkes 1916, vol. I, p. 32) he confidently stated that the building had come down in 1883. ffoulkes was almost certainly not a first-hand observer of this event, being a boy of twelve in 1880.
57 See also Crowther's view of the western end of the Horse Armoury in the same year, which shows a building that was apparently still in use.
58 *The Times* (12 September 1885), p. 7; this is supported by W. J. Loftie's account of the Tower in *The Graphic* (Saturday, 15 August 1885), p. 187.
59 The unexpected discovery of the Wardrobe Tower and an area of Roman wall in the course of the removal of the annexe may well have led to the removal of that section of the Horse Armoury that adjoined the discoveries.
60 In that year the construction of 'An annexe or building adjoining the Horse Armoury on East Side of White Tower but separate from it' was proposed, but was rejected, since 'That part was removed on account of its being unsafe. Being now down it is strongly

recommended not to be rebuilt as it obstructs light and space round the White Tower' (TNA, WORK 14/2/5, fols 62v and 69r).
61 *The Graphic* (Saturday, 15 August 1885), p. 190; according to this source the contents of the New Horse Armoury were moved to the top of the White Tower before the bomb of 1885; but this is certainly not the impression given by the report in *The Times* (26 January 1885) of that event, which describes the west room on the top floor as 'solely devoted to the exhibition of oriental arms and armour'.
62 TNA, WO 94/66/1.
63 See the configurations for access mentioned passim in De Ros 1867; Harman 1867; *The Graphic* (15 August 1885), p. 186.
64 TNA, WORK 31/740, plan in WO 94/66/1; the first edition of Loftie's *Authorised Guide*, of 1886, shows that this was the route that visitors followed.
65 Since the 1860s at least, the eastern annexe had housed the Tower collections of oriental arms and armour (Harman 1867). The conversion of the whole annexe proposed in 1876 was specifically to enable the public to view the Eastern collection more easily (TNA, WORK 14/2/5, fols 59r–60r).
66 *The Times* (3 August 1885), p. 7.
67 *The Times* (26 January 1885), p. 10: 'the racks were empty, and even at the moment of the explosion several wagons were being filled in the Courtyard with cases of rifles for conveyance to Volunteer Armouries'.
68 Loftie 1888; ffoulkes 1939; Barter Bailey 2002.
69 ffoulkes 1916, vol. I, p. 33; Loftie 1894, p. 144. In 1892 this plan was described as 'long been proposed . . . but delayed from want of funds' (TNA, WO 94/49/2, Brian Millman to Sir Daniel Lysons). By February of the following year, however, Lysons remarked that 'The Armouries are now being remodelled and greatly improved' (TNA, WO 94/50/2, Daniel Lysons to the Secretary of State for War).
70 Loftie 1894, p. 144.
71 Loftie 1894, passim.
72 Barter Bailey 2002, pp. 112, 118; C. ffoulkes, 'Dillon, Harold Arthur Lee-, seventeeth Viscount Dillon (1844–1932)', rev. Claude Blair, *Oxford Dictionary of National Biography* (Oxford: Oxford University Press, 2004).
73 TNA, WORK 14/2/6, fol. 5v.
74 TNA, WORK 14/2/6, fol. 28r–v.
75 The creation of the Inspectorate of Ancient Monuments within the Office of Works, following the Ancient Monuments Act of 1882, made this transfer all the more logical (Saunders 1983).
76 TNA, WORK 14/114, 'Notes of a conference', 21 November 1902. In his memoirs, *Arms and the Tower*, Charles ffoulkes reports that the armouries were transferred to the British Museum in 1903, but since this was found to be impracticable for various reasons, they were returned to the War Office's control before passing to the Office of Works in 1904. The original papers in the National Archives make no mention of this.

77 In 1914 there were reckoned to be more than 550,000 visitors per year to the armouries (TNA, WORK 14/125, 'Report on arms, armour and military remains').
78 The incompatibility of storing service weapons, which needed frequent oiling, and the priceless objects in the armouries at such close quarters was compared by ffoulkes (1939, p. 58) to that of storing gunpowder under the records in the previous century; the specific risk of fire, to both the rifles and the armouries, was cited, some years later, as the reason the service weapons were removed (TNA, WORK 14/114).
79 TNA, WORK 14/226, 10 October 1910.
80 TNA, WORK 14/226, Secretary of Office of Works to the Governor of the Tower, 22 November 1910.
81 TNA, WORK 14/226, Governor of the Tower to the Secretary of the Office of Works, 21 November 1911.
82 TNA, WORK 14/226, J. W. Baines minute, 3 May 1912.
83 TNA, WORK 14/4/7, correspondence on this issue: 20 January 1913, 22 July 1913, 3 February 1914.
84 TNA, WORK 14/4/7, 3 February 1914.
85 Progress had been held up by 'the prolonged dispute in the building trade', TNA, WORK 14/226, 1 April 1914; TNA, WO 94/50/4, W. A. Robinson to the Governor of the Tower; *The Times* (7 November 1913).
86 TNA, WORK 14/234, annual report of the Curator of the Tower Armouries, 31 December 1914; TNA, WO 94/50/4, W. A. Robinson to the Governor of the Tower; TNA, WORK 14/226, public announcement of 12 March 1915.
87 TNA, WORK 14/4/7; WORK 14/234, report on the state of the Armouries, 1915.
88 TNA, WORK 14/226, 25 April 1916; WORK 14/183; *The Times* (1 April 1916).
89 TNA, WORK 14/973, report on the state of the Armouries, 1913–1938; Carkeet-Jones 1950, pp. 121–3; Hearsey 1960, pp. 234–5.
90 ffoulkes 1939, p. 58. In December 1913 a scheme had been drawn up of how the White Tower armouries would operate once the basement and entrance floors had been opened, which also made extensive use of the north-east stair, but with the entrance to the building remaining on the south front (TNA, WORK 14/226, 4 December 1913).
91 The Curator's office remained here until 1933, when the office was moved to the first floor of the Martin Tower, and the turret was used instead as a workshop for repairing items in the collection (TNA, WORK 14/973, report on the state of the Armouries for 1933).
92 TNA, WORK 14/234, report on the state of the Armouries, 1916.
93 ffoulkes, unlike Dillon, came to curatorship through academic rather than military training. Nevertheless, he was very much Dillon's protégé, and in his memoirs recorded the moment when he agreed to take on the post at the Tower: 'One afternoon in November 1913 during a walk in the woods at Ditchley,

Lord Dillon stopped, and in his rather abrupt manner asked "will you take over the Tower?"' (ffoulkes 1939, p. 44). He was highly influential in the discussions that led to the creation of the Imperial War Museum in 1920.

94 TNA, WORK 14/125, passim.

95 ffoulkes 1939, p. 64.

96 For details of the rearrangement, see Charles ffoulkes's detailed annual reports for the years 1916 and 1917 in TNA, WORK 14/234, and his revised edition of Loftie's *Authorised Guide to the Tower of London* of 1918. At this time, the figure of Queen Elizabeth and her page, which had been the focus of the Spanish Armoury since the 1770s, was considered unhistoric and removed to the cellars of the London Museum (ffoulkes 1939, p. 67).

97 Goulder 1961, pp. 40–1, shows this arrangement still in place.

98 TNA, WORK 14/2418.

99 See TNA, WORK 14/1497, A. Heasman to Mr Wilson; Carkeet-Jones 1950; Parnell 1998c, pp. 83–100; Hearsey 1960, pp. 236–9.

100 TNA, WORK 14/2418 and 14/1497.

101 Ministry of Works, AM 56174/01 in the care of Historic Royal Palaces Trust. TNA, WORK 14/2418; WORK 14/2764.

102 Ministry of Works, AM 56174/01/B. See Chapter Two, p. 64.

103 See Chapter Two, pp. 54, 63–4.

104 TNA, WORK 14/2764, unfoliated.

105 Ministry of Works, AM 56174/01/B; TNA, WORK 14/2764.

106 Ministry of Works, AM 56174/01/B.

107 TNA, WORK 14/2420.

108 TNA, WORK 14/2420.

109 TNA, WORK 14/2420.

110 Ministry of Works, AM 56174/01/B.

111 TNA, WORK 14/2420.

112 *The Times* (8 December 1964), pp. 8, 14, 22; TNA, WORK 14/2723, A. R. Dufty to K. Newis, 1 March 1965. The great Restoration storehouse to the east of the White Tower, now called the New Armouries, opened (following major works to the building) as an extension to the displays in the White Tower in 1961, which in turn eased the pressure on space when successive parts of the White Tower had to close for repairs (TNA, WORK 14/2702, fols 1–4; *The Times*, 28 June 1961).

113 TNA, WORK 14/2800, notes of a meeting at the Tower, 12 October 1966; WORK 14/2764.

114 *The Times* (8 April 1964); Hammond 1986.

115 TNA, WORK 14/2415, fols 38 ff.

116 TNA, WORK 14/2415, fols 61r, 64r, 64v; WORK 14/2800.

117 TNA, WORK 14/2415, fol. 64r–v.

118 TNA, WORK 14/2415, fol. 94r; WORK 14/2764; WORK 14/2800; *The Times* (5 February 1968).

119 Dr Geoffrey Parnell was responsible for both its identification and for its reinstatement; I am grateful to him for discussing this with me. *The Guardian* (23 March 1998).

120 TNA, WORK 14/226, proposed the access scheme of 1913, which involved an entrance on the south of the entrance floor.

121 TNA, WORK 14/1497, improvements to the Tower, 2 November 1943.

122 TNA, WORK 14/2800; WORK 14/2815. Some changes to the displays were necessary to accommodate this new entrance; the newly configured entrance floor displays were opened by the Duke of Edinburgh in May 1974 (*The Times*, 18 July 1974).

123 See Chapter Two, pp. 47–8.

124 *The Times* (18 July 1974); Blackmore 1976, p. 38.

125 TNA, WORK 14/2764; *The Times* (18 January 1975).

126 The History Gallery (now the Gallery Shop) to the south of the keep was opened to mark this event (*The Times*, 18 January 1978).

127 Draper 1977. The Governor of the Tower was thereafter to answer to the Chief Executive of the Historic Royal Palaces Agency.

128 *Board of Trustees of the Armouries Accounts, 2003–4*, London, 2004.

129 *Royal Armouries Yearbook*, 1 (1996). The plan to move was part of the scheme called 'Strategy 2000'. For a different view of how the White Tower should be shown, see R. A. Brown 1979, pp. 107–8.

130 See 'Review of the Year', *Royal Armouries Yearbook*, 2 (1997) and *Royal Armouries Yearbook*, 3 (1998). The new museum in Leeds opened to the public on 30 March 1996. I am grateful to Dr Geoffrey Parnell for discussing this with me.

131 The redisplay of 1995–8 saw the rooms shown as follows. On the second floor are a temporary exhibition area (east room) and a display on the history of the Ordnance and Armoury offices in the Tower of London (west room). The first floor contains displays on the medieval history of the castle, and of the White Tower in particular (east room), and some of the most important, particularly the royal, suits of armour from the sixteenth and seventeenth centuries (west room). On the entrance floor are a re-creation of the Line of Kings and other related material (east room), material relating to the Small Armoury and Grand Storehouse (west room) and material from the Spanish/Queen Elizabeth's armouries in the south-west room. The ground floor houses objects from the 'Train of Artillery' and tells the story of the destruction of the Grand Storehouse. A large shop is housed in the west room of the basement.

Chapter Nine: The Ancestry of the White Tower

1 See, for example, De Caumont 1853, pp. 408–44.

2 Fayolle-Lussac 1974, p. 122. See also Verbruggen 1950; Flori 1997.

3 De Boüard 1974, pp. 33–9.

4 De Boüard 1974, p. 27.

5 De Boüard 1974, p. 54.

6 De Boüard 1974, pp. 50–53.

7 De Boüard 1974, p. 61.

8 Author's observation, 2001.

9 Early 2004.

10 Helgaud de Fleury, ed. Bautier, p. 92: 'Nam tercia sabbati in oratorio turris Karoli collo-

quens cum quodam familiaritate perfecta sibi conjuncto . . .'; that is, 'The following Tuesday, coming together with one of his most intimate associates in the Oratory of the Tower of Charles . . .'.

11 Héliot 1974, p. 221.

12 Flodoard, ed. Lauer, p. 24: 'Presidii etiam Heriberti turris super Maternam fluvium, ubi Karolus custodiebatur, subitaneo conflagravit incendio.'

13 Flodoard, ed. Lauer, pp. 122–3: 'Regressa Remos regina cum fraterni auxilii pollicitatione, rex Ludowicus Laudunum improvisus aggreditur et noctu muro latenter a suis ascenso disruptisque portarum seris, oppidum ingreditur, capitque custodes, praeter eos qui turrim regiae domus conscenderant, quam ipse ad portam castri fundaverat. Hanc itaque capere non valens, a civitate secludit, ducto intrinsecus muro'; that is, 'When the queen returned from Reims with the promise of her brother's help, King Louis made a surprise attack on Laon. Some of his men having scaled the walls secretly by night and unbarred the gates, Louis broke into the town and captured the guards, except those who had climbed up into the tower of the royal house, which he had himself constructed by the town gate. Being unable to capture the tower, he cut it off by building a wall round it on the inside.'

14 Flodoard, ed. Lauer, p. 70. Flodoard is here describing Louis IV's capture of Laon from Hugh Capet: 'Interea rex Ludovicus evocatus ab Artaldo archiepiscopo regreditur, ingressusque Laudunum, arcem novam nuper inibi ab Heriberto aedificatam obsidet, multisque machinis suffoso eversoque muro, cum magno tandem capit labore'; that is, 'Meanwhile, King Louis returned, summoned by Archbishop Artaud, and entering Laon, laid siege to the new stronghold lately built in that place by Herbert, and with immense labour at last captured it by undermining and overturning the wall with a large number of machines.'

15 Lusse 1992, p. 231.

16 A document of 954 was witnessed 'in palatio Lauduni Clavati, apud monasterium sancti Johannis' (*Recueil des Actes de Lothaire et de Louis V*, no. 1, pp. 1–4). For context, see Lusse 1992, p. 241.

17 Flodoard, ed. Lauer, p. 123.

18 For a history of these events and their chronology, see Lot 1891, p. 244. For the identification of the tower mentioned in 949 with that of 988, see Broche 1900–04, p. 181.

19 Richer, ed. Latouche, vol. II, p.172: 'Nam turrim quae adhuc muris humilibus perstabat, pinnis eminentibus exstruxit fossisque patentibus circumquaque vallavit.'

20 Richer, ed. Latouche, vol. II, p. 176: 'turrim quoque potioribus edificiis intra et extra dilatat ac firmat'.

21 'Anno DCCCCLVIII, castrum Codiciacum quidam fideles Artoldi praesulis clandestina capiunt irruptione. Harduinus, subjectus Tetbaldi, cui Tetbaldus idem commiserat cas-

trum, videns oppidum captum, confugit cum suis in arcem. Erat autem turris illa firmissima' (Flodoard, ed. Lauer, p. 145). On these events, see Lesueur 1963, pp. 163–6.

22 For these events and their context, see Lesueur 1963, p. 160; Barthélemy 1984, pp. 50–51.

23 *Chronique de Saint-Pierre-le-Vif*, ed. Bautier, Gilles and Bautier, p. 82 ('turrim Senonice civitatis'), and p. 104 ('In parte vero quadam ipsis urbis turrim maximam edificavit'). See also Chédeville 1992; Kaiser 1981, pp. 512–15.

24 *Chronique de Nantes*, ed. Merlet, p. 92: 'Praecepit [Alanus] eis terrarium magnum in circuitu ecclesiae facere, sicut murus prioris castri steterat: quo facto, turrem principalem faciens seu reficiens, in ea domum suum constitit.' See also Dunbabin 2000, p. 83.

25 Flodoard, ed. Lauer, p. 127: '. . . Hugo cum exercitu Ambianensem petit urbem, ibique in turri, quam Ragembaldus episcopus tenebat, recipitur; alteram vero turrim, quam Arnulfi comitis homines custodiebant, obsidet'.

26 Hubscher 1986, pp. 52–3, 202; Will 1962, pp. 80–81.

27 '. . . Carnoti turrem et Blesii et Cainonis perfecit' (*Chronique de Nantes*, ed. Merlet, p. 108). The *Chronique* is usually dated to *circa* 1050, although it has also been attributed to the twelfth century, and some parts – this passage excepted – certainly date from the thirteenth century (Professor Michael Jones, personal communication).

28 *Cartulaire de St Père de Chartres*, ed. Guérard, p. 23: Among the property of St Père was a plot '. . . infra quoque civitatem a porta quae dicitur Aquaria usque ad portam Cinerosam. Prisci monachi ac canonici post eos, iuxta murum, sicut via dividebat, ab una porta pergens ad alteram portam, jure hereditario totam possederunt terram; sed a comite in civitate introducto facta turri, ac in circuitu vallis censum subripuit aliosque consuetudinarios usus'; that is, '. . . within the town from the gate called *Aquaria* [Porte Evière] as far as the *Cinerosa* gate [Porte Cendreuse]. The monks of old, and the canons after them, held the whole area next to the wall, as the road divided [?] from one gate to another, and held it by hereditary right. But the Count, on being brought into the town, seized the land within the walls, along with their revenues and other customary rights, and built a tower.' Beyond the fact that the plot was clearly intramural, the topographical interpretation of the passage rests on the positions of the two gates (Chédeville 1973, p. 412). These were destroyed after a larger enceinte was created in the late twelfth century.

29 Metais 1898, passim; see especially pp. 1–15 and pls 2 and 3.

30 Chédeville (1973, p. 410) suggests that this tower was the creation of Theobald's great-grandson Odo II (count 996–1037), on the basis of a reference to the 'Count's tower' in a letter of Bishop Fulbert (1006–29), but there seems no reason to attribute the *turris*

that he mentions, and describes as 'the Count's', to Fulbert's contemporary (*Cartulaire de Notre-Dame de Chartres*, ed. Lépinois and Merlet, vol. 1, p. 53).

31 *Chroniques des églises d'Anjou*, ed. Marchegay and Mabille, p. 248: 'Theobaldus . . . Qui vivens turres altes construxit et aedes, / Unum Carnotum; sed apud Dunense reatum / Non minuit proprium, turritum dans ibi castrum.'

32 Flodoard, ed. Lauer, p. 155: 'Catalaunensem urbem, praesule Gibuino egresso, Heribertus et Rotbertus fratres obsident, explicitisque tandem nundinis, igne succendunt, milites vero in turre quadam loci conscensa liberantur'; that is, 'Bishop Giboin having left it, the city of Châlons was besieged by the brothers Herbert and Robert, and after some weeks had passed, they set fire to it, sparing only the soldiers who had taken refuge in the tower of that place.'

33 For the historical context, see Dunbabin 2000, pp. 95–7; Clause and Ravaux 1981, p. 33. The latter authors provide a reconstructed plan of the Carolingian town (pl. 2) and speculate as to the identity of the *turris*, asking whether it was perhaps a *donjon* or the narthex of the cathedral.

34 Richer, ed. Latouche, vol. II, pp. 196 and 198. See below, p. 235 and note 97. For the context of these events, see Boussinesq and Laurent 1933, vol. I, p. 235.

35 Robert of Torigny, ed. Howlett, vol. IV, p. 106: 'Henricus rex circa turrem Rothomagi, quam aedificavit primus Ricardus dux Normannorum, in palatium sibi, murum altum et latum cum propugnaculis aedificat, et aedificia ad mansionem regiam congrua infra eundem murum parat. Ipsi vero turri propugnacula quae deerant, addit.'; that is, 'King Henry built a wide and high wall with battlements [?] around the Tower of Rouen, which Richard, first Duke of the Normans, had built in his palace, and created a building fit for a king's house beneath that wall'. Jacques Le Maho (1996, p. 66) argues forcefully for the truth of Robert de Torigny's attribution. The *turris* at Rouen is also mentioned by William of Jumièges (*Gesta Normannorum ducum*, ed. Van Houts, vol. II, p. 8), as the place where Duke Richard II (996–1026) imprisoned his rebellious half-brother, William I, Count of Eu.

36 Le Maho 1996, pp. 65–6; Le Maho 2000, p. 74 and n. 3.

37 Robert of Torigny, ed. Howlett, vol. IV, p. 106: 'Turrem nihilominus excelsam fecit in castello Cadomensi'.

38 De Boüard 1979, pp. 101, 103. The tower was demolished in the nineteenth century down to what was then ground level. The substructure was excavated in the 1960s and remains exposed.

39 William of Malmesbury, *Gesta regum anglorum*, ed. Mynors, Thomson and Winterbottom, p. 712: 'Quo concesso, in superiora Rotomagensis turris duxit, iussoque ut late circumposita diligenter ex arcis edito specu-

laretur, sua per hironiam omni futura pronuntians, inopinum ex propugnaculo deturbans in subiectum Sequanam precipitavit, comitibus qui secum aderant pariter impellentibus, protestatus nullam'; that is, 'This being granted he took him up to the top of the tower of Rouen and ordered him to survey the wide prospect from the tower's top, with the assurance – it was a bitter jest – that all would soon be his; they then caught him off his guard, and with help from companions who were with him, threw him from the battlements headlong down into the Seine below.'

40 *Antiquus Cartularius Ecclesiae Baiocensis* (ed. Bourrienne, vol. I, no. ii, p. 3): the charter, confirming a purchase of land by Odo de Conteville, Bishop of Bayeux, was sealed 'apud Rothomagum in Aula Turris'.

41 Le Maho 1996, p. 67 and n. 22. See also Le Maho 2000.

42 'Translatio secunda Sancti Audoeni', in Bollandus et al., *Acta sanctorum* (Augusti), IV, cols 822–3: 'Eadem nocte, qua haec acciderunt, praefato duci Ricardo apud Baiocasse remoranti, ibique palatium sibi et arcem fabricanti, Audoënus pontificalibus insulis redimitus in somnis apparuit.' Later, in a passage addressed to the duke: 'Tu . . . tibi et heredibus tuis palatia et arces construis, mundique praepolles divitiis, et vario vestimentorum ornatu procedis.' See also Renoux 1987, p. 121.

43 Yver 1957, p. 33; of Evreux Yver wrote: 'Here also was a seat of Richard I, and later also a tower.' Neither the evidence for the tower nor its date is discussed; the claim is presumably based on Orderic's mention of a *dangio* at Evreux in his account of the events of 1087 (Orderic Vitalis, ed. Chibnall, vol. IV, p. 114).

44 Impey and Lorans 1998, pp. 69–72.

45 Impey and Lorans 1998, pp. 65–9, pl. VIa.

46 Orderic Vitalis, ed. Chibnall, vol. IV, p. 290: 'magister . . . operis'.

47 Garin le Lohérain, ed. Paris, vol. I, pp. 49–50.

48 Devaux 1887, pp. 11–27; Lot 1899, pp. 274–5.

49 All three paintings are held in the Musée Municipale at Pithiviers. I am grateful to M. Jacques Charles and M. Claude Perron for supplying photographs of the paintings and for much other information.

50 As is clear from the *cadastre* of that date.

51 Orderic Vitalis, ed. Chibnall, vol. IV, p. 290: 'turris famosa, ingens et munitissima'.

52 Impey 2002b, pp. 190–97.

53 Mesqui 1998, passim.

54 Dormoy 1998, passim.

55 Mesqui 1998, pp. 65–125.

56 The results of the study ordered by the Direction Regionale des Affaires Culturelles in 1999 were published in summary by Victorine Mataouchek (2000, p. 441): to date, the full *Etude archéologique du bâti* of 2000 remains unpublished. Mme Mataouchek's attribution of the building's first heightening

to 'about 1030–35', however, has been convincingly challenged by Christian Corvisier (2004, p. 31), who places it in the early twelfth century. I am very grateful to Mme Aline Pouget, M. Frédéric Aubanton and M. Bernard Vella for arranging access to the interior of the Tour de César.

57 The arcades collapsed in 1840, destroying most of the basement vault below (Valéry-Radot 1931, p. 19). The engaged piers at the ends of the arcades and the springing of their arches survive.

58 Author's observation, 2004 and 2006. In 2003–4 the building was thoroughly repaired and a study of its fabric undertaken by Victorine Mataouchek, yet to be published. For brief historical details and description, see Mesqui 1997, pp. 267–9; Siguret 1957. I am very grateful to Mme Françoise Lecuyer for extended access to the site.

59 The remains of this are apparently incorporated in the later building and gatehouse attached to the north side of the main block. Its existence is also claimed by Siguret (1957, pp. 8–9), who also offers a reconstructed plan.

60 Geoffrey's eldest son, Hugh, succeeded his father but disappeared in the mid-1040s (for genealogical and historical context, see K. Thompson 2002, pp. 32–40).

61 Norgate (1887, vol. 1, p. 103) places these events during Fulk Nerra's absence on pilgrimage and Maurice's regency.

62 'Chronica de Gestis Consulum Andegavorum', ed. Halphen and Poupardin, p. 46.

63 'Gesta Ambaziensium Dominorum', Halphen and Poupardin, p. 83.

64 'Gesta Ambaziensium Dominorum', Halphen and Poupardin, pp. 83 and 89.

65 See Boussard 1961, p. 78.

66 Bosseboeuf 1897, pp. 39–40.

67 Hérault du Roy Berry, ed. Stevenson, pp. 352–3: 'une large tour quarree, de la fachon de celle de Londres, ou celle de celle Damboize, se elle estoit entiere'.

68 'Chronica de Gestis Consulum Andegavorum', ed. Halphen and Poupardin, p. 58.

69 Halphen 1906, p. 148.

70 Le Héricher 1845, vol. 1, pp. 11–12; Pigeon 1888, vol. 1, pp. 287–8.

71 Impey 2002a; Nicolas-Méry 2002.

72 Faucherre 2004a, pp. 69–73. See also Mesqui 1991–3, vol. 1, p. 114

73 M.-D. Delayeun (2003, p. 83), author of the most recent study of the building, places the initial construction at the beginning of the century on the basis of its construction and the place of Montbazon in the struggle between Fulk Nerra and Odo II of Blois.

74 Delayeun 2003, p. 83.

75 See Deyres 1969; Delayeun 2003, pp. 77–8. The cartulary of Cormery (*Cartulaire de Cormery*, ed. Bourrassé, no. XXXI, p. 62) shows that Fulk Nerra (died 1040) built a castle (*castellum*) here, but not, of course, this tower.

76 Mortet and Deschamps 1995, p. 7; Aimon, ed. De Certain, p. 139.

77 'Chronica de Gestis Consulum Andegavorum', ed. Halphen and Poupardin, p. 46: 'domus defensabile'.

78 William of Poitiers, ed. Davis and Chibnall, p. 10: 'aulam . . . lapideam . . . arcis usum'.

79 Bocquet and Mastrolorenzo 2001; Renoux 2003, p. 39.

80 For a recent description and plans, see Yvard and Michel 1996, pp. 6–19. The second phase has been dated by dendrochronology to 1075.

81 Mesqui 1998, pp. 70–71.

82 Mesqui 1998, pp. 96–100.

83 See Chapter Four, pp. 132–6.

84 *Chronique de Nantes*, ed. Merlet, p. 92.

85 Helgaud de Fleury, ed. Bautier, p. 92.

86 *Antiquus Cartularius Ecclesiae Baiocensis* (ed. Bourrienne, vol. 1, no. ii, p. 3).

87 Impey and Lorans 1998, pp. 73–4.

88 Impey 2000, pp. 212–13.

89 *Miracula Sancti Benedicti*, VIII, c. xvi (Aimon, ed. De Certain, p. 299): 'Turris ergo in illa in superioribus suis solarium habebat, ubi idem Seguinus cum sua manebat familia, colloquebatur, convivabatur, et noctibus quiescebat. Porro in eius inferioribus habebatur cellarium, diversi generis retinens apothecas, ad recipienda et conservanda humani victus necessaria idoneas'; that is, 'This tower had in its upper part a solar, where Seguinus and his family stayed and met and conversed and ate together and slept at night. Further, it had in its lower regions a cellar comprising various compartments, to receive and store foodstuffs necessary for preserving human life.'

90 'Translatio secunda Sancti Audoeni', in Bollandus et al., *Acta sanctorum* (Augusti), IV, cols 822–3.

91 Renoux 1992, pp. 194–7.

92 For plans and views, see Mallet 1991, pp. 12–14, 27; for a convincing interpretation, see Brodeur, Chevet and Mastrolorenzo 1998, pp. 104–111.

93 Flodoard, ed. Lauer, p. 135.

94 *Chronique de Saint-Pierre-le-Vif*, ed. Bautier, Gilles and Bautier, p. 110: 'Ipse vero comes fugiens nudus evasit, frater autem ejus Frotmundus et quidam milites urbis turrim defenderunt multis diebus: quos tandem rex cepit et victus pietate vivos abire sivit'; that is, 'The count [Rainald II] fleeing defenceless, his brother Fromond and a number of soldiers held out in the tower of the city for many days. When at last the king captured it, he piously let the defeated men escape with their lives.'

95 *Chronique de Saint-Pierre-le-Vif*, ed. Bautier, Gilles and Bautier, p. 82: '. . . in turrim Senonice civitatis'.

96 Flodoard, ed. Lauer, pp. 123–4. The 12th-century *Modernorum regum francorum actus* similarly relates that 'Turrim tamen, quam ipse nuper ad portam castri fundaverat, capere non potuit; quam ideo a civitate seclusit, ducto intresecus muro' (Flodoard, ed. Lauer, p. 217).

97 Richer, ed. Latouche, vol. II, pp. 196 and 198: 'Arnulfus aeque turbatum clamore sese stimu-lat, et fingens metum, turrim petiit atque conscendit. Quem comites secuti post se ostia observere. Karolus Arnulfum perquirens nec reperiens ubinam lateret scrutabatur. Cui cum proderetur in turris cacumine latere, ostio mox custodes adhibuit; et quoniam nec cibum nec arma ante congesserant, Karolo cedunt atque a turri egressi sunt.' For the context of these events, see Boussinesq and Laurent 1933, vol. 1, p. 235.

98 Mesqui 1998, pp. 94–6.

99 Impey and Lorans 1998, pp. 36–7.

100 Impey 2002b, p. 190.

101 See Chapter Ten, p. 273.

102 'Historia Sancti Florentii Salmurensis', in *Chroniques des églises d'Anjou*, ed. Marchegay and Mabille, pp. 217–328.

103 Lesueur 1963, p. 225.

104 Le Maho 2000, p. 74.

105 Chédeville 1973, p. 263.

106 Le Maho 1996, p. 66.

107 'Gesta Ambaziensium Dominorum' ed. Halphen and Poupardin, p. 89–90: 'Erant autem tunc Ambazie tres optimates, quorum nullus alii credebat fore secundus nec erat et quorum nullum servitium alter alteri debebat, habentes singuli domos defensabiles: Supplicius, dominus turris lapidee, et Fulcoius de Torrineio, quem comes Martellus primus ibi hereditaverat, qui dominus domus que mota Fulcoii dicebatur erat; tertius erat Ernulfus, filius Leonii de Magduno, custos domus consulis que vocatur Domicilium, ad cuius ius pars major Ambaziensis castri pertinebat.'

108 De Boüard 1974, p. 102.

109 R. A. Brown 1976, p. 24.

110 See, for example, Oswald, Schaefer and Sennhauser 1966; Fernie 1983.

111 Dieter Barz, personal communication. For a description, see Binding 1996, pp. 92–3.

112 Bur 2002, pp. 76 and 80.

113 Héliot 1974, pp. 229–30.

114 Borger and Oedinger 1969.

115 Hinz 1981, pp. 74–88.

116 Le Maho 1996, p. 67 and n. 29.

117 I am grateful to Kathleen Thompson for advice on this point.

118 Early 2004.

119 See Prigent 2003, p. 19; Vergnolle 1989, 1996.

120 See Chapter Ten, pp. 273.

121 Dixon and Marshall 1993a; Coad and Streeten 1982. This was not the case at Langeais, which, encouraged by the discoveries at Doué, Marcel Deyres saw as having become defendable, and thus in his terms a *donjon*, only *circa* 1100 (Deyres 1974, pp. 8–9, 21).

122 Héliot 1974, pp. 225–6.

123 G. T. Clark 1884, vol. 1, p. 430. See also Chapter Ten, pp. 244–7.

124 See Drury 1982, p. 399, and Stevenson 1982, pp. 409–13.

125 Stevenson 1982, p. 113.

126 Round 1882, p. 26, n. 5.

127 Drury 1982, p. 399.

128 Drury 1982, p. 400.

129 Drury 1984, p. 31 and fig. 12.

130 Paul Drury, personal communication.

131 R. A. Brown 1965, p. 81.

132 Orderic Vitalis, ed. Chibnall, vol. IV, p. 290.

133 Douglas 1964, p. 5.

134 Douglas 1964, p. 90.

135 See White 1948, p. 141 and n. 7.

136 Loyd 1951, p. 52; Musset 1991, p. 92.

137 See Chapter Two, pp. 44–5.

138 Musset 1991, p. 92.

Chapter Ten: The Influence of the White Tower on the Great Towers of the Twelfth Century

1 For example, R. A. Brown 1976; M. W. Thompson 1991. A full account in gazetteer form of the castles, including great towers, of this era has been given by Renn 1965. French examples are summarised by Mesqui (1991–3, vol. I, pp. 89–221), who terms the great tower 'la tour maîtresse'.

2 For example, Fernie 2000, pp. 53–82.

3 M. W. Thompson 1991, pp. 3–15.

4 Thompson's plea is specifically discounted by Dixon and Marshall 1993a. The alternative approach, to treat thematically the roles of the castle, rather than their architectural parts, was used by R. A. Brown in his first edition (1953), and is employed fruitfully by McNeill 1992.

5 The fullest survey to attempt groupings is Renn 1960.

6 'Too big for a chamber (*camera*) and not big enough for a hall (*aula*)': a jest by William Rufus on his new hall at Westminster (Colvin, Brown and Taylor 1963–82, vol. I, p. 45).

7 This has figured reasonably frequently in the literature. The present summary is based on the full account in Higham and Barker 1992, pp. 115–17 and n. 3 on p. 373. See also Chapter Four, pp. 132, 136.

8 See Chapter Four pp. 126–32 and 136–9.

9 Colvin, Brown and Taylor 1963–82, vol. I, pp. 29–32. Further comparisons are discussed by P. Drury (1982, p. 400), who points out that the design of the apse may have derived from the shape of the underlying Roman building, and so have influenced the layout at the White Tower. Fernie (2000, p. 66) believes the influence went from the Tower to Colchester. See also Chapter Nine, pp. 239–40.

10 The following discussion necessarily considers the structure at its finished date of *circa* 1120, since too little remains of the first phase to make a coherent plan. I am grateful to Paul Drury and Eric Fernie for their advice.

11 Drury 1982, fig. 39 and p. 395.

12 In this it would resemble the later phase at Norwich, which seems to be of the same date.

13 Fernie 2000, pp. 65–6.

14 Dixon 1996, pp. 47–56.

15 Notably at all the obvious *comparanda*, the White Tower, Norwich, Castle Rising and Falaise.

16 The charter of Henry I to Eudo is dated 1101, but he was a landholder in Colchester in 1086, and the thirteenth-century Colchester chronicle (unreliable through bias in favour of Eudo, the monks' patron) pre-dated his involvement in the castle to as early as 1072, which is very unlikely (Drury 1982, p. 399). That Eudo was the founder of the castle is emphatically rejected by Colvin, Brown and Taylor 1963–82, vol. I, p. 31, n. 4, but they assume that the building (both Phases 1 and 2) was completed before 1101, and do not consider the possibility of Eudo's finishing the building on Henry I's behalf. The castle was resumed by Henry I at Eudo's death in 1120.

17 For a similar proposition to explain the layout of Henry II's great tower at Orford, see Heslop 1991, pp. 36–58.

18 In an unpublished report by Paul Drury for Norwich City Council, *circa* 1984: this has been rewritten for publication as Drury 2002. Heslop 1994 adds analysis of the dating and the geometry of the design of the building. I am grateful to Paul Drury and Sandy Heslop, and to Brian Ayres, for discussions about the building.

19 What follows is based on Dixon and Marshall 2002.

20 Heslop 1994, pp. 40–41.

21 Drury 2002, figs 4 and 5, pp. 224–5; Heslop 1994, p. 39.

22 Dixon 1996, pp. 47–56; Dixon 1988.

23 Other parts may, of course, have been painted or hung with cloths, but only the 'holding area' (outside the hall door) and the 'waiting room' are treated with carved stonework. This is presumably because these were the areas where people were expected to wait and look around them, rather than focus on the ceremonies or people in the main rooms: all these other rooms are simply finished.

24 Like that in the Tower, the less private approach led to the altar end of the chapel. The royal entrance led to the west end, and one may suspect a dais either here or against the northern wall (the sanctuary itself is orientated aslant the axis of the chapel).

25 The existence of this storey remains controversial. The interpretation of Heslop (1994, p. 49) is that the first-floor rooms were all open to the roof, and that the stair gave access only to the upper mural passageway.

26 For a contemporary parallel for this treatment, compare the narrow tribune galleries that led from the royal upper pew at the west end of the church to the suggested upper chapel in Henry I's church at Melbourne (Donnell 2002).

27 The following analysis is based in part on the account in Bennett, Frere and Stow 1982, pp. 70–88, but differs in the analysis of function of the internal spaces.

28 To avoid confusion, the following description assumes that the longer axis of the building is orientated north–south (rather than north-east–south-west).

29 T. Tatton-Brown in Bennett, Frere and Stow 1982, p. 75.

30 T. Tatton-Brown in Bennett, Frere and Stow 1982, p. 76.

31 Colchester Borough Council 1989, pp. 5, 11; Drury 1982, p. 400, suggests that the period 1081–7 is the most likely time for this threat.

32 One may contrast the treatment given to the keep at Newcastle, when this work was stopped during the Scottish invasion of 1173–4. Here there are no signs of battlementing, but simply a horizontal line in the courses of masonry, and so if any merlons were placed as suggested at Colchester they were still soft enough to be removed when building resumed.

33 Slightly variant accounts are presented by Hull and by Drury in Drury 1982, pp. 317–23 and 398–9. In addition to the possible rebuilding of the entrance door, Hull points out that the failure to reuse all the garderobe chutes provided by the first builders suggests a change of plan (Hull in Drury 1982, pp. 322 and 393). Fernie (2000, p. 67, n. 19), on the other hand, is unhappy about the notion that the doorway and the stair were inserted in Phase 2. He considers that the entrance door and the adjacent staircase were part of the first phase; he uses this as an argument for an original design involving several storeys. The matter remains unresolved, and the present account follows the arguments of Drury.

34 See above, Chapter Two, pp. 30–9, and Chapter Three, pp. 102–5.

35 Drury 2002, p. 212.

36 Dixon and Marshall 2002, p. 235.

37 Heslop 1994, p. 7.

38 Rapidly built *circa* 1097–9 (Colvin, Brown and Taylor 1963–82, vol. I, p. 45).

39 Heslop 1991, p. 8; Drury 1982, pp. 398–9.

40 Drury 1982, p. 399.

41 Armitage 1912, p. 120.

42 Derek Renn (1960a, p. 11) has suggested a start date early in the reign of William Rufus (1087–1100), but only tentatively. He later argued persuasively for a period of construction at some point between *circa* 1085 and *circa* 1125 (D. Renn in Bennett, Frere and Stow 1982, p. 73).

43 Colvin, Brown and Taylor 1963–82, vol. I, p. 39.

44 These are Domfront in Orne and Caen in Calvados (Normandy), and Corfe and Gloucester in England. Domfront and Corfe were of three storeys, and were subdivided by a spine wall, but the other details of the accommodation are sketchy (see below). Caen is now represented by the excavated foundations alone, and Gloucester only by a stylised sketch.

45 Colvin, Brown and Taylor 1963–82, vol. I, pp. 42–3; for details of the site and its excavations, see Hurst 1984; Darvill et al. 1988. The ceremony itself was perhaps held in the ancient palace of Kingsholm near Gloucester (Colvin, Brown and Taylor 1963–82, vol. I, pp. 44–5). For a discussion of this significant ceremony, see Biddle 1986, especially pp. 52–5. The building of the great tower marked a change in the use of Gloucester, with the abandonment of the crown-wearing ceremony and the use of Kingsholm.

46 The effects of a thorough nineteenth-century restoration have recently been greatly exaggerated by a brutal modern rebuilding, which has concealed much of the original interior work and has created several novel features. The best account of the building is still Doranlo 1953. A shorter description is provided by Mesqui 1991–3, vol. I, p. 123.

47 Until recently, this was used to provide access from Henry I's keep to the royal apartments ('le petit donjon'), added at a slightly lower level to the west by his grandson, Henry II. The opening has now been abandoned, and a staircase opened in the frame of one of the original garderobes.

48 The best account is provided by R. A. Brown 1978c; for a full description of the archaeological work on the site and a reassessment of its history, see Morley and Gurney 1997.

49 The design is described and illustrated in Dixon 1996.

50 Morley and Gurney 1997, p. 3.

51 Crouch 1992, p. 255; Hume 1972.

52 The exception is perhaps the scene in which William decides to seize the shipwrecked Harold. Here, perhaps significantly in this military context, the background has been identified as the great tower of Rouen (one of the antecedents of the White Tower). Wilson 1985, p. 177, however, identifies the image as the walls of the town of Rouen.

53 I am grateful to Rick Turner and to Roland Harris for discussions about their recent survey and separate studies of this building. I am more comfortable with an eleventh-century rather than a twelfth-century date for the structure, and would suggest a building period of 1067–71 for perhaps the lower two-thirds of the keep, finished off more slowly.

54 Gem 1986.

55 Stocker and Vince 1997; Stocker 2004.

56 Dixon 1976, p. 104.

57 For example, at the Porta Nigra at Trier, Germany, still standing to its full height, and marked by elaborate blind arcading.

58 Fernie 2001, p. 117. The masonry of Winchester demonstrates the speed of work: it is unusually coarse even for the period, and the construction from the crossing outwards is also unusual, though it allowed simultaneous building of all four arms.

59 Dormoy 1998; Durand 1996. See Chapter Nine, pp. 230–1.

60 Mesqui 1991–3, vol. I; Charbonneau-Lassay 1934, pp. 10–13.

61 Author's observation and conclusion. See also Plant 2006.

62 These and other tall towers of the period before circa 1150 are discussed in Renn 1994b.

63 Watkins-Pitchford 1931. The documentary history is fully described in Mason and Barker 1961. For a discussion of the significance of the tower, see Dixon, forthcoming.

64 Hollister (2001, p. 172) estimates that Robert de Bellême was the richest of Henry's barons, with an annual income in his English lands alone of almost £2,500.

65 Colvin, Brown and Taylor 1963–82, vol. II, p. 576, suggest a period around 1165 for the building of the great tower, relying on the references to 'operation turris de Brug' in the Pipe Rolls. But the design of the roof, the simplicity of the embrasures and the small, square masonry of the ashlars imply a date a generation or two before this time. The raising of the tower and the apparent insertion of an upper floor may belong to the later building period.

66 Cunliffe and Munby 1985, pp. 72–81, 120–22.

67 For a general picture, see King and Alcock 1969, an important paper that sets out clearly the interesting variation in the presence or absence of mottes in castles across England and Wales. For the detail of the timberwork, and the forms that it took, see Higham and Barker 1992.

68 This point, sometimes apparently overlooked, was made clearly by Hamilton Thompson 1912, p. 112, and is picked up by Pounds 1990, p. 20, though his discussion relies too much on his belief that the expense of the buildings limited their construction.

69 Robert of Torigny lists two dozen castles, many with great towers, which Henry had built in Normandy and the Vexin: cf. Colvin, Brown and Taylor 1963–82, vol. I, p. 35.

70 In addition, of course, to his completing the older palatial towers at Norwich, and perhaps Canterbury, Colchester and the White Tower itself, as discussed above.

71 Having paid his brother Robert £3,000, more than half his inheritance, for the privilege (Hollister 2001, p. 49).

72 Decaëns 2001; Cormier 2001. For the extraordinary story of Henry's successful coup de main, see Hollister 2001, pp. 86–7.

73 Decaëns 2001, p. 290; but it seems more likely to have contained fewer storeys: see note 74 below.

74 So Decaëns 2001. The fenestration of the northern side shows that this contained a basement and at least two storeys below the wall-heads. The western side (of which a little more than half survives) seems to show the first-floor hall rising to match the height of two of the northern storeys: its tall window is at the same level as the upper windows of the northern side, but there are no obvious traces of putlog holes or ledges to support an extra floor on this side. In addition, the featureless upper room identified by Decaëns and Cormier seems unlikely. Scaffolding, however, is required to see whether the visible scarcement ledge for the upper floor is in fact a gutter.

75 A date of circa 1105 is as given in RCHM 1960, pp. 57–78. A better guess might be almost any point in the period 1080 to 1120: thanks to John Goodall for discussion of the date.

76 This is suggested by Thackray 1990, p. 24

77 Thackray 1990, pp. 27–35; RCHM 1960.

78 Renn 1994b, pp. 10–11.

79 I am grateful to John Goodall for kindly giving me a sight of his forthcoming text, which convincingly re-dates the building.

80 Goodall, however, points out the similarity in plan to the projecting turrets and stepped plinth at Brandon, a much-ruined keep also on the de Clintons' land.

81 Dixon and Marshall 1993a.

82 Bates 1891, pp. 235–6, relying on the Pipe Roll entry 'in operacione turris de Baenburc', which perhaps relates to the second phase of rebuilding.

83 For a summary of the disputes about the dating, see Colvin, Brown and Taylor 1963–82, vol. II, p. 596, n. 2.

84 Colvin, Brown and Taylor 1963–82, vol. II, p. 595.

85 McCarthy, Summerson and Annis 1990, p. 121.

86 I owe this point to John Goodall.

87 The charter of Henry I making the donation of the perpetual custody of the castle specifically grants Archbishop de Corbeil the right to build a tower, and the building is attributed to him by Gervase of Canterbury, writing at the end of the century (R. A. Brown 1986, p. 9; Colvin, Brown and Taylor 1963–82, vol. I, p. 807). De Corbeil was consecrated in February 1123 and died on 21 November 1136.

88 R. A. Brown 1986, p. 12.

89 R. A. Brown 1986, especially pp. 30–47.

90 R. A. Brown 1986, p. 40; this seems a reasonable conjecture, particularly in view of the former access to the turret of the forebuilding in the northern wall of the mural chamber.

91 The jambs of this door have not been preserved, but similar pairs of openings give access through the spine wall on the level of the basement, the entrance floor and the uppermost floor (where both openings preserve their jambs), and this appears to have been a constant feature of the design.

92 R. A. Brown 1986, p. 41.

93 K. Thompson 2002, p. 11.

94 RCHM 1916, pp. 51–8; M. W. Thompson 1991, p. 77.

95 Dixon and Marshall 1993b.

96 For extended discussion of this, see Dixon and Marshall 1993b, pp. 21–2.

97 Coad and Streeten 1982, pp. 178–82, 191–2.

98 Coad and Streeten 1982, pp. 168–9; the resultant appearance is shown in fig. 16 on p. 182.

99 Stocker 1991, pp. 38–9. This was almost the last of the crown-wearing ceremonies (the final one was held by Henry II at Worcester in 1158), although 're-coronations' with great pomp were later undertaken by both Richard and John: for details, see Bartlett 2000, pp. 128–9.

100 In Colvin, Brown and Taylor 1963–82, vol. I, pp. 64–7.

101 Robert of Torigny, ed. Howlett, p. 104.

102 For discussion of the dating and cost of the work, see Colvin, Brown and Taylor 1963–82, vol. II, pp. 830–31.

103 G. T. Clark 1884, vol. I, p. 189.

104 Chronicles of Stephen, Henry II and Richard I, ed. Howlett, vol. I, p. 104.

105 Colvin, Brown and Taylor 1963–82, vol. II, p. 769, emphasises the king's intention to contain the power of the Earl of Norfolk, Hugh Bigod, and outlines the urgency of the work; for further detail, see R. A. Brown 1952, pp. 127–35; Bartlett 2000, pp. 278–9.

106 Heslop 1991 give a clear analysis of the building, and its designer's intent. For drawings and description, see R. A. Brown 1964.

107 For example, the leaf-shaped *donjons* at Etampes or, earlier, Houdan. The sophistication of Orford's planning lies in the complexity of the mural chambers and passages and their integration in a small footprint.

108 R. A. Brown 1964, p. 16.

109 Colvin, Brown and Taylor 1963–82, vol. II, pp. 746–8; Knowles 1926.

110 Harvey 1954, p. 184; Colvin, Brown and Taylor 1963–82, vol. II, p. 746.

111 Colvin, Brown and Taylor 1963–82, vol. II, pp. 629–33.

112 Most of the windows and fireplaces were rebuilt in the later Middle Ages and afterwards, and the position of the original fireplaces, if different from their successors, is not clear.

113 It is generally assumed that these spine doors, though modernised in the fifteenth century, are in their original positions.

114 A comparison with the enormous and lavish round *donjon* at Coucy, built at a period when circular plans had become almost universal in high-class buildings, shows an internal area of no more than 250 sq. m, in comparison with the 1,230 sq. m of Dover.

115 For a discussion of the developments in the later Middle Ages, see Dixon and Lott 1993.

116 See Chapter Nine, pp. 240–1.

117 Chibnall 1986, p. 11.

118 Atherton et al. 1996, pp. 18–25.

119 See Chapter Two, p. 30.

120 For a discussion of these years of failure and recovery, see Hollister 2001, pp. 61–95.

121 Louise 1993.

122 Renn 1971.

123 Lethbridge 1934, p. 121, who, however, supposes that it was intended to build a keep in the centre of the courtyard.

124 Bradbury 1996, Chapter 6.

125 Bradbury 1996, p. 144; one may doubt Barber's assertion that the reverse 'did little to damp his youthful hopes', especially since it led to two years of inactivity in his father's court (Barber 2003, p. 36).

Chapter Eleven: The White Tower in Medieval Myth and Legend

1 Discussed below, pp. 281–4.

2 Geoffrey of Monmouth, ed. Wright, pp. xv–xvi; see also Crick 1991, pp. 1–2.

3 'Belinus vero in Britanniam reversus est et cum tranquillitate reliquis vite sue diebus patriam tractavit . . . Fecit etiam in urbe Trinovantum ianuam mire fabrice super ripam Thamensis quam de nomine suo cives temporibus suis Belinesgata vocant. Desuper vero edificavit turrim mire magnitudinis portumque subtus ad pedem applicantibus navibus idoneum' (Geoffrey of Monmouth, ed. Wright, p. 30, section 44). Translations are by the author unless otherwise acknowledged. Medieval spelling has been silently corrected for ease of reading with v/u, j/i, i/y and other vowels, and obsolete letters such as thorn and yogh.

4 Tatlock 1950, p. 31; Gransden 1974, p. 207. If this is to be read as a reference to the Tower of London, then the preposition *desuper* must be understood as denoting a horizontal relationship, rather than a vertical one: that is, as meaning 'across from and above', rather than simply 'above'.

5 Geoffrey of Monmouth, ed. Wright, p. 17, section 27; p. 18, section 30; pp. 22–3, section 32.

6 Geoffrey of Monmouth, ed. Wright, p. 35, section 54; p. 42, section 64.

7 Gransden 1974, p. 201; Geoffrey of Monmouth, ed. Wright, p. xix; Gillingham 1990, especially p. 100.

8 Gillingham 1990, p. 101.

9 Gillingham 1990, p. 101; Geoffrey of Monmouth, ed. Wright, p. xix; Shichtman and Finke 1993, especially p. 4; Waswo 1995, especially pp. 277, 278, 282–3; Flint 1979.

10 Gransden 1974, p. 94.

11 'A Londres, sa cité meillur / E u il ert plus a sujur, / Fist une merveilluse porte / Sur l'eue qui navie aporte . . . / Sor la porte fist une tur / Mult grant de laise e de haltur' (Wace, ed. Weiss, p. 82, lines 3207–10 and 3217–18, and translation, p. 83).

12 Wace, ed. Weiss, p. xii.

13 Layamon, ed. Barron and Weinberg, p. 156, lines 3018–21.

14 Pounds 1990, p. 57.

15 Cunliffe 1977a, p. 74; Renn 1973, p. 120; Charlton 1986, p. 1.

16 Tatlock 1950, pp. 69–70.

17 Glare 1968–82, 'castellum' 1.

18 Latham and Howlett 1975–, 'castellum' 2a; Niermeyer 1976, 'castellum' 1; Simpson and Weiner 1989, 'castle' 1.

19 For example, Luke 10.38 and 24.13; Vegetius, ed. Lang, p. 131, Lib. IIII, 5.

20 Simpson and Weiner 1989, 'castle'.

21 Wheatley 2004a, pp. 126–7.

22 Geoffrey of Monmouth, ed. Wright, pp. 28–30, section 43.

23 J. C. Crick has produced a catalogue of more than 200 manuscripts of the *Historia regum Britannie* (see Crick 1991).

24 Dumville 1986, p. 20; Gransden 1974, p. 203; Geoffrey of Monmouth, ed. Wright, p. xviii.

25 There is much debate over the authorship of the *Historia Brittonum*. For recent contributions on either side, see Dumville 1986, pp. 173–92; Field 1996.

26 Gransden 1974, p. 6.

27 Nennius, ed. Morris, pp. 59–60, sections 7–10.

28 See Nearing 1949a, especially p. 895; J. Clark 1981, pp. 139–43.

29 See C. D. Benson 1980; Reynolds 1983, especially p. 378.

30 Crick 1991, p. 2.

31 J. Clark 1981, pp. 141–3.

32 Fitz Stephen, 'Descriptio', ed. Robertson, p. 8, section 12; p. 12, section 18; p. 12, section 19.

33 '[Londonia] habet ab oriente arcem palatinam, maximam et fortissimam, cuius et area et muri a fundamento profundissimo exsurgunt' (Fitz Stephen, 'Descriptio', ed. Robertson, p. 3, section 5). Translated by Jeremy Ashbee. See also Selected Texts: Transcripts of Primary Documents: Medieval, p. 326.

34 Niermeyer 1976, p. 753. Jeremy Ashbee has stressed the importance of understanding the adjective *palatinam* in this phrase as one of three qualifying adjectives: 'arx palatinam, maximam et fortissimam'. This emphasis is very important, although etymologically the first part of the phrase is of most interest in this case (see p. 326).

34 See Hyde 1965–6.

36 Fitz Stephen, 'Descriptio', ed. Robertson, p. 8, section 12; p. 12, section 17.

37 'Brutus ad veteris Troiae recensandam memoriam condidit firmissimam urbem Trinovantum, in ipsa velut Illium ad orientem constituens, ubi Turris Londoniensis est, firmissima munitione palatium circumseptum continens, aqua Tamasis fluvii, quem cotidie ascendentis maris inundatio replet, in ambitu decurrente. Ad occidentem vero Pergama construxit, duo videlicet miris aggeribus constructa castra, quorum alterum Bainardi, alterum baronum de Munfichet, est ex iure successionis' (Gervase of Tilbury, ed. Banks and Binns, pp. 398–400, book 2, section 17). This translation is based on that given by Banks and Binns (ibid., pp. 399–401). The author would like to thank Jim Binns, John Clark and Christopher Norton for recommending this passage. The changes in tense are a normal rhetorical feature of the Latin, but have no English stylistic equivalent, making literal translation difficult. The present participles of the first sentence convey the blending of the past and present in the Tower's setting, which Gervase suggests. Precise grammatical parallels in the construction of the two sentences exactly equate Brutus' founding of the Tower and the other castles. Because of the tense shift, however, it is difficult to translate this exact parallel without resorting to paraphrase. The phrase 'ubi Turris Londoniensis est' should be understood as a continuous present, something like 'where the Tower of London still stands to this day'. The author has consulted Jim Binns in arriving at this interpretation.

38 Niermeyer 1976, p. 753.

39 The stronghold of Ilium often features in medieval descriptions of Troy as a tower, very much like the White Tower and other medieval great tower/citadels, with surrounding defences that separate it from the town. See Wheatley 2004a, pp. 59–66.

40 Binns and Banks 1999, pp. 5–6.

41 British Library, Seal lxviii.18.

42 Cherry 1990, p. 85.

43 Fitz Stephen, 'Descriptio', ed. Robertson, p. 3, section 5. See Cherry 1990, p. 85.

44 Harvey and McGuinness 1996, p. 107, fig. 104.

45 Fitz Stephen also uses this term for London's citizens: 'Habitatores aliarum urbium cives, hujus barones dicuntur'; that is, 'The inhabitants of other cities are called citizens, but those of this [city] are called barons' (Fitz Stephen, 'Descriptio', ed. Robertson, p. 4, section 8). See also G. A. Williams 1963, pp. 3, 44, 204.

46 J. Clark (1981, pp. 147–8) details several medieval cases where the Trojan origins of the city were invoked in legal cases to assert Londoners' rights to special status.

47 British Library, Royal MS 14.C.VII, fol. 2.

48 'La cite de lundres ki est chef dengleterre. Brutus ki primere enhabita engleterre la funda. Et lapella troie la nuvele.'

49 British Library, Royal MS 13.A.III. The date of the sketches in this manuscript is uncertain. It has been suggested that they are by the scribe of the manuscript (Caine 1898, especially p. 319). This seems unlikely, since they are squashed into the margins of the text, rather than placed in specially reserved spaces. They have alternatively been attributed to the fourteenth century through the identification of certain specific buildings (Astley 1903, especially pp. 117–18). The British Museum Catalogue suggests that the drawings are inserted and belong to the early fourteenth century (Warner and Gilson 1921, vol. II, p. 75). This last argument seems the most plausible.

50 British Library, Royal MS 13.A.III, fol. 14. J. Clark (1981, p. 144 and fig. 2) identifies the central church as St Paul's Cathedral.

51 Many medieval castles and buildings within them were associated with Caesar. Other English examples are discussed below, but there are also French ones, such as the great eleventh- to twelfth-century tower at Beaugency, associated with Caesar from at least as early as 1609. The reasons behind this are probably very similar to those behind the attribution of the White Tower to Caesar, discussed below, in Nearing 1948a, 1948b, 1949a and 1949b, and in Wheatley 2004a, pp. 142–5.

52 Nearing 1948a, 1948b, 1949a and 1949b. The author is indebted to Priscilla Bawcutt for help in locating this material.

53 Hartung 1967–98, vol. VIII, p. 2667.

54 Hartung 1967–98, vol. VIII, p. 1501.

55 Hartung 1967–98, vol. VI, p. 154; Nearing 1948b.

56 Nearing 1948b, p. 232.

57 'At postquam Lud, frater Cassibellani qui cum Iuliano Cesare dimicavit, regni gubernaculum adeptus est, cinxit eam nobilissimis muris necnon et turribus mira arte fabricatis' (Geoffrey of Monmouth, ed. Wright, p. 15, section 22).

58 Nearing 1948a, 1948b, 1949b, passim.

59 'Julius Cesar . . . en monstrance de la Conqueste faite sur la terre du Brutaine, q'ore est dit Engleterre, edifa le chastel de Dovre et de Canterburi et de Roncestre et de Loundres' (Trivet, ed. Rutherford, p. 110).

60 *The Parlement of the Three Ages*, ed. Ginsberg, p. 55, lines 405–11.

61 Lydgate, ed. MacCracken, p. 51, lines 26–9.

62 Tatlock 1950, pp. 69–70; Greenhalgh 1989, p. 21.

63 British Library, Cotton Vespasian MS B.XI, fols 72–9.

64 'Iulius Caesar fecit unam turrim in loco ubi nunc est castrum Doverr' ad reponendum illuc thesaurum suum. Quae quidem Turris nunc stat ibidem in Castro Doverr' iuxta ecclesiam' (British Library, Cotton Vespasian MS B.XI, fol. 72).

65 Another reference to this tradition, of a similar date, is mentioned in Nearing 1949b, p. 220: in the *Historia regum Angliae* of John Rous; see also Wheatley 2004b.

66 Impey 1998.

67 Binski 1995, p. 95; Foster 1991, p. 2.

68 *Calendar of Liberate Rolls: Henry III*, vol. II (1240–45), 14.25 Henry III m20. The National Archives (formerly the Public Record Office), C 62/15 m19. The author is most grateful to Jeremy Ashbee for this reference.

69 Thurley, Impey and Hammond 1996, p. 34.

70 Salzman 1952, p. 159.

71 Greenhalgh 1989, p. 129.

72 'Et in fine eiusdem civitatis versus mare est castrum famosissimum et inexpugnabile, duplici muro, fossatis amplissimis, aquarum abissis ac aliis bellicis apparatibus circumdatum, in cuius medio est illa turris famosissima, que Turris Londonie nuncupatur, ex lapidibus quadris et sectis mira altitudine erecta, et inestimabili firmitate constructa' (Symeon Semeon, ed. Esposito, pp. 26–7). The author is grateful to Jeremy Ashbee for this reference.

73 The passages from Matthew Paris's *Greater Chronicle* (*Chronica majora*) are quoted and discussed in Impey 1998, pp. 66–7.

74 J. Clark 1981; see also Rosser 1996.

75 For the negative connotations of the Trojan legend, see Simpson 1998; Federico 1997; Johnson 1995.

76 For example, the 'Alliterative Morte Arthure', ed. Benson, pp. 117 ff., lines 78 ff.; 'The Tale of the Noble King Arthur that was Emperor Himself through Dignity of his Hands' in Malory, ed. Vinaver, rev. Field, vol. I, book 5, pp. 181–247; see Weiss 2002, especially pp. 97–8.

77 *Mabinogion*, ed. Jones and Jones, p. 40.

78 'Penn Bendigeituran uab Llyr, a guduwyt yn y Gvynuryn yn Lundein, a'e wyneb ar Ffreinc. A hyt tra uu yn yr ansavd y dodet yno, ny doei Ormes Saesson byth y'r Ynys honn . . . Ac Arthur a datkudyavd Penn Bendigeituran o'r Gvynnvrynn. Kan nyt oed dec gantav kadv yr Ynys honn o gedernit neb, namyn o'r eidav ehun' (*Trioedd Ynys Prydein*, ed. Bromwich, Triad 37R, pp. 88–19). This version appears in the *Llyfr Coch Hergest* ('The Red Book of Hergest'), a manuscript dating from around 1400 (*Trioedd Ynys Prydein*, ed. Bromwich, p. xxiii). Due to the oral nature of the Welsh legendary material, the content is understood to be of a

much earlier date, perhaps the beginning of the thirteenth century or earlier (*Trioedd Ynys Prydein*, ed. Bromwich, p. cx).

79 *Trioedd Ynys Prydein*, ed. Bromwich, p. 40.

80 *Trioedd Ynys Prydein*, ed. Bromwich, pp. lxxx–lxxxi: the influence of Geoffrey can be detected from the turn of the thirteenth century, and continued throughout the thirteenth and fourteenth centuries.

81 *Vulgate Version of the Arthurian Romances*, ed. Sommer, vol. VI, pp. 326–8; 'Stanzaic Morte Arthur', ed. Benson, pp. 83–4, lines 2994–3001 (the 'towr' is mentioned again on page 85, lines 3034–7); Malory, ed. Vinaver, rev. Field, vol. III, pp. 1228 ff. The French Vulgate cycle represents oral material from the late twelfth century to the early thirteenth, compiled by *trouvères* and surviving in manuscripts of the thirteenth and fourteenth centuries, as well as in some early printed versions. Both English versions are known to have drawn on the French material, and Malory also read the 'Stanzaic Morte Arthur': see L. D. Benson 1986, pp. xvi, xvii.

82 Loomis 1919, especially p. 255; Wheatley 2004a, pp.103–4.

83 'Stanzaic Morte Arthur', ed. Benson, pp. 83–4, lines 2994–3001.

84 Malory, ed. Vinaver, rev. Field, vol. III, p. 1228.

85 In the Vulgate version, the phrase 'tor de Logres' is equivalent to Tower of London (*Vulgate Version of the Arthurian Romances*, ed. Sommer, vol. VI, p. 325).

86 British Library, London, Additional MS 10294, fol. 81v. M. Whitaker (1990, p. 50) identifies this scene as depicting the siege of Lancelot's castle, Joyous Gard, but since the illustration is placed very close to the description of the siege of the Tower of London, it seems more likely to illustrate this.

87 Geoffrey of Monmouth, ed. Wright, p. 132, section 78: 'Set et inclitus ille rex Arturus letaliter vulneratus est; qui illinc ad sananda vulnera sua in insulam Avallonis evectus . . . anno ab incarnatione Domini .dxlii'; that is, 'But even Arthur, that famous king, was fatally wounded, and was carried off to the island of Avalon, so his wounds could be cleaned . . . in the year 542 after our Lord's Incarnation.'

88 'Four hondred wintir and four and fifty acomplivisshed aftir the Passion of Oure Lorde Jesu Crist' (Malory, ed. Vinaver, rev. Field, vol. II, p. 855).

89 See Riddy 1996.

90 Malory, ed. Vinaver, rev. Field, vol. III, p. 1229.

91 Malory, ed. Vinaver, rev. Field, vol. I, p. xxv.

92 Field 1993, Chapter 7, pp. 114–15, 122–3.

93 Shakespeare, *King Richard III*, ed. Ure, Act 3 Scene 4, lines 68–74; *King Richard II*, ed. Hammond, Act 5 Scene 1, lines 2–3.

94 Nearing 1948b, pp. 230–31.

95 *King Richard III*, Act 3 Scene 1, lines 68–74.

96 Nearing 1948b, pp. 228–9.

97 Stow, ed. Kingsford, vol. I, p. 44.

98 Stow, ed. Kingsford, vol. I, p. 44.

99 Stow, ed. Kingsford, vol. I, pp. 43–4.

100 Leland, ed. Hearne, vol. I, pp. lx–lxi. The

author is most grateful to John Clark for this reference.

101 Nearing 1948b, p. 229.
102 Stukeley 1724, pl. 57.
103 See J. Clark 1996.
104 J. Clark 1996, p. 2 and fig 1.2.
105 Milman 1818, p. 4, lines 71–4.
106 Ingoldsby, ed. Barham, pp. 147–55, especially p. 149.
107 Moultrie 1876, vol. I, p. 193, canto ii, stanza lix.

Appendix I

1 See Introduction, p. xiv.
2 Oxford Archaeological Unit Projects TOL64 and TOL72, both of 1997.
3 See Chapter Two, pp. 49, 54–5, 80.

Appendix II

1 English Heritage 1998.
2 Baillie and Pilcher 1973.
3 Hillam, Morgan and Tyers 1987.
4 Miles 1997.
5 Tyers 2001.
6 Miles 1997.
7 Miles and Worthington 1997.
8 Miles and Worthington 1998a.
9 Miles 2006.
10 See Chapter Six, p. 170.

Appendix III

1 See Introduction, p. xiv.
2 Brown and Curnow 1984, p. 60.
3 Worssam and Sanderson 1998.
4 Brown and Curnow 1984.
5 Worssam and Tatton-Brown 1994.
6 Worssam and Tatton-Brown 1994.
7 Hancock 1975; Mégnien 1980.

Appendix IV

1 Cecil Hewett, of course, did take an interest, and illustrated some examples in his works (e.g., Hewett 1980).

2 Works undertaken for Historic Royal Palaces have been monitored by the Oxford Archaeological Unit (now Oxford Archaeology) and reported in a series of client reports for HRPA. Recording work was undertaken by Ric Tyler, Kate Newell and Philip Wallace under the supervision of Julian Munby.
3 Keevill 2004.
4 Robert Chester, personal communication.
5 Miles and Bridge 2005.
6 Miles and Worthington 2002; Miles, Worthington and Bridge 2003; Caple 1999.
7 Miles and Worthington 1998b.
8 'Tower of London, Inspection of the Historic Floor Surfaces of the East and West White Tower Galleries', OAU client report (TOL 64) for Historic Royal Palaces, September 1997.
9 See above, Chapter Two, p. 80.
10 See Chapter Two, pp. 26–31.
11 Unreported excavations by Oxford Archaeology; personal communication, Gustave Milne.
12 Ian Tyers, personal communication.
13 Williamson, ed. Fox, pp. 84–5.
14 Howard and Crossley 1917, pp. 89–95, for late roofs, for example, Bloxham and Ewelme.
15 Miles and Haddon-Reece 1993 list fifty-four tree-ring dates.
16 The joint is apparent in photographs taken at the time of repairs in the 1960s. Hewett (1980, fig. 303) believed the 'barefaced-soffit-tenon-with-diminished-haunch' to have been invented in Cambridge in 1510–12, but it is now known to be used in the Oxford area in the 1430s.
17 These and other historical sources are largely derived from the Chapters by Jeremy Ashbee and Anna Keay; Anglo 1997, pp. 49–51.
18 The National Archives [formerly the Public Record Office], hereafter TNA, SP 1/85, fol. 73r; accounts in Oxford, Bodleian Library, MS Rawlinson D. 777, and Nottingham, Newcastle MS Ne O2. See pp. 163–4.
19 TNA, WORK 31/88 (plan of 1729) and WORK 31.98 (plan of 1754).

20 Waldstein, ed. Groos, pp. 65–71.
21 Simpson and Litton, 1996, Munby 1991 for imported timber, 'Tower of London, White Tower Fire Stair (December 1993) and 'Tower of London, Inspection of Historic Floor Surfaces' (June 1995), unpublished OA client reports to Historic Royal Palaces.
22 Unpublished OAU client report for Historic Royal Palaces.
23 TNA, E 351/3203 (Works accounts, 1565–7).
24 *Calendar of State Papers, Domestic: Edward VI, Mary, Elizabeth*, vol. I (1547–80), p. 312; TNA, SP 12/47, fols 35–6. See p. 169 above.
25 British Library, MS Lansdowne XI, fol. 112, no. 49 (Lord Treasurer to Cecil, 6 May, 1569).
26 *Calendar of State Papers, Domestic: Edward VI, Mary, Elizabeth*, vol. VII (Addenda, 1566–79), p. 311; TNA, SP 13/H/11, no. 14.
27 TNA, E 351/3238 (Works accounts, 1602–3).
28 TNA, E 351/3239 (Works accounts, 1603–4).
29 TNA, E 351/3240 (Works accounts, 1604–5).
30 Stonework examples being, for example, Westminster Abbey (Henry VII's Chapel), Windsor Castle (Curfew Tower bell turret) and Christ Church, Oxford (the lower, Wolsey, part of Tom Tower).
31 TNA, E 351/3252 (Works accounts, 1617–18).
32 TNA, SP 14/156, no. 13, fols 29 ff.
33 TNA, WO 51/300, fol. 160 (Ordnance Office Bill Books, 1781–2), fols 61v, 92, 99–100 (September–December 1781); WO 51/305, fol. 34v (December 1781) (Ordnance Office Bill Books, 1782–3).
34 TNA, WO 51/310, fol. 125v (Benjamin Wilson, painter, 31 December 1782).
35 TNA, E 101/474/12 (Tower works account, June–September 1532).
36 TNA, E 101/474/13 (Tower works account, 24 Henry VIII).
37 Colvin, Brown and Taylor 1963–82, vol. III, p. 265. See pp. 162–3.
38 *Letters and Papers of Henry VIII*, vol. VII (1534), p. 32 (no. 83).

Bibliography

PUBLISHED PRIMARY SOURCES

Acts of the Privy Council
Acts of the Privy Council of England, ed. J. R. Dasent et al., 46 vols, London, 1890–1964

Aimon, ed. De Certain
Aimon, monk of Fleury, 'Miracula Sancti Benedicti', in *Les Miracles de Saint Benoît, écrits par Adrevald, Aimoin, André, Raoul Tortaire et Hugues de Sainte Marie, moines de Fleury*, ed. E. De Certain, Société de l'Histoire de France, Paris, 1858, pp. 90–172

'Alliterative Morte Arthure', ed. Benson
'Alliterative Morte Arthure', in *King Arthur's Death*, ed. L. D. Benson, Exeter, 1986, pp. 113–238

Anglo-Saxon Chronicle, ed. Earle and Plummer
Two of the Saxon Chronicles: Parallel, with Supplementary Extracts from the Others, ed. J. Earle and C. Plummer, 2 vols, second edition, Oxford, 1892

Anglo-Saxon Chronicle, ed. Garmondsway
The Anglo-Saxon Chronicle, ed. and trans. G. N. Garmondsway, London, 1953

Anglo-Saxon Chronicle, ed. Whitelock, Douglas and Tucker
The Anglo-Saxon Chronicle: A Revised Translation, ed. D. Whitelock, D. C. Douglas and S. I. Tucker, London, 1961

Anonimalle Chronicle, ed. Galbraith
The Anonimalle Chronicle, ed. V. H. Galbraith, Manchester, 1927

Antient Kalendars, ed. Palgrave
The Antient Kalendars and Inventories of the Treasury of His Majesty's Exchequer, ed. F. Palgrave, 3 vols, London, 1836

Antiquus Cartularius Ecclesiae Baiocensis, ed. Bourrienne
Antiquus Cartularius Ecclesiae Baiocensis, ed. V. Bourrienne, 2 vols, Société de l'Histoire de Normandie, Rouen and Paris, 1902

Ashmole, ed. Josten
E. Ashmole, *Elias Ashmole, 1617–1692: His Autobiographical and Historical Notes, his Correspondence, and Other Contemporary Sources Relating to his Life and Work*, ed. C. H. Josten, 5 vols, Oxford, 1966

Barnwell Chronicle, ed. Stubbs
The Historical Collections of Walter of Coventry, ed. W. Stubbs, 2 vols, Rolls Series, London, 1872–3

Baudri of Bourgueil, ed. Hilbert
Baudri of Bourgueil, 'Adelae comitissae', in *Baldricus Burgulianus Carmina*, ed. K. Hilbert, Editiones Heidelbergenses, 19, Heidelberg, 1979, pp. 149–85 [for a translation of the relevant passages, see Herren 1988, pp. 167–75]

Bede, ed. Colgrave and Mynors
Bede's Ecclesiastical History of the English People, ed. B. Colgrave and R. Mynors, Oxford, 1969

Bell 1920
W. G. Bell, *The Great Fire of London in 1666*, London, 1920

Bennet 1885
J. A. Bennet, 'Account of Papers Relating to the Royal Jewel-House in the Sixteenth and Seventeenth Centuries in the Possession of Captain Hervey George St John Mildmay', *Archaeologia*, 48, part 1 (1885), pp. 201–20

Bishop and Chaplais 1957
T. A. M. Bishop and P. Chaplais, *Facsimiles of English Royal Writs to AD 1100: Presented to Vivian Hunter Galbraith*, Oxford, 1957

Boccaccio, ed. McWilliam
G. Boccaccio, *The Decameron*, ed. G. H. McWilliam, Harmondsworth, 1995

Bollandus et al., *Acta sanctorum*
J. Bollandus et al., *Acta sanctorum*, Antwerp and Brussels, 58 vols, 1643–1867

Brevis relatio de Guillelmo, ed. Van Houts
Brevis relatio de Guillelmo nobilissimo comite Normannorum, ed. E. M. C. van Houts, Camden Miscellany, 34, Camden Fifth Series, vol. x, London, 1997, pp. 1–48

Calendar of Close Rolls: Edward II
Calendar of the Close Rolls of the Reign of Edward II Preserved in the Public Record Office, 4 vols, London, 1892–8

Calendar of Close Rolls: Edward III
Calendar of the Close Rolls of the Reign of Edward III Preserved in the Public Record Office, 14 vols, London, 1896–1913

Calendar of Close Rolls: Henry III
Calendar of the Close Rolls of the Reign of Henry III Preserved in the Public Record Office, 14 vols, London, 1902–38

Calendar of Close Rolls: Henry VI
Calendar of the Close Rolls of the Reign of Henry VI Preserved in the Public Record Office, 6 vols, London, 1933–47

Calendar of Close Rolls: Richard II
Calendar of the Close Rolls of the Reign of Richard II Preserved in the Public Record Office, ed. A. E. Stamp, 6 vols, London, 1914–27

Calendar of Inquisitions
Calendar of Inquisitions Miscellaneous (Chancery) Preserved in the Public Record Office, 6 vols, London, 1916–63

Calendar of Letter Books
Calendar of Letter Books Preserved among the Archives of the City of London at the Guildhall, ed. R. R. Sharpe, 11 vols, London, 1899–1912

Calendar of Liberate Rolls: Henry III
Calendar of the Liberate Rolls Preserved in the Public Record Office: Henry III, 6 vols, London, 1916–64

Calendar of Patent Rolls: Edward IV
Calendar of the Patent Rolls Preserved in the Public Record Office: Edward IV, Edward V, Richard III, ed. R. C. Fowler, 3 vols, London, 1897–1901

Calendar of Patent Rolls: Henry III
Calendar of the Patent Rolls of the Reign of Henry III Preserved in the Public Record Office, 6 vols, London, 1901–13

Calendar of Patent Rolls: Henry VI
Calendar of the Patent Rolls of the Reign of Henry VI Preserved in the Public Record Office, 6 vols, Norwich, 1901–10

Calendar of Plea and Memoranda Rolls
Calendar of Plea and Memoranda Rolls Preserved among the Archives of the Corporation of the City of London at the Guildhall, ed. A. H. Thomas, 4 vols, Cambridge, 1926–43

Calendar of State Papers, Domestic: Charles I
Calendar of State Papers, Domestic Series, of the Reign of Charles I, ed. J. Bruce and W. D. Hamilton, 23 vols, London, 1858–97

Calendar of State Papers, Domestic: Charles II
Calendar of State Papers, Domestic Series, of the Reign of Charles II, ed. M. A. E. Green, F. H. B. Daniell and F. Bickley, 28 vols, London, 1860–1939

Calendar of State Papers, Domestic: Commonwealth
Calendar of State Papers, Domestic Series, Commonwealth, 1649–1660, ed. M. A. E. Green, 13 vols, London, 1875–86

Calendar of State Papers, Domestic: Edward VI, Mary, Elizabeth
Calendar of State Papers, Domestic Series, of the Reigns of Edward VI, Mary, Elizabeth and James I, 1547–1625, ed. R. Lemon and M. A. E. Green, 12 vols, London, 1856–72; reprinted 1967

Calendar of State Papers, Domestic: Mary I
Calendar of State Papers, Domestic Series, of the Reign of Mary I, 1553–1558, revised edition, ed. C. S. Knighton, London, 1998

Calendar of State Papers: Spain
Calendar of Letters, Dispatches and State Papers Relating to the Negotiations between England and Spain Preserved in the Archives at Simancas and Elsewhere, vol. IV, part ii, ed. P. de Gayangos, London, 1882

Calendar of Treasury Books
Calendar of Treasury Books, 1660–1718, ed. W. A. Shaw, 32 vols in 63, London, 1904–62

Calendar of Treasury Papers
Calendar of Treasury Papers, 1557–1728, ed. J. Redington, 6 vols, London, 1868–89

Cartae antiquae, ed. Conway Davies
The Cartae antiquae: *Rolls 11–20*, ed. J. Conway Davies, London, 1960

Cartulaire de Cormery, ed. Bourrassé
Cartulaire de Cormery, ed. J.-J. Bourrassé, Mémoires de la Société archéologique de Touraine, 12, Tours, 1861

Cartulaire de Notre-Dame de Chartres, ed Lépinois and Merlet
Cartulaire de Notre-Dame de Chartres, ed. E. de Lépinois and L. Merlet, 3 vols, Chartres, 1862–5

Cartulaire de St Père de Chartres, ed. Guérard
Cartulaire de St Père de Chartres, ed. B. Guérard, 2 vols, Paris, 1840

Cartulary of Holy Trinity Aldgate, ed. Hodgett
The Cartulary of Holy Trinity Aldgate, ed. G. A. Hodgett, London Record Society Publications, 7, Leicester, 1971

César de Saussure, ed. Van Muyden
César de Saussure, *A Foreign View of England in the Reigns of George I and George II: The Letters of Monsieur César de Saussure to his Family*, ed. and trans. Mme van Muyden, London, 1902

Chaplais 1964
P. Chaplais, ed., *Diplomatic Documents Preserved in the Public Record Office*, vol. I: *1101–1272*, London, 1964

Chibnall 1982
M. Chibnall, ed., *Charters and Custumals of the Abbey of Holy Trinity, Caen*, London, 1982

'Chronica de Gestis Consulum Andegavorum', ed. Halphen and Poupardin
'Chronica de Gestis Consulum Andegavorum', in *Chroniques des comtes d'Anjou*, ed. Halphen and Poupardin, pp. 25–73

Chronicle of Queen Jane, ed. Nichols
The Chronicle of Queen Jane and of Two Years of Queen Mary, ed. J. G. Nichols, Camden Society, 48, London, 1850

Chronicles of Edward I and Edward II, ed. Stubbs
Chronicles of the Reigns of Edward I and Edward II, ed. W. Stubbs, 2 vols, Rolls Series, London, 1882–3

Chronicles of Stephen, Henry II and Richard I, ed. Howlett
Chronicles of the Reigns of Stephen, Henry II and Richard I, ed. R. Howlett, 4 vols, Rolls Series, London, 1884–9

Chronicon monasterii de Bello, ed. Searle
Chronicon monasterii de Bello, ed. and trans. E. Searle, Oxford, 1980

Chronique de Saint-Pierre-le-Vif, ed. Bautier, Gilles and Bautier
Chronique de Saint-Pierre-le-Vif de Sens, dite de Clarius, ed. R.-H. Bautier, M. Gilles and A.-M. Bautier, Editions du Centre Nationale de la Recherche Scientifique, Paris, 1979

Chroniques des comtes d'Anjou, ed. Halphen and Poupardin
Chroniques des comtes d'Anjou et des seigneurs d'Amboise, ed. L. Halphen and R. Poupardin, Paris, 1913

Chronique de Nantes, ed. Merlet
Chronique de Nantes, ed. R. Merlet, Paris, 1896

Chroniques des églises d'Anjou, ed. Marchegay and Mabille
Chroniques des églises d'Anjou, ed. P. Marchegay and E. Mabille, Paris, 1869

Comptes de l'argenterie, ed. Douët-D'Arcq
Comptes de l'argenterie des Rois de France au XIVe siècle, ed. L. Douët-D'Arcq, Paris, 1851

Coronation of Richard III, ed. Sutton and Hammond
The Coronation of Richard III: The Extant Documents, ed. A. F. Sutton and P. W. Hammond, Gloucester, 1983

Death's Master-Peece
Death's Master-Peece; or, A True Relation of that Great Fire in Tower Street, Friday 4th January 1649, London, 1649

Delaune 1681
T. Delaune, *The Present State of London*, London, 1681

Dockray 1988
K. Dockray, ed., *Three Chronicles of the Reign of Edward IV*, Gloucester, 1988

Doebner 1886
R. Doebner, ed., *Memoirs of Mary, Queen of England (1689–1693) together with her Letters and those of James II and William III to the Electress Sophia of Hanover*, Leipzig, 1886

Dugdale, ed. Caley, Ellis and Bulkeley Bandinel
W. Dugdale, *Monasticon anglicanum*, ed. J. Caley, H. Ellis and the Revd Bulkeley Bandinel, 6 vols, London, 1846

Eadmer, ed. Rule
Eadmer, *Eadmeri Historia novorum in Anglia*, ed. M. Rule, Rolls Series, London, 1884

Early Charters of the Cathedral Church of St Paul, ed. Gibbs
Early Charters of the Cathedral Church of St Paul, London, ed. M. Gibbs, Camden Third Series, 58, London, 1939

Evelyn, ed. De Beer
J. Evelyn, *Diary of John Evelyn*, ed. E. S. de Beer, 6 vols, Oxford, 1955

Eyre of London, ed. Cam
The Eyre of London: 14 Edward II, AD 1321, ed. H. M. Cam, 2 vols, Selden Society, London, 1968–9

Fitz Stephen, 'Descriptio', ed. Robertson
W. Fitz Stephen, 'Descriptio nobilissimae civitatis Londoniae', in *Materials for the History of Thomas Becket, Archbishop of Canterbury*, ed. J. C. Robertson, 7 vols, Rolls Series, London, 1875–85, vol. III, pp. 2–13

Fitz Stephen, 'Vita Sancti Thomae', ed. Robertson
—, 'Vita Sancti Thomae Cantuarensis Archiepiscopi et Martyris Auctore Willelmo filio Stephani', in *Materials for the History of Thomas Becket, Archbishop of Canterbury*, ed. J. C. Robertson, 7 vols, Rolls Series, London, 1875–85, vol. III, pp. 1–154

Flamsteed, ed. Baily
J. Flamsteed, *An Account of the Revd John Flamsteed, the First Astronomer Royal*, ed. F. Baily, London, 1835

Flodoard, ed. Lauer
Flodoard, *Annales*, ed. P. Lauer, Paris, 1905

Flores historiarum, ed. Luard
Flores historiarum, ed. H. R. Luard, 3 vols, Rolls Series, London, 1890

Froissart, ed. Kervyn de Lettenhove
J. Froissart, *Oeuvres de Froissart, Chroniques*, ed. Kervyn de Lettenhove, 29 vols, Brussels, 1870

Gaimar, ed. Bell
G. Gaimar, *L'Estoire des Engleis*, ed. A. Bell, Anglo-Norman Texts, xiv–xv, Oxford, 1960

Garin le Lohérain, ed. Paris
Garin le Lohérain, *Li Romans de Garin le Lohérain*, ed. A.-P. Paris, 2 vols, Paris, 1833

Geoffrey of Monmouth, ed. Wright
Geoffrey of Monmouth, *The* Historia regum Brittannie *of Geoffrey of Monmouth* [Bern, Burgerbibliothek, MS 568], ed. N. Wright, Cambridge, 1985

Gerard, ed. Caraman
J. Gerard, *John Gerard: The Autobiography of an Elizabethan*, ed. P. Caraman, London, 1956

Gervase of Tilbury, ed. Banks and Binns
Gervase of Tilbury, *Otia imperialia: Recreation for an Emperor*, ed. and trans. S. E. Banks and J. W. Binns, Oxford Medieval Texts, Oxford, 2002

'Gesta Ambaziensium Dominorum', Halphen and Poupardin
'Gesta Ambaziensium Dominorum', in *Chroniques des comtes d'Anjou*, ed. Halphen and Poupardin, pp. 74–132

Gesta Normannorum ducum, ed. Van Houts
The Gesta Normannorum ducum *of William of Jumièges, Orderic Vitalis and Robert of Torigny*, ed. and trans. E. van Houts, 2 vols, Oxford Medieval Texts, Oxford, 1992–5

Given-Wilson 1993
C. Given-Wilson, ed. and trans., *Chronicles of the Revolution, 1397–1400: The Reign of Richard II*, Manchester, 1993

Gundulf, ed. Thomson
Gundulf, *The Life of Gundulf, Bishop of Rochester / Vita Gundulfi*, ed. R. M. Thomson, Toronto, 1977

Guy of Amiens, ed. Barlow
Guy of Amiens, *The* Carmen de Hastingae proelio *of Guy, Bishop of Amiens*, ed. and trans. F. Barlow, Oxford Medieval Texts, second edition, Oxford, 1999

Helgaud de Fleury, ed. Bautier
Helgaud de Fleury, *Vie de Robert le Pieux*, ed. and trans. R.-H. Bautier, Paris, 1965

Henry of Huntingdon, ed. Greenway
Henry, Archdeacon of Huntingdon, *Historia anglorum / The History of the English People*, ed. D. E. Greenway, Oxford Medieval Texts, Oxford, 1996

Hentzner 1894
P. Hentzner, *Travels in England during the Reign of Queen Elizabeth*, London, 1894

Hérault du Roy Berry, ed. Stevenson
Hérault du Roy Berry, 'Le Récouvrement de Normendie', in *Narratives of the Expulsion of the English from Normandy*, ed. J. Stevenson, Rolls Series, London, 1863, pp. 239–376

Herren 1988
M. W. Herren, 'Baudri de Bourgueil, *Adelae comitissae*: A Translation', in S. A. Brown 1988, pp. 167–77

Higden, ed. Lumby
R. Higden, *Polychronicon Ranulphi Higden monachi Cestrensis*, ed. J. R. Lumby, 9 vols, Rolls Series, London, 1865–86

HMC: *Fifteenth Report*
Royal Commission on Historical Manuscripts, *Fifteenth Report. Appendix, Part 1: The Manuscripts of the Earl of Dartmouth*, vol. III, London, 1896

HMC: *Seventh Report*
—, *Seventh Report of the Royal Commission on Historical Manuscripts*, 2 vols in 1, London, 1879

Household of Edward IV, ed. Myers
The Household of Edward IV: The Black Book and the Ordinance of 1478, ed. A. R. Myers, Manchester, 1959

Howel 1657
J. Howel, *Londonopolis*, London, 1657

Howes 1615
E. Howes, *The Annales; or, Generall Chronicle of England begun first by John Stow and after him Continued . . . by Edmond Howes*, London, 1615

Hudson and Tingley 1906
J. Hudson and J. Tingley, *The Records of the City of Norwich*, 2 vols, Norwich, 1906

Hugues de Fleury, *Modernorum Regum Francorum Actus* in Flodoard, ed Lauer, Paris, 1905

Hyde, ed. Dunn Macray
E. Hyde, *The History of the Rebellion and Civil Wars in England Begun in the Year 1641*, ed. W. Dunn Macray, 6 vols, Oxford, 1888

Ingoldsby, ed. Barham
T. Ingoldsby, *The Ingoldsby Lyrics by Thomas Ingoldsby*, ed. R. H. Barham, London, 1881

Inventory of King Henry VIII, ed. Starkey
The Inventory of King Henry VIII, ed. David Starkey, London, 2000

Inventory of the Plate in the Lower Jewel House, ed. Brand
An Inventory and Appraisement of the Plate in the Lower Jewel House of the Tower, Anno 1649, ed. J. Brand, London, 1806

James I of Scotland, ed. Norton-Smith
The Kingis Quair: James I of Scotland, ed. J. Norton-Smith, Leiden, 1981

John of Worcester, ed. Darlington and McGurk
John of Worcester, *The Chronicle of John of Worcester*, vols II and III, ed. R. R. Darlington and P. McGurk, Oxford Medieval Texts, Oxford, 1995–8

Jordan Fantosme's Chronicle, ed. Johnston
Jordan Fantosme's Chronicle, ed. and trans. R. C. Johnston, Oxford and New York, 1981

Lanfranc, ed. Clover and Gibson
Lanfranc, *The Letters of Lanfranc, Archbishop of Canterbury*, ed. and trans. H. Clover and M. Gibson, Oxford Medieval Texts, Oxford, 1979

Layamon, ed. Barron and Weinberg
Layamon, *Brut; or, Hystoria Brutonum*, ed. W. R. J. Barron and S. C. Weinberg, Harlow, 1995

Leadam and Baldwin 1918
I. S. Leadam and J. F. Baldwin, eds, *Select Cases before the King's Council, 1243–1482*, Selden Society, 35, Cambridge, Massachusetts, 1918

Leland, ed. Hearne
J. Leland, *J. Lelandi antiquarii de rebus Britannicis collectanea*, ed. T. Hearne, 6 vols, London, 1770

Letters and Papers of Richard III and Henry VII
Letters and Papers Illustrative of the Reigns of Richard III and Henry VII, vol. I, ed. J. Gairdner, Rolls Series, London, 1861

Letters and Papers of Henry VIII
Letters and Papers, Foreign and Domestic, of the Reign of Henry VIII, ed. J. S. Brewer et al., 21 vols, London, 1862–1932

Lydgate, ed. MacCracken
J. Lydgate, *The Serpent of Division*, ed. H. N. MacCracken, London and New Haven, 1911

Mabinogion, ed. Jones and Jones
The Mabinogion, ed. and trans. G. Jones and T. Jones, London and New York, 1949

Magalotti 1821
L. Magalotti, ed., *The Travels of Cosmo the Third Grand Duke of Tuscany though England during the Reign of King Charles the Second, 1669*, London, 1821

Magna Vita Sancti Hugonis, ed. Dimock
Magna Vita Sancti Hugonis Episcopi Lincolniensis, ed. J. F. Dimock, Rolls Series, London, 1864

Malory, ed. Vinaver, rev. Field
Sir Thomas Malory, *The Works of Sir Thomas Malory*, ed. E. Vinaver, rev. P. J. C. Field, 3 vols, Oxford, 1990

Mancini, ed. Armstrong
D. Mancini, *The Usurpation of Richard III / Dominicus Mancinus ad Angelum Catonem de occupatione regni anglie per Riccardum Tercium libellus*, ed. C. A. J. Armstrong, second edition, Oxford, 1969; reprinted Gloucester, 1984

Matthew Paris, *Chronica majora*, ed. Luard
M. Paris, *Matthaei Parisiensis monachi Sancti Albani Chronica majora*, ed. H. R. Luard, 8 vols, Rolls Series, London, 1872–83

Matthew Paris, *Gesta abbatum monasterii Sancti Albani*, ed. Riley
—, *Gesta abbatum monasterii Sancti Albani, a Thoma Walsingham, regnante Ricardo Secundo, eiusdem ecclesiae praecentore, compilata*, ed. H. T. Riley, 3 vols, Rolls Series, London, 1867–9

Matthew Paris, *Life of St Edmund*, ed. Lawrence
—, *The Life of St Edmund by Matthew Paris*, ed. and trans. C. H. Lawrence, Oxford, 1996

Matthew Paris, *Historia anglorum*, ed. Madden
—, *Matthaei Parisiensis monachi Sancti Albani Historia anglorum*, ed. F. Madden, 3 vols, Rolls Series, London, 1866–9

Matthew Paris, ed. Vaughan
—, *The Illustrated Chronicles of Matthew Paris: Observations of Thirteenth Century Life*, ed. R. Vaughan, Stroud, 1993

Maxwell-Lyte 1890–1915
H. C. Maxwell-Lyte, *A Descriptive Catalogue of Ancient Deeds in the Public Record Office: Prepared under the Superintendence of the Deputy Keeper of the Records*, 6 vols, London, 1890–1915

Michel 1840
F. Michel, ed., *Histoire des Ducs de Normandie et des Rois d'Angleterre*, Paris, 1840

Mildmay 1879
H. G. St J. Mildmay, 'The MSS of Capt. Hervey G. St John Mildmay,

RN, of Hazelgrove House, Somerset', in *Seventh Report of the Royal Commission on Historical Manuscripts* (London, 1897), pp. 590–96.

Millar 1972
O. Millar, ed., *The Inventories and Valuations of the King's Goods, 1649–1651*, Walpole Society, 43, Glasgow, 1972

Milman 1818
H. H. Milman, *Samor, Lord of the Bright City*, second edition, London, 1818

Minsheu 1617
J. Minsheu, *The Guide into Tongues*, London, 1617

Mortet and Deschamps 1911–29
V. Mortet and P. Deschamps, eds, *Recueil des textes relatifs à l'histoire de l'architecture et à la condition des architectes en France au moyen âge, XIe–XIIe siècles*, 2 vols, Paris, 1911–29

Moultrie 1876
J. Moultrie, *Poems*, 2 vols, London, 1876

Munimenta Gildhallae, ed. Riley
Munimenta Gildhallae Londoniensis, ed. H. T. Riley, 3 vols in 4, Rolls Series, London, 1859–62

Neininger 1999
F. Neininger, ed., *London, 1076–1187*, English Episcopal Acta, 15, Oxford, 1999

Nennius, ed. Morris
Nennius, *British History and Welsh Annals*, ed. and trans. J. Morris, London and Totowa, 1990

Nichols 1828
J. Nichols, *The Progresses Processions and Magnificent Festivities of King James the First*, 4 vols, London, 1828

Nicholson, ed. Jones and Holmes
W. Nicholson, *The London Diaries of William Nicholson, Bishop of Carlisle, 1702–18*, ed. C. Jones and G. Holmes, Oxford, 1985

Orderic Vitalis, ed. Chibnall
Orderic Vitalis, *The Ecclesiastical History of Orderic Vitalis*, ed. and trans. M. Chibnall, 6 vols, Oxford Medieval Texts, Oxford, 1969–80

Ordinances for the Royal Household
A Collection of Ordinances and Regulations for the Government of the Royal Household . . . from King Edward III to King William and his Queen Mary, London, 1790

The Parlement of the Thre Ages, ed. Ginsberg
Wynnere and Wastoure and The Parlement of the Thre Ages, ed. W. Ginsberg, Kalamazoo, 1992

Pipe Roll 31 Henry I
Magnum rotulum scaccarii vel magnum rotulum pipae de anno tricesimo-primo regni Henrici primi, ed. J. Hunter, London, 1833

Pipe Roll 13 Henry II
The Great Roll of the Pipe for the Thirteenth Year of the Reign of King Henry II, AD 1166–1167, London, 1889

Pipe Roll 18 Henry II
The Great Roll of the Pipe for the Eighteenth Year of the Reign of King Henry II, AD 1171–1172, London, 1894

Pipe Roll 19 Henry II
The Great Roll of the Pipe for the Nineteenth Year of the Reign of King Henry II, AD 1172–1173, London, 1895

Pipe Roll 28 Henry II
The Great Roll of the Pipe for the Twenty-Eighth Year of the Reign of King Henry II, AD 1181–1182, London, 1910

Pipe Roll 29 Henry II
The Great Roll of the Pipe for the Twenty-Ninth Year of the Reign of King Henry II, AD 1182–1183, London, 1911

Pipe Roll 30 Henry II
The Great Roll of the Pipe for the Thirtieth Year of the Reign of King Henry II, AD 1183–1184, London, 1912

Pipe Roll 32 Henry II
The Great Roll of the Pipe for the Thirty-Second Year of the Reign of King Henry II, AD 1185–1186, London, 1914

Pipe Roll 13 John Michaelmas
The Great Roll of the Pipe for the Thirteenth Year of the Reign of King John, Michaelmas 1211, ed. D. Stenton, London, 1953

Platter, ed. Williams
T. Platter, *Thomas Platter's Travels in England, 1599*, ed. C. Williams, London, 1937

Polydore Vergil, ed. Hay
P. Vergil, *The* Anglica historia *of Polydore Vergil, AD 1485–1537*, ed. D. Hay, Camden Society, 74, London, 1950

Proceedings and Ordinances of the Privy Council
Proceedings and Ordinances of the Privy Council of England, 1386–1542, ed. H. Nicholas, 7 vols, London, 1834–7

PRO: *First Report*
Public Record Office, *First Report of the Deputy Keeper of the Public Records*, London, 1840

PRO: *Seventeenth Report*
—, *The Seventeenth Report of the Deputy Keeper of Public Records*, London, 1856

PRO: *Eighteenth Report*
—, *The Eighteenth Report of the Deputy Keeper of Public Records*, London, 1857

PRO: *Twentieth Report*
—, *The Twentieth Report of the Deputy Keeper of Public Records*, London, 1859

Recueil des actes de Charles II le Chauve, ed. Tessier et al.
Recueil des actes de Charles II le Chauve, roi de France, ed. G. Tessier et al., 3 vols, Paris, 1943–55

Recueil des actes de Lothaire et de Louis V, ed. Halphen and Lot
Recueil des actes de Lothaire et de Louis V, rois de France 954–84, ed. L. Halphen and F. Lot, Paris, 1908

Regesta regum anglo-normannorum, ed. Bates
Regesta regum anglo-normannorum: The Acta of William I, 1066–87, ed. D. Bates, Oxford, 1998

Regesta regum anglo-normannorum, ed. Davis and Whitwell
Regesta regum anglo-normannorum, ed. H. W. C. Davis and R. J. Whitwell, 4 vols, Oxford, 1913–68 [vol. I, 1913, ed. H. W. C. Davis; vol. II, 1956, ed. C. Johnson and H. A. Cronne; vols III–IV, 1968, ed. H. A. Cronne and R. H. C. Davis]

Registrum antiquissimum, ed. Foster
The Registrum antiquissimum *of the Cathedral Church of Lincoln*, ed. C. W. Foster, 10 vols, Lincoln Record Society, Hereford, 1931–73

Report from the Select Committee on National Monuments

Report from the Select Committee on National Monuments and Works of Art, London, 1841

Reports from the Select Committee into the State of the Public Records
Reports from the Select Committee appointed to Inquire into the State of the Public Records of the Kingdom, London, 1800

Richer, ed. Latouche
Richer, *Histoire de France*, ed. and trans. R. Latouche, 2 vols, Paris, 1930–37

Robert of Torigny, ed. Howlett
Robert of Torigny, 'Chronica', in *Chronicles of Stephen, Henry II and Richard I*, ed. Howlett, vol. IV, pp. 81–315

Roger of Howden, ed. Stubbs
Roger of Howden, *Chronica Magistri Rogeri de Houedene*, ed. W. Stubbs, 4 vols, Rolls Series, London, 1868–71

Rotuli litterarum clausarum, ed. Hardy
Rotuli litterarum clausarum in Turri Londinensi asservati, ed. T. D. Hardy, 2 vols, London, 1823–44

Round 1899
J. H. Round, ed., *Calendar of Documents Preserved in France, Illustrative of the History of Great Britain and Ireland, vol. I: AD 918–1206*, London, 1899

Sanderson 1658
W. Sanderson, *A Compleat History of the Life and Raigne of King Charles from his Cradle to his Grave*, London, 1658

Sandford 1677
F. Sandford, *A Genealogical History of the Kings of England and Monarchs of Great Britain*, London, 1677

Shakespeare, *King Richard III*, ed. Ure
W. Shakespeare, *King Richard III*, ed. P. Ure, The Arden Shakespeare, fifth edition, London and Cambridge, Massachusetts, 1961

Shakespeare, *King Richard II*, ed. Hammond
—, *King Richard II*, ed. A. Hammond, The Arden Shakespeare, London and New York, 1981

Simeon of Durham, ed. Arnold
Simeon of Durham, *Symeonis monachi opera omnia*, vol. II: *Historia regum*, ed. T. Arnold, Rolls Series, London, 1885

'Stanzaic Morte Arthur', ed. Benson
'Stanzaic Morte Arthur', in *King Arthur's Death*, ed. L. D. Benson, Exeter, 1986, pp. I–III

Stow, ed. Kingsford
J. Stow, *A Survey of London . . . Reprinted from the Text of 1603*, ed. C. L. Kingsford, 3 vols, Oxford, 1908

Stow, ed. Morley
—, *A Survey of London Written in the Year 1598 by John Stow*, ed. H. Morley, Stroud, 1994

Symeon Semeon, ed. Esposito
Symeon Semeon, *Itinerarium Symeonis Semeonis ab Hybernia ad Terram Sanctam*, ed. M. Esposito, Scriptores Latini Hiberniae, 4, Dublin, 1960

Tacitus, *Annals*, ed. Jackson
Tacitus, *The Annals*, ed. J. Jackson, 4 vols, Cambridge, Massachusetts, 1951

Textus Roffensis, ed. Hearne
Textus Roffensis, ed. T. Hearne, Oxford, 1720

Thorpe 1769
J. Thorpe, *Registrum roffense; or, A Collection of Antient Records . . . Illustrating the Cathedral Church of Rochester*, London, 1769

Trivet, ed. Rutherford
'The Anglo-Norman Chronicle of Nicolas Trivet', ed. A. Rutherford, unpublished PhD thesis, University of London, 1932

Trioedd Ynys Prydein, ed. Bromwich
Trioedd Ynys Prydein: The Welsh Triads, ed. and trans. R. Bromwich, Cardiff, 1961

True Relation of the Ceremonies
A True Relation of the Ceremonies at the Creating of the Knights of the Bath the 18 & 19 April 1661, London, 1661

Vegetius, ed. Lang
Vegetius, *Epitoma rei militaris*, ed. C. Lang, Leipzig, 1885

Von Bülow 1892
G. von Bülow, ed., 'The Diary of the Duke of Stettin Pomerania, 1602', *Transactions of the Royal Historical Society*, second series, 6 (1892), pp. 1–69

Von Klarwill 1928
V. von Klarwill, ed., 'A Knight Errant: The Narrative of Lupold von Wedel of Kremzow', in *Queen Elizabeth and Some Foreigners*, London, 1928, pp. 303–43

'Voyage of Don Manoel Gonzales', ed. Pinkerton
'The Voyage of Don Manoel Gonzales, Late Merchant of Lisbon', in *A General Collection of the Best and Most Interesting Voyages and Travels in All Parts of the World*, ed. J. Pinkerton, 17 vols, London, 1808–14, vol. II, pp. 1–178

Vulgate Version of the Arthurian Romances, ed. Sommer
The Vulgate Version of the Arthurian Romances, Edited from Manuscripts in the British Museum, ed. H. O. Sommer, 8 vols, New York, 1861

Wace, ed. Holden
Wace, *Le Roman de rou de Wace et des ducs de Normandie*, ed. A. J. Holden, 3 vols, Paris, 1971–3

Wace, ed. Weiss
—, *Wace's Roman de Brut: A History of the British*, ed. and trans. J. Weiss, Exeter, 1999

Waldstein, ed. Groos
Baron Waldstein, *The Diary of Baron Waldstein: An Elizabethan Traveller in England*, ed. G. W. Groos, London, 1981

Walsingham, *Historia anglicana*, ed. Riley
T. Walsingham, *Thomae Walsingham Historia Anglicana*, ed. H. T. Riley, 2 vols, Rolls Series, London, 1863–4

Ward, ed. Fenwick
N. Ward, *The London Spy by Ned Ward*, ed. K. Fenwick, London, 1955

William of Malmesbury, *De gestis pontificum anglorum*, ed. Hamilton
William of Malmesbury, *De gestis pontificum anglorum*, ed. N.E.S.A. Hamilton, Rolls Series, London and Cambridge, 1870

William of Malmesbury, *Gesta regum anglorum*, ed. Mynors, Thomson and Winterbottom
—, *Gesta regum anglorum / The History of the English Kings*, vol. I, ed. and trans. R. A. B. Mynors, R. M. Thomson and M. Winterbottom, Oxford Medieval Texts, Oxford, 1998

William of Malmesbury, *Historiae novellae*, ed. Stubbs

—, *Willelmi Malmesbiriensis monachi: Historiae novellae: libri tres*, ed. W. Stubbs, vol. II, Rolls Series, London, 1889

William of Poitiers, ed. Davis and Chibnall
William of Poitiers, *The* Gesta Guillelmi *of William of Poitiers*, ed. and trans. R. H. C. Davis and M. Chibnall, Oxford Medieval Texts, Oxford, 1998

Williamson, ed. Fox
A. Williamson, *The Official Diary of Lieutenant General Adam Williamson, Deputy Lieutenant of the Tower, 1722–47*, ed. J. C. Fox, London, 1912

Winchester Annals, ed. Luard
Annales monastici, vol. II: *Annales monasterii de Wintonia*, ed. H. R. Luard, Rolls Series, London, 1865, pp. 3–125

Wood, ed. Clark
A. Wood, *The Life and Times of Anthony Wood, Antiquary, of Oxford, 1632–95*, ed. C. Clark, 5 vols, Oxford, 1891–1900

Wren 1750
C. Wren, ed., *Parentalia; or, Memoirs of the Family of the Wrens*, London, 1750

SECONDARY SOURCES

Ainsworth 1845
W. H. Ainsworth, *The Tower of London: A Historical Romance*, London, 1845

Aldsworth 1990
F. G. Aldsworth, 'Recent Observations on the Tower of Holy Trinity Church, Bosham', *Sussex Archaeological Collections*, 128 (1990), pp. 55–72

Alexander and Binski 1987
J. Alexander and P. Binski, eds, *The Age of Chivalry: Art in Plantagenet England, 1200–1400*, London, 1987

Allibone 1987
J. Allibone, *Anthony Salvin: Pioneer of Gothic Revival Architecture, 1799–1881*, Columbia, Missouri, 1987

Anderson and Quirk 1964
F. W. Anderson and R. N. Quirk, 'Note on the Quarr Stone'; as appendix to E. M. Jope, 'The Saxon Building Stone Industry in Southern and Midland England', *Medieval Archaeology*, 8 (1964), pp. 115–17

Anglo 1969
S. Anglo, *Spectacle, Pageantry and Early Tudor Policy*, Oxford, 1969

Anglo 1997
—, *Spectacle, Pageantry and Early Tudor Policy*, second edition, Oxford, 1997

Anonymous 1740
Anonymous, *The Foreigner's Guide [to] London and Westminster*, London, 1740

Anonymous 1754
—, *An Historical Description of the Tower of London and its Curiosities*, London, 1754

Anonymous 1807
—, *An Historical Description of the Tower of London and its Curiosities*, London, 1807

Anonymous 1815
—, *An Improved History and Description of the Tower of London*, London, 1815

Anonymous 1858
—, *Sketches of the Tower of London*, London, 1858

Anstis 1725
J. Anstis, *Observations Introductory to an Historical Essay upon the Knighthood of the Bath*, London, 1725

Armitage 1912
E. S. Armitage, *The Early Norman Castles of the British Isles*, London, 1912; reprinted 1971

Arn 2000
M. J. Arn, ed., *Charles d'Orléans in England, 1415–1440*, Woodbridge, 2000

Arnold 1988
J. Arnold, *Queen Elizabeth's Wardrobe Unlock'd*, Leeds, 1988

Ashbee 2006a
J. Ashbee, 'Cloisters in English Palaces in the Twelfth and Thirteenth Centuries', *Journal of the British Archaeological Association*, 159 (2006), pp. 71–90

Ashbee 2006b
—, 'The Tower of London as a Royal Residence, 1066–1154', unpublished Phd thesis, University of London, 2006

Askins 2000
W. Askins, 'The Brothers Orléans and their Keepers', in Arn 2000, pp. 27–45

Astley 1903
H. J. D. Astley 'Mediaeval Colchester: Town, Castle and Abbey – from MSS in the British Museum', *Transactions of the Essex Archaeological Association*, 8 (1903), pp. 117–35

Atherton et al. 1996
I. Atherton et al., eds, *Norwich Cathedral: Church, City and Diocese, 1096–1996*, London, 1996

Aubert et al. 1961
M. Aubert et al., *L'Art roman en France*, Paris, 1961

Auerbach 1954
E. Auerbach, *Tudor Artists*, London, 1954

Aylmer 1974
G. E. Aylmer, *The King's Servants: The Civil Service of Charles I, 1625–1642*, second edition, London and Boston, Massachusetts, 1974

Aylmer 2002
—, *The Crown's Servants: Government and Civil Service under Charles II, 1660–85*, Oxford, 2002

Ayton and Price 1995
A. Ayton and J. L. Price, eds, *The Medieval Military Revolution*, London, 1995

BAA: *Anjou*
British Archaeological Association, *Anjou: Medieval Art, Architecture and Archaeology*, ed. J. McNeill and D. Prigent, British Archaeological Association Conference Transactions for the Year 2000, 26, Leeds, 2003

BAA: *Canterbury*
—, *Medieval Art and Architecture at Canterbury before 1220*, British Archaeological Association Conference Transactions for the year 1979, 5, Leeds, 1982

Backhouse 2000
J. Backhouse, 'Charles of Orléans Illuminated', in Arn 2000, pp. 157–64

Baillie and Pilcher 1973
M. G. L. Baillie and J. R. Pilcher, 'A Simple Cross-Dating Program for Tree-Ring Research', *Tree-Ring Bulletin*, 33 (1973), pp. 7–14

Barber 2003
R. Barber, *Henry Plantagenet*, new edition, Woodbridge, 2003

Baring 1909
F. H. Baring, *Domesday Tables for the Counties of Surrey, Berkshire, Middlesex, Hertford, Buckingham and Bedford and for the New Forest, with an Appendix on the Battle of Hastings*, London, 1909

Barley 1976
M. W. Barley, 'Town Defences in England and Wales after 1066', in *The Plans and Topography of Medieval Towns in England and Wales*, ed. Barley, CBA Research Report, 14 [London], 1976, pp. 57–71

Barlow 1983
F. Barlow, *William Rufus*, London, 1983

Barral i Altet and Parisse 1992
X. Barral i Altet and M. Parisse, eds, *Le Roi de France et son royaume autour de l'An Mil. Actes du Colloque Hughes Capet, 987–1987: La France de l'An Mil*, Paris, 1992

Barter 1979
S. Barter, 'The Royal Mint', in Charlton 1978, pp. 117–21

Barter Bailey 1997
S. Barter Bailey, 'J. R. Planché's Rearrangement of the Armour in the Tower of London, 1867', *Royal Armouries Yearbook*, 2 (1997), pp. 137–43

Barter Bailey 2002
—, 'Lord Dillon: Curator of the Armouries, 1895–1912', *Royal Armouries Yearbook*, 7 (2002), pp. 108–18

Barthélemy 1984
D. Barthélemy, *Les Deux Ages de la Seigneurie Banale: pouvoir et société dans la terre des Sires de Coucy, milieu XIe–milieu XIIIe siècle*, Paris, 1984

Barthélemy 1988
—, 'Civilizing the Fortress: Eleventh to Thirteenth Century', in *A History of Private Life, Volume 2: Revelations of the Medieval World*, ed. G. Duby, Cambridge, Massachusetts, and London, 1988, pp. 396–423

Barlow 1955
F. Barlow, *The Feudal Kingdom of England*, London, 1955

Bartlett 2000
R. Bartlett, *England under the Norman and Angevin Kings*, Oxford, 2000

Bates 1891
C. J. Bates, *The Border Holds of Northumberland*, Newcastle upon Tyne, 1891 [also issued as *Archaeologia Aeliana*, second series, 14]

Bateson 1902
M. Bateson, 'A London Municipal Collection of the Reign of John', *English Historical Review*, 17 (1902), pp. 480–511, 707–30

Baylé 1974
M. Baylé, 'Les Chapiteaux de la chapelle Sainte-Paix à Caen', *Bulletin monumental*, 132 (1974), pp. 261–72

Baylé 1979
—, *La Trinité de Caen: sa place dans l'histoire de l'architecture et du décor romans*, Geneva, 1979

Baylé 1982
—, 'La Sculpture du XIème siècle à Jumièges et sa place dans le décor architectural des abbayes normandes', in *Aspects du monachisme en Normandie*, ed. L. Musset, Paris, 1982, pp. 75–90

Baylé 1988a
—, 'Les Ateliers de sculpture de Saint-Etienne de Caen au XIe et au XIIe siècles', *Anglo-Norman Studies*, 10 (1988), pp. 1–23

Baylé 1988b
—, 'Les Origines et les premiers développements de la sculpture romane en Normandie', unpublished Thèse de Doctorat d'Etat, Université de Paris 1

Baylé 2001
—, ed., *L'Architecture normande au moyen âge: actes du colloque de Cerisy-la-Salle*, second edition, 2 vols, Caen, 2001

Bayley 1821–5
J. Bayley, *The History and Antiquities of the Tower of London*, 2 vols, London, 1821–5

Bayne 1910
C. G. Bayne, 'The Coronation of Queen Elizabeth', *English Historical Review*, 25 (1910), pp. 550–53

Bennett, Frere and Stow 1982
P. Bennett, S. S. Frere and S. Stow, *Excavations at Canterbury Castle*, Maidstone, 1982

C. D. Benson 1980
C. D. Benson, *The History of Troy in Middle English Literature: Guido delle Colonne's* Historia destructionis Troiae *in Medieval England*, Woodbridge, 1980

L. D. Benson 1986
L. D. Benson, ed., *King Arthur's Death*, Exeter, 1986

Bentley 1984
D. Bentley, 'A Recently Identified Valley in the City', *London Archaeologist*, 5, no. 1 (1984), pp. 13–16

Bentley 1987
—, 'The Western Stream Reconsidered: An Enigma in the Landscape', *London Archaeologist*, 5, no. 12 (1987) pp. 328–34

Biddle 1986
M. Biddle, *Wolvesey*, London, 1986

Biddle 1989
—, 'A City in Transition, 400–800', in Lobel 1989, pp. 20–29

Bilson 1910
J. Bilson, 'Comment Recorded in Royal Archaeological Institute's Autumn Meeting [4–5 October 1910] at Westminster Abbey', *Archaeological Journal*, 67 (1910), pp. 397–406

Binding 1996
G. Binding, *Deutsche Königpfalzen, 765–1220*, Darmstadt, 1996

Binns and Banks 1999
J. W. Binns and S. E. Banks, *Gervase of Tilbury and the Encyclopaedic Tradition: Information Retrieval from the Middle Ages to Today*, Leicester, 1999

Binski 1995
P. Binski, *Westminster Abbey and the Plantagenets: Kingship and the Representation of Power, 1200–1400*, New Haven and London, 1995

Bishop and Williams 2004
R. Bishop and G. Williams, 'Coenwulf, King of Mercia', *Current Archaeology*, 194 (2004), pp. 56–7

Blackmore 1976
H. L. Blackmore, *The Armouries of the Tower of London*, vol. 1: *Ordnance*, London, 1976

Blair 1994a
J. Blair, *Anglo-Saxon Oxfordshire*, Stroud, 1994

Blair 1994b
—, 'Hall and Chamber: English Domestic Planning, 1000–1250', in *Manorial Domestic Buildings in England and Northern France*, ed. M. Jones and G. Meirion-Jones, London, 1994, pp. 1–21

Blair 2005
—, *The Church in Anglo-Saxon Society*, Oxford, 2005

Blair and Ramsay 1991
—, and N. Ramsay, eds, *English Medieval Industries*, London, 1991

Blockley 1997
K. Blockley, *Canterbury Cathedral Nave: Archaeology, History and Architecture*, Canterbury, 1997

Bocquet and Mastrolorenzo 2001
A. Bocquet and J. Mastrolorenzo, *Sainte-Suzanne. Le Donjon: évaluation archéologique, septembre–décembre 2000*, Service Départementale de l'Archéologie et Musées, Laval, 2001

Bonnassie 1982
P. Bonnassie, 'Les Descriptions des forteresses dans le livre des Miracles de Sainte Foy de Conques', *Mélanges d'Archéologie et d'Histoire*, Geneva, 1982, pp. 17–26

Boreman 1741
T. Boreman, *Curiosities of the Tower of London*, London, 1741

Borg 1976
A. Borg, 'Two Studies in the History of the Tower Armouries', *Archaeologia*, 105 (1976), pp. 316–52

Borger and Oedinger 1969
H. Borger and F. W. Oedinger, 'Beiträge zur Frühgeschichte des Xantener Viktorstiftes', *Rheinische Ausgrabungen*, 6 (1969), pp. 168–85, 203–5

Bosseboeuf 1897
L.-A. Bosseboeuf, *La Touraine historique et monumentale: Amboise, le Château, la Ville et le Canton*, Tours, 1897

Boussard 1961
J. Boussard, 'Le Trésorier de Saint-Martin de Tours', *Revue de l'histoire de l'église de France*, 47 (1961), pp. 61–88

Boussinesq and Laurent 1933
G. Boussinesq and G. Laurent, *Histoire de Reims depuis des origines jusqu'à nos jours*, 2 vols, Reims, 1933

Bradbury 1996
J. Bradbury, *Stephen and Matilda: The Civil War of 1139–53*, Stroud, 1996

Braun 1937
H. Braun, 'London's First Castle', *Transactions of the London and Middlesex Archaeological Society*, 7 (1933–7), pp. 445–51

Brindle and Kerr 1997
S. Brindle and B. Kerr, *Windsor Revealed*, London, 1997

Britton and Brayley 1830
J. Britton and E. W. Brayley, *Memorials of the Tower of London*, London, 1830

Broche 1900–04
L. Broche, 'L'Ancien palais des rois à Laon', *Bulletin de la Société Académique de Laon*, 31 (1900–04), pp. 180–212

Brodeur, Chevet and Mastrolorenzo 1998
J. Brodeur, P. Chevet and J. Mastrolorenzo, 'Construction sur le site du château d'Angers d'après les fouilles récentes', in *La Construction en Anjou en moyen âge: actes du Tableau Ronde d'Angers des 29 et 30 mars 1996*, ed. D. Prigent and N.-Y. Tonnerre, Angers, 1998, pp. 101–12

Brooke and Keir 1975
C. N. L. Brooke and G. Keir, *London, 800–1216: The Shaping of a City*, London, 1975

R. A. Brown 1952
R. A. Brown, 'Framlingham Castle and Bigod, 1154–1216', *Proceedings of the Suffolk Institute of Archaeology*, 25 (1952), pp. 127–48

R. A. Brown 1953
—, *English Medieval Castles*, London, 1953

R. A. Brown 1964
—, *Orford Castle, Suffolk*, London, 1964; reprinted 1988

R. A. Brown 1965
—, 'The Architecture', in Stenton 1965, pp. 76–87

R. A. Brown 1976
—, *English Castles*, second edition, London, 1976

R. A. Brown 1978a
—, 'Architectural Description', in Charlton 1978, pp. 38–54

R. A. Brown 1978b
—, 'Architectural History and Development to *c.* 1547', in Charlton 1978, pp. 24–37

R. A. Brown 1978c
—, *Castle Rising*, London, 1978

R. A. Brown 1979
—, 'Some Observations on the Tower of London', *Archaeological Journal*, 136 (1979), pp. 99–108

R. A. Brown 1981
—, ed., *Proceedings of the Battle Conference on Anglo-Norman Studies, III: 1980*, Woodbridge, 1981

R. A. Brown 1984
—, *The Architecture of Castles*, London, 1984

R. A. Brown 1986
—, *Rochester Castle*, second edition, London, 1986

Brown and Curnow 1984
— and P. E. Curnow, *Tower of London*, London, 1984

S. A. Brown 1988
S. A. Brown, *The Bayeux Tapestry: History and Bibliography*, Woodbridge, 1988

Bur 2002
M. Bur, *Le Château d'Epinal XIIIe–XVIIe siècle*, Paris, 2002

Butcher 1982
S. Butcher, 'Excavation of a Roman Building on the East Side of the White Tower, 1956–7', in Parnell et al. 1982, pp. 101–5

Caine 1898
C. Caine, 'Our Cities: Sketched 500 Years Ago', *Journal of the British Archaeological Association*, 4 (1898), pp. 319–21

Caple 1999
C. Caple, 'The Durham Cathedral Doors', *Durham Archaeological Journal*, 14–15 (1999), pp. 131–40

Carkeet-Jones 1950
E. H. Carkeet-Jones, *His Majesty's Tower of London*, London, 1950

Carpenter 1990
D. A. Carpenter, *The Minority of Henry III*, Berkeley and Los Angeles, 1990

Carpenter 1996
—, 'King Henry III and the Tower of London', in *The Reign of Henry III*, London and Rio Grande, 1996, pp. 199–218

Champion 1911
P. Champion, *Vie de Charles d'Orléans (1394–1465)*, Paris, 1911

Charbonneau-Lassay 1934
L. Charbonneau-Lassay, *La Tour carrée de l'ancienne forteresse de Loudun*, Loudun, 1934

Charlton 1978
J. Charlton, ed., *The Tower of London: Its Buildings and Institutions*, London, 1978

Charlton 1986
—, *Brough Castle*, London, 1986

Châtelain 1973
A. Châtelain, *Donjons romans des Pays d'Ouest*, Paris, 1973

Chédeville 1973
A. Chédeville, *Chartres et ses campagnes, XI–XIII siècles*, Paris, 1973

Chédeville 1992
—, 'Le Paysage urbain vers l'An Mil', in Barral i Altet and Parisse 1992, pp. 157–63

Cherry 1990
J. Cherry, '*Imago Castelli*: The Depiction of Castles on Medieval Seals', *Château Gaillard*, 15 (1990), pp. 83–90

Cherry and Stratford 1995
— and N. Stratford, *Westminster Kings and the Medieval Palace of Westminster*, British Museum Occasional Paper, 115, London, 1995

Chibnall 1986
M. Chibnall, *Anglo-Norman England, 1066–1166*, Oxford and Cambridge, Massachusetts, 1986

Chrimes 1999
S. B. Chrimes, *Henry VII* [1972] (New Haven and London, 1999)

Clanchy 1993
M. T. Clanchy, *From Memory to Written Record*, second edition, Oxford and Cambridge, Massachusetts, 1993

Clapham 1912
A. W. Clapham, 'The Tower of London and its Development', in Clapham and W. Godfrey, *Some Famous Buildings and their Story*, London, 1912, pp. 31–45

G. T. Clark 1867
G. T. Clark, 'Some Particulars Concerning the Military Architecture of the Tower of London', in *Old London: Papers Read at the London Congress* [of the Archaeological Institute of Great Britain and Ireland] *July 1866*, London, 1867, pp. 11–189

G. T. Clark 1884
—, *Medieval Military Architecture in England*, 2 vols, London, 1884

J. Clark 1981
J. Clark, 'Trinovantum: The Evolution of a Legend', *Journal of Medieval History*, 7 (1981), pp. 135–51

J. Clark 1996
—, 'The Temple of Diana', in *Interpreting Roman London: Papers in Memory of Hugh Chapman*, ed. J. Bird, M. Hassall and H. Sheldon, Oxbow Monographs, 58, Oxford, 1996, pp. 1–9

J. Clark 1997
—, 'Pickering Castle', *Archaeological Journal*, 154 (1997), pp. 255–6

Clarke 1994
P. A. Clarke, *The English Nobility under Edward the Confessor*, Oxford, 1994

Clause and Ravaux 1981
G. Clause and J.-P. Ravaux, *Histoire de Châlons-sur-Marne*, Roanne, 1981

Coad and Streeten 1982
J. G. Coad and A. Streeten 'Excavations at Castle Acre Castle, Norfolk, 1972–7: Country House and Castle of the Norman Earls of Surrey', *Archaeological Journal*, 139 (1982), pp. 138–302

Coates 1998
R. Coates, 'A New Explanation of the Name of London', *Transactions of the Philological Society*, 92 (1998), pp. 203–9

Cocke 1996
T. Cocke, 'Change Not Decay: An Account of the Post-Medieval Fabric', in Atherton et al. 1996, pp. 705–27

Colchester Borough Council 1989
Colchester Borough Council, *Colchester Castle*, Colchester, 1989

Collins 1955
A. J. Collins, *Jewels and Plate of Elizabeth I*, London, 1955

Colvin, Brown and Taylor 1963–82
H. M. Colvin, R. A. Brown and A. J. Taylor, eds, *The History of the King's Works*, 6 vols, London, 1963–82

Compton 1881
C. H. Compton, 'Recent Discoveries at the Tower of London', *Journal of the British Archaeological Association*, 37 (1881), pp. 279–84

Cook, Mynard and Rigold 1969
A. M. Cook, D. C. Mynard and S. E. Rigold,. 'Excavations at Dover Castle, Principally in the Inner Bailey', *Journal of the British Archaeological Association*, third series, 32 (1969), pp. 54–104

Cormier 2001
J.-P. Cormier, 'Le Château de Domfront au moyen âge: essai de reconstitution', in Baylé 2001, vol. II, pp. 291–5

Corvisier 2004
C. Corvisier, 'La Tour maîtresse de Beaugency (Loiret) et ses deux états romans', in Faucherre 2004b, pp. 29–34

Cowie 2004
R. Cowie, 'The Evidence for Royal Sites in Middle Anglo-Saxon London', *Medieval Archaeology*, 48 (2004), pp. 201–9

Cowie et al., forthcoming
— et al., *Lundenwic: Archaeological Evidence for Middle Saxon London*, Museum of London Archaeological Service Monograph Series, forthcoming

Crépin-Leblond 1994
T. Crépin-Leblond, 'Le Palais épiscopal de Laon', in *Société française d'archéologie: Congrès de l'Aisne méridionale*, Paris, 1994, pp. 369–94

Crick 1991
J. C. Crick, *The* Historia regum Britannie *of Geoffrey of Monmouth*, vol. IV: *Dissemination and Reception in the Later Middle Ages*, Cambridge, 1991

Crook 1993

J. Crook, 'Bishop Walkelin's Cathedral', in *Winchester Cathedral: Nine Hundred Years, 1093–1993*, ed. Crook, Chichester, 1993, pp. 21–36

Crook 1998

—, 'The Architectural Setting of the Cult of St Edmund at Bury, 1095–1539', in *Bury St Edmunds: Medieval Art, Architecture and Economy*, ed. A. Gransden, British Archaeological Association Conference Transactions for the Year 1994, 20, Leeds, 1998, pp. 34–44

Crook and Harris 2002

— and R. B. Harris, 'Reconstructing the Lesser Hall: An Interim Report from the Medieval Palace of Westminster Research Project', in *Housing Parliament: Dublin, Edinburgh and Westminster*, ed. Clyve Jones and Sean Kelsey, Edinburgh, 2002, pp. 22–59 [special issue of *Parliamentary History*, vol. 21, no. 1]

Crouch 1992

D. Crouch, *The Idea of Aristocracy in Britain, 1000–1300*, London, 1992

Crum and Crum 1933

J. M. C. Crum and M. M. Crum, 'The *Tau*-cross Capitals in the Undercroft of Canterbury Cathedral', *Archaeologia Cantiana*, 45 (1933), pp. 193–200

Cunliffe 1977a

B. Cunliffe, *Excavations at Portchester Castle*, vol. III: *Medieval: The Outer Bailey and its Defences*, London, 1977

Cunliffe 1977b

—, 'Some Problems and Misconceptions', in *The Saxon Shore*, ed. D. E. Johnston, Council of British Archaeology Research Report, 18, London, 1977, pp. 1–6

Cunliffe and Munby 1985

—, and J. Munby, *Excavations at Portchester Castle*, vol. IV: *Medieval: The Inner Bailey*, London, 1985

Curnow 1977

P. E. Curnow, 'The Wakefield Tower, Tower of London', in *Ancient Monuments and their Interpretation: Essays Presented to A. J. Taylor*, ed. M. R. Apted, R. Gilyard-Beer and A. D. Saunders, London, 1977, pp. 155–90

Darvill et al. 1988

T. Darvill, et al., 'Excavations on the Site of the Early Norman Castle at Gloucester, 1983–84', *Medieval Archaeology*, 32 (1988), pp. 1–49

H. W. C. Davis 1949

H. W. C. Davis, *England under the Normans and Angevins, 1066–1272*, London, 1949

R. H. C. Davis 1978

R. H. C. Davis, 'The Carmen de Hastingae Proelio', *English Historical Review*, 93 (1978), pp. 241–61

R. H. C. Davis 1980

—, *The Normans and their Myth*, London, 1980

R. H. C. Davis 1981

—, 'William of Poitiers and his History of William the Conqueror', in *The Writing of History in the Middle Ages: Essays Presented to Richard William Southern*, ed. Davis and J. M. Wallace-Hadrill, Oxford, 1981, pp. 71–100

Davison 1967

B. K. Davison, 'Three Eleventh-Century Earthworks in England: Their Excavation and Implications', *Château Gaillard*, 1 (1967), pp. 39–48

Davison 1974

—, 'Excavations in the Tower of London', *Château Gaillard*, 2 (1974), pp. 40–43

De Boüard 1974

M. de Boüard, 'De l'aula au donjon: les fouilles de la motte de la chapelle à Doué-la-Fontaine, xe–xie siècle', *Archéologie médiévale*, 3–4 (1973–4), pp. 5–110

De Boüard 1979

—, *Le Château de Caen*, Caen, 1979 [special issue of *Archéologie médiévale*]

Decaëns 2001

J. Decaëns, 'Le Château de Domfront', in Baylé 2001, vol. II, pp. 288–90

De Caumont 1853

A. de Caumont, *Abécédaire; ou, Rudiment d'archéologie, architecture civile et militaire*, Caen, 1853

Delaycun 2003

M.-D. Delaycun, 'Le Site castral de Montbazon: étude archéologique de la tour maîtresse', *Bulletin de la Société archéologique de la Touraine*, 49 (2003), pp. 75–84

De Ros 1867

W. De Ros, *Memorials of the Tower of London*, London, 1867

Devaux 1887

J. Devaux, *Essai sur les premiers seigneurs de Pithiviers*, Orléans, 1887

Deyres 1969

M. Deyres, 'Le Château de Montbazon au xième siècle', *Cahiers de civilisation médiévale*, XII année, no. 2 (April–June 1969), pp. 147–59

Deyres 1974

—, 'Les châteaux de Foulque Nerra', *Bulletin monumental*, 132 (1974), pp. 7–28

Dixon 1976

P. Dixon, *Barbarian Europe*, Oxford, 1976

Dixon 1988

—, 'The Donjon at Knaresborough: The Castle as Theatre', *Château Gaillard*, 14 (1988), pp. 121–39

Dixon 1996

—, 'Design in Castle Building: The Controlling of Access to the Lord', *Château Gaillard*, 18 (1996), pp. 47–56

Dixon 2002

—, 'The Myth of the Keep', in Meirion-Jones, Impey and Jones 2002, pp 9–14

Dixon, forthcoming

—, 'The Great Tower of Bridgnorth Castle', *Antiquaries Journal* (forthcoming)

Dixon and Lott 1993

— and B. Lott, 'The Courtyard and the Tower: Contexts and Symbols in the Development of Late Medieval Great Houses', *Journal of the British Archaeological Association*, 146 (1993), pp. 93–101

Dixon and Marshall 1993a

— and P. Marshall, 'The Great Tower in the 12th Century: The Case of Norham Castle', *Archaeological Journal*, 150 (1993), pp. 410–32

Dixon and Marshall 1993b

— and —, 'The Great Tower at Hedingham Castle: A Reassessment', *Fortress*, 18 (1993), pp. 16–23

Dixon and Marshall 2002

— and —, 'Norwich Castle and its Analogues', in Meirion-Jones, Impey and Jones 2002, pp. 235–44

Dobson 1983

R. B. Dobson, ed., *The Peasants' Revolt of 1381*, second edition, London, 1983

Dodd 2003

A. Dodd, ed., *Oxford before the University: The Late Saxon and Norman Archaeology of the Thames Crossing, the Defences and the Town*, Oxford, 2003

Donnell 2002

J. Donnell, 'Melbourne Church, Derbyshire', BA dissertation, University of Nottingham, 2002

Doranlo 1953

R. Doranlo, 'Le Château de Falaise', *Congrès archéologique* (1953), pp. 184–200

Dormoy 1998

C. Dormoy, 'L'Expertise dendrochronologique du donjon de Loches (Indre-et-Loire): des données fondamentales pour sa datation', *Archéologie médievale*, 27 (1998), pp. 73–89

Douglas 1964

D. C. Douglas, *William the Conqueror*, London, 1964

Drage 1987

C. Drage, 'Urban Castles', in R. Leech and J. Schofield, *Urban Archaeology in Britain*, Council of British Archaeology Research Report, 61, London, 1987, pp. 117–32

Drage 1989

—, *Nottingham Castle: A Place Full Royal*, Nottingham, 1989

Draper 1977

P. Draper, *Creation of the DoE*, London, 1977

Drury 1982

P. Drury, 'Aspects of the Origins and Development of Colchester Castle', *Archaeological Journal*, 139 (1982), pp. 302–419

Drury 1984

—, 'The Temple of Claudius at Colchester Reconsidered', *Britannia*, 15 (1984), pp. 7–50

Drury 2002

—, 'Norwich Castle Keep', in Meirion-Jones, Impey and Jones 2002, pp. 211–34

Ducange 1883–7

Ducange, *Glossarium mediae et infimae latinitatis*, 10 vols, Paris, 1883–7

Duchesne 1609

A. Duchesne, *Antiquités des villes et châteaux de France*, Paris, 1609

Dumville 1986

D. N. Dumville, 'The Historical Value of the *Historia Brittonum*', *Arthurian Literature*, 6 (1986), pp. 1–26

Dunbabin 2000

J. Dunbabin, *France in the Making*, second edition, Oxford, 2000

Durand 1996

P. Durand, 'Les Conséquences de la datation dendrochronologique du donjon de Loches pour la castellologie', *Bulletin monumentale*, 154 (1996), pp. 224–8

Durham et al. 1983

B. Durham et al., 'Oxford's Northern Defences: Archaeological Studies, 1971–1982', *Oxoniensia*, 48 (1983), pp. 13–40

Dyson 1978

T. Dyson, 'Two Saxon Land Grants for Queenhithe', in *Collectanea Londiniensia: Studies in London Archaeology and History Presented to Ralph Merrifield*, ed. J. Bird, H. Chapman and J. Clark, London, 1978, pp. 200–15

Dyson and Milne 2002

— and G. Milne, 'The Tradition of a Saxon Palace at Cripplegate', in G. Milne, *Excavations at Medieval Cripplegate, London*, Swindon, 2002, pp. 127–9

Early 2004

R. Early, 'Le premier édifice de pierre du Château de Mayenne', in Faucherre 2004b, pp. 13–22

Ekwall 1960

E. Ekwall, *The Concise Oxford Dictionary of Place-Names*, Oxford, 1960

L. B. Ellis 1948

L. B. Ellis, 'Wardrobe Place and the Great Wardrobe', *Transactions of the London and Middlesex Archaeological Society*, new series, 9 (1948), pp. 246–61

S. M. Ellis 1911

S. M. Ellis, *William Harrison Ainsworth and his Friends*, 2 vols, London, 1911

English 1995

B. English, 'Towns, Mottes and Ring-works of the Conquest', in Ayton and Price 1995, pp. 45–61

English Heritage 1998

English Heritage, *Dendrochronology: Guidelines on Producing and Interpreting Dendrochronological Dates*, London, 1998

Faucherre 2004a

N. Faucherre, 'La Tour de Broue (Charente-Maritime): l'œuvre du Comte d'Anjou', in Faucherre 2004b, pp. 69–73

Faucherre 2004b

—, *Tours seigneuriales de l'Ouest: travaux récents sur quelques tours maîtresses de la Normandie à la Catalogne. Comptes rendus des seminaires de l'équipe en 2001–3: Centre d'études supérieures de civilisation médiévale*, Poitiers, 2004

Faulkner 1958

P. Faulkner, 'Domestic Planning from the 12th to the 14th Century', *Archaeological Journal*, 115 (1958), pp. 150–83

Fayolle-Lussac 1974

B. Fayolle-Lussac, 'Les Châteaux des territoires du "Ducatus Francorum" et de l'Eglise de Reims de 840 à 996. Recherches d'après les chroniques sur les dates d'apparition et le vocabulaire', Mémoire de Maîtrise, University of Caen [typescript]

Federico 1997

S. Federico, 'A Fourteenth-Century Erotics of Politics: London as a Feminine New Troy', *Studies in the Age of Chaucer*, 19 (1997), pp. 121–55

Fernie 1982

E. Fernie, 'St Anselm's Crypt', in BAA: *Canterbury*, pp. 27–38

Fernie 1983

—, *The Architecture of the Anglo-Saxons*, London, 1983

Fernie 1993

—, *An Architectural History of Norwich Cathedral*, Oxford, 1993

Fernie 2000
—, *The Architecture of Norman England*, Oxford, 2000

Field 1993
P. J. C. Field, *The Life and Times of Sir Thomas Malory*, Woodbridge, 1993

Field 1996
—, 'Nennius and his History', *Studia Celtica*, 30 (1996), pp. 159–65

Fleury 1891
G. Fleury, 'Les Fortifications du Maine: La Tour Orbrindelle et le Mont-Barbet', *Revue historique et archéologique du Maine*, 29 (1891), pp. 137–54, 279–303

Flight 1977
C. Flight, *The Bishops and Monks of Rochester, 1076–1214*, Kent Archaeological Society Monographs, 6, Maidstone, 1977

Flight and Harrison 1978
— and A. C. Harrison, 'Rochester Castle, 1976', *Archaeologia Cantiana*, 104 (1978), pp. 27–60

Flint 1979
V. J. Flint, 'The *Historia regum Britannie* of Geoffrey of Monmouth: Parody and its Purpose. A Suggestion', *Speculum*, 54 (1979), pp. 447–68

Flori 1997
J. Flori, 'Châteaux et forteresses aux XIe et XIIe siècles: étude du vocabulaire des historiens des ducs de Normandie', *Le Moyen Age*, 103, no. 2 (1997), pp. 261–73

Forbes 1929
A. Forbes, *A History of the Army Ordnance Services*, 3 vols, London, 1929

Foster 1991
R. Foster, *Patterns of Thought: The Hidden Meaning of the Great Pavement of Westminster Abbey*, London, 1991

ffoulkes 1916
C. J. ffoulkes, *Inventory and Survey of the Armouries of the Tower of London*, 2 vols, London, 1916

ffoulkes 1939
—, *Arms and the Tower*, London, 1939

Fournier 1964
G. Fournier, 'Le Château du Puiset au début du XIIe siècle et sa place dans l'évolution de l'architecture militaire', *Bulletin monumental*, 122 (1964), pp. 355–74

Frankl 1926
P. Frankl, *Die frühmittelalterliche und romanische Baukunst*, Potsdam, 1926

Frere 1978
S. Frere, *Britannia: A History of Roman Britain*, revised edition, London, 1978

Gaimster and Bradley 2002
D. Gaimster and J. Bradley, eds, 'Medieval Britain and Ireland, 2000', *Medieval Archaeology*, 46 (2002), pp. 146–264

Galbraith 1925
V. H. Galbraith, 'The Tower as an Exchequer Record Office in the Reign of Edward II', in *Essays in Medieval History Presented to Thomas Frederick Tout*, ed. A. G. Little and F. M. Powicke, Manchester, 1925, pp. 231–47

Gem 1981a
R. D. H. Gem, 'The Romanesque Rebuilding of Westminster Abbey', in R. A. Brown 1981, pp. 33–60

Gem 1981b
—, 'Chichester Cathedral: When Was the Romanesque Church Begun?', in R. A. Brown 1981, pp. 61–4

Gem 1982
—, 'The Significance of the 11th-Century Rebuilding of Christ Church and St Augustine's, Canterbury, in the Development of Romanesque Architecture', in BAA: *Canterbury*, pp. 1–19

Gem 1986
—, 'Lincoln Cathedral: *Ecclesia Pulchra, Ecclesia Fortis*', in *Medieval Art and Architecture at Lincoln Cathedral*, ed. T. A. Heslop and V. A. Sekules, British Archaeological Association Conference Transactions for the Year 1982, 8, Leeds, 1986, pp. 9–28

Gem 1987
—, 'Canterbury and the Cushion Capital: A Commentary on Passages from Goscelin's *De Miraculis Sancti Augustini*', in *Romanesque and Gothic: Essays for George Zarnecki*, ed. N. Stratford, Woodbridge, 1987, pp. 83–101

Gem 1990
—, 'The Romanesque Architecture of Old St Paul's Cathedral and its Late Eleventh-Century Context', in *Medieval Art and Archaeology in London*, ed. L. Grant, British Archaeological Association Conference Transactions for the Year 1984, 10, Leeds, 1990, pp. 47–63

Gibson 1978
M. Gibson, *Lanfranc of Bec*, Oxford, 1978

Gillingham 1981
J. Gillingham, *The Wars of the Roses*, London, 1981

Gillingham 1989
—, 'William the Bastard at War', in Harper-Bill, Holdsworth and Nelson 1989, pp. 141–58

Gillingham 1990
—, 'The Context and Purposes of Geoffrey of Monmouth's *History of the Kings of Britain*', *Anglo-Norman Studies*, 13 (1990), pp. 99–118

Given-Wilson 1986
C. Given-Wilson, *The Royal Household and the King's Affinity: Service, Politics and Finance in England, 1360–1413*, New Haven and London, 1986

Glare 1968–82
P. G. W. Glare, *Oxford Latin Dictionary*, 8 vols, Oxford, 1968–82

Goldingham 1918
C. S. Goldingham, 'The Navy under Henry VII', *English Historical Review*, 33 (1918), pp. 472–88

Gomme 1887
G. Gomme, 'Boley Hill, Rochester', *Archaeologia Cantiana*, 17 (1887), pp. 181–8

Goulder 1961
L. Goulder, *London: The Tower Pilgrimage*, London, 1961

Gower 1902
R. Sutherland Gower, *The Tower of London*, 2 vols, London, 1902

Gransden 1974
A. Gransden, *Historical Writing in England, c.550 to c.1307*, London, 1974

Greenhalgh 1989
M. Greenhalgh, *The Survival of Roman Antiquities in the Middle Ages*, London, 1989

Greenway 1996
D. Greenway, *Henry, Archdeacon of Huntingdon*, Oxford, 1996

Hallam 1979
E. M. Hallam, 'The Tower of London as a Record Office', *Archives*, 14, no. 61 (Spring 1979), pp. 3–10

Halphen 1906
L. Halphen, *Le Comté d'Anjou au XIe siècle*, Paris, 1906

Hamilton Thompson 1912
A. Hamilton Thompson, *Military Architecture in England during the Middle Ages*, Oxford, 1912

Hammond 1986
P. Hammond, *The Royal Armouries: Official Guide*, London, 1986

Hammond 1999
—, 'Epitome of England's History: The Transformation of the Tower of London', *Royal Armouries Yearbook*, 4 (1999), pp. 144–74

Hancock 1975
J. M. Hancock, 'The Petrology of the Chalk', *Proceedings of the Geologists' Association*, 86 (1975), pp. 499–535

Harben 1918
H. A. Harben, *A Dictionary of London: Being Notes Topographical and Historical Relating to the Streets and Principal Buildings in the City of London*, London, 1918

Harman 1867
A. Harman, *A Guide to the Tower of London*, London, 1867

Harper-Bill, Holdsworth and Nelson 1989
C. Harper-Bill, C. J. Holdsworth and J. L. Nelson, *Studies in Medieval History presented to R. Allen Brown*, Wolfeboro, New Hampshire, 1989

Hartmann-Virnich 1996
A. Hartmann-Virnich, 'L'Escalier en vis voûté et la construction romane: exemples rhodaniens', *Bulletin monumental*, 154 (1996), pp. 113–28

Hartung 1967–98
A. E. Hartung, ed., *A Manual of the Writings in Middle English, 1050–1500*, 8 vols, New Haven, 1967–98

Harvey 1950
J. Harvey, *The Gothic World, 1100–1600*, London, 1950

Harvey 1954
—, *English Medieval Architects*, London, 1954

Harvey and McGuinness 1996
P. D. A. Harvey and A. McGuinness, *A Guide to British and Medieval Seals*, London, 1996

Haslam 1988
J. Haslam, 'Parishes, Wards and Gates in Eastern London', in *Minsters and Parish Churches: The Local Church in Transition, 950–1200*, ed. J. Blair, Oxford, 1988, pp. 35–44

Hearsey 1960
J. E. N. Hearsey, *The Tower: Eight Hundred and Eighty Years of History*, London, 1960

Héliot 1969
P. Héliot, 'L'Evolution du donjon dans le Nord-Ouest de la France et en Angleterre au XIIe siècle', *Bulletin Archéologique du Comité des Travaux Historiques et Scientifiques*, nouvelle série, 5 (1969), pp. 141–94

Héliot 1974
—, 'Les Origines du donjon résidentiel et les donjons-palais romans de France et d'Angleterre, *Cahiers de Civilisation médiévale*, 17 (1974), pp. 217–34

Heslop 1991
T. A. Heslop, 'Orford Castle: Nostalgia and Sophisticated Living', *Architectural History*, 34 (1991), pp. 36–58

Heslop 1994
—, *Norwich Castle Keep: Romanesque Architecture and Social Context*, Norwich, 1994

Hewett 1980
C. A. Hewett, *English Historic Carpentry*, Chichester, 1980

Hewitt 1841
J. Hewitt, *The Tower of London: Its History, Armouries and Antiquities*, London, 1841

Higgott 2004
G. Higgott, 'The Fabric to 1670', in Keene, Burns and Saint 2004, pp. 178–81

Higham and Barker 1992
R. Higham and P. A. Barker, *Timber Castles*, London, 1992

Hill 1996
D. Hill, 'A Gazetteer of Burghal Hidage Sites', in *The Defence of Wessex: The Burghal Hidage and Anglo-Saxon Fortifications*, ed. Hill and A. R. Rumble, Manchester, 1996, pp. 189–231

Hillam, Morgan and Tyers 1987
J. Hillam, R. A. Morgan and I. Tyers, 'Sapwood Estimates and the Dating of Short Ring Sequences', in *Applications of Tree-Ring Studies: Current Research in Dendrochronology and Related Areas*, ed. R. G. W. Ward, British Archaeological Reports, International Series, 333, Oxford, 1987, pp. 165–85

Hiller and Keevill 1994
J. Hiller and G. D. Keevill, 'Recent Archaeological Work at the Tower of London', *Transactions of the London and Middlesex Archaeological Society*, 45 (1994), pp. 147–81

Hind 1922
A. M. Hind, *Wenceslaus Hollar and his Views of London and Windsor in the Seventeenth Century*, London, 1922

Hinz 1981
H. Hinz, *Motte und Donjon: zur Frühgeschichte der Mittelalterlichen Adelsburg*, Zeitschrift für Archäologie des Mittelalters, 17, Cologne and Bonn, 1981

Hiscock 1994
N. Hiscock, 'Platonic Geometry in Plans of Medieval Abbeys and Cathedrals', unpublished PH.D thesis, Oxford Brookes University, 1994

Hogg 1963
O. F. G. Hogg, *The Royal Arsenal: Its Background, Origin and Subsequent History*, 2 vols, London, 1963

Hollister 1973
C. W. Hollister, 'The Misfortunes of the Mandevilles', *History*, 58 (1973), pp. 18–28

Hollister 2001
—, *Henry I*, New Haven and London, 2001

Holmes and Sitwell 1972
M. Holmes and H. D. W. Sitwell, *The English Regalia*, London, 1972

Honeybourne 1965
M. B. Honeybourne, 'The Reconstructed Map of London under Richard II', *London Topographical Record*, 22 (1965), pp. 29–76

Hope 1911
W. H. St J. Hope, 'The Discovery of the Remains of King Henry VI in Saint George's Chapel, Windsor Castle', *Archaeologia*, 62 (1911), pp. 533–42

Horrox 1989
R. Horrox, *Richard III: A Study in Service*, Cambridge, 1989

Hotson 1954
L. Hotson, *The First Night of Twelfth Night*, London, 1954

Howard and Crossley 1917
F. E. Howard and F. H. Crossley, *English Church Woodwork*, London, 1917

Howell 1998
M. Howell, *Eleanor of Provence*, Oxford, 1998

Hubscher 1986
R. Hubscher, ed., *Histoire d'Amiens*, Toulouse, 1986

Hume 1972
K. Hume, 'The Concept of the Hall in Old English Poetry', *Anglo-Saxon England*, 3 (1972), pp. 63–74

Hurst 1984
H. Hurst, 'The Archaeology of Gloucester Castle: An Introduction', *Transactions of the Bristol and Gloucestershire Archaeological Society*, 102 (1984), pp. 73–128

Hutchinson 1997
M. Hutchinson, 'Edward IV's Bulwark: Excavations at Tower Hill, London, 1985', *Transactions of the London and Middlesex Archaeological Society*, 47 (1997), pp. 103–44

Hyde 1965–6
J. K. Hyde, 'Mediaeval Descriptions of Cities', *Bulletin of the John Rylands Library*, 48 (1965–6), pp. 308–40

Impey 1996
E. A. Impey, 'La Demeure seigneuriale en Normandie entre 1125 et 1225 et la tradition Anglo-Normande', in *L'Architecture normande au Moyen Age*, ed. P. Bouet and M. Baylé, Caen, 1996, pp. 219–24

Impey 1998
—, 'The Western Entrance to the Tower of London, 1240–1241', *Transactions of the London and Middlesex Archaeological Society*, 48 (1998), pp. 59–75

Impey 2000
—, 'The *donjon* at Montrichard, Loir-et-Cher: Observations on its Date and Function', *Revue archéologique du Centre de la France*, 39 (2000), pp. 199–214

Impey 2002a
—, 'The *donjon* at Avranches (Normandy)', *Archaeological Journal*, 159 (2002), pp. 249–57

Impey 2002b
—, 'The *Turris famosa* at Ivry-la-Bataille, Normandy', in Meirion-Jones, Impey and Jones 2002, pp. 189–210

Impey and Lorans 1998
— and E. Lorans, 'Langeais, Indre-et-Loire: An Archaeological and Historical Study of the Early *Donjon* and its Environs', *Journal of the British Archaeological Association*, 151 (1998), pp. 43–106

Impey and Parnell 2000
— and G. Parnell, *The Tower of London: The Official Illustrated History*, London, 2000

James, Marshall and Millett 1984
S. James, A. Marshall and M. Millett, 'An Early-Medieval Building Tradition', *Archaeological Journal*, 141 (1984), pp. 182–215

James and Robinson 1988
T. B. James and A. M. Robinson, *Clarendon Palace*, London, 1988 (Reports of the Research Committee of the Society of Antiquaries of London no. 45)

Johns 1989
H. Johns, 'Introduction to the Maps', in Lobel 1989, pp. 57–62

Johnson 1995
L. Johnson, 'Return to Albion', *Arthurian Literature*, 13 (1995), pp. 19–40

Kahn 1991
D. Kahn, *Canterbury Cathedral and its Romanesque Sculpture*, London, 1991

Kaiser 1981
R. Kaiser, *Bischofherrschaft zwischen Königtum und Fürstenmacht*, Bonn, 1981

Kantorowicz 1946
E. H. Kantorowicz, *Laudes Regiae: A Study in Liturgical Acclamations and Medieval Ruler Worship*, Berkeley and Los Angeles, 1946

Keats-Rohan 1999
K. S. B. Keats-Rohan, *Domesday People: A Prosopography of Persons Occurring in English Documents, 1066–1166*, vol. I: *Domesday Book*, Woodbridge, 1999

A. Keay 2001
A. Keay, *The Elizabethan Tower of London: The Haiward and Gascoyne plan of 1597*, London, 2001 (London Topographical Society no. 158)

J. Keay 1991
J. Keay, *The Honourable Company: A History of the English East India Company*, London, 1991

Keene 1985
D. J. Keene, *Survey of Medieval Winchester*, vol. II, Oxford, 1985

Keene 2003
—, 'Alfred and London', in *Alfred the Great: Papers from the Eleventh-Centenary Conferences*, ed. T. Reuter, Aldershot, 2003, pp. 235–49

Keene 2004
—, 'From Conquest to Capital: St Paul's, *c.* 1100–1500', in Keene, Burns and Saint 2004, pp. 17–31

Keene, forthcoming
—, *London, 500–1300*, forthcoming

Keene, Burns and Saint 2004
—, A. Burns and A. Saint, eds, *St Paul's: The Cathedral Church of London, 604–2004*, New Haven and London, 2004

Keene and Schofield 2004
— and J. Schofield, 'Before St Paul's', in Keene, Burns and Saint 2004, pp. 2–4

Keevill 2004
G. Keevill, *The Tower of London Moat: Archaeological Excavations 1995–9*, Oxford, 2004

Kelsey 1997
S. Kelsey, *Inventing a Republic: The Political Culture of the English Commonwealth, 1649–1653*, Manchester, 1997

Kendrick and Radford 1943
T. D. Kendrick and C. A. R. Radford, 'Recent Discoveries at All Hallows Barking', *Antiquaries Journal*, 23 (1943), pp. 14–18

Keynes 1998
S. Keynes, 'King Alfred and the Mercians', in *Kings, Currency and Alliances: History and Coinage of Southern England in the Ninth Century*, ed. M. Blackburn and D. N. Dumville, Woodbridge, 1998, pp. 1–45

King and Alcock 1969
D. J. C. King and L. Alcock 'Ringworks of England and Wales', *Château Gaillard*, 3 (1969), pp. 90–127

Kingsley Porter 1917
A. Kingsley Porter, *Lombard Architecture*, 4 vols, New Haven, 1917; reprinted New York, 1967

Knight 1842
C. Knight, *London*, 6 vols, London, 1842

Knowles 1926
W. H. Knowles, 'The Castle, Newcastle upon Tyne', *Archaeologia Aeliana*, fourth series, 2 (1926), pp. 1–51

Körner 1964
S. Körner, *The Battle of Hastings: England and Europe, 1035–1066*, Lund, 1964

Lander 1965
J. R. Lander, *The Wars of the Roses*, London, 1965

Lanfry 1928
G. Lanfry, 'Fouilles et découvertes à Jumièges: le déambulatoire de l'église romane', *Bulletin monumental*, 87 (1928), pp. 107–37

Latham and Howlett 1975–
R. E. Latham and D. R. Howlett, eds, *Dictionary of Medieval Latin from British Sources*, Oxford, 1975

Le Héricher 1845
E. Le Héricher, *Avranchin monumental et historique*, 2 vols, Avranches, 1845

Le Maho 1996
J. Le Maho, 'Autour d'un millénaire: l'œuvre architecturale à Rouen de Richard Ier, duc de Normandie (d. 996)', *Bulletin des amis des monuments rouennais* (October 1995–September 1996), pp. 63–83

Le Maho 2000
—, 'La Tour-de-Rouen, palais du duc Richard Ier', in F. de Beaurepaire and J.-P. Chaline, *La Normandie vers l'An Mil*, Rouen, 2000, pp. 73–6

Lesueur 1963
F. Lesueur, 'Thibaud le Tricheur, comte de Blois de Tours et de Chartres au xe siècle', *Mémoires de la Société des sciences et lettres de Loir-et-Cher*, 33 (1963), pp. 225–9

Lethaby 1906
W. R. Lethaby, 'The Palace of Westminster in the Eleventh and Twelfth Centuries', *Archaeologia*, 60 (1906), pp. 131–48

Lethaby 1925
—, *Westminster Abbey Re-examined*, London, 1925

Lethbridge 1934
T. C. Lethbridge, 'Excavations at Burwell Castle', *Proceedings of the Cambridge Antiquarian Society*, 36 (1934), pp. 121–36

Levalet 1977
M. Levalet, 'Les Fortifications d'Avranches', *Art de Basse Normandie*, 71 (1977), pp. 17–23

Lindley 2004
P. Lindley, ed., *The Early History of Lincoln Castle*, Occasional Papers in Lincolnshire History and Archaeology, 12, Lincoln, 2004

Lobel 1989
D. M. Lobel, ed., *The City of London from Prehistoric Times to c. 1520*, The British Atlas of Historic Towns, 3, Oxford, 1989

Loftie 1886
W. J. Loftie, *Authorised Guide to the Tower of London*, London, 1886

Loftie 1888
—, *Authorised Guide to the Tower of London*, abridged second edition, London, 1888

Loftie 1894
—, *Authorised Guide to the Tower of London, second edition, revised . . . with an appendix on the Armoury by the Viscount Dillon*, London, 1894

Logan 1990
F. Logan, *Norman London by William Fitz Stephen, with an Essay by Sir Frank Stenton*, New York, 1990

Loomis 1919
R. S. Loomis, 'The Allegorical Siege in the Art of the Middle Ages', *American Journal of Archaeology*, 23, no. 3 (1919), pp. 255–69

Lot 1891
F. Lot, *Les derniers Carolingiens*, Paris, 1891

Lot 1899
—, 'Heloïse de Peviers, soeur de Garin le Lorain', *Romania*, 27 (1899), pp. 273–7

Loud 1982
G. A. Loud, 'The *Gens Normannorum*: Myth or Reality?', in *Proceedings of the Battle Conference on Anglo-Norman Studies, IV: 1981*, ed. R. A. Brown, Woodbridge, 1982, pp. 104–16

Louise 1993
G. Louise, 'Châteaux et pouvoirs dans le Domfrontais médiéval, ixe–xiiie siècles', *Le Domfront médiéval*, 9 (1993), pp. 15–17

Loyd 1951
L. C. Loyd, *The Origins of Anglo-Norman Families*, Harleian Society Publications, 103, Leeds, 1951

Lusse 1992
J. Lusse, *Naissance d'une cité: Laon et le Laonnois du Ve au Xe siècle*, Nancy, 1992

Lyons 1982
F. Lyons, 'Aspects of the Knighting Ceremony', in *The Medieval Alexander Legend and Romance Epic: Essays in Honour of David J. A. Ross*, ed. P. Noble, L. Polak and C. Isoz, Millwood, New York, and London, 1982, pp. 125–9

McCann 1993
B. McCann, ed., *Fleet Valley Project*, interim report, Museum of London, 1993

McCarthy, Summerson and Annis 1990
M. R. McCarthy, H. R. T. Summerson and R. G. Annis, *Carlisle Castle: A Survey and Documentary History*, London, 1990

McNeill 1992
T. McNeill, *Castles*, London, 1992

McKisack 1971
M. McKisack, *Medieval History in the Tudor Age*, Oxford, 1971

Maddicott 1994
J. R. Maddicott, *Simon de Montfort*, Cambridge, 1994

Maitland 1756
W. Maitland, *The History of London from its Foundation to Present Times*, 2 vols, London, 1756

Mallet 1991
J. Mallet, *Angers, Le Château: Maine-et-Loire*, Nantes, 1991

Marsden 1980
P. Marsden, *Roman London*, London, 1980

Marshall 2004
P. Marshall, 'The Architectural Context of the Medieval Defences', in Lindley 2004, pp. 53–65

Marshall and Foulds 1997
— and T. Foulds, 'The Royal Castle', in *A Centenary History of Nottingham*, ed. J. Beckett, Manchester, 1997, pp. 43–55

Mason and Barker 1961
J. F. A. Mason and P. A. Barker, 'The Norman Castle at Quatford', *Transactions of the Shropshire Archaeological Society*, 57 (1961), pp. 37–45

Mataouchek 2000
V. Mataouchek, '"La Tour César": chronique des fouilles médiévales en France en 2000', *Archéologie médiévale*, 30–31 (2000), p. 441

Maurice and Salvèque 1992
B. Maurice and J.-D. Salvèque, 'La Charpente de l'Hospice de l'Abbaye de Cluny, ou "Ecuries de Saint-Hugues"', in *Les veines du temps: lectures du bois en Bourgogne*, Autun, 1992, pp. 176–8

Mégnien 1980
C. Mégnien, ed., *Synthèse géologique du bassin de Paris*, vol. 1: *Stratigraphie et Paléogéographie*, Mémoire Bureau de Recherches Géologiques et Minières, 101, Paris, 1980

Meirion-Jones, Impey and Jones 2002
G. Meirion-Jones, E. Impey and M. Jones, eds, *The Seigneurial Residence in Western Europe, AD c. 800–1600*, British Archaeological Reports, International Series, 1088, Oxford, 2002

Mesqui 1991–3
J. Mesqui, *Châteaux et enceintes de la France médiévale: de la défense à la résidence*, 2 vols, Paris, 1991–3

Mesqui 1996
—, 'Les Ensembles palatiaux aux XIVe et XVe siècles', in *Palais royaux et princiers au Moyen Age*, ed. A. Renoux, Le Mans, 1996, pp. 51–70

Mesqui 1997
—, *Châteaux forts et fortifications en France*, Paris, 1997

Mesqui 1998
—, 'La tour maîtresse du donjon de Loches', *Bulletin monumental*, 156 (1998), pp. 65–125

Messent 1932
C. J. Messent, *The City Churches of Norwich*, Norwich, 1932

Messent 1936
—, *The Parish Churches of Norfolk and Norwich*, Norwich, 1936

Metais 1898
C. Metais, 'Château de Chartres et Place Billard', *Revue des Archives historiques du diocèse de Chartres* (1898), pp. 3–84

Meyrick 1826
S. R. Meyrick, *A Critical Enquiry into Ancient Armour*, 3 vols, London, 1826

Miles 1997
D. H. Miles, 'The Interpretation, Presentation and Use of Tree-Ring Dates', *Vernacular Architecture*, 28 (1997), pp. 40–56

Miles 2006
—, 'The Tree-Ring Dating of the White Tower, HM Tower of London (TOL99 and TOL100)', English Heritage Research Department Report Series, 2006

Miles and Bridge 2005
— and M. C. Bridge, *The Tree-Ring Dating of the Early Medieval Doors at Westminster Abbey*, Centre for Archaeology Report, 38, 2005

Miles and Haddon-Reece 1993
— and D. Haddon-Reece, 'List 54: Tree-Ring Dates', *Vernacular Architecture*, 24 (1993), pp. 54–60

Miles and Worthington 1997
— and M. J. Worthington, 'Tree-Ring Dates', *Vernacular Architecture*, 28 (1997), pp. 159–81

Miles and Worthington 1998a
— and —, 'The Tower of London', in *Proceedings of the International Conference Dendrochronology and Environmental Trends: Kaunas, Lithuania, 17–21 June 1998*, ed. V. Stravinskiene and R. Juknys, Kaunas, 1998, pp. 37–45

Miles and Worthington 1998b
— and —, 'Tree-Ring Dates', *Vernacular Architecture*, 29 (1998), pp. 111–29

Miles and Worthington 2002
— and —, 'Tree-Ring Dates', *Vernacular Architecture*, 33 (2002), pp. 81–102

Miles, Worthington and Bridge 2003
—, — and M. C. Bridge, 'Tree-Ring Dates', *Vernacular Architecture*, 34 (2003), pp. 109–21

Mills 1996
P. Mills, 'The Battle of London, 1066', *London Archaeologist*, 8, no. 3 (1996), pp. 59–62

Milne 1995
G. Milne, *Roman London*, London, 1995

Moore 1918
N. Moore, *The History of St Bartholomew's Hospital*, 2 vols, London, 1918

Morley and Gurney 1997
B. Morley and D. Gurney, *Castle Rising Castle, Norfolk*, East Anglian Archaeology Report, 81, Gressenhall, 1997

R. Morris, no date
R. Morris, *Chester in the Plantagenet and Tudor Reigns*, Chester, no date [c.1893]

Mortimer 1989
R. Mortimer, 'The Baynards of Baynard's Castle', in Harper-Bill, Holdsworth and Nelson 1989, pp. 241–53

Morton and Muntz 1972
C. Morton and H. Muntz, eds, *The Carmen de Hastingae Proelio*, Oxford, 1972

Munby 1991
J. Mundy, 'Wood', in Blair and Ramsay 1991, pp. 379–405

Musset 1991

L. Musset, 'Autour du château d'Ivry', *Annuaire des cinq Départements de la Normandie*, 149e Congrès (1991), pp. 89–93

Museum of London Archaeology Service 2000

Museum of London Archaeology Service, *The Archaeology of Greater London: An Assessment of Archaeological Evidence for Human Presence in the Area now Covered by Greater London*, London, 2000

Nearing 1948a

H. Nearing, Jr, 'Caesar's Sword' *Modern Language Notes*, 63 (1948), pp. 403–5

Nearing 1948b

—, 'Julius Caesar and the Tower of London'. *Modern Language Notes*, 63 (1948), pp. 228–33

Nearing 1949a

—, 'The Legend of Julius Caesar's British Conquest', *Publications of the Modern Language Association*, 64 (1949), pp. 889–929

Nearing 1949b

—, 'Local Caesar Traditions in Britain', *Speculum*, 24 (1949), pp. 218–27

Newton 1980

S. M. Newton, *Fashion in the Age of the Black Prince*, Woodbridge, 1980

Nicolas-Méry 2002

D. Nicolas-Méry, 'Le Donjon d'Avranches: redécouverte d'un monument médiéval', *Revue de l'Avranchin et du Pays de Granville*, 79, fasc. 391 (June 2002), pp. 87–150

Niermeyer 1976

J. F. Niermeyer, *Mediae Latinitatis lexicon minus*, 2 vols, Leiden, 1976

Norgate 1887

K. Norgate, *England under the Angevin Kings*, 2 vols, London, 1887

Norgate 1902

—, *John Lackland*, London, 1902

Oman 1906

C. Oman, *The Great Revolt of 1381*, Oxford, 1906

Orlandi 1996

G. Orlandi, 'Some Afterthoughts on the *Carmen de Hastingae Proelio*', in R. I. A. Nip, et al., *Media Latinitatis: A Collection of Essays to Mark the Occasion of the Retirement of L. J. Engels*, Instrumenta Patristica, 28, Turnhout, 1996, pp. 117–27

Oswald, Schaefer and Sennhauser 1966

A. Oswald, L. Schaefer and H. Sennhauser, *Vorromanische Kirchenbauten*, Munich, 1966

J. J. N. Palmer 1995

J. J. N. Palmer, 'The Conqueror's Footsteps in Domesday Book', in Ayton and Price 1995, pp. 23–44

R. C. Palmer 1982

R. C. Palmer, *The County Courts of Medieval England, 1150–1350*, Princeton, New Jersey, 1982

Parnell 1978

G. Parnell, 'An Earlier Roman Riverside Wall at the Tower of London', *London Archaeologist*, 3, no. 7 (1978), pp. 171–6

Parnell 1980

—, 'Tower of London: Inmost Ward Excavation, 1979', *London Archaeologist*, 4, no. 5 (1980), pp. 69–73

Parnell 1981

—, 'The Tower of London: The Reconstruction of the Inmost Ward during the Reign of Charles II', *Transactions of the London and Middlesex Archaeological Society*, 31 (1981), pp. 147–56

Parnell 1983

—, 'The Western Defences of the Inmost Ward, Tower of London', *Transactions of the London and Middlesex Archaeological Society*, 34 (1983), pp. 107–50

Parnell 1985a

—, 'Five Seventeenth-Century Plans of the Tower of London', *London Topographical Record*, 25 (1985), pp. 63–82

Parnell 1985b

—, 'The Roman and Medieval Defences and the Later Development of the Inmost Ward, Tower of London, Excavations, 1955–1977', *Transactions of the London and Middlesex Archaeological Society*, 36 (1985), pp. 1–79

Parnell 1993

—, *The Tower of London*, London, 1993

Parnell 1994

—, 'The King's Guard Chamber: A Vision of Power', *Apollo*, 140 (August 1994), pp. 60–64

Parnell 1998a

—, 'The White Tower, The Tower of London', *Country Life* (9 July 1998), pp. 86–9

Parnell 1998b

—, 'Ordnance Storehouses at the Tower of London, 1450–1700', *Château Gaillard*, 18 (1998, for 1996), pp. 171–80

Parnell 1998c

—, *The Tower of London Past and Present*, Stroud, 1998

Parnell et al. 1982

— et al., 'The Excavation of the Roman City Wall at the Tower of London and Tower Hill, 1954–76', *Transactions of the London and Middlesex Archaeological Society*, 33 (1982), pp. 85–133

Parsons 1991

D. Parsons, 'Building Stone and Associated Materials', in Blair and Ramsay 1991, pp. 1–27

Pigeon 1888

E.-A. Pigeon, *Le Diocèse d'Avranches: sa topographie . . . ses châteaux*, 2 vols, Coutances, 1888

Pilbrow 2002

F. Pilbrow, 'The Knights of the Bath: Dubbing Knighthood in Lancastrian and Yorkist England', in *Heraldry, Pageantry and Social Display in Medieval England*, ed. Maurice Keen and Peter Coss, Woodbridge, 2002, pp. 195–218

Planché 1901

J. R. Planché, *Recollections and Reflections*, London, 1901

Plant 2006

R. Plant, 'Gundulf's Cathedral', in *Medieval Art, Architecture and Archaeology at Rochester*, ed. T. Ayers and T. Tatton-Brown, British Archaeological Society Conference Transactions, 28, Leeds, 2006, pp. 38–53

Poole 1955

A. L. Poole, *Domesday Book to Magna Carta, 1087–1216*, second edition, Oxford, 1955

Popescu 2004

E. Popescu, 'Norwich Castle Fee', *Medieval Archaeology*, 68 (2004), pp. 209–19

Popescu 2006

—, *Norwich Castle: Excavations and Historical Survey, 1987–1998, Part I: Anglo-Saxon to c.1345*, Norwich, 2006

Pounds 1990

N. J. G. Pounds, *The Medieval Castle in England and Wales: A Social and Political History*, Cambridge, 1990

Prigent 2005

D. Prigent, 'Evolution de la construction médiévale en pierre en Anjou et Touraine', in BAA: *Anjou*, pp. 14–33

Pugh 1966

R. B. Pugh, 'Charles Abbot and the Public Records: The First Phase', *Bulletin of the Institute of Historical Research*, 39, no. 99 (May 1966), pp. 69–85

Raby and Baillie Reynolds 1987

F. J. E. Raby and P. K. Baillie Reynolds, *Framlingham Castle*, London, 1987

Rahtz 1979

P. A. Rahtz, *Saxon and Medieval Palaces at Cheddar*, British Archaeological Reports, British Series, Oxford, 1979

RCHM 1916

Royal Commission on Historic Monuments, *The County of Essex*, London, 1916

RCHM 1930

—, *An Inventory of the Historical Monuments of London*, vol. V: *East London*, London, 1930

RCHM 1960

—, *The County of Dorset*, vol. II, part 2, London, 1960, pp. 57–78

Redknap 1983

M. Redknap, 'The Pottery', in Parnell 1983, pp. 120–49

Reid 1964

W. Reid, 'Commonwealth Supply Departments within the Tower, and the Committee of London Merchants', *Guildhall Miscellany*, 2, no. 6 (October 1964), pp. 319–52

Renn 1959

D. F. Renn, 'The Anglo-Norman Keep, 1066–1138', *Journal of the British Archaeological Association*, third series, 22 (1959), pp. 1–23

Renn 1965

—, *Norman Castles*, London, 1965

Renn 1971

—, 'The *Turris* de Penuesel: A Reappraisal and a Theory', *Sussex Archaeological Collections*, 109 (1971), pp. 55–64

Renn 1973

—, *Norman Castles in Britain*, London, 1973

Renn 1982a

—, 'Canterbury Castle in the Early Middle Ages', in Bennett, Frere and Stow 1982, pp. 70–77

Renn 1982b

—, 'The Decoration of Canterbury Castle Keep', in BAA: *Canterbury*, pp. 125–8

Renn 1994a

—, 'Burgheat and Gonfanon: Two Sidelights from the Bayeux Tapestry', in *Anglo-Norman Studies*, 16 (1994), pp. 176–97

Renn 1994b

—, *Old Sarum, Wiltshire*, London, 1994

Renoux 1987

A. Renoux, 'Châteaux et résidences fortifiées des Ducs de Normandie aux xe et xie siècles', in *Actes du 11ème Congrès International d'Archéologie médiévale tenu à Caen, le 2, 3 et 4 octobre 1987*, pp. 113–24

Renoux 1992

—, 'Evocation morphologique des palais normands et capétiens à la fin du xe et au début du xie siècle', in Barral i Altet and Parisse 1992, pp. 193–200

Renoux 2003

—, 'Entre Anjou, Ile-de-France et Normandie: les donjons du Comte de Maine du dixième au début du treizième siècle', in BAA: *Anjou*, pp. 34–51

Reynolds 1983

S. Reynolds, 'Medieval *Origines gentium* and the Community of the Realm', *History*, 68 (1983), pp. 375–90

Riddy 1996

F. Riddy, 'Contextualizing the *Morte Darthur*: Empire and Civil War', in *A Companion to Malory*, ed. E. Archibald and A. S. G. Edwards, Arthurian Studies, 37, Cambridge, 1996, pp. 55–73

Rivoira 1933

G. T. Rivoira, *Lombardic Architecture: Its Origin, Development and Derivatives*, 2 vols, second edition, London, 1933

Rokéah 1990

Z. E. Rokéah, 'Money and the Hangman in Late 13th-Century England: Jews, Christians and Coinage Offences, Alleged and Real, Part 1', *Jewish Historical Studies*, 31 (1990), pp. 83–109

Ross 1981

C. Ross, *Richard III*, London, 1981

Rosser 1996

G. Rosser, 'Myth, Image and Social Process in the English Medieval Town', *Urban History*, 23, part 1 (1996), pp. 5–25

Roth 1935

D. Roth, 'Norman Survivals in London: The Tower of London and the London Buildings of the Military Orders', *Journal of the Royal Institute of British Architects* (8 June 1935), pp. 863–70

Round 1882

Round, *The History and Antiquities of Colchester Castle*, Colchester, 1882

Round 1892

—, 'Tower and Castle: Appendix O', in *Geoffrey de Mandeville: A Study of the Anarchy*, London, 1892, pp. 328–46

Rowley 1997

T. Rowley, *Norman England*, London, 1997

Rumble and Morris 1994

A. R. Rumble and R. Morris, 'Translatio Sancti Ælfegi archiepiscopi et martiris: Osbern's Account of the Translation of St Ælfheah's Relics from London to Canterbury, 8–11 June 1023', in *The Reign of Cnut, the King of England, Denmark and Norway*, ed. Rumble, Leicester, 1994, pp. 283–315

Ruprich-Robert 1884–9

V. Ruprich-Robert, *L'Architecture normande au 11e et 12e siècles*, 2 vols, Paris, 1884–9; reprinted London, 1971

Ruud 1989

M. Ruud, 'Monks in the World', *Anglo-Norman Studies*, 11 (1989), pp. 245–60

Salway 1981

P. Salway, *Roman Britain*, Oxford, 1981

Salzman 1952
L. F. Salzman, *Building in England to 1540: A Documentary History*, Oxford, 1952

Sands 1912
H. Sands, 'Spring Meeting at the Tower', *Archaeological Journal*, 69 (1912), pp. 219–25

Sankey 1998
D. Sankey, 'Cathedrals, Granaries and Urban Vitality in Late Roman London', in *Roman London: Recent Archaeological Work*, ed. B. Watson, Journal of Roman Archaeology, Supplementary Series, 24, Portsmouth, Rhode Island, 1998, pp. 78–82

Saunders 1967
A. D. Saunders, *Upnor Castle*, London, 1967

Saunders 1983
—, 'A Century of Ancient Monuments Legislation', *Antiquaries Journal*, 63 (1983), pp. 11–33

Saunders 2004
—, *Fortress Builder: Bernard de Gomme, Charles II's Military Engineer*, Exeter, 2004

Schofield 1993
J. Schofield, *The Building of London from the Conquest to the Great Fire*, revised edition, London, 1993

Schofield 1994
—, 'Saxon and Medieval Parish Churches in the City of London: A Review', *Transactions of the London and Middlesex Archaeological Society*, 45 (1994), pp. 23–145

Schofield 1999
—, *The Building of London from the Conquest to the Great Fire*, third edition, Stroud, 1999

Scottish Record Office 1996
Scottish Record Office, *Guide to the National Archives of Scotland*, Edinburgh, 1996

Sellwood and McKerrow 1974
B. W. Sellwood and W. S. McKerrow, 'Depositional Environments in the Lower Part of the Great Oolite Group of Oxfordshire and North Gloucestershire', *Proceedings of the Geologists' Association*, 85 (1974), pp. 189–210

Seymour 1734
R. Seymour, *A Survey of the Cities of London and Westminster*, London, 1734

Sharpe 2002
R. Sharpe, 'Martyrs and Saints in Late Antique Britain', in A. Thacker and Sharpe, *Local Saints and Local Churches in the Early Medieval West*, Oxford, 2002, pp. 75–154

Shichtman and Finke 1993
M. B. Shichtman and L. A. Finke, 'Profiting from the Past: History as Symbolic Capital in the *Historia regum Britannie*', *Arthurian Literature*, 12 (1993), pp. 1–35

Siguret 1957
P. Siguret, 'Le Château Saint-Jean de Nogent-le-Rotrou', *Cahiers Percherons*, 2 (1957), pp. 5–47

Simpson 1998
J. W. Simpson, 'The Other Book of Troy: Guido delle Colonne's *Historia destructionis Troiae* in Fourteenth- and Fifteenth-Century England', *Speculum*, 73 (1998), pp. 397–423

Simpson and Litton 1996
G. Simpson and C. D. Litton, 'Dendrochronology in Cathedrals', in *The Archaeology of Cathedrals*, ed. T. Tatton-Brown and J. Munby, Oxford University Committee for Archaeology, 42, Oxford, 1996, pp. 189–90

Simpson and Weiner 1989
J. A. Simpson and E. S. C. Weiner, *The Oxford English Dictionary*, second edition, Oxford, 1989

Smirke 1836
S. Smirke, 'Remarks on the Architectural History of Westminster Hall: In a Letter from Sydney Smith, Esq. FSA, to Sir Henry, Ellis, KH, FRS, Secretary, read 28 May 1835', *Archaeologia*, 26 (1836), p. 411

Smith 1943
R. A. L. Smith, 'The Place of Gundulf in the Anglo-Norman Church', *English Historical Review*, 58 (1943), pp. 257–72

Smuts 1989
R. Malcolm Smuts, 'Public Ceremony and Royal Charisma: The English Royal Entry in London, 1485–1642', in *The First Modern Society*, ed. A. L. Beier, D. Cannadine and J. M. Roosen, Cambridge, 1989, pp. 65–94

Stalley 1971
R. A. Stalley, 'A Twelfth-Century Patron of Architecture: A Study of the Buildings Erected by Roger Bishop of Salisbury', *Journal of the British Archaeological Association*, third series, 34 (1971), pp. 62–83

Stenton 1965
F. Stenton, *The Bayeux Tapestry*, second edition, London, 1965

Stenton 1971
—, *Anglo-Saxon England*, third edition, London, 1971

Stenton 1990
—, 'Norman London: An Essay', reprinted in Logan 1990, pp. 1–45

Stewart 1996
R. W. Stewart, *The English Ordnance Office: A Case-Study in Bureaucracy*, Woodbridge, 1996

Stocker 1991
D. Stocker, *St Mary's Guildhall, Lincoln*, Archaeology of Lincoln, London, 1991

Stocker 1992
—, 'The Shadow of the General's Armchair', *Archaeological Journal*, 149 (1992), pp. 415–20

Stocker 2004
—, 'The Two Early Castles of Lincoln', in Lindley 2004, pp. 9–22

Stocker and Vince 1997
— and A. Vince, 'The Early Norman Castle at Lincoln and a Re-evaluation of the Original West Tower of Lincoln Cathedral', *Medieval Archaeology*, 41 (1997), pp. 223–32

Stoll 1967
R. T. Stoll, *Architecture and Sculpture in Early Britain: Celtic, Saxon, Norman*, London, 1967

Storey 1998
R. Storey, 'The Tower of London and the Garderobae Armorum', *Royal Armouries Yearbook*, 3 (1998), pp. 176–83

Stukeley 1724
W. Stukeley, 'Londinium Augusta', in his *Itinerarium curiosum; or, An Account of the Antiquitys and Remarkable Curiositys in Nature or Art, Observ'd in Travels thro' Great Britain*, London, 1724

Sturdy 1979
D. Sturdy, 'Nine Hundred Years of The Tower', *London Archaeologist*, 3, no. 10 (1979), pp. 270–3

Tanner and Wright 1934
L. E. Tanner and W. Wright, 'Recent Investigations Regarding the Fate of the Princes in the Tower', *Archaeologia*, 84 (1934), pp. 1–26

Tatlock 1950
J. S. P. Tatlock, *The Legendary History of Britain: Geoffrey of Monmouth's* Historia regum Britannie *and its Early Vernacular Versions*, Berkeley and Los Angeles, 1950

Tatton-Brown 1980
T. W. T. Tatton-Brown, 'The Use of Quarr Stone in London and East Kent', *Medieval Archaeology*, 24 (1980), pp. 213–15

Tatton-Brown 1986
—, 'The Topography of Anglo-Saxon London', *Antiquity*, 60 (1986), pp. 21–7

Tatton-Brown 1990
—, 'Building Stone in Canterbury, c.1070–1525', in *Stone: Quarrying and Building in England, AD 43–1525*, ed. D. Parsons, Chichester, 1990, pp. 70–82

Tatton-Brown 1993
—, 'Building Stones of Winchester Cathedral', in *Winchester Cathedral: Nine Hundred Years, 1093–1993*, ed. J. Crook, Chichester, 1993, pp. 37–46

Tatton-Brown 1994
—, 'The Medieval Fabric', in *Chichester Cathedral: An Historical Survey*, ed. M. Hobbs, Chichester, 1994, pp. 25–46

Tatton-Brown 2001
—, 'The Quarrying and Distribution of Reigate Stone in the Middle Ages', *Medieval Archaeology*, 45 (2001), pp. 189–201

H. M. Taylor 1965–78
H. M. Taylor, *Anglo-Saxon Architecture*, 3 vols, Cambridge, 1965–78 [vols I and II with J. Taylor]

P. Taylor 2004
P. Taylor, 'Foundation and Endowment: St Paul's and the English Kingdoms, 604–1087', in Keene, Burns and Saint 2004, pp. 5–16

Thackray 1990
D. Thackray, *Corfe Castle, Dorset*, London, 1990

Thomas and Watson, forthcoming
C. Thomas and B. Watson, *The Mendicant Houses of Medieval London: An Archaeological and Architectural Review*, Museum of London Archaeology Service, forthcoming

K. Thompson 2002
K. Thompson, *Power and Border Lordship in Medieval France: The County of the Perche, 1000–1226*, Woodbridge, 2002

M. W. Thompson 1991
M. W. Thompson, *The Rise of the Castle*, Cambridge, 1991

M. W. Thompson 1992
—, 'A Suggested Dual Origin for Keeps', *Fortress*, 15 (November 1992), pp. 3–15

M. W. Thompson 1995
—, *The Medieval Hall: The Basis of Secular Domestic Life, 600–1600 AD*, Aldershot, 1995

M. W. Thompson 1998
—, *Medieval Bishops' Houses in England and Wales*, Aldershot, 1998

Thurley 1993
S. Thurley, *The Royal Palaces of Tudor England: Architecture and Court Life, 1460–1547*, New Haven and London, 1993

Thurley 1995
—, 'Royal Lodgings at the Tower of London, 1216–1327', *Architectural History*, 38 (1995), pp. 36–57

Thurley 1998
—, *Whitehall Palace*, London, 1998

Thurley 2003
—, *Hampton Court Palace*, London and New Haven, 2003

Thurley, Impey and Hammond 1996
—, E. Impey and P. Hammond, *The Tower of London*, London, 1996

Tomlinson 1979
H. C. Tomlinson, *Guns and Government: The Ordnance Office under the Later Stuarts*, London, 1979

Tout 1920–33
T. F. Tout, *Chapters in the Administrative History of Mediaeval England*, 6 vols, Manchester, 1920–33; revised edition, 1937

Tout 1934
—, 'Firearms in England in the Fourteenth Century', in *The Collected Papers of Thomas Frederick Tout*, vol. II, Manchester, 1934, pp. 233–75

Tronzo 1997
W. Tronzo, *The Cultures of his Kingdom: Roger II and the Cappella Palatina in Palermo*, Princeton, New Jersey, 1997

Turner 1912
G. J. Turner, 'William the Conqueror's March to London in 1066', *English Historical Review*, 27 (1912), pp. 209–25

Tyers 2001
I. Tyers, *Tree-Ring Analysis of Coffin Timbers Excavated at the Church of St Peter, Barton on Humber, North Lincolnshire*, English Heritage Centre for Archaeology Reports, 48, 2001

Tyler 2000
K. Tyler, 'The "Western Stream" Reconsidered: Excavations at the Medieval Great Wardrobe, Wardrobe Place, City of London', *Transactions of the London and Middlesex Archaeological Society*, 51 (2000), pp. 21–44

Valéry-Radot 1931
J. Valéry-Radot, *Beaugency: église Notre-Dame et donjon*, Orléans, 1931

Van Houts 1989
E. van Houts, 'Latin Poetry and the Anglo-Norman Court, 1066–1135: The *Carmen de Hastingae Proelio*', *Journal of Medieval History*, 15 (1989), pp. 39–62

Van Houts 1997
—, 'Wace as Historian', in *Family Trees and the Roots of Politics: Britain and France from the Tenth to the Twelfth Century*, ed. K. S. B. Keats-Rohan, Woodbridge, 1997, pp. 103–32

Van Houts 2000
—, *The Normans in Europe*, Manchester, 2000

Vaughn 1987
S. N. Vaughn, *Anselm of Bec and Robert of Meulan*, Berkeley, California, 1987

VCH Essex
A History of the County of Essex, Victoria History of the County of Essex, vols I and II, London, 1903–7

Verbruggen 1950
J. F. Verbruggen, 'Note sur le sens des mots *castrum*, *castellum* et quelques autres expressions qui désignent des fortifications', *Revue belge de philologie et d'histoire*, 28 (1950), pp. 147–55

Vergnolle 1989
E. Vergnolle, 'Passages muraux et escaliers: premières expériences dans l'architecture du xie siècle', *Cahiers de civilisation médiévale*, 32 (1989), pp. 43–60

Vergnolle 1996
—, 'La Pierre de taille dans l'architecture religieuse de la première moitié du xie siècle', *Bulletin monumental*, 154 (1996), pp. 229–34

Vince 1984
A. Vince, 'The Aldwych: Mid-Saxon London Discovered', *Current Archaeology* (July 1984), pp. 23–7

Vince 1990
—, *Saxon London: An Archaeological Investigation*, London, 1990

Wallenberg 1934
J. K. Wallenberg, *The Place Names of Kent*, Uppsala, 1934

Warner and Gilson 1921
G. F. Warner and J. P. Gilson, *Catalogue of the Western MSS in the Old Royal and King's Collections in the British Museum*, 4 vols, London, 1921

Waswo 1995
R. Waswo, 'Our Ancestors, the Trojans: Inventing Cultural Identity in the Middle Ages', *Exemplaria*, 7, no. 2 (1995), pp. 269–90

Watkins-Pitchford 1931
W. Watkins-Pitchford, 'Bridgnorth Castle and Ethelfleda's Tower', *Transactions of the Shropshire Archaeological Society*, 46 (1931), pp. 3–12

Watson 1992
B. Watson, 'The Norman Fortress on Ludgate Hill in the City of London, England: Recent Excavations, 1986–1990', *Château Gaillard*, 15 (1992), pp. 335–45

Watson, Brigham and Dyson 2001
—, T. Brigham and T. Dyson, *London Bridge: 2000 Years of a River Crossing*, Museum of London Archaeology Service Monograph, 8, London, 2001

Weale 1854
J. Weale, ed., *The Pictorial Handbook of London*, London, 1854

Weiss 2002
J. Weiss, 'Emperors and Antichrists: Reflections of Empire in Insular Narrative, 1130–1250', in *The Matter of Identity in Medieval Romance*, ed. P Hardman, Woodbridge, 2002, pp. 87–102

Wernham 1956
R. B. Wernham, 'The Public Records in the 16th and 17th centuries', in *English Historical Scholarship in the 16th and 17th Centuries*, ed. L. Fox, London and New York, 1956

Wernham 1966
—, *Before the Armada: The Emergence of the English Nation, 1485–1588*, New York, 1966

Westlake 1923
F. H. Westlake, *Westminster Abbey*, 2 vols, London, 1923

Wheatley 2004a
A. Wheatley, *The Idea of the Castle in Medieval England*, Woodbridge, 2004

Wheatley 2004b
—, 'King Arthur Lives in Merry Carleile', in *Carlisle and Cumbria: Roman and Medieval Architecture, Art and Archaeology*, ed. M. McCarthy and D. Weston, British Archaeological Association Conference Transactions for the Year 2001, 27, Leeds, 2004, pp. 63–72

Wheeler 1935
R. E. M. Wheeler, *London and the Saxons*, London, 1935

Whitaker 1990
M. Whitaker, *The Legends of King Arthur in Art*, Arthurian Studies, 22, Cambridge, 1990

White 1948
G. H. White, 'The Household of the Norman Kings', *Royal Historical Society Transactions*, fourth series, 30 (1948), pp. 127–55

White and Cook 1986
P. White and A. Cook, *Sherborne Old Castle*, London, 1986

Whitelock et al. 1966
D. Whitelock et al., *The Norman Conquest: Its Setting and Impact*, London, 1966

Wickham Legg 1901
L. G. Wickham Legg, *English Coronation Records*, London, 1901

Will 1962
E. Will, 'Recherches sur le développement urbain sous l'empire romain dans le nord de la France', *Gallia*, 20 (1962), pp. 79–101

G. A. Williams 1963
G. A. Williams, *Medieval London: From Commune to Capital*, London, 1963

P. Williams 1979
P. Williams, *The Tudor Regime*, Oxford, 1979

Wilson 1985
D. M. Wilson, *The Bayeux Tapestry*, London, 1985

Wolstenholme 1855
J. Wolstenholme, *Two Lectures on the History and Antiquities of Berkhamsted*, London, 1855

Woodman 1981
F. Woodman, *The Architectural History of Canterbury Cathedral*, London, 1981

Worssam 1995
B. C. Worssam, 'Regional Geology', in D. Tweddle, Martin Biddle and B. Kjølbye-Biddle, *Corpus of Anglo-Saxon Stone Sculpture*, vol. iv: *South-East England*, Oxford, 1995, pp. 10–21

Worssam and Sanderson 1998
— and R. W. Sanderson, 'Geology of the White Tower South Elevation', unpublished Report to Historic Royal Palaces, Hampton Court Palace, 1998

Worssam and Tatton-Brown 1994
— and T. Tatton-Brown, 'Kentish Rag and Other Kent Building Stones', *Archaeologia Cantiana*, 112 (1994, for 1993), pp. 93–125

Younghusband 1918
G. Younghusband, *The Tower from Within*, London, 1918

Younghusband 1921
—, *The Jewel House*, London, 1921

Yvard 1994

J.-C. Yvard, 'Sur l'existence d'un "domicilium" (fin du XIe siècle) au donjon de Lavardin (Loir-et-Cher)', *Bulletin de la Société archéologique, scientifique et littéraire du Vendômois* (1994), pp. 27–31

Yvard and Michel 1996

— and A. Michel, *Le Château féodal de Montoire, XIe–XVe siècle*, Vendôme, 1996

Yver 1957

J. Yver, 'Les Châteaux forts en Normandie jusqu'au milieu du XIIe siècle', *Bulletin de la Société des Antiquaires de Normandie*, 53 (1957), pp. 28–115

Zarnecki 1979

G. Zarnecki, 'Romanesque Sculpture in Normandy and England in the Eleventh Century', in *Proceedings of the Battle Conference on Anglo-Norman Studies, I: 1978*, ed. R. A. Brown, Ipswich, 1979, pp. 168–89

Illustration Credits

Index

Lord *Lumley's* House sometime
belonging to *Crutched Fryers*

The New Brick Wall

AC

AE

The Nine Gardens

At this time a broken Tower as the rest of the Wall

Pikes Garden

TOWER HILL

The Posts of
the Scaffold

Post

SEMPER EADEM

The DESCRIPTION of the TOWER
of LONDON with all the Buildings
and the Outermost Limits thereof
together with all such places adjoyn
ing as do confine and abound the
said Liberties. made by the direction
of Sr John Peyton Knt

The Cage

Barkin Church

The Houses betwixt the Church Yard
and the Hill are St Katherines Rents.

TOWER STREET

AH

E

F

D

TOWER
of
LONDO

THAMES STREET

The Bulwark Gate

The Lyons Gate

The Lyon's Tower

Petty Wales

A

The Lieutenᵗˢ
Lodgings

B

C

AB

T

THE

W

S

V

HAR